First Fruit

For Len —
with warm thanks
from new
friendship
Warmly,

First Fruit

A Whizin Anthology
of Jewish Family Education

Edited by Adrianne Bank and Ron Wolfson

The Shirley and Arthur Whizin Institute for Jewish Family Life
Los Angeles, California 1998

Address editorial correspondence to:
The Shirley and Arthur Whizin Institute for Jewish Family Life
University of Judaism
15600 Mulholland Drive
Los Angeles, California 90077

ISBN 0-9646836-1-X

Editor-in-Chief: Adrianne Bank
Design and Production Staff: Lisa Johnson and Martha Tocco, *Backyard Graphics*
Cover Design: Lisa Johnson, *Backyard Graphics*

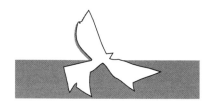

Contents

V   Breaking New Ground

Preface

As the first—and surely not the last—Whizin anthology focused on the emerging field of Jewish family education, *First Fruit* brings together thirty-six outstanding articles by authors associated with the Shirley and Arthur Whizin Institute for Jewish Family Life.

Each author has been connected with the Whizin Institute for a number of years, usually in more than one role. All have been either regular or visiting faculty or participants at the nine Whizin Institute Summer Seminars or Think Tanks and all have experienced the excitement, the exhaustion, and the exhilaration of the annual four days of text study, lectures, workshops, affinity groups, music, dance, and field trips. In addition, all work during the year in their own communities and institutions doing family education, often influenced by their Whizin experiences.

Each author's connection with Jewish family education is deeply personal as well as professional, and this intensity saturates the collection. As well as sharing with you their observations about the families they teach, the authors bring to you their own struggle to define themselves in relation to their own families. Each author's ideas have many roots—most certainly, in their own experiences in working with many kinds of families in many different settings. But to a greater degree than in most fields, over the past decade the authors of this collection have been engaged with one another in ongoing dialogues. Through these articles, you are able to eavesdrop on the years of conversation compressed into these pages.

As a group, the authors are teachers, administrators, social workers, lay leaders, rabbis, and academics. Often they are two or three of these at the same time, or they may have switched from one role to another in the course of their professional lives. Whatever their present involvements, they have had eclectic and diverse career paths.

One important thread that they have in common—in life as well as between these covers—is that they are each pathfinders in family education. As Jewish family educators, they are at the forefront of the struggle to figure out how to create enough time and space in busy American lives so that more families can savor the rituals and learnings that their Jewish heritage provides. They are finding new ways of reaching out to families; of inviting them to learn about and experience the joys of Shabbat; of helping them appreciate the ever-changing, ever-recurring cycle of the holidays; and of supporting them as they make for themselves the connections between accumulated Jewish wisdom and their everyday world.

You are not likely to read this book in one sitting or from beginning to end. Rather you will probably sample from the various parts and revisit them, each time coming to understand better the many possibilities of this specialty area of family education—a specialty similar to and different than other types of Jewish education. As you dip into the articles, you may find that the same people are referred to by different authors or even that the same story or event is described several times. It will become apparent that these authors share with one another a neighborly knowledge.

In *Part I, Whizin Landscapes*, Ron Wolfson, Bruce Whizin, and Adrianne Bank roam through the past of the Whizin Institute to describe how it arose, was formed, and took shape. They show how the Institute evolved and continues to evolve as a dynamic response to particular needs strongly felt in the American Jewish community. They tell of how, simply by its existence, the Institute has reshaped aspects of this community.

We know that this community—composed of all the Jewish people in America—is filled with stories. The act of telling stores and listening to stories grabs our past and brings it, with all its baggage, into the present. In *Part II, Personal Paths*, Diane Tickton Schuster, Chana Silberstein, and Jo Kay demonstrate the importance to family education of telling and listening to stories. They write about how adults retrieve and reconstruct their own and their families' experiences, and how, in turn, they create family stories for their children's future. Shelley Silver Whizin, Jo Kay, Lucy Y. Steinitz, and Risa Munitz-Gruberger relate to us portions of their personal stories. And we feel we are witnessing their experiences.

Our American Jewish community exists not in a single location but wherever it is that we come togetherin homes, schools, and synagogues; in community centers, camps, and museums; and on trips to Israel. And so it is that Jewish family education occurs on many sites and has many sounds. Although all of it is Jewish and for families and for education, Jewish family education looks and sounds different in different places. In *Part III, Many Sites and Many Sounds*, Victoria Koltun Kelman and Joan Wolchansky write of family education as it occurs in the living rooms of people's homes. Cindy Dolgin and Jeffrey Schein describe synagogues grappling with decisions about how to do family education. Jo

Kay, at one school, and Mark Loeb, Eyal Bor, and Fern Cohen, at another, explain how they combined the teaching of parents with the teaching of children so that the mixture became the education of families. Esther Netter, Judy Israel Elkin, and Victoria Koltun Kelman connect family education to discoveries that can happen in museums, to intimacies that can happen in camp, and to pilgrimage experiences that can happen on trips to Israel.

Jewish networks in American cities are activated by federations and other associations of people interested in achieving common goals. In many cities, Jewish family education has come to be regarded as a vehicle for bringing adults and children together around their Jewish heritage and for insuring the continuity of a Jewish presence into the next generation. In *Part IV, Community Ventures,* Joan Kaye provides an analytic introduction to the family education efforts in eight cities. Detailed descriptions of the history and structure of this work are supplied by Harlene Winnick Appelman for Detroit, Marilyn Vincent for Chicago, Nancy Bloom, Marion Gribetz, Sharon Jedel, Barbara Penzner, and Harvey Shapiro for Boston, Jeffrey Schein for Cleveland, Carol Pristoop for Baltimore, Cecile Jordan for San Diego, Sandy Dashefsky for Hartford and Victoria Koltun Kelman and Nechama Tamler for San Francisco.

New insights into how to educate families have become a staple of the Whizin Institute. The articles of the eight authors in *Part V, Breaking New Ground,* do indeed break new ground and bring variegated seeds to the family education field. Joel Grishaver brings Torah texts and life texts. Susan L. Shevitz brings educational evaluation perspectives. Harlene Winnick Appelman and Joan Kaye bring educational curriculum thinking. Sally Weber forges links between social workers in social agencies and Jewish family education. Diane Tickton Schuster brings an adult development point of view, while Betsy Dolgin Katz brings an adult education frame of reference. From two very different settings, Rachel Sisk and Esther Netter bring the wisdom they have distilled from working on funding and program development. And in the *Postscript,* Bruce Whizin acknowledges the contributions made by his parents to the family education work of the Whizin Institute.

We want to acknowledge everyone whose hard work has made this book possible, particularly Ellen Franklin, Jill Rosenberg, and Risa Munitz-Gruberger. Very special thanks go to Lisa Johnson and Martha

Tocco of *Backyard Graphics*, who designed and produced this volume.

As the Whizin Institute approaches the tenth anniversary of its work, we have taken great pleasure in assembling and editing these "first fruits." We recognize that the decade has been a fertile one, and we celebrate the authors who have seeded and planted, sowed and reaped, and finally seen Jewish family education become an established field. We believe that, all over the country, Jewish family education is becoming a vast ecological system where the growth of each part is interdependent with the growth of other parts. *First Fruit: A Whizin Anthology of Jewish Family Education* presents some of what we know now. We are confident that it will spur new growth in the years to come.

Adrianne Bank
Ron Wolfson

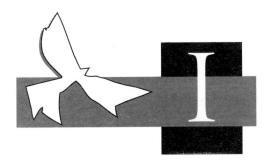

Whizin Landscapes

Introduction: Whizin Landscapes

These initial articles view Jewish family education through the lens of the Shirley and Arthur Whizin Institute for Jewish Family Life, established in 1989 at the University of Judaism. The authors frame the sweep of the Whizin landscape from three points of view: Ron Wolfson, as creator and director of the Institute; Bruce Whizin, as its founder and funder; and Adrianne Bank, as the long-term evaluation consultant documenting its growth over time.

Ron's story, *Growing a Field of Dreams*, tells of the confluence of his own life and the life of Jewish family education. He reveals how, for himself and for many people working in this area, images and dreams inspired each step of the way. A new field based on an old idea, Ron's title accurately describes how the neglected space of inside-the-home Jewish family learning became, within a very few years, the focus of a national educational endeavor involving schools, synagogues, and community agencies. He chronicles the people, the institutions, and the communities who made major contributions along the way. In an extensive overview, he describes for us, with clarifying detail, the principles, strategies, programs, and infrastructures that currently characterize Jewish family education, and he speculates on future directions the field might take.

Bruce starts his very personal story, *Weathering the Storms*, with the birth of "Whizin," flashes back to his childhood in the San Fernando Valley, and then takes us on his own tumultuous adult spiritual journey. He describes how his Jewishness is becoming deeper every day, driven by the intensity of his own learning and by his activities as what he terms a "tzedakah professional" in the Whizin Institute for Jewish Family Life.

2

Adrianne's title, *The View from Mulholland Drive*, refers both to the actual location of the Whizin Institute, which sits in the University of Judaism's building high atop Mulholland Drive in Los Angeles and to the David Hockney painting with a similar name. As the resident observer-participant, consultant-evaluator, and outside-insider, she sees the Whizin Institute from many points of view. She uses Hockney's image as a metaphor for describing the overlapping and intersecting collage of the Whizin landscape: the planning and execution of the annual Whizin Summer Seminars; the reactions of participants while there; and their activities when they return home.

These three articles, together with those in the rest of the volume, illustrate the central characteristics of the work of the Whizin Institute and of the emerging field of Jewish family education: innovation, dedication, and energy. People bring to this work their passion, their experience, and their previous knowledge. In it they combine the personal and the professional, the expert and the novice, the diverse and the similar; and they join all of this with the richness of the Jewish tradition. As a result of their work, they are confident that—whatever variations exist among Jewish individuals, families, and institutions—the resources of Jewish family education can help revitalize American Judaism for the next century.

Ron Wolfson credits his family, his activities in a Conservative synagogue and in United Synagogue Youth, and his summer camp experiences for leading him into a career in Jewish education. He first learned how to celebrate Jewish holidays in Omaha, Nebraska, where, yes, there are Jews—6,500 of whom make up one of the finest small Jewish communities in North America.

Ron Wolfson

Ron received his Ph.D. in Education from Washington University in St. Louis. Coming west to the University of Judaism for further study in Judaica, he was invited to join the UJ faculty in 1975. After serving as Dean of Education, Ron is now vice president, William and Freda Fingerhut Assistant Professor of Education, and director of the Shirley and Arthur Whizin Center for the Jewish Future. He directs the Whizin Institute for Jewish Family Life and is a principal investigator of Synagogue 2000: A Transdenominational Project for the Synagogue of the 21st Century.

Ron is the author of The Art of Jewish Living, *a series of books on the celebration of Jewish holidays in the home, sponsored by the Federation of Jewish Men's Clubs and the University of Judaism. Books in the series include* The Art of Jewish Living: The Shabbat Seder *(1985),* The Art of Jewish Living: Hanukkah *(1988/1990),* The Art of Jewish Living: The Passover Seder *(1988, translated into Russian, 1990), and* A Time to Mourn, A Time to Comfort *(1993).*

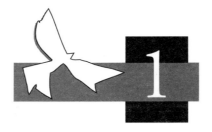

Growing a Field of Dreams
Ron Wolfson

Once upon a time...
It was twenty years ago today...
In the beginning...

Storytelling is a root experience of the Jewish people. Our sacred texts, particularly the Bible, are filled with stories. Our most observed Jewish holiday, Passover, is designed to tell the master Jewish story of our redemption. Our daily lives are filled with the telling of stories—about our families, our work, and our community.

I want to tell you a story. It is a story about families, work, and communities. It is a story about the challenges that have swept through the Jewish community of our time. And it is a story about the subsequent emergence of a new field of Jewish education—Jewish family education—a bold response to the challenges to Jewish continuity in the last quarter of the twentieth century. In our work in the Shirley and Arthur Whizin Institute for Jewish Family Life, we have learned that the process of telling our stories is fundamental to the practice of Jewish family education. Stories are our way of sharing the experiences of our journey through life, helping us to clarify their meaning through the telling.

I have chosen to tell this story of Jewish family education (JFE) intertwined with what I know best—my own story. It is not the only story: this volume and other accounts of the pioneering work in Jewish family education offer other viewpoints. I am blessed, as director of the Whizin Institute, to have witnessed the beginnings of the field and its evolution from a front row seat. For twenty years, my personal family life and my professional work have intersected at the nexus of Jewish family education. Thus, b'r'shut, with your permission, my story.

5

Introduction

Vishinantam levanekha v'dibarta bam: you shall teach them deliberately and you shall speak about them. My reading of this most famous phrase from Jewish liturgy, taken from the Shema and the Ve'ahavta is this:

> You parents, you should carefully teach God's instructions to your children. It is your responsibility to tell them the stories of our people. When? All the time. Not just when dropping them off at religious school, but when you wake them and when you read to them at bedtime; in the morning when you prepare their lunch boxes and in the evening at the dinner table; when you celebrate Shabbat at home and when you celebrate with portable candlesticks in your room during the family vacation at Disney World.

There is no clearer mandate in Jewish life. The parent is to be a child's first teacher of Judaism. It is the dining room where Shabbat is first to be observed, the backyard where the sukkah is first to be built, the home where the Passover Seder is first to be celebrated. But what if the parent cannot tell the story, does not know God's instructions, is not comfortable celebrating the ritual?

For the post World War II families who built the suburban Jewish communities of the 1950s, the answer to this was, "Take the children to the synagogue," or more specifically, "Send them to religious school." There they would learn the details of Jewish living, the reasons for the customs and ceremonies many of them still saw at Bubbie and Zadie's (grandma and grandpa's) house, if not in their own home. Walking to afternoon classes past neighborhood kosher butcher shops and Jewish bakeries, they would feel the vibrant Jewish community. This was a golden age of Jewish education. By the mid-1960s, the baby boom had produced more than a half million Jewish children who flooded into classrooms bursting at the seams. But, it was an education centered on teaching children how to be competent "synagogue Jews." Most instructional time was devoted to teaching Hebrew language skills for comprehending the prayer book and the Bible. The ultimate goal of Hebrew school became bar and bat mitzvah, the opportunity to showcase the skills required for "public" Jewish observance. Jewish educators assumed that their students' families provided them with a Jewish environment in which to celebrate holidays and learn Jewish values. But such was not always the case.

In fact, the parents of these students, many of them second generation American Jews uncomfortable with religious requirements which seemed to impede speedy assimilation into American society, were gradually replacing the private Jewish practice of the home with the public Jewish practice of the synagogue. To be Jewish, one went to the synagogue—to late Friday night services, High Holy Day extravaganzas, and life-cycle celebrations. Synagogues responded by transforming what had been primarily a place of worship into what Mordecai M. Kaplan called "the synagogue center," a multifaceted provider of activities for every constituency: adult education, social action projects, youth groups, and preschools.

By the end of the tumultuous sixties, surveys of the Jewish community revealed disturbing indicators of what was to come: a steady decline in key indicators of personal Jewish observance; the signs of cracks in the foundations of the "nuclear" Jewish family; and most ominously, the increasing rate of divorce and intermarriage. While Jewish summer camps and youth groups seemed to be successful vehicles, supplemental religious schools were perceived to provide unexceptional educational experiences.

As with the protests against the conduct of the war in Vietnam, it was students who questioned the status quo; in this case, Jewish students, products of a Jewish educational system that seemed to them woefully under-funded, unimaginative, and unsuccessful. When a group of Jewish college students demonstrated and demanded a hearing at the 1969 General Assembly of the Council of Jewish Federations (CJF), the Jewish community heard their call to make Jewish education a higher communal priority. The CJF responded by creating the Institute for Jewish Life, originally a well-intentioned but later an under-funded and ill-fated attempt to address the Jewish content of the communal effort. The Institute's most successful initiative was to recruit students interested in becoming Jewish communal workers, educators, and rabbis. The college students themselves sponsored a conference on alternatives in Jewish education at Brown University in 1976, which was the forerunner of the Coalition for Alternatives in Jewish Education and the present-day Coalition for the Advancement of Jewish Education (CAJE).

My Life and Work

I begin with this background because it paints the backdrop upon which we might understand the emerging picture of Jewish family education in the 1970s, and because it is, in fact, my own story. I was born to second-generation American Jews, a baby boomer, and a product of an afternoon Hebrew school. If not for an excellent experience with a teenage Jewish youth group, I might easily have entered college in the mid-60s with less Jewish commitment than my parents. Instead, with the guidance of my mentor, Rabbi Bernard Lipnick, I found my way into Jewish education.

In 1974, upon completing a Ph.D. in Education at Washington University in St. Louis, I received a mid-career training fellowship for leadership in Jewish education from the Institute for Jewish Life. This fellowship enabled me to enroll in a master's degree program in Judaica at the University of Judaism (UJ) in Los Angeles. The following year, I was invited to join the UJ faculty as an Assistant Professor of Education, specializing in teacher training. And in 1976, two important events occurred which had a substantial impact on my life and career.

On January 29, 1976, my wife Susie and I welcomed our daughter Havi into the world. As most first-time parents, we now considered ourselves a family. We reveled in Havi's growth and surrounded her with an environment in which Jewish celebration was pervasive. It soon became clear to me from watching Havi experience Shabbat and the Jewish holidays and imitate the ritual behaviors she observed us doing, that, as a context for Jewish education, the family and the home were paramount.

In the summer of 1977, I attended the second Conference on Alternatives in Jewish Education at the Rochester Institute of Technology. One of the hundreds of workshops on creative innovations in Jewish education was a session on a Jewish family program created by Cherie Koller-Fox at the Harvard Hillel Children's School in Boston. Cherie had come to believe that her job as an educator of children had to be expanded to include the family, especially those parents who were looking for additional ways to celebrate Jewish life in the home. Cherie's pioneering work with families was a revelation to me.

The next year, two important papers assessing the effectiveness of Jewish schooling appeared. Harold Himmelfarb's scathing analysis of afternoon religious schools climaxed with the assertion that for most students who received less than a minimum threshold of contact hours (4,000 in his study), the experience was "a waste of time." Himmelfarb was no more kind in his assessment of the families sending their children to these schools, claiming that they had "culturally deprived" their children of the richness of Jewish expression in the home. Among his recommendations was this call for action:

> [W]ithout the encouragement and reinforcement from the home, it is extremely unlikely that Jewish schools will have any lasting impact on their students. If the home provides the necessary encouragement and reinforcement, Jewish schooling can increase the level of Jewish commitment achieved in the home. These two institutions need each other and the efforts of one without the other are likely to produce only slight results.[1]

Despite later questioning of Himmelfarb's methodology and agenda, his paper added to the growing belief that religious schools were in need of major rethinking. Although Geoffrey Bock's paper that same year came to a somewhat different conclusion about the effectiveness of afternoon schools—he claimed that 1,000 hours was the minimum threshold for the school to have an impact—he, too, posited that the "religious identity of the family is the major predictor of future adult Jewish identity." He stressed the impact of the family in the following way:

> Personal Jewishness (such as religious observance, Jewish self-esteem, participation in informal social networks and cultural perceptions) is mainly influenced by Jewishness of home background. To the extent that Jewish schooling is important, home background is 1.3 to 2.4 times more important.[2]

As I became more convinced that the family was an essential factor in creating individuals who felt themselves to be Jewish, I began to search the literature and the community for individuals and programs educating the family in the ways of Jewish living. While there was some discussion of parent involvement programs, such as the Parent Education Program (PEP) in the Conservative movement, these were mostly forms of adult education for parents. The literature was empty of reports of Jewish educators working with families. Professor Gerald Bubis, in the forward to his fine volume *Serving the Jewish Family*, published in 1977, lamented that he could not find any article by a Jewish educator to include in his anthology. Although his colleagues in the Jewish communal service field were developing programs called Jewish Family Life Education, most of these centered around teaching Jewish adults better parenting skills.

One additional influence was critical in my own thinking about this issue. In 1978, we moved to Encino, a suburb of Los Angeles, in part to be close to one of the most dynamic congregations in the American

Jewish community, Valley Beth Shalom (VBS). Its spiritual leader, Rabbi Harold Schulweis, had come to VBS in 1970 with a new vision of the synagogue and a perceptive analysis of the "psychological" Jew. Schulweis, too, argued that the Jewish family had lost its role as the first and most important place of Jewish learning. He called on the families of his congregation to join in small groups of family ḥavurot and encouraged parents to engage in Jewish study so they could, once again, become Jewish teachers of their children. It was a call that resonated within me as a congregant, as a parent, and as a Jewish educator.

With the arrival of our son, Michael, that summer, our family was complete. As confident as we were of the importance of creating a Jewish home, we were just as convinced of the need for our children to receive the best Jewish education we could find. Whereas most members of our generation had started programs of Jewish education with Hebrew school at age eight, our children entered Mommy and Me programs in Jewish pre-school at age eighteen months. Although the classes were good, we became keenly aware, as parents, that the resources to guide families to a life of Jewish celebration were meager at best.

In a conversation Susie and I had with a close friend and creative colleague, Judy Bin-Nun, then director of the first Reform Jewish Day School in the country—Temple Emanuel Community Day School—we developed the idea for a Jewish family magazine. I had found several publications for families in the Christian community and thought we could create something similar for Jewish families. We envisioned this as a way to reach parents of young children with ideas for celebrating Jewish holidays in the home, including the basics of ritual observance, information on the holiday, creative crafts, kitchen activities, stories, and games. It would be, to use the terminology of that day, "hands-on," printed on brown Kraft paper, with cute illustrations, and written in a light, accessible, and warm manner. We called it *Chicken Soup: To Nourish Jewish Family Life. Chicken Soup* was published from 1980 to 1986 and eventually reached more than 10,000 families. Although many schools did purchase copies of the magazine in bulk to distribute to their school families, it was difficult to convince some Jewish educators of its intended purpose. Teachers would use the creative ideas for holiday projects in their classrooms rather than send the magazine home. Some never quite understood that the target audience was the parents not the children.

The concept of families learning together was very new, and although the magazine was a success on many levels, it was clearly ahead of its time.[3]

As a faculty member at the UJ, I had begun to speak about the need to reach and teach Jewish families during my public lectures and scholar-in-residence appearances. In 1983, Dr. Max Vorspan, vice president of the University of Judaism, asked me to write a monograph for a University Papers series. In the paper, "Shall You Teach Them Diligently?" I outlined the forces of change buffeting the Jewish family and analyzed the challenges and opportunities facing parents who still aspired to be Jewish teachers of their own children. I addressed the relationship between the school and the home, arguing that, while the community had done an excellent job building the institutions of Jewish religious life—the synagogue and the school—Jewish educators had ignored the family as a locus for Jewish learning. They had assumed that the families who sent their children to their institutions also knew how to create homes filled with Jewish celebration and learning. However, David Schoem, in his ethnography of a suburban afternoon religious school, had observed that, for most parents in the school he studied, to be Jewish meant to step out of their daily lives to enter temporarily the Jewish world of the institution.

The myth of Jewish families living consciously Jewish lives in a mythical Jewish neighborhood community misled school professionals to assume something that simply did not exist. In reality, Jewish families had become dependent on the synagogue and on the school as the primary places in which to "be Jewish." Harold Schulweis put it another way: If the family can visit the synagogue's sukkah, why build one in their own backyard? I called for the creation of a two-way street between the institution and the home, envisioning the synagogue and school as resource centers for Jewish families to learn how to "do Jewish" in their homes. And, in a wistful idea that was luckily prescient, I outlined a university-based research and development institute for Jewish family education.

The following year, in 1984, I was approached by Jules Porter, then incoming president of the Federation of Jewish Men's Clubs (FJMC), to help conceptualize a project to follow-up the success of their Hebrew Literacy Campaign. Jules had in mind a program for teaching Jewish literacy, an initiative that would, like the Hebrew Literacy Campaign, depend on lay people teaching other lay people. I told him of my thinking and of my work with Jewish families and suggested a program centered on the teaching of holiday ritual skills for family celebration. The curriculum would include material for adults, designed to help them introduce or enhance Jewish holiday celebration in their homes. When asked which holiday to begin with, I unhesitatingly replied, "Shabbat."

Thus, *The Art of Jewish Living* series was born. Focusing on the Friday night table ritual in the home, the first book, *The Shabbat Seder*, created the model for the program. Using photographs and interviews of Jewish families and single people demonstrating and discussing their own experiences with the ritual, the book detailed very specific steps in organizing and celebrating a Shabbat dinner. Several principles guided the development of the material; principles, as we shall see, that ultimately became standard practice in the work of Jewish family education.

1. Don't assume any knowledge on the part of the learner.
2. Offer easy access into the texts and ritual behaviors.
3. Explain everything in great detail.
4. Give permission for the creative expression of ritual behavior.
5. Respect the diversity of family structures.
6. Encourage the adoption of small steps towards observance.
7. Emphasize the warmth and joy of the holiday.
8. View Jewish ritual time as Jewish family time.

With the support of Jules Porter and the creative input of my editor and friend, Joel Grishaver, *The Art of Jewish Living: The Shabbat Seder* was published by the Federation of Jewish Men's Clubs and the University of Judaism in 1985. We also produced an audio tape of the chants of the blessings, a table "bentscher," and a detailed leader's guide. Under the direction of Rabbi Charles Simon, the director of the FJMC, clubs throughout North America began to offer courses in the Art of Jewish Living, taught by lay people for lay people. It touched a nerve in the community and enjoyed an excellent reception. By 1988, a second course, book, audio tape, and leader's guide on the Passover Seder was published. Over the next ten years, three additional books appeared: *The Passover Seder* (in Russian), *Hanukkah*, and *A Time to Mourn, A Time to Comfort*.

The material found an audience eager for ways to enhance Jewish living in the home. Moreover, a growing number of Jewish educators found the series an effective tool in early work of Jewish family education. This encouraging response seemed to validate the idea of Jewish family education. The question remained: Could the idea grow into a field?

Seed the Field: The Whizin Experience

What is a field of educational practice? If we think of any well-recognized field in education, such as special education or adult education, we think of components such as:

A. A body of knowledge including conceptual definitions, theories, and research

B. Curricula, programs, methodologies and strategies for the practice of the field

C. A group of experts and specialists who devote their professional lives to the development and dissemination of the work in the field

D. Professional development and training opportunities—conferences, seminars and workshops on how to do the work

E. Practitioners—those who become "Jewish family educators"—the front-line professionals in the field

Jewish family education, to be considered a field, needed to develop all of the above. How do educational fields with these components develop? Sometimes, an academic researcher sparks the creation of a new field. For example, Piaget virtually invented theories of learning, and Lawrence Kohlberg founded the field of moral development. Alternatively, it is the practitioners who create the new approaches for solving the educational problems they encounter. Sometimes it is a single gifted practitioner who develops the important solutions. For example, Maria Montessori was a teacher of young children who developed from her own experience a unique approach to early childhood education. The field of Jewish family education developed from the practice of Jewish education; but it developed as a result of many people working simultaneously and independently. While I was pursuing my work, other pioneering Jewish family educators were making contributions to the emerging field.

Cherie Koller-Fox was working in Boston. Harlene Winnick Appelman, a Jewish educator in Detroit, was creating a program for families in a major Conservative synagogue, Shaarey Zedek, called "Jewish Experiences for Families" (JEFF). Using savvy marketing and creative programming which emphasized children and parents experiencing Jewish life together, JEFF quickly mushroomed into a city-wide effort, adopted by major synagogues and supported by lay leader Mandell "Bill" Berman and the Detroit Jewish Federation. In New York City, Jo Kay, a

Jewish educator at Rodeph Sholom, a large Reform temple, introduced the idea of parents learning Jewish content at the same time as their children were studying in religious school. The model came to be known as parallel learning and quickly spread throughout the Reform movement.

Other Jewish educators began attaching family education to their curricular work. Vicky Kelman, a curriculum writer for the Melton Research Center, wrote a series of materials designed for families entitled *Together* to be used with the Melton afternoon school curriculum. Joan Kaye, a consultant with the Bureau of Jewish Education in Boston, developed a reading-aloud program for parents and children called *The Parent Connection.* Joel Lurie Grishaver created "family homework" for his *Life Cycle Workbook* and expanded on the idea when he and his colleagues at Torah Aura Productions developed a series of materials for parents and children called *Building Jewish Life.* Janice Alper compiled an anthology of the new programmatic models in her book, *Learning in the Jewish Family.*

These pioneering efforts emerged from educational practice not from policy. These talented Jewish educators were problem solving. The problem: Jewish parents were not informed supporters of Jewish education and the Jewishness of many families was under siege. Harlene Appelman used parents' interest in visiting the planetarium as a hook to get families to experience havdalah. *Chicken Soup* emerged from the need to share creative ideas for home celebration. Audrey Friedman Marcus told Joel Grishaver he needed to explain what circumcision was to parents whose children would be reading his workbook. Vicky Kelman knew that parents and children could learn about Judaism together. In a sense, these practitioners were educational entrepreneurs, developing new approaches, models, and strategies to respond to a new educational reality.

Searching for a way to share with educators the growing body of experimentation in family education, I began to offer a course entitled "Reaching and Teaching the Jewish Family" in the annual Summer Institute for Jewish Educators at the University of Judaism. The first course, in 1988, attracted seven participants, mostly principals and teachers from local religious schools. I invited a few colleagues to make guest appearances in the course and to teach about the work they had been doing. Response to the course was encouraging. Simultaneously, the number of educators gathering at the annual CAJE conferences to discuss family education was steadily growing. Nearly everyone reported that their initial efforts at working with families were meeting with success.

A watershed in the evolution of Jewish family education as a field occurred in 1989. Arthur Whizin, his son Bruce, and Bruce's wife Shelley, created an endowment at the University of Judaism in Los Angeles to establish the Shirley and Arthur Whizin Center for the Jewish Future. Envisioned as a network of three institutes based on the three pillars of the future Jewish community—the family, the synagogue, and the community—Dr. David Lieber, then president of the University of Judaism, asked senior staff members to propose a program to launch the center.

I had just returned from a thrilling week with my family at the first Jewish Family Camp at Camp Ramah in Ojai, California, directed by Vicky Kelman. Having shared the week with some forty other Jewish families in that remarkable environment, and having watched and interviewed families who were profoundly effected by the experience, I was more than ever convinced of the need to create an address for the nascent field. Based on my initial concept put forward in the 1983 monograph *Shall You Teach Them Diligently?* and on the experience of an additional five years of work, I wrote a detailed proposal for an Institute on Jewish Family Education. After the idea was presented to the Whizin family, and upon the recommendation of Dr. Lieber, the Shirley and Arthur Whizin Institute for Jewish Family Life was created in the Spring of 1989.

A conversation with Joel Grishaver led to the first initiative of the new Whizin Institute. Joel had met Harlene Appelman at a General Assembly session in the Fall of 1988, and they concluded that it would be a good idea to gather together people experimenting with Jewish family education, perhaps as a pre-conference to CAJE. During the course of our work on *The Art of Jewish Living* series, Joel mentioned the idea. I replied that I might have the funding for such a meeting and suggested we convene a Think Tank to meet simultaneously with the course in Jewish family education I was teaching during the summer. Thus, the first Whizin Think Tank on Jewish family education was convened in June 1989, during the University of Judaism's Summer Institute. In an expansion of the "Reaching and Teaching the Jewish Family" course, the twenty Jewish educators invited to participate in the Think Tank met over four days, teaching in the mornings and deliberating in the afternoons, assessing the status of the field. Although they held different opinions about what constituted Jewish family education, they were unanimous on the need to continue meeting and to develop further a model for disseminating the work to an ever broader audience of institutions and communities.

Later in 1989, the Jewish Educational Service of North America (JESNA) sponsored a conference on Jewish family education in Newark, New Jersey, which attracted nearly two hundred participants. Speaking in the name of the Whizin Institute Think Tank, I argued that Jewish family programming should not be viewed as some sort of educational fad of the moment. Rather, we believed that a new specialized field of Jewish family education should emerge. Such a field would require research, curriculum development, and dissemination. It should also develop models of training, not only for Jewish educators, but also for rabbis, cantors, social workers, teachers, early childhood specialists, communal organizers, and perhaps most uniquely, lay people—parents, who it seemed clear, had to be brought into partnership with the professionals. The conference acted as a lightning rod, attracting a flurry of interest. Who knew that within a few short months a bombshell would hit the Jewish community that would explode the rate of development of Jewish family education programming in the last decade of the twentieth century?

The bombshell was the 1990 *National Jewish Population Survey.*[4] Its findings confirmed what many already knew—that the Jewish community was undergoing rapid change. An intermarriage rate of fifty two percent reflected the number of first marriages of born Jews to persons not born Jewish. This high rate explained the increasing numbers of Jews-by-choice and of non-Jewish members of Jewish families. The study offered the startling statistic that only seventeen percent of Jewish families in the sample were traditional nuclear families—two parents, both born Jewish, living and raising children in their first marriage. These statistics revealed the extent of the diversity of contemporary Jewish family structures.

A new call for initiatives to ensure Jewish continuity spread throughout the land. Although it was clear that Jewish education for children had to be intensified, the advocates of Jewish family education argued persuasively that these new facts of Jewish life made the task of equipping families with the information and skills to live Jewishly even more urgent.

Suddenly everyone wanted to know how to reach and teach Jewish families. Synagogues and community centers, facing precipitous drops in affiliation, sought to become "family friendly," offering family services and family holiday dinners. Although few principals and even fewer teachers knew how to educate families, schools began to get the message that the need to move beyond parent involvement in schools to family education was critical. Jewish family service agencies, many of which had already developed programs of Jewish family life education emphasizing parenting skills, saw an opportunity to broaden their work. Summer camps suddenly found a new market for their successful blend of informal education and residential experience with total Jewish living, and they began to offer "family camps." Nursery schools expanded into "parenting centers." Dozens of Federation communities, following the early example of Cleveland, created Jewish Continuity Commissions. Often their first task was to develop funding for new initiatives for Jewish continuity. In nearly every community, strengthening Jewish families was ranked at or near the top of the priority list. With newly-available community dollars and a newly-developed attitude about Federation-synagogue relationships, conditions were ripe for rapid growth in the field.

Several communities made significant commitments to Jewish family education. Cleveland's Jewish Continuity Commission ranked Jewish families high on the agenda and, with characteristic gusto, created a Jewish Fellows program at the Cleveland College of Jewish Studies with a special emphasis in Jewish family education. Graduates of the program were placed in newly-funded positions as Jewish family educators in local synagogues. Boston began its initiatives with targeted grants for congregations that developed programs for Jewish families. Detroit adopted the Jewish Experiences for Families (JEFF) program as a city-wide effort. In Los Angeles, the Bureau of Jewish Education created an office of Family Education and began to develop materials and models. Baltimore turned to The Jack Pearlstone Foundation for Living Judaism, which engaged the Whizin Institute to help conceptualize a variety of approaches, including a city-wide program of grants to local schools and congregations, wide-spread training opportunities, and a series of community events. The Institute also developed an insert for Jewish families that was placed in the *Baltimore Jewish Times*. A number of Bureaus of Jewish Education secured funding for a consultant in Jewish family education to assist constituent schools with programming. Chicago hired a consultant at the central agency for Jewish education to develop a communal approach.

Within the first five years of its existence, the Whizin Institute collaborated with Bureaus of Jewish Education and Federations to offer short-term training in Atlanta, Boston, Chicago, Detroit, Hartford, Metro West (New Jersey), New York, Philadelphia, the San Francisco Bay area, Seattle, and St. Louis. The leadership of Jewish educational institutions and Jewish communities rapidly warmed to the new field. Early programming was innovative, experimental, and exciting. Creative flair characterized the early pioneers and captured the imagination of the leadership of major Jewish communities. But would Jewish family education capture the hearts—the Jewish hearts—of the families themselves? Would they respond to the challenge to make their families the primary setting for Jewish education? Or would parents continue to depend on institutional settings as the place where Jewish learning took place?

The Importance of Jewish Families in Educating Jewish Children and Grandchildren

As the recently-popularized old African folk saying argues, "it takes a village to raise a child," and one of the most important components of the village is its families. In a time when both the Jewish village and the Jewish family appear to have lost their preeminent role in the raising of Jewish children, Jewish family educators have begun to sense that institutions alone—be it the school or the synagogue; the Jewish community center or the summer camp or the youth group—could not replace the family unit as the most important locus for Jewish learning and experience. As a result, there was now lots of work to be done. Why had so many Jewish homes ceased to be environments that were conducive to Jewish learning? How could the contemporary American family become an agent for Jewish education? How could the family provide the context for Jewish education? How could it also become Jewish education's client?

During the early 1990s, the creative efforts in Jewish family education developed against a backdrop of rapid change in American Jewish family life. When the idea of family education first began in Jewish education, many people in the Jewish community held what might be thought of as the "myth of the Jewish family." Reinforced by nostalgia and by images of the family of Tevye and Golde in the story Fiddler on the Roof, this myth implied that the Jewish family of the late-twentieth century resembled the normative Jewish family of the late-nineteenth century: one where a mother and a father, both born Jewish, both in their first marriage, bore children and created a family unit.

From the late 1960s on, the so-called traditional nuclear Jewish family was giving way to new family structures: single people, both young and old; blended families; single parents raising children; families with one parent converted to Judaism; intermarried couples; parents with adopted children; grandparents raising grandchildren; and other family structures of every conceivable type. The contemporary Jewish family had clearly become something other than the mythological family. It became evident that Jewish educators who wished to work with families would have to learn what was for most a whole new discipline: family systems.

Furthermore, new family structures are only one distinctive characteristic of the 1990s Jewish family. An even more pervasive characteristic of the family today is its tremendous busyness. Children are scheduled from early morning to night with every conceivable kind of program—lessons, athletics, orthodontics, and other appointments. Parents often work in fast-track jobs and must manage their careers while shuttling their children back and forth to any number of extracurricular activities. Daily life in many families today is so fragmented and hurried that during the week parents and children can rarely find the time to eat together.

And the parents of young children in the 1980s and 1990s are also very different than parents of earlier generations. Now both women and men pursue careers, and this results in a later average age of marriage. Couples are no longer getting married in their early twenties; by 1990, the average age of Jewish marriage was twenty-six, and there are many instances of people remaining unmarried well into their thirties and sometimes into their forties, delaying marriage until they have completed their educations and established themselves in good jobs. In keeping with these sweeping changes, many women now face the daunting task of pursuing a career and running a family at the same time.

Successful in their businesses and professions, many couples are also trend-setters and leaders in their social circles. As well-educated and accomplished as most of today's parents are in things secular, the Jewish background of many of these baby boomers is elementary and superficial.

Sophisticated and intelligent in most settings, when visiting the synagogue or confronted with Jewish practice, some parents feel intimidated, uncertain, and perhaps even embarrassed that their children know more than they do. These parents need more Jewish information and skills. Other parents, who may remember their Jewish education with distaste or aversion, think that they do not want any more of this education as adults. These parents need to be persuaded that there is different Jewish information and skills to be acquired than those to which they were exposed as children.

Families of the late-twentieth century lack another major component of earlier American Jewish life: a close Jewish community. The tightly-knit Jewish neighborhoods of an earlier time have disbanded, dispersed by sub-urbanization. Today extended families living close to one another are the exception rather than the rule. Many young people who go away to college do not return. Instead, they establish their own families in far-away cities; while grandparents, seeking relief from cold winters, often remove to the far-away sun-belt cities of Florida and the Southwest.

The pioneers in Jewish family education understand these families and their needs. In some cases, they are *them*: baby boomers who face the same challenges in their own young families. While their Jewish backgrounds might have been stronger, their understanding of the position of today's parents led them to offer learning opportunities that provided quality family time, excellent Jewish content, an opportunity to strengthen family and parenting skills, and a supportive network of other learning families to learn with.

Why is the family an important provider of context for the Jewish education of children? Because the task of Jewish education is enculturation. I, along with other Jewish educators, particularly my colleague Isa Aron, view the task of Jewish education as enculturation—the transmission of Judaism from one generation to the next.

In contradistinction to acculturation, the adaptation of one culture to forces introduced by exposure to another culture, enculturation is "the process of learning and being trained in a culture from infancy."[6] Enculturation is more specific than the broader phenomenon of socialization. Anthropologist Margaret Mead distinguished between the two in this way: "It is important to reaffirm the difference between the study of enculturation—the process of learning a culture in all its uniqueness and particularity—and the study of socialization—the set of species-wide requirements and exactions made on human beings by human societies."[7] Thus, while all children experience socialization into the family of humankind, Jewish children—if they are to grow up with a Jewish identity—must learn the norms of Jewish culture. How will such enculturation happen? There are three distinctive ways a person learns the behaviors and attitudes of a particular culture: observation, participation, and explicit communication.

A child's first learning comes from observation. A baby constantly explores the world around her, watching and eventually imitating that which she sees. I learned this first hand from an incident that set me on the path to becoming a Jewish family educator. Our eleven-month-old daughter Havi, seeing a patio candle in an Italian pizza restaurant, promptly began circling her hands over the flame, imitating the traditional motions of blessing the Shabbat candles. Most toddlers presented with a similar stimulus would blow out the candle or sing "Happy Birthday" because those are the cultural associations with candles that they observe as children. But Havi, having observed her parents lighting Shabbat candles in her home every week, had learned one norm of Judaism before her first birthday. She knew candles were for blessing. The creation of a Jewish environment in the home, with parents who engage in Jewish behaviors, creates opportunities for the child to observe Jewish living, and this is their first step in the process of Jewish enculturation.

Participation is the second step in the enculturation process. If a parent models how Jews behave, the child imitates this model, especially if the parent encourages the child's active participation. Thus, the emphasis in early childhood education is on teaching children to participate in the songs and movements of Jewish ritual practice, including lighting candles, chanting Kiddush, breaking ḥallah, and practicing the Four Questions at a model Seder. Play-acting is also evidence of enculturation through participation. One day, using wooden blocks, our children constructed a synagogue complete with pews, a bima, a Holy Ark in which they placed a stuffed Torah, and of course, a parking lot near the front entrance. We found them sitting next to this construction, wearing kippot (head coverings), wrapped in long winter scarves which doubled for tallitot (prayer shawls), and holding siddurim (prayer books).

When children are taken to the synagogue and their parents sit with them, or when they go to Jewish life-cycle events, or attend Jewish schools and camps, they have opportunities, not simply to observe Jewish settings, but also to participate actively in them.

Explicit communication is the third way enculturation takes place. The earliest, most central Jewish sources emphasize explicit communication as a way for one generation to tell the story to the next.

You shall tell your child on that very day: "This is what God did for me when I went out from Egypt . . . ." Exodus 13:8

"And you shall teach your children diligently, speaking of them when you are home and away, morning and night." Deuteronomy 6:6

Thus, the Passover Seder is the prototypical opportunity for communicating the master Jewish story. In daily life, parents and teachers who offer explicit instruction in how Jews behave engage in this step of the enculturation process.

Notice the degree to which the process of enculturation depends on knowledgeable adults who can model behaviors, encourage participation, and offer explicit information about Jewish living. Yet, we have already seen that many Jewish parents need to learn the norms of Judaism themselves before they can transmit them to their children. If one of the major tasks of Jewish family education is to equip parents with the information and skills of Jewish living, then the adults themselves must engage in the process of enculturation. In many families, both parents and children will be learning the norms of Jewish living simultaneously.

If Jewish norms are to be the content of this enculturation, then the following steps toward commitment represent the sequence in which this enculturation process takes place, particularly for adults. The first step in this process is characterized by compliance with the norms of Jewish living. Herbert Kelman, in his groundbreaking paper "Processes of Opinion Change," establishes criteria for the antecedents and consequences of compliance. The antecedents include accepting the normative power of a way of living. Judaism is a system of normative behaviors that calls for certain standards of conduct. When an individual agrees to respond to that call, that individual begins to comply with that normative system. Often this means "trying on," or experimenting with Jewish celebrations, rituals, and behaviors. Compliance with Jewish norms is usually selective. Behaviors and celebrations which seem "do-able" are attempted first. Kelman suggests that commitment to new behaviors is often tentative, needing oversight from others and continuing reinforcement. In short, compliant behaviors usually depend on external pressure. I light Shabbat candles at the synagogue's Friday-night communal dinner because everyone else does. Compliance is an initial step toward adopting norms as one's own.

The second step along the continuum of commitment is identification. Kelman posits that identification occurs "when an individual adopts behavior derived from another person or a group because this behavior is associated with a satisfying self-defining relationship to the person or group." Identification does not mean that the individual adopts these norms because they are intrinsically satisfying; rather, they are adopted because the individual recognizes that they are important to the group of which he or she wants to become a part. Identification differs from compliance because the individual does actually identify with the norms she or he adopts, and, here, the individual's behavior does not depend on whether others are doing the same thing at the same time. I light Shabbat candles in my home because the act identifies me with a culture and a people of whom I count myself a part.

The last step in enculturation is the internalization of the norms of the culture. According to Kelman, internalization occurs when an individual accepts these norms into her or his own value system. Unlike compliance or identification, the individual who internalizes behavioral norms absorbs the content of the norms and adopts them as her or his own. At this stage, the norms of Jewish culture are perceived to be similar to and contribute towards the maximization of his or her own individual values. When enculturation is complete, I not only comply with the norms and identify with others who share them, but I also believe in them. They are one and the same with the values I myself hold. I light Shabbat candles because I believe that by doing so I am demonstrating my commitment to Judaism and affirming my belief in Jewish norms. I light the candles regularly, even if I am alone, because I have internalized this act as normative behavior in my own life. The act defines me personally as a member of the Jewish people.

If the task of all Jewish education is enculturation, then the family must be seen as providing the context for all Jewish education. It is not sufficient to offer children only formal schooling, no matter how effective. It is abundantly clear that, if Jewish enculturation is to happen for children, it must first happen for the adults in children's families. Parents and grandparents make the important decisions about how Jewish a child's home will be: what holidays will be celebrated and in what manner; what blessings will be said and rituals performed; what involvement in the synagogue will be endorsed; and what kind of formal Jewish schooling and informal Jewish education will be made available. Adults in the family make all these crucial decisions. If they themselves are intimidated by, unprepared for, or uninterested in their role as enculturating agents, then the Jewish enculturation of children will not take place in the family.

What, then, is the difference between Jewish family education and adult Jewish education? While adult Jewish education is essential to the process of Jewish family education, until very recently the offerings of adult Jewish education had been designed only for the personal edification of the individual learner, not for the broader purpose of becoming a teacher to one's children. In Jewish family education, however, the education of adults has two purposes. The first is to engage the adult's interest. The second is to have the adult take whatever is learned back into their own family setting and teach it there.

To illustrate this difference, consider that an adult education course about the Shabbat is very different than a family education workshop that teaches adults how to conduct a Shabbat dinner experience in the home. In another example, a close friend attends a seminar on the Passover Seder. The teacher, a talented rabbi, offers an informed overview of the haggadah and an inspirational call for the participants to make their Seder more participatory and meaningful. Unfortunately, the rabbi does not take the next step and detail specific strategies for creating such a Seder. Although adult learning, "l'Shma," learning for its own sake, is an ideal all Jewish educators strive for, it is different than family education. For many adults, Jewish family education may open the doors of Jewish learning for the first time, but Jewish learning for adults does not, by itself, produce Jewish families.

Jewish family education represents a sea of change in the way many view the task of Jewish education. As noted earlier, in the 1950s, the synagogue religious school was seen as the appropriate arena for Jewish education because educators' assumed that a large percentage of the families sending their children to these schools actually performed in their homes the Jewish customs, ceremonies, and holidays that formed the basis of the school's curriculum. By the 1960s, it was clear that this assumption was no longer valid. Parents sent their children to synagogue religious schools so that they could become Jewish.

Once it became evident that the Jewish character of the Jewish home was no longer a given, educators adopted a new strategy: get the children away from the family and into a controlled Jewish environment. Summer camps, weekend retreats, youth group conventions, and Israel experiences provided total Jewish living situations (see Bernard Lipnick, An Experiment That Works in Teenage Religious Education) where Jewish educators could exert maximum influence over Jewish youth. However effective these experiences were—and evidence exists to support that they are among the most effective of Jewish educational experiences for children and teenagers—the programmers did little to ease the transition from these peak experiences to regular Jewish life at home and in the synagogue. In some cases, the exposure to such intense Jewish experiences actually caused religious rifts in Jewish families, for instance, in those cases where children returned home from summer camp far more religiously observant than their parents.

Jewish family education, in contrast, takes a different tack. It seeks to restore to the family its role as providing the predominant context for Jewish learning and experience. Although formal schooling and informal educational programming are indispensable to children's well-rounded Jewish educational experience, the family is missing from these contexts. Jewish family education is not a substitute for these; neither is it a substitute for quality adult education. Rather, it augments both by providing the context within which all of them fit.

The Nature of Jewish Family Education

As indicated earlier, an educational field requires conceptual definitions, goals, principles of practice, curriculum, content, instructional targets, program models, and an infrastructure. In many ways, Jewish family education is still evolving as a field, yet we can already discern the outline of several of its essential aspects, and we can review both the essential characteristics of Jewish family education and the key elements of family education programs.

We have said that Jewish family education establishes for families the context for all other Jewish education. Thus Jewish family education is not simply a series of programs for parents and children. In the Whizin Institute, we encourage practitioners to "think family," to look at all programs, all religious services, and all other events to see how they can all be made "family friendly."

Given this broad perspective, it is not surprising that, when the first Whizin Institute Think Tank meet in 1989 and addressed the task of defining "Jewish family education," the group had difficulty reaching agreement. What qualified as education? Who constituted a family? Did family education require only that parents and children come to the same event? Or did it mean that they would actually learn together?

We reviewed several activities called "Jewish family education" that did not meet our criteria for what we meant by Jewish family education. For example, in many model seders, even though parents and children might be in the same room, the children perform from a script while the parents observe their performance. But parents and children do not engage in a learning experience together, and it is doubtful whether the parents themselves feel empowered by this to create a better seder experience at home. Likewise, families may gather together for a Shabbat retreat in a camp setting but almost never engage in a Jewish learning experience. In short, we felt that simply getting parents and children together in the same place at the same time did not constitute family education.

We also reached consensus on expanding what we meant by "family" to include single parents, blended families, grandparents raising grandchildren, even singles who belong to a family of origin and have not yet established their own family. It was clear to us that, whatever our ideological or denominational position, the increasing number of Jewish families experiencing the impact of intermarriage or the outing of a gay family member or the adoption of a child or any one of a variety of other situations necessitated the broadest and most inclusive definition of the family if JFE was going to be responsive to its many constituencies in the Jewish community.

In retrospect, it seems obvious that any attempt to establish rigid definitions in this new field of educational practice would have been more limiting than helpful, especially if it were to be successful. Then as now, we understood that during these heady, early days of Jewish family education, the field required experimentation and innovation rather than one simple formula or structure. Innovation, experience, and practice would come to define the field.

So, the Think Tank arrived at a strategy, and the repercussions of that strategy are felt to this day. First, we agreed not to make definitions but to keep on discussing what might be good goals, good strategies, good principles, and good program models for Jewish family education. The following represents some of what we believed then and believe now.

Goals: Jewish family education seeks to—

1. Empower the family as an essential agency for Jewish learning
2. Strengthen the ability of family members to enhance the "Jewishness" of their homes
3. Increase the "familyness" of the family system, no matter what the family composition
4. Foster relationships between the home and Jewish institutions
5. Strengthen Jewish institutions by forming teams of professionals and laity to implement family education agendas
6. Connect Jewish families one to another

Strategies: Jewish family education aims to

1. Provide parents with the skills, information, props, and repertories for Jewish living
2. Emphasize doing rather than talking about Jewish behaviors
3. Offer access to a variety of paths leading to Jewish choices and commitments
4. Be free from ideological boundaries
5. Center activities around Jewish content and text
6. Take into account the complexities of family life
7. Stress the transference of the practice of Judaism from the institution to the home

Principles: As our experience working with families increased, and our insights grew, the following ten principles on good ways of work with families began to emerge—

1. Invite families in
2. Remove the obstacles
3. Offer family time together
4. Build programs around what families already like and know how to do
5. Watching children perform is not Jewish family education
6. Provide scaffolding
7. Encourage small steps
8. Jews need other Jews to be Jewish; it is very difficult to be Jewish alone
9. Jewish education is a retail business
10. Teach for transfer

Programming: Based on our experience working with families, Jewish family education programming has begun to change. The major changes in programming have involved these basic areas—

1. Program content
2. Program format
3. Program modalities

Experience and insight helped us to establish our ten principles of Jewish family education. We learned that you must invite families in because families need to feel welcomed in order to participate in the process of Jewish education. Too often the message still sent by our institutions is the old one: "Send us your children and we will make them Jewish." As a result of this message, we have created two generations of "drop-off" parents, for whom the most regularly practiced Jewish behavior is driving in a carpool. The question now is, Even when a new invitation is extended, how do we convince parents to get out of the car?

Jewish family educators must remove the obstacles because fear is one of the primary reasons parents will not engage in Jewish family education. Many Jewish parents are highly educated, intelligent, and successful human beings. They have graduated from good colleges, secured good positions in the workplace, and are high achievers. Accustomed to feeling in charge of themselves, capable and effective in most aspects of their lives, they enter Jewish settings and suddenly find themselves in an environment where they are neither knowledgeable nor capable nor effective. Their own religious school training—if any—may have ended at age thirteen. Many are only occasional visitors to the synagogue. While they may engage in Jewish customs at life-cycle events or during major holidays, it is rare that these parents feel competent to be in charge of the celebration. Although Judaism stresses that parents are to be teachers of their children, most parents have, until now, depended on paid professionals in the Jewish community to be their surrogates.

Our response as educators must be to create safe places for families to learn to be Jewish. For a school, synagogue, or center to be regarded as a safe Jewish place, it must accept people as they are; it must provide easy access to new learning; and it must be open to inquiry. Many parents will begin conversations with something like, "I'm not a very good Jew." This defensive statement anticipates negative judgments by the Jewish educator. To counteract this, Jewish educators must create a climate of acceptance. A second common conversation starter is, "I know this must be a stupid question, but…" In most circumstances, it is difficult to admit it when you do not know something you think you ought to know. This is particularly true when parents are standing next to their own children, who may know a lot more about things Jewish than they do. What can appear to educators as parental apathy may simply be parents' attempts to cover up their lack of knowledge. Unfortunately, it is sometimes easier to say, "I don't care," than "I don't know."

We have to offer families the opportunity to spend time together. The most precious commodity in today's culture is not money. It is time. Today's families operate at a frenetic pace and are desperate to find time to be together. Most parents work and struggle to find the time to shuttle children to school and to all sorts of activities. Sometimes the family dinner table is the back seat of a minivan. Many parents view the two hours children are in Sunday School as precious free time to catch up on their own errands. They have no time to undertake to the task of preparing a traditional Shabbat dinner. Yet parents actively hunt for opportunities to engage with their children in a shared meaningful activity. Thus, when a Jewish family education program can be seen as providing "quality family time," an obstacle can be turned into an opportunity.

Building on this, Jewish family education programs need to structure programs around what families already like and know how to do. What do families like to do together? How do they spend time with one another now? How can what they like to do now be turned into Jewish family time? In Detroit, Harlene Appelman used this principle to develop one of the most popular Jewish family education programs. Her objective was to teach families the havdalah service that separates Shabbat from the rest of the week. She started by noticing that what one needs to celebrate the havdalah ritual is wine, spices, a multi-wicked candle, and stars—three stars, to be precise, which indicate the Shabbat day is over. Then Harlene thought about where it was that families liked to go to see the stars. Her answer was the planetarium. Thus she devised a Jewish family education program entitled When Three Stars Appear, which attracted hundreds of families to the Detroit Planetarium to view stars through telescopes and then to learn how to conduct the havdalah ceremony.

What do families already know how to do? Well, perhaps the most fundamental family educational activity of all is reading aloud. The vast majority of Jewish parents reads to their children at least until their children learn to read on their own. So why not convince our families to read good Jewish children's literature together? This is precisely what programs such as Sefer Safari and The Parent Connection do: they get Jewish books into the hands of Jewish parents and provide them with discussion questions for the family to talk about while reading together. The brilliance of this program strategy is simple: by putting the considered, well-crafted words of a Jewish author into the mouths of parents, parents are given the script to become Jewish teachers of their own children.

One axiom of Jewish education is that when children perform, parents come. Yet watching children perform is not family education; school performances do not constitute family education. But performance-based programs, such as the Model Seder program, could be transformed into a family education experience if parents sit next to their children and participate with them, sharing a text or creating something to bring back to their own Seder table at home. We do not object that performance motivates parents to come to the school; we object to the limited vision of the model Seder, where children perform and parents observe them.

Provide scaffolding because many Jewish parents do not see Jewish living as accessible to their families. The Hebrew language is unfamiliar, Jewish rituals seem arcane and difficult, and three thousand years of accumulated Jewish literature is intimidating even to those with strong intellectual training. The Jewish family educator must find ways to provide unintimidating access to Jewish tradition and practice. At the beginning of the process, this often means depending on translations and transliterations. Unintimidating access to Jewish tradition and practice requires programs which coach, mentor, and model—programs which emphasize the experiential over the purely intellectual. This means finding ways to introduce Jewish living to the family.

Vicky Kelman contributed the notion of "scaffolding" to the field of Jewish family education. Citing Lev Vygotsky's theory of a zone of proximal development, "the distance between the actual developmental level (of the learner) as determined by independent problem solving and the level of potential development as determined through problem solving under adult guidance or in collaboration with more capable peers," Kelman thinks of scaffolding as the support required by families who are ready to take charge of their Jewish life as a family.[8] These supports may take numerous forms—encouragement, psychologically and physically safe space, invitations to move forward, and the props the family needs to experience Jewish living. Good family education programs provide appropriate scaffolding to move the family along its own unique path.

Encourage small steps because, for many families and the individuals within them, the journey into Jewish living can seem overwhelming and arduous. The process of enculturation outlined earlier involves stages of commitment that can take years to develop. It is difficult for those deeply involved in Jewish life to remember what it feels like to take the first tentative steps to introduce Jewish practice into the home. To the novice, the simple act of lighting Shabbat candles can seem quite complicated.

Thus, many family educators have adopted what might be called "the Rosenzweig Gambit." Franz Rosenzweig was a famous nineteenth century German Jewish philosopher and educator who was about to convert to Christianity. On Yom Kippur, at his intended final visit to a synagogue, he had a transformational experience which led him to reconsider his Jewish heritage. Rosenzweig came to the realization that he and his contemporaries had not truly learned the depth and complexity of Judaism. Rather than converting, he went on to establish the first modern program of adult Jewish education, the Lehrhaus Judaica, where he encouraged his peers to take their next steps on the path to Jewish awareness and practice. In a famous (and probably apocryphal) story, Rosenzweig was once asked by a skeptic curious about the progress of Rosenzweig's own Jewish journey, "Dr. Rosenzweig, do you keep the laws of kashrut?" To this question Rosenzweig replied, "Not yet."

"Not yet" implies a process, an approach that encourages taking the next step into one's zone of proximal development, a process rooted in the understanding that one traverses the Jewish path one step at a time and takes on new Jewish practices only when ready. "Not yet" keeps open the possibility of adopting a more demanding Jewish practice in the future.

The metaphor of "walking a path" resonates with biblical motif and rabbinic insight. From God's call to Abraham, "Lekh lekha," go out, to the naming of the system of Jewish practice "halakha," the Hebrew root word "holekh," to walk, reveals the nature of this understanding. It is a task of Jewish family education to empower families to get on the path and to help them take the next step. It does not matter that families, and the individuals within them, will always be at different points along many different paths, there will always be a next step for each family.

Jews need other Jews to be Jewish; it is very difficult to be Jewish alone. The Jewish liturgical system virtually mandates that prayer be in the presence of others, the minyan, the quorum of ten. Likewise, the adoption of Jewish practice in the home requires ongoing support and encouragement. Unfortunately, with the disappearance of cohesive Jewish neighborhoods, many Jewish families feel isolated and have little sense of Jewish community. Jewish family education recognizes the power that can come from gathering families together for learning and celebration. Joining families for mutual celebration of holidays and Shabbat dinners, matching families to form havurot, and linking families into learning communities are Jewish family education initiatives that extend beyond the limits of institutional settings.

In a society dominated by mass-merchandising, cookie-cutter franchises, and impersonal malls, families are in search of intimacy and personal attention, and Jewish education must become a retail business. In many large Jewish institutions, families often feel like just another "membership unit," with little opportunity to know the rabbi or other professionals. Many families report that the only time someone from the synagogue visits their home is when the congregation needs money. We have not yet developed within our institutions a Jewish practice that provides a system of personal or family counseling and mentoring. Yet, it seems clear that Jewish growth happens most often when individuals and families are influenced by the personal example of another. To offer families this kind of attention would require a rethinking of the professional and parapro-fessional laity in reaching out to marginal members of the community, as well as reaching in to the core families. Jewish families need personal attention—from their initial welcome into a community and throughout the lifetime of their association with the institution.

Jewish family education must teach for transfer if one of its major objectives is to effect personal Jewish knowledge and expression. Much of what happens in the public arena must be designed to empower the fam-ily to engage in Judaism back home. Therefore, take-home materials are de rigueur in most Jewish family education public programming. Vicky Kelman calls these materials "portable scaffolding," the support mecha-nisms that will assist the family in being Jewish. Portable scaffolding are supports provided by institutional programs that go home with the fam-ily to help the it take its next steps. Portable scaffolding may include texts, tapes, instructions, materials, ideas, enthusiasm or mentoring. Written material, crafts, audio tapes, and books are the most common portable scaffolding. Although the home is the family's personal, often private, space, the possibility of actual presentations or interventions in the home pushes the boundaries of what Jewish educators might do to involve Jewish families.

Based on the foregoing principles, our experience in building the field of Jewish family education has led us to begin to reshape educational pro-gramming. As a result, program content is changing. In the early years of Jewish family education, programs often centered on the celebration of holidays. With the experimentation of the past decade, however, virtual-ly every aspect of Jewishness—God, spirituality, prayer, ethics, Bible, social justice, healing, life-cycle events, tzedakah, history, and Israel—has become part of Jewish family education. Sometimes programs have com-bined Jewish content areas with more secular content, particularly around parenting and family dynamics. For example, in a curriculum developed by the Whizin Institute for Hadassah entitled Training Wheels, the les-son plans for each session include a section on the concerns of parents of toddlers: separation anxiety, nighttime fears, sharing possessions with others, etc. A program for families with teenagers in Detroit called Hazak v'Ematz incorporated the study of classic Jewish texts on defending one-self with actual instruction in martial arts from a self-defense expert.

Program formats are changing, too. Beginning with Jo Kay's pioneering model PACE—Parent and Child Education—parallel learning has become part of family education formats. Religious schools have begun to offer parents the opportunity to engage in Jewish learning parallel to their children. In this format, parents are invited to come into the school once or twice a month to study the same subject matter that their children are learning but on their own level. Often, parents and children conclude the day's study by engaging in a joint family activity.

Intergenerational learning is the most intrinsic form of Jewish family education. When the entire family is involved in the learning experience, learning is, by definition, intergenerational. At schools and synagogues, siblings of many different ages may come together with parents to engage in a program or a series of programs. Handling such a diverse group presents a considerable challenge to the program provider, who must create learning experiences that work for learners of widely varying abilities.

Might the Jewish family educator actually conduct programs in the home? Home-based programs are emerging. At the Whizin Institute, Vicky Kelman transferred the work of Roman Catholic family educator, Kathy Chesto, whose program FIRE: Family Intergenerational Religious Education, inspired Kelman's home-based curriculum for Jewish families' education, Family Room. After three years of development and field-testing, the Whizin Institute published Family Room in 1995. Family Room, is specifically designed to link Jewish families by working with them in their homes. Valley Beth Shalom sends "para-rabbinics" into the homes of bar/bat mitzvah families for individual counseling about the nature of the experience. The Parent Connection and Sefer Safari are examples of Jewish family education programs that reach into the home by offering Jewish books for parents to read to their children. Joan Walchansky's program in St. Louis, where educators go into individual homes, is another model of a home-based program.

Now program modalities are changing as well. Celebrations are one of the most popular forums for family education. They provide family quality time through celebratory experiences of Jewish holidays and life-cycle events. Shabbat dinners, havdalah ceremonies, Succot progressive dinners, Tu B'Shevat seders, and family services all offer the family the opportunity to worship and celebrate together. Workshops are a successful and often preferred method for families seeking to introduce or improve the level of Jewish expression in their homes. Workshops that teach the hows and whys of Jewish celebration are not theoretical. There is not much talking about the holiday. Rather, these workshops emphasize skills and behaviors to empower the family to "do Jewish"—to celebrate the holiday, to practice the ritual, to use the behavior.

Extravaganzas, pioneered by Harlene Appelman's Jewish Experiences for Families program in Detroit, may be institution-wide or community-wide events which attract, instruct, and entertain large numbers of families. Such an Extravaganza might be a Purim carnival featuring "stations" which offer families the opportunities to do a craft, hear a story, play a game, practice a ritual, dance, sing, or otherwise engage in Jewish experience together. Extravaganzas and other program modalities are described in Appelman's book Jewish Experiences for Families: A Manual, published by the Whizin Institute and the Detroit Jewish Federation in 1995.

Family camps, retreats, and trips are widely recognized as a most effective form of Jewish education. Camping offers participants a total Jewish living experience. Following the successful models of recreational family camping, Jewish summer family camps offer opportunities for families to come to camp together. On a local level, congregations can sponsor weekend Shabbat retreats that attract families. These experiences combine family celebration, study, parallel learning, workshops, and Jewish living in a natural environment. Vicky Kelman's model of Jewish family camp, first offered at Camp Ramah in California, is described in her book Jewish Family Retreats, co-published by the Melton Research Center and the Whizin Institute in 1993. Perhaps the ultimate form of Jewish family camping, a family trip to Israel, is described later in this volume.

Because ongoing Jewish family education must also take place at home, home materials are essential to serve as resources and supports for family celebration and learning. Jewish family educators and publishers of Jewish educational materials have developed books, tapes, celebration kits, magazines, newsletters, even computer programs designed for use by families in the home.

Creating an Infrastructure for Jewish Family Education
I believe that the development of Jewish family education represents a turning point in the history of Jewish education in America. Responding to the new realities of family life and the dissolution of Jewish neighborhoods and communities, the pioneers of Jewish family education have

begun to create a comprehensive vision of the tasks of Jewish education.

This vision of Jewish family education requires of Jewish educators a knowledge base and a set of skills in areas most have never studied. Jewish teachers, principals, and curriculum specialists with academic degrees and credentials from Jewish educator preparation programs in North America know about Judaism and about the classic areas of education: subject matter, classroom teaching methodologies and management, and school and classroom administration, with a heavy emphasis on elementary education. What have Jewish educators been taught about organizational theory and family dynamics? What were they taught about management, teamwork, community organization, and the politics of advocacy and grantsmanship? Very little; and as a result, a sustaining infrastructure for Jewish family education must include support in the following three areas: professional development, educational entrepreneurship, and defining new roles and responsibilities.

Professional Development

Family education has broadened the vision of Jewish education beyond schooling to enculturation, and few Jewish professionals were prepared for this change. The need to prepare a cadre of professionals and laity to implement Jewish family education became of paramount importance. What should be the content of such training? Who would be the trainers? What mechanisms existed or could be created to deliver the training? Who would pay for it? In our work at the Whizin Institute, a number of principles have guided our approach to the professional development of Jewish family educators:

1. Create an intensive opportunity for professional learning.

The annual Summer Seminar of the Whizin Institute became our "laboratory" for creating our model for professional development. Convened over a five day period, the seminar features a packed program of learning experiences, including plenary presentations, program workshops, mini think tanks, resource sharing sessions, study opportunities, team planning time, prayer experiences, and celebrations. Strictly limited to 130 participants, the Institute creates a feeling of intimacy and sharing. All sessions emphasize practical skills that can be immediately applied in the participants' own settings. A group of approximately fifteen

Whizin Institute consultants act as the core faculty, lending stability and continuity to each subsequent year's seminar.
2. Be as role-inclusive as possible.
Learning from the CAJE model, the Whizin Institute decided to be as inclusive as possible in terms of who could attend the annual summer seminar. Anyone with a desire to work with Jewish families was welcomed. In fact, specific outreach effort were made to recruit not just Jewish educators and teachers, but Jewish Community Center staff, early childhood educators, resource specialists, Jewish family service counselors, and others who did not necessarily fit the job description "Jewish educator."
3. Encourage teamwork to create a sea of change.
The Whizin consultants agreed that it would be difficult for any single person in a school, synagogue or center to create what they saw as a "sea change" in Jewish education. Particularly in synagogue religious schools, still the most predominant setting for children's Jewish education, the need to involve the rabbi, classroom teachers, and lay leadership seemed crucial for the new effort family education to succeed. Likewise, if a community seized upon Jewish family education as their response to the call for programs enhancing "Jewish continuity," then interagency teams representing the various institutions and stakeholders of a community might come to the Summer Seminar. In December of 1990, the Whizin consultants decided to offer incentive grants for "teams" from synagogues and communities to attend the 1991 Summer Seminar. The response to the call for applications was overwhelming.

In subsequent years, the Whizin staff promoted additional alliances and collaborations within the Jewish community that were unusual and imaginative: social workers and educators, publishers and teachers, day schools and congregations. The Whizin Institute explicitly rejected an institutional turf model in favor of collaboration across existing boundaries, both within institutions and between institutions.
4. Reach trans-denominationally; reach beyond denominational boundaries.
From the very beginning, the Whizin Institute was committed to

reaching beyond denominational boundaries. Teams from Reform, Conservative, Orthodox, and Reconstructionist congregations were awarded grants. Small ḥavurot and alternative communities were encouraged to attend the course. Diversity in religious expression was respected. The guiding principle was: "At Whizin, we teach methodology, not ideology."

5. Stimulate knowledge in many areas.

This new field demands a new set of information and skills, plus a spirit of creativity and experimentation, beginning with Jewish content. The centerpiece of the Summer Seminar course was Torah L'Shma, Jewish learning for its own sake. Whether rabbi or lay person, everyone was expected to study Jewish texts. "Jewish," after all, is the first name of the field.

- Increase educators' knowledge of family systems. With an audacious and possibly invasive attitude toward intervention into home and family life, it was clear that an enhanced knowledge of families as systems was of paramount importance to practitioners.
- Devise educational methodologies for the entire family. Devising strategies for intergenerational learning was a new challenge for most Jewish educators trained to work with children, or adults, but not both, together, in the same room at the same time.
- Study organizational dynamics. Schools, congregations, and communities are organizations that can be viewed through a variety of frames. The principles of organizational behavior and institutional change and transformation are not well-known in the Jewish education community. Building collaborative relationships and working with multi-role teams presented particularly sensitive challenges.
- Study marketing. In an environment where families are inundated by multiple messages and diverse demands for their attention, the need for Jewish family educators effectively to market their programs was essential.
- Study evaluation techniques. Broadly conceived, evaluation techniques can range from needs assessment to

determining the outcomes of programs, the effects of family education on family behavior, and the ways institutions change.

- Explore new sources of funding. New initiatives demand new sources of funding. Jewish family education was a prime candidate for grants, continuity agenda funds, and foundation awards. Techniques of grantsmanship were high on the list of new knowledge for many Jewish family educators.

- Gather in new thinking from new sources. The creativity evident in early forms of Jewish family education stemmed in part from a willingness to incorporate new ideas from sources new to Jewish education. In the early years of the Whizin Institute, a Roman Catholic family educator from Connecticut, a Mormon professor of family dynamics from the University of Southern California, and two psychologists specializing in the role of ritual in the family from Washington, D.C. brought their unique expertise about families to the Summer Seminar.

Educational Entrepreneurship

As an emerging field, the early years of Jewish family education demanded of educators an entrepreneurial spirit. Guided by the mantra "think family," programmers began to develop new approaches, revise tried and true models, and search for new ideas in related fields of practice. Many entirely new approaches, such as the Extravaganza described above, became the most popular programming models. Others were new takes on well-known forms of Jewish education, such as Jewish camping—universally recognized as one of the most effective forms of Jewish education, which became newly popular as resorts and universities promoted the idea of family vacations. Other models were versions of programs adapted from other religious traditions and translated into the Jewish educational milieu. As Jewish family educators discovered such family educators in the Christian community as Kathy Chesto, Margaret Sawin, and Dolores Curran, they sought to create programs for Jewish families that utilized some of the methodologies developed by these pioneers.

This notion of educational entrepreneurship presented a challenge for

Jewish educators and rabbis, who often thought of Jewish education for children as schooling and Jewish education for adults as simply courses and lectures. Jewish family education demanded something entirely new—new thinking, new strategies, new vision. As with most entrepreneurial efforts, some of these hit while others missed, but the overall effect was to infuse the field with a sense of excitement and challenge that was infectious and stimulating.

New Roles and Responsibilities

As the field has grown, a new job title has emerged in schools, synagogues, centers, and central agencies for Jewish education, that of Jewish family educator. Stimulated by Federation grants, most synagogues in Cleveland and Boston had a position for a Jewish family educator by the mid-1990s. Many Jewish community centers recruited Jewish educators to work with their families. These positions created new roles and responsibilities within the organizational framework of the host institutions.

In most cases, the Jewish family educator was responsible for the new family education programming to be introduced into the activities of the institution. In synagogue settings, this often meant developing grade-level programming for families in the school and synagogue-wide family events such as Shabbat dinners and other holiday celebrations. In centers, the new professional family educator developed programs for families in the pre-school, for youth programming, even for the senior populations.

As vital as these new positions were to the growth of family programming, they also presented challenges to the leadership of the institutions. For example, who would supervise the new Jewish family educator—the rabbi or the school principal? Would the Jewish family educator have a new committee of lay leadership? What would be the relationship between the Jewish family educator and the classroom teachers? A recent Ph.D. thesis at Stanford University by Lisa Malek investigates these and other issues facing institutions as they plan their work in the field.

In addition, nearly every major Bureau of Jewish Education had employed a "community Jewish family educator" by mid-decade. These senior consultants were responsible for advising bureau-affiliated schools and institutions on the development of family education programs, creating resources for family-educator training, and often implementing city-wide family education programming. Some professionals managed grants programs designed to stimulate the work with Jewish families. Jewish education had established positions or portfolios for Jewish family educators. By the time of the 1995 Whizin Institute Summer Seminar, a new "reference group" was added to those of rabbis, principals, social workers, teachers and lay people, that of Jewish family educator. That year, sixteen community Jewish family educators gathered during the Whizin Institute Summer Seminar for the first of what may be an annual meeting to develop further that network of professionals. The reports of many of these outstanding Jewish family educators are in this volume.

Agenda for the Future
The idea of Jewish family education is less than twenty years old, but during those twenty years, an educational novelty, some might even have called it a "fad," has become an educational field. Returning to our list of the components needed to establish a field of educational practice, we can now summarize, from our perspective, where the field stands today and where it might develop in the future.

Creating a Body of Knowledge
This volume of collected writings represents one attempt to gather together what we, at Whizin, know about Jewish family education. It is clear that one of the most important tasks for the future is the development of research and the documentation of practice. Fortunately, Jewish family education is currently the subject of a number of Ph.D. dissertations at major universities. The Whizin Institute has been engaged in studying the impact of attendance at its annual Summer Seminar. Some communities with major investments in Jewish family education, such as Boston, Cleveland, MetroWest (New Jersey), and New York, are assessing the effects of their funding upon constituent institutions.

Studies of how Jewish family education programs and experiences influence the Jewishness of the families who participate in them have yet to appear, although a group of family educators in Cleveland is doing research on what parents have to say about their own views of Jewish family education. We need to study more about how interventions are received by the family as a unit and by individual members of the family. We need to learn how Jewish experiences in the institutional setting transfer to the home. We need to attempt the difficult task of peering inside the family structure to test out the theories of enculturation which inform the work of the field. What we learn from these studies will help shape the Jewish family education programs of the future.

Developing More Experts

A number of talented individuals have devoted much of their professional lives to the practice of Jewish family education. Those who have served as Whizin Institute consultants—Janice Alper, Harlene Appelman, Adrianne Bank, Joel Lurie Grishaver, Risa Munitz-Gruberger, Jo Kay, Joan Kaye, Vicky Kelman, Esther Netter, Susan Shevitz, Rachel Sisk, Sally Weber, Bruce Whizin, and Shelley Whizin have graced the field with their talent, sensitivity, and enthusiasm for Jewish family education. Throughout the years, a coterie of outstanding educators, counselors, and academics has joined the core consultant group and lent expertise to the field. These and additional experts must come along and be drawn from many fields within the Jewish and the secular worlds.

Curricularizing Jewish Family Education

A creative potpourri of Jewish family education programs and curricula have come into being over the years. Yet much more work remains to be done in this area. Two specific interrelated challenges confront the field: a more consistent linking of Jewish family education experiences to the school curriculum, and the development of a spiral curriculum for Jewish families. This last point is particularly difficult. Ideally, a family entering a child into a Jewish preschool would begin a program of Jewish family education that would be carefully sequenced throughout the child's school experience until the child graduated from high school. But even if such an ideal sequence could be conceived, what should be done about families who begin at different points? Will they all have to start at the same entry level? And what is the family to do when the second child enters the system? Are they to encounter the same experiences over and over again with each child? We will need some creative thinking to deal with these issues.

Another challenge is the systematic development of what might be called level two Jewish family education. Excellent models exist for bringing what might be called the novice Jewish family into the start of Jewish living. What is the next step to keep the seriousness of such families? Here we might look to opportunities for in-depth family learning in ḥavurot-style groups or in family retreats and encampments. Encouraging in-depth adult learning and assisting parents with the smooth transition back and forth between their own adult Jewish education and their family's Jewish education may be another promising strategy. It has been started by the linking of Jewish family education programs with adult learning opportunities such as in the Florence Melton Adult Mini-School and the Wexner Heritage Foundation's adult learning programs.

Expanding Professional Education

One of the first tasks of a new field is to offer professional development opportunities to those who hope to be practitioners. A number of excellent programs have emerged on the local and national and even international levels. Communities mounting extensive professional education programs include Cleveland, Boston, New York, Chicago, Washington, D.C., and Hartford. Virtually every major Jewish community in North America and England has sponsored short-term conferences and seminars in Jewish family education. The Whizin Institute's annual Summer Seminar, "Reaching and Teaching the Jewish Family," continues to attract full enrollments. The University of Judaism's Fingerhut School of Education offered a Certificate in Advanced Graduate Studies in Jewish Family Education over two summers. Professional associations of Jewish educators such as CAJE, the Jewish Educators Assembly, and the National Association of Temple Educators continue to schedule workshops at their annual conferences.

Most of this activity has been devoted to retraining current professionals. There is clearly a need to expand these opportunities. Simultaneously, courses in Jewish family education should be required in the curricula of pre-professional preparation programs at the colleges, universities, and seminaries producing the majority of Jewish educators, communal service professionals, rabbis, and lay leadership for the Jewish community.

Job Opportunities

A field provides jobs for those who wish to work in it. During the past decade, the Jewish community has witnessed the creation of new professional opportunities for Jewish family educators. We look forward to continued growth in the jobs available in day schools, religious schools, synagogues, Jewish community centers, Jewish family service agencies, Jewish camps, and central agencies for Jewish education.

At the local institutional level, many congregations are creating positions of Jewish family educator on their professional staffs. In Cleveland, Boston, in funding these new jobs. Evaluative studies indicate greater success in implementing Jewish family education programming when someone on the professional staff carries this specific portfolio. When it is difficult for congregations to afford a full time staff position, some assign the task to an assistant rabbi, a head teacher, a youth group director, or engage a lay volunteer to coordinate Jewish family education activity.

The Jewish community center movement has also moved into Jewish family education. More than forty Jewish community centers across the continent have created a position of Jewish family educator. Likewise, a number of Jewish family service agencies have staff assigned to coordinate the work of Jewish family life education. The Whizin Institute has hosted specialized groups of JCC and JFS workers at the Summer Seminar.

Recently, Jewish day schools have discovered Jewish family education. Many day school leaders assumed that the families sending children to the most intensive form of Jewish education would not need programs of Jewish family education. Of course, the reality is quite different. The development of Jewish family education programming for the day schools is a major task for the future.

Finally, Jewish family camps have now been established in many of the major denominational summer camps across the country. Most have engaged Jewish family educators to direct these programs. An interesting and as yet underdeveloped area for Jewish family education are educational trips to Israel for families. Many institutions take family groups to Israel, but much work remains to be done in encouraging vendors of experiences in Israel to better organize for intergenerational family programming and in developing pre-trip and post-trip follow-up for families once they return home.

As for the Whizin Institute for Jewish Family Life, much remains on our own agenda for the immediate future, specifically:

1. Research on the impact of Jewish family education on institutions and families
2. Expansion of professional development opportunities to additional regions of the country
3. Continued relationships with the Jewish communities in England, Australia, and Israel as they further develop their

work in the field
4. Dissemination of community organization models such as JEFF and curricular models such as Family Room
5. Development of level two Jewish Family Education programming
6. Creating an Internet site for sharing resources among Jewish family educators
7. Convening the networks of Jewish family educators in central agencies of Jewish education, Jewish community centers, Jewish family service agencies, Jewish preschools, and Jewish museums
8. Collaborating with Synagogue 2000, a transdenominational project for the synagogue of the 21st century, to develop pilot sites of excellence in Jewish family education

Epilogue: A Concluding Story

In the fall of 1994, our family traveled to Ann Arbor to take Havi to the University of Michigan. On the drive back to Omaha, where we celebrated Rosh ha Shanah with the extended mishpaḥa, we noticed a sign near Dyersville, Iowa, that read, "Visit the Field of Dreams." One of my all-time favorite films, *Field of Dreams* was the story of a man, played by Kevin Costner, who hears a voice tell him: "Build it and they will come." He learns that "it" is a baseball field and, although nearly everyone considers him crazy, he plows valuable commercial crop land in order to build a baseball diamond, for exactly what, he has no idea. But, in the end, the ghosts of the infamous Shoeless Joe Jackson and his Chicago White Sox teammates emerge from the midst of the corn to seek redemption for their misdeed of throwing the 1919 World Series. As for the Costner character, his vision is rewarded in the memorable final scene when hundreds of cars appear in a line that stretches for miles waiting to visit this field.

We turned right on Lansing Road, named after Don Lansing, the owner of the farm on which the *Field of Dreams* movie was filmed, and after transversing several undulating acres of corn, we saw it. The white house, the small bleachers, and the shining diamond in the front yard, literally cut out of the crops, with the tall stalks forming the outfield fences. And, like thousands of other tourists, we made our pilgrimage: we walked the base paths, stood on the pitcher's mound, and yes, walked into the corn, imagining that Shoeless Joe might be hanging around, waiting for another game.

Those of us who envisioned a new form of family-centered Jewish education wondered, "If we build a new field, will they come?" Would parents get out of their cars and come into our synagogues and centers, our schools and camps, for opportunities to learn with their children? Would our institutions see the value in creating teams of rabbis, principals, teachers, and lay people to learn the strategies of family education? Would communities strive to overcome the turf battles among their constituent agencies and build collaborative efforts to reach and teach Jewish families? The answer to all of these questions is an unqualified "Yes."

This book and the stories within it are testimony to the power of the idea of Jewish family education. Yet, relative to other forms of Jewish education—religious schools, day schools, summer camps—family education is a very new field. It is a diamond in the rough, and it requires further polishing to reveal its brilliance. It is a field where the positions of leadership, both professional and lay, still await clear articulation. It is an activity where the rules of the game await further refinement. It is an adventure that begs to be undertaken.

As I stood on the pitcher's mound on Don Lansing's farm, I marveled at the mystery of hearing a "calling," that still, small voice within us that tells us to do something, to make a change, to follow a dream. Jewish family education has been a field of dreams—a field that has demonstrated its potential to make a significant contribution to ensuring the Jewish future. It is a field still abuilding—a field of dreams to make Jewish continuity a reality.

Endnotes

1. Harold S. Himmelfarb, "Jewish Education for Naught: Educating the Culturally Deprived Jewish Child," *Analysis* 51 (September 1975):4.
2. Geoffrey E. Bock, *Does Jewish Schooling Matter* (American Jewish Committee, 1977).
3. The publication of *Chicken Soup: To Nourish Jewish Family Life* was supported by a grant from Florence and Samuel Melton and the Arnold and Kay Clejan Educational Resources Center of the University of Judaism.
4. Council of Jewish Federations, with the Mandell Berman Institute, North American Jewish Data Bank, the Graduate School and University Center, CUNY, *Highlights*

of the *CJF 1990 National Jewish Population Survey* (New York: 1990).

5. For a discussion of enculturation, see Ronald G. Wolfson, "A Description and Analysis of an Innovative Living Experience in Israel," Ph.D. diss., Washington University, St. Louis, 1974 and Isa Aron, "The Malaise of Jewish Education," *Tikkun* 3 no. 4 (May/June 1989): 32-34.

6. Felix M. Keesing, *Cultural Anthropology* (New York: Holt, Rinehart and Winston, 1958), 35.

7. Margaret Mead, "Socialization and Enculturation," *Current Anthropology* 4 (April 1963): 187.

8. Lev Vygotsky, *Mind in Society: The Development of Higher Psychological Processes* (Harvard University Press, 1978) 85.

Bruce Fabian Whizin, with his wife Shelley, is the co-creator of the Shirley and Arthur Whizin Center, Dedicated to the Jewish Future at the University of Judaism in Los Angeles. Bruce has lived the true meaning of "partnership" and is directly involved in two institutes of the Whizin Center, the Institute for Jewish Family Life and Synagogue 2000, a Transdenominational Project for the 21st Century.

Bruce is executive vice chair of the University of Judaism and serves on many boards: the Whizin Center, Camp Ramah, the Jewish Community Foundation of the Los Angeles Federation, the American Technion Society, the Chaim Sheba Medical Center in Israel, and the Jewish Funders Network. He also serves on various committees, such as American Youth in Israel and the Department of Continuing Education at the University of Judaism. He manages the Whizin Foundation and the Whizin Shopping Center.

Bruce will listen to practically anything anybody wants to talk to him about. He has had two complete careers, that of restauranteur and that of hypno-therapist/Shamanistic healer. He loves to travel and write poetry and is looking forward to making time for Torah study and learning Hebrew. He swims a mile a day. His favorite television show is X Files. *He has four sons, four grandchildren, and is blessed with his wife, Shelley, and daughter, Sarah.*

Bruce Fabian Whizin

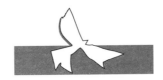

48

Weathering the Storm
Bruce Fabian Whizin

The Beginning of Whizin

I will never forget that sunny day in early February of 1989 when Whizin was born. As with any birth, it seems like only yesterday that my wife, Shelley, and I were sitting in the University of Judaism (UJ) board room with the chairman, Jack Ostrow, and with Irving Brott and Rabbis David Lieber, Max Vorspan, and David Gordis, discussing what might be the initiating body of work for our newly created Shirley and Arthur Whizin Center, Dedicated to the Jewish Future. We felt that for there to be a Jewish future, there would need to be three pillars of strength: the family, the synagogue, and the community. What we did not know was what we could create in order to support this notion.

Previously, we had heard presented two options for how to proceed, and we were about to listen to a third. Dr. Ronald Wolfson, a faculty member at the UJ, sat down in front of us and pulled out a stack of papers about a foot high. I thought to myself that they must be the copies he intended to distribute to all of us. To my great surprise, they were Ron's own copies, and we were each given our own foot-high stack of papers. As Ron began to talk about the importance of families to the Jewish future, little shivers of goose bumps began to break out on the back of my neck, and I found out later that Shelley had had similar feelings about what we were hearing. We felt we were on the right track. And so began the Whizin journey.

The Shirley and Arthur Whizin Institute for Jewish Family Life is a culmination of experiences that span many lifetimes. Thinking about this Whizin journey takes me into my past, to reflect on the various experiences I had while growing up with parents who were very much

49

involved in the "corporate" Jewish world while not ever having a "real" Shabbat dinner at home. So, as I look back, I remember...

My Growing Up

The Valley Jewish Community Center (VJCC) was conceived in 1937. My parents, along with several other families, had been meeting for some time to create the first synagogue in the San Fernando Valley, just north of Los Angeles. The Valley, then, had a population of less than 10,000 people along with thousands of walnut, orange, grapefruit, and other fruit trees. The Los Angeles River was in my back yard, where I hunted for crawdads and threw rocks at trout. It was beautiful. It could have been the garden of Eden.

This group of Jewish families were determined to purchase a building of their own; in the meantime, they were occupying several temporary spaces. Finally, a building was found and (VJCC) was transformed from a gambling hall and speak-easy (a term used during prohibition for a bar) into a synagogue. I remember my dad and others mixing concrete in wheelbarrows and pouring the cement slabs that became the foundation of our Temple. We kids were always getting in the way, of course, but we were first in line for the sandwiches and sodas passed out for lunch. That synagogue is known today as Adat Ari El, in North Hollywood, the home of over 1,000 families.

My Rudimentary Jewish Education

Some of my fondest memories are of standing with my friend Chukka—even though our names were Charles and Bruce, we called one another Chukka and Brukka—and singing at the top of our lungs. We knew the entire prayer book by heart, and we used to see who could go through the whole service without having to refer to the book. We had no official Hebrew school, only Sunday school, so we learned all the Hebrew by the transliterations of the text and chants. I thought it was great fun, and I guess that's where my deep feeling for our tradition began to take root. I didn't know at the time that I was being raised as a Conservative Jew, or even what that meant. Without an adequate Jewish education or knowledge of Hebrew, however, I lacked what would make me comfortable as an adult in shul. I realize that, for most of my life, the only time I have been truly comfortable in shul is when I do not use the siddur. When I'm fully engrossed in the atmosphere, the chanting of people around me, the music, and my own internal meditative state, only then do I really feel at "home" during services. And also, when I am holding the Torah.

In 1944, during the Second World War, I was one of those "ninety-day wonder-kids" who became a bar mitzvah without knowing any Hebrew at all. I was given a transliteration of the prayers and I memorized them. Wallets and fountain pens were very popular then, and I got so many wallets that I didn't have to buy a new one until I was thirty-eight years old. It was during that time period that every bar mitzvah boy—there were no bat mitzvah girls during that time—rehearsed his speech with the words, "Today, I am a fountain pen." So, was that all there was to my Jewish spirit, my Jewish soul?

Inspiration and Deviation Along the Way

I was inspired by a few teachers and rabbis who influenced me. I think the best part of my Jewish education was listening to Rabbi Max Vorspan's sermons at High Holy Days for twenty-five or thirty years. Max showed me the part of Judaism that makes you think. The High Holy Days have always been a special time for me—a time of reflection, a time of spiritual reconnection, a time when I could alter, or change the direction of my psychological, emotional, and spiritual life. It's the only time and place I can write poetry in my mind, remember it word for word, and write it down later—without missing a beat.

rosh hashana 5742

> *once more G-d we are here, together, you and me...*
> *what a year, so much growth, so much change*
> *I thank you for your help, for your guidance,*
> *I would not have made it, without you...*
> *your light has given me strength, love, and happiness*
> *you are truly my friend, you are no longer someone,*
> *or something, up there...*
> *you are with me, always, you are the best of me,*
> *I am the best of you*
> *I cannot tell where you end in me and where I begin in you...*
> *when I love others, you are loving them too,*
> *when I love me, I feel you loving me...*

I am so full with what I am receiving from you,
that it spills out to all I see...
I am you now, that is the bond we have forged together...
on this the first day of rosh hashana 5742,
the birthday of the world,
I celebrate my birth, my union, with you...
I pledge myself in service, to you...to do your work,
now and forevermore...
G-d is the strength, in which I love...
G-d is the love, in which I trust...
9/29/81

In 1968, at the tender age of thirty-seven, I went back to college and majored in anthropology. It seemed that all my earlier education had been such a disaster that I felt I had just begun to open myself for higher learning. I was not one of those "A" students most of my life; I graduated from high school with a C- average. I remember doing home work in only one class, civics. We had a twenty-question quiz each Friday, and a two-hundred question constitution test for our final, and I never missed an answer the entire semester. So, somewhere lurking inside me was a scholar just dying to get out.

While in college, I was meditating and doing Yoga and my "temple/shul" became the outdoors: camping, backpacking, and writing poetry. This was, of course, during the height of student activism around social and political issues brought on by the civil rights movement; the assassinations of JFK, Bobby Kennedy, and Martin Luther King; the psychology therapy explosion; and the Vietnam War. I was right in the middle of it. I was a student organizer and wound up being the Peace and Freedom Party's candidate for treasurer in the 1968 California general election. Not much Judaism, but a lot of social action, and after all, that's what Judaism stood for, wasn't it?

During this time my Jewish life consisted of celebrating the holidays and leading the family seder. I had taken over that role when my father handed it over to me when I was fifteen. And, of course, being in shul for the High Holy Days. I have to admit that synagogue life for me was bereft of anything spiritual, except for the poetry that "came through me" during High Holy Days. Other than the holidays, I don't think I even walked into a synagogue from 1968 to 1989, although I did attend bar and bat mitzvahs, and picked my kids up at Hebrew school. Organized Jewish life held nothing for me, despite the fact that during the fifties and sixties I was a "Ten Year Key Man" with the United Jewish Appeal, an award they give to individuals who've spent ten years as a division chair. Outside of being and feeling intensely Jewish, the only deep spiritual connection I felt was during High Holy days.

I spent a lot of time with many Jewish young men and women who became Buddhists or Sikhs or joined the Moonies. During this self-oriented period of time, whenever someone asked me what religion I was, I would say, "I'm more than Jewish." I couldn't understand why our tradition, which had such a richly contemplative and personal connection with ha Shem, was almost completely cut off from any personal connection with G-d through meaningful practice. I found it terribly sad for our people, our culture, and our religion that we lost so many of our brightest and best to other faiths and practices because of the religious priorities in what we chose to expose our children to. Since being involved with the Whizin Institute, I have heard many wonderful stories that inspire the heart, but somehow back then, we just weren't aware that they existed, and many of us looked elsewhere for answers.

We lost many young people during what I refer to as "the time I left the organized Jewish community." I want to emphasize "organized," because for me, while I was not active Jewishly, those years contained many rich Jewish experiences, mostly because of what I brought to the table, not because of what was brought to me. The paradox was that we had one of the most deeply spiritual of traditions, one that was supposed to be filled with a mystical, spiritual connection to the universe, one that was richly contemplative, and established a personal connection to G-d, Kabbalah, Jewish mysticism, and other spiritual practices, so how come we couldn't have "grabbed these young people" and held them within this rich tradition? It was quite disturbing.

Returning to Rooted Rituals

After the creation of the Whizin Institute for Jewish Family Life, I became more intrigued with the multitude of brilliant Jewish teachers, scholars, and rabbis. Shelley and I attended Jewish family camp at Ramah and spent weekends with various scholars in residence. One of the most incredible experiences I ever had in shul took place at a Camp

Ramah Academy weekend with Rabbi Yitz Greenberg. I shared my feelings of inadequacy with Yitz and told him that the only time I felt comfortable during services was when I put the siddur aside. And he said "Don't open the prayer book, there are many ways of davening, each person has to find their own way." So, I left my siddur unopened, and as luck would have it, I was given the honor of Hagbah that Shabbat.

I will remember lifting the Torah, and what happened then, for the rest of my life. As I grasped the handles, a pulse went threw my hands. I sat down, and when the Torah was wound or "dressed," I held it in my arms, and I felt each Hebrew letter enter each cell of my body, my mind, and my spirit. Every cell "smiled and cried with tears of joy." I sat there enraptured, with tears running down my cheeks, until someone touched me on the shoulder and indicated that it was time to "give up" the Torah. The only description I can give for the feeling was, "a state of total oneness" with the Torah. Torah was me and I was Torah, there was no separation.

The Shabbat Queen Appears

I mentioned at the beginning of this chapter that I never had a "real" Shabbat dinner growing up. In fact, my very first Shabbat dinner was shortly after we had our first Whizin board meeting in February 1989. Ronnie and Susie Wolfson invited us to their house for Shabbat dinner. I remember looking at Ron and seeing his week of work "drain away," and as the Kiddush and motzi were chanted, the stress of my week also drained away. I'm old enough to remember the old gas pumps that had a ten gallon glass tank on top, and as you filled your car with gasoline, the fuel in the glass tank, which was a reddish-orange color, drained away. That's exactly what the feeling was like at the Wolfson's Shabbat table.

Shelley and I looked at each other. Tears filled our eyes, and even though nothing was said, we knew our home life would change. We immediately started having Shabbat dinners, and until the 1994 earthquake, we celebrated the coming of Shabbat at our dinner table or those of our friends on most Friday nights. It took about a year for me to stop working on Saturdays. Not working on Shabbat has been wonderful, since I worked weekends for the first forty-three years of my life, often working all seven days of the week. I started working when I was nine, mowing lawns and other stuff until the age of thirteen, when I started working in our restaurants and ice cream parlors. So, to take off one day a week, and the same day at that, for over six years now, has made me envious of Jews who have been raised since birth with this behavior. At the beginning of Shabbat I, too, now feel my week "just drain away."

It is strange to me that I had to wait until I was fifty-eight years old to experience what so many Jews feel when Shabbat begins. In looking back at Friday night dinners at home when I was growing up, my mom did light candles, but it was something she did privately before we came to the dinner table, and we never did Kiddush nor the motzi. This was even stranger, considering that my mom was raised in an Orthodox home, always went to shul, and her maiden name was Cohen. I don't mean to demean my mom. She is responsible for the deep love and affection I have for our tradition, but it is just one of those strange examples of how many of us Jews are raised with bits and pieces of our tradition.

Filling a Need, Personally and Professionally

These stories represent some of the reasons we were so excited about establishing the Whizin Institute for Jewish Family Life. A change needed to happen to light the spark for families to help them kindle their candles—and for me to kindle my own—and celebrate their Jewishness together, forming memories that would last lifetimes. We were thrilled to be part of what seemed to be an ever-growing entity which is genuinely feeding and nurturing the Jewish community in a way never done before, looking at the family as the context for Jewish learning/experiences.

Ron filled us with information about the field of Jewish family education—what it lacked, what he thought we needed to do, and the people we needed to brainstorm with. That first year, the deadline had already passed for the Institute for Jewish Family Life to be included in the University of Judaism's Summer Seminar catalog, so Ron called together fifteen educators interested in Jewish family education and invited them to come and spend four and one-half days with us at the UJ. They were to teach those who would come to the Summer Seminar, as well as to participate in a Think Tank, and envision what an Institute devoted to Jewish Family Life Education would look like. Twenty-eight people enrolled for the session in addition to the fifteen invited Jewish family educators, and so the saga began. Even though Whizin was not to begin officially until July 1, we actually held a first summer session at the end of June 1989.

That first Think Tank was exciting and challenging. The participants mostly knew each other, but Shelley and I were meeting them for the first time. During the introductions, I remember saying that the Whizin Institute would be successful to the extent we could each let go of "turf" issues. I added that "lay persons" would have to let go of the sole right to dictate policy and that "professionals" would have to let go of their sole right to create content and curriculum. For me, this is what enabled everyone to begin to take ownership of Whizin and make it a unique and successful partnership, growing in depth and breadth, a working model in the Jewish community. These "official" Jewish family educators gathered together for over eight hours each day for five days. In the past they had only been able to meet, as they often said, "over stale coffee at midnight, during conferences and workshops where we are teaching." And so, from this day forward, our lives would be changed forever.

Why the Whizin Institute Works

For me, there are six components essential to the success we have had with the Whizin Institute for Jewish Family Education. First of all, it's the faculty. These are the most talented, creative people I have ever worked with. Without them Whizin would not be Whizin. There are others out there in the universe, many of whom I have met, who may be just as talented, but I have not worked with them as intimately as I have with the Whizin faculty. They are led by Ron Wolfson, and I simply do not have words to describe what I feel about Ron. The neshuma of this human being is awesome. He generates excitement the moment he begins to speak. His enthusiasm and passion for his work reflects in the ambiance that is immediately created by his presence.

Secondly, it's the participants who come to the Summer Seminar every summer. They are among the most dedicated people I have come across in my sixty-six years of inhabiting this planet. They are bright, energetic, and thirsty for knowledge; and they love what they do. They come with a wide range of experience, wisdom, and ruach, which they share with everyone. They are always willing to learn more, more, and then more, and share, share, and share again. In the final analysis what we, as faculty, learn from them continually enables us "to raise the level of our game."

Thirdly, our organizational structure enables us to be extremely flexible when it comes to the delivery of our teaching and training. We have turned the organizational pyramid upside down, onto its apex. We see ourselves as consultants and resources for the people who come to us and those we service in their own environments. One memorable example, for me: during the 1991 Summer Seminar, at the conclusion of the first day's program, we knew that what we had designed was not meeting the needs of the ninety-eight people who were attending. At our 6:00 P.M. staff meeting, we completely redesigned the remaining three and one-half days of programming in about thirty minutes.

We believe that policy and programming is best created by having an organizational structure immediately responsive to the population being served. So, policy is determined by what is happening. Policy needs to result from action, rather than action and content resulting from policy. I think, more than anything else, this is what drives Whizin, and it is gratifying to be involved with people who are aligned with this notion.

Also, because we have let go of our own turf issues, we have now developed a common language that enables us, not only to finish each other's sentences, but also to not have our egos tied up in having to finish our own sentences. This has come more easily than expected but not without some pain. It has emerged slowly out of the deep respect for the integrity, experience, and wisdom we hold for each other. While this may sound like a Pollyanna description, it is not. Good communication has only come because of a strong dedication, on the part of everyone involved, to get the job done. We have become an integrated, focused team.

Fourth, the University of Judaism, home of the Whizin Center, Dedicated to the Jewish Future, of which the Whizin Institute for Jewish Family Education is one part, has provided an environment that is totally supportive of our work. The Summer Seminar is the "engine" that drives the Whizin Institute for Jewish Family Education. By 1992, at our third Seminar, we had one hundred and thirty-five participants and twenty-two faculty members, and we've purposely kept it at that number ever since. The Seminar is four days of non-stop learning, sharing, teaching, and being, in an atmosphere that is indescribably delicious. Delicious? Yes, delicious is the only word I can come up with.

Fifth, is the idea of teams. As we worked through issues of ego and turf in order to accomplish a job bigger than each of us, we realized if we were really going to get the job done, we needed to bring teams to Whizin— teams which can transform institutions. Teams can only work when the participants put aside "turf issues" in order to get the job done.

I want to draw a distinction between being competitive and the idea of competition. While on the surface there does not seem to be much difference, I believe there is because of what I have learned about the root of the word *competition*. Competition comes from the Greek word *compartier*, which means *to seek together*. This concept was the philosophy behind the original Olympic games. Athletes sought together in order to achieve athletic harmony of the mind, body, and sprit. When I learned of this concept, it put a whole different spin on the way I looked at competition, and I coined the term intentionally cooperative for what I meant. That is the spirit behind the team concept at Whizin.

In preparation for our second Summer Seminar, we began to invite teams to participate, and to give modest grants to those teams. The first teams were to be composed of a rabbi, a senior educator, and a lay person. The following year, we requested that a classroom teacher be added to the teams coming from schools and synagogues. We also began seeing requests from community teams that wanted to come to the Seminar. Community teams have ranged in size from four members from one city to the twenty-five-person inter-agency team that came from San Diego.

And the sixth aspect of our success is also something that came up very early. I began to take exception to the term "lay person." After much playing around with words, I came up with the term "tzedakah professional." It seems to me that dividing Jewish communal workers into professionals and lay persons just perpetuates some of the turf issues, and is not an accurate description of what "lay people" bring to the table. Everyone is a professional in their own right, and they bring professional skills to the institutions they serve. So, Shelley and I are "tzedakah professionals," and Ron and the faculty of family educators are "professionals who do tzedakah." I know this is a play on words, but in my work as a therapist, I emphasize changing language. I teach that when you change even one word, a whole new world opens up in front of you, and your perception of what you see, and what you get, changes dramatically.

My Own Jewish Work

As I became more involved in the Whizin Institute for Jewish Family Education and the University of Judaism, I learned more about Judaism. One of the most vivid memories I have is when I first heard the story of what happened with Moses, when G-d told him it was time for him to die. I was at family camp and Rabbi Eddie Feinstein told us this midrash of Moses drawing a circle around himself, starting to pray, and in effect saying to G-d, "No, I won't go." When I heard that Moses's prayers were so powerful that G-d couldn't shut them out, and that the very fabric of the universe was in danger of being ripped asunder, I started to cry. Here I was, fifty-nine years old, and I had never heard this story before. I also got angry. Why didn't my kids ever hear this midrash and other stories that would have made a tremendous difference in their Jewish lives? Incidentally, Moses didn't "want to go" because he was alone. G-d took care of that. Perhaps there's a lesson here for us?

My thirst for knowledge has grown immeasurably. Shelley and I enrolled in classes at the University of Judaism, attended three or four Ramah Academy weekends per year, and started reading Jewish books and getting involved in study groups. Shelley enrolled in the undergraduate program at the University of Judaism's liberal arts college, but unfortunately, our studies were interrupted by the earthquake. We had to bulldoze our ninety-four-year-old home. But from the ashes rose a phoenix, and we built a new house with a kosher kitchen.

Who would have ever thought that Bruce Whizin would have a kosher home? I wonder what my mom and dad would think about that? Shelley has returned to school and is presently working towards her bachelor's degree in Jewish Studies, and my own studies are continuing. I intend to start writing more Jewish poetry and more Jewish commentary. I was even invited to do a d'var torah one Shabbat at my synagogue, Adat Ari El, and I've begun to learn Hebrew. I've been asked to do another d'var in the Fall. My goal is eventually to read our sources and be able to translate Hebrew from original texts. That may take me ten or fifteen years, but seventy-five or eighty seems like a good age to start doing something that is exciting, challenging, and productive.

All in all, whatever else the Whizin Institute for Jewish Family Life has given to other people, I feel that it has enabled me to come full circle. I was born from a Cohen mother named Sarah, with a father whose Hebrew name was Abraham; I was bought back in a pidyon ha'ben by my uncle Irwin Cohen, after a suitable brit m'lah; and I am, after many years of doing other things, now doing that which I was called to do, G-d's work in the Jewish world.

Adrianne Bank has been the evaluator for the Whizin Institute for Jewish Family Life almost from its beginning. Currently, she works as a consultant helping many Jewish federations, bureaus, schools, synagogues, and agencies do the strategic planning, program evaluation, and change management which will serve them and the Jewish people well during the next century. She is an adjunct faculty member in the Master's in Business Administration program at the University of Judaism, teaches at the Center for Non-Profit

Adrianne Bank

Management, and spends time on many boards and committees. Her most recent publication is Pathways: A Guide to Evaluating Programs in Jewish Settings, *published by JESNA.*

In a former life, Adrianne was involved with many public school reform projects as associate director of UCLA's experimental University Elementary School and of UCLA's Center for the Study of Evaluation. She has a Ph.D. from UCLA, a very knowledgeable spouse, three well-informed adult children, and two precocious grandchildren.

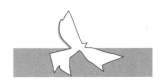

View from Mulholland Drive
Adrianne Bank

Whizin: The Metaphor

Mulholland Drive winds along the spine of the Santa Monica mountains for about fifty miles. I travel a short way along this road whenever I go to 15000 Mulholland Drive, the Whizin Institute office, housed at the University of Judaism. The view from Mulholland changes at each turning in the road; even after eight years of making this trip, I am surprised by the vistas offered by the close-in hills, the craggy outcroppings, and the distant landscape.

David Hockney, the British-born, LA-resident artist, has captured my sense of continuing surprise in the painting he calls simply *Mulholland Drive*. The painting is vivid and alive in oranges, reds, greens, and blues. Each object is recognizable, but overall the impression is of a fantastic, alive, moving, and incredibly interesting scene—one that makes you feel energetic and somehow inside of it. The perspective in the painting shifts as you look at it. Sometimes you see things whole, sometimes partially, sometimes hidden or only hinted at. Sometimes you seem to be looking straight on, other times peeking from around a hill.

This painting has come to be, for me, a metaphor for the ever-changing work of the Whizin Institute and for the complex landscape of Jewish family education. As in the painting, what you see at Whizin and what you see from Whizin shifts when you look from different angles or at different times. What seems first obscure may come into focus; what may once appear as background moves into foreground; what you once thought prominent may recede.

In this article, I sketch in broad strokes how I currently see the salient features of the Whizin Institute and its work. These are my own interpretations, and as with the Hockney painting, one's perspective shifts depending on where you stand, so others may have different interpretations of this landscape. I describe here what I see as the guiding themes in Whizin's work and suggest how they manifest themselves in the structure and functioning of the Institute, in the evolution of the Summer Seminar, and in Whizin views about and for the field of family education.

Whizin: The People

From small, second-floor offices in the University of Judaism, Ron Wolfson, Director of the Whizin Institute for Jewish Family Life, along with Associate Director Risa Munitz-Gruberger, work on the phone and at their computers. Bruce and Shelley Whizin, founders of the Institute —one part of the larger Shirley and Arthur Whizin Center, Dedicated to the Jewish Future—also spend many hours there. Faculty members in Los Angeles often come to the office to talk about family education. Yet the work done there is only a small segment of the whole of Whizin.

Everyone involved with Whizin—a word now used as either a noun or adjective replacing, even for Bruce, his own last name—have different images of Whizin. For Ron, Bruce, and Shelley, it is an all-consuming, life-time calling and passion. For the dozen or so members of the faculty, it is also a calling and a passion, but a part-time and intermittent one. The permanent Whizin faculty meet together three or more times a year, interrupting their everyday work as educators, administrators, teachers, social workers, writers, and consultants to focus on family education.

Their first get together of the year is a relaxed three-day January Think Tank where they catch up on each other's personal and professional lives, evaluate the previous Summer Seminar, plan the next one, and think about shaping the future of family education. Next comes a one-day session to review applications for the Summer Seminar. Finally, there is the frantic four-day Summer Seminar where they teach, learn, and interact fifteen hours a day with approximately 130 participants drawn from the United States and a number of other countries. In-between and afterwards, many teach at Mini-Whizin Seminars held around the country.

For the Whizin Summer Seminar participants, Whizin usually means an event requiring a substantial commitment of effort. They have to find the money to come, make home and work arrangements to free up a week of time, perhaps meet with others who form their institutional or community team. They fly to LA and navigate the many options at the Seminar—networking, studying, making action plans—and commit themselves to more work upon returning home. Many find their experience at the Summer Seminar transformative—life-changing as well as work-changing—one that renews their own sense of vocation in a form of Jewish education they see as vital to the Jewish future.

For those attending the local or regional Mini-Seminars, Whizin provides an introductory, tantalizing sampling of what family education might become in their community—small tastes of how to do community Extravaganzas, grade-level intergenerational programming, multifamily Shabbat dinners, or family text study. For the many Jewish professionals and lay leaders in the field of family education not directly connected with Whizin, the Whizin Institute is viewed as a stimulant, a catalyst, a motivator, and an advocate for family education. They see the Summer Seminar as a place for family educators to either get inducted into the field or refresh their repertoire of ideas.

As for me, I have been on the part-time Whizin faculty since 1990 as an outside-insider, consultant-evaluator, participant-observer. My primary responsibilities are to evaluate, and sometimes teach at, the Summer Seminar, to periodically take the pulse of the field through surveys and phone calls, and to contribute to the January Think Tank planning sessions. It is from this vantage point, then, that I look out from Mulholland Drive at the national sweep of family education and the up-close features of the Whizin Institute. For me, these views of family education are much like the views from Mulholland Drive portrayed in the Hockney collage: each distinct element, uniquely important in its own right, frequently appears to change as it is brought into relationship with other elements. The scene forms a dynamic whole which feels in continual motion.

Whizin: Guiding Themes

Many themes hold together the separate elements of the Whizin Institute's work, forming an ecology of interdependent parts. These guide Whizin's operations both behind-the-scenes and at the Summer Seminar. The themes are phrased differently and with different emphases at different times. Understanding them is important for understanding Whizin.

In the 1989 proposal for the Whizin Institute for Jewish Family Life, Ron Wolfson set forth a number of objectives, including a statement of three guiding themes he thought should form the Whizin Institute's contribution to shaping the field of Jewish family education. These were first, to provide high quality training for Jewish family educators; second, to encourage change through the integration of educational, experiential, and spiritual elements; and third, to be inclusive, collaborative, and creative. These initial objectives shaped the Institute's subsequent work.

Commitment to High Quality Training

The Whizin Institute's training occurs at annual four day Summer Seminars and at periodic two-day local or regional Mini-Seminars. Such short-term training is clearly different from that provided by a one or two year master's program or by a multi-session certificate program. The Summer Seminar, sometimes referred to as the Whizin Summer Institute or abbreviated to the Whizin Institute, is neither pre-service nor in-service training. Rather, it is a stand-alone single course intended for people coming from many backgrounds who are either interested or experienced in the field of family education. It is unique in combining motivation with direction-setting, immediate and practical how-to-do-it techniques with mind-blowing, big-picture ideas for the future.

The Whizin Institute intends that its June Summer Seminar be a personal growth experience, connecting or reconnecting participants to their own passions for Jewish family education. Whizin is intentional about wanting to reinvigorate people's sense of dedication, vocation, meaningfulness in the work they do. The Seminar purposefully seeks out and sets before those who attend exciting teachers, who nourish them emotionally, spiritually, and intellectually and make them feel part of something bigger than themselves. Whizin sees this vital energy to capture and channel. This energy will create and sustain Jewish family education, especially in circumstances where the people involved feel overworked, underpaid, or under-acknowledged and where the payoffs for their effort may be invisible and long-term rather than immediate and high profile.

In addition to being a turn-on, Whizin knows that its Summer Seminar is only a teaser. Since it is not possible in only a few days to provide family educators with in-depth understanding of the many areas about which they should be knowledgeable, the Seminar simply arrays possibilities. Whizin faculty have faith in the power of ideas and experience to inspire people to seek out the additional knowledge and skills they need in their work. Whizin sees family educators as facing an enormous challenge: to bond serious Jewish knowledge with sophisticated organizational competence and in-depth psycho-social understandings. Learning how to do this is likely to become a life-long preoccupation. In addition to these turn-on and teaser characteristics, Whizin emphasizes collegiality. Many people come to the Summer Seminar as part of an institutional or community team. If they do not, they are urged to form such a team when they arrive back home. Whizin believes that only teamwork can supply the critical mass of individuals, skills, creativity and sustaining energy to move family education into a place of importance for families.

Lastly, Whizin is action-oriented. The Summer Seminar tries to insure that people leave with a specific plan of action—a concrete way of channeling motivation and newfound techniques and ideas into specific tasks and activities for the coming year. The Whizin faculty understands that not everything participants experience at the Summer Seminar will transfer into back-home activities, and they acknowledge that even the best-laid plans may be interrupted by unexpected opportunities or constraints. Nevertheless, they try to arrange it so that people leave the Summer Seminar knowing what they want to do with what they have learned.

Interest in an Integrated Approach to Change

The changes envisaged by the Whizin approach to Jewish family education are multi-level and ambitious. Whizin believes that family education will change those who provide it and that the educators, clergy, and lay people who deal with families will expand their own horizons by doing such work. The Jewish families who experience family education will also change by becoming more serious and intentional about their Judaism whether that seriousness and intentionality is expressed in new attitudes, greater observance, more study, increased attendance at synagogue or heightened participation in the Jewish community. Whizin believes that those Jewish institutions which provide family education will themselves become more integrated and interactive as will those Jewish communities which take on family education as a serious commitment.

The sequence and nature of how these anticipated changes will occur are not yet fully defined by Whizin faculty. They do sense that such personal, family, institutional and community changes among Jews are already being propelled by current forces within American society and culture. They believe that, at the grass roots, Jewish families are yearning for intimacy, for roots, for ritual, and for connection to community. They also believe that the professionals and lay leaders who are drawn to family education experience similar yearnings. Because the providers of Jewish family education are empathetic with the families they work with, Whizin believes, they can shape Jewish family education events, classes, activities to meet the needs of families. As providers and families experience change, Jewish institutions such as schools, synagogues, community centers and agencies, will in turn, be changed. Whizin's self-assumed role, therefore, is to act as an agent of change, a convener and catalyst for all those who want to experience family education.

Proponents for Inclusive, Collaborative, and Creative Relationships
The Whizin Institute operates on the assumption that Jewish family education programs, policies, and activities will develop in institutions and communities nationwide in a decentralized fashion. Whizin faculty believe that we are now in an early stage of family education, one which bears more resemblance to an inspirational movement than to a full-fledged professional field. Whizin is therefore interested in stimulating Jewish family education within and across denominations, institutions, and roles. Whizin wants to unleash the creative energy that they believe happens when people move across and beyond their customary boundaries. One key to unlocking that creative energy is communication. Whizin believes that everyone involved in Jewish family education, whatever their other expertise, must be able to bring to the table their own experiences, to speak their own stories and listen to the stories of others. Everyone must learn how to collaborate, how to produce new win-win solutions, and use everyone else's talents constructively.

These three themes of short-term training, multi-level change and comprehensive inclusiveness have manifested themselves in the operations of the Institute and in the Summer Seminar over the past nine years. The ongoing experiences of Whizin faculty in operationalizing these themes has produced what might be called a Whizin vision of the transformative power of Jewish family education. That vision, ultimately, is a radical one, audacious in its expectation that family education can transform contemporary Jewish life and influence the American Jewish future. That vision was articulated by the Whizin faculty in their January 1997

Think Tank and took the form of ten statements:

1. Jewish family education should be grounded in knowledge of Jewish text and tradition and be informed by contemporary insights from education, psychology, sociology, management, history and the arts.
2. Jewish family education should aim at families becoming life-long Jewish learners, connected to one another and to the community.
3. Family is an important lens through which activities of a Jewish institution should be refracted.
4. Everyone involved with Jewish family education—children, parents, grandparents, educators, rabbis, lay leaders, funders—should regard themselves as teachers of one another and as learners from one another.
5. The ambiance surrounding Jewish family education—in the synagogue, school, home, camp, museum, or on trips—is as important as the instruction or the program in communicating what JFE is about.
6. Jewish family education work is multi-disciplinary, non-hierarchic, partnered, and collegial. It requires teamwork.
7. Jewish family education should dissolve the boundaries between roles formerly defined as lay and professional. Everyone together does these sacred tasks.
8. Good things happen when you bring good people together.
9. Outside-the-box thinking and diverse perspectives should be encouraged and honored by those working in JFE.
10. Jewish family education has the potential to change the way Jewish institutions function. Family education is everyone's job, not just the job of the Jewish family educator.

Whizin: Operations

As noted above, the Whizin Institute for Jewish Family Life does its training, its change agency, and its inclusive collaborative work primarily through the annual four-day Summer Seminar. In addition, the Institute presents at conferences, conducts local or regional Mini-Seminars, does one-on-one consultations, and holds workshops. In its early years, Whizin faculty worked in Chicago, Baltimore, MetroWest (New Jersey),

Atlanta, Houston, Philadelphia, San Diego, and the San Francisco Bay area. Recently, other types of consultations and collaborations have been initiated. For example, a Whizin consultant facilitated the adaptation by MetroWest of the JEFF model, developed in Detroit. Baltimore's Beth El congregation initiated Project Mishpacha, its school-within-a-school, with consultation and evaluation from Whizin faculty members. The Cleveland College of Jewish Studies collaborated with Whizin on a research project for their advanced Cleveland Fellows.

To the degree that the Whizin Institute for Jewish Family Life is an organization, it consists of Bruce and Shelley Whizin, founders, Director Ron Wolfson, Associate Director Risa Munitz-Gruber, and semi-permanent faculty members, among whom have been Janice Alper, Harlene Appelman, Adrianne Bank, Joel Grishaver, Jo Kay, Joan Kaye, Vicky Kelman, Esther Netter, Susan Shevitz, Rachel Sisk and Sally Weber.

The Whizin Institute can be described in terms of its structure, its human relationships, its political features, and its culture, using the four-frame approach to organizational analysis suggested by Lee Bolman and Terrence Deal in their book, *Reframing Organizations: Artistry, Choice and Leadership* (1991). Such an analysis suggests that the way in which Whizin functions internally seems very close to the way Whizin organizes the Summer Seminar and the way which Whizin suggests is desirable for the field of family education as a whole. One might say that the Whizin Institute is a hologram and contains within its own small setting that which is writ somewhat larger during the Summer Seminar and then magnified again for the entire field of Jewish family education.

Whizin Structure

In structural terms, the faculty responsible for mounting the Summer Seminar comes together in an individualistic, decentralized, and non-hierarchic team with a minimum of formal structure and few job descriptions. The team operates within a context of shifting roles and distributed leadership tasks which are constantly being renegotiated.

Responsibility for carrying out the various activities of the Summer Seminar is informally delegated. While common convictions about family education are hammered out at the Think Tank, the specifics of planning the Summer Seminar, the on-site workshops, the publications of the Institute, and its evaluation and research activities are primarily left to those who will do the work. Whatever coherence exists among the Whizin faculty derives from a collective body of shared understandings. Beyond these common understandings, everyone has a great deal of latitude about specifics.

The Whizin faculty were originally recruited because of their different backgrounds and teaching strengths—some in text study, some in curriculum, some in instructional formats and programmatics, some in community organizing, some in organizational development. As a result, the leadership responsibilities for accomplishing any particular task move around depending on the nature of the task. Authority at any given moment derives from the expertise needed at that moment.

The creation of such a loosely-coupled, low-structure operation was conscious and deliberate. Ron has written, "In planning the Whizin Institute for Jewish Family Life, our intention was to create a new paradigm for building a field within Jewish education. Central to this notion was the turning of the usual pyramid for top down thinking on its head. Rather than 'command and control' planning, the Institute was to be designed so that there would be bottom up thinking, where a broad coalition of voices from diverse segments of the professional and lay community would inform all of its activities. The core faculty of consultants would therefore be listening and responding and facilitating the emergence of the field."

In addition to this ideological preference for bottom-up thinking, the structure of the Whizin Institute is a practical accommodation to the realities of its situation. For most of its existence, no one has worked full time at Whizin, including Ron who, even as its director, has also had a full load of other teaching and administrative responsibilities. The faculty all had full time jobs when they were brought together by Ron and continue to be so engaged. Each faculty member has a great deal of experience in some combination of Jewish education, public education, schools, synagogues, or Jewish agencies. Each has a path breaker personality as well as expertise in particular areas. Although their energy and ideas are boundless, each has only limited time to devote to Whizin administration. A system for encouraging personal responsibility for carrying out broadly-defined tasks, with only minimum supervision and coordination, was a more realistic management strategy than trying for a tighter delegation and reporting structure.

Beyond these considerations of ideology and practicality, the structure of Whizin has been importantly influenced by the personalities of the convening leadership. Ron's natural leadership style—that of assembling a highly-motivated and skilled team, of respecting and glorying in the differences among the players, of pushing for agreement only on broad general goals rather than on specific objectives, and on maintaining a high tolerance for openness and for ambiguity—has became characteristic of Whizin operations. Bruce and Shelley, as founders and funders, coming from unconventional backgrounds and interested in hands-on involvement, strongly support that style. Thus, the founding leaders who shaped the structure of the Whizin Institute welcome creativity even at the expense of efficiency. Spontaneity is valued somewhat more than planning. Serendipity is trusted more than system. Celebration is as important as cerebration.

Whizin Relationships

In looking at the Whizin Institute from a human resources perspective, the values of inclusion, collaboration, and creativity are clearly manifested. A simple communication technique known as the "check-in" is used at the Think Tank and at the Summer Seminar and is advocated as a vital technique to be used in all family education settings. Check-ins encourage people to bring their whole selves into the conversation by sharing their personal, their professional and their Jewish experiences in a safe and bounded manner.

Each Think Tank begins with a go-around—each person reporting on personal and professional activities that are relevant and important for the team to know about. Faculty have been very reluctant to shorten this activity even when time is limited. People say that they vividly remember past check-ins and anticipate for much of the year what they will say at future check-ins. They report learning from these go-rounds a great deal not only about one another but about the entire Jewish enterprise in America. The check-ins have become an important mechanism for group bonding as well as for developing new ideas.

Even with check-ins, the Whizin team has discovered that it has taken a great deal of time for faculty to share enough about themselves and their convictions so that they can communicate easily. As a Whizin faculty person observed, "In the early years, people couldn't finish a sentence. They were interrupted by others who disagreed wholeheartedly with what they thought was being said. In recent years, people still can't finish their sentences. They are interrupted by others who agree completely with what they think is being said." The Think Tank has given Whizin faculty first-hand and direct experience about both the rewards and the difficulties of functioning as a team.

Another aspect of the Whizin view of human relationships percolating through the Think Tanks, Summer Seminars, and Mini-Seminars, which is suggested as useful for the field at larg, is an ambiance of welcoming. Everyone is treated as an honored guest, greeted at the door, introduced, and inducted into whatever is happening with care and sensitivity. Many times while working together people will ask one another the equivalent of, "How is it going for you?" "Are you OK?" "Is there something you would like to say?" This reflects a deep recognition that people enter professional, educational, and social situations, particularly those related to Jewish family education, with varying levels of prior understanding of what is going on. It also reflects the awareness that many people may remain silent because they feel ill-at-ease or because they are concerned about how their comments may be interpreted. The welcoming ambiance conveys a sincere desire to make all spaces where Jewish family education is discussed or conducted "safe space" for everyone involved.

With regard to human relationships and how human resources are utilized, another characteristic of Whizin work is a high level of attention to process. Whizin faculty understand the necessary and desirable balance between attention to process and attention to task. Nevertheless, the optimal process/task balance sometimes erodes during Think Tank discussions as it sometimes does during the Summer Seminar. Time allocated to processing may exceed that allocated to deciding. For some, this is a comfortable ratio, for others not. As a participant-observer, it sometimes seems to me that the Whizin faculty operates more like a family than like a formal work group. This means that outcomes of discussions are more often implied than stated. Closure may consist of reaching agreement on direction rather than on specific next-steps.

These experiences in working as a team in Think Tank sessions give the Whizin faculty first-hand knowledge of what they teach about teams at the Summer Seminar. They know about the barriers impeding open communication and the importance of reestablishing, over and over again, "safety" for those involved in family education. They are cognizant of the need to respect privacy and not to become invasive. They recognize that it takes a great deal of effort, as well as skill, to tell one's own story and listen to the stories of others with empathy and a non-judgmental ear.

Whizin Politics

Looked at from a broad political perspective, the Whizin Institute has been very attuned to the territorial aspects of Jewish communal life. At every opportunity, Whizin tries to convert political issues into problem-solving issues. Instead of dividing up the available family education "turf" and protecting their own piece, Whizin tries to expand the "turf" by creating inter-institutional alliances, collaborations, joint ventures, and win-win activities. Whizin's outreach to all denominations, roles, and institutions to fully participate in educating Jewish families Jewishly can be seen as an all encompassing political statement. Much of politics is destructive if the objective is to win at any cost. However, much of politics can be constructive when the objective is to unite to achieve a common goal. Bolman and Deal observe that "politics can be the vehicle for achieving noble purposes...through fashioning an agenda, building a network of support and negotiating effectively both with those who might advance and those who might oppose the agenda."

Whizin Culture

The culture of a group is defined by Edgar H. Schein in *Organizational Culture and Leadership*, (1992) as "the pattern of shared basic assumptions that the group learned as it solved its problems of external adaptation and internal integration, that has worked well enough to be considered valid, and therefore, can be taught to new members as the correct way to perceive, think and feel in relation to those problems." The Whizin culture is quite apparent to those who come in new to the Whizin faculty or who attend a Summer Seminar or a Mini-Seminar for the first time. According to Schein, the culture of any organization can be understood at three levels: the taken-for-granted level of basic underlying assumptions, the declared level of espoused values, and the observable level of artifacts.

So far, we have looked at some of the underlying assumptions and the espoused values that define Whizin and its approach to Jewish family education. Among those that we have already mentioned are: continuing

interest in text study and tradition as well as in contemporary social science; a sense that everyone is simultaneously a teacher and a learner; a
willingness to dissolve role relationships and to entertain new thinking;
a respect for individuals and for their diverse points of view; a push for
broad agreement on goals while leaving details to be worked out later;
distributed leadership responsibilities; preferences for creativity, spontaneity, and celebration.

The "artifacts" or behaviors and actions which embody these assumptions and espoused values can be observed in several places. The first place
is in the publications of the Whizin Institute. These include this anthology along with *Family Room: Linking Jewish Families into a Learning
Community* by Victoria Koltun Kelman, *JEFF-Jewish Experiences for
Families: A Model for Community Building and Family Programming*, by
Harlene Winnick Appelman and *Jewish Family Retreats: A Handbook*, by
Victoria Koltun Kelman. The second place is in the on-the-road work of
the Whizin Institute consisting of Mini Seminars, one-on-one consultations, day-long workshops, and Jewish Family Educator in Residence
weekends. And the third and most apparent place they can be observed
is at the annual Summer Seminars.

Whizin: The Evolution of the Summer Seminar

At the Think Tank in January 1991, the Whizin faculty decided to initiate a small grants program to encourage even more teams to attend the
June 1991 Summer Seminar. The grants were intended to provide incentives for the formation and continuation of teams in a school, synagogue,
agency, or community. Applications for grants were solicited from synagogues and schools already involved in family education which agreed to
send their rabbi, their principal, a lay leader, and a classroom teacher.
Applications were also solicited from interagency community teams to be
composed of people from some combination of Bureaus of Jewish
Education, Jewish Family Services, Jewish Community Centers,
Federations and denominational movements. Although Whizin permit-
ted the grants to be used to defray transportation expenses, the primary
purpose of the funding was to encourage individuals to plan and work
together during the year following their attendance at the Seminar.

In the 1991 Summer Seminar, there were over one hundred participants:
some independents and four inter-agency teams—from Baltimore,

Houston, Wilkes-Barre and Hartford—and eleven synagogue teams. Three separate "tracks" or homerooms were formed to accommodate the different needs of the attendees.

By 1992, the Summer Seminar attracted an even larger attendance. Seventy cities were represented, along with three countries—Israel, England, and Australia—for a total of 140 rabbis, educational directors, communal workers, and lay people. There were five synagogue teams and four large inter-agency teams from Kansas City, Seattle, Columbus, and San Diego. But it became apparent that the interagency teams were teams in name only. Although the individuals had come together to Whizin, they had not yet started to function as teams. Their work began at Whizin, where they spent several hours each day in their inter-agency homeroom track trying to define for themselves what being an inter-agency team really meant. People occupying different roles in different institutions began to discuss what they had in common. They then formed themselves into role-alike groups to try to articulate the unique features of their particular disciplines. Finally, these jigsawed groups brainstormed what they saw as stumbling blocks to collaboration and proposed incentives for stimulating further inter-agency collaboration.

During that year's Summer Seminar, outside experts from a completely different field added to Jewish family educators' knowledge about the positive role of ritual in families. Steve and Sybil Wolin reported on their research with children growing up in families with alcoholic parents and concluded that the children in families which had rituals did better than those in families without such rituals: "Ritual life in families is important because it reinforces the family identity and gives all members a shared and necessary sense of belonging."

Although everyone felt that the 1992 Institute had been successfully experimental, the large numbers of participants taxed the facilities and the faculty, resulting in a loss of intimacy and a sense of scatter. Consequently, two decisions were made at the 1993 Think Tank: future enrollment would be held to 125 even though that would mean painful choices about rejecting people who wanted to attend; and the Seminar would become more focused and deal with issues at a deeper level. Whizin intentions were clarified and restated: one, family educators should have an understanding of the variety of instructional techniques appropriate for adult and intergenerational learning and become more familiar with techniques of marketing, public relations, and program evaluation; two, they should come to understand better the developmental stages of family life and concepts such as "scaffolding and layering;" three, they should be better able to operationalize their sensitivity to diverse family structures and think about the development of customized family education curricula; and four, they should see family education as a transformative change agent for institutions.

So, in June 1993, several intensive two or three day workshops were added to the Summer Seminar schedule. New single session workshops on program evaluation and on strategic planning were introduced. Guest faculty included Kathy Chesto, the author of a highly successful Catholic intergenerational program called F.I.R.E, and Peter Pitzele, a pioneer in the use of psychodrama in biblical text study. In key-noting the Summer Seminar, Ron Wolfson provided an overview of the Whizin orientation to Jewish family education by listing the "Top Ten" Whizin words. His choices clearly expressed the basic assumptions and the espoused values of the Whizin Institute. His words—transformational, cutting-edge, collaboration, team-work, sharing, marketing, access, alternatives, scaffolding, continuity. These Top Ten evidently did not adequately capture what he really wanted to say, and so he added an eleventh injunction "Fly."

At the 1994 Summer Seminar, there were fourteen teams from synagogues, two from day schools, and two interagency teams from St. Louis and MetroWest (New Jersey). A new session was introduced in an attempt to create a structure for talking about Whizin concepts: the core plenary. Each day, before homeroom, all participants gathered to explore a different key word in the phrase Jewish Family Education—on Monday, "Jewish," on Tuesday, "family," on Wednesday, "education." Thursday's session culminated with comments on the concept of "change."

After this Summer Seminar, the Whizin faculty was still not certain that they had adequately conveyed their complex message about what family education really was. They needed to alter the still-prevailing view of incoming participants that family education consisted primarily of single events where parents and children together learned something about Jewish holidays or Jewish rituals. So, for the 1995 Summer Seminar, the guiding metaphor of a "Journey" was adopted. The program notes were formatted as a trip-tik. The core plenary sessions were organized thematically around the journey metaphor. Monday focused on personal journey stories.

On Tuesday, several Whizin faculty revealed their own family journeys, powerfully and poignantly illuminating their own family diversities. On Wednesday, presenters described community journeys towards family-oriented practices. Thursday's session, as it had the previous year, dealt with change, this time as the essential component of every journey.

In 1995 and 1996, the field of Jewish family education had matured sufficiently so that more than a dozen outstanding Jewish family educators responsible for their community's family education efforts could come to the Summer Seminar. During the time they spent together, they shared their work and deliberated about the challenges they and their communities faced as they attempted to do Jewish family education.

The 1996 Summer Seminar adopted the theme of "Stories." During the plenary sessions, Rabbi Ed Feinstein presented the Jewish Master Story and others told their own Jewish stories on successive days. An evening innovation was introduced: laboratory demonstrations of guided conversations in which real families were observed as they, too, told their stories. In this 1996 Seminar, about a dozen individuals including administrators, social workers, and Jewish family life educational directors from Jewish Family Service agencies, nationwide, came together for the first time ever to share experience and develop skills of interdisciplinary collaboration, program development, and training. They met with the community educators to discuss how educational and social work expertise might be harnessed together in productive-partnered efforts.

The theme of the 1997 Summer Seminar was linked with the forthcoming book, *First Fruit: A Whizin Anthology of Jewish Family Education.* Ron Wolfson's opening-night introduction analogized family education and gardening: even with great care and attention there is no guarantee that growth will occur because unexpected things may intervene. Nevertheless, as with gardening, the pursuit of family education is a spiritually fulfilling life-time calling. In this Seminar, two innovations demonstrated additional examples of Whizin's espoused values of experimentation, risk-taking, and openness to new possibilities. One worked well, the other was less successful. The first, very successful experiment was inviting dancer and choreographer Liz Lehrman to the Summer Seminar. Starting with a Sunday evening introduction to movement, she linked the content of the core plenary sessions to one another with audience-suggested dance choreography. She modeled a new and creative way to combine dance with Jewish family education.

The second, less successful experiment was contracting with SkillPath, a leading national provider of training to businesses and non-profit organizations to facilitate an intensive workshop in team-building. From the beginning, Whizin had been committed to using teams as a way to spur intra- and inter-institutional collaboration. During previous Summer Seminars, discussion about the nature of teams, about team-building mechanisms, and about the communication challenges posed by teaming had been insufficient to reduce the frustration some experienced when working in teams. By 1997, it had become clear that family educators needed more in-depth understanding of forming and maintaining synagogue, school, and community teams. Since team-building is currently a much-discussed topic in management literature, it seemed appropriate to bring in a professional trainer. Although the presentation had helpful ingredients, the gap between the trainer's business world and the participants' Jewish education world was too wide. Most people could not make the bridge, and many participants were disappointed in the session. For the most part, however, they were able to look upon the experience as an example of risk-taking programming from which to learn.

Over the eight-year span of Summer Seminars, the day-by-day details have changed in order to make the experience broader, deeper, and more lasting for participants. The various elements of the Seminar have been readjusted in order to strike the most workable balance between didactic and experiential learning; between Jewish and general knowledge; between beginning and advanced information; and between personal fulfillment and professional growth. Underlying these changes, however, there has evolved an enduring model.

Whizin: The Model of the Summer Seminar

As noted earlier, the Summer Seminar is, in actuality, a stand-alone course called *Reaching and Teaching the Jewish Family*—one of several concurrent courses offered by the University of Judaism's Hertzmann Summer Institute. The Summer Seminar begins on Sunday afternoon, and immediately establishes a personalized and welcoming ambiance. There are a number of interactive get-acquainted ice breakers and context setting activities. Official activities start at 8:00 Monday morning and continue through Thursday afternoon. It is possible to see the many assumptions and values of Whizin embodied in the "artifacts" of the schedule, which includes a dizzying number of assigned or elective settings—large groups, small groups, team meetings, role-alike discussions, interest-related or skill-building workshops, program sharings, consultations, laboratory demonstrations, music, and field trips to LA sites such as the Skirball Cultural Center, the Museum of Tolerance, and My Jewish Discovery Place Children's Museum. Prayer services are available every day.

Tracks serve as the "homeroom" for the course. Based on information from their applications and from pre-Seminar welcoming phone calls, participants are pre-assigned to tracks facilitated by one or two Whizin faculty. Group learning experiences, consulting time, and planning time for teams are supplemented by discussions during which individuals think about how to apply what they are learning to their home situations. Every team using an Action Plan form thinks specifically and in detail about what their family education agenda will be for the coming year.

Daily core plenaries are the required large group learning experiences. They usually are built around a theme or metaphor which links three successive presentations by guest speakers or Whizin faculty. After each presentation, some processing format is arranged, such as individual journal-writing or conversations in dyads or facilitated small groups.

Lehrhaus workshops are elective, hour-long sessions dealing with specific programs or skills, usually taught by Whizin permanent or guest faculty. Lecture-discussion formats are used from time to time, but more often, small group work, case studies, and videos are the instructional modality. In order to make appropriate choices, participants are informed in the program guide as to what they can expect of content, format and level of difficulty. Whizin has discovered that adult learners have strong views about their preferred teaching and learning styles.

Intensive workshops are elective double-session classes which cover topics in more depth than the single Lehrhaus session. Whizin faculty introduced these for people who wanted to choose depth over breadth. Torah L'Shma are daily text study sessions, where "study for its own sake" is dedicated to the spiritual and educational needs of family educators and contributes to their personal growth. Scholars and inspiring teachers from the Los Angeles area teach what they are passionate about, and participants choose a teacher with whom to study for the entire week.

Reference groups, sometimes called affinity groups, enable people with something in common—whether it is their role (rabbi, lay leader, administrator, educator) or the type of institutional affiliation (synagogue, day school, community center, bureau, federation) or region of the country—to process the Seminar through that lens. Programs that participants develop are shared at a Shuk, set up at mealtimes, so that participants can explain their programs to one another and distribute materials. Two tiers of evening activities are scheduled, including concerts, demonstrations, labs, and games. Participants carry home handouts and materials in a three-hole binder with the Whizin logo and Seminar date. They also bring home Whizin T-shirts and formal group pictures.

Whizin: Soliciting Feedback

One of the strongly held values of the Whizin Institute is that of learning by doing. Whizin faculty encourage Summer Seminar family educators to try the new, to be unafraid of failure, to be creative and "fly" (Ron's 1993 eleventh word), to reflect on their own experiences, and to seek feedback from others. There are many devices to get participants to reflect variously on their Summer Seminar experience and provide feedback to the Whizin faculty. These include personal journals, written reaction forms, and end-of Seminar evaluations. There are mid-year check-back phone calls. Two state-of-the-field surveys have been distributed.

On a day-to-day basis, the Summer Seminar is a high-energy, non-stop event involving upwards of 150 people as participants, faculty, guests, and assistants, each trying to cope with residential dorms, cafeteria food, transportation, phone calls, elective and required classes, meetings with strangers and friends. To try to forestall frustrations and debug arrangements, Whizin provides many opportunities for immediate feedback both orally or in writing. Participants are encouraged to complete and hand in short checklists on their classes and daily journal pages. Ron, Bruce, Shelley, and the entire Whizin faculty frequently ask participants about how things are going. As the in-house evaluator, I drop in on many sessions and have a lunch table for people who want to register compliments or complaints.

Typically a high percentage of participants, about one-half of the group, complete their daily feedback forms. I quickly review them to look for discernible patterns—for example, whether returnees have different reactions from newcomers, whether rabbis are responding differently than educators, whether any of the tracks are having difficulty, whether particular teams need assistance. If patterns occur or there are pressing individual needs, the daily five o'clock staff meeting usually produces instant responses for the next day, such as clearing up schedule confusions, providing additional consultation for teams or individuals, or adding explanations or clarifications during sessions.

Over the years, the daily feedback forms have revealed recurring patterns and have led to permanent alterations in subsequent Seminars. For example, there has frequently been an after-lunch loss of energy. The Whizin programming response is to provide individual and small group optional activities in that time slot. Also, there has typically been a temporary second-day dip when jet lag and a sense of being overwhelmed produces fatigue. Alerting participants to this likelihood in advance is often enough to help people anticipate and mitigate their own reactions. Recurring requests to which the Summer Seminar tries to respond in different ways each year include: better explanations of the overall context for family education and the Whizin point of view; more concrete examples of family education successes; more program suggestions for specific populations; and sufficient processing time for individuals to think through the at-home applications of what they are learning.

Participants complete an end-of-Seminar evaluation form giving us data on the roles, denominations, and institutions represented at each Summer Seminar. These help us understand the overall impact of the Seminar on participants' knowledge, skills, and attitudes and on their anticipated behaviors in relation to family education.

Two formal surveys were distributed to the 100 individuals and teams who had received Whizin grants between 1990 and 1994, and to the 125 participants at the 1995 Summer. With an approximately fifty percent response rate, respondent answers further documented the range of institutions and roles attending the Summer Seminar. They explored how teams at the Summer Seminar functioned afterwards, the kinds of family education activities occurring in participating institutions, and what family educators thought they most needed to continue their work. Several informal, mid-year phone check-backs asked respondents about the impact of grants on their institutions, the status of their teams, and their suggestions for topics they wished to discuss at the Summer Seminar. The findings from these data-collection activities have influenced policy and programming for subsequent Summer Seminars and for the longer term. A few highlights are summarized below.

Whizin: Findings from the Field

Small Grants are Valuable.

In the early 1990s, as the Whizin grants program was being organized, I queried participants about whether and how such small amounts of grant money—somewhere up to $2000, depending on location and other circumstances—made a difference. The responses were surprising. The grants were highly regarded by the recipients for both their symbolic and economic value. Many synagogues, schools, and agencies saw winning the award as outside validation of the importance of family education and as adding prestige to individuals advocating it. In many cases, the grants jump-started other contributions and encouraged lay and professional leaders to find additional sources of support to enable a team of people to come. If there was money left after paying for transportation and registration, it was used to support family education programs. With the shoe-string budgets available for family education, even several hundred dollars were welcome to pay for refreshments, xerox paper, phone calls, or craft materials.

Teamwork is Important but Complex to Initiate and Sustain.

Almost since its inception, Whizin has urged institutions and communities to send teams to the Summer Seminar. Synagogues were required to send some combination of clergy, educators, teachers, and lay leaders who would work together on family education activities upon their return home. Community teams were to be composed of individuals from different organizations and agencies who had been or might in the future develop partnered family education activities. This request reflected Whizin's expectation that such teams would become the future core of family education advocates and supporters who would work together on family education projects once they returned home and advocate family education with their colleagues and peers.

Feedback from phone, survey, and face-to-face interviews indicates that there are many issues still to be resolved before this expectation is fully realized. Intra- and inter-institutional teams are more complex to organize and sustain than Whizin first anticipated. Consistent with Bolman and Deal's analysis of organizations, teams—as as small organizations—

must also have well-functioning structures, relationships, politics, and culture. We found that teams coming to Whizin differed from one another in the extent to which they possessed these attributes.

Teams varied in the amount of time members had previously spent working together, the kinds of work they had done, and the degree to which they regarded themselves as a team. Some had formed only in response to the Whizin request, and individuals were not even acquainted with one another. In others, the various team members had worked as colleagues on particular projects, but had not previously considered themselves a team. A few teams had met prior to the Summer Seminar, gotten to know one another, and decided on some common purpose.

Most teams had not previously developed a way of working together nor had they evolved shared group norms. They had to use track time during the Summer Seminar to do this. In general, developing a workable sense of team often proceeds in recurring stages—forming, storming, norming, performing, reforming. At the Summer Seminar each year, many teams found themselves in the storming and norming stages. Role and temperament differences among team members surfaced around such issues as leadership, decision making, and communication. Discussing these differences was very important, even though, in some cases, it led to tension or conflict.

Resolving such tensions and moving the team into the performing stage requires time and group process skills. With consultation, some teams were able to deal with difficulties and accomplish a great deal of planning. For others, more intensive individual and collective skill- building was required, and they could only make a beginning. At this point, despite a number of workshops and consultation devices, the Summer Seminar has not found an ideal way to provide sufficient time, guidance, or customized support to all the teams that attend.

Nevertheless, many teams do leave the Summer Seminar with a written plan and the motivation to implement it. The 1995 Whizin Survey revealed that many teams had met two or three times after attending the Summer Seminar. They thought it was very useful to have come as a member of a team and shared a common experience. The many ways the teams function once back home needs more clarification to be better understood by Whizin faculty. For example, sometimes individuals move ahead with family education activities and keep other team members informed. In some cases, several team members act as family education advocates and garner funding and political sponsorship within the institution to support specific family education activities. In others, team members incorporate Summer Seminar learnings into their usual routines: rabbis talk about family learning from the pulpit; administrators organize programs; and teachers make assignments to children asking them to ask parents about their views. Summer Seminar participants would welcome more structure and guidance from Whizin faculty so that they could think more clearly about how their teams might function in their own work settings.

Single-Session Programming Still Dominates Family Education.
Since 1989, the Whizin faculty has been advocating for a conceptualization of Jewish family education that is comprehensive, serious, creative, and more intensive than the programs with which the field began. Many participants arrive at the Summer Seminar with some experience in conducting intergenerational programs, usually for grade-level families. Some have experience with parallel learning, where parents and children study separately but are encouraged to discuss together what they have learned. Very few have experience with formulating a multi-year curriculum for family education or for creating formats through which parents become Jewish teachers of their own children or in helping families join with each other in learning communities.

Participants report that they leave the Summer Seminar with many good ideas about organizing community-wide, multi-institutional programming; creating specific programs for families with pre-schoolers or adolescents or older parents; or for single parent families, gay and lesbian parent families, and interfaith families. They note, however, that in four short (even if packed) days, they may not have been able to acquire the necessary knowledge and skills to act on those ideas.

In the 1995 and 1996 surveys, respondents overwhelmingly said that, as a result of their Whizin Summer Seminar experience, they now understand that family education goes "beyond programs." They note that in most of their institutions the idea of family education is welcomed and well received both by families and by program providers. In many places, they suggest that family education is on its way to becoming institutionalized, supported by permanent, hard-money in the budget rather than by temporary, soft-money grants. Still, it is sobering news that many reported that one-shot programs are still the predominant form of family education in their institutions. Sixty percent said that single family education sessions, either grade-level, school-wide, synagogue-wide, or community-wide, were the norm. The subject matter was usually related to a holiday, Shabbat, or life-cycle theme; family oriented services and Tot Shabbats were the most frequently reported synagogue activities.

Institutions Experience Common Roadblocks to Doing Jewish Family Education.

Forty percent of respondents to the 1995 Whizin Survey said that three major obstacles impede further development of family education activities at their institutions. These are: lack of sufficient funding for family education; lack of sufficient knowledge about family education; and lack of personnel trained to carry out family education. Fewer than twenty percent of respondents reported problems with lack of interest by families or lack of lay leadership.

Whizin: Next Steps

Based on feedback from the field, Ron, Bruce, Shelley, and the Whizin faculty initiated their own strategic thinking and planning process at the Think Tanks of 1996 and 1997. Everyone had become acutely aware that family education, as a rapidly growing field, required careful and continuous cultivation and reseeding. The eight years of building support for the idea of family education had been persuasive. The Whizin Institute could take much satisfaction from the important part they had played in convincing many in the Jewish community of the importance of educating not only children and adults but entire families. Now they knew that there remained a great deal of work to do to expand family education and deep-root programs, activities, policies, and planning. Change had been successfully initiated within the Jewish community, but how should it be sustained and what part should Whizin play in this effort?

The Think Tank discussions generated ideas and new thinking. In Whizin fashion, directions were indicated while decisions were left open. The faculty restated their vision of family education by articulating the ten principles given earlier in this article. They also elaborated clusters of questions for themselves and others interested and involved in family education to address. The question clusters they articulated include:

How do we make it possible for family education to supplement rather than supplant other educational opportunities? Given limited resources, how do we best advocate for Jewish family education perspectives within an institution and get resources increased?

How do we encourage interested institutions to move beyond programs to new thinking about changing perspectives, policies, and practices? How would a synagogue/school that "thinks family" and "does family" look different than it does now? What would an institution-wide Family Education Plan look like?

How do we connect a family's personal experience and feelings to subjects such as holidays, ritual observance, and text study? How do we make it legitimate for professionals to bring their personal Jewish journey stories into family education? How do we make it safe for parents to share conflicts, ambivalence, or ignorance in family education settings? How do we deal with the family dynamics provoked by these discussions?

How do we make connections with existing educating entities? How can we connect Israel trips, havurot, or camps with family education?

How do we go beyond the "basics" of family education to individualize family education for different kinds of families? How do we move families along when they have several children in a school and many years of prior experience with family education or when they already have a very Jewish home?

How do we support and expand the job market for family educators, including community family educators within bureaus and Jewish community centers; family educators within synagogues; and Jewish family life educators within Jewish Family Services? How do we address differing professional needs? For example, community educators need to understand how to do consulting, coordinating, planning, and technical assistance. Synagogue educators need to clarify roles and relationships to other professionals in the synagogue and to the families in the congregation.

How do we build advocacy? How do we encourage institutions to put family education in their mission statements and get denominational movements to "think family?" How do we encourage JESNA and CAJE to "think family" as part of policy and practice, not simply as special programming or have pre-service educator and rabbinic programs include training in family education?

How do we expand continuing education/training for family educators and develop local and national support systems?

Sparked by these questions, the Whizin faculty then outlined four possible areas for future Whizin activities—advocacy, deep-rooting, professional development, and generation of new knowledge.

1. Advocacy activities to help to maintain Jewish family education as a high-profile community agenda item include: upgrading the Summer Seminar's offerings for lay leaders; expanding Whizin's funding partnerships; explaining Jewish family education at Federation General Assemblies, the Jewish Funders Network, and other meetings; developing ways to get permanent, stable funding; urging that communal and institutional mission statements and the formation of synagogue or school committees concerned with the Jewish growth of families reflect a commitment to family education.

2. Deep-rooting activities to help deep-root Jewish family education include: doing more regional Seminars and working with Jewish Family Service agencies, Jewish Community Centers, and Bureaus of Jewish Education as well as with synagogues and schools. This might include stimulating inter-organizational dialogue and team building, creating stronger post-Seminar networks of materials, E mail, Websites, and the like, and developing techniques to help families initiate their own "Jewish growth plans" and attend to the Jewish ambiance of their homes and their connections to other families.

3. Professional development activities include promoting pre-service or continuing education for family educators, teachers, lay people, and rabbis by convening those currently responsible for such activities and discussing the possibilities for more, better, and different types of training.

4. New knowledge generating activities to actively seed the field include expanding its "think-tank" activities on a local or national basis, inviting new people onto the faculty, encouraging

research activities, and creating additional publications. Funders, academics, experts from all fields are seen as an untapped resource to be brought into multi-disciplinary collaborative efforts, encouraged to share their knowledge of the literature and their own experience, and, with Whizin encouragement, to do additional marketing research, program evaluations, and longitudinal studies.

At the end of the Think Tank, instead of producing a mission statement, the Whizin faculty reverted to a familiar device. They listed for themselves a new set of "Top Ten" descriptors of the Whizin roles they were choosing for themselves: Leaders in…. Catalysts for…. Cutting-edge-thinkers about…. Capacity-builders of…. Advocates for…. Seeders of…. Trainers/educators of…. Support-base for…. Resource-producers for…. Authors/publishers of….

Whizin: The Metaphor Revisited

The physical landscape, as viewed from Mulholland Drive, appears to be ever-changing, always in motion, different at each turning of the road even though its rocks and trees, peaks and valleys have existed and remained stable for a long time. The figurative landscape of country-wide Jewish family education, as seen from the Whizin Institute offices on Mulholland Drive, is similarly dynamic, fluid, and multi-hued yet grounded in the basic elements of family, of Jewish, and of education. The same goes for the Whizin Institute and its Summer Seminar.

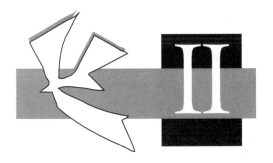

Personal Paths

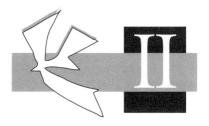

Introduction: Personal Paths

The seven accounts in this section are stories of personal journey from authors who understand that their own and their families' life experiences, changes, conflicts, ambivalences, and challenges infuse and inform their professional journey as Jewish family educators.

Diane Tickton Schuster writes that, at a point of profound change in her own Jewish life, she turned her "re-search" into a "me-search," and started listening to other people's Jewish stories. In *Telling Jewish Stories/Listening to Jewish Lives*, she urges all Jewish family educators to become good "story listeners." She shares three life stories, and using the constructs presented in *Women's Ways of Knowing* by Belenky and others, she gives us valuable clues as to what matters most in people's lives.

Shelley Silver Whizin's *My Jewish Journey* is a story that we think we often hear: "the one," Shelley says, "about Jews who go away from Judaism and then return to find their roots in their own heritage." But Shelley's universal story is also unique. She tells of her journey into self discovery with the voice of one who has questioned Judaism since childhood. She relates a spiritual quest filled with a yearning to belong and of a desire to find God in everyday life. Her narrative about personal struggle and strong determination is also a story of the life of a lay person very active in the Jewish community. By revealing herself to us, Shelley allows us to share her struggles with Jewishness and experience what is truly "a story of hope."

The next article, *One Family's Jewish Road Map*, is an account of Jo Kay's personal and professional journey into Judaism and how it affected her life, her family, and her work as a Jewish family educator. Jo's story sheds light on how decisions made by one family member alter the lives of the others. Jo links her two perspectives—the personal and the professional—to provide bits of wisdom for family educators.

We are coming to understand, from our families and those of our friends, that the many types of American Jewish family structures described by demographers are now part of our own homes. They are the norm rather than the exception. Yet, we are only starting to probe what this means for our sense of who we are. We are trying to clarify what should be proposed in terms of the policies for, and the boundaries to, Jewish communal life. In *Celebrating Our Jewish Diversity*, Lucy Y. Steinitz writes not only about the data but also about her own complex family circumstances. She movingly describes the challenges and opportunities that reside in our multiplicities.

Chana Silberstein reflects on the role that memories of the past play in Jewish identities of the present. In *Building Jewish Memories*, she describes how her family education programs in New York City encourage both those who conduct the programs and those who participate in them to create intentionally the positive Jewish memories which will suffuse their children's lives.

Developed by Jo Kay in 1978 at Temple Emanu-El, East Meadow, New York, the PACE program—an acronym for Parent And Child Education—is a nationwide family education model that combines separate-but-parallel learning experiences for adults and children with interactive family learning experiences. Jo interviewed four of the original PACE families many years after their experiences in the program. She presents a glimpse into what that experience meant to them at the time and how it continues to affect their lives today.

Risa Munitz-Gruberger draws on first-hand experience to tell the story of what can happen to a Jewish family educator when he or she begins on a course of program innovation. In *Bumps on the Way*, Risa tells of her high hopes for a new program of her own design and the unexpected opposition she encountered when she set out to implement this program. In this article, she distills from this experience a dozen lessons to make the road of program innovation less bumpy for other family educators.

Diane Tickton Schuster

*D*iane Tickton Schuster, Ph.D., is a developmental psychologist currently writing a book about the growth and learning of contemporary American Jewish adults. An adjunct faculty member at the Claremont Graduate School and California State University, Fullerton, Diane has taught and consulted for numerous Jewish adult learning programs. Her book, Women's Lives Through Time: Educated American Women of the Twentieth Century (1993), reflects her ongoing interest in adults' life stories, career and family development, transitions, and patterns of lifelong learning. She and her husband, Jack, have raised two daughters, Jordana and Ariana, in Claremont, California, and maintain an active involvement with Temple Beth Israel of Pomona.

Telling Jewish Stories/Listening to Jewish Lives
Diane Tickton Schuster

Introduction
The theme of the 1996 Whizin Summer Seminar was the power of story telling in Jewish family education. Together we learned how story telling nurtures the spirit and enlarges one's sense of being part of a community that values the most basic human bonds of caring and communication. Collectively we considered the role of story telling in Jewish tradition and the ways that the Jewish story has both changed and remained the same from generation to generation. Each of us reflected on our own stories, and we collected stories to tell when we returned home. At the Seminar, I had the opportunity to comment on some ways we can better understand Jewish stories in the context of modern life and how we can reframe the stories we hear and thus broaden both our roles and our goals in Jewish family education. This article expands upon those comments.

My Story
My work over the past twenty-five years as a developmental psychologist and adult educator has led me to appreciate the significance of stories in the lives of adults who are in the process of growing and changing. During this time, first as a social worker, then as a career counselor and college instructor, and recently as a researcher and writer, I have gathered stories about the huge number of American adults whose lives are in transition. And throughout these years, in these roles and in my roles as a wife, a mother, a daughter, and a member of various communities, I have told many stories about lives in transition—especially my own.

One story that I tell is about my personal shift from doing intellectual, academic work about women's lives to doing very personal work about

Jewish adult learners. Indeed, about four years ago, when I had finished Hulbert and Schuster's book on the lives of educated American women (1993), I felt the need to change, to discard the skin I had worn for many years. I was entering a new time in my life and wanted to attend to neglected, scattered, even ragged parts of myself which, for reasons I did not exactly understand, I labeled Jewish. In what psychologists might call a mid-life crisis, but what I called a spiritual journey, I began to think more deeply about what being Jewish meant to me, how being Jewish affected my work and family life, and what kind of Jewish community I wanted for myself. I questioned what my Jewish legacy would be and how I wanted to sustain a sense of continuity from my aging parents, who treasured Jewish life and learning, to a range of younger adults who now looked to me for education and guidance. I found that I had many questions about myself as a Jew and about Jewish text and Jewish history, Jewish law and Jewish practice. I realized that in most areas of my life, I had basic feelings of competence and authenticity, but in my experience as a Jewish adult I felt less adequate and far from complete.

In response to discomfort during a time of questioning and transition, I did what most Americans do when confronted with a major life change: I began to look for new education. Indeed, as Aslanian and Brickell reported in a major study by the College Board called *Americans In Transition* (1980), it is typical for people who have benefited from higher education to assume that even more education will help them cope with changes in jobs, social roles, and other unanticipated shifts in adulthood. In our learning society, lifelong learning has become a way of life for many people, and adults today tend to see themselves as capable of new learning and even of new and different lives and opportunities. Research indicates that college-educated adults are especially receptive to new educational opportunities because higher education has demonstrated increased personal and professional gain. Adult learners tend to be especially motivated at transition points in their lives—at times when they or their society are changing and new learning can help them adjust or grow. And there is evidence that the more people learn, the more they want to learn. All of these findings are particularly relevant to the experience of contemporary Jewish adults, especially those who already have benefited from American higher education programs and have achieved the economic success concomitant with advanced learning.

But where was I going to get the education for my "Jewish journey"? My first reaction was to go to a bookstore and assemble a library about Judaism and Jewish life to acquire the basic vocabulary missing from my earlier education. My second response was to take courses from excellent teachers at the University of Judaism and in programs in my own synagogue and the larger community. I also sought out my rabbi, and his response, was to ask me to head the temple's adult education committee.

Ultimately, because of who I am and how I learn, I started a research project, "Jewish Lives/Jewish Learning" so I could do some research on my own issue. I would systematically ask other Jewish adults about their lives, their transitions, their concerns, and their learning as Jews. I turned questions about myself into questions about them, doing something many researchers unwittingly do: I let my "re-search" become "me-search."

My research work is that of a phenomenologist: someone who starts with people's experiences and only later moves to thinking about hypotheses or categories or ways of explaining data. Phenomenologists care less about statistics than we do about the intricacies of people's lives. Our primary research tool is the interview, and we tend to focus in depth on a limited number of people whose subjective experiences may suggest issues or trends that can be studied later on a larger scale. Phenomenologists ask for—and like to hear—people's stories. It is in the stories that we look for patterns, get new ideas, come up with recommendations, and build theories about what matters in people's lives. And, thus, while phenomenologists ultimately may be story tellers, first we are story listeners.

Story Listening

Story listening is what I want to address here. It is, I believe, the skill that brings many people into the work of Jewish family education. Educators like to do people-centered work and are genuinely interested in hearing and responding to people's needs. But because of the demands of their jobs—activity-centered demands, budget planning, curriculum planning, supervision, evaluation—Jewish family educators often fall out of their story listening mode. They end up cultivating the skills that meet the programmatic aspects of their work and gradually pay less attention to keeping their story listening skills in shape. And when educators focus on programs rather than the people in them, they risk losing touch with the most meaningful and growth-producing dimensions of their work.

Teachers as Listeners

What is it that we, as teachers and former students, really remember about our best educational experiences? If you think back to your favorite times of learning, my hunch is that you likely will recall a situation with teacher gifted at listening, someone who, beyond his or her ability to organize and convey information, quietly, sensitively, and thoughtfully listened to you, heard something you were trying to say, and found ways to mirror back to you your ideas so that you felt acknowledged and affirmed. By listening to your story, it is likely that this teacher let you know that you were a worthy companion on a shared intellectual quest, and that you brought to the quest a perspective or set of questions meriting respect. Moreover, because of that respect, you grew as a learner and felt more empowered to help others learn too.

We have all experienced teachers who were not good story listeners. We have memories of educators who never heard us, never understood what we were trying to say, never affirmed what we knew. In my own work with adult learners, I frequently hear about the scars that people carry with them from such experiences. I am always startled in my college courses when I hear from students how insecure they are about their ability to learn because their third grade teacher told them that they really didn't have what it took to do fractions or play softball or share ideas coherently with their fellow classmates. And I am struck in Jewish adult education settings by the high percentage of men and women who report that they carry "negative baggage" from early Hebrew or religious school experiences, and who describe having no voice in their education or feeling that their questions received no response.

Learners as Knowers

In both secular and religious education settings, I meet adults who feel intellectually inadequate and reluctant to take learning risks. They have little sense of themselves as "knowers"—as people who have the capacity to learn or to be able to turn knowledge into ideas or opinions or perspectives for reflection or debate. These "walking wounded" have become what Mary Belenky, et al., in *Women's Ways of Knowing* (1986) have described as either *Silent Knowers*, people who do not yet have any sense of their own voice in the world of learning, or *Received Knowers*, people who want to write down everything the teacher says and then try to replicate the information without any embellishment or interpretation.

Jewish Adult Learners as "Knowers"

Received Knowers see knowledge as coming from outside authorities, are dependent on others when forming opinions, prefer lecture and "facts."

> Example: *I will go to the lecture about Pesach and will do all the things the rabbi says so that I can do the seder the right way.*

Silent Knowers don't know they have the right to know, don't know how to begin to acquire knowledge; they are silent observers.

> Example: *I'll attend the seder, but I won't feel comfortable asking what it all means.*

Subjective Knowers rely on personal experience as the basis for knowledge, have strong convictions that their knowledge is correct, use intuition.

> Example: *The only meaningful way to do seder is to go to my parents' home and do what we've always done. My gut tells me that that's what will work best for everyone.*

Procedural Knowers recognize the value of multiple perspectives, develop tools to analyze data, able to conceptualize an debate opposing views.

> Example: *I'll learn Hebrew so I can participate more fully at the seder.*

Constructed Knowers develop own knowledge base after careful analysis, push back boundaries of own perspectives, create new ways of seeing old ideas, take risks in teaching others..

> Example: *At the seder, I will present a creative interpretation of what each item on the seder plate symbolizes for American Jews today.*

Silent Knowers and *Received Knowers* have a hard time acquiring a sense of personal authority in their learning and are reluctant to become self-directing in their education; they tend to remain dependent on the expertise of others and do not engage in the inquisitive dialogue that could help them to grow. Professor Belenky and colleagues investigated what helps such knowers increase their confidence and sense of participation as learners and have found that story telling and story listening are key ingredients to the learner's developmental process. They report that when *Silent* and *Received Knowers* are asked to talk and receive feedback about their lives as learners, they begin to invest in their learning and to see themselves as knowers who can grow and change. Moreover, when these knowers are able to find their own interests and values within their personal stories, they discover dormant or unacknowledged aspects of themselves that they may wish to enrich or explore. Belenky advises educators who want to help their students to feel more authoritative and confident about what they know to create a learning climate that, first, acknowledges the value of the learner's own experience by inviting them to enlarge their stories, and second, challenges the learner to attempt new ways of knowing. Educators who create such a climate enable students to discover what it's like to make their knowledge "their own" and also help them to find a sense of personal meaning through learning.

Listening to Jewish Adult Learners

Creating a genuine story-listening climate is critically important in Jewish family education. It is, I believe, one of the most compelling and exciting aspects of our work with Jewish adults today. I came to this awareness in the past couple of years when I began to interview Jewish adults about their developmental experiences. Although most of my interviewees were people who had already embarked on a course of sustained Jewish learning, I quickly realized that previously many of them had been *Silent* or *Received* Jewish knowers.

In other aspects of their lives, these men and women were extremely self-directing, self-starting, and capable adults; they were resourceful, critical thinkers who managed busy lives, juggled multiple roles, and coped well with competing demands. Yet, with respect to Jewish identity or practice or learning, they felt very uninformed. They told me stories that showed that as Jews they were self-conscious and insecure, fearful and defensive. They described experiences of having felt shut out—by parents who didn't care or rabbis who were rigid or other Jews who made them feel unworthy. Some, as children or teenagers, had received a Jewish education, but they remembered themselves as passive learners, accepting others' definitions of what they were supposed to learn or not learn. Their stories described their journeys of overcoming feelings of being Jewishly stuck, unknowing, even developmentally delayed.

In listening to the stories of these adults, I was sobered and intrigued—what, I pondered, had the Jewish community done to damage itself from within? But at the same time, I was uplifted and encouraged, for within the stories were messages about what had prompted these adults to find new meaning in Jewish study and had brought them in closer to Jewish life. Given my training in psychology and education, I was interested in the kinds of developmental "tasks" these people had been dealing with, and I was curious about the people and environments that had supported them in their experiences as Jewish adult learners.

Below are some stories I heard in my interviews, and my comments on how I listened to these stories and what I learned by analyzing them. Within these stories are themes that I believe are especially relevant to the diverse population of adults who now become involved with Jewish family education activities. Each story sheds some light on how Jewish adult learners today perceive and participate in the building of Jewish knowledge. In this respect, I find the Belenky theoretical model helpful for assessing the learning orientation of a variety of adults.

The stories also provide insight into how Jewish family educators can help adult learners to grow. All too often, Jewish family educators (like other adult educators) fall into the practice of telling learners what the educator thinks the learner needs to learn rather than helping the learner to discover what will promote his or her individual growth and change. The process of "facilitating" learner development has been described by various adult education experts (e.g., Knowles 1984; Cross 1982; Daloz 1986; and Brookfield 1986) who have found that the most engaged adult learners are individuals whose teachers helped them—using story listening techniques—to elicit their learning objectives, strategies, and needs. Facilitators of learning are student-centered and collaborative; flexible and willing to design curriculum based on learners' needs; process-oriented and attentive to learners' feedback; committed to helping students define and organize their individualized learning goals; and open to accommodating a variety of learning orientations and styles.

Although facilitators of learning bring expertise and content to their work with adults, they see themselves as resource people whose primary goal is to help adults become more active, initiating, and self-directed in their learning and their lives. It is my position that the vast majority of Jewish family educators already see themselves as committed to the principles of facilitating adult learning, However, to become more genuinely attuned to who Jewish adult learners are and what they need, Jewish family educators need to listen with new ears to Jewish adult learners' stories.

Listening to a Subjective Knower:

Fred's Story

Take, for example, the story of a man I'll call Fred, a thirty-five-year-old lawyer who attends family education classes in conjunction with his son's enrollment in a synagogue preschool. When I asked Fred to tell me something about his Jewish life—his Jewish journey—he said no one had ever asked him that question before. He told me that he had grown up in a social action oriented Reform Jewish household, but when he went to a "Waspy" undergraduate college, he separated himself from active Jewish life. His wife, also Jewish, is a corporation executive, and when they had their first child, they decided to join Fred's parents' synagogue, even though both of them felt relatively removed from Jewish practice. Fred is suspicious of people who get too caught up in religious fervor, and in the early part of the interview, he seemed very detached from his Jewish identity. He commented that his main link to Judaism these days comes when he goes to a family education holiday program or when he has quick snatches of conversation with his son's preschool teacher. However, once Fred mentioned the preschool, he began to talk about his son's Jewish life—and his whole tone changed. With a measure of wonder, he said:

> My child is more religious than I am....He observes Shabbat. At preschool, they do prayers, they get _hallah_, he knows the brachot. He knows the Shabbat....he has a sense that Shabbat is special, it's like a day in the week that's different from the others. He knows songs, he knows candles. And for him, through the school, it's become—as I think it should be—a day where, ok, stop, take a breath, be with your family. You know, you don't necessarily have to, you know, be real.....do something particularly religious. 'Cause he does not go to services; after a while, he gets tired. But....for him, it's part of his life.

As Fred's story unfolded, I learned that while Fred saw his son's experience as the primary motivator for his own involvement in Judaism, actually he had another important connection. In talking about holidays, he suddenly remembered his mother's family's tradition of constructing a family Passover haggadah. His face lit up when he described how each year family members brought new readings to the haggadah about contemporary ways that we seek and know freedom; he speculated that this

year there would probably be readings about Yitzhak Rabin. And, he said
with pride, he now uses his computer skills to enter and merge new material into the family's ever-changing book. "Oh, yes," he said, "I am the
keeper of the haggadah." And he told me how he looked forward to sharing this tradition with his son and to contributing to future generations.

Implications

As a story listener, what did I understand from Fred's story? When I first
started asking him about his Jewish life, Fred seemed unconnected—even
wary—and my reaction was, "Uh oh, this guy really has a chip on his
shoulder about himself as a Jew." But as a story listener, I kept him talking, asking about his own Jewish story and values—and what had contributed to those values. The more he told his story, the more it became
clear to me that Fred loved being Jewish and was eager to build on the
Jewish traditions that already existed in his family. Moreover, because
Fred was clearly an independent thinker who was used to planning and
constructing ideas in a systematic fashion, it was evident that he was capable of identifying the elements of a Jewish learning curriculum that would
mesh well with his personal interests and needs.

As a Jewish adult learner, Fred is what Professor Belenky called a
Subjective Knower, someone whose personal or intuitive experience is the
primary basis for explaining phenomena in his life. *Subjective Knowers*
hold on tightly to meaningful events and sometimes are reluctant to
think about things in new or innovative ways; nonetheless, their personal investment in honoring their own experience typically makes them
willing to pass their ideas on to others.

In Fred's story, I discovered the voice of a *Subjective Knower* who
expressed a deep interest in perpetuating two traditions from his past: the
use of the family's own haggadah and the incorporation of current material supplied by a variety of family members. I also heard Fred's need to
chart his own course, perhaps to create a curriculum related to whatever
is going on in his Jewish family life at this moment.

As a family educator, what can I do with these discoveries? First, I must
take Fred's wariness seriously and accept that his guardedness is understandable and legitimate. As many his age, Fred doesn't feel a strong sense
of commitment to the Jewish community, and when he comes to Jewish
family education, he needs to be "won over"—to be brought into Jewish

life and learning with genuine warmth, solicitousness, and respect. In welcoming Fred, I would take special steps to acknowledge how far this man has come; I would endeavor to help him see that for someone who didn't even think he had a Jewish story to tell, he is a virtual storehouse of Jewish experiences and ideas. I would encourage Fred to honor those stories and see how rich his Jewish journey already has been. Second, I would invite Fred to become a resource to other parents who might be looking for ways to develop family traditions. I would ask him to tell his story to others or to help me in a pre-Passover workshop. I would arrange for him to share his understanding of Passover from a very personal point of view. I would help him see that he has the capacity to educate others Jewishly and that his experience is valuable to his Jewish community.

At the same time, however, I would not ask too much of Fred. From a developmental point of view, he is at a stage of life where he is fitting Judaism into an already crowded timetable. He and his wife are busy putting together the pieces of early career and young family, and it is likely that he will opt to learn in small segments how to do this. He probably is willing to participate in short-term activities; like his young child, he has a fairly short attention span in Jewish life. But, also like his son, he is building skills, and accumulating information, and enjoying rituals.

Ultimately, as Fred's Jewish family educator, I would recognize that this is a man who is an independent learner who likes challenges. Accordingly, I would ask him what he would like to learn Jewishly over the next few years and would offer to help him chart his own learning agenda. I would tell him that I want to stay in close touch with him as he adds on to his Jewish knowledge base because I know that this man can become an important resource for other families in the congregation. I would continue to ask for and listen to Fred's story because through his story I may have discovered a future colleague—a paraprofessional Jewish family educator—and Fred doesn't even know it!

Encouraging a Procedural Knower:

Joan's Story

A different kind of story comes from Joan, a forty-year-old high school art teacher, who grew up "not knowing one holiday from the next." Joan's parents never rejected Judaism, but they were not interested in synagogue affiliation and never arranged for Joan or her siblings to receive a Jewish education. And, yet, Joan longed for involvement with a Jewish community and as a college student sought out Jewish groups. When she married an equally assimilated Jew, she opted to construct a deliberately Jewish home. Together, she and her fiancé wrote a marriage ceremony that incorporated traditional Jewish rituals. Later, when their children were born, they arranged for brit and naming ceremonies. Recently they joined a synagogue and participated in an adult b'nai mitzvah class. Reflecting on her bat mitzvah preparations, Joan said:

> *My husband and I went to Hebrew class every Sunday together. And we already have a wonderful marriage, but it definitely added a new dimension. We studied together in the evening. After our kids went to bed, we would read the Hebrew prayers together. And we would laugh—we would have the best time. It was always a fun experience for me.... And those two years, they were also a stressful time for my husband at work. And I found myself using my Torah portion like it was a mantra. Sometimes in the middle of the night, if was I was anxious, I'd find myself chanting it; loving to chant it.*

When Joan told me her story, she was very animated about her growth as a Jew, and I got caught up in her excitement about all she was learning. However, on another level, I was listening to a story about Jewish life in contemporary times. Here was an adult who had a lot of catching up to do, who knew she had a lot of gaps in her Jewish education and identity. Joan is part of a generation of highly secularized Jews who come into the tradition with limited Jewish literacy.

Like many of her peers. Joan was very surprised to learn that Judaism offers adult opportunities for growth and change—indeed, that one of the hallmarks of Judaism is the value of learning as an ongoing, life-long process. She was deeply moved by the welcome she had received at her synagogue and by the willingness of her teachers to take her seriously as a learner—without shaming her for what she did not yet know. As an artist and teacher, she made profound connections between her secular life and her new learning. And when Joan discovered the relevance of Jewish study to her life, she became especially motivated to bring her whole family in close to the learning experience. For her, Jewish learning was an intergenerational phenomenon, and the "reverse direction" of her generation-to-generation activity was emblematic of a large number of Jewish adults today. Look at how her story about her bat mitzvah unfolded:

For my bat mitzvah, I had to figure out my Hebrew name. My mother remembered hers for some reason; my father could not. He didn't have a clue. So the rabbi said something to me that was very special. He said, "Why don't you give your father a Hebrew name?" And my parents, for the first time in their life said, "We'll give you a Shabbat dinner." That was a first. "Tell me the menu you want, and we want to have it there with you that night, and they did this beautiful dinner. And it was after I lit the candles, I turned to my father, and I blessed him. And he didn't know it was coming. I was just getting choked up. "Dad," I said, "this is such a pleasure. I'm gonna be naming you. I mean, you name the child, you hope they reach the name that you've given them. But I'm naming you because I know you. And this is the name you deserve." And tears all around. I named him Raḥamim, which means "one who has compassion...."

Joan's story tells me that over the past few years this woman has moved tremendously in her sense of herself as a Jew. She is no longer a *Silent Knower* in her Jewish life, and she has moved beyond being a *Received Knower*, blindly following what her teachers' define as Jewish knowledge. Joan has realized that there are many ways to find meaning in Judaism, and she has equipped herself with important tools for feeling more authentic Jewishly. She is quickly becoming a *Procedural Knower*—one who grapples with differences, tries out solutions, and comes to understand herself as an active explorer of Jewish ideas.

Implications

In listening to Joan's story with a Jewish family educator ear, I heard that she is ready to move forward and broaden her Jewish learning beyond "Hamentashen 101." However, given her background, it is likely that she will need help to understand how to take her skills to a new level and how to become a Jewish adult learner in an ongoing and committed way. She needs guidance to alternatives in learning and support for pursuing the kind of study and practice that are right for her. If I were Joan's Jewish family educator and I was listening to her story, I would reflect back to Joan that she, like all Jewish adult learners, needs connection, needs intimacy, needs community for learning. She also needs to be challenged and stretched—and from her story I can hear that she is ready to branch out, try new teachers, and explore alternative learning modes.

Developing a Constructed Knower

Sheila's Story

Let me share a third story—about a woman named Sheila, a fifty-three-year-old social worker long active in synagogue leadership who now finds that because one of her adult children has married a non-Jew and is becoming quite remote, she is feeling uneasy and finds herself questioning her effectiveness as a Jewish parent:

> *I feel very proud to be Jewish; it's a very rich tradition, and that's why it breaks my heart that my son, Mitch, doesn't see it that way. And sometimes it makes me feel: how did we—you know—is it something we did wrong to not communicate it to him? And yet I have this daughter who lived in the same family, but who came out with a very rich appreciation of it all. Maybe it isn't my fault, our faults.... And I have to say that an area that's certainly close to my own heart is parenting adult children—parenting them Jewishly. I sure need to learn that.*

In my view, Sheila's story is about the contemporary changing Jewish family, and thus it merits special attention by Jewish family educators. Here is a strong, dynamic woman who has been a leader in her congregation, a role model to others, and a confident adult, fully at ease with her Jewish identity. For her, Jewish family life has been a matter of course. But, now, her son's choices are upsetting the world as she has known it. She is surprised by the intensity of her reactions to Mitch's choices, and she feels unequipped as she looks to the future.

> *I don't want to get into heavy-duty conversations about religion, but I know Mitch and his wife are looking for something religiously. They have been cooperative enough that as each child was born, they would come for a visit and allow our rabbi to bless the child. They did not give them Hebrew names, and I do know that they went to an Episcopal church a little bit when they lived in the East. Now that they've moved back to southern California, I'm trying to give them room, but I think I'd better not give them too much room. Because we need to say what we have to say. He went to Temple with us last year, but he didn't come for the Holidays this year. It's so upsetting, and I can see that it could lead to one big furious conversation.*

When I listen to Sheila's story, I hear a Jewish adult learner asking for help. Despite all this woman knows Jewishly, at age fifty-three, she is struggling with questions and concerns about Jewish family life across time. As a parent and grandparent, she is worried that what she has known before may not be enough to help create a comfortable Jewish atmosphere authentic for herself and acceptable to her son. Like other parents whose children don't conform to family expectations, Sheila feels the need for new ways of understanding her situation. She wants ideas and alternatives. She is up against something that feels like a major problem, and, like all adult learners, she wants help in solving it—right away.

Implications

What challenges does this woman present to us as Jewish family educators? What should we offer her? As an adult developmentalist, I am especially sensitive to three dynamics in this story. First, Sheila is grappling with loss: the family world as she has known it is threatened, and she feels that she may be losing a part of her Jewish dream. The outcome of her Jewish story is unknown, and because it is so unclear, she is vulnerable, both psychologically and spiritually. Sheila is in transition, and as such, she needs to know that she can tell her story in safe and welcoming places in the Jewish community. As Jewish family educators, we are not psychotherapists. Sheila is not asking us to fix her problem. We just need to be present to her and maybe even learn something from her story.

Second, even though Sheila's major preoccupation right now is what is going to happen to her son Jewishly, on another level she is having to come to terms with who she is as a Jew. Now that her world has been up-ended, it is likely that she will begin to have questions about her Jewish identity and values, as well as questions about the meaning and purpose of her Jewish life. She also may become intensely interested in issues of outreach and diversity within the Jewish community. Sheila is becoming an adult learner of topics she has never had to think about before. And despite her despair, she is fully capable of intellectual growth and change. At this time of change, Sheila needs lots of resources—people, programs, classes, books, and the like—to support her as she re-frames her understanding of her changing roles as a Jewish parent and grandparent.

Third, as an adult, Sheila wants to feel, in Erik Erikson's (1950) terms, generative—able to transmit what she's learned to future generations. Although Sheila feels stymied because her son doesn't seem open to her

106

as a teacher and role model, she hopes that she can be generative with her grandchildren, sharing with them the best of her Jewish life and wisdom. And because Sheila is a bright woman and used to being an effective problem-solver, she has the potential to become a *Constructed Knower*— someone who takes what she has learned and pushes back the boundaries to make new possibilities come alive. *Constructed Knowers* redefine old meanings and find ways to broaden their understanding of complex situations. For Sheila, the challenge now is to construct new ways of conveying her Judaism to the next generation. She is treading into murky waters, but the more she explores her own Jewish values and assumptions, the more likely it is that she will find ways to communicate those values effectively to her son and his family.

Celebrating the Constructed Knower Who Teaches Others:
Ron's Story

This last story is, for me, what Charles and Anne Simpkinson (1993) call a sacred story: one that is powerful and tells us about ourselves and simultaneously connects us to our fellow human beings. According to the Simpkinsons, sacred stories move us; they get us thinking about what is important; they communicate through symbol and metaphor deep truths about the mysteries of life. Upon hearing a sacred story, even if we don't understand the message intellectually, we are aware that some profound lesson has been imparted.

The story I share is about a *Constructed Knower*—an individual who pushed the boundaries of his own understanding and ultimately, under the most difficult circumstances, was able to help others in Jewish learning. I first listened to this story in December 1994, when I had just begun interviewing Jewish adults about their lives and their learning. I had the privilege of meeting Ron, a forty-two-year-old man living with—and dying of—AIDS. During his decline, Ron had found incredible joy and intellectual stimulation in learning Hebrew, developing a spiritual discipline, and studying text. An Ivy League graduate with an extraordinary talent for languages, Ron had never appreciated that Hebrew was a living language or that text study could take him into layer upon layer of interpretation and insight. In his professional life, Ron had been a prize-winning film maker, and he had a wonderful way of reporting events.

As we sat in his warm, and sunny home, he spun story after story about various aspects of his Jewish journey and told me how he had come to make meaning of his Judaism and his growth in adulthood. One of the things that pleased Ron about his entry into Jewish study was that it had enabled him to help his parents and siblings find ways to be more connected with Judaism and with one another. He said, "One of the exciting things about all this has been that I've gone back to my family and re-imbued them, or imbued them for the first time, with my religious passion....It's brought us all closer. Our family celebrations now are less about eating and more about talking about what they mean."

More poignant, however, was Ron's experience with another group of people—a group that had in many ways become family to him as he struggled with his illness. Listen to his version of Jewish family education:

I would go to Torah study on Monday nights, and more and more I would take what I learned there and apply it on Tuesday nights in my AIDS support group. I would find that it was not only a way for me to frame my experience and understand what was going on— because a lot of people were dying—but I was able to give so much to other people. Especially my sense of faith. None of the others were Jewish, but I would very much frame my thoughts in a Jewish context, and what was behind them was always so universal that they kind of appreciated that it came from somewhere. In California you've got this whole new age kind of religion, which is all a big mishmash. And nothing in it is untrue, but nothing is earned. And I was just so grateful that I had a spiritual discipline and tradition to connect with that was thousands of years old.

Ron's story is one I tell, but each time I tell it I find myself listening to it anew. It is a story that has taught me about the human capacity to grow and to learn and ultimately to teach, no matter what the obstacles. It is a story about learners and teachers and the wonderful ways that we pass our legacy on to others. It is a story about Jewish lives and Jewish learning— in an unexpected and very powerful form. It is, for me, a painful story. Ron died just a few weeks after he told it. And, yet, it holds great joy because it was told with so much love.

Jewish Adult Learners and Jewish Family Educators

Silent Knowers, Received Knowers, Subjective Knowers, Procedural Knowers, Constructed Knowers: these are the learners found in all family education settings. We walk into a room to meet with a group of parents, grandparents, "stand-in" parents, and we know that, in the 1990s, we are likely to find fairly well-educated, highly motivated adults competent and purposeful in many areas of their lives. And yet, when these adults come into contact with Jewish learning, many seem confused, uncomfortable, unsure of themselves. They may be, in the language of the theory I've been describing, *Silent* or *Received Knowers*. They will look to Jewish family education to tell them how to "do Jewish." They will invite us to be "the Authority," and often, in our anxiety, we will talk at them, structure for them, exert control over them—and even enable them to remain passive and detached as Jewish knowers. How do we work with people at all levels of knowing when we ourselves, while knowledgeable about the Jewish tradition, feel confused, uncomfortable, and unsure in dealing with such psychological diversity? What can we do to help these adults—whose lives may seem so removed from our own Jewish-centered reality—to become more actively engaged in Jewish learning and Jewish life?

In my work with Jewish adult learners, I have developed a number of strategies for eliciting Jewish stories. In individual interviews, I typically begin with one basic question: "Could you tell me about your life—your journey if you see it that way—Jewishly?" This question tends to surprise people, because few of them have constructed their autobiographical reflections from a distinctly Jewish point of view, and the idea of being on a Jewish journey is quite intriguing to many disaffected or questioning Jewish adults who now seek to find a place for themselves in Jewish life. The benefit of this strategy is that it provides the story listener with a lot of information from which to identify the learner's needs and interests and to make recommendations for future steps on the learner's journey.

In group settings, I frequently ask people to draw their stories—to represent graphically their growth and development in terms of both their secular and Jewish experiences. I assure them that this is not an art project, but rather a visualization exercise; it is not a graded activity—and there is no right or wrong way to talk about one's life. I give group members permission to put boundaries on the amount of personal information they disclose; the pictures will be used to prompt discussion of the many ways Jewish adults have navigated their journeys, and the drawing process is meant to help people to get a lot of historical information out in a hurry. I find that once group members overcome about thirty seconds of resistance to putting crayons and pens to paper, they tend to become wonderfully creative and expressive in depicting their histories. I give them about twenty minutes of drawing time, ask them to pin their pictures on the wall, and then invite them to circulate in the newly created "gallery" of Jewish lives. This strategy always opens up extraordinary commentary on the diversity of Jewish lives, as well as the various commonalties shared by fellow travelers on the Jewish journey.

With groups of parents who are new to Jewish family education, I sometimes offer a several-session workshop that focuses on participants' family immigration and migration stories. This activity highlights that the Jewish journey is ongoing in all Jewish families across time. I have found that Jewish families need to see where they have come from and what kinds of communities their families have lived in before; this consciousness raising is a good starting point for helping groups of parents to consider how to begin building and solidifying their own Jewish community here and now. This strategy is especially effective when parents have the time to assemble evidence from their own family's Jewish journeys, such as photos, maps, books, family trees, or memorabilia. This technique can be adapted to include the journeys of Jews-by-choice, as well as Jewish adults whose Jewish backgrounds initially seem vague or sketchy. The emphasis is on the collection of materials that can contribute to one's own sense of being on the journey—whenever it has begun.

Why Begin?

My view is that by getting Jewish adults to tell us their stories—and by listening seriously to those stories—we begin a process of welcoming, affirmation, and encouragement for people who may never have felt listened to before. When we ask Jewish adults to tell us their stories, we acknowledge that they have a Jewish past that has shaped their attitudes, expectations, and readiness to learn. When we show interest in their stories, we help them to discover that they have a story—and sometimes they discover hidden, forgotten, personally significant Jewish parts of their lives. When we honor their stories, we demonstrate respect for the diversity of their needs, and we create a safe place for them to articulate these needs. When we thoughtfully listen to their stories, we discover what they are grappling with and what might help them activate a useful curriculum for their learning. When we help them to probe their stories, both we and they can begin to identify the skills and interests they bring as Jewish knowers. And with that shared information, we can become learning partners who have an ongoing dialogue with them as they begin to explore and develop more meaningful Jewish lives.

As storyteller Peninnah Schram (1994) has pointed out, "There is comfort and meaning in stories, there is form and beauty in stories, there is wisdom and power in stories. there is identification and safety in stories, there is healing and friendship in stories, there is the personal and the universal in stories. There is a shared experience between the story teller and the story listener."

I urge you to have such shared experiences. Become a story teller. Become a story listener. Invite stories. Honor stories. Encourage stories to grow. Help them to change. Pay attention to their themes. Let them teach you about what Jewish learners want and about how Jewish teachers can do a really good job. Listen to stories. You will be richer for what you hear.

References

Aslanian, C., and Brickell, R. (1980). *Americans in Transition.*

Belenky, M. F., Clinchy, B., Goldberger, N., and Tarule, J. (1986). *Women's Ways of Knowing: The Development of Self, Voice, and Mind.* New York: Basic.

Brookfield, S. (1986). *Understanding and Facilitating Adult Learning.* San Francisco: Jossey-Bass.

Cross, K. P. (1982). *Adults as Learners: Increasing Participation and Facilitating Learning.* San Francisco: Jossey-Bass.

Daloz, L. (1986). *Effective Teaching and Mentoring: Realizing the Transformational Power of Adult Learning Experiences.* San Francisco: Jossey-Bass.

Erikson, E. (1950). *Childhood and Society.* New York: Norton.

Hulbert, K.D., and Schuster, D. T. (1993). *Women's Lives Through Time: Educated American Women of the Twentieth Century.* San Francisco: Jossey-Bass.

Knowles, M. (1984). *The Adult Learner: A Neglected Species.* Revised. Houston: Gulf.

Schram, P. (October 14, 1994). "The Voice is the Messenger of the Heart." *Sh'ma,* 25/479.

Simpkinson, C., and Simpkinson, A. (1993). *Sacred Stories.* San Francisco: Harper San Francisco.

Shelley Silver Whizin is the co-creator, with her husband Bruce, of the Shirley and Arthur Whizin Center, Dedicated to the Jewish Future, established in 1989 at the University of Judaism in Los Angeles. She is actively involved in the Whizin Institute for Jewish Family Life and in Synagogue 2000, a Transdenominational Project for the 21st Century, both under the umbrella of the Whizin Center. Shelley serves on the boards of the Whizin Center, Making Marriage Work, the Bureau of Jewish Education, and on the

Shelley Silver Whizin

Communications Advisory Committee for the American Technion Society. Her inquisitiveness has brought her back to school as a student majoring in Jewish Studies at the University of Judaism.

Shelley's professional background is in advertising and marketing design. She was the advertising director of a national rental franchise and started two businesses: Lighthearts, designing and manufacturing European bedding, and SSW, hand-painting one-of-a-kind wearable art. She is a Yoga teacher. Her love of theater took her first into acting and then into producing an award-winning original musical play, Pepperstreet, *in Burbank, California. She is an adventurer at heart and a seeker on a never-ending quest for the meaning of life. Shelley is the mother of Sarah, a multi-talented writer, artist, visionary, and creative spirit.*

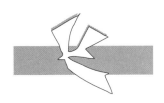

My Jewish Journey
Shelley Silver Whizin

I am a perfect example of Jews who go away from Judaism for one reason or another. And, I am probably a perfect example of how someone can return to being Jewish after so many years of searching elsewhere for their spiritual sense of being....

"Malachoooooo oooooto ohonu vo necha, eh eh eh ehli, oh oh nu vo necha"

Were these the actual words and what did they mean anyway?

That was my solo in the children's choir when I was eight or so. Most Friday nights, I stood up as tall as I could and belted out those words with all my strength.

I joined the choir, just so I could sing the solo.

I thought Hebrew was a written language we sang or read, but never spoke. It wasn't until much later when I actually heard people speaking Hebrew that I discovered I was wrong.

I have fond memories of attending our temple in San Rafael, California, where I grew up.

To tell you the truth, I don't remember the name nor do I know if it was Reform or Conservative.

The men did wear kippot, come to think of it.

I remember loving the rabbi and my beautiful Sunday school teacher, who looked just like Shirley Temple.

My Jewish journey as a child was filled with mixed messages.

I'm having a hard time remembering anything Jewish, and I'm not exactly sure why I'm bereft of Jewish memories, so, what these mixed messages were, I will try to articulate the best I can.

My perception of what I remember learning in Sunday school was that being Jewish somehow meant a lot suffering, like our ancestors did in Egypt and continued to do throughout time.

Not to mention the day off I could have had to play!

Oh sure, there were miracles: the staff turning into a snake, the plagues, the parting of the Red Sea, Jacob's ladder, Elijah and the angels, etc. etc., but people always seemed to be dying, and God seemed to be extremely judgmental, killing thousands of people at will. Just look at the book of Joshua.

This didn't leave me with a great desire to be Jewish nor did I want anything to do with such a judgmental God, I was afraid of Him. Here's where one mixed message came in. I pictured God, like any other child, as an old wise man with a long white beard, wearing a long white robe, sitting on a Golden throne. How could He (yes, He) look so wise and kind and kill people just like that?

I never had a clear picture of what God was supposed to be to us, even though I prayed to Him every night after my grandma died when I was five, asking Him to take care of her because she was so nice, and I missed her so much. I also found myself talking to God on occasions when I was sad or in pain, trying to find answers to so many questions. And so, I was left with mixed messages about God—that He was tough and mean and nice and wise….Which was it? I often wondered what the celebration and joy was in being Jewish, and why didn't we kids feel it?

Why didn't we talk about God in our home? What was God's word, and what did God want from us anyhow? Why weren't we nicer to each other? Why did we fight all the time? How come God didn't help us be kinder, more understanding, more empathetic? Somehow, I missed that part.

In pre-school, I learned how to sing "Let My People Go," while circling around our classroom tables humped to the ground, imitating the slaves of Egypt, holding on to the person in front, pretending to carry big rocks on my back. Thirty years later, I saw my own daughter, Sarah, perform this same song at her nursery school.

As I watched her, I felt a sudden sadness rush through my body, realizing we were still passing this same sense of suffering to our next generation. I didn't really understand the impact of this experience until years later. Where were the songs of jubilation?

114

When Sarah was in the fourth grade at her Jewish Day School, I noticed that she would come home knowing how to say the prayers, but when I asked her what they meant, she didn't know. I guessed that her teacher had neglected to say why we were supposed to pray and how God was connected to all this and must have felt uncomfortable talking about God to her students.

I wanted to talk about God, but I didn't know how to relate God to Jewish life.

I asked her teacher why she didn't talk about God in this private "Jewish" school. She didn't have an answer, so I asked the Hebrew teacher, the vice principal, and the principal. They all said the same thing, "We don't know how, we won't touch the subject with a ten foot pole. Everybody's notion of God is different, and we don't want parents angry with us." Something was wrong with this picture, I thought. We have a great opportunity to spark our young children, and somehow we're not doing it.

I did it in the only way I knew how, which was more from a universal perspective of God, but I certainly couldn't relate to anything Jewish that Sarah was learning in school. Why don't our Jewish educators know how? The Christians seem to know how to raise the consciousness of God in their children. They feel comfortable talking about God being inside your heart, and all you have to do is look there. I wondered if just being born Jewish was enough to keep us wanting to be Jewish.

The highlight of my Jewish youth was watching my parents perform in "Jewish parodies" of various Broadway shows. I'm not sure who sponsored them, but I think several temples were involved. I remember sitting in the audience, feeling so proud that my mom and dad were up on stage, singing, dancing, and participating in the community. I can even recite some of the words to these parodies.

It's amazing what the selective memory will hold on to…

In 1962, when I was eleven, we moved from Northern California to a small community near Los Angeles, called Thousand Oaks. We were practically the only Jewish family in the area and attended one Friday night service in a church with a few other families.

I thought this was awfully weird, the service being held in a church. *Where was the community, the synagogue, the rabbi, the friends, the Jewish parodies?*

That was the only service I remember attending. It was the end of our "formal" Jewish/social/community experience with other Jewish families.

All my new friends from school were Christian. It was the first time I shared the experience with families having Christmas trees—

—even though I learned all the Christmas carols in the elementary schools up north, where I grew up.

We even played "I Saw Mommy Kissing Santa Claus" on our record player at home.

I loved that song.

As I look back, each of the five children in our family (I'm the oldest girl with two sisters and two brothers) have an entirely different Jewish life experience from the same household.

Two years later, we moved back to Los Angeles. I remember my mother lighting the candles on Friday nights, while singing the blessing, but I don't remember doing haMotzie or the Kiddush.

I didn't know why she covered her eyes, while lighting the candles.

We did not go to Friday night or Saturday morning services. Basically, we were "Jewish" on the High Holy Days, where we all got dressed up and went together to a huge impersonal service held in a movie theater in Los Angeles, where thousands of people were singing and chanting words I couldn't understand. All the tunes were unfamiliar and made me feel uncomfortable, unwelcome, and foreign.

I was totally bored, and I wasn't even singing the solos in the choir. Why did we have to go to a theater to pray, anyway? What were we there for?

I became disenchanted with being Jewish, since the whole thing felt hypocritical.

Something was definitely lacking. What went on in my house didn't align itself with what I thought we were supposed to be like as a "Jewish family." I did not know what this meant exactly, but I knew we could be relating to each other differently, if we only knew how.

Yes, we observed Rosh ha Shanah and Yom Kippur and had big dinners.

I loved my mother's cooking, but I didn't understand why the Jewish rituals were so important. Why did I think that's what made us Jewish?

Of course, we had Passover seders, which nobody was into and everybody could care less about. We all complained about when were we going to eat (and still do) so, we just read from the Maxwell House Haggadah, and that was that.

Oh, I just remembered I was once on a local television program, singing "Dayenu" at a "mock" seder. That was fun.

We celebrated H̲anukkah and lit the menorah and sang the blessings, and my mom made great latkes!

At least my sense memory is still intact. Her food was yummy.

But looking back, our family never discussed how Jewish values or Jewish ethics related to our everyday lives, and we didn't talk about God, so I thought, what's the point of being Jewish? I could be anything.

If we didn't have a connection with God, why abide by the traditions? What was so important in doing the rituals? Maybe my parents didn't know the meanings themselves, so how could they teach them to us?

I liked the idea of being Jewish and saying that I was Jewish, but I never felt like I belonged religiously, nor did I know what this actually meant. Since I never read any enlightening or spiritual stories about being Jewish, or how we connected with our Jewish God or angels or souls, I was determined to find my spiritual self somewhere else. My solace was my poetry. I lost myself in writing—questioning everything—and read all kinds of "spiritually-oriented" books. On the top of my reading list was Siddartha by Herman Hesse. I'd read it fifteen times by the age of sixteen.

Was I suppose to be Indian to find myself?

I read Edgar Cayce's book, *There is a River,* and wondered if I was supposed to be a "psychic" to find myself.

Who was I supposed to be, and where did I belong?

I certainly didn't feel that it was in Judaism. Nothing made sense to me…only a longing to search where I belonged.

I bought a one-way ticket to Europe with my best friend when I was nineteen. The only Jewish thing we did in the six months of hitch-hiking throughout Europe was visit an ancient Babylonian synagogue in Rome. It was astonishing, quite beautiful and very ornate. It was strange to see gold laminated into the walls, like a Catholic Church.

I had a negative experience staying in a youth hostel when we attended the Octoberfest in Munich, Germany. The hostel was run by what I imagined had to be a "nazi-like figure," tough, mean, and rigid. I was so scared, I didn't want to stay in Germany nor go near any of the concentration camps. Since my girlfriend was a child of Holocaust survivors, she too, wanted to stay far away from these camps, and we left Germany as quickly as we could. We traveled from one country to another with no time barriers, no restrictions…just freedom to explore life's adventures.

I have to say this was one of the best experiences I have ever had, but I often wondered why I didn't feel a pull to go to the concentration camps, even though I knew it would be "good" for me. Was I too young or too frightened of what I might see? I guess I had seen enough World War II movies to last a lifetime and wanted no part of it.

And then…IT happened, the beginning of a transformation inside of myself…the becoming. We were traveling in Morocco and were faced with a decision to live with some new friends in Marakesh or "try out" Israel first. We chose Israel. I'm not sure why we even thought about going there, since I never really had a great desire to go, but all that changed one star-lit December night in 1969, flying from Rome to Israel on El Al Airlines with my two girlfriends. The "black hatters" were davening in the back of the plane. All I could hear was a low rumble, not knowing what they were praying. The inside lights were turned down so that as we landed we could clearly see the lights of Tel Aviv glimmering, shining, as if calling out…something. "Hatikva" was playing on the loudspeaker. Suddenly, I had tears in my eyes. It was 1969.

Could there have been any more ambiance for a first-time visitor to Israel?

No question about it, I was awestruck by the overwhelming sense that I was about to set foot on the land of Abraham, Isaac, and Jacob. Where this came from, I do not know.

OK, so Sunday school wasn't a total waste, I did remember who our ancestors were.

I was actually going to walk the land where our history took place.

How was I to know I would be captured by the spirit of Israel in a matter of hours? Would I finally belong to this great land of our own people? Why did I suddenly feel so attached?

Upon landing, I found myself crying and kissing the ground. A friend of my family's met us at the airport and took us to her house in Zahala, just outside of Tel Aviv. She told us about her life, being raised on a kibbutz in the North with her husband, a general in the army, and I was enraptured. The whole thing sounded incredibly important, the reason for building up the borders agriculturally, strengthening the Israeli side, populating the perimeters to prevent the "enemy" from encroaching on the land. Since I was definitely a romantic at heart, I wanted to serve in whatever capacity I could to help this country and "our" people of Israel.

Of course, I didn't even know what that meant.

I could see myself as a pioneer, staking out the ground, digging my hands into the earth, planting the crops, fighting the enemy, and healing the wounded.

Suddenly, I felt proud to be Jewish, proud to see everyone being Jewish, the baggage person, the taxi driver, the store-keeper, the police, the army, everyone! I couldn't believe my eyes. Young soldiers my age, both boys and girls, walked down the streets with rifles slung on the their backs. The minute they stuck their hand out to catch a ride they would be picked up immediately by an Israeli car. These soldiers were absolutely beautiful, strong, mature with a wisdom far beyond their years, and they were Jewish. I just couldn't get over this fact.

The day after we arrived we went to a kibbutz agency looking to volunteer our services. We entered the office and asked for a kibbutz with a swimming pool.

After all, we were still middle-class American Jewish girls.

The woman told us about a kibbutz that "desperately needed girl volunteers," and then she said, "but it's on the border of Jordan and Israel and there might be bombing." We looked at each other with a moment of hesitation and said, "oh God—"and then we said, "We'll go anyway, we want to go where we are needed."

We were also naive American girls who had no idea what war meant on our own homeland.

The next day, we entered an Israeli bus heading for the Jordan Valley, and the bus ride was amazing. Several hours later, the bus dropped us off on a road, and we walked about a quarter of a mile to this beautiful kibbutz, with avocado trees, banana trees, grapefruit trees, orange trees, cows, and acres and acres of grape vines. It looked like, what I imagined the Garden of Eden to be. The strangest thing I saw, however, were bomb shelters, covered in flowers.

So there I was, waking up at 4:30 in the morning, digging my nails into the earth, clipping the grape vines, chopping the banana trees, driving a tractor, working in the fields, cleaning the big dining hall, the kitchen, the children's quarters, and being part of a big family working together to make the kibbutz a thriving entity. I was experiencing a sense of camaraderie like never before, being "adopted" by kibbutz families, feeling home at last. We got dressed up every Friday night for Shabbat dinner, but never had a service.

It didn't matter, this was the Israeli way, they didn't have to be religious to be Jewish, they lived it every day, they were committed to the land of Israel.

After only two weeks, something I never expected happened. I saw this incredibly handsome soldier walk through the doors of the dining hall.

Could this be my Israeli hero?

I spotted him from across the room. He was dressed in a khaki uniform with big black boots, a burgundy beret (which meant he was a paratrooper), an uzi on one shoulder and a guitar on the other. He was stationed on the kibbutz and in charge of military radio operations.

I could envision this handsome Israeli man serenading me, while he protected me, swooping me off my feet and holding me in his arms, while he sang to me....this Jewish knight in shining armor, guarding the country of our people, standing proud and tough, while being the father of my children. Whoah, was there no stopping me?

He stood there with those dark eyes, dark hair, dark skin, and "one eyebrow" that reached from one side of his face to the other. He was Iraqi, I had never seen anyone like him before. I was hooked and determined to do whatever it took to make him like me.

I wasn't kidding, I think I became exactly what he wanted me to become and left a lot of "me" somewhere I wasn't conscious of at the time.

"I'm going to marry that guy," I said to my friends, as I kept my eyes glued. Several months went by and we were a solidified couple, living together on the kibbutz.

One day I received a phone call from my mom telling me that she was sending my younger sister for me to take care of. She thought it was "safe" with me, not realizing we lived on the border of Jordan and Israel. So, I, the "big sister" took the responsibility and picked her up from the airport. I laughed when I saw her wearing her maxi coat and false eyelashes. Little did my mother know that my sister and I would later be bombed and "wounded" on the same arm. Little did she know that her daughters would both marry Israeli men.

Eight months passed and my "Israeli hero" finished his army service and was accepted into the Hebrew University in Jerusalem. I returned to California to avoid getting in the way of his education.

My mother was so relieved, she thought I would "get over him" by being home.

About 30 days later, I received a letter from him, "Come back to me, you are the blood of my life, you are my heart, I need you…"

Well, what else could I have done but return?

I bought a ticket back to Israel, arrived with a suitcase full of levi's, just a handful of money. I lived with his family in Jaffo, outside of Tel Aviv, while he lived in Jerusalem.

Let me see if I can accurately describe my new "shangri-la." We lived on the roof of an old building, built by the English in the forties, with five flights of stairs, stone walls, a metal corrugated roof, no washer, no dryer, no heat, and no phone! Across the street from our "penthouse" was a tire yard and Laundromat.

I had to shlep wet laundry up five flights of stairs. My mother came to visit, and was horrified when she saw how and where I was living and begged me to come home, but I was sacrificing myself for LOVE and ISRAEL.

Even though I only saw my boyfriend on Shabbat, and his brothers also wanted his attention when he got home, I was committed to making my life work. Even though, according to his brothers, I was the last on the totem pole of priorities, I tried to understand. Even though I couldn't speak of word of Hebrew, I "ate" the dictionary for breakfast, lunch, and dinner.

I cried a lot to myself, not being able to communicate my
feelings with anyone, but I was still determined.

So, my Jewish life took hold in Israel, and I worked hard to belong to
something bigger than myself. I started to feel connected to my Jewish
soul, not religiously, but in my everyday life.

—just like an Israeli.

I took a bus to work like everybody else and was now becoming assimilated, preparing to make aliyah. I was even becoming "Iraqi" and could
easily make kubbah (bulgar meatballs) and shuweet (green bean stew).
The most challenging test, however, was figuring out how to make tea
five minutes before his father would ask me for it.

That was a real trick.

I learned many of the Sephardic traditions, one of which was witnessing first born males being named after their living grandfather, rather
than in the Ashkenazi tradition of naming a child after a dead relative. I
got a chuckle when the grandchildren would run around the grandfather,
taunting him tirelessly, as he just sat there watching his future generations
with an eternal smile on his face, mumbling words in Aramaic.

Then, after a year and a half of taking care of his family, we decided to
be married. The night before the wedding, I experienced the mikveh.
"Ooooochlaaaaa, oooooochlaaa," the women shouted with their
tongues rolling in the back of their throats, throwing candy at me when
I emerged from the holy water.

I was definitely in another world....was it third world or
what?

They colored my hands and feet with henna, and I sat there watching
in amazement.

I didn't even know this was a Jewish thing.

After our honeymoon, we immediately moved to the States to save my
immigration status, because we had no money to buy anything, while we
had been living in Israel. Now we were in my American homeland, my
culture, my way of life, living with my family for the first six months. It
was a dramatic change from living in Israel. We didn't observe Jewish rituals in our home nor did we celebrate Shabbat.

Somewhere in my psyche was the belief that if I married an
Israeli man, I would instantly become the Jewish person I thought
I was supposed to be, but this was a fallacy.

Was it because we were in America now without the daily life or influ-ence of Israeli life that our relationship was not the same? After all, being in Israel was not a religious experience, the majority of people living there just focused their lives on living. The religious right had their perspective, while the religious "bereft" just worked hard to survive.

He wanted me to be different, and I wanted him to be different, and so the story ended—

Three years later my life changed, and like so many cross cultural mar-riages, we divorced.

Several years passed, and I was still searching for meaning with no Jewish life *per se.* I didn't embody the practices of Judaism myself, nor had I found anything that would inspire me within the Jewish world. I didn't expose myself to anything Jewish, I was happier and interested in all kinds of other things. My career was flourishing, and I had worked hard to become a young, successful advertising executive for a national company, feeling quite comfortable with who I was (even with no Jewishness) and quite prolific in my marketing/design abilities. I was free to explore my spiritual essence, finding God in different places, not within the Jewish realm. I read books on self-hypnosis, universal mind-sciences, and wrote more poetry, still questioning life and all its meaning.

But was I satisfied deep down?

Still determined to find my place in life, I married a very handsome man I had known since high school. I was attracted to him for all the rea-sons my mother told me to look for: he was Jewish, good-looking, fami-ly-oriented, with strong values, and I concluded, "he was the one." He was a child of Holocaust survivors, and frankly, I thought his pain and his parent's plight far outweighed my own insignificant life.

I was faced with the suffering of our people once again, the memories of concentration camps and the horror it brought to so many. I felt I had a purpose, I wanted to help, I wanted to keep the light burning bright, but was I equipped with a level of understanding to deal with the anger, the guilt, the adverse effects the nazi's had left on the children of these miraculous Holocaust survivors?

I felt a definite affinity, since my best friend's parents were also Holocaust survivors. I spent my teenage life growing up with them and empathized deeply with their pain and their strong determination to live life in spite of their suffering. I admired and loved their whole family so very much—and still do.

He and I traveled to Israel together before we were married, and I shared my experiences of the land with him. He loved the country and saw a need to repopulate the Jewish world. A couple of years later, we married, and our Jewish life began to take shape. We lit Friday night candles and had a baby naming ceremony for our beautiful daughter, Sarah, at the Temple.

As time went on, our spiritual lives grew in different directions. Everything changed. My life turned one-hundred-eighty degrees all at once—I closed my business and ended my marriage when our daughter was three and one-half. I felt completely lost. I stripped myself of my personality to find out who I really was. I met "a group of people" that I thought I could relate to. They prescribed certain "truths" that seemed to make sense to me at the time.

I later admitted it was a cult.

This was a crucial period in my life, a definite major transition, filled with pain and anguish, freedom and self-expression. I remember standing on a mountain top and screaming "Noooooooo!" The depth of my soul was crying out, "no more empty rituals, no more trying to be someone I'm not, no more…." I vowed never to do another personally empty ritual again as long as I lived, even if that meant never to be involved in Judaism. This was the hardest period of time in my life. I was groping for survival.

I always believed people left Judaism due to a lack of spirituality, not feeling the sparks of God that kindle the heart and light the soul on fire—and I wondered why it was like this.

I found through experiences, other than Jewish ones, that God was universal, loving and kind, taking care of all kinds of people's needs, and I was definitely one of them. I yearned to belong somewhere, and it seemed I couldn't quite find my place in Judaism. I felt it in other philosophies and hungered for clarity in my life. I took a "mind-psy-biotics" course, a Yoga teacher's training course, aura-reading classes, channeling classes, and read every self-help, soul-enlightening book I could get my hands on, and I studied "A Course in Miracles." Everything I learned made sense to me. There was a God, and if I meditated, I could "hear" his guidance, I could reach into my heart and find something there.

So, if anyone would have ever told me that my life's work would be focused in the Jewish world, I would have said they were crazy. I could see myself as a yogi or a goddess or a channel or a psychic or something like that, but to be thrust right smack dab in the middle of the Jewish world, and have the opportunity to make a difference in people's lives through Judaism—not to mention my own—that was a real surprise.

It was beshert and just goes to show we don't always know what our destiny holds.

And now, this long story brings us to the present time. You see, God sent me a guardian angel, named Bruce, who didn't fit any of my images at all. He wasn't an Israeli hero or a high school sweetheart or any con-jured-up image, he was simply my soul mate, the one that I had been looking for all my life. We connected on a very spiritual level and con-ducted our own marriage ceremony after our first date. Then, we were married by a judge, and three months later, we were married by a rabbi connecting our families. Two years later, we were married by an Indian Shaman in Peru.

I knew this was the man for me.

Sarah was six years old when Bruce and I got married in 1986, and it wasn't until Bruce and I became involved in the Jewish world in 1989 that we started incorporating some Jewish rituals into our home. Sarah attended Jewish Day School for the first twelve years of her life, having more Jewish education than I ever did, and I felt totally incompetent as a Jewish parent. I had a strong desire to "be more Jewish," but I didn't know how.

In 1989, Bruce's **father, God** rest his soul, endowed the University of Judaism with a sum **of money** to create "something Jewish, dedicated to the Jewish future," but he didn't know what. Bruce told his dad that he wanted to help make his parents' dreams come true and wanted to assure their legacy.

Pop was truly blessed, when Bruce became Trustee, because Bruce has been an incredible steward of his family affairs and, not only has an innate ability to find solutions in a holistic way, but has an incredible memory and is an articulate speaker.

In February of 1989, Bruce and I became the co-directors in creating the "Shirley & Arthur Whizin Center, Dedicated to the Jewish Future." I remember the first meeting with Rabbi David Lieber, the residing

President of the University of Judaism, the Chairman of the Board, other rabbis, and scholars. We were sitting in the board room around a huge conference table.

I felt like this tiny little person sitting in a big chair, and I questioned myself, what was I doing there, and who did I think I was getting involved in something way over my head? After all, my Jewish education ended when I was eleven, and I didn't even finish my bachelor's degree. These men were scholars, I was a marketing designer for God's sake, what did I have to contribute?

I felt totally intimidated by this situation, but something happened. It took me about five minutes to get over this overwhelming sense of intimidation, when I suddenly realized that I was THE perfect example of Jews that go away from Judaism for one reason or another, and that's why I was there, if we could get to ME, we could get to ANYONE!

When Rabbi Lieber introduced us to Dr. Ron Wolfson, and I heard his notion that the *home* was the place Judaism thrived, and if we didn't reach the *family*, we would be missing the heart of the Jewish future, goose bumps started to appear on my arms. When he explained to us that many parents feel competent as parents in general, but incompetent as "Jewish parents," even inept and ashamed, I thought somehow he knew my background and was talking about me. He kept on explaining that some parents don't know the Jewish rituals, their meanings or how to conduct them in order to share them with their children and that some of these parents didn't even have Jewish memories of their own to rely on, as if their Jewish memory banks were empty. It was his contention that it was up to "Jewish family education" to help them feel competent Jewishly, especially for those parents of children who attended Jewish day schools.

Well, I thought he had to be talking about ME.

Chills ran up my spine, and I knew this was IT. Bruce and I looked at each other, and everyone agreed that we would create the first Institute for Jewish Family Life.

My theory was right, if we could get to ME we could get to anybody.

Not too long after we met Ronnie, he and his wife, Susie, invited us to their house for our first real Shabbat dinner.

I have to tell you, this was a big deal for me!

Ronnie explained why we circle our hands over the candles three times, why we close our eyes, why we hold the wine cup a particular way, why the ḥallah is covered, and what the significance of Shabbat means.

No more empty rituals for me, now they had meaning.

As we sat down, after singing Shalom Aleichem, I could see the stress from Ronnie's week drain from his face, to be replaced by the genuine joy of being home with his family and friends, celebrating Shabbat.

Wow, this was amazing, I never experienced anything like it, even his children liked each other and shared loving words. I had found my role models, Ronnie, Susie, Havi and Michael Wolfson, were the ideal Jewish family in my eyes, and still are. Bruce, Sarah, and I were inspired and delighted.

I was definitely on the right path, and to my surprise, it was the path of my own heritage.

Imagine that!

I didn't have to go back to Peru and become a shaman or a goddess to feel a sense of belonging. I didn't have to find myself in someone else's tradition. There were actually mystical qualities I could discover in Judaism. I could return to my roots and explore all there is to know about my own religion. I was inspired, so inspired, we even started having our own Shabbat dinners.

Will wonders never cease!

I have taken steps towards my quest for knowledge and am one of those "returning students" finishing my bachelor's degree at the University of Judaism, majoring in Jewish Studies.

My life certainly has taken a shift that I didn't expect.

Being surrounded by brilliant professors and students in an atmosphere that encourages the love of study, I am continually stimulated and challenged. My first two classes, which I took simultaneously, were "Ancient Jewish Civilization" and "Ancient Western Civilization." I felt I was growing up for the first time, learning how Jews were the basis of our entire western society.

Amazing. I didn't know that. I learned so many things I never knew at forty three years old. I guess it was appropriate that I was studying with nineteen-and twenty-year-old kids, I felt just like them.

I became obsessed with learning, hungry for every piece of information.

I love to study and look forward to completing my degree and going further.

I may be eighty by the time I finish, but I guess, what's the hurry. I'll be older anyway, and I'm making good use of my time.

I have a new found love for the study of Torah and enjoy sharing with other people in study groups. I love to light the candles and welcome the Sabbath Queen. I'm getting better at resting on Shabbat, even though I still drive, but there's something to be said about taking the day to contemplate, rejuvenate, and recharge our batteries that are used constantly. I have a new "Jewish" hobby too, hand painting kippot, which I love to give away as gifts. I still have a lot to learn and am far from being the Jewish maven, but my consciousness is growing. I thank God for Camp Ramah in Ojai: Sarah has had life experiences that will stay with her forever, being a camper for eight years, going to Israel with her Ramah group, and even becoming a counselor in regular summer camp, as well as family camp, and we've even been going to family camp now for the past eight summers.

Bruce and I have taken baby steps to bring authentic rituals of Judaism into our home. Since I am committed never to do another empty ritual again, it is not always easy to discipline myself, it takes great intention and determination. At the Whizin Summer Seminar, I learned, among so many things, that you could "intend" to have your family a certain way, whereas, I always thought that life "just happened," and you had to deal with whatever was occurring.

We even have a kosher kitchen now.!

Looking back on my life, I realize that I was desperately trying to find the truth of my inner core, my "God," whether it was Jewish or not…my meaning, my reason for living, my journey to find my truth. I know that being Jewish meant something to me, but I truly did not know what. As I write this part, I'm thinking of what I believe now. All of these experiences that I had, going from one extreme to the other, are a part of what brought me to my life today. It's still a constant struggle and challenge to "be what I believe in, walk my talk," to live each day by embodying the precious Jewish spiritual practices that give me and my family a place of learning, peace, and serenity.

I have always longed for harmony and believe we can have it, if we only open ourselves to the deeper part of our souls…to seek and find those places inside that resonate love, which I know comes from God. I pray that I have the strength to keep pursuing these values and embracing them into my life, as I awaken and as I go to sleep. I pray that my awareness and consciousness stay awake to recognize the values put forth through our traditions. Saying the Shema at night reminds me that we are mortal, that our souls and bodies belong to God. Our precious rituals remind me of our fragility and bring me back home...home to the spirit of God. Praying in Temple on High Holy Days has new meaning for me, a way of reflecting all that I am, the mistakes that I make, and the ability to be forgiven and start anew. As long as we live, we are given a new chance.

I am truly blessed and wake up every morning saying the blessings for my body, my soul, my family, and my environment. Here's to the future of our people, one life at a time, starting with ME.

Jo Kay is Religious School director at Congregation Rodeph Sholom, a large Reform congregation in Manhattan. For ten years she had been director of Judaic Studies at the Rodeph Sholom Day School. Jo created the PACE (Parent and Child Education) model of Jewish family education almost twenty years ago in Temple Emanu-El, East Meadow, New York, and is among the pioneers of Jewish family education.

A former fellow of the Melton Center of the Hebrew University in Jerusalem, where she lived with her family for a year, she holds both Teachers' and Principals' Certification from the Union of American Hebrew Congregations and a master's degree in Hebrew Culture from New York University. Jo lives in East Meadow, New York, with her husband, Alan, and their three daughters, Corinne, Lisa, and Adina.

Jo Kay

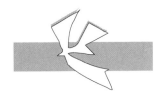

One Family's Jewish Road Map
Jo Kay

My Jewish journey began over thirty years ago with my decision to convert to Judaism. As I continue to journey, I am mindful of how what I learn and integrate into my life sets off a series of actions and reactions within me and my family and others with whom I share my life. My journey—spiritual, religious, and cultural—continues to affect me, my family of origin, my immediate family, and the family into which I married.

Family educators must keep in mind when working with intermarried families and/or families where one spouse has converted to Judaism, that Judaism-by-choice is a journey that never ceases to affect the one making the journey and all those who are in some way a part of that journey. And if statistics published recently in *The Jewish World* are accurate, there were 34,000 intermarriages in the North American Jewish community in the year 5755 (more than double the number of Jewish couples marrying), then this Jewish journey is being taken by an unprecedented number of men and women—far too many to be ignored.

With my conversion to Judaism, an act of faith, I began my Jewish life preparing for the rest of my life with my husband, Alan.

In the beginning, there was our Jewish wedding. My dad had died just two years before my marriage. I was very close to my family and wanted desperately to keep it that way. My mom clearly felt this same need when she pleaded with me not to elope, and said, "I want to see you married in the eyes of God, and it doesn't matter to me if it is in a church or in a synagogue." (I didn't realize it then, but that statement, unusual as it may sound, framed my relationship with my family in a very significant way. My mom was, if not accepting, at least acknowledging my decision to be Jewish, and I was being given the chance to share that part of me with my

131

family—which would enable me to stay close.)

So…Uncle Rocco, my dad's brother, led me to the ḥuppah in the sanctuary, and all my Italian uncles wore kippot. The food was kosher, which meant chicken without Parmesan cheese. The music, however, blended both cultures, which meant horas and tarantellas. On the threshold to the rest of our lives, Alan and I had defined our new family as committed to Judaism while accepting and facing the challenges of remaining close to both families.

It is my personal experience that I draw upon when working with inter-married couples and their families or with Jewish couples and their non-Jewish extended families. For me, being able to share cultures, while not compromising the religion of either, maintains the dignity of both sides of the family and fosters shalom bayit—a peaceful home.

Next…there was our Jewish home. We invited our parents to the first Shabbat in our home after returning from our honeymoon. My mom arrived with ḥallah and my in-laws with Italian bread. We cherished the moment and their loving support. But it would be quite a long time before this home would be the "Jewish Home" we dreamed about creating.

I had formally studied Jewish history, Bible, life cycle, holidays, and rituals. I had completed a formal conversion process, and Alan and I had entered our marriage as a "Jewish couple." Yet, as with all learning, while the classroom has its purpose, it is the practical, the actual doing, which enables one to have a "transformative" experience.

During the first several years of our marriage, Alan and I actually did very little doing! My husband's parents created the Jewish living experiences for all of us. My own awkwardness, unfamiliarity with Jewish ritual, and my secret fear of acting foolishly, held me back. On the holidays, we accompanied my in-laws to their synagogue, attended seders at their home, and had many Shabbat dinners with them. I felt distant and unsure, although never unloved. Without actually doing for ourselves, for myself, I felt empty and unconnected. I was a "spectator Jew." I never told Alan how I felt. And that made me feel even more unconnected.

Having grown up in an Italian-Catholic home, I carried memories into our marriage of dozens of customs and rituals in which I participated as a child. The excitement, the talk, even the smells of each holiday were distinctive. The void which had been left now needed to be filled.

Recent converts have often approached me with the question, "Don't you miss Christmas?" My answer is always the same, "No, I don't miss Christmas because there are no 'holes' in my life." One of our duties as family educators is to help families find ways to fill the "holes" created when the religious practices of Judaism are not observed.

Our home had not yet taken on the special characteristics that had made my parents' home so special to me. I needed to become personally involved, and I did not know how. I was just like so many of the families with whom I now share my Judaism. I was looking for a "safe" way in.

Jewish family educators must be constantly aware of creating safe opportunities for families to experiment with what it means to live a Jewish life. This is true for all families attempting to bring Judaism closer. What can we do to provide them with the means to practice with us and, thereby, help strengthen their confidence to practice without us in their own homes?

When Cory, our first daughter, was born she became our reason for reclaiming our Jewish life. We began lighting candles in our home on Friday night. Our rabbi (who with his wife had become close friends and mentors to us) introduced us to Shlomo Carlebach, whose music soon became all we chose to listen to as we prepared for Shabbat. Together with friends we learned to bake ḥallah, prepare festive chicken dishes, and many other delicious "goodies." We were creating a personal Shabbat observance filled with family, friends, flowers, stories, and songs. Surely, a two-month old could not possibly know what we were doing; nevertheless, the need to create our own Jewish family rituals compelled us to act.

The change was gradual but, ultimately, monumental. The process was made up of small steps toward a big goal. We were turning our home into a mikdash ma'at, a miniature sanctuary. We were "removing the obstacles" and filling the void. We were taking responsibility for creating a Jewish life for ourselves. This is what I had longed for. What a gift we gave ourselves, and, of course, our one daughter then, and our three daughters today. What a spiritual experience, so many years after my conversion. My journey into the world of Judaism had taken a side-trip for a period of time and now was back on the main road again.

Today, when I speak with Jewish couples in which one partner is a convert—or not—or where both are born Jewish but have not taken Jewish living into their own hands, I emphasize that they do not have to wait to have children to begin taking responsibility for their own Jewish living.

Alan and I did not have "role models," that is, couples like ourselves, with one partner a convert; and so, not knowing what to do, we waited until our child was born. The American Jewish community today has changed a great deal in the thirty years since Alan and I married. Today, a Jewish family may be one person or two or seven. And there is no reason to wait if one is ready to live Jewishly.

Not long after our decision to light candles, we invited both of our families to a Purim dinner party as an announcement that our home was to be a place for the celebration of our Judaism. From that point, it became clear to both of our families that Judaism was "serious business" to us. Also at that point, we received greater support from the non-Jewish side of our family and questioning looks from the Jewish side.

My family could understand and value what was becoming so intrinsic to our lives while my husband's family began to feel threatened. We seemed to be too involved. After all, my in-laws had never built their own sukkah, nor was weekly synagogue attendance or havdalah a regular part of their Shabbat observance. Were we trying to show them how to "be Jewish?" Nothing was said, but we sensed their question. With careful and sensitive planning every step of the way, things changed over time. Slowly but surely, the questioning looks disappeared and were replaced with smiles and voices of approval.

Many of the families in our schools and community centers are experiencing these same struggles. We must help them find ways to remove the obstacles which stand in the way of their journey towards creating a meaningful Jewish lifestyle for themselves without alienating their extended families.

Early on this new road, it was clear to us that we could not succeed alone. We had created a meaningful Jewish home, had succeeded in helping Alan's family feel comfortable in that home, and had also maintained a close relationship with my family of origin. We wanted our children to have close relationships with all of their grandparents, while having a clear, strong, positive sense of their own Jewish identities. This all seemed to be going well until an incident that occurred late one afternoon while we were driving on the Belt Parkway in Brooklyn. At the time, Cory was in kindergarten in a local elementary school in Brooklyn, where we lived. She and her teacher were the only Jewish people in her class. We lived in a two-family house, owned by people who were not

Jewish. My mom lived close by, and we visited often. Except for our family of four (our second daughter, Lisa, had been born almost three years before), and my husband's parents, and his extended family (sister, aunts, uncles, and cousins), who lived outside our community, the world was not Jewish for our children.

One day, during the Christmas holiday season, while driving on the highway, Cory, then almost six years old, looked up at the Verrazano Bridge, and seeing it lit from one end to the other with what looked like strings of Christmas lights, asked, "Mommy, is the bridge Catholic?" Alan and I looked at each other and said, "It's time to move."

We needed to find more Jewish children for our children to play with and more Jewish families for all of us to spend time with. We needed to change the balance for our daughters. While continuing to maintain the special relationship with my family, we needed more support for our Jewish side. Inside, our home was intensely Jewish: Shabbat, synagogue attendance, and holiday celebrations in our home and in the synagogue were an integral part of our lives. But we needed and wanted more. We needed a Jewish community, so we moved to a suburb of New York City, amidst a large Jewish population and joined a local synagogue.

Family education programs bring families together and help create community. Each program must contain a component which enables families to meet and interact. Jews need other Jews to support their Jewish living. Worshipping as a community is only one means of creating community; for some, it is the beginning of community; for all, it cannot be the only occasion to meet and interact with other Jews. Family education programs are, in fact, family education occasions.

As our family journey continued, and our Jewish identity strengthened, our family increased to five. With three daughters (by whose names one could measure our Jewish growth: Corinne Michelle, Lisa Miriam, and Adina Caryn) our search took us to the world of Jewish camping and took me into the world of Jewish education.

Neither Alan nor I had ever gone to sleep-away camp as children. Alan's family had spent summers at bungalow colonies in New York's Catskill Mountains, and my family had taken many auto trips during the summers. The thought of being totally immersed in Jewish life as a family was intriguing. And as teachers, we had the opportunity to choose our summer experiences. Our daughters were aged two, seven, and nine when Alan and I both obtained jobs working at Cejwin Camps in Port Jervis, New York. Cejwin (Central Jewish Institute) was a pluralistic Jewish camp, that had its roots in Mordecai Kaplan's Reconstructionist movement. Nevertheless, the camp was structured to be accessible to Jews from all movements. It had a strict kashrut policy, various daily minyanim, Shabbat sichot (discussions) and Friday evening "staff-onegs." Participating in life at camp enabled us to engage in regular debates on Jewish topics ranging from Israel to personal choices of observance.

Those years at Cejwin were wonderfully enriching and came to figure largely on the road map of our Jewish journey. Both extended families came to camp on visiting day each summer. This gave them the opportunity to witness the Jewish cultural and religious growth we were now living. They celebrated with us and saw, first-hand, the direction our lives were taking. These visits helped our families understand our latest decision to begin to explore the world of kashrut.

Having grown close to so many people who observed kashrut, our first step was to make our home (like camp) accessible to all Jews. We had decided to eat only kosher in our home. Although we had not yet decided to refrain from eating in either family's home, this decision still meant no more "care-packages" from either mom. We were once again challenged to be sensitive and understanding of both sides, while remaining strongly committed to our personal Jewish journey.

Change is a process. It happens over time—slowly. The Jewish and non-Jewish families (both sides) are threatened when children will no longer accept food from parents. We must help our families learn to move slowly and sensitively. not only with respect to food, but in all aspects of life. Change is a process.

For me, Cejwin served yet another purpose. It was the catalyst for my own renewed study. During those years at camp, I had begun to take courses in Judaica at Hebrew Union College, while also teaching in several religious schools. I had no idea where this road would lead me, but I was sure I needed to learn more.

When it came time to enroll Adina in school, it seemed quite natural for us to consider Jewish Day School. We never actually made a conscious decision to enroll Cory and Lisa in public school—we just did it. Now it was quite different. We were different. We were actively involved in Cory's and Lisa's religious school (as parents and as teachers); I had just begun teaching at the Rodeph Sholom Day School in their Jewish Studies Department, we had increased our home observance. We had already spent four summers at camp, and we had been invited to attend the siddur and Tanach ceremonies at the day school our friend's children were attending. That did it! We were ready to become a day-school family, and we enrolled Adina in the Solomon Schechter school closest to our home.

When Cory was about to become a bat mitzvah, and both extended families were to be brought together in Jewish celebration once again, my children wanted to find ways to honor all their grandparents. Naturally, the non-Jewish grandparent could not have an aliyah to the Torah, but she could offer the toast at the party following the synagogue service.

Cory spent weeks with my mom (at mom's request), helping her learn to say L'Chaim. At the conclusion of her toast, at the bat mitzvah party, the joy in the hearts of my children was expressed by how they jumped up and kissed her. Everyone cheered, and that moment—when Grandma Agnes raised her glass and said L'Chaim—is preserved forever in our memories, along with Grandma Rose's and Grandpa Milton's aliyah, and Grandpa Milton's motzi before dinner. At our celebration after the service, we were once again able to blend our two cultures through music and dancing. Everyone in both families felt included and we were able to be who we needed to be.

Finding ways to include non-Jewish family members in synagogue services, in particular, those for bar and bat mitzvah, requires the greatest of sensitivities. In consultation with the rabbi, families will find there are opportunities to participate for those who are not Jewish, whether it is at the service, at the party, or in the planning.

During my years at Rodeph Sholom, I completed a master's degree in Hebrew Culture and Judaica at New York University. At the same time, I was appointed director of the Jewish Studies Department at the Rodpeh Sholom Day School. The more I studied, the greater became my desire to learn. One road led to another as my journey continued.

Our decision to spend a year in Israel with our children produced the greatest pressure and tension we experienced in relation to our extended families. We had gone to Israel two summers before on a JNF program for families: "Jewish Living Experience in Israel." That summer had affected each of us in a palpable way. Israel had become deeply entwined in our own Jewish identities. The following summer, Cory returned to

Israel to work on a kibbutz. Now, after graduating from high school, Cory wanted to spend her first college year in Israel. Lisa was entering tenth grade, and Adina was entering fifth grade at the Solomon Schechter Day School. Alan and I knew living in Israel would be a life-changing experience we could not let pass. Alan was granted a sabbatical from college teaching, and I was able to take a leave-of-absence from my job at the Rodeph Sholom Day School to accept a fellowship to study in the Melton Center's Senior Educator's Program at the Hebrew University.

The five of us were thrilled about going, but our families were not. How could we think about living so far from home? And for so long? How could we think about putting ourselves and our children in such danger? No, they would not visit. We were tearing the family apart. We had gone too far. We were saddened, yet we needed to continue our journey—and a year in Israel seemed to us the natural continuation of that journey. So, we went—without the blessings of our extended families, but with their prayers for our safe return.

Not two days after our arrival in Jerusalem in July, my sister called informing us that my mom had been hospitalized but was already released and at home. I was assured that she was fine and that heat exhaustion had probably caused her to faint. Yet, when I spoke with my mom on the telephone that same day, she insisted her "little episode" was a reaction to our leaving her for the year. Who said Jewish mothers had a monopoly on inducing guilt?

We wrote to our families regularly and called often. Our first month's telephone bill was $700.00! In our letters and on the telephone, we shared our experiences and tried to understand what was keeping them all so removed from us. It wasn't until we returned that we really understood what was happening. This very close family, both sides, who had been so understanding and cooperative had drawn the line. They were so terrified we would choose to remain in Israel, that they could not offer us their blessings. To have done so, in their minds, would have made it okay for us to stay. So they remained aloof for the year we were away. Yes, they did write, and they did call, but they would not visit. It was quite painful, regardless of how right we felt it was for us, to be there for the year.

Sometimes growth is painful. A friend once told me. "Just because it hurts, does not mean it's wrong." It hurt. But we healed. Our families were hurt too. And they, too, healed. Alan and I are certain that because we did not judge our families or become defensive in any way, we allowed for the healing. Living in Israel for a summer or for a year is one opportunity for Jewish families to enrich their Jewish lives. It is not the role of the family educator to define a Jewish family journey: it is the role of the Jewish educator to open Jewish families to the possibilities available on a Jewish journey.

When we returned from Israel after our year there, we had to rebuild relationships with both families. We were moving too fast for the rest of the family. We were not able to share completely what the year had meant to us all. Slowly, our relationship to Israel became clear. The children continued to speak of their desire to return—and returning each summer, thereafter, was like going home. They returned to be with friends who had become family. We have each returned eager to speak the language, to eat the foods, to be with friends—to support the country. Today, our families more fully understand the place Israel holds in our hearts. They recognize that Israel is inextricably connected to who we are. And, they more frequently accompany us on our continuing Jewish journey.

And now for the latest stories…. A few years ago, five years after our year in Israel, Alan decided to enter rabbinical school, and attend a seminary which would allow him to study part-time, the Academy for Jewish Religion in Manhattan, so that he could continue to teach full-time in his college, New York City Technical College of the City University of New York. Our children were supportive, and I thought it was a wonderful way for him to continue his own spiritual journey. Both of our families were baffled but not obstructive. Yet, none of us were ready for what it would mean for us individually or collectively.

As Alan studied—and continues to do so—and was exposed to new rituals and new ways of observance, we found ourselves struggling about what it would mean for us as a family. Sometimes Alan seems to be traveling on a side road, in his own car. Sometimes I ride with him, at other times I take my own car. It is a new challenge, and one which surprised us both. Yet, we are prepared to understand the other's needs, and we are open to the new challenges.

Sometimes the members of the families with whom we experience Jewish family education have different responses to what they are learning. One parent may be more receptive than the other. A child may be more receptive than a parent, or a parent more receptive than a child. We must encourage each family member to be sensitive to the needs of the others. This may be difficult to achieve, but it must be a goal.

My daughters first understood what their dad's rabbinic studies would mean for them when, during a wedding celebration at which he co-officiated, the bride's parents (whom we all had known for many years) introduced Cory, Lisa, and Adina as "the rabbi's daughters." My girls gasped, "Does Dad's new adventure change who we are? Does it change who we must be? What are the expectations?"

Journeys prompt questions; questions prompt further journeying. Jewish family educators do not have all the answers families need. And clergy may not have the answers either. Sometimes families have to find their own answers, and sometimes. there may not be an answer. Family educators must remember that families are constantly changing and that family journeys affect the entire family. Just as family members must "hold on," so too must family educators "hold on."

Because she had been an active Young Judaean ever since our return from Israel, we all knew that our youngest daughter, Adina, would spend the year between high school and college in Israel on Young Judea's One-Year Course. Unlike the time Cory had asked to spend a year in Israel, this time we would not be going as a family. We were facing the reality of the "sandwich generation." At the time of Adina's high school graduation my mother was—and still is—dependent upon us for her care. We could not leave her for a year. And Alan was not prepared to leave his mother. (His father had died the year after our year in Israel.) But we knew Adina had to go, and we wanted her to have the experience.

Meanwhile, Lisa had graduated from college a month before. Our graduation present to her was a ticket to Israel, so she could attend an Israeli girlfriend's wedding. The trip was planned so she could return in time for Adina's graduation. She expected to begin teaching in the fall. After a month in Israel, she did return, but again, an Israel experience had stirred something within her. She had become reacquainted with a young Israeli man whom she had met during the year we all lived in Israel. At Adina's graduation, Lisa told us she had decided not to begin teaching here in the fall, but to return to Israel to live and work instead. She wanted to "try it out." She felt pulled and needed to follow her heart. Neither Alan nor I were surprised, although we knew we would be terribly lonely with two daughters in Israel for the year. But they, too, needed to continue their journeys.

Adina came home to attend college in New York, but with plans to return to Israel for her junior year. Lisa came home with a more permanent decision. She will be making aliyah upon completing her master's degree in Teaching English as a Second Language. And we are planning her wedding!

Once again, we realize our lives are changing as our family's journey continues. Sometimes we break the speed limit, at other times we need to follow detour signs. And at still other times, we are no longer on the same road, but rather all on our own roads, roads which sometimes run parallel to each other and at other time head off in another direction. Still, we are always in sight of each other.

Lucy Y. Steinitz

Lucy Y. Steinitz has spent most of her professional career in Baltimore as the executive director of the Jewish Family Services of Central Maryland. In 1997, desiring to pursue a life-long dream, she and her family left the United States to do "Peace Corps-like" work in Windhoek, Namibia (formerly Southwest Africa). She holds a Ph.D. in Social Service Administration from the University of Chicago and an M.A. in Jewish Communal Service from Brandeis University. She has published and lectured extensively on issues related to contemporary Jewish life, social work, and her previous experiences in the developing world.

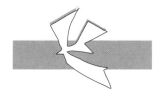

Celebrating Our Jewish Diversity
Lucy Y. Steinitz

Two themes guide this chapter. The first is that family diversity has become normative within the Jewish community—often where you would least expect it. The second is that, although this diversity is a rich source of creativity and strength within contemporary Judaism, it also poses unprecedented challenges. I shall illuminate the first theme through a short autobiography. This will be followed by a discussion of several broader concepts and historical perspectives. Finally, I call for a deeper understanding of diversity and its implications for our collective future.[1]

Autobiography
I am a New Yorker by birth and personality—the only child of German Jewish Holocaust survivors. Although my parents rarely mentioned their World War II experiences, I was always aware of the compensatory role that I filled to ensure that they had not suffered in vain. No one needed to say this directly. It was simply there, like the air we breathed.

We lived modestly but were not poor. As in most immigrant families, I matriculated through the public school system, which my parents supplemented with gymnastics and Girl Scouts and regular trips to the city's cultural institutions. They were liberal Jews: liberal in politics as well as religion. And so, at my parent's insistence, I also attended weekly Hebrew school classes and joined two Reform Jewish youth groups, both affiliated with local German Jewish synagogues.

When I left New York for college, I reveled in the free-thinking and political-protest movements of the late sixties and early seventies. Although my family's legacy and values successfully steered me away from the "hippie" lifestyles prevalent during that era, I still worried my parents about what "new cause" I would take up next. My father, in particular,

fretted that, as a Jew, I should never take a take a lead role in any contro-
versial activity because he feared that disagreement with the leadership
would unleash an anti-Semitic outburst. In the end, I did nothing to
cause them long-lasting concern. As the years passed, I spent time on a
kibbutz in Israel, graduated from college, enrolled in the Hornstein
Program in Jewish Communal Service at Brandeis University, (Class of
'74) and then returned to live and work in New York City. Throughout,
my so-called "Jewish credentials" grew accordingly: as a campus activist
and writer; as a member of H̲avurat Shalom in Somerville,
Massachusetts, and then the New York H̲avurah; as an author and co-editor of *Response Magazine*; as a founder of New York's West Side Minyan;
and ultimately, as a professional at the City College of New York, working with some of our country's most inspirational Jewish teachers, including Rabbi Yitz Greenberg and Elie Wiesel.

I had found myself, or so I thought. And I felt terrific. In time, I also
began dating a very Jewish young man from Brooklyn and then followed
him to Chicago, where in 1976, I began doctoral study. Unfortunately,
the relationship soon soured, and I eventually left him—fortunately
before marriage. Soon afterwards, when my doctoral professors unexpectedly rejected the dissertation proposal on which I had been working
for months, I felt as if my world had suddenly caved in.

To keep my sanity, I realized that I had to do something for myself,
something radically different and completely uplifting. My bank account
had $800 in it. I spent every cent of it on the most radical, uplifting, and
"different" thing I could find: a two-week camping trip in Iceland.

I arrived in Reykjavik and found myself booked into a German-lan-
guage tour where—as if emerging from a fog—I met a simply incredible, thoughtful, gentle, and wonderfully caring man. It is important for
me to assert that the absolutely last thing I had ever expected was to fall
in love and marry a non-Jew, especially a German gentile. Yet, after
months of internal wrestling and several trips back and forth to Europe,
this is exactly what I did. Even with my parents' support, which I had, it
was the most difficult decision I have ever made.

I am not telling this story to advocate my choice to anyone. Although
my husband—who is a humanist, not a Christian—fully supports and
even participates in our family's active practice of Judaism, this aspect
of our lives is a recurring struggle. I believe that it is only because our

marriage is so strong and mutually supportive in every other way that we have been able to maintain the degree of consistency, depth, and loving-kindness on these issues that we have. While I realize that some may consider our decision detrimental to Judaism in a broad, existential, and religious sense, our relationship is, nevertheless, an extremely caring one that contributes positively to our surroundings and to the Jewish community. In fulfilling this commitment, despite our so-called "non-traditional structure," we are not alone. Quite the contrary. Increasingly, our family's heterogeneity is what contemporary Jewish life is all about. Diversity is here; it is part of us.

I contribute in other ways to the context of Jewish diversity. It happens that I am also an adoptive parent—twice, in fact. Historically, Jewish law has no mechanism for the adoption of children. Although foster care was prevalent in olden days (as in the case of Moses, our culture's most famous foster child), adoption—and especially cross-racial or cross-cultural adoption—is relatively new as a way of building families within Judaism. As with my marriage, this was not the course I had imagined my life would take. The decision to adopt children required deep soul-searching. For years I struggled with infertility and my notions of how I thought family life was supposed to be. As it happens, however, my husband is also adopted. Building our own family through adoption turned out to be the best decision we ever made.

The foregoing has been hard for me to write. It is not my usual style to be so personal. But I have chosen to do it in order to make three points: First, to underscore that, while my own story is about intermarriage and adoption, it could just as easily have been about being lesbian or gay or being a single mother by choice or being in some other non-normative situation. Second, I wanted to take you behind the headlines about "The Changing Jewish Family" to illustrate how a community-wide perspective on "what is good or bad for the Jews" sometimes stands at odds with the experience of particular individuals, with "what is good or bad for them as individual Jews." Such dissonance challenges us to consider, and ultimately to design, a multi-variant response to the growing diversity of the American Jewish family—one that is responsive to individual situations and can also operate on an organizational or communal level. Third, within this context, I want to argue for a position of maximum inclusiveness. Thus, while you may reject or even condemn particular decisions that I have made, I hope that you will not reject me or my family. Moreover, while neither we nor others who have followed a "non-traditional path" may be accepted by all segments of the Jewish community, being a true community means that we ensure that all the Jews among us have some place in the community where they can feel at home.

Concepts and Historical Perspectives

To a large degree, a Jew's life journey today contains many more possibilities than were available a generation or two ago. Much depends on circumstance, on chance, and on events beyond our control. Diversity—within our families and within our community—is a certain by-product of these expanding possibilities. Now, we must find constructive, inclusive ways to deal with it.

Not everyone understands diversity and its implications for the Jewish community in the same way. Let me describe a presentation undertaken in the spring of 1996, when I had been asked to respond to Dr. Steven Bayme, director of the William Petschek National Jewish Family Center at the American Jewish Committee. Dr. Bayme began his talk to a group of family life educators by citing the Bible—Genesis in particular—as a paradigm for Jewish perceptions of family and family ties. While recognizing that Genesis in no way suggests an idyllic portrait of the family, he described the stories in Genesis as didactic in several areas.

First, Bayme said, the families of Genesis serve as a corrective to the "me first" syndrome so prevalent today. While our personal needs and drives are natural and understandable, according to Bayme, Genesis teaches the limits to unchecked individualism.

Second, these stories in Genesis describe the family as a mediating institution between the individual and the broader society. The family is the setting in which individuals learn social responsibility to others. Learning social responsibility inside the family prepares members for good citizenship in society, broadly.

Third, said Bayme, the stories suggest the importance of family for ensuring the future of the Jews as a people. While it is assumed that conflict will take place within the family, the rehabilitation of Cain after murdering his own brother, and the wisdom of Judah as he emerged from the sale of Joseph to leadership among the sons of Jacob, are important teachings for us. They teach us that it is in the willingness to

pursue struggle in the commitment to family and to be steadfast in iron-
ing out conflicts and in building relationships that reconciliation and
unity can ultimately be achieved.

On first blush, this analysis sounds on-target and very appealing. But
after fifteen years of affiliation with Jewish Family Services, I live in a very
different world than Steven Bayme. Therefore, while I accept and even
applaud the biblical lessons that Bayme draws from Genesis, I read the
Bible with a different slant. To me, a key lesson from our First Families is
how we, as a people, were born into dysfunctional relationships and survived—even thrived—despite them. To understand this, I believe that we
have to look beyond the household tensions that led to the expulsion of
Hagar and Ishmael in the face of Sarah's demands. Similarly, we have to
look beyond the sibling rivalries between Rachel and Leah and, even
worse, those between Cain and Abel. We have to accept and even forgive
Jacob's weaknesses as a father in bestowing legacies to his children, and
perhaps most challenging of all, we have to forgive Abraham's willingness
to commit the ultimate form of child-abuse towards his son Isaac.

Many thoughtful interpretations of these stories have been offered
through the years. In particular, traditional Jewish texts contain vast
tractates about the nature and quality of family relationships, especially the sanctity of marriage. Throughout Jewish history, however, the
structure of the family has changed dramatically. Changes have
occurred in the composition and roles of the family, in who constitutes
the core economic and social unit of people living together, in who raises the children together, and in who cares for the other during periods
of illness or dependency. One reason I believe that the dysfunctional
aspects of our biblical legacy do not inhibit us today is because our
shared families-of-origin, if that's what we call them, were not limited
to the nuclear relationships that these husband-wife, sister-brother, or
parent-child tensions initially suggest.

In the days of our foremothers and forefathers, our families consisted
of wandering clans, near-tribal groups of people, working and living
together as a single unit. Even after we became an agricultural people or
later settled in small towns, we still lived in vast extended families, often
spanning multiple generations, with grandparents and aunts and uncles
and cousins to whom we could turn when dysfunction or tragedy

occurred. In fact, the nuclear family—mother, father, children living at home—the family we now erroneously tend to call "traditional," dates back only a 120 years or so, to the beginnings of the Industrial Revolution and to the great migration of Jews and others to urban life. While our family structures have evolved many times since our earliest history, most recently the pace of change has quickened, and major demographic shifts have produced a new, broad range of family forms. Academicians offer many reasons to explain this rapid rate of change in the lifestyles and structure of twentieth-century American Jewry. Increasingly, American Jews exhibit diverse demographic behaviors indistinguishable from other American ethnic groups given similar socio-economic status.

Perhaps you need to isolate only one factor—that Jewish women are the most highly educated group of women in the United States—to see that virtually the entire sociology of North American Jewry falls into place. What are some examples?

The Relatively Late Date of First Marriage
For Jews, this is about five years later than for the American public in general: age twenty-nine for Jewish men and age twenty-six for Jewish women.

The Divorce Rate
About one in three Jewish couples divorce (more frequently if it's the second or third marriage), compared to about one in two nationally. The fact that we marry later may well account for much of this.

The Rate of Child-Bearing
More education correlates with later marriage, correlates with fewer children. Statistically, Jewish women average only about 1.8 children each, considerably less than the 2.1 number needed for maintaining community size. This has enormous implications, possibly no less than intermarriage,in terms of our national Jewish continuity agenda.

The Rate of Intermarriage
This also correlates with education—the more, the more. So it is no wonder we're at the fifty-two percent rate or higher.[2] But the story doesn't end here. Especially in those intermarriages where

the woman is the identifying Jewish partner—or if she is Gentile but does not belong to any other religion—then it is likely that the children will be raised as Jews. How Jewishly they are being raised is another question, for which we don't yet have longitudinal data but Jewish, nevertheless.

The Fertility Rate

Late marriage and delayed childbirth also correlate with higher rates of infertility. No wonder that Jews adopt at twice the national average—at about three percent, instead of the usual one-and-a-half percent. This may also speak to the high priority Judaism places on family and child-rearing.

The Proportion of Alternative Relationships

We also find "no marriage" relationships, single-parents-by-choice, and a variety of other lifestyles in the Jewish community that correlate with high educational achievement.

Finally, the Proportion of Elderly

American Jews have the largest group of people over sixty-five, as a percentage, of any ethnic or religious group in the United States. This is only partly because we live slightly longer, on average, than non-Jews. The major reason is that, proportionately, we have fewer children, so that our generational graphic looks like an inverted pyramid. Overall, we have more aged Jews (sixty plus) than "core" Jewish children under age eighteen, which points dramatically to our declining numbers over time and also to the stresses facing the "sandwich generation," who increasingly have to care for young children and frail elderly relatives simultaneously.

In a somewhat different statistical comparison, about 16.5 percent of American Jews are aged sixty-five or over, which comes to about one-third more elderly than white America in general (which is about 13.5 percent aged sixty-five and over). Once again, the implications of these figures are enormous, and it should come as no surprise that our communal responses in serving the elderly—pioneering efforts in health care, social welfare services, and federation-supports—are often regarded as models of what our country, as a whole, needs to do.

Understandings and Implications

What is important about these scenarios is that they make it difficult to wax nostalgic and wish simply for the old days to return. To do so would condemn both freedom-of-choice and women's educational achievement in the same breath. And so, despite the major consequences, here we are: a very different Jewish community from our parents' and grandparents' and great-grandparents'—one that is more precarious in some ways, to be sure, but also far richer in opportunity, diversity, and creative expression. A graduate student I taught at the Baltimore Hebrew University once put it this way. "We may be losing many of our young people to intermarriage and other things," she said, "but the pay back has been an entire generation of Jewish women in leadership positions, both within and outside the Jewish community. It's worth it."

Previously in this essay, I briefly highlighted a subgroup of Jewish women, that of single Jewish mothers by choice. They make an interesting case study. *Lilith* magazine featured this group as their spring 1996 cover story. Their premise, confirmed by the United States Census Bureau, is that more and more middle-class white women are choosing to have—either biologically or through adoption—children without partners. Not surprisingly, Jewish women are over-represented in this new crop of financially solvent, single mothers by choice. Overwhelmingly, I might add, this was not the mothers' first choice. "I would rather have been married," one woman is quoted as saying, "but I couldn't find a mate and I wanted a child."

Psychologist Ann Wimpfheimer notes that most of the research on the lives of children in households headed by unpartnered women has looked at mothers who are much younger, much poorer, and with considerably less education and fewer skills than the children of these single, middle-class mothers. Wimpfheimer, a Ph.D. candidate, indicates that the children she has studied, aged two through six, show no behavioral or developmental differences from their biological peers raised in two-parent families. While we don't know what will happen when the children get older—say, when they move into their teenage years—it appears, at least during the formative years, that if the mother is secure and feels in control of her situation, the children feel similarly.

To me, this example is instructive because of the way it takes us, once

again, behind the surface meaning of statistical data—behind family dissolution, divorce, or dysfunction to those islands of strength on which to
build for the future, affirming that personal courage, Jewish identity, and
a meaningful Jewish life need not be lost simply because family structures
are changing. The same is true for many intermarried families, co-habi-
tating, and same-gender families, and other so-called "new family con-
stellations," many of which are filling our congregations, agencies, camps,
voluntary organizations, and educational institutions.

This brings us back to the family diversity debate, and back to Steven
Bayme and others who offer the notion of a preferred Jewish communal
policy in the face of growing family diversity. Most recently, Bayme put
it in terms of Jewish family values. "What are the normative statements
we make concerning family," he asked, "that are relevant to today's Jews?"
In his presentation to family educators he went on to suggest that:

> [W]e respect personal choice but at the same time articulate
> communal norms. [W]e operate on an inclusive basis reaching
> out to all Jews interested in leading a Jewish life, yet we articulate
> statements that are ideologically exclusive, restoring the primacy
> of the in-married two-parent home as the Jewish ideal and pre-
> ferred model. This position has the virtue of remaining true to
> Judaic traditions, articulating normative statements, yet, con-
> versely, we remain able to include operationally all interested in
> leading a Jewish life but who, for whatever reason, do not meet
> this family script.

Bayme makes a good case for what, in my experience, is currently the
predominant position held by many of our communal leaders and policy makers. I can accept this position when applied in a particular situation, institution, or denomination within Judaism. As a community-wide
philosophy, however, its negative impact far outweighs any positive benefit that might be achieved.

The reality of applauding families composed of a married couple and
their biological children, but not those families who embrace alternate
lifestyles, is heard and experienced as a turn-off by anyone who, whether
by choice or otherwise, is in the latter category. Such a philosophic value-
statement is likely to motivate very few people to pursue a nuclear in-
married family structure who were not already oriented in that direction.

But for those people who have made difficult and sometimes unpopular personal choices, or who find themselves in such categories for reasons beyond their control, sentiments of exclusion or rejection of who they are will be experienced as negative and will cause them to go elsewhere. Gone forever. Another Jew lost. Can the Jewish community afford this?

In contemporary America, we know that virtually every door is open to us as Jews. By contrast, for the vast majority of our history, Judaism was not an option; it was a condition. It was not chosen; it was assigned. Today, we are all Jews by choice. Young people today—and increasingly, all of us—can enter the great American super market of life and select there at will, often oblivious of the nostalgic attraction of the goods stacked in the Jewish aisle. Why should they spend discretionary income on Jewish merchandise when other options, usually lower-priced and more seductively packaged, beckon the shopper instead? Leonard Fein asked this question rhetorically at the 1995 annual conference of the Association of Jewish Family and Children's Agencies.

To such questions, the leaders of the Jewish community usually respond in the same way as they did a generation or two ago—with lessons about Israel or halakha or the Holocaust or even with ones about the American experience of anti-Semitism and struggle. These answers may work for some, but clearly they fall short out there in the competitive market-place, where buyers, particularly young buyers, don't want a Judaism consisting only of nostalgia and memory and past history.

Instead, these young buyers want nourishment, validation, healing, and a sense of fulfillment. They want relationships with meaning. They want Judaism to be a source for comfort, joy, and personal renewal. They are willing to work for these goals—to invest in them—but they need an assurance that their investment will pay off. In her wonderful, heart-warming, and ever-inspiring book, *Finding a Home for the Soul*, a book by and about people who have converted to Judaism, written by a Jewish Family Services social worker who leads a Jews by Choice group in Baltimore, Cathy Myrowitz lists personal contact and openness as the two key ingredients in the Jewish community that helped her inter-viewees choose affirmatively to become Jewish.[3]

Permit me to stand rhetorically on this soap-box a little longer—to illustrate what can happen if we, as a community, do not consciously activate attitudes of sensitivity and openness to the diversity of contemporary Jewish experience. Once again, I'll draw from my own experience. Last year, for a fourth-grade session on European Jewish emigration at my children's Jewish supplementary school, my daughter was asked to draw a family tree. To assist the students, the teacher presented a classic genealogy grid, the kind where you are supposed just to fill in the blanks, where the lines connecting families presumed a direct descent from prior generations. The grid did not contain spaces for divorce, remarriage, adoption, single parenthood, intermarriage, or a variety of other family-relationship patterns which are so common today.

My daughter, who is adopted and from Guatemala and is converted to Judaism and who identifies ethnically as a Mayan Indian and religiously as a Jew, was very upset. She felt that the family tree—as delineated by the teacher—did not "speak to her family origins." Understandably, she did not want to deny or ignore her Guatemalan heritage, even as she willingly described the European heritage of her adoptive parents. After much discussion with us, she turned in a revised form of a "family tree" with both roots and branches—the roots from Guatemala, and the branches from my husband's family and my own. Fortunately, my daughter's teacher was receptive to this adaptation—but how much better it would have been if the original assignment had allowed for variation, according to each child's own family heritage?

Since my daughter's experience, I have written or spoken with dozens of colleagues across the Jewish spectrum—rabbis, school principles, and family service professionals—all of whom agree that, with rare exceptions, curriculum design and teaching methods in Jewish schools have yet to catch up with a 1990s understanding of "Klal Yisrael."

To be clear: for me this example stretches out beyond genealogy charts, halakhic interpretation, or even religious pluralism. It calls for inclusivity—for finding a home for all Jews, and for making all Jewish children in our schools feel welcome and a part of the rich tapestry of contemporary Jewish life, without first having to raise their hands and ask if their personal situation is an exception that meets with the teacher's or the school's approval. It's about training teachers, across denominations, to describe not only how the Friday evening Shabbat meal is generally observed in a traditional two-parent family but also to volunteer—without being asked by a student who feels left out—how this can be done when only one parent is present. It's about creating pictures for Hebrew school textbooks and children's haggadot and posters for the wall that show a range of family compositions and appearances. And it's about acknowledging and celebrating the diversity that characterizes contemporary Jewish life, rather than making the child who does not fit the assumed norm feel like the odd kid out.

Unfortunately, because we have not yet sufficiently concerned ourselves with the implications of the changing Jewish family in our development of organizational membership policies, school curricula, and professional training within the Jewish community, we are turning off families who do want to affiliate with the Jewish community, who have made the commitment to a Jewish education for their youngsters, but who do not fit the "traditional" nuclear-family norm.

In a society where people have choices about their identity and where Judaism is defined by consent, issues of diversity confront us everywhere. This is not to suggest that every sector within the Jewish community should be asked to accept all individual life choices. Subgroups within the community are free to create or enforce their own membership boundaries. But our survival as a strong community relies on a broader definition of acceptance, where each Jewish individual and family is helped to find a viable anchor such as a synagogue or other affiliation, which offers acceptance, nurturance, and the opportunity for Jewish expression, learning, and the support of others.

The diversity of our families and community offers us a rich texture and blend of sources from which new expressions of Jewish celebration, creativity, meaning, and life-cycle rituals will inevitably emerge. But it also generates thorny questions of conflicting values and trans-personal boundaries. Given the pace of change in our society, we will be hard pressed to find long-term answers; rather it is the process of debate and struggle itself that will likely survive as our most enduring norm. Such a process is as dynamic as it is critical, and it requires the joint efforts of Jewish educators, writers, family service professionals, synagogue leaders, and parents. In contrast, if we collectively fail to adapt to the new diversity in our communities, our efforts to enhance our own and our children's Jewish identity will result in the disintegration or alienation of vast sectors of American Jewry. And we will have only ourselves to blame.

Endnotes

1. This chapter has been adapted from a June, 1995 presentation at the Whizin Summer Seminar, University of Judaism, Los Angeles, California. The author gratefully acknowledges the helpful suggestions of Norman Linzer, of the Wurzweiler School of Social Work, Yeshiva University, in the preparation of this work.

2 A fifty-two percent rate of intermarriage means that whenever four Jews marry, on average two will marry each other (= one marriage) and the other two will marry non-Jews (= two marriages). My source for this statistic and the other demographic data in this chapter is the 1990 *National Jewish Population Study* by the Council of Jewish Federations in New York.

3: Catherine Hall Myrowitz, *Finding a Home for the Soul: Interviews with Converts to Judaism*, Northvale, NJ, Jason Aronson Inc. 1995.

Chana Silberstein is director of the Division of Community Organization/Education and Family Education at the Board of Jewish Education of Greater New York. Chana supervises Mishpacha, a progressive series of three year-long family education programs beginning with preschool and continuing through Hebrew School. Over one hundred Mishpacha programs are currently in synagogues and community centers throughout the city. To address the needs of émigrés from the former Soviet Union, Chana instituted the Shibbolim

Chana Silberstein

Educators Institute, a dual track year-long program for Jewish educators and volunteers working in Russian-speaking communities.

Chana holds master's degrees in Psychology and Education from Hebrew University, Jerusalem, where she taught family education and was a field work supervisor at the Baerwald Graduate School of Social Work. She directed a pilot family Headstart program in Israel and instituted a training program for directors of day care programs. She has certification from the Institute for Not-for-Profit Management for Jewish Communal Workers at Colombia University.

Building Jewish Memories
Chana Silberstein

A profound discussion on religion, exile, and survival takes place at a historic meeting in Dharamsala, India, between the Dalai Lama, the spiritual leader of the Tibetan Buddhists, and a group of American rabbis and Jewish scholars. The Tibetan monks are eager to learn about how Jews survived for so long in the Diaspora. The Jewish leaders say that Jewish continuity occurs through study and scholarship but especially through the family, which transmits Jewish culture and religion from previous to future generations.

Memories, then, are the life blood of a people. Roger Kamenetz, in his book, *The Jew in the Lotus*, wrote, "We construct memory in the present, and by constructing memory, we build our identity. What we remember constructs who we are."

Because I believe this so strongly, I always begin our Jewish family education training programs in New York City with a workshop on self-awareness. I ask family educators two questions: Who are we? and What of ourselves do we bring to our work? Together, we recall significant memories and describe for one another how they inspired us and how they influence our lives and our work.

I would like to tell you about some of my own early memories and about the impact they have had on my life. Beginning at the age of two, I remember my mother lighting Shabbat candles. I am standing by her side imitating her movements, covering my eyes, playing hide-and-seek with the burning flames—what magic they held.

I was brought up in Israel during the fifties. It was a time of tzenna—of rationing. Food was scarce, and unemployment was high. The country was populated by newly-arrived immigrants. There were many beggars and peddlers who came to our door, especially before Shabbat. One particular peddler stands out in my mind—the Alte Zachen Man (the schmata man). He would drag a cart and sound out loudly, "Alte zachen, shiuch, hamdech, mantels...." ("Old articles, shoes, shirts, coats....")

My parents gave him all sorts of articles to sell; and my mother would feed him regularly. He would look forward to her delicious Shabbat meal, eaten on Friday afternoon. I asked my parents, "How do you know when and to whom to give?" My father answered, "It is written, 'When a hundred people ask for tzedakah and ninety-nine do not need, and only one is in need, give to all so that the one who really needs will be certain to get it.'"

The last memory I will share with you was of an experience repeated on different occasions. The reciting of the sheheheyanu, a prayer of thanks for having arrived at a special moment. We had ten fruit trees and a vegetable patch in our garden. When the first fruit or vegetables of the season ripened, we would pick them and then before eating recite the sheheheyanu. This prayer applies to any first event of the year or season. When a relative was reunited with my family for the first time after the Holocaust—and we received notice of her coming—we recited the sheheheyanu.

How did these memories shape my life? I was sensitized to the wonder and the grandeur of the world and its creator. I learned about the richness of our sources, about our Jewish values of loving-kindness, charity, hospitality and communal responsibility. I learned about rituals in the home which provide order, stability, security—linking us to our past and connecting us to our future.

I learned not to let wonderful, teachable moments slip by. They are opportunities to introduce concepts because every thing has a Jewish connection. I learned that role modeling is important—that in order for learning to occur, one needs emotional as well as cognitive readiness—and that timing is critical.

My memories of my childhood are the building blocks for what will become my own children's memories. Parents are the conveyers of Jewish memories. The memories they pass along and the memorable experiences they create for their children will influence their children's self-identity.

Building memories, then, is a major focus of our work in family education. The Bureau of Jewish Education (BJE) has developed a series of programs designed and tailored to meet the specific needs of different populations, such as families of nursery school- and kindergarten-age children, Hebrew school-age children, immigrant families, and interfaith families. I would like to introduce you to three women and their families who have been Jewishly inspired by our programs.

Olga

Olga is an immigrant from the former Soviet Union. I met her at BJE's first Intergenerational Family Education Program for Immigrants held at the Shorefront 'Y' in 1989. It began on Tu B'Shevat, the New Year of Trees. We called the workshop Planting a New Seed in a New Jewish Life. I asked the group, "What does this mean to you?" And Olga said, "It means not having Hebraica written on my passport." Her mother took over at that point and said, "It means having a B'rit if my daughter gives birth to a boy."

Needless to say, Olga's early Jewish memories were painful. She was still ambivalent about her identity. I'll never forget the first time we lit Shabbat candles: she went to draw the shades down, an instinctive reaction of fear from growing up in the former Soviet Union—where no one should see that this was a Jewish event. She had to overcome her fears and her justifiable paranoia gradually.

Despite mixed emotions, Olga continued to come to our Sunday program. She became an active participant in the group. During our Shabbaton at the end of the year, surrounded by her family, she recited the blessing over the candles on Erev Shabbat. She gave birth during the summer, and her son had a B'rit, which I attended, together with most of the families from the group.

Susan

Susan is a mother of two young children, ages three and six. She lives on Long Island. She grew up in an unaffiliated family and never received any form of Jewish education. Her first significant Jewish memory was a seder at her great aunt's house when she was a child.

When her second daughter was born, one of her friends asked her when she planned to have a baby-naming. She replied, "What do you mean? My daughter has a name, *Jennifer*." It never occurred to Susan that her daughter might receive a Hebrew name in a synagogue.

Fran, the friend who asked her about the baby naming, invited Susan to a Mishpacha program in their local synagogue. The group consisted of ten families, thirty-two people. They were very warm and welcoming to Susan and her family. Susan and Mike, her husband, and their two daughters attended the Mishpacha program regularly. They enjoyed learning about Shabbat, holidays, and life cycles through hands-on experiences of arts and crafts, music, drama, storytelling, and cooking. Susan and Mike also participated in a discussion group led by the rabbi, while their children were engaged in a cooking activity with the Mishpacha leader. After the discussion, the parents joined their children for a snack and a story that reinforced the day's topic.

During that spring, Susan and Mike celebrated a baby-naming in the synagogue. They named Jennifer *Yona*, which in Hebrew means dove. The group continued with the program for a second year, where they focused on Bible stories and Jewish law. In the third year, most of the families became members of the synagogue. They formed a ḥavurah and continued to explore Judaism through adult education courses. Today, at home, Susan and Mike celebrate holidays that they learned through participation in Mishpacha.

Yehudit

Yehudit, an Israeli, grew up in a kibbutz in the Upper Galilee. She now has two boys. Yehudit's most significant Jewish memory was a Shavuot celebration on the kibbutz when a display of fruits and vegetables were brought on decorated wagons to mark the celebration of the harvest. For Yehudit, Shavuot was a secular holiday and did not hold religious significance. Her kibbutz, she explained, did not dwell on religion. "We didn't count the omer." (Omer is both a grain of wheat and the period of fifty days when we count down from Passover to Shavuot, the harvest.) Nor was Shavuot a commemoration of Matan Torah (the time of receiving of the Torah from G–d on Mt. Sinai.)

Yehudit, like most Israelis, is educated in Jewish history, culture, and the Bible, yet she views her Jewishness as nationalism. Jewishness is synonymous with Israel to her. Having been raised in a Jewish state, she was not concerned about her Jewish identity. Once outside of Israel, she had to redefine that identity.

Yehudit wanted to transmit to her children her Israeli heritage and culture, yet she did not understand that to maintain Judaism in the Diaspora, she needed a Jewish home. Yehudit and several other Israelis in the community were the pioneers of the first Israeli supplementary school, named Etgar, at the Central Queens 'Y.' The school's curriculum included Israeli culture, Hebrew language, Bible history, and literature. Once a month, a family education workshop was held focusing on Jewish culture. The second year of school, a bar mitzvah program was instituted. Every year more Jewish living was introduced. The school is now twelve years old and thriving. Both of Yehudit's boys became bar mitzvah at the age of thirteen. The family has joined a synagogue and are active in many of its community programs. Their oldest boy is a leader in USY.

I have described three women: an immigrant from the former Soviet Union, an unaffiliated American, and an Israeli. Although they did not share a common cultural background, they did share ambivalence towards or alienation from Judaism. Our programs are all about finding ways to connect them Jewishly, inspire them spiritually, arouse their curiosity to explore and learn further, and motivate them to live Jewishly.

For these women and their families, the building blocks began with the loving-kindness extended to them when they were welcomed to this program. They were made to feel comfortable in the synagogue and in Jewish community centers. The programs spoke to their hearts, touched them, and related to their past experiences. They became partners in the educational process; every one of these women became active in their advisory committees.

I believe that inviting them to participate in the planning of these programs gave them a sense of ownership and validation as people and as Jews. They enjoyed the informal atmosphere and the variety of activities offered within the workshops. They enjoyed the quality time spent with their families. The other families in the group became their extended family, and they formed a mini-community.

This experience became a wonderful entree into the larger Jewish community. They were stimulated by the Jewish ambiance in the room, by the displays of symbols, posters, and crafts. They welcomed the opportunity to place comments or questions in the suggestion box in the room, and these questions were used in planning future programs. They engaged in the process of Jewish living and were captivated by its richness. They began constructing their own Jewish memories.

Both of the programs previously described, Building Memories for Émigrés of the Former Soviet Union and Outreach to Israelis, were funded by grants from the UJA Federation. So was another project called Mishpacha.

Mishpacha is a three-phase program. Phase one is geared for nursery- and kindergarten-age children and their families, but can be adapted to suit any age. It focuses on holidays, Shabbat, and life-cycle rituals.

Phase two bridges the gap between early childhood programs and supplementary Hebrew school. This phase, called From Covenant to Covenant, focuses on Bible stories and Jewish law, beginning with Abraham and ending with the giving of the Torah on Mt. Sinai.

Phase three is called "Roots/Jerusalem 3000." It takes a journey through Jewish history and traces family roots connecting people back to Jerusalem. The BJE conducts monthly regional Mishpacha workshops for family educators. The training programs combine text and program planning. There are over one hundred Mishpacha programs throughout the New York metropolitan area, with over 3,500 people participating in them.

With a Target Population Grant from the Federation, the BJE has recently developed the Shibbolim Family Education Institute. This program offers a dual track institute to train professionals and volunteers who work with émigrés from the former Soviet Union. The goal of the Institute is to provide these professionals/volunteers with the specific skills they need to work effectively with this specific population. An integrated curriculum of theoretical and practical work covers three areas of course work: Jewish studies, social work, and a practicum. The participants meet twice a month for a full day. One day is a colloquium devoted to theory and one day is a practicum for planning and sharing programs. There is also a field work requirement of a minimum of four hours per month, supervised by BJE staff.

The Institute was named Shibbolim because of its rich significance to

Judaism. Shibbolim means ears of grain, which symbolizes bread flour, the basic staple that one needs to live. It is also one of the symbols of charity and communal responsibility, for at Shavuot, the holiday of the harvest and the gleaning of the wheat, we are instructed to set aside ten percent of the crop for the needy. It is also the time when we were given our Torah, which gives us spiritual sustenance. It is written, "Ihm ain kemach, ain Torah." If there is no flour, there is no Torah.

We hope that the Jewish community will continue to provide us with flour so that we can continue to transmit Torah.

Jo Kay is Religious School director at Congregation Rodeph Sholom, a large Reform congregation in Manhattan. For ten years she had been director of Judaic Studies at the Rodeph Sholom Day School. Jo created the PACE (Parent and Child Education) model of Jewish family education almost twenty years ago in Temple Emanu-El, East Meadow, New York, and is among the pioneers of Jewish family education.

Jo Kay

A former fellow of the Melton Center of the Hebrew University in Jerusalem, where she lived with her family for a year, she holds both Teachers' and Principals' Certification from the Union of American Hebrew Congregations and a master's degree in Hebrew Culture from New York University. Jo lives in East Meadow, New York, with her husband, Alan, and their three daughters, Corinne, Lisa, and Adina.

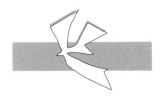

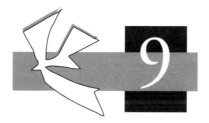

Fifteen Years Later: PACE Families Revisited
Jo Kay

How Pace Began

It was 1978. I had been working at Temple Emanu-El's Religious School for nearly a year. My youngest of three daughters, Adina, was only six-months old; Lisa was almost six years old and in kindergarten; and Cory was eight years old and in the third grade. We were a close family, new to this suburban community of East Meadow, Long Island, and in search of support for our growing Jewish identity.

I had converted to Judaism many years earlier, and we had successfully maintained a close relationship with my husband's parents and with my family of origin. We wanted very much for our children to have close relationships with both sets of grandparents. We felt that our family had a strong, positive Jewish identity until late one afternoon on the Belt Parkway, when we were returning home to Brooklyn after visiting with friends on Long Island. I share that story elsewhere in this book in my essay, *One Family's Jewish Road Map*.

As a result of our need to find more Jewish children for our children to play with and more Jewish families for us to spend time with, we moved to a suburb of New York City to live amidst a large Jewish population and joined a local synagogue. When Cory was about to enter fourth grade, the rabbi at Temple Emanu-El, where I was teaching and where we had become members, approached the principal with an idea that grew out of a United Synagogue program called PEP (Parallel Education Program), that offered parents an opportunity to study while their children were in religious school. It was a side-by-side program which followed its own curriculum. Our rabbi's idea was to bring parents and children together for study, and his question was, "Who will do it?"

The principal, who knew my history, my observance, my search, my struggles, my skill, and my commitment, felt certain I could manage the task. My own confidence was initially less secure. Nevertheless, I was very excited about a teaching opportunity that was new and mine to mold. Yet I remember telling the rabbi I had one condition before I would consent to this challenge—he had to promise to study with me on a regular basis. He accepted my condition, the principal promised her guidance and support, and I agreed to discuss the program with my family, who would become students in my "family education class."

That summer I wrote a course outline, reviewed it with the principal, and began to plan units, trips, art projects, special programs, a schedule for guest speakers, and films, worship services, etc. The principal accepted my outline, shared it with the rabbi, and they began to make the necessary contacts. We were a team, and we worked well together. The curriculum grew out of the text for the course and my own interests.

During this same year, Alan and I were the curriculum coordinators for a temple-wide retreat weekend. We were leaving one of the meals singing, when our rabbi approached us and asked, "Have you guys ever thought about going to camp? You'd love it!" This simple suggestion of total immersion in Jewish life for the summer had us sold. (Alan and I had never gone to camp as children. "Sleep-away camping" was a world unknown to both of us.) So during our interview with the director of Cejwin Camps, a pluralistic Jewish camp which had its roots in Reconstructionism, we were asked why we wanted the jobs, and we replied, "Because we want to go to camp!" He loved the answer; we were hired, and I became a Jewish culture counselor. Adina was two years old, Cory was entering fifth grade, and Lisa was entering second grade—we all went to camp. Lisa and Adina were day-campers in the staff camp, and Cory was a full camper.

We worked at Cejwin for five summers. I became a Head Counselor, and all while we were continuing with PACE during the year. Camp provided me, and our family as well, with an opportunity to grow Jewishly in new and special ways. Although we consider ourselves observant Reform Jews, in the camp setting we lived with and were exposed to Jewish life from all perspectives. There was a regular Orthodox minyan and a large Orthodox staff to whom we grew quite close. They were wonderfully enriching years, and ones that seemed to fit naturally in the development of our family's Jewish identity.

In PACE's second year at Temple Emanu-El, it moved from Sunday morning to Shabbat morning. The program began with a service and was followed by the study of the life cycle. Simultaneously, I began a second fourth-grade PACE class on Sunday mornings. I was now teaching two PACE classes at one time. The second group of families was as excited as the first group had been. This time, it wasn't my family in the class; it was the rabbi's family instead. It was a wonderful dynamic for all of us.

Four Families in Pace

Now it is eighteen years later. I am no longer teaching in Temple Emanu-El's Religious School. Today I am the principal of Congregation Rodeph Sholom's Religious School in Manhattan. Recently I spoke with four families from the original PACE class—including my own family— about their PACE journeys.

Miriam, Frank, and Their Son, Max

Miriam and Frank are Max's parents. Max, the fourth of six children, was not particularly interested in his secular school studies, but remained in the PACE program and graduated with his class at the end of the twelfth grade. Miriam answered my question "Why did you join PACE?"

I wanted to learn more about Judaism. When I registered Max for the fourth grade, I was told there was a PACE option, a class in which I could learn with the children while they were learning. The only Jewish activities I did at home were lighting candles on Friday evening and saying the blessing. I knew the holidays, Rosh ha Shanah and <u>H</u>*anukkah only a little. I was not proud about that and I wouldn't have been able to admit that to anyone but I found the PACE class to be made up of adults very much like me. They were safe to be with, non-judgmental and non-threatening.*

I learned so much about being Jewish. For example, I had never heard of a Tu B'Shevat seder. PACE helped me become aware of beautiful fun things. Everything you feel about life, joy, and beauty, you can feel as a Jew. I remember when we first helped you build a sukkah at your house. Alan said to us, "I'll give you the cinder blocks so you can build your own." We did!

You know, sometimes a temple is hard to be in. It doesn't have the warmth and closeness of home. When I first joined Temple Emanu-El,

I didn't know if we could really be a part of this congregation. PACE help,ed because in PACE, people bonded. I remember when Frank and I couldn't go on the Ellis Island trip. You and your family "adopted" Max for the day so he could go with a family. That's what PACE did for me and for my family. It gave us "belonging."

If it weren't for PACE, we wouldn't have studied and learned and celebrated together as a family with other families. And because we did everything together as a family, we could share what we learned, not just tell each other about it. PACE strengthened us as a family, not just as a Jewish family.

Harriet, Elliott, and Their Son, Michael

Elliott was the PACE parent in the family, although Harriet attended many of the special events, such as trips and holiday services. Michael, the second of three children, graduated with his class. This family experienced the PACE program twice, since Michael's younger brother, Matthew, entered the fourth grade two years later, along with my daughter, Lisa. Matthew and Lisa graduated with their class. Elliott explained:

When I heard Michael say he would be happy to be with his father in religious school, I knew I had to join PACE. When we went to the Eldridge Street Synagogue on the Lower East Side, I learned what it meant for a child to study with his parent. And what it meant for a parent to study with his child.

The Eldridge Street visit was a powerful experience because of the history of the synagogue. When we stood in the sanctuary, it seemed all time had stopped.

On the way home on the bus that evening, and for a long time afterwards, Michael and I talked about the visit. He related to the synagogue because it reminded him—and me—of his grandfather's synagogue; so he could relate to the shamas, Mr. Benjamin Markowitz. Like his grandfather, Mr. Markowitz was old and religious and happy to be with young people. The visit blended personal history with Jewish history.

And the visit to the mikveh! PACE was surely becoming an interesting experience. At the mikveh, we, the adults, were learning about a place and a ceremony we had only heard about. We were fascinated. You know, children don't usually relate to things that don't touch their lives, but here, the kids were watching us as much as they were watching you as you taught. In the interest we were showing, I think they heard us, even if we didn't actually say the words, "It's important to us, even if you don't fully understand." Our children not only learned as we learned, they learned from watching us learn.

I would do it again in a minute! The PACE experience has made me a more knowledgeable and confident Jew. Actually, I became a happier person and a more positive—and active—member in the synagogue. Why I even became president of the congregation!

PACE worked for us because of the specialness of the teacher and the support, encouragement, and active participation of the principal and the rabbi. There was a team. As a family in PACE, we were also a team.

Sandy, Paul, and Their Daughter, Fayth

Sandy and Paul are Fayth's parents. Fayth, the youngest of three children, graduated with her class. There was no PACE program at the time her brothers, Michael and David, were in religious school. Both boys left religious school after becoming b'nai mitzvah.

Before Sandy, Paul and I talked, Sandy went to her refrigerator and pulled off a speech given by Alan at the first PACE high school graduation, and said, "It's been here ever since. Every so often, I pull it off and read it and put it back." Alan had spoken about how difficult it was for him to let go of this class of parents and children after being together for nine years. He recounted the many wonderful experiences we had all shared and gave a personal blessing to each student. Sandy went on:

I became involved with PACE because I wanted to support my daughter. She wasn't interested in spending too much time in religious school. I needed to encourage her even though I wasn't religious.

There's so much to remember. Ellis Island. It was immediate. Very real. Life-cycle events, Torah study, holiday celebrations. PACE made it clear it was "okay" to be Jewish. I never had a place where I could do these things before, where I could talk about what it means to be Jewish, and where I wouldn't be judged for what I didn't know or what I didn't do.

I remember that first class. We broke into groups trying to find a name for the program. I was in the group that chose PACE: Parents

*and Children for Education. I cried when we agreed on the name.
I remember our trip to Crown Heights in Brooklyn to spend the
day in the Lubavitch Hasidic community. At one point in a small
sanctuary in their headquarters on Eastern Parkway, the men put on
tefillin. Paul was crying. I began to cry. The Lubavitch were so excited for us, so eager to impart to us their knowledge, to share with us
their beliefs. They weren't talking down to us; they embraced us with
their enthusiasm. And in some way, they helped us connect to our past.
I remember when we delivered food packages in Coney Island
before Passover. We went into the homes of elderly Jews, and they all
blessed us. One woman took my face in her hands. I began to cry. It
was a good feeling, human tears, caring, doing a good deed. Everyone
was so happy about what they were doing. The children pleased me
the most. They were working so hard; those shopping bags were heavy,
full of wine bottles and matza and jars of gefilte fish. They learned
a lot, that life is not all suburbia, and that many people lived alone.*
"Would you do it again?" I asked. *Paul answered quickly: "Yes! It
was an experience for parents and children. What could be better?
Learn, develop, discuss together, be a family together."*

*Sandy said, "PACE added meaning to me and my family. PACE
and my family was a marriage made in heaven. It was beshert. And
my involvement with PACE brought me into greater involvement in
the Temple. PACE got me on the Temple Board. PACE gave back to
the Temple. PACE didn't stop at the classroom door. And PACE keeps
on giving to me."*

Jo, Alan, and Their Daughter, Corinne

Alan and I are Cory's parents. Alan was the parent and I was the teacher
in the original PACE class through the sixth grade, when the temple began
a second PACE program with a fourth-grade class, and I became the
teacher, with Lisa as one of my students. Alan was also a parent in that
class. Alan and Cory continued as students in the original PACE class. In
the eighth grade, Alan became the PACE teacher. The following year,
because both PACE classes met at different times, I was able to join Alan
and Cory, with Alan continuing as the teacher, while I became the parent.

Our third daughter, Adina, who was one-and-one-half years old when
the original PACE class began, went on to attend a Jewish day school,

yet enrolled in Temple Emanu-El's PACE program when she entered the fourth grade.

Cory's PACE experience was enriched by several factors. Since I began a new PACE class each year, my family always joined me on PACE trips with the other classes; also, when Cory's younger sister Lisa entered fourth grade, both children were involved as a family in both PACE classes which later combined to form a ḥavurah. Alan said,

> *I remember the year PACE began as a remarkably exciting time. I remember how full of enthusiasm and energy you were, and how ready I was to start. I was relieved I was not the one in front of the classroom; on the other hand, I felt I had a special role to play as your husband, as well as a parent in the class, and I knew I would have to serve as 'both' parents for Cory when you were the teacher.*
>
> *It was also exciting to begin to become acquainted with some of the new people in the congregation, and to give our daughter an opportunity to feel part of an extended congregational family.*
>
> *I had no problem being a student of yours and I felt it was important for me, as a parent, to be with my daughter, to have this wonderful opportunity I never had as a child to study with my parents. And it was fun to do this together on a Sunday morning: getting up early, having breakfast, going to the Temple, and doing it again with Lisa, when she began her PACE experience.*
>
> *I recall how willing everyone was to participate, to volunteer, to give of themselves, so we could celebrate life-cycle events, both inside and outside the congregational setting. I remember the PACE trip to Ellis Island. I really felt I was on a mission very early that Sunday morning traveling to New York Harbor, to be first on line to purchase tickets for the ferry ride.*
>
> *Whenever we see people today who were members of the first PACE class or the second, there's always, either spoken or unspoken (usually a long hug), acknowledgment of just how wonderful those years were. In the second PACE class with Lisa, when we created our ḥavurah with the other families, we were doing what PACE was created to do: extend Jewish family into everyday living. That ḥavurah kept us going outside the temple setting and after high school graduation.*
>
> *That I became a religious school teacher myself is directly related*

to my experience as a student in the PACE class. I learned new information and how to share that information, how to facilitate discussion among adults, and among adults and children. I would not have been able to begin teaching that PACE class myself in the eighth grade had it not been for the fact that I had the experience of being a student in the PACE class from fourth through seventh grades.

Cory said,

When I think of PACE, I think of how often the PACE experiences were part of our conversations at home. PACE certainly made us closer as a family. There were also some pressures for Dad and me in the beginning. We always had to be the first to initiate the stories, share the feelings, answer the questions. But all that gave me more confidence. It was also cool that Dad was required to have homework, too.

I remember when PACE families participated in worship services. Not only was the preparation—and the doing—fun, it made worship attainable. When you were doing it, you understood it more; it became your language. And I remember all the crafts projects we did, for examples, the mezuzah and the havdalah candle. Making these with our parents was fun and real. We were having more than a textbook education.

My relationships with the other students were very close and stayed that way through high school. We were very fond of each other. Together, we gained a greater understanding and respect for Jewish education, for our Jewish heritage, for Israel, for our own family. I would want my children to have the experience in religious school I had. And I would want to be a part of their experience because a family must support a child's education. PACE keeps working for me.

What Have We Learned About Pace?

The families with whom Alan and I and our daughters shared the PACE and havurah experiences loved being with my entire family. Having my own husband and children actively involved gave the PACE program a special hekhsher: "It must be good if her children are here." But the teacher's own family does not have to be actively involved to make a PACE program succeed as long as the teacher appreciates her role as being also a member of the PACE community, as a student as well as a teacher.

PACE offers opportunity for the teacher and the class to transcend the traditional teacher-student relationship. Whether the PACE teacher is married or not, married with children or not, she is still part of a family—beginning with a family of one. PACE does not define what makes a family: people do.

Whoever is the teacher, she must listen and respond to every need and feeling of her students. One PACE member said, "When we ask you a question, you look us straight in the eyes and listen; that's why you almost always have the answers we seek. You don't just hear us, you listen to us."

Because the PACE teacher is responsive to the needs of the families—needs necessary to their success as PACE families—the depth of the families' commitment to PACE is greater. Another PACE member acknowledged, "We would do anything you ask because you do what we ask." PACE works in the same way successful families work.

Initially, it was difficult for most interviewees to remember specifics from fourteen to fifteen years ago. However, once particular incidents were recalled, memories began to pour forth.General feelings were quite strong for all. In some cases, people remembered similar events differently, and in other cases, people remembered different things.

This experience of interviewing and reflecting on that period in my own life was both validating and emotional for me. It was the first time I had done such work with this population, even though I have been teaching about PACE for years! It seems to have borne out what I have been feeling all along. Successful family education programs should strive to be:

1. **Affective**
   It was a very emotional experience.
   People cried remembering the program.
   It had a powerful impact.

2. **Cognitive (Provide Skills)**
   I did things I'd never done before.
   Learning, experiencing Jewish life was exciting.

3. **Communal (Democratic Learning Process)**
   It felt like an extended family that supported each other. It was like a ḥavurah. We learned from each other.
   We grew together like a family.

4. **Personal**
   We all felt committed to the program.

We were truly invested in its success and continuation. It was tied to the successful interaction of our own families—and our personal connections to the teacher.

5. Supportive

Studying as a family, being with the family, supported and strengthened the family. There was better communication as a result. The program connected families to their past and their history.

6. Fun

The program was fun!

7. Empowering

The program was experiential, hands on, not a textbook experience. Doing what was studied helped families do it for themselves.

8. Comforting

The PACE experience was safe, non-judgmental and non-threatening. It was okay to be Jewish regardless of how much or how little you knew.

I never had a place to talk about being Jewish before.

9. Transferable

The PACE experience had an impact on the synagogue experience. It made synagogue more approachable, due to having friends, and more accessible, due to having knowledge. It added another dimension to synagogue life—it brought it home.

PACE helped several participants become involved in synagogue life. They became more visible, more knowledgeable, more confident, more comfortable.

The PACE experience created a desire on the part of some parents to continue their own studies, thus becoming role models for their children.

10. Special (Ownership)

PACE made participants feel special. We always got positive feedback from the entire PACE team, the rabbi, the teacher, the family, etc., and that created a momentum which kept us coming back.

A true sense of belonging developed.

The PACE experience is "sharing a way of life." For the teacher, it is not just teaching a class, it is sharing a class. For the families, it is not just learning in a class, it is sharing in a class. When a PACE teacher reaches her students, they reach back. When she touches them, they touch back. PACE keeps pace with the changing needs of Jewish families, and the changing needs of Jewish families are met by PACE. PACE may have been revolutionary when it first began. Today it is evolutionary.

Risa Munitz-Gruberger

Risa Munitz-Gruberger is associate director of the Whizin Institute for Jewish Family Life. She was director of Family Education at the Conejo Valley Jewish Center for Early Childhood and Family Education. Earlier she was director of Education at Shar'arei Am: The Santa Monica Synagogue.

Risa specializes in teaching bar and bat mitzvah programming and the connection between early childhood and family education. Her work is included in the A.R.E. Bar and Bat Mitzvah Handbook *and she writes for Torah Aura Productions. Risa earned a bachelor's degree in Elementary Education from California State University, Northridge and a master's degree in Jewish Education from the University of Judaism. She lives in the Conejo Valley with her husband, Don, and two children, Brittney and Michael.*

Bumps on the Way
Risa Munitz-Gruberger

Sometimes we learn more from our mistakes than our successes. The story I want to tell happened several years ago. I can reflect on it now with amusement, but at the time, I was not quite so sanguine. I hope this story and what I learned from it will help others involved in family education prepare for the bumpy process of innovative programming.

The Story: A Good Family Educator

Once I directed an afternoon Hebrew school at a small synagogue with mostly young families. It was an active place, with innovative programs that attracted good participation. As far as family programming went, the synagogue was well on its way before I arrived. The rabbi had instituted Family Days by grade level some ten years earlier. He also hosted monthly parent education coffees where everyone studied Torah. There were the usual Tot Shabbat programs as well as grade level Shabbat Dinners. Eager to add to this panoply of family education events, I decided to start what I thought was a creative and exciting new program, Family Time.

In the fall, we held an annual dinner-meeting of the Education Committee, composed of the teaching faculty and parents of children in the school. This was an opportunity for the two groups to mix, get to know each other, and discuss school issues. They were not there to set policy. After dinner and schmoozing, everyone gathered for my presentation.

Homework had been an issue in the school for several years. The Education Committee was in favor of homework because they set high standards for learning. Many parents, however, complained of lack of time. They felt that their children were already overburdened with work from public/private school and did not have enough time also to do Hebrew homework. The teachers favored homework; they felt it was the only way their students could meet the goals of the curriculum. Most students agreed with the "not enough time" faction. I had a different point of view and thought I had an innovative solution. We would change the nature of homework all together. I orchestrated a detailed demonstration with props and graphics to dramatize my new concept. I started by listing on the board educational goals that the committee and the faculty shared. The list looked like this:

We have specific learning goals for our children.

Learning should be reinforced in the home.

Homework can help students meet educational goals.

Then came my program recommendation, Family Time, a new way to have our students combine doing Hebrew homework with spending time with their families. I gave examples of this type of homework. For example, our first grade curriculum included Bible heroes. So, the teacher might send home a story to be read by the family and discussion questions that emphasized the hero and his or her special qualities. The family would then draw a picture together of the hero performing an act of bravery. Another example was for fourth grade, the year we introduce Hebrew reading and writing. The Family Time activity might be to identify how many times five new letters appear in a given prayer. Such homework would always include a transliteration to guide parents at home.

I explained that all the at-home activities would say Family Time on the top page so that families would become familiar with the concept. My suggestion was to offer Family Time assignments once each month. Reactions varied. The teachers loved the idea, although some were concerned about the time required to come up with appropriate projects and put the packets together. One teacher thought it was a good idea but did not feel qualified to create home projects for families. Committee members were less than impressed. Here were a few of their comments: "What if the family doesn't do the work?" "How long would each project take?" "Would the work be graded?" "I'm not sure I could get my seventh grader to actually sit with us and do work. One parent, not happy at all with the idea, delivered a three minute monologue about why, at the end of a long day at work, the last thing she had energy for was sitting with her kids doing more work.

After I quickly assessed that my presentation was not going as smoothly as I had hoped, I creatively wrapped up the discussion, leaving the decision wide open. We tabled Family Time for future discussion. The meeting was not a total disaster because I had saved dessert for last, after the presentation. This was the smartest thing I did that night. Everybody went home savoring the flavor of New York cheesecake and coffee.

The Question: How Could This Happen To Me?

Here it is—I did not have a clue about what I was doing. This may be hard to believe when you hear my credentials. I have an undergraduate degree in Elementary Education and a masters' degree in Jewish Education. When I presented my Family Time program, I had already spent thirteen years as a successful teacher and administrator in the field. I had a family of my own. I thought I understood the process of effectively solving a problem with a new program. You may have already seen that I was doomed to fail because there were no stakeholders invested in the program or its creation. I had just assumed that reestablishing the home as the center for Jewish learning and living was everybody's goal. I had not created any partnerships. I might have brought the faculty around with discussion and support; but, the parents presented a much more formidable challenge. At the time I didn't know why. Now I do.

I had not taken family dynamics into consideration. An understanding of the minimal basics of family systems theory would have been useful. The study of family process develops concepts such as relational space, family boundaries, family stratification, change models, and child socialization. With this knowledge, many issues could have unfolded differently. To intrude on family space and time is risky business. Families protect and defend the boundaries they create.

Today, I am aware that introduction of family education is more complex than I naively believed a few years ago. There is great demand for family education, but if we introduce it into our institution before we recognize the challenges and obstacles, we are at risk. We are in danger of not succeeding before we have really begun.

The Analysis and the Revision:

What I Wish I Had Known Before I Introduced Family Time; And What, If I Had, I Would Have Done Instead

In order to design family programs we need to learn about "the family." We will not all become experts, but for the majority of practitioners in the field, we need basic, practical information: we need to understand the development of the family, family processes, and family systems. We should also be familiar with curriculum development specifically for family education, organizational theory, and adult learning. Let's revisit the planning of Family Time to illustrate each general point below.

1. Know Before Whom You Stand

I was new to the position of Director of Education. Getting to know congregants takes time. I might have consulted with the rabbi, the president, and the chair of the Education Committee to gather more information about the families and their interests. Here are some suggestions and questions you might consider if you are new to an institution.

Ask to see enrollment forms. You can begin to learn about families by their answers on membership or school enrollment forms. Meet with lay leaders, i.e., the chair of the Education Committee, and ask general questions about congregants. Some questions might include: What kind of events interest congregants most? What has been the most successful event at the synagogue? The least successful? Other than the synagogue, how are our families involved in our community? Do we have many interfaith families? Blended families? What is the average age of the children in the synagogue? This is not gossip. It is information that will assist you in getting to know the families you will be working with. Then schedule the same kind of meeting with the rabbi, cantor, and teachers, to gain perspective from both professionals and lay leaders.

Each family is a unique, complex system, one we need to learn about. Knowing how and why a system functions is important for our work, and knowledge and understanding makes a family feel important too. Caring about a family goes a long way. This is a time consuming task, especially in very large institutions. But, if more time is not devoted to knowing families we will continually fail to reach our goals.

2. Create Safe Spaces

Although the home environment is considered to be "safe," it is only comfortable when families are asked to do what feels right to them. Whatever is to be sent home needs to be non-threatening and designed with success in mind. Families have boundaries—limits that each family determines based on time and space. We need to be aware of the vast and varied levels of family limitations. There are many elements that have an impact on the choices families make about what they will or will not let into "their space." Families protect their time and space both physically and emotionally.

Unfortunately, much of our work is a guessing game. The safest bet is to ask a family directly, "What works best for your family? Would you have time to work on a family project together?" Creating safe spaces is critical, and our families must be included in determining what is considered a safe space. One family's safe space is another's danger zone. Some programs work better if tailor-made to fit individual family needs.

3. Create Different Paths to Get to the Same Location

The shape of Family Time could have varied according to families' needs and abilities. For one family, assignments could have been bi-monthly; for another, they could have gone home once a month. Individualizing curriculum is an accepted academic approach for teaching students. Why not for families? All families don't learn in the same way. Using the word "options" as a constant reminder can be helpful. Try using the image of a "sun diagram" to approach developing the concept of multiple options. In the center of a circle write your program goal. Then begin drawing lines, creating rays of the sun, and list as many ways as you can think of to reach your program goal. If possible, do this exercise with a team. Revisit your rays of multiple ideas when you implement the program.

4. Listen First, Then Talk

The first meeting should have been spent listening to the committee's feelings about the current homework policy, and time should have been spent generating new program ideas. It would have been helpful initially to hold a gathering simply to meet the parents and hear their stories. We gain tremendous knowledge about each other when we listen to each other's stories. You might begin with some trigger questions to open the discussion, questions like: "Where are you from?" "How did you come to join this congregation?" "Tell us about your family, your kids, your husband, your wife." "Tell us a funny story about your family."

5. Always Think in Terms of Team Effort—Plan Collaboratively

It is important to regard the program as the team's creation, not your own. With Family Time, the program should not have been brought to the table, but created around the table. Without committee investment, the program was doomed to fail. Ownership is a key ingredient for success. To create a sense of ownership, some of these phrases may be helpful: "I need your input." "Your thoughts and ideas will help shape and build this school." "Together, we can create a dynamite program."

6. Combine Your Needs with Those of Others Invested in the Plan.
If all voices have an opportunity to be heard, needs are combined rather than prioritized. Prioritizing implies that some ideas are more important than others. Creating a list together of educational goals would have been more prudent than simply providing a list from the parent manual.

7. Take Baby Steps.
A new position does not require that all programs must be new. Every program or idea does not need to be mammoth. Family Time would have been a smart program to attempt in the spring, after I had had time to "bond" with the families. Change takes time. It may sound simple, but it is not so easy. Slowing down can make us feel unproductive. Several critical steps along the way may at first appear to be unproductive, but if they are skipped, the end goal will move further and further away. In order to inspire change, we need to approach cautiously, not frivolously.

Here, the Carl Brodrick model for change is helpful. His model employs three elements, affect, behavior, and cognition. They form a triangle with arrows pointing in every possible direction indicating movement between each concept. To fostering change, it is important not to judge. First, begin with passive acceptance of all three of Broderick's elements (listen and show that you care.) Second, show support for the client as a person. The beginning stages allow you to establish rapport. Third comes intervention. Finally, the follow-up stage is very important, it provides an opportunity to reinforce change. The first two steps are referred to as joining. Change will not work if you do not join first. People will not do things for people they do not like. Diagnosis exists between steps two and three. Diagnosis shapes the intervention to fit the situation. The suggestions from this family systems theorist are to listen and enlist.

8. Answer the Questions Others Are Asking, Not Only Your Own
As the committee members shared comments and concerns, each point should have been confronted and answered. It is not unreasonable for someone to question the viability of any program.

9. Consider All Stakeholders.
It is simple to set up task forces for any kind of program idea or concern. A Family Education Task Force composed of a variety of members and

staff would be beneficial for any institution that considers family education a main ingredient. In this case, a Homework Task Force could have been a subcommittee of the Education Committee. Every organization has a structure. Some are easier to work with than others. Most are complex because they are forever changing. Still, it is important to look within a system to see how it functions, especially if you have a key role in it. Gathering information about how the synagogue functioned in the past would have been helpful to me. It is as important to get to know the institution as it is to get to know its families. Drawing a sketch of the organization's framework could be helpful. What this does the framework of the organization tell you about who the players are and where they play?

10. Seek Advice.

Today's information highway is vast. Networking is a must. Do not be too shy to ask others about what they are doing and what they think about your ideas. Bottom line: get an e-mail address quickly.

11. Remember, We Learn from Every Kind of Experience.

After everything you do, ask yourself, "What did I learn from this experience?" Evaluation should be the stronghold of this field. But it is often over looked because it requires time. Yet, how can we improve ourselves and our work if we don't take the time to ask, "How did it really go?" "What worked, what did not, and why?" "Why did some families participate and others choose not to?" There are many important evaluation questions we should ask. It is critical to program in time for evaluation.

12. Serve Dessert Last!

In the End: Risks Worth Taking

We are all pioneers in a new field. The Jewish community has given us a mandate. It is time to move forward and enable families to teach and practice Judaism on an everyday basis at home. As educators, we should take risks, but only risks that are carefully thought out, and we should involve our families as full participants. I come now to answer my own question, "How could this happen to me?" My answer is, "It can happen to anyone." We can do everything right, and still, things may not work out as we want them to. But we can get smarter each time we attempt something, and we can learn from our experience. As for me, I have come to understand that the important thing is to keep trying, keep listening, and keep experimenting.

Many Sites, Many Sounds

Introduction: Many Sites, Many Sounds

Jewish family education can take place wherever Jewish families are. The nine articles in this section are outstanding examples of how family education might happen at home, in synagogues, in schools, in museums, at camps, and on trips to Israel.

At home is where families used to live their Jewishness and where family educators hope that they will do so once again. Victoria Koltun Kelman's article, *Home is Where the Heart Is: Families in a Jewish Learning Community*, describes the program that she has developed where families meet regularly in one another's living rooms for several years to learn together and to share the joys and sorrows of life events. She explains how such small, organic Jewish communities, which give families support, the comfort and structure of ritual and time for a spiritual dimension as well as shared fun, can be brought into being and sustained even in large urban settings.

Joan Wolchansky adapted to Jewish circumstances the successful Missouri Parents-as-Teachers program. *In Our Jewish Home: Educators in the House*, she describes how interested parents invite visiting educators into their homes four times a year before different holidays to help them create Jewish celebrations just right for their own family situation.

Synagogues are a frequent site for family programs. Since providing family education differs a great deal from providing education either for adults or children, new roles and relationships must be developed. Cindy Dolgin in *Team Spirit: Congregation in Partnership* describes the challenges of this kind of all-synagogue team effort.

As a rabbi, an educator, and a consultant for the Reconstructionist movement, Jeffrey Schein frequently visits synagogues which are developing family education programs. *Theme and Variations: Jewish Family Education in a Gay/Lesbian Congregation* is his thoughtful account of a synagogue team wrestling with how to use text study as an educating experience for the many different family configurations making up their community.

Jo Kay, in *Parallel Learning and Parent Empowerment*, describes a classic form of family education, one in which parents and children both engage in Jewish study but not at the same time or place. The parents' course of study is conducted to encourage them to understand how their own learning helps them become Jewish teachers of their children.

A large Conservative synagogue recently took a bold step when it created an optional family track within their existing supplementary school. In *Project Mishpacha: A School Within a School*, Mark Loeb, Eyal Bor, and Fern Cohen chronicle these efforts. When they subtracted one afternoon of formal student instruction and added family services, family field trips, and family programs, they found that these changes increased everyone's Jewish interest and Jewish knowledge increased.

Esther Netter's article, *My Jewish Discovery Place: A World of Imagination*, takes the reader to a unique museum where interactive environments, costumes, music, food, arts, and crafts engage entire families in engrossing discoveries about their past. Her account is filled with ideas for local or traveling mini-museums that can be created anywhere.

Many adults have vivid and enduring memories of their own childhood camping experiences. Judy Israel Elkin, in *Family Camp: Temporary Communities, Permanent Changes*, describes the policy and programming challenges faced when creating, at a Jewish family camp, those unforgettable moments which can affect individuals' lives forever.

Israel tours usually are either for teens or for adults. Even those trips called "family tours" have largely separate programs for different age groups. Victoria Koltun Kelman, in *Back to the Future: The Family Israel Pilgrimage*, details what can be done before, during, and after a family trip to Israel to change what might be only a refreshing vacation experience into a transformational pilgrimage.

Victoria Koltun Kelman began her journey into Jewish education the summer that her parents announced that she and her sister would be going to a "Hebrew speaking camp" (Ramah) because they had been awarded scholarships by their synagogue. Exactly thirty summers later, she created and directed the first Family Camp at Ramah in California. In between these summers, she collected three degrees, made a specialty of teaching teenagers in Jewish schools, and became a curriculum developer for the Melton Research Center.

Victoria Koltun Kelman

Her long work in classrooms led her to realize the urgency of engaging parents in the Jewish educational enterprise. Her first foray into this then-nameless field was Together: A Child-Parent Kit, *published by Melton in 1984, followed by* Windows *and five summers of Family Camp at Ramah in California. She is a founding member of the faculty of the Whizin Institute, which published with Melton* Jewish Family Retreats: A Handbook *and* Family Room: Linking Families into a Jewish Learning Community. *She is now director of the Jewish Family Education Project, a collaboration between the Jewish Community Federation and the Bureau of Jewish Education of the San Francisco Bay Area, a capacity-building project nurturing and mentoring family education in synagogues, JCCs, and day schools. She lives in Berkeley, California with her husband. They are the parents of four young adults.*

Home Is Where the Heart Is:
Families in a Jewish Learning Community
Victoria Koltun Kelman

Freeze frame: Eight families. Three parents—one mother and two fathers—are Jewish by choice. Two are blended families. In one family the parents are a lesbian couple. One mother is president of the synagogue. One child has cerebral palsy and is in a wheelchair much of the time. Eight children attend the congregational school and eight attend the community day school. One family lost their home and everything they owned in a fire; they lived in three different homes over the three years their home was being rebuilt.

These eight families, thirty lively souls—half parents and half children from newborn to ten years old—are gathered in the overflowing living room of a modest home. They share "good news" that has happened in their families in the month since the last group gathering. The following contributions come tumbling forth:

Tamar, age six: *We went to Disneyland.*

Alex, age seven: *I won an art contest at school.*

Diane, mother: *We've been saying berakhot at the dinner table every night. We have always said prayers at bedtime but now we've added dinner time prayers.*

Mike, father: *I have cut back on my work hours so that I can get home in time to have dinner with the family.*

Ariella, age eight: *I'm selling Girl Scout cookies. They are kosher. I'm taking orders tonight.*

Tina, mother: *I started a new job on Friday.*

After each report—a burst of applause.

One notable aspect of this exchange is that participants of all ages offered responses. This is a community where everyone is invited to

189

share—everyone listens and everyone counts. A second is that responses reflect the gamut of family life. The third, and the most important for this article, is that two of the six responses indicate changes that Jewish family educators would consider good changes. The addition of berakhot before meals (which is a "take-home" idea from a previous get-together) and a parent's decision to spend more time at home both reflect conscious choices in the direction of stronger family ties and a more Jewish family life. Over three years of monthly get togethers, these eight families have become a community, an extended family, for each other.

In this chapter, I will examine, reflect, and most of all, make a case for this kind of intensive, ongoing model of family education. What I write is based primarily upon my experiences while creating and developing *Family Room: Linking Families into a Jewish Learning Community.*[1] Family Room is a two-year curriculum designed for a group of five to ten families who commit to meeting once a month for shared Jewish experiences. The learning component in Family Room concentrates on the spiritual and Jewish components of everyday life. In the course of its development, I observed and tracked three Family Room groups and facilitated a group myself. My current position as director of a community-wide Jewish family education project has also added to my knowledge about and insight into the power of an ongoing group in multi-session programs. Personal observation and data collection from a variety of family programs have made me a very staunch advocate for such intensive models. While I use Family Room as my primary example, I intend for it to stand for intensive models in general.

Family Room began as a way to package the transformative power of family camp for use during the year. More flexible and less expensive than camp, it takes some of the magic of camp and sprinkles it throughout the year. Camp offers total immersion—no phones, no TV, no malls, no office. Monthly, city-based models cannot provide that kind of intensity. Families come straggling in from birthday parties, piano recitals, and soccer games. Sometimes, someone is "on call" and a beeper sounds. But in the hours spent together, families tune out the outside world and tune in to one another. They laugh, sing, create, study Jewish text and weave it into their lives; break bread and chant birkat hamazon together. Everyone leaves with something new to work on: look for miracles, try to say a berakha once a day before eating, add the Shma to your bedtime ritual.

What this ongoing, intensive experience offers that camp does not is exposure over time—sharing the new job or the lost tooth; seeing a baby grow from one month old to toddler and then to three years old; sitting in the circle and contributing to the conversation; parents sharing what it felt like to "try on" saying a berakha before meals; talking about choosing schools or about Girl Scouts and how they "do" Christmas. The gathering provides a monthly booster shot. It is successful because it helps families be Jewish on their own, in their own home, on their own time, and in their own way. These families are now a part of an ongoing community which supports their growth. As a model, Family Room meets five common needs of Jewish families.

1. Families Hunger for Community

"To get to know other families better"

"Close interaction with a small constant group of other families"

"In our constant search to make and maintain a Jewish community for our family we thought this would be ideal"

"To be with and get to know other Jewish families better"

"To have the opportunity for my family to meet with other families in a Jewish context"

"We appreciate the chance to meet other families with children similarly interested in learning about Judaism"

These comments represent a cross section of families' answers when asked why they registered for Family Room. Several elements are reflected in them, but need for community is clearly a common denominator. We know that hurried lifestyles, single and working parents, the feeling that kids can't play safely in neighborhoods without supervision, the mobility careers require, and the distance from extended family all contribute to the isolation families with young children feel. For many, synagogue membership or attendance at a Jewish school does not meet this basic need.

In *Habits of the Heart*, an important book for understanding the America we live in and the families we work with today, Robert Bellah and his co-authors argue that American society has finally reached the end of its long romance with the culture or cult of the individual.[2] Americans yearn for "something," although they are not quite able to express in words just what that "something" is. Growing up is defined as leaving home and standing on one's own two feet. "Self-reliance" has been the measure of successful adulthood, "finding oneself" an ultimate goal. Research done for *Habits of the Heart* reveals that, when pushed to think beyond this "first language," most Americans, albeit inarticulately, express an awareness that they cannot devote their lives only to "finding themselves." Very few Americans really believe that the good life can be lived alone. There is a "second language"—a language of commitment to community—which is rarely spoken aloud. It is not the language of popular media or public rhetoric. Americans struggle with it as if it were a foreign language. Family Room speaks directly to this unexpressed need.

2. Families Need Support as They Grow Jewishly

I have found many parents who seek to raise their children more Jewishly than they were raised, but because they are novices at Judaism themselves, they find that they cannot do it without help, encouragement, and support. A one-time event, be it a workshop, study session, or Jerusalem 3000 Faire, often leaves such parents with a sweet taste in their mouths, wanting more, but unsure of where to go next and unable to incorporate that experience into their daily life. A more intimate, ongoing setting such as Family Room acts as a laboratory where families can try things out, and reduce "Judaism" writ large into baby steps which are achievable one by one.

3. Families Need the Comfort and Structure of Ritual

It's not necessary to go further afield than the *New York Times* to read about modern families' need for rituals. "Rituals most intimately affect families, giving them a common focus, bringing them together in a way that everyday activities cannot," writes Gina Bria (New York Times, Thursday, July 13, 1995) as she describes her family's "discovery" of the potency of rituals and how that discovery has led them to create their own. Family Room families, probably a lot like Bria's, have been gathering monthly to learn the wisdom of Jewish tradition, and receive the gift of rituals which they can inherit, adapt, and pass along.

4. Many Parents Seek Development of the Spiritual Dimensions of Personal and Family Life

They seek "something more" than the largess granted them by successful life in America. Meaning. Ultimate meaning. God. Purpose. As Wade Clark Roof points out in his book *A Generation of Seekers*: "Members of this generation are asking questions about the meaning of their lives, about what they want for themselves and for their children...religious and spiritual themes are surfacing."[3]

Roof details the impact that growing up in the Vietnam era—those born post-1946—has had on the spiritual questions and religious affiliations of the baby boom generation, the parents in the families we work with today. Their search questions tradition and traditional institutions. They seek God and meaning in more personal ways than did the generation which preceded them. Commitment to a faith is seen as a personal choice rather than as an inheritance—something which changes and grows and develops rather than something static. Roof calls this "journey theology." He uses the Jungian archetypes of the "wanderer" and "orphan" to describe the baby boomer generation and sees their religious quests as "seeking shelter" and "coming home." And, in describing parents who return to religion "for their children," he quotes an astute pastor who notes, "The(ir) children become a safe vehicle for them to come without ever admitting that there is something in it for them." This is something Jewish family educators see every day.

5. Families Want to be Good Families

This can mean many things—strong families, cohesive families, open families, sharing families. Whatever it is, many families need help figuring out "how to do it" as they battle the centrifugal force of American culture, which spins family members outward and away from one another.

Debbie Friedman wrote a song which begins "Miracles don't just happen. They need people to help them along."[4] When I think about intensive and continuing community models of family education, I paraphrase those lines for myself and say, "Communities don't just happen. They need people to help them along."

There are a number of critical ingredients we can marshal which help community happen: time, structure, at-home gatherings, communal meals, learning and fun.

The first ingredient is time. In all the small groups I have studied, the third get-together has been the point at which separate families become a group.[5] This is true even in those groups in which people had known each other before. This "third-time phenomena" is a very important finding for family educators. If three times of being together are needed for a small group to "jell" into a community, this has profound implications for all the other models of family education that we work with to provide community. Whereas a big event can introduce people to a community and can entice them to come in the door, it cannot produce actual community. That takes more time. Another song comes to mind here: "You can't hurry love. You just have to wait."

Another aspect of this kind of time is its duration. The length of time—the two years plus which families commit to Family Room, one year or six months for other programs—permits lives to be shared. The triumphs (first piano recital, success in the city-wide spelling bee, bar or bat mitzvah, new job or home, first sleep-over away from home) and the tragedies (death, divorce, hospitalization, illness, bankruptcy) can be shared. These are the strands which weave authentic community. These natural ups and downs provide the opportunity to experience traditional Jewish responses to life. Community ties are strengthened by sheheheyanus shared and cooked meals delivered. Families so graced have the opportunity to make a shiva call, write a condolence note, shop for and deliver a book or game to a home-bound friend, usher or hand out the candy at a bar mitzvah, cheer on the parent reading Torah for the first time. This is the experience of organic Jewish life lived in community. Only sustained time can provide this. These children will never need a course entitled "Life Cycles" to learn Jewish life-cycle rituals. They will have learned it from living it with their families and their community of families.

The second ingredient is structure. A repeating structure helps people connect through community-building activities during which they learn about each other and uncover what they share. These might include sharing family "good news;" warm-up activities that create fun and whole-group interaction; singing; activities that require collaboration between individuals and families; and sharing ideas and feelings. Topics can be selected and ordered in accordance with the development of the group, with more factual topics preceding more abstract or self-revealing ones.

The third critical ingredient is that meetings take place in the homes of member families. Hosting people in your own home and being a guest in someone else's home are acts which foster trust and friendship. If you have not been inside someone's home, there is a way in which you do not really know that person, a subtle barrier to a deeper kind of friendship. Reciprocal host/guest roles connect people in a more intense way than seeing each other in a public place can.

The fourth ingredient is the communal meal. Breaking bread and thanking God together has long been recognized as a pivotal experience in the building of communities. Eating together provides the glue for a community. This communal potluck, with its attendant blessings of haMotzi and birkat hamazon, forges group bonds. The fact that the meal and blessings are shared and each family contributes part of the meal reinforces the idea that we each have a responsibility to feed one another.

The remaining two ingredients, real Jewish learning and real Jewish fun, round out this recipe. I link them because I see them as complementary and overlapping. Opportunities for substantial Jewish learning in a context which is also fun offers an irresistible package. Study should be as "real" as possible—the Torah text itself, the midrash itself, a Hasidic story, a tefillah, a section of the Talmud. Not summaries, real text. Conversations about text are the conversations which build meaning and family. When family members have talked about how each of them is created in God's image, about how to make shalom bayit, about what "Asher Yatzar" is saying about the human body, about daily miracles or sheheheyanu opportunities, Judaism is alive.[6] The family is nurtured by immersion in Jewish concepts. Interesting conversations about worthwhile things strengthen respect and connection among family members. Mary Pipher, in her book *The Shelter of Each Other,* points out that the power of family therapy may lie in the fact that families take time to talk together. "Time talking together is often all that needs to happen for things to improve. Talking and listening are healing."[7]

And that last ingredient. Fun and laughter supply the leaven which enables all the other ingredients to blend and rise.

"We have attempted to integrate some of the activities into our daily lives, especially those that bring Jewish mindfulness into our daily practice (i.e., prayer before meals, thinking and talking about our relationship to God and with one another, thankfulness)"

"This has provided us with opportunity to participate and reflectupon Jewish observance as a family."

"Our participation as a family has motivated us to participate more fully in Jewish rituals and to come together as a family for those special times when secular concerns pull us in differing directions."

"We're more aware of Jewish 'content' in daily life; increased sense of community; we tend to use occasional berakhot which we didn't use previously except on holidays or Shabbat."

"I've especially enjoyed tying 'thankfulness' and 'the G-word' into the things we do. I think it will become more of a discussion for J (husband) and myself about the issues we tend not to discuss because of our differences. I liked the berakhot poster we made—it hangs in our dining room, and even if we don't remember to make a berakha every time we eat, it is a reminder."

"This program has dovetailed well with my own efforts to bring a sense of God and living Judaism into our family life. I particularly liked the specific ways of thinking about God— saying the blessings before meals, looking at nature as a gift from God."

These are some of the answers to the survey question posed at the end of the first year of Family Room: "What difference has participating in Family Room made in your family's life?" It's clear that families did weave threads of Judaism into their daily lives, and that for them, this was a very positive addition to their family life.

These answers show also that families have taken home—and to heart—something of the study component from each gathering. Their daily Jewish lives, the choices they make about family life and Jewish family life are informed, shaped and sustained by their encounters with the great Jewish ideas and by their membership in a Jewish mini-community.

The families' actions support this observation: Families return to a mifgash having done their homework and having made a list of God's treasure which they are ready to read aloud and share. A family tells how their daughter took her framed copy of the Shma on the family camping trip and kept it in her sleeping bag. A four-year-old proudly announces that he has memorized the names of the four guardian angels mentioned in the bedtime Shma. A family has made a decision about a better way of organizing their Hanukkah gifts based on a reading shared at a mifgash. Another family enrolls their children in Jewish school, inspired by an informal discussion between parents over dinner during a mifgash.

Participation in Family Room or another ongoing program is a kind of proactive stance vis-a-vis family health. Families have made a future-oriented choice about how they will spend their meager discretionary time. They have set aside time to attend to their families. They are learning and getting better at talking together and working together.

In *The Good Society*, Robert Bellah and his co-authors point out that if American society is to be healthy and continue to flourish, it is necessary that someone pay attention to the family as a family: "Families require a good deal of attention to function successfully...[T]here is a crisis with respect to giving and receiving attention in the family. The care of everything and everyone, especially children, is suffering because there is not enough time."[8] A community is only as strong as its component families. A Jewish community will only be strong if its component families are strong and Jewish. Both aspects of family need to be strengthened for the continuity of the Jewish people.

In his discussion of the evolving American family, David Elkind describes the modern family—the kind of families many people reading this grew up in—as a haven, and the post modern family—the kind of families many of us have now, and with whom we work—as a railroad station.[9] Neither Jewish life nor family life can take place in a railroad station. An intensive group setting for ongoing Jewish family education is the context which can make a difference. The railroad station can become a haven. In baby steps.

Endnotes

1. Victoria Koltun Kelman, *Family Room: Linking Families into a Jewish Learning Community*. Published by the Whizin Institute for Jewish Family Life (Los Angeles: California, May 1995).
2. Robert Bellah, et al., *Habits of the Heart* (Berkeley: University of California Press, 1985).
3. Wade Clark Roof, *A Generation of Seekers: The Spiritual Journeys of the Baby Generation* (San Francisco: Harper Collins, 1994).
4. Debbie Friedman, *Miracles and Wonders* (Sounds Write Productions, Inc., San Diego, California, 1992).
5. These include Family Room groups as well as other kinds of ongoing (5-10 sessions) family programs.
6. Peace at home, a peaceful home A berakha (blessing) which is part of the morning blessings section of the daily service which talks about the miraculous functioning of the body.
7. Mary Pipher, *The Shelter of Each Other* (New York: G.P. Putnam's Sons, 1996).
8. Robert Bellah, et al., *The Good Society* (New York: Knopf, 1991), 256-260.
9. David Elkind, *Ties That Stress* (1996).

Joan Wolchansky is director of Family Education and School Services, Central Agency for Jewish Education, St. Louis, Missouri. She is co-founder and co-coordinator of Our Jewish Home, and currently serves as director of Family Education and School Services at the Central Agency for Jewish Education in St. Louis.

Joan Wolchansky

Before moving to St. Louis, Joan was assistant director of Planning and Budget, American Jewish Joint Distribution Committee in New York City. She also worked in Kiryat Shmona, Israel, as a community out-reach worker after the Yom Kippur War and at the 92nd Street 'Y' and the New Orleans Jewish Community Center. Joan holds a master's of arts in teaching (M.A.T.) degree from Teachers' College, Columbia University, and a master's of social work (M.S.W.) from Wurzweiler School of Social Work, Yeshiva University.

Our Jewish Home: Educators in the House
Joan Wolchansky

As befits residents of the largest city in the "Show Me State" of Missouri, Jewish parents in St. Louis have asked "to be shown" how to create a Jewish home and become more knowledgeable Jewish parents. Responding to this request, the Jewish community of St. Louis established an innovative program of in-house, at-home Jewish family education called Our Jewish Home (OJH).

Our Jewish Home (OJH) began as a "meeting of the minds" between a staff member of the Central Agency for Jewish Education (CAJE) and a staff member of the Jewish Community Centers Association (JCCA), both of whom saw an opportunity to create a Jewish version of a popular secular educational program for parents of preschool children, Missouri Parents As Teachers (PAT).

Parents As Teachers, founded eleven years ago in St. Louis by a visionary secular educator with funding from the Danforth Foundation, provides parenting skills and developmental testing to parents of children from birth to three years old. Although the program was funded through a private foundation, it was implemented through each public school district in St. Louis. In the past eleven years, the program has not only extended its purview to include children up to the age of five but has also expanded to over a thousand sites throughout the United States, Canada, England, and New Zealand.

The Parents As Teachers program helps parents "to become their children's best first teachers." Trained parent educators make four to six home visits per year to families who choose to be in the PAT program. Parent educators are able to detect children's learning problems that show up at an early age, and at the same time, model parenting skills. Parents As Teachers started as a program for inner city and lower income families, but quickly spread to include middle- and upper-class families including many Jewish families. Because Jewish families in St. Louis were already familiar with the concept of having a parent educator come into their homes, they were receptive to having that same educational methodology transferred to a Jewish program. One mission of Our Jewish Home, then, is to "enable parents to become their children's best first Jewish teachers."

After conceptualizing Our Jewish Home, we wrote a grant to the Jewish Federation of St. Louis. Our Jewish Home received a planning grant in September, 1993. Just as the concept of the program was well regarded by the Federation Allocations Committee and the Board of Directors, so, too, was the cooperative effort between CAJE and the JCCA seen as a positive model for other community programs. Within several months after receiving the $8,000 grant, the program was up and running with twenty families enrolled and seven family educators hired.

From the beginning of Our Jewish Home, there were several critical components. First, the Our Jewish Home family educators needed to be role models and mentors to their families. We felt that the relationship between the educator and the family was the central element of the program. That belief has remained constant throughout the program. Accordingly, our seven educators were hired on the basis of their communication skills, their own personal commitment to a Judaic lifestyle, and their educational and professional backgrounds. They came from diverse Judaic backgrounds. Several had preschool children. One was an educator in the Parents As Teachers' program. Before the program had even been funded, we had received applications for these parent educator positions. Many more applications for family educators were received than could be accepted.

A second and equally important element of the program was the training of the educators. New staff are trained and returning staff are retrained each year before the new year starts, and mandatory staff meetings before each curricular unit continue the training process. Because the methodology of our home visits was modeled on the methodology of Parents As Teachers, a Jewish social worker who was both an educator and a trainer in the PAT program was hired to train Jewish educators in the dynamics of conducting educational home visits. In addition, she helped coordinators concretize the concept that evolved into Our Jewish Home. The Jewish component was added by the CAJE coordinator of the program.

A third important component of the program was the development of an Advisory Committee of both lay and professional leaders from diverse backgrounds and parts of the community. One of the first tasks of the Committee was to find a name for the program. Initially, our thought was to call the program "Jewish Parents As Teachers," but the national Parents As Teachers program felt that it would be important to differentiate between the two programs so we looked for a different name. After much discussion, we decided on "Our Jewish Home" as representing the message of the program. From the beginning, the Advisory Committee played a strong role in publicizing the program, recruiting families, and advocating for the program among synagogues and various organizations in St. Louis, as well as in setting program policy.

Currently, the Our Jewish Home program consists of four home visits occurring between February and December. The four curricular areas covered are Pesach, Shabbat, the Fall holidays, and Jewish values/mitzvot. When Our Jewish Home was being planned, it was felt that the curriculum should start with the Jewish New Year; however, since funding was not received until September, it was impossible to get the program up and running before the fall holidays that year. Passover was then chosen as the topic for the first home visit because the seder was cited in the Council of Jewish Federations 1990 National Jewish Population Study as the most frequently attended Jewish celebration. What started out as a function of the timing of funding ended up as effective educational planning. After the complexities of Passover, the Shabbat rituals seemed the natural next step in the families' learning.

Each home visit consists of an hour of instruction and discussion that includes background information and activities for the families to do together. The challenge for the educator is to balance the needs of the entire family at once. A "juggling act" takes place as she deals with the family as a family unit, the adults as adults, the adults as parents, and the children as children. Several dynamics happen at once, which is why appropriate training of parent educators is so critical. For example, if an educator is teaching the berakha for Shabbat candle lighting, she will strive within a five minute period to do all of the following: reinforce the knowledge of the berakha that the preschool children sometimes have, support the parents in whatever knowledge they already have, share information about the ritual and how-to of lighting Shabbat candles, and enable the family to recite the berakha together. In this way, she not only provides information about Judaic practices, observances, and rituals, but demonstrates to parents how they might interact with their children around Judaic issues. It takes skill and practice to integrate all these elements at the same time, and ongoing staff training deals with the complexity of doing this.

The whole family is served during the hour visit. Whether the educator brings a Jewish story to the home and reads it aloud to the family, teaches a berakha (blessing), braids ḥallah, or plays a game about Succot, the purpose of the activity is to show parents how to do it for themselves with their children. Because the family educator does these activities in the familiar atmosphere of the families' own home, usually at the kitchen or dining room table, parents recognize that "doing Jewishly" is possible for them as well.

Parents are also shown the wide array of Jewish resources available through our community Jewish library, Educational Resource Center, and Judaic and secular bookstores. They come to realize that they do not need vast Judaic knowledge or expensive ritual objects to engage in meaningful Jewish observances and activities with their children.

The families who participate in Our Jewish Home come from a variety of backgrounds and different geographic areas of St. Louis, including interfaith couples who are raising their children Jewishly. Some families are involved in their synagogues and in the larger Jewish community; others have no ties to the organized Jewish community; some come from the New American community.

Our Jewish Home has proven to be an especially powerful tool in the Jewish education of New American families. A trained educator who moved to St. Louis from Kiev twenty-one years ago has given these families the confidence to take the first steps in exploring their Jewish roots. Because this process is at-home, with Jewish activities appropriate for their preschool children, the New American parents sometimes have their first positive experience with Jewish rituals right in their own kitchens or living rooms.

As expected, families who have little or no Judaic background and observe few, if any, rituals in their home display the greatest degree of growth. Nevertheless, because there is a strong emphasis on individualizing the curriculum to meet the specific needs and interests of each family, families who have been involved in their synagogue and regularly participate in home rituals and observances find that Our Jewish Home provides them with what they need—an even deeper and richer level of understanding and involvement. For example, learning about the search for chametz before Pesach, incorporating havdalah, and blessing the children have enhanced the families' weekly Shabbat celebration.

To recruit families, an outreach program has been initiated to reach the Jewish preschools, synagogues which do not have preschools, secular preschools wherever allowed, and individual families through word of mouth. Many families now involved in the program heard about it from other families who recommended it. An unexpected by-product is that being in Our Jewish Home has now become "the thing to do."

One of the reasons why the program has been so successful is that virtually every obstacle to learning and to family participation has been removed. Because the visits take place at home, there is never an issue that the location of the program is inconvenient. Because the home visits are held at a mutually agreed upon time by the family educator and the family, there is no problem that the time is inconvenient. If a family has to cancel due to illness or a last minute scheduling change, the visit is always rescheduled. Because the children are involved in each home visit, there is no babysitter problem. And, even though the activities are geared to preschoolers, younger and older children are encouraged to participate as well.

Finally, and most importantly, because the curriculum is individualized, there is no problem of embarrassment at not knowing something. In the house, with a caring family educator, a comfort zone for the family is provided which allows for learning at the most optimal level. We hope that families will be involved in Jewish learning sessions and programs after their experience in Our Jewish Home. To that end, Our Jewish Home educators provide information and resources to families about educational Jewish programs that are occurring in the community.

Tracking Our Jewish Home "graduates" is part of our evaluation process. A pre-program inventory is distributed to each family and filled out by one or both parents. Parents answer questions about their current practices, rituals, and observances, and several months after the program ends, families are asked to fill out a shorter form of this inventory.

Families are also questioned at different times after the program has ended to determine whether there is a continuation of the observances started during the program.

The fourth year of operation presents new challenges to the staff. With funds from a 1996 Covenant Grant, the program is now being piloted in two communities outside St. Louis: Indianapolis and Montreal. Additionally, securing a steady funding base for the continuation of the local program in St. Louis is being explored to enable a greater number of families to participate in the program, and to provide the opportunity to modify the curriculum on an ongoing basis.

At the request of "graduate" families, additional ways of involving families once the official program has ended are being sought. Group programs throughout the year for current and "graduate" families help promote that continuity. Adult members of "graduate" families have been added to the Advisory Committee. Additionally, in 1997 an "Our Jewish Home: Next Steps" program has been implemented with a grant received from United Synagogue Youth. The format will consist of either a fifth home visit on a new curriculum topic or the development of additional curricular materials and activities.

Partnerships with congregations have always been a goal of the program, and that goal will be realized with a family education grant from a local foundation, the Henry and Gladys Crown Charitable Income Trust, to five Reform and Conservative congregations. In 1998, these congregations will be starting OJH's for their families with first, second, and third graders. While new curriculum is being developed to suit the needs of this particular age group, the methodology of home visits with trained educators will continue to be the model of program implementation.

Our Jewish Home has become an important part of the St. Louis Jewish community in the four years of its operation. Our Jewish Home is the only Jewish community-sponsored program of its kind in the country that we know about using the format of individualized home visits to promote, teach, and support families in their quest for Jewish knowledge. Based on the recognition that Jewish identity begins at home, Our Jewish Home assists parents in acquiring the educating tools they need. This home-based, personal visit educational model is designed to supplement, not replace, other forms of Jewish education currently in place. Assessment to date indicates that the impact of this concentrated one-on-one program goes far beyond the one-year enrollment period in meeting the families' Jewish needs. Our Jewish Home provides young Jewish families with, not only a tangible curriculum, but a lasting foundation of Jewish knowledge.

Cindy Dolgin

Cindy Dolgin recently completed six years as educational director at the Huntington Jewish Center on Long Island, New York, where she gained a reputation as an innovative, hands-on educational leader, teaching students of all ages, from toddlers to senior citizens. Cindy earned a bachelor's degree from the University of Michigan in 1982 and a master's degree in Jewish Education from the Jewish Theological Seminary of America in 1996.

For seven years, Cindy lived in Israel with her husband Moti, where their two children, Yonatan, age ten, and Maya, age nine, were born. After years as a computer programmer and systems' analyst, Cindy happily returned to the field of Jewish education, first in Tel Aviv and now on Long Island, where the Dolgins make their home.

Team Spirit: Congregation in Partnership
Cindy Dolgin

The meaning of Jewish family education (JFE) varies from institution to institution, as does the way of implementing such education. Wise providers of JFE should evaluate their own institutional needs in relation to the myriad models available before adopting, adapting, or experimenting. But no matter which programs are used, the success of JFE is due to the dedicated work and commitment of a broad group of interested stakeholders, representing both the professional and volunteer leaders of the institution. Consider for a moment the following scenario:

I don't understand what went wrong. I came back from CAJE with a fabulous idea for an intergenerational family program. I thought through the details of each self-explanatory station, sent a beautiful flyer to the whole congregation, made a poster for the lobby, ordered delicious and thematically appropriate food, spent a fortune on art supplies, and came at 6:30 in the morning to set up. After all that work, only seven families showed up. I'm disappointed, exhausted, humiliated, and I'll never run a family program again!! Tamar

After planning a fool-proof, top-notch, educationally sound and fun intergenerational program, how could such a disaster have befallen this well-intentioned, talented educational director? What could she, and we, learn from this experience? What is missing from Tamar's method of making JFE a priority for her congregation?

The missing element is collaboration. Tamar assumed that since she so passionately believed in her program, the families in the congregation would share her vision and excitement. Tamar worked herself to the bone for the sake of the congregation she cares about, but she worked in a vacuum, taking all the responsibility upon herself, and not investing others in her vision. Where were volunteers to help shop, make posters, make reminder phone calls, set tables, and develop the concepts and projects for each of the stations? Where were the other professionals from her synagogue staff? Did they help promote Tamar's program through nursery school, adult education, the daily minyan, or youth group?

Why We Need Professional/Volunteer Partnerships

As a result of the challenging statistics about the increasing rate of assimilation contained in the CJF 1990 *National Jewish Population Survey*, Jewish education has been changing, and the community's expectations of formal and informal educational institutions are rising. It is clear that new leadership patterns must now emerge, with greater sharing of responsibility between professional Jewish educators and actively involved volunteer leaders. If such sharing of responsibility does occur, three important objectives will be achieved: first Jewish education will adapt its operating style to be more in tune with the needs of Jewish families; second, more heads, hands, and hearts will be involved in a greater variety of Jewish educational programming; and third, additional financial resources will be generated to upgrade the quality of Jewish education.

We know that Jewish education and Jewish educators do not yet have sufficient support or resources to face the challenges of Jewish continuity. Jewish education is not to blame for the recent and current erosion of commitment, but it is certainly expected to come forth with solutions for the future. Jewish education including day school, summer camp, youth group, and Israel trips have produced "soul-touching" experiences strongly correlated to positive Jewish identification throughout adulthood. We want to add family education to this list.

Most people enter into Jewish education, whether as children or as adults, through their local synagogue. Because more Jews cross through its portals than through any other institution, the synagogue is an important entry point for Jewish education. Synagogues are beginning to understand that they must come to be compelling educating communities. A collaborative lay and professional planning process is essential to creating such an educating community. And a supportive relationship based on mutual respect among volunteer leaders, rabbi, religious and nursery school directors, programming or family life directors, youth advisor, and teachers is key to a collaborative planning process.

Why We Are Telling Our Story

This article describes the volunteer-professional and intra-professional links in our synagogue-based family education. In part, we are telling the story of one congregation which has consciously and actively implemented JFE; in part, we are offering a general comment about healthy, even if imperfect, lay-professional links in any synagogue.

In order to understand how this article came about, the reader should be aware that a two-page questionnaire was sent to families active in sewing JFE into the fabric of our congregation over the past few years. Their responses were incorporated into this article and then edited by several volunteers and professionals. The end product reflects the collective voice of partners who have been involved in the implementation of JFE within our synagogue. Had I written a description of the volunteer-professional relationship from my own perspective as Religious School director, it would have been an inaccurate, one-dimensional picture of the professional/volunteer partnership that has evolved in our setting.

We have been implementing JFE for the past eight years. Efforts have become achievements, and we have become more and more collaborative, expanding our circle of stakeholders over time. According to Susan Shevitz, "Five years is the minimum amount of time it takes to institute significant change. Only when the flurry of activities and excitement associated with the change subsides can it be known whether the innovation has staying power." Although activity has not yet subsided (hopefully, it never will) we feel that enough significant change has occurred to begin reflecting upon and sharing our experiences.

We are profoundly fortunate to have been recipients of a UJA Continuity Grant to fund experimental synagogue programming in JFE. Federations, emerging from their previously distant relationship with synagogues, are coming to recognize the critical role synagogues play in reaching large numbers of American Jews. In many parts of the country, Federations are now supporting bold and original structural changes within synagogues which demonstrate genuine collaborative relationships among the professional and volunteer leadership.

Perhaps this article will be helpful for synagogues with the same ideas who are interested in creating collaborative environments for experimentation and innovation. But if the importance of professional-volunteer collaboration in the Jewish communal world is already well established, why should we focus specifically on collaboration as it occurs in Jewish family education?

As we noted earlier, JFE within synagogues can touch the seventy to eighty percent of American Jews who are members of synagogues at some point in their lives. Only twenty five percent of these members would say that Jewish activity is a very important component of their lives. The others can be described as "marginal" or "intermittent" Jews who seek a religious school education for their children in order to get them "bar mitzvahed," a social norm of contemporary Jewish life. Getting the parents of these religious school children out of the car and into synagogue-run JFE workshops and classes is one way to reach, teach, and touch Jewish lives. It is a second chance to draw in those who are apathetic or dejected by memories of their childhood Jewish education. Those who are touched by JFE may in turn become volunteer leaders to help with the ideas, efforts, and funding of future JFE endeavors. This is really important.

The Whizin Institute's Influence

The Whizin Institute, recognizing the significance of the relationship between professionals and volunteers, makes grants for synagogues seeking funding to offset the cost of their participation in the Whizin Summer Seminar only if they commit to sending a full "team," including the rabbi, the educational director, a teacher, and a volunteer leader. Once the team meets together and spends five intensive days at Whizin, bonds among team members are likely to become strong. The team, representing different aspects of synagogue life, returns home united and enthusiastic, ready to roll up their sleeves and get to work. This diverse group shares a vision of reinvigorating the synagogue. They work in partnership to share responsibility for implementing their vision. Over time, additional stakeholders within the synagogue are added to the JFE cause.

In the summer of 1992, our synagogue sent a team to the Whizin Summer Seminar, and indeed, the magic happened. During "Whizin Team Time," intended for defining short and long term goals for each individual institution, we agreed that the religious school sub-community was the most logical starting point for implementation of JFE programming, We planned that over time, a kindergarten through seventh grade family education curriculum would be phased in. Other existing synagogue programs, services, and activities beyond the scope of the religious school were also identified as possessing "potentially teachable moments," where JFE components could be added to enhance the Jewish skills and knowledge of participating families. All phases of programmatic development were to be divided among team members, with the bulk of the educational tasks undertaken by the professionals and significant portions of the planning and implementation to be handled by volunteers.

We noticed that our group was beginning to behave like a team. The rabbi served as captain, and each player filled his or her position. As in any team sport, a deep sense of mutual appreciation and respect develops for one's teammates when one realizes that a squad will never emerge triumphant if a superstar hogs the ball or if someone quits playing in the middle of the game. All team players must be flexible enough to cover for others, and to think fast on their feet. And, as any coach will tell you, a winning team is only as good as its bench. Therefore, in order for JFE to permeate and transform our synagogue, we recognized that we would need to add additional potential players, investors, and cheerleaders.

During the first year, the core team would put on a few exhibition matches, that is, run a few Whizin-style razzle-dazzle and fool-proof JFE programs for limited captive audiences, and along the way, gain enthusiastic support and identify additional stakeholders. Perhaps, after building this diverse squad, based on a sound philosophy, ample talent, and mutual respect, our entire congregation would emerge a winner.

Josh Elkin has written that, "For the most part, professionals meet their lay counterparts within a context marked by a severe lack of reflection. When a productive working relationship does seem to exist, energy rarely exists to think systematically about the components contributing to that positive collaboration. Few, if any, case records exist which document successful working relationships such that someone could analyze them in the future and derive some useful guidelines for others." But at the conclusion of his article, written within the context of day-school education, Elkin states that he "resisted the temptation to present a recipe for successful lay-professional collaboration. No two settings are the same and there exists more than one potentially successful course of action." Each institution needs to nurture and develop its own individual tradition of partnership between the professionals and volunteer leaders, and to refine and nourish that relationship as it evolves.

211

After three years of implementing JFE and going as far as we could in the religious school sub-community, a recomposed synagogue team returned to the Whizin Summer Seminar in June of 1995. The members of this team reflected an expanded vision of family education as a lifelong pursuit, not just a grade-school one. After several years of JFE aimed primarily at the religious school, our synagogue's efforts had begun to move down into the nursery school, out to the day school, up to the high school, and beyond to the empty nesters. With our new and wider field of vision, the 1995 Whizin team included the educational director, nursery school director, a teacher who leads many family workshops in the religious school, a volunteer leader from the family life committee with nursery and school aged children, and a volunteer leader with high school and college aged children, who co-chairs the family-life committee.

Revisiting the Whizin Summer Seminar without the rabbi, who had very much been our JFE visionary from the beginning, and without the Family Life Educator, who was on maternity leave at the time, forced the other participants to clarify their own vision of the synagogue and to relinquish their natural turf in deference to "the common good."

We came to certain realizations, which now seem obvious, but which we had overlooked in the past. For example, we had paid very little attention to the fact that nursery school is the most common entry point into synagogue life, and that its director and teachers are the window through which many families get their first glimpse of synagogue life and Jewish living in general. When the nursery school director joined the JFE team, everyone began to realize that the nursery school years are ones when families are establishing the social contacts that often last a lifetime. Families are open to adopting and adapting rituals while their children are pre-schoolers. Therefore, we saw that those entry-level holiday and home-ritual family workshops usually offered to families in the primary grades in the religious school should be revised and moved into the nursery school program. Likewise, we saw that certain issue-based family programs, like an inter-dating and intermarriage workshop, currently part of the seventh grade family education curriculum, should be offered to the families of older teenagers, when dating is an even more relevant issue.

It did not take much discussion before these five individuals realized that their participation in the Whizin Summer Seminar did not give them the right to make decisions for the rest of the congregation, because they were just representatives of a much larger team back home, which included the other professionals (especially the rabbi and family life coordinator) and volunteer leaders from all branches of synagogue life. Since family education beyond the religious school is a very complicated matter, with repercussions for populations represented by nursery school, sisterhood, men's club, youth group, adult education, and others not part of a particular interest group within the synagogue, the team could not come back with a whole new game plan, as had been the case the first time around. Instead, the Whizin team brought back with them a wide-angle vision and suggestions for expansion of programs throughout the synagogue. An ongoing dialogue with myriad stakeholders seemed to be the most effective way to bring the team spirit back home.

Part of the ongoing dialogue was to be organized through the Family Life Committee, the group responsible for those JFE programming initiatives which fall outside the domain of the religious school community. Part would happen at staff meetings, and further discussions of a more philosophical nature would be ongoing among the Whizin participants.

Who are the Team Players and How do they Interact?

Several teams now operate simultaneously within our setting. The professional team meets bi-weekly to discuss common issues, especially those which pertain to JFE. The volunteer-professional team, which evolved from the Whizin participants, has developed into a think-tank, and comes together periodically to discuss the philosophical issues of achieving life-long Jewish learning. The family life committee plans and implements most JFE programs. The religious school and nursery school boards meet regularly and part of their discussions pertains to JFE programs. Each of the educational committees includes members of the professional staff. All other synagogue arms, from the most narrowly focused right up to the board of trustees and executive board, discuss goals for involving each individual in lifelong Jewish learning and living.

Susan Shevitz has written of the failure of "congregational teams" to work effectively together and the difficult process of re-examining and adjusting long-established rules, roles, and relationships. As an example, she notes that professional teams made up of rabbis, principals, and family educators that have been meeting for two or more years sometimes flounder because they are uncomfortable exposing dilemmas and dealing with issues pertaining to process. I have to ask myself, if so many congregational teams are falling short for the reasons that Shevitz indicates, how can our own very positive experience be helpful to others who seek to overcome barriers which prevent honest and constructive communication within a professional team?

We have no magic "one size fits all" formula, and our team is far from perfect. Nevertheless, I offer general job-descriptions of the individual professional positions, a method of intra-professional communication, and a few hypotheses about why this approach works. Rather than profiling the individual players in our congregation, I highlight those qualities which make for collaboration and consensus building. I will first introduce the professional roles, and then the volunteer roles.

The Rabbi

As spiritual leader of the congregation, the rabbi sets the tone for priorities and may be inclined or disinclined to promote innovation and experimentation. The rabbi sees "the big picture," while others in the synagogue are more focused on the specific areas in which they are involved. Since JFE is still an unproved area, with no firm statistics demonstrating that JFE impacts the lives of those who participate, some rabbis may be ready to jump on the bandwagon while others may have a wait-and-see attitude.

Different rabbis not only have different reactions to JFE itself; they also have a variety of responses to the question of who sets the JFE agenda. Rabbis whose style is to be consensus builders recognize the potential in responsible, trustworthy, creative individuals, whether professionals or volunteers, who bring new ideas to the table and can be instrumental in making successful JFE a reality. On the other hand, a rabbi who wants things done his or her way may not encourage stakeholders to venture into uncharted territory to pursue areas for which they feel passion. If such a rabbi is not committed to JFE, JFE will not establish deep roots in the congregation. In some cases, a rabbi may favor JFE but insist that ideas be implemented just as he or she envisions the program. In such settings, those lay leaders who revere the rabbi may adopt his vision, and contribute to its success, without having entered into shaping the vision.

In our case, the rabbi had a vision of JFE before anyone else in the congregation had heard of it. In 1988, at his recommendation, the congregation took a financial gamble and hired a new religious school principal with the added title and salary, of "Family Life Coordinator." Like the buds and shoots of early spring, signs of life soon began to emerge in this new area. The rabbi and principal shared a vision, and were determined to sell it to the congregation. But after two years, the new principal/coordinator left, and the congregational leadership withdrew their commitment to paying a family life professional.

At this time, the volunteer leaders had not yet bought into the rabbi's vision, and the next principal hired was once again a part-timer without the added title and responsibility for family education. The rabbi, a patient man and a believer in the centrality of the family as the conduit of Jewish continuity, did not lose his commitment to JFE, and over the years he raised the leadership's awareness. Undoubtedly, our first visit to the Whizin Summer Seminar aided the spread of grass roots enthusiasm among professional and volunteer leaders. Whizin left us on an emotional high, full of enthusiasm and hope. It also left us fearful, especially about the amount of work that lay ahead. The rabbi helped alleviate our fears because he was one hundred percent committed and would take upon himself responsibilities for programs and courses for which he felt himself particularly well-suited.

Though I have colleagues who disagree with me, I believe that JFE will not take root and make a major impact on the whole congregation without the support and enthusiasm of the congregation's rabbi, even though it may be possible to establish a meaningful religious school or nursery-based JFE program without the weight of the rabbi, if the director is well-established, respected, and highly motivated.

Our model for success depended upon the rabbi playing the part of team captain: leading the team and playing in the game.

The Nursery School Director and Staff

Before I left for the Whizin Institute, I assumed I would return with a notebook full of new family programs that the parents of the nursery school would benefit from. Instead I returned with something much more meaningful. The Whizin Institute helped me reconfirm my belief that "no man is an island." I no longer look at how the nursery school will benefit from the JFE programs, but see that all of us are interconnected at the deepest level. Each congregant needs to be reached to understand that with a mutual commitment to bringing

Judaism closer to our lives, we can turn personal hopes into shared
responsibilities and communal celebrations.   Susie

For many young families, the nursery school director is the first point
of contact in the synagogue, a fact not frequently enough acknowledged
and appreciated in congregational life. It is not unusual for the nursery
school to operate in a vacuum, removed from the pulse of the synagogue,
and many congregations are reluctant to even open a pre-school. If the
primary focus of Jewish education in the congregation is bar and bat
mitzvah preparation, then little regard will be paid to the importance of
a strong Judaic presence in the nursery school. Those who fear the
encroachment of a nursery school are not up-to-date on the latest
research in child development indicating that the values acquired by the
age of five are the values retained throughout a person's life. Those who
are serious about Jewish continuity should extend great "kavod" to the
pre-school staff of the synagogue.

Nursery school teachers and directors dispense parenting advice and
offer informal counseling every day. Parents consult with the pre-school
staff on issues such as separation, trust, bed-time, nutrition, and potty
training, and they feel secure that the staff has their child's interests at
heart. Parents are very eager to do right by their young child and are creating family rituals as they go along. Why shouldn't the nursery school
staff also be helping parents infuse Jewishness into their family life? If it
is true that what you learn by age five forms the bulk of what you learn
in a lifetime, why wait until fifth grade to have a family sukkot program?
Who is more likely to take the plunge and build a sukkah, the family of
a four year old or the family of a ten year old?

There are many reasons why a synagogue board should value a good
pre-school director, not the least of which is the potential for feeding synagogue membership. When our congregation re-examined the pre-school
dues and tuition structure and decided to create incentives for nursery
school families to join the synagogue, many did just that. Once the nursery school and religious school directors teamed up to rework the primary grade registration process and put it into the nursery school domain,
the religious school enrollment swelled. In many cases, families registered
their children for religious school, not because they had previously
planned to do this, but because everyone else seemed to be doing it.
Parents with older children in religious school volunteered to work on

recruitment and registration; old trends reversed because of their hard work and enthusiasm. Staffing considerations were re-examined, and the star nursery school teachers were hired by the religious school to replace the kindergarten and first grade religious school teachers.

We have hit some unanticipated potholes because of our collaborative initiatives. As a result of the new tuition structure, pre-school revenue decreased, and for the first time the nursery school operated at a loss. Many congregants were enraged that our one and only money maker was now in the red, and there were some who believed that the nursery school should be shut down. The critics were not looking at membership numbers, only at tuition dollars; they were forgetting that many young families were paying lower tuition because they were also now paying synagogue dues, albeit at reduced rates. Over time, a handful of families have left our synagogue to become members at other congregations offering fewer hours of religious school, but a far greater number have remained, including many who never dreamed that they would belong to and be actively involved in a Conservative synagogue. Only time will tell if the influx of young families will maintain their affiliation once they graduate up to full dues. In the meantime, these young families are taking advantage of and enjoying the variety of family programming available to them, and are melding into the synagogue mainstream.

The second unanticipated and disturbing bump in the road is the drop in new day school enrollment from our synagogue. The high cost of day school education has always been a deterrent for many families, but a new factor has now arisen. Parents have established such warm ties and friendships as a result of their involvement in the synagogue's nursery school that many are reluctant to separate themselves out of the mainstream. Ten years ago when some of the most committed families began sending their children to day school, the religious school community suffered because of their absence. Today, thanks in part to strong and ongoing family education, the nursery school families are more committed and more connected than ever, and they perceive that (1) socially, they'll be on the outside if their children do not attend religious school together as part of the majority, and (2) they and their children will learn about Judaism in religious school and in the family and parent education add-ons.

In response, the director recently hosted a Pre-K parents' breakfast to discuss "The future of your child's Jewish education after nursery school."

She invited the rabbi and principal to come and answer questions. Day school was suggested as the natural extension of the warm, holistic, nurturing Jewish environment of the nursery school. Parents were surprised to be hearing such praise from the principal of the religious school.

Empathy and long-term vision go a long way in smoothing the seams between professional jurisdiction and turf issues. I am not always happy to hear the "bad news" from the nursery school director that her enrollment is expanding and that she will need to share just one more religious school classroom. I do lose sleep wondering how furious the religious school teachers will be when "little tike" equipment appears in the corners of their classrooms. Then I take a deep breath and dream about the day when today's four-year olds will be tomorrow's eleven year olds, and God willing, roles will be reversed and the principal will have to come tell the nursery school director the "bad news" of needing to share more nursery school space.

The Religious School Principal

As mentioned above, our previous educational director had been a full-time employee serving as both principal and family life coordinator. In 1991, when I was promoted from teacher to principal, I knew nothing at all about JFE. As a young mother, I was personally not interested in working full-time. As luck would have it, this was a perfect "shiduch" for a congregation that was re-evaluating its philosophical and financial commitment to JFE.

Once our congregation sent a professional-volunteer team to the Whizin Summer Seminar in 1992, the rabbi's vision of family education was back on the table, this time drawing a larger group of enthusiastic stakeholders. Our first Whizin game plan focused on the religious school community, although several programs also had broader appeal. That Whizin Summer Seminar inspired me to re-envision the future of the school by having it evolve into a place where the primary focus is on the child within the context of his or her family.

In order to do a proper job of getting JFE up and running, I had to put in many extra hours, in effect working close to full time. JFE and all we learned at the Whizin Summer Seminar had presented us with a tremendous challenge, and the response to family education led to a surge of enthusiasm among the parents. Everyone knew that we were all in this transformational experiment together. This sparked an outpouring of volunteerism. I never asked parents to give a hand with something I myself was not willing to do, whether it was shopping ("I'll do the food, you do the paper goods"), table setting ("Are you available to set tables with me on Friday afternoon?"), or self-study in order to co-lead a session.

JFE evaluations were handed out at every program, and parents quickly realized that the staff was taking their comments and suggestions about structure, style, and content very seriously. The depth of their responses increased year by year. Parents were valued and appreciated, and most came to understand that they were the key to their child's Jewish identity. Rather than moaning and complaining about how rotten Jewish education was "when we were kids," we all joined hands, lifted our chins, and set out to do our best to make religious school a positive and meaningful experience for the whole family.

The down side? My time was so stretched that I sometimes felt on the verge of collapse. Something had to give, and the volunteer leadership and rabbi worked with me to determine priorities. More of the time-consuming details such as "KP" (kitchen patrol) were handled by volunteers as the JFE schedule became busier. Some parents expressed their dissatisfaction with the content of particular programs. Others complained about "being forced" to give up their Sunday morning freedom.

These issues have subsided over the years as we have come to feel more comfortable with the programs. The content has evolved in response to parent feedback, parents and teachers have come to appreciate the benefits of JFE, the workload has been spread among many professionals and volunteers, and JFE has become a way of life in the school community. Having lived through the early stages, we can understand why so many schools give JFE a first chance, and then give up. Like any new enterprise, the startup is an enormous burden, but the end results justify the early aches.

The Religious School Teaching Staff

After returning from our first Whizin experience in 1992, eight grade-level family education programs were implemented on Sunday mornings during religious school hours. Those workshops were co-led by the religious school director and the teacher who had attended Whizin. At first, some teachers were hostile to the idea of having the parents present in their classes and were suspicious of our "holy crusade" for involving the whole family in the religious school. They felt that the previous school-year had ended just fine; but when the teachers returned for staff meetings in August, they found a principal who seemed to have gone mad, a fellow teacher who was going to be teaching a few of their Sunday classes, and a whole new philosophy which they did not understand or share.

Twelve hours of in-service during the 1992-93 school year were spent educating the teachers about family education, thanks to the United Synagogue Department of Education's U-STEP program. During the first year of implementation, teachers were not expected to come up with their own ideas for family education sessions, but were to observe and participate. Our hope was that once a teacher saw how valuable these parent-child sessions were, they too would become believers. Most teachers' attitudes did change, although some remained resistant. (Once they saw how appreciative parents were and how this translated into better classroom management.) Over time, several teachers became interested in taking a more active role in family education. Some began attending JFE teacher-training sessions on their own, and two enrolled in a two-year certification program being offered at the local BJE/SAJES (The Suffolk Association of Jewish Educational Services).

In the meantime, religious school committee members came to appreciate the value of the first year's experimental programming, and at the recommendation of the rabbi and principal, agreed to relieve the participating teacher of her own Sunday morning classroom duties for the following school year, so that she would be available to facilitate more family education programs. The principal and family education teacher developed a very close working relationship, a partnership which gave birth to a successful, grade-by-grade, K-7 family education curriculum.

After four years of JFE in the religious school, the teachers noticed the increased participation of families in school as well as synagogue and community programs and the increase in student motivation. Now it is rare for a child show up alone on a Sunday when a parent-child session is scheduled. Yet most teachers can remember back to the days when they rarely met their students' parents.

What snags have we run into? Some parents complain that teachers have taken advantage of the Sunday family involvement to "corner them" about problems that have erupted during the week in the classroom. Some teachers feel that increased participation has led to unrealistic expectations on the part of parents. Involving the rest of the teaching staff in developing and facilitating family education workshops has been slower than anticipated. Time, or rather the lack of it, is the main obstacle in getting other teachers more involved.

One of our next goals is to turn responsibility over to teachers for modifying current JFE curriculum and developing new pieces. Both the educational director and the family education teacher will be available to assist those teachers who wish to "take the plunge," and participating teachers will be paid per diem for the additional workload.

The Family Life Coordinator

If our congregation had not received a Continuity grant from UJA, we might have had to wait a few more years to hire a JFE professional. The unique twist of our grant proposal was to build beyond our already strong JFE program in the religious school by striving towards a "womb to tomb" JFE program based on a different theme each year. The annual theme would permeate the congregation and shape our choice of family programming. Narrow definitions of "family" would become more inclusive, and the family life coordinator and committee would offer programs of interest to families with pre-schoolers, grandparents, single parents, day school families, families of teen-agers, and empty-nesters. While the world of JFE within the religious school community was a known entity with a built-in audience, the areas to be covered by the family life coordinator were vast and uncharted.

After receiving word that we had been awarded the UJA grant, the congregation was fortunate to hire a newly ordained rabbi who had been a rabbinic intern in our synagogue during her senior year at the Jewish Theological Seminary. The new coordinator was already familiar with the congregation, had worked on programming for a family retreat as part of her rabbinic internship, and had a strong personal interest in Jewish educational and JFE in particular. As part of the effort to share the JFE vision with the entire congregation, the family life coordinator gave the Kol Nidrei sermon during her first year on staff.

Even with these advantages, it took time for this talented young rabbi to make herself known to the congregation at large and establish JFE as an organic entity with a life outside of the captive audience of the religious school community. The job description of family life coordinator had not been clearly defined; rather, it became a work-in-progress, with no physical or programmatic turf of its own. Overlapping interests caused friction as greater emphasis was placed on the concept of family life education. These tensions were natural growth pains. They occur in many congregations employing JFE directors and subside with time, patience, planning, and good will.

I have heard laments from many religious school principals who feel bitter that they had personally brought JFE into their religious schools and congregations, only to have that part of their job taken away and handed over to a "new kid on the block," the newly hired JFE director. In our case, also, had personnel changes resulted in a diminished role for the principal, I suspect that good will would have been sacrificed and cooperation hampered. This problem was avoided by the congregation's decision to define the family life coordinator's responsibilities as "everything BUT religious school." This helped focus new initiatives on new markets, and fostered creative brainstorming between professionals, both in thinking about the alternative venues for JFE within the congregation, and in strengthening the religious school program. The result: the family life coordinator facilitates some of the religious school family education programs, and the religious school director helps staff family life programs, each doing so on a voluntary basis.

Partnership between professional and volunteer leaders results in many outstanding programs and multi-session courses, enjoyed and appreciated by those who participate. It would have been impossible for a professional working alone to offer the variety and quantity of programs that our congregation now offers, without this partnership between the staff and volunteer leadership.

The most difficult obstacle for planning congregational JFE programs is not knowing who will show up and how many participants to expect. RSVP-ing in a timely manner is a foreign concept in our congregation, and this has generated enough stress to make many volunteers swear to never again chair an event. For the professional who is involved in all the workshops, events, and courses, the stress is multiplied. When a family workshop is offered for a specific grade in the nursery or religious school, the pool of potential participants is finite and parents can be phoned. Synagogue-wide events present greater logistical challenges. Another challenge is that synagogue-wide "extravaganzas" are very labor intensive and are not repeatable. Over time, it has become apparent that while extravaganzas serve an important purpose in generating community spirit and attracting newcomers, the number of such programs must be limited to cut down on professional and volunteer burnout.

The Cantor

Why is it that in the emerging JFE literature, the cantor is almost never mentioned as a significant player? Until this year, our cantor was simply not in the loop of JFE activity, and I know of only a few congregations where the cantor is actively involved in JFE. Once our cantor was asked to participate in JFE staff meetings, however, wonderful new ideas began flowing. And why not? For many adolescents, the cantor is the last point of close contact with the synagogue. While the nursery school director may become the key to getting an early start, the cantor may be equally important in turning the tide of the post bar/bat mitzvah dropout.

Intra-Professional Communication

Bi-weekly staff meetings, attended by the rabbi, family life coordinator, religious school principal, and nursery school director, focus specifically on the JFE agenda. A time for these staff meetings changes periodically from morning to evening to include the cantor and youth director. Although the idea of regularly scheduled staff meetings seemed simple enough, it was difficult for everyone to find time for these meetings. They proved invaluable, however, in ways we had not anticipated. For example, the nursery school director, herself the mother of teenagers, had many insights about that age group. So did the cantor. Overlapping areas were identified. Duplication and over-programming were reduced. Eventually we found ourselves each "volunteering" to take on tasks which were not in our job description, but were also not anyone else's specific responsibility.

At times there are disagreements between staff member. Nonetheless, everyone trusts that disagreements will remain behind closed doors. We have agreed to resolve our intra-professional debates away from the public. Each professional has his or her own job to do, but by taking the time to put our heads together, we work toward smoothing over the cracks through which congregants often fall.

The Family Life Committee

I am not Jewish, but my husband and I have decided that as a family we are Jewish and our sons are being brought up as Jews. The rabbi and members could not have been more supportive, but the synagogue as an institution remained somehow impenetrable. My own and my family's "synagogue confidence" has been fostered by the Family Life Education Program and my involvement in the committee. At the first meeting I was greeted warmly and given a task to do. I was made to feel useful and it would have been impossible not to respond to such inclusion.   Patricia

After returning from the Whizin Summer Seminar in 1992, the rabbi called for the establishment of a volunteer "Family Life Committee" responsible for implementing JFE programs. The first committee chair was a volunteer leader who had been a member of the Whizin team. This began the conscious process of vesting synagogue members as true partners in this new frontier.

By building on existing strengths and capitalizing on "teachable moments," a few congregation-wide holiday and Shabbat programs were enriched with family activities. But the success story coming from the work of the early days of the Family Life Committee was a well planned and well attended family retreat weekend. The committee chairperson, a social worker, co-chaired this retreat with her husband, who had had strong youth and camping experience in his young-adult life. Together they did a superb job in coordinating this effort, found more volunteers to share the load, and worked hand-in-hand with the professionals in planning the schedule, structure, and content of our weekend getaway. JFE, outside the rubric of the religious school, had finally taken firm root in the minds of the volunteer leadership of the congregation.

The continuing role of the Family Life Committee has been to plan non-religious school family experiences. Over the years, each chairperson has been a highly-respected, motivated person, who also serves on the board of trustees. This gives the committee high visibility. (One of the current co-chairs is also a synagogue officer, sitting on the executive committee.) Since the 1994 grant from the UJA Federation of New York and the hiring of the part-time Family Life Coordinator, the influence of the Family Life Committee has grown. Although the work-load is sometimes overwhelming, it continues to attract top-notch volunteers representing many sub-communities of the synagogue. The Family Life Committee's policy is to recruit representative members from the other important committees and organizations, such as the religious and nursery schools, youth group, sisterhood, men's club, chai club, UJA, and adult education. Overall responsibility for the religious school's family education curriculum remains with the religious school committee, by that committee's choice. The two groups overlap and cooperate.

One "hiddush" from our 1995 Whizin experience was to invite all members of the Whizin team to join the Family Life Committee, including the religious school and nursery school directors, and the religious school family education teacher. This has proved to be valuable in coordinating "joint ventures," spreading and lightening everyone's workload, improving channels of publicity, and increasing the turnout at family education events, programs, and courses.

The Whizin Team Becomes the Core of the Family Life Study Group

We started out as five individuals with very separate perspectives on the synagogue, and different objectives in attending Whizin. We learned so much about the different arms of the synagogue that each of us represents, and developed a tremendous appreciation of each other. We cooperate, we disagree, we support each other, and have developed trust and respect for each other. From this group experience, I suddenly saw myself as an able participant, a consensus builder, and at times a leader. I learned that our "plan" could be something that evolves, that it did not have to be etched in stone. And I learned that we could work hard and laugh hard, and still be very productive.   Elaine

Let's look at the formation of the Whizin team of 1995. The rabbi, the leader who sees "the big picture" could not attend, nor could the family life coordinator and family life committee co-chair. Nonetheless, we were able to take a great deal away from the Whizin experience. Each of us learned to abandon our own personal or professional agendas in favor of a more holistic approach for reaching and teaching families, at whatever stage they might be. Since so many of the professional and volunteer stakeholders were not present, what we were unable to accomplish at Whizin was to come up with a long-term game plan, While members of the Whizin team might have felt frustrated, it was more productive to take this unfinished task back home.

Our first post-Whizin meetings included the five members of our team, plus the rabbi, family life coordinator, and the committee's second co-chairperson. This group of eight met several times before expanding to include other members of the executive board and Family Life Committee and evolving into the Family Life Study Group. The purpose of this "think tank" was to examine the emerging literature, evaluate our successes and failures and dreams, and set future goals.

A feeling of safety and trust has developed between and among the volunteer leadership and professional staff. Although the rabbi is the spiritual leader, and his opinions carry a great deal of weight, he is in a sense "first among equals," making everyone else feel important and valued. Trust makes everyone feel free to express their own opinions; synergy makes the sum of our efforts more than each individual achievement; and collaboration has improved almost every good idea.

The one and only programmatic responsibility that the Family Life Study Group took upon itself was planning a series of Family Life Stakeholders' Forums beginning in June, 1996. The first forum, facilitated by Jo Kay, a Whizin consultant, brought together six representatives from each of ten synagogue sub-divisions for the purpose of formulating and articulating a long-term, synagogue-wide commitment to JFE. After several years of the Family Life Committee and synagogue professionals providing the agenda for JFE, it was time for broader synagogue leadership to take responsibility for offering family-friendly programs. These forums provided an opportunity to brainstorm ideas to be co-sponsored and co-funded by collaborating representatives, which would limit competition for resources, manpower, and participants, and reduce duplication on the synagogue's bulging calendar. Despite the elimination of outside funding, the synergy between professional and volunteer leadership at these forums has led to a rich, rewarding JFE agenda and synagogue calendar. JFE has truly seeped into every nook of this synagogue.

The Pitfalls of Consensus

Being involved in planning JFE programs sends the message to our kids that the synagogue and Judaism are important parts of who we are as a family. I think they have gotten that message. The only negative is that I sometimes feel that the pool of volunteers is too small and we risk burnout at the same time we are trying to expand the scope of our programming.   Anonymous

At all levels, collaboration and consensus decision making have increased the commitment of a broader base of stakeholders and has created many varied synagogue programs for families at all stages of life. Without volunteers willing to help, the professionals would simply not be able to offer adequate quantity and quality of JFE programs.

The greatest drawback in working by consensus is the amount of time it consumes. Leadership by consensus can be counter-intuitive and inefficient. It sometimes seems simpler and more efficient to just do the job alone; it is nerve-wracking to wonder if everyone will hold up their end. It is essential, however, that the professionals not get bogged down in all the implementation details and that volunteers be stimulated and enriched by their involvement. Sharing and rotating responsibilities promotes a feeling of ownership among participants and helps avoid burnout of volunteer and professional leaders.

Conclusion

On the surface, close collaboration and working by consensus between professional and volunteer leaders might seem cumbersome. It is certainly not the fastest way to introduce and implement JFE in a congregational setting. We believe, however, that teamwork forms the strongest and most enduring foundation for long-term systemic change. Collaboration in generating ideas and spreading the workload beyond the scope of the professional staff expands the pool of stakeholders, allowing for increased quantity and quality of JFE programs; and it guarantees the involvement of interested participants.

Only time will tell if our hypotheses are correct and enduring. Somehow, we have a strong hunch that our collaborative modus operandi deserves careful consideration as a model for other congregations seeking to refocus Jewish education as a family-centered, life-long pursuit.

Helpful Tips for Promoting Team Spirit in Congregational Family Education.

The following ideas may promote greater collaboration and cooperation in a congregation, and avoid common problems associated with implementing JFE.

1. Make up the team with individuals who respect each other and who can work together. The team's sum will only be

greater that each individual's worth if there are good feelings amongst its members. Personal animosities will ruin the team.

2. Avoid alienating staff and volunteers when introducing JFE. JFE should supplement, not replace, existing structures.

3. Even though topics for JFE programs may be suggested by professionals, final choices should be made by the Family Life Committee made up of both professionals and volunteers. This increases everyone's personal commitment and enthusiasm.

4. Limit the responsibilities of even the most enthusiastic volunteers to chairing one or two programs each year. This broadens the base of stakeholders, diminishes the perception that the leadership ranks are impenetrable, and protects the leadership from burnout.

5. Chairs for specific programs should feel passionate about the importance of their program. When planning the yearly calendar, avoid topics which no one feels vested in and no one cares to chair. Rotate responsibilities to avoid boredom or feelings of being taken for granted.

6. Give out evaluation forms at each program, and analyze the responses in preparing subsequent events. This avoids making the same mistake twice. It also gives participants the opportunity to let you know what their interests are and which topics might draw them in to lend a hand.

7. Assign simple "bring with you" assignments to participants. This cuts the shopping burden and the expense of running programs. It also makes participants feel vested.

8. Plan for all types of families and all ages, both in program content and committee membership.

9. Keep the batteries charged by offering learning opportunities for teachers and lay leaders through readings, in-service, conference participation, and courses at local institutions of higher learning.

10. Professionals should provide the scaffolding to facilitate the personal growth of lay leaders.

11. The synagogue Family Life Committee should avoid taking over programming responsibilities which logically belong

elsewhere. In order to help the other synagogue arms to "think family," events could be co-sponsored by Family Life.

12. Laugh often and enjoy each other's company. Everyone wants to have some fun, especially when facing challenging moments.

13. And last but not least, the best advice we learned from Ron Wolfson and his Whizin Summer Institute consultants, "Plan long journeys. Take short steps!"

The road to changing a congregation into a multi-generational learning community may stretch in front of us. When our journey is broken up into small steps, our goals are achievable.

References

Cindy Dolgin, "The Establishment of an integrated Family Education Curriculum for all Grades (K-7)," Master's Thesis.

Joshua Elkin, *Lay-Professional Relations in the Jewish Day School, in Curriculum, Community, Commitment,* Daniel J. Margolis and Elliot Salo Schoenberg, eds. West Orange, NJ: Behrman House, 1992.

Bernard Reisman, *The Role of Lay People in What We Know About Jewish Education,* Stuart L Kelman, ed. Los Angeles: Tora Aura Productions, 1992.

John Ruskay, "From Challenge to Opportunity: To Build Inspired Communities," in *Journal of Jewish Communal Services,* Fall/Winter, 1995/96.

Susan Shevitz, "An Organizational Perspective on Changing Congregational Education," in *A Congregation Of Learners,* Isa Aron, Sara Lee, Seymour Rossel, Eds. New York: UAHC Press, 1995.

Jeffrey Schein

Jeffrey Schein received his rabbinical ordination from the Reconstructionist Rabbinical College in Philadelphia in 1977 and his doctorate in education from Temple University in 1980. Between 1971 and 1991, he was principal for three different religious schools in Philadelphia and California. Between 1991 and 1993 he developed Project Mishpacha, the Philadelphia community's initiative in Jewish family education. He is presently associate professor and director of Community Family Education programs at the Cleveland College of Jewish Studies. He also serves as National Education Director for the Jewish Reconstructionist Federation.

Theme and Variations: Jewish Family Education in a Gay/Lesbian Congregation
Jeffrey Schein

The Reconstructionist movement is committed to a policy of full and complete acceptance of gay and lesbian Jews as members of the Jewish community. As the education director of a movement with such a policy, it is not surprising to me to be working with Bet Haverim, a gay/lesbian congregation in Atlanta seeking to develop its educational resources. But each congregation and every consultative relationship is a story unto itself. And in the context of this two year old consultation, there have been more than a few challenges to my accustomed ways of thinking about the Jewish family and Jewish family education.

Consider my latest visit to Bet Haverim. My first activity with the congregation comes at the Kabbalat Shabbat family service. I am on the verge of self-congratulation as we reenact the classical Jewish folk tale, "Joseph the Lover of the Sabbath," in such a way that Joseph's wife has become "parent #2" rather than remaining simply "Joseph's wife." In the end, I am prevented from enjoying my clever recognition of diverse family structures because, as a straight Jew, I am still sorting through my own attitudes towards Judaism and its relationship to homosexuality.

My ambivalence can be quickly ignited, as it is when I look into the kahal during the Yedid Nefesh prayer praising God as our soul mate and see several gay and lesbian couples holding hands. Not only my own sexual orientation but the emerging orientations of my three teenage children flash before my eyes and shape the reality in front of me. My own issues both frame and cloud what I see, which is exactly what you would want any piece of Jewish poetry and song to achieve: a correspondence between Godly images and human enactments of those images.

On Sunday of this same weekend, the more customary challenges of teaching and consulting take over until, in my final session, working with teachers to develop musar/moral education lessons, I learn of a real-life dilemma for Bet Haverim that has arisen because two children on the playground are teasing one another. This otherwise usual kid behavior holds a particular barb because one child is calling the other child "gay."

History of Bet Haverim

Congregation Bet Haverim in Atlanta would be a complex and interesting consultancy under any circumstances. The intensity is heightened, however, because this gay/lesbian congregation is now going through profound changes in its institutional and spiritual character. Once a small, lay-led havurah of several dozen members founded by gay men, Bet Haverim is now a congregation with a membership of 130 households and a growing number of straight members. A woman rabbi, a professor at nearby Emory University, is challenging the congregation to utilize her spiritual leadership in ways that will preserve the congregation's original ethos of lay involvement and empowerment.

Over the past two years, the Bet Haverim board has started a religious school to provide for the educational needs of the children of both gay and lesbian parents and the growing numbers of straight parents in the congregation. This has presented the members of Beth Haverim with new colors and materials from which to weave their new fabric of intergenerational learning. The potential for either an educational coat of many colors or one of twisted, knotted fabric are equally real.

The school is a magnet for the growth of Bet Haverim, and this growth poses new questions. Will a parent who is attracted to Bet Haverim because of the educational quality of its school understand the broader context and history of the congregation? Ought children and parents of straight families new to the congregation be expected, encouraged, or required to participate in gay pride activities? Should gay and lesbian parents be encouraged or required to engage in some activity that sensitizes them to the needs and commitments of the straight families? Only occasionally does this ring in my ear as being connected with a need to be "politically correct." Bet Haverim, I have come to understand, is deeply committed to living out the ambiguities and challenges of their own evolving understanding of Jewish pluralism. Finding effective responses to these and other challenges occupy the mind, spirit, and time of a significant percentage of the membership of Bet Haverim.

The Emerging Reality

The discussions about the evolving character of Bet Haverim are both formal and informal. At an oneg Shabbat you can hear gay/lesbian and straight members earnestly asking one another, "So, after we have acknowledged our differences—that you are a lesbian and I am straight, what do we do? What does pluralism and inclusivity mean after we've accepted one another?" More formally, as I read through the minutes of the design team meeting which lay out the process that will chart a future course for Bet Haverim, I re-experience a Hillel and Shammai debate that I hope is l'shem shamayim, for the sake of heaven:

Bob: *"Bet Haverim ought to anchor its identity around the notion of being a Reconstructionist congregation with special outreach to the gay/lesbian and progressive communities."*

Jeri: *"We are nowhere near living in a post-queer liberation era. First and foremost we need to be a place that is safe for gays and lesbians to be fully Jewish."*

Bob: *"Reconstructionism has already challenged us to be a kehillat mekabelet, a welcoming congregation. The principles of diversity and inclusiveness are already part of the Jewish pluralism we gain as we study Jewish tradition from multiple perspectives and honor and respect each person's uniqueness. It's only guilt and shame that keeps us from embracing this broader identity."*

Jeri: *"I have no quarrel with that. It's an important second element of our identity. But most of all, I want and need Bet Haverim to be the kind of place where my child thinks that it is perfectly fine to be the Jewish daughter of a Jewish lesbian."*

Jewish Family Education at Bet Haverim

Three facets of Jewish family education have special twists and turns at Bet Haverim: first, the working definition of the Jewish family; second, the creation of a learning community; and third, the emotional and spiritual investment of the community in the education of its children.

Bet Haverim is currently responding to each of these challenges. Although I have tried to review my understanding of these issues with the people I work with at Bet Haverim, my presentation still feels rough and rudimentary. I believe these issues to be worthy of greater refinement, one that can come only through additional dialogue and clearer analysis of the changing Jewish family.

Defining The Jewish Family

The conventional definition of the American Jewish family is stretched in a gay/lesbian congregation. The "hidden diversity" issues that often surprise family educators—the remaking of family trees to allow for blended, divorced, and gay/lesbian families—are not at all surprising here. The challenge that Bet Haverim takes upon itself is to treat this diversity in family constellation as "text" rather than "context." To present children with a wide variety of images of the Jewish family is an educational goal in itself rather than simply a means to other Jewish knowledge objectives. The thrust is proactive: Bet Haverim wants to establish a large initial canvass for painting different portraits of the Jewish family rather than constantly explain why the conventional definition of family is too narrow. As Bet Haverim develops its full curriculum, members raise important issues about how to move beyond "Political Correctness" in imagining and understanding the Jewish family.

My early discussions with the faculty and education committee around this issue focused on several tensions. The first was how to be intellectually and spiritually honest in presenting diversity in family structures while, at the same time, representing "our understanding of Judaism" without distorting the plain meaning of key biblical and rabbinical texts that do not embrace diverse family structures. A framework on sexuality in Jewish life has been laid out in educational materials developed for adult learning in the Reconstructionist movement. This method involves searching for the underlying values in Jewish tradition in order to understand what kedusha (holiness) says about loving relationships. Distinguishing between context-specific and underlying meaning in Jewish tradition requires extraordinary knowledge and judgment. It is an even more complex challenge to help teachers develop such judgment for themselves and then transmit it in developmentally appropriate ways to children![1]

Further, if we make an a priori commitment to educating rather than to indoctrinating children, then selecting the most obvious of Jewish textual materials might prove counterproductive. On the surface, surveying Jewish images of sexuality with an eye towards diversity would make much of the loving and erotic relationship between David and Jonathan in the Bible. In one sense, this is a template for the reality of diversity in relationships. Yet, including this text in a curriculum might be more advocacy than education.

After deliberating with the faculty and education committee, we agreed that it might be better to turn to those verses in Hosea that are recited as the conclusion of the ritual of putting on tefillin, which speak of loyalty, compassion, and knowledge as the hallmark of a relationship. These qualities could be applied as a measure of the Jewish worth of any relationship—gay, lesbian, straight, platonic or sexual. Such a selection reinforces the Bet Haverim understanding of sexuality as being less a matter of specific sexual behaviors and more a form of personal and Jewish identity.

In a later conversation with Bet Haverim's rabbi, I realized that the challenges of creating a Jewish understanding which gives tradition a "vote but not a veto" can cut in many different directions. For I myself had chosen—and then encouraged teachers to choose—to abstract from the biblical text of Hosea those verses compatible with my own understanding of loving relationships. Had I also alerted the teachers to the anger and misogyny of Hosea expressed in his choice of the metaphor of Israel as the whoring wife of God? A fine question which revealed how some of my own fixed assumptions might guide or subtly misguide the consultation with Bet Haverim.

A Framework for Congregation-Wide Learning

Bet Haverim members are drawn to a framework of "intergenerational learning" partly because of a deep concern that "family education" may be full of images of nuclear, "normative" families removed from the realities of Bet Haverim. Therefore, the notion of becoming an intergenerational congregation of learners holds particular promise for Bet Haverim.

Intergenerational learning at Bet Haverim also functions as a strategy for finding commonalty amidst the various diverse populations of the congregation. My work as consultant has been to provide Bet Haverim with programs through which they can first experience and then appropriate for themselves the sweetness of Jewish learning.

My earlier visit to Bet Haverim marked one of the first times that the gay/lesbian and straight populations of this congregation had come together to explore consciously their own learning processes. I chose to focus their learning on the broad issue of partnerships for Jewish learning, because the role of the children in the religious school needed much more communal focus than it was receiving within the narrow confines of the education committee. For study, we used "A Journey of Three Thousand Years Through Four Jewish Texts," in *Targilon: A Workbook for Charting the Course of Jewish Family Education*.[2] Much of the work was done in paired ḥevruta. People were asked to team up with a person they knew only casually and had never studied with before, rather than forming pairs in terms of common or different sexual orientation.

My second visit to Atlanta was in early December of 1996. In the intervening six months, Bet Haverim had realigned its learning programs for both adults and children so that there was a fifteen minute overlap each Sunday morning to allow children and adults to share with one another what each had been learning. My goal for this visit was to help plan an intergenerational learning/celebration day for Shavuot later in the year. The first half of our day together was spent in study as we experienced and analyzed different understandings of matan Torah, the giving of the Torah. We paid particular attention to aseret ha-dibrot, the role of the ten commandments in Jewish tradition.

The second half of the day was devoted to unpacking the learning we had just done, presenting James White's theory of intergenerational religious programming, and brainstorming about possible projects and activities for the Shavuot learning day.[3] A committee was formed to execute the next stages of planning; for professional support, the committee would turn to the director of Jewish Educational Services in Atlanta for general guidance and to myself for particular Reconstructionist input. The ultimate goal for Jewish Family Education programming is to help Bet Haverim develop their own educational resources so that they can independently sustain intergenerational Jewish learning.

The Favored Role of Children In The Educational Process

There was another important piece of the learning that took place during my December visit. After engaging in our own adult study, we observed a group of Bet Haverim children discuss two midrashim about the giving of the Torah. This corresponds to the parallel learning segment of the White model of intergenerational learning. We wanted to give adults who did not have children in the religious school a glimpse of what the children might be doing while the adults were engaged in their own learning.

The children were at their very best. They asked great questions, said outrageous things, and generally absorbed the message of both midrashim. Parents and non-parents alike evinced considerable pride and nachas as they commented on how "their kids had been learning." It was also a moment of affirmation for the Bet Haverim faculty who were participating, as learners, in the adult learning segment of the day.

It struck me at that moment how many and convoluted are the paths along which family education moves. For many of us, at least judging from our rhetoric, the curse of the American Jewish community has been the emphasis on Jewish education fur der kinder (for the children), which has removed adults and families from the center of the educational process. But at Bet Haverim, in my estimation, there is no issue more critical than developing a strong sense of communal responsibility for all of the "children" of the congregation. It is, to use an Eriksonian phrase, the very "generativity" of caring about learning fur der kinder as well as caring about their own learning that will produce the caring that builds community across differences. In my experience, congregations which develop from intensive adult learning havurot represent the mirror image of the more common Jewish family education dilemma of getting adults to transcend their role as parents once they have come through the synagogue door for their children's sake. At Bet Haverim as well as at other such congregations, the goal is to have the congregation as a whole accept parental responsibility for all the children's Jewish education.

Paradoxes and Postscripts

Bet Haverim will continue to struggle with defining what kind of Jewish community it is and aspires to become. At the same time, it will deal with the very mundane challenges of educating children—developing curricula, ordering textbooks, communicating with parents.

The Reconstructionist movement has asked Bet Haverim to join its Cooperating Schools Network, a group of twenty congregations devoted to integrating adult, family, and child-oriented Jewish education. Within this Network, it will be one of several congregations dealing with the educational side of diversity and inclusiveness.

Is it realistic to ask such a young, developing congregation to carry such heavy responsibilities? Sometimes it must seem to the remarkable lay principal of Bet Haverim's religious school that it would be dayenu—

quite enough—to simply get through the next day. Yet, the great energy and capacity for self-reflection possessed by this congregation promises something larger. As Bet Haverim members are fond of saying, "may God in all her wisdom" grant us strength and guidance.

In the meanwhile, the process of exploring the "family-ness" of a congregation with as much diversity as Bet Haverim continues. Bet Haverim has identified its two core Jewish values as embracing Jewish pluralism and becoming an intergenerational, learning congregation. If that is Bet Haverim's educational Torah, there is much midrash waiting to be created around the synergies and dissonances of these two values as they interact in the Jewish life of this community.

Endnotes

1. Publications of the Jewish Reconstructionist Federation's Commission on Homosexuality and Judaism. The two most valuable publications are *Homosexuality and Judaism: The Reconstructionist Position* and *Homosexuality and Judaism: A Reconstructionist Workshop Series.*

2. Leora Isaacs and Jeffrey Schein. *Targilon: A Workbook for Charting the Course of Jewish Family Education.* (New York: JESNA and JRF, 1996) 7-12.

3. James White. *Intergenerational Religious Education.* (Birmingham, Alabama, Religious Education Press, 1988) 264.

Jo Kay is Religious School director at Congregation Rodeph Sholom, a large Reform congregation in Manhattan. For ten years she had been director of Judaic Studies at the Rodeph Sholom Day School. Jo created the PACE (Parent and Child Education) model of Jewish family education almost twenty years ago in Temple Emanu-El, East Meadow, New York, and is among the pioneers of Jewish family education. A former fellow of the Melton Center of the Hebrew University in Jerusalem, where she lived with her family for a year, she holds both Teachers' and Principals' Certification from the Union of American Hebrew Congregations and a master's degree in Hebrew Culture from New York University. Jo lives in East Meadow, New York, with her husband, Alan, and their three daughters, Corinne, Lisa, and Adina.

Jo Kay

Parallel Learning and Parent Empowerment
Jo Kay

If a parent wishes to study Torah, and he has a child who must also learn—the parent takes precedence. However, if the child is more insightful or quicker to grasp what there is to be learned, the child takes precedence. Even though the child gains priority thereby, the parent must not ignore his own study, for just as it is a Mitzvah to educate the child, so, too, is the parent commanded to teach himself.
Maimonides, Mishna Torah (Laws of Torah Study 1:4)

Maimonides thus defines Jewish study as a concern for both parents and children. The parent must provide for the study of the child while also attending to his own study. It is a "family Mitzvah," a family "commandment and concern." Thus throughout Jewish tradition, beginning with the commandment to retell the Passover story to our children, there is repeated concern for education of the entire family; or, to put it another way, for "family education."

Jewish family education occurs when family members, either parents and children together or in parallel settings (apart from each other), are involved in experiences that have learning as the primary objective. Most family education opportunities now offered in synagogues and schools or in informal settings such as Jewish community centers, Jewish family camps, or Jewish museums are interactive, parent-and-child programs.

One very popular interactive family education program format is structured around a series of stations. While focusing on one particular theme, the parent and child move from station to station performing a series of different tasks. The family engages in discussion, study, fun, and celebration together. This format is frequently used during holiday workshops for families.

Family programs for large groups or for family classes also utilize the age-old technique of Jewish study known as ḥevruta, studying in pairs with a study partner. In these instances, the parent and the child are given a particular text with a series of guided study questions to work through together. Each family unit, that is, each ḥevruta pair, works independently and then rejoins the larger group and often shares some of the discussion and discovery. Families with children of all ages have found ḥevruta study to be both exciting and meaningful.

Each of these programs generally involves the entire family learning or experiencing the same subject, at the same time, in the same room. This format for fulfilling the Mitzvah of family study puts into practice only one response to Maimonides' vision of meaningful Jewish education.

Parallel learning is an alternative format for fulfilling the Mitzvah of family study and another response to Maimonides' vision of meaningful Jewish education. Parallel learning, while designed for parent study, still keeps the family unit in sharp focus. (Many Jewish Day Schools have begun their relationship with family education through the creation of Parent Education programs, or, in other words, parallel learning programs.) There is correlated adult study, as in the PACE (Parent and Child Education) program; or non-correlated adult study as in the PEP (Parallel Education Program). In both approaches, the parent and the child engage in Jewish study, but not in the same room at the same time.

It should be noted here that family education, in this case parallel learning, is not adult education as we know it. Dr. Norman Linzer, in his book, *The Jewish Family,* says that in adult education, the subjects are taught to adults with the purpose of educating them Jewishly, as individuals. In family education, the same subjects could be taught to the same adults (even without their children), but the purpose is different. The teacher's perception shifts from the students as adults to the students as parents and as members of families. The focus is on the transfer of learning to the family setting, and the emphasis is on family values and family issues as they relate to the curriculum.

PACE, while bringing families together for interactive study, also brings the parents together, usually at a different time, for adult study. The parallel learning components of PACE, the adult-only segments, however, are specifically designed to correlate with the children's classes. For a fifth-grade studying the life cycle, parallel learning classes focus on in-depth study of the development of the rituals associated with each life-cycle event, similarities and differences in rituals among various movements, sharing of personal ritual experiences, and development of new rituals.

PEP, developed by the Conservative movement, is designed to bring parents into the synagogue for non-correlated adult study on a Sunday morning, while their children are in school. PEP has its own curriculum, one that is not related to what the children are studying. The idea governing this type of family education is that both parents and children are engaged in Jewish study, and both are aware of what the other is doing and are sharing the Mitzvah, the value and the experience of Jewish study.

Since the success of religious education for children is to a great extent dependent upon the positive attitude and the observable behaviors of the parents, parents must begin to make certain commitments about their own behavior if they are serious about their children's Jewish learning. They must try living the Jewish tradition and actively continuing their own Jewish studies. Through parallel learning experiences, the parent can prepare to join with his or her child in living Jewishly. A positive change in the Jewish lifestyle of the family (greater observance, greater involvement in and commitment to Jewish living) may develop.

Advantages of Parallel Learning for Parents

Parallel learning experiences for the parent address the intellectual excitement of study, Jewish study in particular. The parent, exposed to mature Jewish thinking, begins to appreciate the value of the guidance inherent in Jewish tradition and comes to respect and draw from it.

In a seventh-grade parallel learning session, parents read and discussed the biblical text (Genesis 22) dealing with the parent-child interactions between Abraham and Isaac as Abraham prepared for the akedah. Who is this child? How do the two characters relate to one another? Where is Sarah during the preparation and interaction? What home scenarios might be compared to this one? How have you interacted similarly or differently with your child? What do the commentators have to say about Isaac? About Abraham's effect upon Isaac's psychological development? What do psychologists say about dealing with adolescents? What frustrations have you as parents experienced in dealing with your seventh graders? These questions enable parents to study and become conversant with biblical text; at the same time, they offer parents an opportunity to

Esther Netter is executive director of My Jewish Discovery Place Children's Museum and Cultural Center of Jewish Community Centers of Greater Los Angeles, an innovative and interactive museum for children and families which has become a model for the nation. During 1997, its traveling exhibits were in more than thirty Jewish communities including London and Warsaw. Esther also serves as the assistant executive director of Jewish Community Centers of Greater Los Angeles.

Esther Netter

Esther is on the faculty of the Whizin Institute for Jewish Family Life at the University of Judaism and a member of the clinical faculty of the Rhea Hirsch School of Education at Hebrew Union College. She lectures and teaches about museum education and informal education in North America, Europe, and Israel.

Esther received her undergraduate degree in Jewish studies from the University of California, Los Angeles, and her master's degree in Jewish education from the Jewish Theological Seminary in New York. She is the mother of three innovative and interactive children, Elisheva, Moshe, Shira.

parents are encouraged to recapture their roles as primary teachers (Jewish teachers) of their children. The school becomes relevant to the home environment. More parents are likely to join synagogue committees. At Temple Emanu-El of East Meadow, graduates of family study classes for parents and children, both together and in parallel learning programs, went on to become the presidents of the Men's Club, the Sisterhood, and the synagogue itself. These parents were actively involved in the ritual committee, the school committee, and cared about the synagogue as a whole. On a community level, parents from this program became involved in Jewish communal organizations like Ort, B'nai B'rith, Hadassah, Federation.

Advantages of Parallel Learning for the Children

Parents of students in congregational schools have children who attend secular public or private schools. The secular day schools are their children's primary educational institutions and in most cases, are the institutions where these parents place most of their energies. It is the primary schools' Parents Associations and School Committees which receive their primary attention and where they feel compelled to volunteer and to offer support. Religious school and Hebrew school fall into another category for most parents. The challenge for Jewish educators working in congregational schools is to find a way to help parents equalize their attention. Involving parents in family study of any kind can begin to shift the balance.

Parents new to the congregational school world are generally more flexible and willing to extend themselves for their children. Thus, beginning family study programs at the earliest point of entry (nursery school, kindergarten, alef classes, etc.) may insure for the child many years of parent involvement and shared experiences. By creating opportunities for parents to develop more positive attitudes towards their own Jewish studies, children learn to value what their parents value. And, as parents acquire new skills and understanding, these skills are more likely to be integrated into home and synagogue life. Common experiences help to cement wholesome parent-child relationships and draw the family closer to the school, to the synagogue, and to each other.

In a family bar/bat mitzvah program, which has parents and children engaged in interactive and parallel learning classes, parents and children were asked independently to reflect on the meaning of the bar/bat mitzvah experience. After much consideration and an opportunity to reflect in writing, parents and children were brought together to share their reflections. Time and again, I have seen parents quite moved by what their children have shared. They are impressed by the seriousness and depth of feeling with which their children have approached their bar/bat mitzvah preparations. But more importantly, they are often awed by the mere fact of the conversation! Parents have shared that they might never have spoken about these issues or feelings with their children. They might never have had this discussion if not for the family study experience, if not for the parallel (parent education) study experience, if not for the opportunity to reflect and then discuss with their children. Facilitating a meaningful discussion between parent and child and enabling the child to get in touch with deep feelings and then to share those feelings related to this Jewish "right of passage," is powerful for the entire family.

Organization of Parallel Learning Opportunities

In a parallel learning program, the parents' class schedule may or may not be identical to the children's schedule. The organization of parallel learning takes many forms. It is the nature of each individual community that is generally the defining factor. Who are the parents? When are they available to study? Where will the parent classes take place? What will the parents study? Should the parents' course of study be related to the children's course of study? Asking questions such as these begins the assessment process (the necessary homework) all educators must engage in before embarking on any new educational adventure. Parallel learning programs or parent education programs, in their many forms, are relatively new initiatives.

The PACE program's parallel component (a program designed with related parent and child study) has taken many different forms. In one school, the parents and children study at the same time, on a Sunday morning, in two different classrooms. This same program, in a different setting, holds the parents parallel class on an evening when the children are not in school. Some schools organize the program so that the family classes and the parallel classes are equal in number and always related in content. Other schools organize the program with more flexibility, allowing for the parents' interests to be reflected. In all cases, however, the parents and the children study similar subjects and at similar times, providing families with numerous opportunities for healthy discussion and sharing of views and experiences at home.

In a PEP-style program, of parallel but unrelated parent study, the course may or may not be offered at the same time as the children's classes and may or may not be for the same number of hours. The parent courses may begin later in the year and continue well beyond the close of religious school. Nevertheless, both the parents and the children are aware of each other's involvement in Jewish study. Educators and psychologists stress the value of experiences commonly shared by family members. And it is a common educational venture that parent and child have undertaken together, even if it is at different times and in different subjects.

In other parallel learning formats, parents may be invited in for a series of lectures in the evening or to engage in a home-study project or to attend a study-weekend away. Parallel learning takes many forms, yet the focus remains the same. The parent (student), viewed as a member of a family, is challenged to raise his or her own level of Jewish self-esteem and then bring the new Jewish learning into the home. Parents who become comfortable with their own Jewish study are more likely to become involved in intensive or ongoing learning experiences with their children.

Parallel education teachers should be experienced members of the synagogue or school faculty, familiar with the program's objectives and curriculum. They should be capable of interpreting the program to the parents intelligently and convincingly. They should be able to serve as role models for change, the kind of Jewish family life involvement the program seeks to effect. They should be comfortable with the behavior the program is encouraging and they should be capable and comfortable sharing their own Jewish family-life experiences with the group.

Most Jewish parents, having gone to schools of higher learning, need to respect the parallel learning experience if it is to be meaningful for them. Not all excellent teachers of children are also excellent teachers of adults. Therefore, rabbis, cantors, educators, experts in a particular area of study, can be great resources or teachers of these programs. The excitement of Jewish study must be preserved for the parents, who are our adult students. Parallel learning programs are seeking to empower these parents with the role of primary Jewish teacher of their children.

Mark Loeb has been senior rabbi at Beth El Congregation, Baltimore, Maryland, since 1976. Currently, he is also president of the Baltimore Board of Rabbis; vice-chair, Board of Trustees, Baltimore Hebrew University; board member of the Institute for Christian-Jewish Studies; and national chairman of Mazon—a Jewish Response to Hunger—the central Jewish organization that mobilizes support for the hungry and the homeless. He has been a member of the Commission on Human Sexuality of the Rabbinical Assembly; program co-chair of the National Christian-Jewish Workshop; and chairman of the National Rabbinical Assembly Convention Resolutions Committee.

Mark Loeb

Eyal Bor

Eyal Bor was born in Israel and is a fifth generation Sabra. Upon completion of his army service, he came to study in the United States, graduating from the University of Southern California School of Music, with a B.M., majoring in clarinet. He holds a master's degree in Educational Administration from the University of Judaism, Los Angeles, California. Eyal received his Ph.D. from the Baltimore Hebrew University in Political Science, where his specialty concerned the relationships between the Israeli and the American Jewish communities—the two largest in the world. Eyal is director of Education at Beth El Congregation in Pikesville, Maryland. He is married to Dr. Hana Bor and the father of four children.

Fern Cohen, a native of Miami, has lived and worked in Baltimore for the past eight years. For four years, Fern was the Jewish family educator at Beth El Religious School and the coordinator of Project Mishpacha. Fern is a graduate of the Baltimore Institute of Jewish Communal Service and holds master's degrees in Social Work and in Jewish Studies. A life-long learner, Fern is currently working on a master's degree in Jewish Education from Baltimore Hebrew University.

Fern Cohen

Project Mishpacha: A School Within a School

Mark Loeb, Eyal Bor, Fern Cohen

On the surface, in the spring of 1990, Beth El Congregation's Religious School appeared to be "a success," as supplementary schools go in the Conservative movement. Part of a large synagogue of 1,700 families, the Beth El school embraced students from pre-school through Confirmation and was serving more than 900 students. The retention rate following bar/bat mitzvah was nearly eighty percent. A significant number of graduates were continuing their studies either at Beth El or at the local communal Hebrew High School, which was run by the Board of Jewish Education.

Below the surface, however, some fundamental things were amiss. For one thing, the parents of the children were not involved in the life of the school. This was especially challenging at Beth El because a number of the parents had themselves been educated there and, not atypical of their generation, had some memories which were not overly positive. Therefore, they had little motivation to be tolerant of the sometimes negative experiences of their own children, which seemed all too familiar to them.

Another challenge was that the received tradition of an afternoon Hebrew school, originally conceived in the image of public elementary education, had become outdated and was ineffective, even at Beth El, in transmitting a passion for Jewish identification. The sense of a "school after school" which focused on academic subjects, assigned homework, distributed report cards and otherwise operated in the same mode as the schools the children attended during the major part of the day, lacked a sufficiently imaginative or emotionally warm ambiance either to garner parental support or to inspire children.

Perhaps more troubling was the sense that, like many other Hebrew schools, there was not a lot of "feeling" in the school's approach to Jewish education, the kind of affective energy that creates positive emotional connections between home and school and between teacher and student. This was the challenge Beth El's school faced as it confronted a new generation of parents whose relationships to Jewish educational institutions had been complicated by major changes in the structures of family life— working fathers and mothers, competition for children's and parents' available time, a "consumer" mentality whereby children are delivered to institutions for a purpose (in this case to "Judaicize" them and prepare them for bar/bat mitzvah), and the inability of parents to be Jewish role models for their children due to their own inadequate Judaic knowledge.

Rabbi Mark Loeb: *I had long been unhappy with what seemed to be the stodginess of Jewish school culture. For me, it lacked creativity and seemed resistant to addressing the complaints of parents. Especially because Beth El is a multi-generational congregation, I could sense the ambivalence, perhaps even guilt, that some parents felt at sending their children to a school that they felt had been oppressive to them when they were children. I also believed that our school's focus on cognitive learning needed to be changed. Particularly for Jews in our day, the real need is to foster positive affective attachments to Judaism and the synagogue. Without such attachments, academic learning will fail either to have any meaning at all or will be insufficient to assure Jewish survival. In short, we needed to do something, but what to do was not clear.*

Beth El's Religious School had a noble history, but it was clearly time to move in new directions. Beth El's school principal, Joseph Lipavsky, had served devotedly for thirty-three years. His sudden passing in the summer of 1990 left a great void and created an unsought but necessary duty to rethink the direction of the school under new leadership. Eight months later the congregation elected a new director of education, Dr. Eyal Bor, who was anxious to make his own imprint upon the school. He brought in some dynamic new faculty members, showed himself open to program innovation, and began to update the school technologically. Of most significance, he began to bring parents and grandparents back into the building for what were advertised as family programs. These, it appears in retrospect, had the inadvertent effect of planting the seeds for what would become a very far reaching reform.

Dr. Eyal Bor: *When I arrived at Beth El, I noticed that, notwith-*

standing its many strengths, the school was in need of reinvigoration. Some of the faculty had been retained due to inertia. There were virtually no parents on the premises. And the number of assemblies and supplementary programs that involved the entire family was nil. Interestingly, the School Committee members seemed to know all this, and were prepared—indeed anxious—to branch out into new directions. This provided a real opportunity for change.

By chance, in 1992 The Pearlstone Coalition for Jewish Family Education, an endowed fund of Baltimore's Federation, convened a conference on Jewish family education for local congregational and day schools. Its purpose was to arouse interest in developing family education programs and models in Baltimore's religious schools. The Pearlstone people had contacted Dr. Ronald Wolfson at the University of Judaism, in Los Angeles, two years earlier and had come to see family education as a possible vehicle for transforming and reviving some of Baltimore's religious schools. High-profile talent, many on the staff of the Whizin Institute at the University of Judaism, were brought in for the conference held at Beth El. As a follow-up to the conference (its message enthusiastically received by those attending), schools were invited to submit grant proposals for "special programs," with the clear implication that all worthy ideas would be funded. Nevertheless, after discussion between Dr. Bor and Rabbi Loeb, Beth El decided not to submit a proposal. Instead, they told the Pearlstone people that the synagogue would develop a significantly more comprehensive program than a one-time family education event.

The Pearlstone Coalition, directed by Carol Pristoop, who was committed to the idea of family education, was amenable to this idea. Dr. Bor and Rabbi Loeb visited with a number of Jewish educational luminaries. Professors Joseph Riemer and Susan Shevitz at Brandeis, for example, were helpful in suggesting ways of engaging parental participation in the planning stages. Dr. Ronald Wolfson helped in formulating the programmatic ambiance. Harlene Appelman provided useful ideas on how to reorient the teaching staff to a new program. Local Baltimore communal educational leaders such as Dr. Chaim Botwinich, Rabbi Joseph Braver, and Dr. Shulamith Elster provided needed reality checks, especially since it became apparent that the plans were moving towards a program that would be a substantial break from past tradition, a stance alien to Baltimore's usually conservative instincts.

Rabbi Loeb: *In order to secure support from Beth El's laity, it seemed both politically and educationally advisable to garner expressions of support and cooperation from local and even national educational experts, expressions which would allay any anxieties as to the value of some of the proposed changes.*

After a good deal of thinking, Dr. Bor and Rabbi Loeb concluded that what Beth El's Religious School needed was to be divided into two separate tracks: the first, the traditional three-day-a-week Hebrew School already in place; and the second, a new family education model. At first, they imagined that they could move the entire school into the new tract but quickly revised their thinking in the face of thoughtful disagreement from lay leaders and some parents.

The Family Education program would be based on several principles.

1. Children would come on Sundays and on one midweek afternoon rather than two. This was a major structural change.

2. The parents would come to school with their children one Sunday morning per month for Parent Adult Education while their children were in class.

3. The parents would commit themselves to attending, with their children, Shabbat services eight times per year; and when they came on Shabbat mornings, both the parents and children would have separate forty-five-minute learning sessions before the service, followed by a service in which parents, as well as students, took on leadership roles.

4. There would be required family Tikkun Olam projects.

5. The school would offer family day trips of Jewish interest that included participation by grandparents.

6. The school would encourage home-based family observance events, such as at-home havdalah get-togethers and Erev Shabbat havurah-style dinners with groups of other families, thus providing a meaningful socio-religious component to the overall program, something quite important in a 1700-family synagogue, which can easily come to feel impersonal.

7. Families would be required to attend four family education programs per year to be held on Sunday mornings in lieu of regularly scheduled classes.

8. Students had to attend Religious School consistently. If their

absences exceeded five per year, they would have to complete makeup assignments.

The basic point of the program was to create a model of learning wherein parents would be participants and come to invest more in their child's Jewish education, where their own intellectual lacunae could be unthreateningly filled, and where lost formal schooling time (for children) could be replaced with more stimulating, informal educational experiences for the entire family that might have an enduring impact.

These ideas seemed to be attractive, perhaps dangerously so, with the offer of one less day of class. Dr. Bor and Rabbi Loeb wondered whether people would sign up merely to reduce the demands on their children, who tended not to want to be in Hebrew School any more than they had to be. Also, since the parents had no real history of participation in the school, would they really buy into the new program? The biggest question of all: Would the children be able to learn in two study days a week, on the cognitive level, what they had in three study days? What would this cost? And, could it be done at all? Would the synagogue's lay leadership be receptive? What would be their concerns?

Dr. Bor: *My greatest concern was whether we would be creating a self-perpetuating monster. If the program came to be seen as a popular easy way out for a child's Jewish education, it might take on a life of its own and be impossible to undo. In effect, we were gambling with the school's integrity. Also, we had no idea as to whether the parents would receive positively the experience of Jewish learning for themselves. In short, we were sailing into uncharted waters.*

Well before these ideas were broached with lay leaders, Dr. Bor and Rabbi Loeb tried to develop the concept as fully as they could. In addition to outside consultations, locally and beyond, a key appointment to the Beth El staff was made by hiring Fern Cohen as a full-time family educator. Ms. Cohen had been hired one year earlier to create school-wide and grade-specific family education programs and assemblies. Since they had stimulated significant positive parent and grandparent responses, these became the groundwork for the changes that were envisioned. Ms. Cohen thus became the third partner, along with Dr. Bor and Rabbi Loeb, in the team which began to create, implement, and in the end, direct what they came to call Project Mishpacha, admittedly not an original name, but a useful one in terms of the school's purpose.

Ms. Cohen: *I came to the project with professional training in two fields, Jewish education and social work. My orientation was to be very positive to the concept of parental involvement especially in the planning stage of a new program. I had already been developing a series of family education programs in the school on all grade levels, which was a departure from Beth El's status quo, and which had garnered much enthusiastic response. These programs helped to prepare parents for the more elaborate program we were to develop.*

The team began to think through the politics of involvement, persuasion, and participation of Beth El's lay leaders. The rabbi and Dr. Bor began with the lay officers of the congregation, who were unexpectedly easy to convince. Perhaps they had long recognized the rumblings of parental dissatisfaction and wanted to find a better way to educate Beth El's children. Two past presidents of the synagogue, one a nationally-regarded expert on middle-school education, the other a proponent of family education who had been to the Whizin Summer Seminar with the Pearlstone staff, added their support and offered many valuable ideas.

The outgoing and incoming School Board chairs were approached. They were open to being convinced. They participated in several thoughtful discussions, and based on their input, earlier ideas were significantly refined. The School Committee was consulted and added their own caveats and suggestions. As noted above, the original thinking of Dr. Bor and Rabbi Loeb had been to make the entire school over in the Project Mishpacha mode, but the lay people cautioned against this, and they were right to do so. After all, there were many parents who liked the current model, and to force them into another schedule might provoke resistance. If Project Mishpacha proved itself, reasoned the Committee, then these parents would join of their own accord.

Next, and of crucial significance, a delegation of six individuals went to the fifth Whizin Summer Seminar in Los Angeles both to get ideas for the program and to develop a strengthened faith in, and understanding of, the concepts of Jewish family education. This proved to be an enlightening experience for the delegation, which included the rabbi, the president of the synagogue and his wife, the family education director, and the incoming and the outgoing chairs of the School Committee, a most salutary mix in terms of influencing the synagogue's laity.

From that point on, gaining the approval of the Beth El Board of

Trustees to undertake a two-year pilot program was fairly simple, since so many of the constituencies had already bought into the idea. One key contribution of the board was to affirm the school's decision to keep the tuition of the two school tracks equal, even though it was already clear that Project Mishpacha would cost the school a great deal more per pupil.

Since the School Board had urged parent involvement in the planning process, an Ad Hoc Advisory Committee of Interested Parents was convened to ask questions, especially about the Sunday morning adult study sessions. Would the sessions pay attention to parent interests? Would they coincide with what the children were learning? Would there be a systematic curriculum? How would people be selected for the program, since a pilot program with a fixed budget could only take a limited number of students and families? The Committee proved to be politically helpful: it both promoted the interest of potential families for the program and gave those parents who felt that no one had been listening to them reason to buy into a Beth El Religious School program with enthusiasm. All of this had a salutary effect on its subsequent implementation.

> Ms Cohen: *It was a pleasant challenge to find ways to connect with the parents. It was important to include them in planning programs in which they were to be involved. Also, we worked with our School Committee in ways we never had done before—namely, encouraged Committee members to communicate directly with parents and interpret Project Mishpacha to them after parents had submitted their applications.*

Next in the planning process were major investments of energy and thought. First, we had to redefine the curriculum to compress the essence of the three-day-a-week curriculum into the two-day structure. Obviously, some things had to go and others needed to be restructured, especially teaching Hebrew reading. Second, we had to create a curriculum for parents. Should it be the same for all parents? Different for parents of children at each grade level? We had to orient to the new program. We brought in a master teacher-trainer, Harlene Appelman from Detroit, as a regular visitor and consultant. We recruited teachers based on their ability to relate to parents as well as students. We needed to work out space requirements for the Sundays when parents were studying, and we had to requisition non-school rooms for that purpose. We had to plan family-style programs, including field trips and Tikkun Olam projects.

We had to devise a method of accountability lest some families use Project Mishpacha as a convenient alternative to the rigors of the three-day program. We needed to design an application brochure, which came to include a written application and an oral interview. We had to set up pre-program sales meetings for parents, which helped to set the right tone for the new program. We also planned spirit-building events and promotions, including a special concert, t-shirts and coffee mugs. We needed to devise special communication links. A special Project Mishpacha newsletter, with articles by children, parents, and teachers, began to appear regularly. We had to find master teachers, in addition to the school's regular faculty, to teach the parent classes. And finally, we had to establish budgets and undertake fund raising.

All in all, Project Mishpacha evolved into quite a large set of administrative challenges. They drew the school staff together through a sense of common quest. Shabbat services began to involve parents and children as active participants. Parents were now interested in Jewish learning. Those who applied to the program, it turned out, were not slackers but, on the contrary, the most motivated families in the school—those who had long wanted to be "turned on" Jewishly.

> Dr. Bor: *The process was enormously demanding, but it did create an invigorating new avirah (atmosphere) for the staff and drew forth their creativity. It also built their pride and professional self-esteem as they were called upon to be co-creators of this venture.*

But one nagging question remained: Was all of this really doing any good? To answer the question with as great a degree of certainty as possible, the school was able, thanks to a grant from the Jacob and Hilda Blaustein Fund for Jewish Education, a project of Baltimore's Federation, to retain the services of Dr. Adrianne Bank of Los Angeles, who developed an evaluation strategy to cover the initial two-year period of the pilot program. Dr. Bank met with Beth El's staff and proposed a series of instruments to determine whether the level of Hebrew language achievement was the same, less, or more for Project Mishpacha students compared to students in the mainstream, three-day-a-week program. Evaluation also measured the level of parental and student satisfaction in the two programs and asked for reports of observable "Jewish behavioral changes" in the lives of the Project Mishpacha families. It also was to determine if Project Mishpacha was working, and if so, which elements were the key to its success and which might need modification.

Dr. Bank made several trips to Baltimore, developed and administered evaluative instruments, and spent time interviewing students, teachers, and parents before the program began, during it, and at the end of a two-year period. She submitted a comprehensive report that, in the main, validated what the school had done through Project Mishpacha. She concluded that, by the end of the pilot period, Project Mishpacha had been successful in achieving its goals. From the political point of view, she helped to shape the congregation's willingness to invest in Project Mishpacha by meeting personally with the synagogue's lay leaders and even addressing its Board of Trustees. Since it is they who are footing the bill—Project Mishpacha turned out to cost fifty percent more per-pupil than the three-day-a-week program—her participation helped to reinforce lay support and pride in what the school was doing.

Rabbi Loeb: *Dr. Bank saw that this was a front-line program whose potential applications were very far-reaching. Her role was crucial because it provided us with information from which we could gain insight as to desired modifications and improvements.*

The bottom-line result is that Project Mishpacha has become a permanent Department of Family Education in the Beth El School, engendering a new culture of Jewish learning for close to half the families served by the school. It has facilitated the development of new positive attitudes among parents and students. It seems to be accomplishing its goals without any apparent loss of educational content when compared to the three-day-a-week program. But a school-within-a-school remains a constant challenge, evoking a continuing need to create new experiential programs for the entire family. In the years ahead, we know we must answer some really important questions, among them: Can Project Mishpacha work effectively for the entire six-year stretch of the child's stay in the school? Will it be as useful for the upper grades as it appears to be for the lower? Will it require fine-tuning as families approach the bar/bat mitzvah year? What will we do with and for parents when their children move on to post-elementary school, when joint parent-child programs may provoke resistance in adolescents beginning to individuate?

It is clear that we have much to learn as we go. But we have made a beginning and the road ahead looks to be a very interesting one for us, and perhaps for others, to travel.

Esther Netter is executive director of My Jewish Discovery Place Children's Museum and Cultural Center of Jewish Community Centers of Greater Los Angeles, an innovative and interactive museum for children and families which has become a model for the nation. During 1997, its traveling exhibits were in more than thirty Jewish communities including London and Warsaw. Esther also serves as the assistant executive director of Jewish Community Centers of Greater Los Angeles.

Esther Netter

Esther is on the faculty of the Whizin Institute for Jewish Family Life at the University of Judaism and a member of the clinical faculty of the Rhea Hirsch School of Education at Hebrew Union College. She lectures and teaches about museum education and informal education in North America, Europe, and Israel.

Esther received her undergraduate degree in Jewish studies from the University of California, Los Angeles, and her master's degree in Jewish education from the Jewish Theological Seminary in New York. She is the mother of three innovative and interactive children, Elisheva, Moshe, Shira.

My Jewish Discovery Place:
A World of Imagination
Esther Netter

Close your eyes and imagine—
Holding the hand of your six-year old child. Walking together through a magic curtain. Entering a time machine room. Being greeted by Moses Ben Maimon and Don Isaac Abravanel, who introduce themselves to you and describe the journey you are about to begin. Finding costumes, turbans, scarves, jewels, belts and shoes to adorn you on your journey "back into time."

You and your child follow the instructions and, in the blink of an eye, you pass through another magic curtain and find yourself standing in a Sephardic home in Spain in the early 1400s. You visit the surrounding neighborhood, synagogue, and outdoor marketplace. The smells of the fruits, vegetables, and flowers, the conversations with people you meet along the way, the songs and sounds of your Sephardic journey, are wonderful.

No sooner have you and your child left Spain, than you find yourself standing in the sandals of Judah Maccabee when he led the revolt against the Syrians. And then your child is transformed into Colonel Uri, who fought to liberate Jerusalem in the Six Day War in Israel. Just moments later, you board an El Al plane and fly to Israel, with your child as the captain. You fasten your seat belt and the flight begins. The views from the plane as you begin your descent are spectacular.

In Israel, your travels know no bounds. From Safed to Eilat, you meet new Israeli friends and discover how much you have in common. Your last stop is Jerusalem, the City of Gold. There you write special notes and prayers and put them into the cracks of the Kotel, the Western Wall.

This has been an afternoon at My Jewish Discovery Place Children's Museum in Los Angeles, California. Our museum provides Jewish

experiences for children and families who do not have the natural rein-
forcements that used to support the Jewish identities of earlier generations: neighborhoods with the sights, sounds, and smells of Jewish lives;
grandparents with memories of Jewish culture from around the world;
family members who may have experienced the suffering of the
Holocaust or the thrill of the creation of the State of Israel. In their place,
we can give our children and grandchildren glimpses and experiences of
what living a Jewish life has meant in the past. Museums, when thought
of as centers for experiential learning, can provide such experiences.

My Jewish Discovery Place Children's Museum

My Jewish Discovery Place Children's Museum (MJDPCM or MJDP) of
the Jewish Community Centers Association of Greater Los Angeles was
established to simulate some of the experiences, for children and adults,
which have been lost in contemporary daily life. This museum is an interactive adult-child learning environment where the participation of parents and families in the Jewish education of their children reinforces
everyone's joy in living a Jewish life. The concept of MJDP was developed
by the Jewish Community Centers Association of North America and
funded by the Avi Chai Foundation as a demonstration project. In Los
Angeles, additional grants were obtained for exhibits designed by experts
familiar with interactive education, educational gaming, computer programming, and interior design.

Since opening in July 1992, My Jewish Discovery Place Children's
Museum has been a highly effective tool for Jewish education and outreach to families. By 1996, more than 74,000 people had passed through
our doors. Four hundred seventy community institutions have brought
groups to the museum. Fifty-five docents have been trained to help guide
visitors through it. The Council for Initiatives in Jewish Education
(CIJE) has featured MJDP in its Lead Communities Best Practices
Project in Early Childhood Education. In addition to extensive coverage
in the international Jewish and general press, articles about MJDP have
been published in the Coalition for the Advancement of Jewish
Education and Jewish Community Center newsletters.

The Idea Behind the Exhibits

The exhibits and learning areas operate on two levels: first, as interactive
experiences introducing aspects of Jewish life to children in a sensory-

intensive, joyful, manner; and second, as a teaching resource instructing adults by reinforcing and structuring their own Jewish learning.

Museums are transformed spaces, creatively designated environments where families learn together. Environmental learning, using space to teach, is key to the impact and success of the museum. Walls, ceilings, and floors are all teaching tools immersing the visitor in total environments. During a two-hour visit, the museum visitor experiences Spain in the 1400s, Egypt as a slave, or a flight to Israel. The immersion theory behind museum education is similar to that of summer camps and Israel experiences, which gain power through intensity and fullness. The museum, in a small time and space, creates a "slice" of a trip or a day at camp.

My Jewish Discovery Place's self-directed, self-paced environment is non-judgmental and allows learning to take place on any level at any age. People visiting the museum do not feel "incompetent" when they come in the door. The museum is a "safe" space for children, and especially for adults, "to do Jewish" and "learn Jewish" by roaming free, exploring, discovering, and questioning.

Jewish self-confidence and self-esteem bubble up in children, parents, grandparents, teachers, museum docents, and all who work with and visit MJDP. Adults are empowered to be teachers. Parents and grandparents are given the explanations and answers they need so that they can become Jewish educators of their children and grandchildren. Bolstering the adult visitor's Jewish parenting ability is a powerful outgrowth of a visit to the museum. These considerations guide the design of all museum elements, including the training of volunteer docents. We try to create in the museum a trusting environment where fear is unknown and discovery is unlimited. The child, like the adult, becomes an independent learner constructing his or her own experience.

Our museum setting flip-flops the usual relationship between children and adults. The child acquires adult-like autonomy, while the adult's experience becomes more child-like in that it is immediate, direct, and playful. Open-endedness in the museum encourages reciprocal learnings. We normally think of the adult as teacher, but at the museum one sees the opposite—a child opening a window so the adult can learn. Children are willing to imagine, to suspend reality, and to prompt adults to rediscover the child inside themselves. When a child asks a parent or teacher to put on a costume or to put on a seat belt so as not to "fall" out of the plane, the adult is encouraged to be creative, playful, and inquisitive.

This meeting of the minds, hearts, and hands of adults and children occurs throughout the museum, encouraging the creation and the telling of stories. Telling stories is central to the museum experience and it forms the core of the "Family Routes and Roots" exhibit on genealogy, where families talk about journeys and travels. More storytelling unfolds when families stand in front of the Giant Torah Scroll. In the center of the Torah Scroll is an ark. Inside the ark are felt-board Torahs, a beautiful Sephardic Torah, kippot (head coverings), tallitot (prayer shawls) and many sets of tefillin (phylacteries), each in its own special embroidered bag. The tefillin, in particular, stimulate family storytelling. One day a mother describes to her daughter her memory of her grandfather, who used to put on tefillin each morning. She tells how, as a small girl, she used to watch her grandfather secretly from the other room. On another day, a son asks his father to help put the tefillin on his arm. The father recalls the last time he put on tefillin, which was twenty-three years ago at his bar mitzvah. The father remembers that his tefillin are packed away and promises that they will go home and find them. Another day, a group of women and their young children, who had never seen tefillin up close and certainly had never tried to put them on, attempt to strap on the tefillin and practice wrapping them around their arms and hands, while they exchange stories of their fathers and grandfathers and talk about growing up as young girls in religious homes. The museum is full of symbols, objects, and experiences that, like the tefillin, prompt visitors to become tellers of their own Jewish stories.

Current Exhibits

As I write, a new exhibit, "Our Sephardic Communities: Through the Eyes of Children," is on display in our museum. As children and parents or school, synagogue, and community groups enter, they pass through a giant archway designed as a Spanish tower and surrounded by latticework woven with vines and flowers. The first section is a three-room odyssey, "Back in Time." The first room, with beaded curtains and a telephone time machine, has two life-size, child-size, talking dolls, Moses Ben Maimon and Don Isaac Abravanel. They introduce themselves and instruct everyone to select costumes from three overflowing trunks filled with clothing, head coverings, accessories, jewelry, purses and shoes.

In the second room, museum participants are greeted by a doll, Dona Grasia Nasi, a famous Marrano. She welcomes everyone to her home, invites them to sit on the pillows and rugs, to fix food, to set the table, and to complete the beautiful tapestry on the wall. She asks them to join her as she sings her favorite Ladino melodies. The home is full of Sephardic ritual objects, household items, and child-size furniture typical of the time. After leaving her home, they go to the synagogue, complete with specially designed benches, the hekhal in the center of the synagogue, an aron kadosh filled with Sephardic Torahs, tallitot, and kippot. This room is surrounded by a replica of a marble balcony found in Sephardic synagogues of the time. Above is an eternal lamp, and along the bottom of the synagogue walls are ritual object-puzzles for children to complete and decorate their synagogue. A doll identified as a rabbi describes the synagogue, shares prayers and melodies, and asks the children and adults about what they are seeing and hearing. Each area is covered with murals, backdrops, colorful ceilings, and floor coverings designed from photos and descriptions of the architecture of the time.

In the open area next to this exhibit is a re-creation of an outdoor market, Plaza Maimonides, complete with platform, mural, roof covering, and large baskets overflowing with fruits, vegetables, flowers, eggs, and jewelry. Smaller baskets, bags, and pots stand ready for children and adults to fill. More costumes are set up in the marketplace. And as the families play, they can view themselves on a television monitor focused on this plaza. Adjacent to the marketplace is an audiovisual exhibit with six telephones, each connected to a cassette recorder playing a continuous tape that guides listeners as they view a 180-degree mini-mural of Sephardim with scenes depicting life-cycle events and everyday life. Nearby, six four-foot-high dolls stand in an area called Shticky City. With Velcro, museum-goer participants dress and adorn these dolls. Mixing and matching costume tops, bottoms, and hats allows the children to dress new "friends" and incorporate them into their imaginative play.

Our rubbing table is a Sephardic one. Children use crayon and paper to uncover hidden symbols and letters and use the border designs to create pieces of art. Efo Eitan, our hidden picture exhibit, challenges families to find and identify over fifty characters, symbols, and situations. A beautiful, one-of-a-kind picture overflowing with ritual objects is another opportunity for educational hide-and-seek to engage both adults and children. This Sephardic experience is a rotating exhibit in one area of the museum. Other rotating and permanent exhibits housed at the museum include:

Happy Birthday Dear Jerusalem, where you magically journey to Jerusalem and learn about the city, its history, and how people of different cultures and religions live together as neighbors.

The exhibit People Helping People focuses on the Jewish mitzvot (commandments) of tzedakah, righteousness; pikua<u>h</u> nefesh, the saving of lives; and bikur <u>h</u>olim, visiting the sick. Through the exhibit, you learn about these values and how to make them part of your life.

A Spectrum of Jewish Experience: The Rescue of Ethiopian Jews reenacts the rescue and resettlement of Ethiopian Jews in Israel. "A Spectrum of Jewish Experience" focuses on immigrant journeys and raises questions such as, "Is one's community defined by race, religion or geography?"

My Family's Roots and Routes: Genealogy Exhibit encourages families to explore their histories and immigrations against the backdrop of the Statue of Liberty and Ellis Island. This exhibit teaches the importance of the family, the connections between generations and the passing on of traditions by presenting Jewish communities and cultures world-wide.

Back in Time: The Exodus from Egypt. Visitors travel to Egypt, through the Red Sea and into the wilderness of Sinai where Moses leads the people. This exhibit teaches and reminds us about the Exodus story, presenting concepts of freedom, leadership and personhood.

Noah's Ark: A Rainbow and A Promise exemplifies kindness and respect for other living things, humanity's relationship to the environment, and our Jewish responsibilities to build a better world, do Tikkun Olam.

Honi the Circle Drawer: It's the Tree of Life also challenges visitors to think about their responsibility for the environment and its future.

Bendigamos: The Blessing of Sephardic Life. Bendigamos means *blessings* in Ladino. The celebrations shown in the exhibit depict the blessings of this Sephardic family, the Ben-Simons, of their family home on the eve of the Sabbath and Fortuna's wedding. "Bendigamos" teaches about comparative cultures and about community and life-cycle events.

The Art of Words: Discovering Calligraphy & Illumination. Artistic interpretations and creative techniques of calligraphy, modern and ancient, encourage visitors to create their own illuminated art pieces and letters, explore different alphabets, learn about the work of the scribe. The centrality to our tradition of text and "words" forms the core of this exhibit.

You, Me & Dignity. This exhibit helps children and adults learn about themselves, about people with special needs, and about how everyone fits into our community, emphasizing that each of us is special and should be treated with respect and dignity.

Family guides and materials are in all exhibit areas, with suggestions for questions and activities to do together. In-depth background information about the exhibits is posted for adults and older children. Take-home family activity sheets provide creative ways for the museum learning experience to continue at home. Teacher resource materials make it easy for schools to prepare for and follow up on the museum experience.

Museum activity kits expand the capability of the museum to serve large school, camp, and family havurot groups. The Jewish Activity Kit, JAK-In-The-Box, promotes positive, interactive Jewish learning experiences in the museum. Each is self-facilitating, self-directed, and self-paced. The fifteen to twenty kits in the museum rotate every three months. Titles include: "What's the Grog in the Grogger?" (matching the sounds that the groggers make), "Oy, I'm Stuffed" (Jewish foods that have other foods inside them), "The Touch Box" (identifying Jewish objects in a covered box by touch), "Make a Face" (drawing faces to match hats from Jews around the world). Other kits focus on the holiday sequence, Shabbat rituals, and sorting games for Kosher/non-Kosher foods.

Who Visits the Museum?

My Jewish Discovery Place, serving the Jewish and general communities of Los Angeles, is for children three and up and their parents. Schools, camps, and synagogues with pre-schoolers, kindergartners, and first and second graders also visit MJDP. So do families—from the unaffiliated to the ultra-Orthodox. In addition, MJDP is available to the general public through public and private school visits so that the multi-ethnic Los Angeles community can come to know the many ways of being Jewish. MJDP demonstrates how even diverse communities share much in common. Teacher materials for Jewish and non-Jewish school provide more information and emphasize the the beauty and richness of different traditions and the importance of preserving them all.

Museum Infrastructure

The museum has an executive director, a museum director and three full-time staff. Additional part-time staff are hired as needed; graduate student interns work with the museum staff, Everyone is involved in developing and evaluating exhibits, recruiting and training lay leadership, and promoting the museum. Professional staff are essential to the success of an institution, as is their partnership with the ever-growing treasure trove of volunteers, patrons, and lay leaders. It is a priority of the museum to educate and involve every volunteer in meaningful, worthwhile Jewish educational work. From the onset, the role of the chairperson of the museum's Board of Directors was of utmost importance. The chair served as an anchor in securing community support and as a magnet for involving others on the museum's board and committees. Together with staff, the chair, and the board have successfully articulated the museum's vision. The board and its committees include Jewish community lay leaders, donors, program participants, representatives of other community organizations, educators, artists, and museum experts.

Enthusiastic and dedicated lay involvement in the museum has been a key to its success. Together, the board and staff raise the funds necessary to operate and expand the museum. An annual membership campaign to defray operating costs began when the museum opened. Founding grants and endowment funds have helped the museum build a strong financial base. Fund raising events raise needed additional dollars. Fees from family and group visits are another source of income.

An Executive Board coordinates the work of the Board of Directors and all board committees. Each board member serves on at least one committee. Committees include: Patrons and Membership, Fund raising

Events, Public Relations, Program Events, Multi-Ethnic Outreach, Community Events, Docents, Fine Arts Programs, Cultural Arts Programs, Newsletter, Artistic Advisory Board. The large number of committees has made it easy for lay people to find the niche within which they want to work. This structure has also created opportunities for people of different Jewish backgrounds, ages, stages in life, and social groups to meet, work, and develop relationships. Board and patron events also support building and educating board members. Celebrating havdalah together, coming to an evening of Jewish learning with a visiting scholar, or attending a concert of Jewish music, are all opportunities to build a sense of community among lay leaders, their families, and friends.

Museum Docents

One amazing success of the museum's lay structure is the docent program. Early in the first year of the museum, it became clear that the museum needed to expand its hours and find more trained people to work with groups and serve on the museum team. The museum began its docent training program to meet this need. A docent committee was formed with the help of the docent chairperson to establish criteria for recruiting and selecting docents, to develop the training program, and to identify potential docents. It has been a tremendous success.

Current docent training is a six-hour course, given in two sessions, covering the history and logistics of the museum, group dynamics and Jewish study. It reviews early childhood education, learning styles, and behavior management. After attending, docents receive a manual with resources and review materials. Before they begin to work alone, they apprentice with a staff person. Once experienced and confident, they begin to work with other docents to run particular areas of the museum. All are committed to Jewish education and to working with children and families, and each adds a unique, personal perspective to visitors' experience.

Docents are an intergenerational mix: grandparents, parents, singles, adults, and teens. Each brings a different type of knowledge, background, education, and professional experience. Most docents are also learners; many had no previous Jewish background. Because of their training, docents often makes changes in their own Jewish lives. Although the program began as a way to expand hours and serve more visitors, it has evolved into a rich adult educational experience. Docents have become more connected to the Jewish community, and for some, this is their first positive Jewish connection. For others, it is a first opportunity to work with families and to teach and learn. For still others, it has presented an opportunity to use professional skills to enhance what the museum offers. And many simply enjoy working with children and families. Docents share their joy in their work with museum visitors. The words docents often use to evaluate and reflect upon their work are "transforming," "rewarding," and "satisfying." These are some responses of docents and lay leaders involved with the museum:

The museum has filled me—an empty and dry vessel—on a spiritual level and on many other levels as well.

The museum is more than a museum—I feel like I am coming home. I want to be a Jew again.

I ask questions about Judaism. I don't know anything. The museum, because it is a children's museum, has the level brought down so I myself can walk in and learn.

When I introduced myself at the Board, I said I'd never really been involved before. Before, I just wrote checks. Here they want me. They want me.

I never felt like a Jew before. I didn't know how.

In my heart it is frustrating to be a Jew, to be affiliated and not to know. I want to learn so much.

My husband converted. He said the best compliment to me 'You make Judaism fun.'

I'm looking forward to the holidays for the first time. I'm going to make a special holiday dinner, for the first time, because of the museum.

The docent program, which recruits, trains, empowers and rewards these volunteers, is also a wonderful vehicle for involving and educating lay volunteers in other aspects of the museum.

What Next?

Inspired by My Jewish Discovery Place's success, many Jewish community centers and communal institutions are eager to have similar resources in their communities, either on a permanent or traveling basis. Their interest has led to the National Traveling My Jewish Discovery Place Children's Museum. Communities can readily accommodate a traveling museum with exhibits similar to those that have made MJDP so success-ful. The National Traveling My Jewish Discovery Place Children's Museum, operating in collaboration with local synagogues, boards of Jewish Education, and other Jewish institutions, helps communities orga-nize exhibits on their own sites. The National Traveling My Jewish Discovery Place does research, design, and fabrication of new interactive learning exhibits which are easily transportable and can be assembled in various spaces. There are additional supports for each of the traveling exhibits along with kits and materials for families to use at home. Communities receive pre-installation consultations and seminars for coalitions of professionals and lay people to inform them about how to use the exhibits to build or enhance ongoing family education programs in their own communities.

Although the traveling museum stays in a community for one month at a time, the exhibits, the training sessions, and materials are intended to have long lasting effects on the community's capacity to engage families in long-term Jewish educational activities. Pre-arrival consultations deal with establishing and maintaining community-wide coalitions to maxi-mize participation by affiliated and non-affiliated members of the Jewish community through publicity, marketing and outreach, fund raising, building lay support for the museum and family education programs, and the technical aspects of using the museum. When the traveling muse-um is installed, the project director visits and leads sessions for the pro-fessional staff and the volunteer docents who will help families use the exhibits, and other professionals who might use the museum.

As the museum continues to grow and establish itself as a resource for families, centers, schools, synagogues, camps, and the community, new areas are under development. The concept of a "museum without walls" envisions the museum as a home base for fine arts, cultural arts work-shops, and classes for children and families. This started in Los Angeles with a summer series of storytelling and intergenerational art classes. In the fall and winter, a series of performing arts programs (drama, music, dance) culminated in performances in the museum's theater area (a convertible space).

The "museum without walls" includes small transportable exhibits to take to schools—Jewish and non-Jewish, private and public—throughout Los Angeles. The notion of portability has become a key consideration for all new museum exhibits in order to include as many as possible regular museum exhibits in the "museum without walls programs."

Summary

The creation of a museum-like space is a powerful way to reach and teach families with young children and to offer positive Jewish experiences. The concepts behind the development of MJDP have application to a variety of community institutions. For example, if a Jewish community center or other institution has a permanent space which can be utilized, the Los Angeles museum can be replicated, in full or in part, and establish a relationship to share exhibits and cooperate on the creation of new experiences. If space can only be assigned on a temporary basis (i.e., one month per year), specially designed exhibits can transform that space temporarily. Even if a community does not have any single large space to allocate to exhibits, there are ways to transform small spaces to create family learning environments—in a classroom, in a center or school lobby, or in a corner of a synagogue foyer.

At a time when our families need strengthening and our communities need more opportunities to celebrate living and learning Jewishly, the museum model provides us with positive answers. Many secular youth museums already provide experiences that educators use to complement school lessons. Many adult museums are seriously dedicated to education are adding elements suited for individual and family learning. The museum is a new vehicle for Jewish education. Our museum is not intended to inspire only one-visit. Families can return together again and again to build Jewish self-confidence and Jewish understandings.

My Jewish Discovery Place Children's Museum of Jewish Community Centers of Greater Los Angeles started with less than one thousand square feet, twenty-three exhibits, a $50,000 annual budget and a part-time museum director. By year two, the director had become full time and additional museum programs were added. At the end of year three, MJDP had moved into its new 4,500 square foot site, with expanded staff, exhibits, and museum hours.

In its first year, the National Traveling Museum visited thirty-four communities and demand is increasing. This national network may begin to function as "franchise museums," in order to share, exchange, and maintain high-quality, innovative educational exhibits.

My Jewish Discovery Place Children's Museum focuses on Jewish themes and values for Jewish children and adults. MJDP is opening windows and doors to many previously uninterested Jewish learners. MJDP is an innovative work in progress—a drama ready to unfold, a script that is being written, with new characters stepping on stage every day.

Now Imagine Once Again—

You and your family have just spent Sunday afternoon with Abraham, Joseph and Sara. You participated in an archaeological dig and you attended two bar mitzvahs and a wedding. You spent time talking to Arabs, kibbutznikim, soldiers and new immigrants, all of whom you met in Israel. Luckily, they all spoke English. You visited the Statue of Liberty and met Jewish families from around the globe. Bubbie Rachel showed you her favorite candlesticks. You found hidden objects everywhere but you know you did not find them all.

The museum was your stage—the drama began when you became the actor, director, producer, and audience all at once. It was full of props and tools that allowed you to travel across boundaries of time and space. It helped you discover the joy of living Jewishly through the celebration of Jewish values, culture, and traditions. The museum opened many doors for you and you left through a different door than you entered. John Holt writes in *How Children Fail*:

Not many years ago I began to play the cello. Most people would say that what I am doing is "learning to play" the cello. But these words carry into our minds the strange idea that there exists two very different processes: (1) learning to play the cello; and (2) playing the cello. They imply that I will do the first until I have completed it, at which point I will stop the first process and begin the second. In short, I will go on "learning to play" until I have "learned to play" and then I will begin to play. Of course, this is nonsense. There are not two processes, but one. We learn to do something by doing it. There is no other way.

We learn to do something by doing it. There is no other way. My Jewish Discovery Place Children's Museum allows us to learn something by doing it over and over again.

Judy Israel Elkin

*J*udy Israel Elkin lives in Boston and is a family education and professional development consultant at the Bureau of Jewish Education. Judy is also director of Ramah Family Camp in Palmer, Massachusetts, an adjunct lecturer at Brandeis University and Hebrew College, and a participant in the Teacher Educator Institute of CIJE. Together with her husband Josh, she has three wonderful children who provide some of the best material a family educator could want.

Family Camp: Temporary Communities, Permanent Changes
Judy Israel Elkin

Introduction

Sometime this past winter I ran into a woman at the supermarket who had attended that summer's Ramah Family Camp in Palmer, Massachusetts, which I had directed. She told me that as a result of family camp her family now keeps kosher. She has just kashered her kitchen and bought what she needed to separate milk and meat dishes. She emphasized that the experience of family camp had transformed her and her family. It was just what they wanted. I was surprised by what she told me. We had not even touched on kashrut at family camp. The whole experience had lasted only five days. What happened for this family? What did they bring with them to family camp, and what did we provide that led them toward this decision?

To some extent, we know that attending family camp is self-selective. Adults who come are often seeking a Jewish experience to enrich their family in some way. But not always. Sometimes a family comes because family camp is an easy vacation—no decisions about kids' activities or restaurants or hotels. Some come because they loved camp as kids and want to have that experience again as adults. Others want to get their children to experience what they remember as uniquely happy moments. Each year, some parents risk part of their family's vacation on family camp because they are starving for Jewish connection, study, and prayer. And still others are brought by friends who have "seen the light" and want them to share it. Most frequently, people come for a combination of reasons.

For children the issue is less one of motivation than expectation. Many children are not involved in the family's decision about summer plans.

Still, for those young people who have already attended family camp, their desire to return may influence parents' plans for future summers. Children attending for the first time, typically half the population, frequently have anxieties: What will it be like to be at camp with my whole family? Will it be a family vacation or will it be lonesome for me? Will I make friends? What if I don't find a friend? Where will my parents be when I'm with other kids playing? What if I don't have nice counselors? For the other half of the children who have been to family camp before, expectations predominate. This group wants assurance that this year's camp will be as good as before, or even better.

Whatever their motivation or expectations, everyone comes together—with all their family baggage and luggage—and they become a community. And in so doing, they often leave with more than when they came. Friendships carry over into their city life with progressive sukkot parties and sleep-overs for kids. Despite their initial reasons for attending camp, the family shares an experience together that often is transformative. The five-day camping experience is quite powerful. The intensity comes from being immersed in a total environment with other people who share important commonalties. Many parents feel isolated and alone in their task of Jewish parenting. Many families come from small towns where there are few Jewish communal supports. For them, and even for families from cosmopolitan areas such as Boston, family camp acknowledges their role as Jewish parents and offers them time for serious exploration of issues of Jewish concern and parenting.

Camp provides the opportunity for real growth through the living-together experience. For example, the workshop parents attend on Talking to Children about God continues informally over lunch or on the beach or in front of bunks while watching kids play. The environment promotes these discussions as part of the natural order. And, there are plenty of other adults to talk to.

Immersion is not enough, however. As director, I must facilitate their transformation by creating opportunities for it to occur in every aspect of the program. And the staff, who will be having the most contact with the families, must work hard at the same task. I look for enthusiastic, warm, talented, and self-aware madrikhim, counselors, who understand how to connect immediately with campers. Unlike a children-only summer camp, we do not have the luxury of easing a child into the group over a period of weeks. We must make the connection immediately. If children don't feel that the group wants them, that camp is a fun place to be, that the counselor knows their names, then they won't separate, adults won't go to their programs, and the total experience is jeopardized. We take the work of blending new and returning children and their families very seriously, and preventing cliques is of great concern.

As for program and content: I seek extensive feedback from families and use their many suggestions. At the same time, I am of the "give-them what-they-should-have" school as opposed to the "give-them-what-they-think they-want" school. People may not know what they want or they may be mistaken. Even if they sense what they want, they may not be able to articulate it clearly. I have found that families who come to camp usually want more than they say they do. For example, I intentionally do not provide detailed descriptions of the program in advance. I simply invite people to a "unique family activity" or to a "special adult program" and then jump right into it when everyone is together.

This article will describe three aspects of the Ramah family camp experience that I believe illustrate why it is so powerful. First, I will describe a successful program, unpack its components, and examine its effect on participants. Next, I will review the schedule and goals of Ramah Family Camp and tell how they nourish the needs of families. In the third section, I will describe the philosophy that lies behind my role as camp director.

A Successful Program: Heroes and Sheroes

The hero making program was one of the most powerful, cathartic, and spiritual programs we have ever done at Ramah Family Camp. To introduce the theme of heroes/sheroes—Maya Angelou's term—we started the project on the second day using artist Farrel Haddari's idea of making a hero. Farrel has perfected a two-hour art project which culminates a longer discussion of personal heroes/sheroes. I had chosen this theme at a time when televisions were bombarding America with the O. J. Simpson trial. "A hero has fallen," said the commentators. "Why," I asked, "was he a hero? What would our traditional Jewish commentators say about heroes? Is there a difference between a hero and a celebrity?"

I decided to explore this concept through activities, discussion, art, and music. The first activity on the first night was designed with my assistant Naomi Katz Mintz as a get-to-know-you activity. It was hero/shero bingo blackout. Families were given a sheet of paper divided into twelve squares; in each, families were to answer a series of hero-related questions, "Who is your family's favorite biblical hero? Israeli hero? Sports hero? Professional hero?" I wanted families to identify their most common heroes/sheroes, such as Golda Meir, Moshe, or Magic Johnson. Once a family answered these questions, they had to find other families who had written the same answers and have them initial the square. No family could initial more than one square of another families' card. That way each family would meet at least twelve other families. We talked about these heroes/sheroes and shared the most common responses. My first goal was to extract from each family what they initially thought about when they heard the word hero. That had to be done so we could stretch our definition of a hero/shero during the camp experience. Eventually, I wanted to move from an understanding which places the hero/shero outside of ourselves to one which places the hero/shero within ourselves.

After looking at the responses on the Bingo sheet, we could ask ourselves, "How many of us have those attributes? Can we be those kinds of heroes/sheroes?" Using the many definitions of heroes/sheroes, I began to expand the theme. For example, I printed on the daily schedule quotes like, "Who is the greatest of heroes? He that makes his foe a friend," by Avot DeRabbi Natan. Also the quotation by Rabbi David Wolpe in his book *Why Be Jewish*, "Heroism is realizing the highest potentials within us....One is only a hero for using one's gifts in ways that improve the world." And also, from the poet Maya Angelou, "A Hero/Shero encourages people to see the good inside themselves and to expand it...We can develop the heroic in ourselves by seeking to do right by others." We began to understand that heroes/sheroes weren't only those who were amazingly talented or courageous but were also people like ourselves who could do extraordinary things. My intention to examine the idea of the hero/shero as being within each of us was central to having people understand that we each have the potential to be heroic in someone else's life.

With that in mind, I invited two of Danny Siegel's "mitzvah heroes" to come and share with us what they do and how they got involved. Danny describes the work of these individuals in his books: *Munbaz II and Other Mitzvah Heroes* and *Good People*. One of the people who visited with us was a college student who had founded an organization that brought leftover food from bar/bat mitzvahs or weddings to shelters or shut-ins. He talked about his idea and how he had to work through the amazingly thick red tape in order to achieve it. The other was a woman who had used her skills as an attorney to set up an organization in the Boston area called Bet Zedek which offers free legal counsel to those who can't afford it. These two people had stretched beyond themselves to help make the world a better place. What better heroes/sheroes could there be?

Later, in the separate children's program, some groups approached the theme through drama, creating and acting out skits dealing with hero/sheroes or with heroic moments. They reenacted the crossing of the Red Sea, Abraham arguing with God, and classroom scenes where one child defended another against a group of bullies. Counselors read heroic stories in Jewish literature to the children, and they in turn acted out the story to other groups. The theme was given music by our song leader David Paskin, who taught songs like *David Melech Yisrael* to the younger children and Debbie Friedman's *Miriam's Song* to the older ones.

In separate adult workshops, the psychologist spouse of our art specialist offered a workshop on Heroes Today. He dealt with the issue of heroism in the 1990s by asking, as parents, "Can we be, should we be, are we our children's heroic models?" Another workshop for parents, led by a rabbinic spouse, introduced biblical heroes through art. Using colored Xeroxes of biblical heroes taken from slides from the Skirball Museum in Los Angeles, and descriptive texts in Hebrew and English, he asked questions to stimulate conversation about biblical heroes, heroism in general, and differences in criteria for heroes/sheroes then and now.

On the second day at breakfast, everyone was told that we would be doing something unusual after lunch. I asked each family to think about some of their new definitions of a hero/shero, and to talk about one individual who had influenced their family—someone who had made a real difference in their lives. They were to come to lunch with that person in mind. During lunch, I explained that we would actually be bringing into our midst their family's hero/ shero. Our art specialist demonstrated how to make this happen. We moved to the art area, a huge tent set up ready for families to work with newspaper, plaster strips (to make a cast), water, and paint. Counselors, who had made their own hero/shero the week before, were stationed at every table. For two hours, each family worked, talked, and laughed together as they gave shape to very important people in their lives. Each figure stands approximately nineteen inches high.

Many families made relatives: a zayde that the children had never met but was present in the family through legend and lore now became an actual presence, stimulating discussions about him, "What should we put in his hand?" "Well, a telephone, he was so involved in Jewish life, always talking and helping someone or giving advice." In went a plaster phone to the hand. "Would he wear a tallit? Did he love to daven? Was his hair curly or straight? Was he bald like you, daddy? What color eyes did he have?" In two hours—a concentrated amount of time—more was shared about the zayde the children had never met than had accumulated in all the bits of stories they had heard over the years. Another family made Joan Davenny, the teacher who had been killed in Jerusalem by a terrorist bus attack over the summer. One of the children of this family would have had her as a teacher at the start of school—two days after family camp ended. This child had been looking forward to being with her. It was going to be a great year. The family's thinking that went into the props accompanying her figure was evident. She was given an Israeli flag to carry. She held a book as if teaching from it and gazed out into the future with a look of hope. For this family, bringing their hero into physical being was particularly powerful and cathartic.

The children in one family decided, without hesitation, to create their sibling who had died at a very young age. From this young child, the others had learned about courage and getting the most out of life, lessons they felt they might not have known otherwise. In some way, this departed child was becoming connected to family camp itself, making this family's experience truly complete and whole. Some families chose biblical heroes; some chose historical figures like Hannah Senesh and Henrietta Szold. Others chose their rabbi or a family friend. In two hours, the figures were finished, painted, and labeled. People said: "The experience of making the Hero statues was overwhelmingly exciting—I have never been involved in any project like this before—what a thrill for all of us." "Making Hero statues was a great project!" "The Hero art project was a ten."

I had never attempted a whole camp-wide art activity before and was overwhelmed by its success. I discovered that many factors contributed to that success. First, the art activity was the climax of a great deal of learning and exploration. Second, everyone had something to do regardless of age or generation. Third, the creative activity was meaningful and personal, even intimate, for some people. Fourth, working together encouraged conversations that might not have otherwise taken place. Fifth, the product was aesthetically beautiful and worth bringing home. Lastly, the project made no demands artistically, Hebraically, or Judaically on the participants. Everyone could succeed, and they did!

Only one family chose not to participate. The mother was quite angry that the waterfront wasn't available during this time. She told me that this should not be the only thing offered—that her children did not like art and they did not need another "chotchke" in the house. When someone confronts you this directly it gives you pause. I thought: "Was I mistaken to make this a required activity, with no alternative? Was this an unreasonable expectation? What if it didn't work? Shouldn't everyone's preferences be accommodated?" Then I had to remind myself that Camp Ramah is not Club Med for Jewish families. It has an educational and religious agenda. Everyone knows that in advance. I also had to accept what I believe is a good parenting model: not everything will please everyone or make them happy. That should not be my primary goal, though it is nice when it happens. What I had to feel comfortable with was my idea that this project was the focus of the entire camp experience and that I thought it appropriate that everyone be part of it. If I had allowed competing activities, I would have sent a different message. What I had to do was convey that this project was do-able and this experience was worth having.

As director, I had to claim the authority to craft the experience so that it made sense both from an educational and a recreational point of view. I must say that if half of the families had come to me with a similar request for swimming, I would have been somewhat shaken. Knowing the power of the project, I would probably have persisted, with humor and good spirit, but it certainly would have been more difficult. Drawing on my experience with mentors like Vicky Kelman, I felt empowered to follow through with my own perception of the program "Trust me," I felt myself conveying to parents, "it will be worth it." And it was.

So what happened in that tent on Thursday afternoon? Many things. Whole families engaged in a meaningful art project together, perhaps for the first time ever. Families were thinking together as a family and talking to each other, sharing their feelings and sense of connection to other human beings whom they may not have previously recognized as being important to their family. Parents understood that they were not to monopolize the project. Families worked together with everyone doing something. Before Shabbat, a museum of these heroes/sheroes was set up in the Hadar Okhel and stayed up until camp was over on Sunday afternoon. And then, the hero/shero from family camp went home with each family to keep on reminding them of their full family experience.

The hero theme continued throughout the camp in subtle and not-so-subtle ways. Two unsubtle activities deserve mention here. On Friday night, as part of the adult oneg Shabbat, adults listened to a panel of counselors talk about themselves and their own heroes/sheroes. Specifically, the panelists addressed the question: "Who were the individuals and what were the events that most influenced your own positive Jewish identity?" The young panelists were from thirteen to twenty-two years old, from both day school and public school settings. Parents asked questions at the end. At times you could have heard a pin drop and at other times, there were tears and laughter. Interestingly, for the majority of the panelists, their parents had been their models for constructing a solid Jewish identity. One young man talked about his journey back to Judaism and how his parents had weathered it, always being there and offering the anchor of a Jewish life even when he did not appear to accept it.

In summarizing the evening, I suggested that our task as parents was to be clear about our own Judaism before trying to convey it to our children. As a child I had never understood why the flight attendant would instruct parents to put their own oxygen masks on first. How heartless I thought. But my work and experience as a parent has taught me that in order to "save" my children I have to take care of myself first. This seems like a good metaphor for our role as Jewish parents. The family who builds a sukkah *for* the children does it in a different way than those parents who do it *with* the children because it matters to them as parents and as individuals. And the panelists were saying that they respected their parents' commitment to Jewish life and were positively affected by their various expressions of that commitment. It was also evident that the panelists had been shaped by watching their parents actively pursue their own Jewish journey. These young people were profoundly affected because their parents were seekers rather than people who had already found all the answers profoundly affected these young people.

A second link to the hero theme was not a program but a gift. At family camp each year, we give each family a gift when they leave to make concrete the notion that family camp is a gift the family gives itself. One year, for example, we gave each family a trophy inscribed with their name, the date, and the title of camp. This year we wanted to tie the gift into our theme and the new definitions of heroes/sheroes we had learned. The first gift was a cassette tape and book of songs sung at family camp as well as other songs about heroes. We wanted families to drive home with the sounds of family camp filling their ears. Our musician and song leader, David Paskin, had recorded most of the songs. The others were from different artists who had given us permission to use their songs. The second gift was a framed picture of themselves that we presented to each family. The picture was a Polaroid, taken when they arrived. It was surrounded by two mats. The first mat was dark green (also the color of our camp t-shirt and cassette cover) and had on it the quotes by Maya Angelou and David Wolpe, noted earlier, about realizing the good inside ourselves, expanding it, seeking to do right by others, and using our gifts to improve the world. The other mat was white, on which they as a family, wrote the attributes of each family member. The gift was a total surprise.

How did we make it happen? When families arrived, they were asked to get out of their car and pose for a Polaroid picture to be available at a later time. After lunch one day, families were asked to spend a few minutes decorating a white piece of paper (which was later to become the inside mat) with the names and attributes of each family member in response to the question, "What do you appreciate about the members of your family?" Later that night, a few of the staff cut out the white frames, inserted the Polaroid picture, fit the white designed frame onto the green matting, and put the whole thing in an inexpensive but nice black frame. Each family at the end of the program received a framed picture of their own heroic family and their cassette tape.

To return to the beginning of camp: the theme of heroes /sheroes had been announced in a pre-camp mailing along with an excerpt from David Wolpe's book, *Why Be Jewish,* about the Jewish concept of a hero:

> Heroism is realizing the highest potentials within us. Skill, talent, magnetism, charisma—these are all morally neutral. No one is a hero for being born with certain talents. One is only a hero for using one's gifts in ways that improve the world. There is an everyday heroism that comes from the attempt, in normal life situations, to do what is good and what is right. Not only grand historical figures are heroes. The Jewish tradition also sees as heroic

those who strive continually to improve the world in small incremental ways, in acts of everyday goodness.

Soon after the mailing I received a phone call from a parent who had never been to family camp. I didn't write her name down during the call so I wasn't able to identify her during camp, but here's what she had said on the phone, "This theme of heroes/sheroes is just for the kids isn't it?" "No," I answered calmly and confidently, "it's for everyone." "Oh," she replied, "that's unfortunate, it sounds so juvenile and pedestrian. I can't imagine what you could do that would be of value for the adults." "Well," I replied "when you come, you'll see. I think you'll find it quite appealing."

At the end of family camp, this person came up and introduced herself to me as the person who had made that phone call. She now wanted me to know that she was an enthusiastic and satisfied customer, and she apologized for not having recognized the potential of the theme. But why should she have known? When else or where else would she have experienced something like this? Although she belonged to a small ḥavurah, it didn't yet offer family programming, and for her—as for many others— this kind of experience was totally new.

Schedules: Families Together and Apart

Not everything at Ramah family camp is thematically related. Transformation happens in many other ways. The schedule on a typical day is t'fillot (prayer), breakfast, adult study with a scholar and in workshops, children with peers in a day camp setting, open family time, lunch, adult/child separate time, family time, dinner and a full family experience for everyone, bedtime for children, and an adult activity.

Each day's periods are approximately two hours. Adults spend one period with the scholar in residence and one period selecting from four to five workshops or just hanging out or playing sports. Workshops offered include: Shofar blowing; z'mirot (Shabbat songs) I Missed Along the Way; Jewish Parenting 101; God; Torah Trope; Hebrew Ulpan; How to Make Shabbat Last Longer than Friday Night. These workshops provide a variety of opportunities: something intellectual, a skill to learn, discussion of Jewish parenting or spiritual matters. Though everything is optional, most families want to participate. What is transformative is how the program works as a whole. There's magic when it all comes together.

Family time consists of four hours in two blocks, one in the morning and one in the afternoon, and it needs structuring. Not every family is comfortable planning for themselves. Some families appreciate having options so they can avoid the painful discussion which begins, "What should we do now?" Often, if it's extremely hot, the activity of choice is swimming or boating. Otherwise we offer a variety of craft activities such as mezuzah making (the container is a test tube decorated with paint) or making Shabbat decorations for the Ḥadar Okhel. In another session, inspired by Vicky Kelman, I have offered an activity on miracles where families have a bag of miracle clues to help them discover the small miracles they see every day. Family nature hikes as well as family baseball games are also options, because at family camp our mission is to reinforce the family and help them be together in fun and meaningful ways.

After dinner there is a family program, scavenger hunts with Jewish trivia clues, campfires, relay races, Israeli dance, and sing downs. Since it is important to bring the family together before bedtime for a fun experience, each program concludes with singing either Rad Hayom, or Craig Taubman's Lailah Tov in a big circle. Once children are asleep, parents participate in the adult program while our madrikhim (counselors) supervise the housing areas. This adult time is critical to forming an adult community. During the day, adults are divided into smaller groups for study. At night we come together and get to know one another more intimately. Some programs have Jewish content, others are sheer entertainment. One successful night was spent doing Karaoke. It was so hysterical that parents didn't want it to end. They took up a collection, on the spot, to pay for another hour, and four parents offered to relieve the madrikhim who needed to go to sleep. One staff member, Rob Scheinberg, typically takes half of an evening program to form the parents into an adult choir. They learn two songs, with incredible harmony, to sing to their children on the last day. Even parents who claim they cannot sing, do sing, and love it. It's a very emotional and exciting experience.

The schedule and structure of Ramah Family Camp is influenced by my mentor and family education shero, Vicky Kelman. Her work as the pioneer of Ramah Family Camp in Ojai, California, informs and inspires me always. When the staff made their heroes/sheroes, I made Vicky. For more details on setting up a retreat or family camp, I recommend her book *Jewish Family Retreats: A Handbook*, published by the Melton Research Center and the Whizin Institute of the University of Judaism.

The Family Educator at Family Camp

The last point I want to discuss is that of the role of a family educator in making family camp a success. I take my role very seriously. I feel privileged to be in that role, and I see how much it is appreciated and needed.

I believe it is important to ground family camp in the notion that families, especially Jewish families, need to be nurtured and nourished as families and as Jews. Do I think family education is the only answer for Jewish survival and Jewish continuity? No. Do I think it is one answer and a powerful one? Yes. The first reason is that it keeps us honest: everyone hears everything together. In the car ride home, families can now ask each other different questions. Instead of "What did you learn today?" they can say "What did you think of the program?" Such a shared experience can't help but draw families together. Second, addressing the family as a system makes sense. When a therapist treats a young child, often part of the treatment involves bringing the entire family into the session. One individual affects the other individuals in a family and lasting change occurs. Lastly, family camp deepens family connections on two levels: between children and parents and between families and Jewish institutions. Creating a common language helps create meaningful, long-lasting bonds. When we use a common Jewish language, one of shared experience, we develop a sense of belonging complete with emotional expressions and opportunities to study and to celebrate.

One way I move toward a common language of shared experience is by distributing to families a small booklet entitled, *The Wisdom of Ramah Family Camp; Parenting At a Glance.* For two years, in advance of family camp, I have asked families to send me their parenting wisdom. Their ideas or suggestions were then published in a bound booklet that was in their packet when they arrived.

Many families lack confidence as Jewish parents and family camp might even exacerbate their problems because parenting styles are out there for everyone to witness. As director, I must deal with this issue. My entire family comes to camp with me: three young children, my husband, and my mother-in-law. I am very aware of people watching how I parent and how my children behave. As a family, we do a bit of preparation before we arrive at camp. Just by going over the fact that they won't see me much and that daddy or Bubby are on duty for them helps a lot. I had occasion to comment on families being observed at t'fillot one morning when an agitated parent complained that she felt some children had mis-behaved the previous night. Though my children were not the ones in question, they could have been. I used the comment as an opportunity to discuss with the whole group how hard it is to create a community even though it's what we all want most. It's important to be generous with each other and realize it is hard for the kids too. We should all cut ourselves some slack and pat each other on the backs. Parenting is a tough job even under the most relaxed circumstances. Being thrown together in a tight community may add some strains for some even while alleviating them for others. The talk seemed to work for them and for me.

Creating community is crucial. The community must be user friendly: non-judgmental, nurturing, warm, and challenging. Humor and laugh-ter are central to making it that way. People need to be relaxed in order to be open to new growth. Jewish growth for adults is often intimidating, and we have to work extra hard to facilitate it. Laughter is an intimate expression; so are tears. I am thrilled when I have provided for both.

As a family educator, I feel it is important to teach at family camp as well as administrate. I try to offer at least two chugim (workshops) for adults on topics of interest to me personally. I've enjoyed leading discus-sions on Talking with Your Children About God, Enhancing Shabbat at Home, Ethical Will Writing, and Jewish Parenting. Being involved allows me to get to know the adults in a way I could not otherwise. Teaching and facilitating are critical to the definition of this position.

As a family educator, I realize that people need Jewish books. Many families do not live near Jewish bookstores, so I bring one to them. For the last few years, I have brought a local Jewish bookstore, Kolbo, to camp. They bring a wide variety of listings including those that tie into the camp theme. They also bring an array of tapes and CD's, which may be scarce in most communities. With music playing in the background all day, families have a chance to see what is out there in the Jewish world of books and music and add to their libraries.

In the last few years of family camp we've seen about a fifty percent returnee rate. Each year half of the camp is returning families and half is new. I am not certain whether this is a good thing or not. I ask myself, "Should family camp be experienced only once? Would we better meet our goals if we touched a larger number of people? Should we be the year-ly Jewish reunion experience for families? Can people continue to be touched by family camp year after year? If people keep coming back, is it because they experience a need for their own family that only family camp can meet? Have we failed in turning them on to other experiences in their own communities and homes? Should people drop out of where they are if they find some other programs or institutions that better meets their needs?" I grapple with these questions and look forward to exploring them with other family educators. I think about these questions each year as I prepare to send out brochures. One way I address the reality of so many returning families is by selecting new material, new themes, and a different scholar-in-residence each year.

Through my role at camp, I have found that parents are very interested in text study and in sharing their own experiences. They like to know at the end of the session that they have covered a certain amount of text. Their emotional connection to the material is important. When adults study together and in the midst of it laugh, cry, feel close to others, or have an Aha! moment, their text study has been successful. Text is a great unifier because it can be approached by everyone, regardless of prior knowledge and background. Everyone has access to Jewish texts. Our own life experiences inform our connection to the words. For many, this is the first positive Jewish study experience in their lives. We are confronted with the "Hebrew School Ghost" all the time. Adult learners are always surprised to learn that we Jewish educators are not shocked by their announcements that they hated Hebrew school. In fact, many of these same Jewish educators hated it too! As guides for these adult learners, we have to be mindful of that experience and tread lightly. We should also recognize that not everyone has had a negative Jewish education. Some adults enjoyed their schooling, whether it was day school or Hebrew school, and are looking either to enhance their background or reconnect to it. Being sensitive to these attitudes to past Jewish educational experiences is certainly a challenge, but I have no interest in making a homogeneous community.

I am interested in allowing the reluctant adults or those who were turned off by childhood Jewish experiences to "save face." In some ways, I feel they expect me or someone with authority to say, "See, I told you so—isn't Judaism rich and worthwhile?" Instead, I empathize. Since I happen to be one of those people who did not particularly enjoy my early Jewish education, I can share that experience as well, highlighting the difference between the way I was taught as a child and the way I now experience Jewish learning. There is no one road leading to a committed Jewish life. That realization is both humbling and inspiring. Everyone learns from everyone else and we are often surprised to do so. That is worth everything all by itself.

Epilogue

So, back to the woman in the supermarket who is now keeping kosher. First of all, she is not alone. As a result of family camp, other adults have also made profound life changes. One woman I know began studying every Shabbat with a small group of women, another changed her career and began training to be a Jewish educator. Families began taking Shabbat more seriously—singing zmirot (Shabbat songs) and setting time aside for family and community. Others instituted new rituals into their family life. I have heard many families report, as one father did, that they now send their children to Jewish camps rather than secular camps because they realize that immersion in a Jewish way of life, attached to the concept of fun, is critical to their identity as Jews. And they say it was because of family camp. This cannot be: it's too easy. If it were really so easy, we would be able to convince philanthropists and foundations to fund only retreats and family camps, and that would do it!

What I think happened to these families and others like them is that they come to family camp experiences ripe for the next step on their Jewish journey. Family camp is a catalyst for change. If these experiences are successful, they motivate people to take whatever plunge they have been contemplating. Alternatively, if the experience is not a pleasant one, it repels, and confirms their worst fears about organized Judaism.

If family camp is accepting, welcoming, and nurturing, then families will be more likely to seek for their sense of belonging in a more committed way back home. My goal is clear: that families and individuals within the family come to see themselves on a life long path of Jewish learning and living. Affirming and reaffirming one's commitment to Jewish life is a powerful experience. Although it is a personal one, it most often happens in the context of community. Creating that sense of community and helping families recreate that sense of community back home is what family camp is all about.

Victoria Koltun Kelman began her journey into Jewish education the summer that her parents announced that she and her sister would be going to a "Hebrew speaking camp" (Ramah) because they had been awarded scholarships by their synagogue. Exactly thirty summers later, she created and directed the first Family Camp at Ramah in California. In between these summers, she collected three degrees, made a specialty of teaching teenagers in Jewish schools, and became a curriculum developer for the Melton Research Center.

Victoria Koltun Kelman

Her long work in classrooms led her to realize the urgency of engaging parents in the Jewish educational enterprise. Her first foray into this then-nameless field was Together: A Child-Parent Kit, published by Melton in 1984, followed by Windows and five summers of Family Camp at Ramah in California. She is a founding member of the faculty of the Whizin Institute, which published with Melton Jewish Family Retreats: A Handbook and Family Room: Linking Families into a Jewish Learning Community. She is now director of the Jewish Family Education Project, a collaboration between the Jewish Community Federation and the Bureau of Jewish Education of the San Francisco Bay Area, a capacity-building project nurturing and mentoring family education in synagogues, JCCs, and day schools. She lives in Berkeley, California with her husband. They are the parents of four young adults.

288

Back to the Future:
The Family Israel Pilgrimage
Victoria Koltun Kelman

Can Israel be an important venue for Jewish family education? Should the community support this effort? No: "It's too expensive for the community to encourage; it's too far, too complicated, too staff intensive, and much too expensive for most families; it's too much time on a bus for kids; it will spoil the freshness of the experience when they go as teens or adults." Yes: "It's Israel."

While logic and logistics weight the negative answer to these questions, emotion, feeling, and the 2000 years of connection push most of us to answer in the affirmative. The question that follows for those who answer, "Yes," turns out not to be, "Can Israel be an important venue for family education?" but rather, "How can Israel become an important venue for family education?" The obstacles are real. Therefore, before embarking on such an endeavor, we should be clear that the value inherent in the experience outweighs the impediments. In other words: What could happen in Israel for a family that could not happen anywhere else? How do we define that? Then, how do we make it happen?

A family vacation trip, no matter where the destination, can be a positive, powerful, and energizing family experience. For the Jewish community to become involved in encouraging, organizing, and supporting family trips to Israel, however, it is critical to figure out how we move beyond the scrapbooks, the photos, the souvenirs, and the suntan lotion. From the point of view of community priorities and planning, we, as Jewish family educators, need to delineate what a family trip to Israel can offer that adult trips or teen trips cannot.

In this article, I will make the case that a family Israel experience is something uniquely worthwhile and worthy of our attention, our energy, and our funding. As a community, we have a great deal of experience with trips to Israel. Most such programs are designed for teenagers and university students. Twenty-five percent of all participants in programs are high school students and eighty-five percent of all participants are under thirty years of age. Adult "missions" are organized by federations and other Israel-oriented national organizations.

In addition, there have always been family tours to Israel. Until very recently, almost all were characterized by separate programming for adults and children, typified by parents in the front of the bus listening to the tour guide and children in the back of the bus being entertained by a counselor; or parents at Massada and children at the Waterpark. These trips are recreational and patriotic and inspirational. A fair amount of Jewish learning might take place on the better ones, but in general, they are not characterized by attention to the soul of the family in any way reflective of thoughtful Jewish family education.

The hallmark of thoughtful Jewish family education would be that families are guided to think about integrating their Israel experience into their subsequent home life, that they gain an understanding of the struggle to be a Jewish family in the American milieu as contrasted with the Israeli milieu, and that the liminal or threshold of a journey far from home serves as an opportunity to strengthen family bonds. Jewish family educators should always want to know how a family will be different after the program, event, retreat, or trip they attend. What will they know and feel and be ready and able to do that was not the case before they walked in the door? How will the program transform them? How can we as educators provide them with the scaffolding they need in order to incorporate these changes into their daily lives? These questions are the same whether the program is a two-hour event or a two-week trip to Israel.

In *A Home for the Heart*, Bruno Bettelheim, in discussing the creation of the special environment of the Orthogenic School, points out that change of milieu is an age-old component of any therapeutic experience. The two classic types which he singles out are the pilgrimage and the spa. For Bettelheim, the spa offered an alternative experience that worked by providing a change of environment designed to serve the body, not the soul. (And it's interesting to note that an aspect of this, parallel to

Bettelheim's complimentary pairing of spa/pilgrimage, is restated in Turner's point that pilgrims traveled for festivity and trade as well as for solemnity. At pilgrimage centers there was also feasting and dancing, entertainment, markets, and fairs.)

> Pilgrimages seemed to work as a combination of escaping the customary setting and at the time experiencing a more rewarding and stimulating new one. Leaving the accustomed environment with its demands and routines...escaping burdensome emotional involvements...formulating stimulating new associations; concentrating on one's inner voices and feelings, as in religious contemplation—all this renewed the spirit and gave strength for returning with new vigor to meeting the tasks of living.[2]

This observation by Bettelheim provides the metaphor to frame our thinking about the family Israel trip. It should be a pilgrimage.

Anthropologists tell us that a pilgrimage is "a journey made to a sacred place as an act of religious devotion." The pilgrim starts in a familiar place, goes to a far place, and returns to a familiar place, theoretically changed. The geographic site of a pilgrimage represents a "liminal place" (a threshold), a place and moment "in and out of time," and the pilgrim expects to have a direct experience of the sacred, invisible or supernatural order at that place.[3]

A dominant characteristic of the pilgrimage experience is communitas—the creation by shared common experience of a community of feeling not related to blood or locality. "Pilgrimages seem to be regarded... both as occasions on which communitas is experienced and as journeys toward a sacred source of communitas, which is also seen as a source of healing and renewal." Jews traveling to Israel are often aware that the journey is to the source of community, but I believe attention to the details of the journey itself can strengthen the experience by creating community along the way.

The metaphor of pilgrimage gives shape to the design of such a trip because it answers two challenging questions such an enterprise faces: How is the family Israel trip different from the family vacation to Mexico, Paris, Plymouth Rock, or Yosemite? and What does a family Israel trip offer that a peer group Israel trip cannot?

The pilgrimage image frames what we know American Jewish families are seeking in particular experiences and more broadly as well. They are seeking to be grounded in tradition, something that contemporary American life does not offer them. They are seeking respite from the stress and rush of everyday life. And many of them are seeking answers to spiritual questions. They want to unite, heal, and nurture their families. Turner's phrase "familiar place," as used above, speaks to this yearning. The family starts out from their family place, journeys together, and then returns home with their family in a new place.

It is clear that for educators to transform the Israel trip or the Israel tour or the Israel experience into an Israel Pilgrimage is a major endeavor and requires new perspectives on the pre-liminal phase (recruiting and pre-trip preparation), the liminal phase (activities during the trip) and post-liminal phase (follow-up or aftercare upon return home).

Pre-Liminal—Still in the Familiar Place

A pilgrimage frame requires that the journey toward communitas begin well before boarding the airplane.[5] Community building may start with name games and other structured group-building exercises as well as with discussions of why people are choosing to go, what are their goals and dreams for the trip, and what are their fears for the trip. Communal study sessions could focus on some of the classic texts/statements of the relationships of the Jewish people to Israel, along with a consideration of the concept of pilgrimage and the notion of a sacred site. Preparation could also include intra-family and inter-family exercises which involve collaborative decision making, compromise, and problem solving. Families will be making choices and decisions and adjustments in their own plans as the trip unfolds. Families might also prepare for the trip with family study activities—of geography or basic Hebrew, or of songs, stories, and poetry. Susan Wall, who directs Family Experiences in Israel for Camp Ramah, suggests pre-trip preparations such as collaborating on making an inventory of Jewish ritual objects which the family already owns and then deciding what to buy in Israel to add to their collection.

Although any good land-provider in Israel has the experience and know-how to draft an appropriate itinerary, if at all possible, families should have a say in some aspects of the trip.[6] For example, is jeep-riding in the Negev important enough to be worth the bus ride there? Is Yad VaShem suitable for all ages? Such discussion and consensus building are part of becoming a trip community. Design of the elements of the trip should be shaped by the age-range of participants. Experiences should be selected for their potential impact on families' Jewish lives when they return home. Families need to have fun together. For a family pilgrimage, an afternoon at the local park may be more valuable than yet another museum or archeological site. The land-provider, the family educator, and the families should all be partners in designing the experience.

Liminal—In the Far Place

First and foremost, the Israel pilgrimage should bear the hallmarks of constructivist and interactive learning, "hands-on" and "minds-on." The tour-guide should be just that, a guide. The information provided should be enough for participants to be able to make sense of what they are see-ing, experiencing, and feeling. Models for this kind of learning are found in some excellent family education programs being developed in the United States which can be adapted for the Israeli scene.[7] Some examples: family storytelling or a family tree activity preceding a visit to Bet HaTfutzot, family text study of the creation story or of the berakha sys-tem before a nature hike.

There are interactive programs developed in Israel, based on scavenger hunts where participants fan out in a locale looking for specific things. Even newer on the Israeli scene is a model close to our Colonial Williamsburg or Sturbridge Village, in which an entire bygone world is recreated.[8] There will be times when participants teach each other. Of course, there will be times for parallel learning. And children and par-ents benefit from some "peer-group" time and the subsequent sharing of their divergent experiences. This way of learning stimulates discussion at home and has the potential to help families learn to share their day's experiences with one another.

Israel is a laboratory for the many flavors of Jewish religious expression. Part of any Israel experience has to include sampling them. The major challenge is in selection. Families should be able to immerse themselves in Shabbat. This is the time and the place to "try on" new observances. What better place than Israel to try out what it feels like to wear a kippah all day or walk every where on Shabbat? In many ways. these form the scaffolding to support trying subsequent Jewish experiences.

"A site is a text," says Sally Klein-Katz, who works with family pro-grams for the Melitz-Oren project. Each site is a text for Jewish learning.

She suggests three categories of sites: the "must sees;" the sites that raise themes relevant for today; and the places that encourage interaction with the site. Then she adds a fourth category: the favorites of the group leader—because the powerful attraction the leader feels for a particular site provides the energy to connect families with that site.

Decisions about these aspects of the trip-community's life should be made in relation to the wishes of the group about balancing the familiar and the strange. Experiences and settings should be selected so as to challenge families to reflect on their own Jewish observance, to gently push them to consider new possibilities for growth. For example, Kibbutz Sa'ad might be a better choice than Kiryat Mattersdorf or a secular neighborhood in Haifa precisely because, in atmosphere and approach, it seems accessible, familiar, and yet it is within the zone of proximal development—neither overwhelmingly alien, exotic, "other," nor like an American suburb on a Saturday.

An act of tzedakah and G'milut Hasadim should be part of every family pilgrimage, either as a group activity or one for individual families. It should build in something begun at home, in the familiar place. For example, a family pilgrimage group might adopt a school or community center where Ethiopian immigrants need school supplies or sports equipment. The home activity might have been collecting tzedakah in a sponsoring institution, raising tzedakah by holding a bake-sale or a walk-a-thon, buying and bringing school supplies or sports equipment. Families could have prepared skits or songs to present to the students. Once in Israel, the site would be on their itinerary. The students, having been asked in advance, might present songs and crafts they had made.

For reasons both practical and educational, a visit to a kibbutz can be an ideal component of the family's Israel pilgrimage.[9] On the practical side, a stay on kibbutz enables families to "stay put" for a few days eliminating the daily bus rides and the packing/unpacking cycle of hotels. It is also likely to be less expensive, perhaps making a sizable difference in the total cost of the trip. In many ways, the kibbutz is also a more "family friendly" environment: Children can run around outside and come and go freely. No elevators or traffic. Other children to meet. Exciting places (such as barns, hydroponic tomato hothouses, chicken coops, avocado groves, or fish ponds) to explore. The possibility of participating in the ongoing work of the kibbutz (folding laundry, serving soup, collecting eggs, or cleaning chicken coops). On the educational side, a kibbutz stay offers a new view of community, of family, and of social engineering. As a historical-social experiment, it can guide a family to consider the elements of its own lifestyle back home in the familiar place. What do they like and not like about kibbutz life? In what ways would their life be different if they lived on kibbutz? How does it enrich or challenge their notions of community? What elements of kibbutz life can they take home with them?

Post Liminal—Return to the Familiar Place

The post-liminal phase is as critical as the other two phases in sustaining the impact of the pilgrimage experience, but it may not be attended to by the Jewish family educator. This phase is the equivalent of ending a knitting or weaving project in a way that prevents unraveling. There is no defense against unraveling if the ending is not tight.

The definition of pilgrimage given at the beginning explicitly assumed that one attribute of a pilgrimage is that the returnee has been transformed in some way. As new or differently shaped pegs, family members may have trouble fitting smoothly back into their old holes. The return from the peak experience of a pilgrimage can be quite choppy. The first challenge is the let-down and "post-partum blues," exacerbated by jet lag. The next challenge is readjustment to home and prior routines. The third challenge is the biggest, takes the most time, and requires the most support—figuring out how the experience of the liminal place fits into the familiar place.

What are the responsibilities of the Jewish family educator for re-entry and for post-pilgrimage scaffolding? The date for the group's first reunion, about a month after returning home, should be set and agreed upon before leaving Israel. That first reunion should include sharing family scrapbooks (and videos if there are any) and reminiscing. Group study that picks up some aspect of the pilgrimage could be an important component.

Just as families were encouraged to keep a pilgrimage journal, they should be encouraged to keep a coming-home journal, perhaps sitting together before Shabbat to make their weekly entry. Ideally, the pilgrimage group might become a ḥavurah and commit to regular get-togethers for study and celebration. This ḥavurah might find ways to save for children's future trips to Israel or for another family trip. They might want special savings accounts, future birthday gifts, and bar/bat mitzvah gift plans. They could also recruit other families for subsequent family pilgrimages. A weekend or one-day retreat to mark the six-month anniversary with reflection, study, and stocktaking would be a powerful way of extending and strengthening the power of the trip.

A Case Example

Ron Wolfson, director of the Whizin Institute for Jewish Family Life in Los Angeles, has led three family group trips to Israel. He began community building before each group's departure for Israel. His pre-departure meetings included group building, study, and discussion about Israel, as well as dealing with pre-trip details. When each group boarded the airplane, they were no longer nine distinct families but had become a single community composed of nine families.

While still at home, each family had been given an assignment to prepare something for that community. A paradigmatic example is the group's preparation for visiting the Chagall windows at Hadassah Hospital in Jerusalem. Several months before the trip, each family had been assigned one of the Chagall windows to research. When everyone arrived at the chapel at Hadassah Hospital, each family taught the group about "their" window. This technique is not a programmatic "gimmick." It is a carefully layered experience whereby the family actualizes their responsibility to the larger group of which it is a part. Every family has a similar responsibility. They recognize that the success of the event rests on each family's contribution. This interdependence builds community.

Each of Ron's groups kept a trip diary. Every day a different family took responsibility for recording the significant events of the day. At the end of the trip, the journal was photocopied so each family had a complete journal. This group project was an effective community builder.

Ron believes that the family trip to Israel resembles family camp in some ways, but that it is much more intense. He attributes the intensity to the preparation for the trip. Families do not prepare for family camp in any special way. Preparation increases the sense of anticipation about the trip to Israel. For many young people, this may be their first trip abroad and for many parents this may be the realization of a life-long dream. The length of the experience is also an important difference: the two-week Israel trip is more than twice as long as even the longest family camp stay.

In Ron's experience, the impact of the trip on the adults is that "they come home Zionists." For the younger children, the trip is like going "to the Israel-land section of Disneyland if Disneyland had one." Everyone wants to return and expects that they will. The Israel trip has been a pilgrimage from which pilgrims return with different experiences. Israel has become a prominent thread in the tapestry of the family's Jewish life.

Conclusion

Israel should be a venue for American Jewish family education and is well worth the effort and the expense if it is seen as a pilgrimage, rather than just another vacation. In this article I have tried to show what a pilgrimage might be like. I have chosen not to take an Israel/Diaspora relations approach to the trip, although such a case can also be made. This paper argues that an Israel pilgrimage strengthens the American Jewish family unit and enhances their Jewish life. The power of pilgrimage and communitas, the intensity of the experience, and the total immersion in Jewish life have extraordinary power to touch the heart and soul of the family.

When Israel is shared in this way it enters the consciousness of all family members. Israel is not merely in the news or in the siddur. It activates an otherwise-dormant part of American Jewish life. Return visits may become part of the family's Jewish plan. Future trips, whether with the family or with peers, will be reinforced by these earlier connections. Teen trips can build on the earlier Israel experiences with families. A family Israel pilgrimage appeals to all ages. Connections with Israel made in childhood can become a deeply rooted part of one's lifelong Jewish identity.[10]

Currently, the age group that visits Israel least is between thirty-five and fifty years of age—the age of parents who might choose to become part of this family adventure. We do not know why this is, but one reason may be that parents of young children aren't aware that Israel can be a family undertaking.

In the past few years the American Jewish community seems to have decided that Israel is a "teen thing," putting almost all of its Israel "eggs" in the teen "basket." Now it is time to diversify. Family Israel trips are an ideal vehicle for weaving Israel, as a component of Jewish identity, into young children's formative years. Israel family trips should become as much a part of the American Jewish family life cycle as the already established American Jewish life-cycle event of "sending" a teenager off to Israel. Such reorientation has the potential to re-shape the teen Israel trip because many teens would then be returnees, not first-time tourists. On a community level, a rise in the number of thirty-five too fifty year-olds traveling to Israel might translate into a stronger voice for Israel in the community, more community activism, and enriched perspectives on what it means to be an American Jew.

Our educators struggle with the question, "How to teach Israel?" Their answers are social studies curricula and Jerusalem 3000 celebrations. but teaching about Israel should not be like teaching about Japan or cele-brating Chinese New Year. Israel is a category of Jewish life which must be experienced. The time has come to understand that, just as Israel is not necessarily a "teen thing," it is probably not a "school thing" either.

I look forward to the time when the family Israel pilgrimage is as much a part of the landscape of American Jewish life as the teen trip is today. And is as well funded.

Endnotes

1   The term scaffolding indicates the supports to be provided to a participating family as they extend themselves. It is a metaphor originated by Wood, Bruner and Ross as a complement to Lev Vygotsky's theory of the zone of proximal development. A scaf-fold, much as in building construction, "has five characteristics: it provides a sup-port; it functions as a tool; it extends the range of the worker; it allows the worker to accomplish a task not otherwise possible; and it is used selectively to aid the work-er where needed." Patricia Greenfield, *A Theory of the Teacher in the Learning Activities of Everyday Life, Everyday Cognition*, eds. Rogoff and Lave, Cambridge, MA: Harvard University Press, 1984, 117-134.

2   Bruno Bettelheim, *A Home for the Heart*, Chicago, University of Chicago Press, 1985 paperback edition, 202.

3   Victor Turner, "Pilgrimages as Social Processes" in *Dramas, Fields and Metaphors*, edited by Victor Turner, Ithaca, NY, Cornell University Press, 1974, 166-228. Wade Clark Roof, *A Generation of Seekers: the Spiritual Journeys of Baby Boom Generation*.

4   *Ibid*, 203.

5   Experience with other intensive models tells us that the group should meet a mini-mum of three times before embarking together on their pilgrimage.

6   For these reasons, the selection of the Israel partner (the land provider) for a family Israel trip is critical. To my knowledge, there are three educational groups with expe-rience in planning for families in Israel. All three have an educational rather than a tourism approach. They are: Camp Ramah in Israel; the Melitz Center, in collabo-

ration with project Oren, and the Israel Study Institute; the Museum of the Diaspora in Tel Aviv

7 For example: "The Old City Game" and the "Jerusalem Neighborhoods Game" developed by Ross Culliner. "The Tzfat Game" developed by Mark Rosenstein of Makom ba Galil.

8 At the national park at Tzippori in the Galilee, the era of Rabbi Yohanan ben Zakkai has been faithfully recreated under the direction of Joyce Klein.

9 David Leichman at Kibbutz Gezer has developed an innovative and meaningful experience for families based upon their participation in developing a corner of the kibbutz developed as a park / botanical garden rather than having to fit them into the ongoing work of the rest of the kibbutz. Project Oren, which is part of Oranim the School of Education of the Kibbutz movement, offers the Kibbutz Family Adventure, a seven to fourteen day kibbutz-based experience.

10 David Mittelberg, *The Israel Visit and Jewish Identification*, Issues Series #4, the Institute on American-Jewish-Israeli Relations, the American Jewish Committee.

Community Ventures

Introduction: Community Ventures

The eight communities chronicled here have all engaged in pioneering efforts in the systematic development of Jewish family education. Their work provides valuable information to those doing or wanting to do similar work in their own communities. There are many success stories and a few cautionary tales for cities around the country that wish to move along the same path. Educating contemporary Jewish families so that parents and children together come to know their heritage has become a major goal of federations, bureaus of Jewish education, synagogues, schools and other Jewish agencies. Methods for achieving this goal differed from city to city, but there are also many similarities.

Joan S. Kaye, in *Building Blocks and Kaleidoscopes,* outlines the routes followed by twenty communities in conceptualizing and implementing family education since the late 1980's. She analyzes four components of family education structure that exist in most places: involvement of federation continuity groups; service provision by central agencies; grants to synagogues or schools for local programming; and training for family educators. Next, Harlene Winnick Appelman in her article *Detroit: Jewish Experiences for Families* describes the history and features of the now widely-disseminated JEFF model. She discusses consultant assistance to synagogues and schools for on-site programs and the production of well-publicized community-wide holiday extravaganzas.

Marilyn Vincent, in *Chicago, The Action Plan,* analyzes why there were such feelings of urgency about the need for family education throughout the country and in Chicago during the 1980s. She explains the now well-developed and widely-known Chicago family education system for direct service, training, program development and evaluation. In Boston, Federation planning initiatives for family education led to many new start-up efforts: the creation of new synagogue positions for family educators; the development of new training programs to equip people to fill those positions; and the establishment of new networks for professional exchange and psychological support to nurture these pioneering individuals during their first years of role clarification. Nancy Bloom, Marion Gribetz, Sharon Jedel, Barbara Penzner, and Harvey Shapiro, co-authors of *Boston: Planning, Supporting, Training*,describe their different roles in this effort.

Jeffrey Schein traces the family education activities in Cleveland which led up to the 1986-88 Commission on Jewish Continuity Planning Process. He documents the dramatic expansion of Jewish family education efforts as a result of their report, which stimulated the infusion of new resources to a variety of institutions to support programming, training, retreats, curriculum development and scholarship. Carol Press Pristoop's *Baltimore: How it Goes* tells of the process of conceptualizing a family education delivery system "from scratch." She describes the chronology, and the players, particularly The Pearlstone Coalition, and details the challenges to getting such a system up and running.

In 1992 in San Diego, the Continuity Task Force of the United Jewish Federation and the Agency for Jewish Education began work on Jewish family education. Three people came to the Whizin Summer Seminar as a small team. The next summer a twenty-six person team attended. By 1997, as Cecile Jordan notes in *San Diego: Collaboration, Outreach, Inreach*, family education has become a buzz word for interactive, multi-generational Jewish programming. Sandy Waldman Dashefsky in *Hartford: Collaborative Endeavors*, describes how Hartford's family education efforts include community-wide celebrations, in-service education, a family education network and a grant process requiring collaboration among Jewish institutions. In *Strategy and Serendipity: The San Francisco Story*, Victoria Koltun Kelman and Nechama Tamler report on the intensive and extensive planning process which led to the 1994 initiation of the Jewish Family Education Project in San Francisco. They describe its rapid growth and continuing rebalancing.

Joan S. Kaye, an original member of the Whizin faculty, graduated magna cum laude and Phi Beta Kappa from Boston University and completed an M.A.T. at the Harvard Graduate School of Education. Her first experience with Jewish education was as chairperson of the school committee of Congregation Beth El of the Sudbury River Valley. Many years, many ulpanim, and many courses in Jewish studies later, she became director of the Brandeis Jewish Education Program.

Joan S. Kaye

In 1981, she went to the Boston Bureau of Jewish Education (BJE) as director of High School Programs. In her five years in that position, she established the BJE as the foremost producer of Jewish high school materials, co-authoring six curricula including Why be Good? *and* The Power to Lead. *In 1986, Joan became director of the BJE's newly formed Division of Community Education and Planning, through which she created one of the first Bureau family education departments. She also authored* The Parent Connection. *In 1991, Joan moved to Newport Beach, California, to become executive director of the Orange County Bureau of Jewish Education and is currently engaged in a community-wide professional development initiative funded by the Covenant Foundation.*

Building Blocks and Kaleidoscopes
Joan S. Kaye

In 1987, when I was given the assignment of creating a Jewish Family Education (JFE) Department at the Boston Bureau of Jewish Education, there were few resources available. There were no training programs; no examples of community planning for JFE; no published curriculum or programs; and the only central agency to have a JFE department was in the process of phasing it out. In 1997, ten short years later, family education had become a "household word." (Pardon the pun.)

Now, more than twenty central agencies in North America have established family educator positions.[1] In Columbus and Boston, matching funds are provided to place full-time family educators in any synagogue willing to meet the established criteria. In communities with a planned communal effort in place for more than three years, every synagogue in the community is currently engaged in some type of family education programming. In addition to the Whizin Institute's annual Reaching and Teaching the Jewish Family, which has trained more than 1000 educators over the past eight years, a number of Jewish colleges offer master's degrees in Jewish family education. In-service education takes place in a variety of formats, ranging from single sessions with visiting experts to one- and two-year courses such as those conducted by the New York Board of Jewish Education and Boston's Hebrew College. Senior family educators in Cleveland are entering the second year of an advanced seminar arising from a collaboration between the Cleveland College of Jewish Studies and the Whizin Institute. Millions of dollars have been and continue to be dedicated to Jewish family education.

This article is designed to provide an overview of what has taken place, to discern patterns within the abundance of work that has been done, and to raise questions for the future. I begin with a comparison of three communities: pioneers who developed models and created the building blocks for other communities which, in turn, rearranged and improved on them and, in many cases, created kaleidoscopes of entirely new structures. I will look at these communities (their full stories can be found in the following pages) to see how they got started, the source(s) of their funding, their initial approach to their tasks, and the agencies and stakeholders who played the major roles in their development.

The first community-wide program was JEFF, Jewish Education for Families, established in Detroit, Michigan in 1986. JEFF was created through the combined vision of Harlene Appelman, who produced family programs in one synagogue, and Bill Berman, who saw the potential those programs had for the entire community. He provided the funding to make community-wide development a reality in Detroit. Over the course of its existence, JEFF has been housed in the Fresh Air Fund, which supports camping, and in the Jewish community center. Currently, it resides in the Detroit Agency for Jewish Education. It was conceived as a direct service project, with the director providing individual programs as well as large-scale community events for synagogue members. JEFF staff initially approached each synagogue through its rabbi, but in order to become part of the project, each synagogue then had to establish a lay committee to work with the JEFF professional who would implement the program.

Boston came on the scene in 1987 with a project developed in response to a Federation Task Force on Supplementary Jewish Education that established a curriculum expansion fund. The Boston Bureau was asked to develop a process to provide grants to supplementary schools in the area of family education in consultation with educators and rabbis. Once the process was in place, the BJE staff established the Family Education Deliberation Forum where scholars, social workers, and educators talked together in an effort to develop a theoretical underpinning for the work of JFE and to create a network through which those implementing family education programs could exchange ideas.

The Cleveland Commission on Jewish Continuity published its report in 1986, although the family education programs arising from that report did not begin until 1990. They worked from a "let a thousand flowers bloom" approach, funding three efforts housed at three different agencies: a retreat center at the JCC; a curriculum development project (which, while not created primarily for family education, was to incorporate family elements into their projects); and a master's program in JFE at the Cleveland College of Jewish Studies designed to create full-time family educators for synagogues. In addition, congregations were encouraged to use an existing grants program run by the Federation for family education initiatives.

The next communities to enter the JFE arena adopted structures similar to the Central Agency model established by Boston, with the following elements:

- Special Federation funding from money raised specifically for "continuity," or from money taken off the top of the campaign and allocated to "continuity" projects
- Grants to schools, usually non-competitive, from that funding source
- Administration of the grant program and consultation to schools by the Central Agency
- Focus on program development
- Focus on synagogue schools and synagogue educators as implementors
- Lay leaders involved, if at all, only in the grant approval process

Training was the next element to be added to this model. When the Chicago Central Agency, working with their long-range planning committee, determined that family education should become a priority, their initial focus was on training.[2] Their realistic estimate of current and future resources led them to train existing educational directors to do family programming rather than to attempt to add a new professional position to synagogue structures. After attending the Whizin Institute's Summer Seminar, Chicago's JFE consultant, in consultation with Whizin, developed a full-year series of seminars for Chicago educators.

The Whizin Institute has played an important role in JFE training in many communities. The process usually begins with a summer visit by the Central Agency consultant to the Whizin Summer Seminar, and then continues in one of three ways: (a) the consultant returns to a subsequent Whizin Summer Seminar accompanied by community and/or synagogue teams; (b) Whizin faculty, either individually or as a group, are invited to the community to spearhead training; or (c) a combination of these two methods. In Chicago, the entire Whizin faculty, over a one-year period, worked with educators. San Diego took the opposite route, bringing over thirty-five people, representing every agency and synagogue in town, to a Whizin Summer Seminar. After a community team from Baltimore studied at the Summer Seminar, individual members of the Whizin team went to Baltimore to offer seminars; then the entire faculty followed to provide a two-day conference for synagogue teams on site.

In the summer of 1995, to recognize the emergence of family educators working in bureaus or other central agencies, Whizin instituted a special track to provide a forum for the dissemination of ideas among communities and an opportunity for continued professional growth.

Another smaller group of communities chose the direct service model initiated by JEFF. Elements of this model include:

* Special funding, either from a single donor or through the "continuity" process
* Large-scale family events (extravaganzas) open to the entire community and drawing hundreds of people
* Central role for lay leadership
* Programming in individual institutions provided by the central agency
* Extensive use of media, particularly community Jewish newspapers

As more people were exposed to Whizin thinking, and through Whizin, to each other, two things happened: elements of the original models were refined and improved as they moved from one community to another; and new communities embarking upon JFE ventures were free to choose from more than one model. A wonderful example is the way in which each new community learned from the experience of earlier ones as they developed grant criteria. When Chicago was developing their grants program, they consulted with Boston. Baltimore, in turn, had the advantage of Chicago's experience when they established their criteria; and San Francisco, one of the newer communities, was able to benefit from all the previous experience.

Most communities have used the existing building blocks to create new structures. They have combined elements from the Central Agency and from the Direct Service models, usually emphasizing one or the other, but freely adapting from both. San Diego chose to focus on outreach and large community events, while retaining an element of consultation to synagogues. Philadelphia uses consultation but also runs large community events. Southern New Jersey and St. Louis both emphasize outreach and extravaganzas, but both also facilitate professional development through family educators' networks. Columbus is one of the most interesting amalgamations because they have combined the JEFF model of direct service and extravaganzas with the Cleveland model of training full-time family educators.[3]

Four factors are common to each community variation on JFE. First, in every case, the funds to initiate family education programming comes from something other than the normal funding process. In three cities, those funds came from individual donors or from individuals in charge of family foundations; in all the others, the money comes from special Federation continuity funding. The second factor is that the initial focus is on programs, most likely ones designed for families with elementary-school-age children. A third similarity is the establishment of family education networks in each community. These involve regular meetings where practitioners can grow professionally and share their successes and frustrations. Finally, in almost every community there is a publication of some sort. These run the gamut from newsletters distributed to professionals to splashy monthly insertions in the community's Jewish newspaper. The major differences, therefore, among these twenty communities are the relative emphasis placed on outreach versus consultation, the role of lay leaders in the JFE project, and the direction in which the community moves after its initial foray into the field of JFE.

As we survey the field, we discover that, with one exception, the differences among communities grow greater the longer a community is involved with JFE. The older communities have been adding new elements to their work.[4] In Boston, there are two new initiatives: full-time family educators for synagogues, centers, and day schools and Me'ah, an intensive adult education program. JEFF has begun replication projects in other cities. Within Detroit, JEFF staff have been working on outreach to special populations such as single mothers and new Americans. In Cleveland, a two-year seminar for senior family educators is in its second year. New grants are being targeted for small family groups. And a secular agency has been invited to partner in work creating connections between home, school, and community. Chicago has developed six different models of family schools, ranging from an optional program within a school to a school which offers only family education. They find that families are willing to make longer commitments to their ongoing education. In St. Louis, family educators are going into homes to teach families the skills of creating Jewish celebrations. In Hartford, planning for JFE has led to initiatives in planning for synagogue change.

As JFE grows and prospers in North America and abroad, we should ask: What pieces are still missing? What are the needs being created and not yet met? What questions are being raised that are not yet answered? One glaring need we see is for curriculum materials. While publishers, led by Torah Aura, have begun to address this, these twenty communities are also producing programs, classes, and courses which should be shared. Existing materials need to be disseminated, and practitioners should be taught to put their materials into formats that can be used by others.

When community family educators meet, the one word heard over and over again is "evaluation." It is now time to find out exactly what effect all our work has had, time to discover what works and what does not. We need methods for evaluation, and beyond that, we need serious research efforts ranging from Jewish identity formation to understanding how communities make choices when they embark on new projects. We need to know if there really is a connection between the level of previous grass roots activity and the success of community-wide JFE efforts. And we need to know about funding. Can JFE be funded only through an infusion of "soft" money? What will happen when the excitement wears off? Where will the funding come from to enable JFE to grow both in breadth and depth in these twenty communities? Will continuity continue to fuel the entrance of new communities into the JFE field?

Despite these questions, the tremendous success and unprecedented growth we have seen over the past ten years should be cause for great optimism. Whereas, in 1987 there were two Central Agency family education consultants, now there are twenty. Then, there were a few isolated pockets of individuals doing great work, now there are whole communities. Perhaps what is most exciting of all is that no one is working in isolation. The ideas, projects, and plans in one community spark new creations in other communities. The kaleidoscope of Jewish family education continues to turn.

Endnotes

1. These communities are Baltimore, Boston, Chicago, Cleveland, Columbus, Detroit, Hartford, MetroWest (New Jersey), Miami, Montreal, New York, Philadelphia, Providence, San Diego, San Francisco, Southern New Jersey, St. Louis, Springfield/western Massachusetts, Suffolk, and Toronto.

2. Chicago is the first city in which the initiative for family education came out of a Central Agency rather than a Federation planning process.

3. It is particularly interesting to note that the Cleveland model came to Columbus through Boston, which had adapted the concept of full-time family educators, but with a totally different training model. Where Cleveland does a pre-service master's degree program complete with internships to train its full-time family educators, Boston provides intensive in-service education through its Hebrew College. Columbus' training is provided by the Central Agency consultant and visiting Whizin faculty.

4. The exception is in the area of training. Every community, whether they began with it or not, has now incorporated some form of professional development for family educators. In the communities just beginning, it is built in from the beginning; in the communities with JFE history, it is intensified. San Francisco incorporated it into their initial project as a requirement for receiving a grant; Hartford has added a recently-developed two-year academic certificate program in JFE to its existing training programs.

Harlene Winnick Appelman

Harlene Winnick Appelman is director of Field Services for the Whizin Institute for Jewish Family Life. She has created and directed many family education programs in Detroit, Michigan. Among them are the highly regarded Jewish Experiences for Families, affectionately known as JEFF; Family Camp; and Jewish Acculturation Programs for Russian Newcomers. Currently, she is director of Community Outreach for the Detroit Federation and consultant to the Appelbaum Family Center of Detroit's Shaarey Zedek Congregation. She received the Covenant Award from JESNA for her outstanding contributions to Jewish education.

Detroit: Jewish Experiences for Families

Harlene Winnick Appelman

Jewish Experiences for Families (JEFF) is a community model for initiatives in family education. The JEFF model creates lay-professional partnerships among Jewish agencies and collaboration between federations and synagogues. Synagogues reach people whom themselves can build strong communities. Federations reach other people whom synagogues see infrequently, if at all. When these two institutions join to provide creative experiences for families, everyone benefits. The other partnership, that between lay people and Jewish professionals, is an important key to keeping many Jewish institutions vital. Mutual respect is renewed when people learn together and work to complete tasks. JEFF's history, methodology, and implications for the future are explained below.

History

Jewish Experiences for Families began in metropolitan Detroit in 1986 with the involvement of marginally affiliated Jews as its primary objective. This objective, combined with the idea that the Jewish family is the primary transmitter of Judaism, has made JEFF an effective force within the metropolitan Detroit community. Also, JEFF has become an excellent Federation-agency-congregation partnership. The congregations build mini-communities of families who have already identified themselves as interested in the larger Jewish community. For its part, the Jewish Federation of Metropolitan Detroit reaches out to these mini-communities by offering to them the strengths of its agencies in formal and informal education.

JEFF provides the structure through which federated agencies can channel their expertise to congregants. It has been a galvanizing force in the non-congregational community. With programs and events attracting pluralistic audiences; it presents Jewish education and "edutainment" appropriate for the entire spectrum of Jews in Detroit.

JEFF aims to involve more Jewish families in the larger Jewish community and at the same time strengthen the Jewish family's educating structures by pursuing the following objectives:

- To create non-threatening environments where families, regardless of "Jewish competency," can participate in a meaningful way, have a good time, and look forward to returning again
- To give families the tools to take newly-learned (or relearned) Jewish behaviors and integrate them into their lives
- To create gateways and/or easy points-of-entry into the organized Jewish community, recognizing that once families form one strong Jewish connection, that bond may spill over into other institutions and affiliations
- To train both lay and professional leaders to perpetuate Jewish family education within their institutions
- To create partnerships—among synagogues, between congregations and federated agencies, and between Jewish organizations and private enterprise

On-Site Administration: Congregational Lay Committees

Jewish family education and programming must be a team effort. Because the issues are complex and the total family becomes the *student* or *client*, it is important to draw on many resources—teachers, principals, rabbis, mental health professionals, physicians, and others—when designing family education programs or curricula. In addition, lay people should always be incorporated into planning family education programming. They form the core idea group for determining the appropriate starting point for family programming and can identify the natural target population for a particular program. If family education is ever to be a major thrust of the community, agency, or congregation, a lay committee must advocate, validate, and plan it. Ultimately, this lay committee will help recruit both participants and sponsors for the endeavor.

Each institution or agency participating in JEFF has a lay committee staffed by a professional from the congregation or the agency whose function is to help create, implement, and endorse family programming. This committee enables each congregation to maintain ownership of family education while utilizing the organizational skills of the JEFF consultants. During the formation of each new lay committee, a JEFF consultant works closely with committee members, helping them create their own unique vision, budget, and series of programs. The JEFF staff person acts as a facilitator, not a legislator or executor. This means that every time a new congregation, agency, or organization embarks on JEFF, a JEFF consultant invests considerable time in helping this unit to function. This staff person attends the first three or four meetings of a new committee and then continues to keep in regular contact with the committee chair and others.

Establishing Congregational Lay Committees

Each of the Detroit congregations began using JEFF's services in the following way. First, a JEFF professional approached the rabbi of the congregation with the idea of family education. After the rabbi agreed that this would be an added benefit to the congregation, the rabbi assembled appropriate lay leaders and professional staff to take the second step. This involved organizing a visioning process to explore how family education programming might enhance the congregation and strengthen the family. This session was usually attended by a wide variety of congregation leadership from the school, pre-school, sisterhood, brotherhood, and youth commission. The appropriate professionals joined in, and the beginning of a family approach for the congregation was defined. Next, a smaller JEFF committee to advocate and implement family education was formed, and the congregation began a planning process to examine the potential for family education in their institution.

Many institutions first convene JEFF committees as focus groups. They try to recruit a cross-section of the congregation members so that different needs can be identified and met. Further, this committee becomes a wonderful training ground for future leadership. Participants view this committee as a place where personal contributions will have impact and make a difference.

The JEFF professional remains involved in the process until congregational leadership takes over. The leader may be rabbi, education director, program director, or lay person.

A programmatic inventory and a needs assessment is carried out by the JEFF committee so that each institution develops a vested interest in the planning and implementation of the programming. In addition, this process helps the congregation identify gaps in existing programming for populations which may have been overlooked. The committee simultaneously creates, helps to implement, and endorses family programming. Each congregation thus maintains ownership over its JEFF programming while utilizing the organizational skills of the JEFF staff. Further, the JEFF consultant involves as many members of the agency or congregation staff as possible, and as a result, informally trains them to work in family education. JEFF contacts with professional and support staff vary from congregation to congregation, but throughout JEFF's evolution, we have found that a professional contact at each site is extremely helpful. In the majority of the congregations, JEFF has not been maintained solely by volunteers and lay leaders.

What JEFF Brings to the Process

JEFF consultants bring their expertise in family education and funding to enable each congregation to carry out their plans with quality and visibility. In Detroit the congregation does not pay for initial JEFF services but agrees to assume increasing responsibility for costs and staffing of the program as the institution expands its family programming. The goal is that each congregation will ultimately add a JEFF line to its budget and assume all the costs of JEFF programming. As the program continues and family programming becomes entrenched in the congregation structure, JEFF staff assume a background role. They help with new programming as the congregation maintains what is already in place. JEFF does not provide either grants or family educators. Instead JEFF serves as a catalyst to encourage each congregation to consider how family education can best be adapted to its own unique environment.

The JEFF Community Structure

In Detroit, JEFF is a joint venture involving the time, energy, and resources of the three agencies who handle formal education, informal education, and camping. Over the years it has been housed at each of its partners: at the Fresh Air Society, the Federation's year-round camping agency committed to informal Jewish education; at the Jewish Community Center, an institution that reaches both affiliated and unaffiliated Jews with young families; and at the Agency for Jewish Education, which offers families a wide variety of formal and informal experiences.

By being able to provide different settings for JEFF, these agencies have exposed congregations to new program opportunities and made them aware of agency resources. Nevertheless, coordinating the efforts of three agencies and working on projects as a team is most challenging. When possible, it is important that staff from all three agencies meet on a regular basis. In Detroit it was common to have a JEFF staff person meet with each agency individually to discuss agency-specific programs.

Governing Bodies

JEFF is built on a pyramid of lay committees. There is a lay committee in each congregation to spearhead JEFF programming that meets about once every two months. The chair from each committee, two lay representatives, and a professional from each of the three sponsoring agencies form an Agency Committee which shares information about programming in their respective congregations, helps determine policy that all congregations can live with, and provides help with community events. It meets about five times a year.

A third committee, called the Community Advisory Committee, which is made up of Federation leadership, the rabbis from each of the participating congregations, and the executive directors of each of the sponsoring agencies, serves as another forum in which to assess community needs. This committee is also the forum through which the community's top lay and professional leadership keep informed about issues and challenges facing the contemporary Jewish family. It meets two or three times a year. Finally, the coordinator of JEFF is a member of the Educators' Council, so educators are kept informed of the ongoing evolution of JEFF

Essentials in JEFF Program Philosophy

In Detroit JEFF did not replace formal Jewish education. It simply added an important dimension to it: involving families in using the principles and values that are the core of Judaism—naaseh v'nishma—parents and children together become more willing and better able to understand.

JEFF has also provided programs to particular populations for which a single congregation has insufficient numbers or funding. Today, the Institute for Single Jewish Mothers, Outreach to New American Jews, and Stepping Stones to a Jewish Me are also under the JEFF umbrella. The challenges facing single parents and their children, immigrants to the community, and interfaith families have a common thread: through JEFF these groups can take their Jewish futures into their own hands.

Many of the programs and events offered through Detroit JEFF have been extremely successful. They have attracted large numbers (from 150 to 1500 participants) and participants have returned for programming many times. When interviewed, participants have acknowledged that the materials distributed through JEFF have enhanced their Jewish lifestyles.

The philosophy underlying the development of JEFF programs is that they should be comprehensive. While Jewish holidays and life-cycle events are central to JEFF programming, so, too, are contemporary issues and Jewish history. In addition, programs are based on things that families already see as valuable. A trip to the zoo becomes a Jewish trip to the zoo to locate animals from the Bible. Reading to children becomes a Jewish reading program where parents read Jewish books to their children. Family walks become a Jewish walking program with other Jewish families. One of the chief organizing principles of JEFF is that Jewish education should not take place only in the classroom. Families should engage the whole world as their Jewish text. If we limit our learning activities only to our own institutions, then we are doing both families and institutions a disservice. Some families on their first step into things Jewish find it easier to come to a secular location: a zoo, museum, or park. We must take advantage of our own institutions, but not limit ourselves to them.

The Multi-Layered Program

Research shows that people attended JEFF programs in Detroit for a variety of reasons. Some attended because they wanted to learn about Jewish customs; others because they wanted to have quality time with their children; and still others because the program looked like fun. Most attended for a combination of reasons. JEFF programs, by design, build in many layers: educational, recreational, social, spiritual, and more. One-dimensional education does not work for families since there are so many personalities, learning styles, and motives for attending. Our contemporary society offers many choices for how we spend our time; it therefore behooves us to offer Jewish programs that compete successfully against other choices. Along with Jewishness, our programs must demonstrate care, quality, and attractiveness.

The most valuable commodity for most Americans today is not real estate, jewels, oil, or furs. It is time. When we ask families to spend time together Jewishly, we are asking them to make an important investment. Ask most people today, and they will tell you that they just do not have enough time to do what they need and want to do. Therefore, when we, as Jewish educators, invite parents and families to become involved with their Jewishness, it is incumbent upon us to offer them a multi-layered minute when they will get a high return for their investment of time.

Who Is the Learner?

Identifying the primary learner at JEFF programs is always an adventure. Is it a parent reading an explanation aloud to a child? Or is it a child asking a parent an important question? Or is it the lay group who organizes the experience? One of JEFF's trademarks is to use lay people as teachers in their areas of expertise. For example, in preparation for a program in which physicians were asked to examine children's stuffed animals in order to reduce children's fear of physicians, several of the doctors wanted detailed explanations of the concepts of bikkur holim (visiting the sick) and b'tzelem Elohim (being created in God's image). This resulted in a class for the physicians. Again, a mental health professional wanted to understand better the concepts of t'shuvah and mechillah when, before the high holy days, he participated in a panel called Teaching Your Kids to Say I'm Sorry. JEFF continually watches for opportunities to emphasize that Judaism touches every moment of life.

Multi-Site Startup

Where do we start? How much should we do? and What's realistic? are questions frequently asked about JEFF. JEFF began on many levels almost simultaneously. This was not by chance. In order to root something in the community rapidly, we wanted wide exposure. When JEFF was first launched in the Detroit metropolitan area, we had community-wide events and family education programs going in several congregations. The *Jewish News* initiated a family section in its publication. Thus, within the same month, people participated in family education in the community, in their congregations, and by reading about it at home.

The *Jewish News* and JEFF created a monthly family supplement, *L'Chayim: A Toast to Jewish Living*, which focused on family celebration, contemporary issues, and informal education. In addition to this supplement, the *Jewish News* continues to help underwrite major community family events. It also provides free advertising for the events. That the *Jewish News* became an integral part of the communal thrust for family education was an extremely important element in JEFF's success.

How JEFF Differs from Other Community Family Education Models

JEFF has not been built by giving grants or training family educators but by providing services. The Federation has helped congregations develop programming by supplying each congregation with the services of skilled consultants and with other tools that congregations can use to reach their own goals. JEFF also has been involved in the entire spectrum of Jewish living: congregational affiliation, education, life-cycle opportunities, family camping, and Jewish community celebration. It has supported these experiences with written guides and materials. JEFF actively seeks community partners—in other Jewish agencies as well as in the private sector—to further family education. While JEFF's primary mission is to help marginally affiliated Jews become more embedded in the Jewish community, its primary target is not necessarily the unaffiliated, although community programming does provide safe, easy access for them to the Jewish community.

Community Pre-requisites for Using JEFF as a Model

Application is not duplication. Because every community has unique characteristics, replicating JEFF in a "cookie cutter design" will not work. Instead, as Adrianne Bank noted in her evaluation of JEFF in Detroit, there are some basic conditions that must be present for a JEFF-like model to work. In order for JEFF to take root, flourish, and be effective in achieving its goals, it requires the following:

1. An hospitable attitude towards family education
The first and most essential condition which must be present in any community thinking about a JEFF model is a sense of welcome and encouragement for such a venture. A critical number of key players, namely the Federation, the congregations, coalition partners such as the Bureau of Jewish Education, the Jewish Community Center, and possibly other groups must be interested in family education and in formulating its own version of the

JEFF model. They must see it as having advantages for each of their institutions and for their community as a whole. Potential advantages include expansion and retention of synagogue membership, revitalization of the involved organizations, and a helpful spill-over into other programming.

2 Supportive leaders

General endorsement of a JEFF model is not enough. There must also be individuals who will function as "idea champions" for the program. Among these should be both lay and professionals who have influence among the leaders in the community and who can marshal the political and financial resources, not only to start up the program, but to see it through the difficulties expected during its infancy and toddler stages.

3. Availability of Jewish knowledge, programming talent and organizational skill

Not all of these talents need reside in one individual, but this collection of essential skills must be available within or to the JEFF staff. Essential skills include Jewish content knowledge, an understanding of experiential education, expertise in mounting programs and acquiring resources, political savvy, and organizational skills. It is helpful if there is a "sizzle person," someone whose passion about Jewish family education is contagious, someone who is entrepreneurial and has the magnetism to involve, excite, and inspire passion in a group.

4. New financial resources

Although JEFF is not an expensive program, it does require new money. In Detroit this new funding was provided by a generous endowment from Mandell Berman. Diverting money from other programs into family education is not likely to contribute to congregational feelings of ownership or generate collective goodwill for the project. Because JEFF is based on coalitions and team building, it should not compete with other programs to procure funding. One important factor contributing to JEFF's success in Detroit was that JEFF staff could plan high-quality programs with congregations and initially pay most of the costs for the services and materials to mount them. The new money had a multiplying effect, because other institutions became eager to contribute in-kind services, to find new sources for partnership dollars, and to allocate additional dollars from their own budgets.

5. Careful attention to structural arrangements
JEFF is designed to be pluralistic and to build bridges across institutional boundaries. JEFF requires partnerships. It is therefore important to house JEFF in a setting where partnership is valued and supported. Detroit respondents agreed that the particular agency within which JEFF is located is less important than that there be compatibility between JEFF and its managing partners about work style, policies, and procedures.

6. Feedback loops and open channels of communication
In any start-up endeavor there are bound to be mishaps and misunderstandings. It is important to have both formal and informal mechanisms to resolve small difficulties before they become large and to manage the inevitable conflict and turn it into creative rather than destructive energy. Communities which already possess such mechanisms are well suited to the JEFF orientation. In the start-up period, JEFF requires much discussion and committee time. Making this investment in the beginning can insure a program that does not fizzle after initial monies are terminated.

7. Program assistance from experienced JEFF personnel
In the early days of thinking about replicating educational innovation, it was assumed that written manuals and guidelines were sufficient. While it is true that written materials are an important part in helping others understand complex programs, we are now aware that they play a necessary but not sufficient supporting role. The people who are knowledgeable about the nuts and bolts of the program and motivated to make it successful are often the keys to successful program replication. People familiar with JEFF are invaluable in orienting the community to the essential elements of the program and in assisting with their assessment of whether the program is appropriate and suitable to meet a new community's needs. This role requires a sensitive blend of talents: facilitation as well as promotion. Experienced JEFF consultants should also provide assistance in the start-up

phase so that activities are sequenced appropriately and training can be provided to all those involved. They should be available for technical assistance and support—providing a "hot line" for problems and a "warm line" for encouragement.

Moving JEFF from Detroit

The first site outside of the Detroit metropolitan area to try JEFF was MetroWest, New Jersey. As in Detroit, MetroWest has successfully used the JEFF model to help congregations create family education initiatives through mobilizing lay people. In addition, it has had excellent community programs that have brought thousands of people out to learn, have a good time, and view the Jewish community as welcoming and accessible.

MetroWest, New Jersey, has had JEFF successes unique to its community. JEFF staff have compiled and distributed an impressive collection of family education programs. They are developing a consortium for training family educators and an initiative that will touch families in their own homes. Due to its unique geography, regional community JEFF programming is being developed to touch even more people.

JEFF principles are now being applied in Columbus, Ohio. Again, a network of lay committees and family education teams is being developed. Enthusiasm and interest in family education remains high. JEFF appears to be a force for galvanizing a Jewish community around an issue rich with opportunity: the Jewish family.

What is JEFF Success?

Based on program evaluations, attendance figures, testimonies, and continued community investment, Jewish Experience for Families appears to have achieved the following. First, it has provided an easy point of access to the Jewish community for some who would not otherwise have found their way in. Second, it has empowered lay people to take charge of their own Jewish lives and to become involved in the Jewish community in professional roles or as leaders in congregations or the Federation. And third, it has a created an awareness of the positive potential for congregational-federation partnerships, an alliance once fraught with suspicion. JEFF's over-arching success is as model that can energize a community and bring together Jewish education and Jewish families.

Marilyn Vincent is currently director of Family Education at the Community Foundation for Jewish Education in Chicago, where she has worked for the past twelve years. Her portfolio includes providing direct services in family education programming to over sixty congregational schools and day schools.

Marilyn Vincent

In the field of Jewish education for the past nineteen years, she has extensive experience with family education, curriculum development, the facilitation of community wide grants, the Kids on the Block Disability Awareness Program, and the Artists in Residence Program. Marilyn is responsible for the development of a Family Education Program Bank, which disseminates programs, including Family School models, on a community-wide and international basis. Marilyn has also been a teacher, an educational director of a religious school, and a director of a preschool. She holds a B.A. in Education from Northeastern Illinois University and a master's degree in Judaica from Spertus College of Judaica, Chicago, Illinois.

Chicago: The Action Plan
Marilyn Vincent

Bereshit—in the Beginning—
One morning shortly after they had been driven out of Gan Eden,
Eve looked at Adam and said thoughtfully: "You know, Adam, we
are living in critical times."

There is hardly a family in Jewish history about which this could not be said, including families today. Over the past ten years, however, Jewish family education, as a newly-energized field, has brought to these times an openness and awareness about the critical state of the American Jewish family which will have possibly far-reaching effects on the strength of the family and the American Jewish community into the twenty-first century.

Attention to the importance of the family unit is not a new phenomenon in Jewish tradition and focusing on educating the family is not a new concept for the religious schools and synagogues of Chicago. The Community Foundation For Jewish Education, (CFJE), Chicago's current central address for Jewish Education, has embraced, expanded upon, and broadened the scope of the earlier initiatives of one of its founding partners, the Board of Jewish Education (BJE). In 1993, a partnership between the BJE and the Reform, Conservative, and Reconstructionist movements in Chicago resulted in the establishment of the Community Foundation For Jewish Education, an affiliate of the Jewish Federation of Metropolitan Chicago, for the purpose of "ensuring the continuity and quality of Jewish life through Jewish Education." (Mission statement, CFJE 1993)

Previous work in Chicago, during the 70s and 80s, in the field of family education, included family education newsletters containing suggestions for involving families as partners in their child's Jewish education.

These suggestions encouraged parents to volunteer in the school and to be an appreciative audience for performances in which their child was involved. At that time, so-called family education programs brought parents and children together to view, for example, a slide presentation about Soviet Jewry or to learn songs and prayers sung in different Jewish communities around the world. In addition, some schools began to experiment with family programs and family retreats to give families Judaic experiences in the hope that they would carry-over into the home.

One of our Chicago schools had a part-time family educator on staff as early as 1970, perhaps the first position of its kind in the country. Another created a "family school" in which parents had the option, during their child's third-, fourth-, and fifth-grade years, to study on an adult level the curriculum offered in their child's grade level and also to join their children in class for parallel learning experiences twice a month. In response to increasing rates of divorce, family newsletters contained articles such as "Divorce And The Jewish Child." It was evident, even then, to Chicago Jewish educators that our Jewish families had undergone radical changes since the 1940s and 1950s, when the American Jewish nuclear family seemed intact and the Jewish home played the central role in teaching Jewish traditions and values.

The 1970s brought a turn-about in Jewish education. Many Jewish educators moved from reinforcing and supplementing what they had thought was taking place in the home to teaching what, in many cases, they knew was not taking place in the home. Our Jewish parents, in the 1970s, had come to rely on the religious schools to do it for them: to make their children Jewish. Jewish educators had become the primary teachers of Judaism, separate from and, in some cases, in spite of parents. This role continued into the 1980s and 1990s. As one educator put it, "We know that the interest many of our parents have in religious education stops at making sure that their children are exposed to it." Many parents seemed to be saying, "Here are our children. It's your job to fill them up with Jewish knowledge. It's your job, not mine, to make them Jews." This kind of apathy became known as the "drop off" syndrome. Parents dropped their children off at Hebrew or religious school but rarely came into the building themselves and rarely thought more about their children's Jewish education.

The decade of the 1990s witnessed an increase in both intermarriage and divorce. In addition, as have other American families, Jewish families have become more mobile both socially and geographically. Many of our Chicago families are single parents trying to raise a family and work full time or they are two-career parents. The rhythm of family life has been and continues to be fast-paced and frenzied for these modern families: sleep, wake, get the kids off to school, and get to work. In between, they have to eat, fight traffic, and try to squeeze in "quality time" together. Then they have to do it all over again tomorrow and the next day.

Where does being Jewish fit into this hectic lifestyle? The sad fact is that increasing numbers of families were not making any time or room for Judaism in their lives and many parents were themselves weak in their Judaic knowledge. Educators in Chicago had earlier hoped that school-based programs would infuse non-active families with the spirit of Judaism. Over the years, however, we had become painfully aware that when there is little Judaic knowledge or observance at home, Jewish formal education for children is not likely to change the family's situation.

So educators began to revise their views. After all, parents are the primary "value transmitters" in our American society. More than any teacher or rabbi, Mom and Dad are in a position to give their children extraordinary experiences in Jewish learning right in their own homes. From ḥallah to charoset, from the brit and naming ceremony to the bar/bat mitzvah and from simḥa to simḥa, our tradition provides us with a never-ending supply of holidays, life-cycle celebrations, and mitzvot. It seemed reasonable for us to think that, if Jewish parents only had the tools and the motivation, they could become a powerful educational force for their children.

This kind of educational thinking was reinforced by an emerging national focus which emphasized that the key to Jewish continuity was informed, educated, and practicing Jewish parents. The phrase *Jewish continuity* swept across the American Jewish community in the early 1990s accompanied by the term empowerment, which was sweeping across American education communities. Together, these catch-words encouraged us, as Jewish educators, to look at Jewish families in terms of the positive strengths they offered and not in terms of the problems they presented. The central tenet of the phrase *Jewish continuity* is to empower parents and foster their own expertise so that they, in turn, can provide an environment for their children which will foster Jewish family life and encourage ongoing Jewish learning.

A "Home Start" for Families

In 1985, our agency joined forces with the Chicago Jewish Federation in a campaign designed to reach non-affiliated families as well as affiliated ones. The Home Start Program was one of the outcomes of this campaign and happened to be my first job with the agency. The goal of Home Start was to connect families, in a meaningful way, with their synagogue community and to give parents a way to bring Jewish knowledge and practice into their own homes. At the time, as a religious school principal and as the director of a Jewish Early Childhood Center, I became very involved in bringing parents and children together for family education experiences, even before it was common to refer to such experiences or programs as "family education." I was excited about working with the Home Start Program, which was to help me reach large numbers of families in the greater metropolitan area of Chicago.

The original Home Start series consisted of holiday packets to be used at home for young children. These had been written by the Baltimore Board of Jewish Education under the direction of Hyman Channover. In 1985, Behrman House Publishing Company purchased the rights, made additions, and converted the program into a family subscription series. This meant that *Home Start Jewish Holiday Packets* containing information, materials, and suggestions for family Jewish holiday activities arrived by mail at the homes of subscribing families prior to each Jewish holiday throughout the year.

In Chicago, we used the series to reach unaffiliated as well as affiliated families by offering parent-child family education holiday-centered programs as well as separate parent education and empowerment sessions. I taught about the Jewish holidays at programs designed for parents and children together. Each program included an interactive activity or a Jewish craft project that parents and children created together and then took home. At times, Jewish storytellers or puppeteers participated in these programs. I also was part of parent education and empowerment sessions where panels of specialists—for example, a child psychologist along with a rabbi and other Jewish educators—conducted sessions such as "Christmas and the Jewish Child," or "The Making of a Jewish Home."

These programs were marketed in synagogue bulletins and Jewish newspapers and at the Jewish Community Centers. To reach unaffiliated Jewish families, an advertising campaign was launched in major Chicago newspapers and in local community newspapers. In addition, posters and flyers were circulated in community libraries, grocery stores, and other public places. Chicago synagogues and religious schools welcomed and supported these outside programs they were happy to house, because the programs brought parents and children into their buildings on a monthly basis throughout the year.

In order to encourage synagogue affiliation for non-affiliated families, a publication with information and descriptions of Chicago synagogues was made available to families attending programs and subscribing to the series. These families were invited to visit synagogues and attend services to learn more about what the affiliated Jewish community had to offer. Although the Home Start Program was introduced in several communities across the country with mixed results, the response in Chicago was excellent and participation was high. Thousands of our families subscribed to the series and participated in their local Home Start family education programs. Eventually, Behrman House converted the series to direct classroom use for schools to order and send home to families.

A Central Address for Family Education

We can see that Chicago was offering family education experiences to families early on. The concept of family education is not new to us. What is new today, however, is that family education in the Chicago metropolitan area commands a central role on the agenda of the Community Foundation For Jewish Education, and the CFJE is the central address of family education for Chicago's Reform, Conservative, and Reconstructionist schools and synagogues.

In 1990, the centrality of family education in Chicago became evident when a separate Family Education Department was established in the agency. This department was to provide family education assistance and direct service to schools and synagogues. A concentrated effort was to be made to develop innovative programs and models for family education and to provide schools and synagogues with supplies, materials, resources, plans, supervision, training, and seed money. The goal of this new department was to assist these institutions in helping their families make

Judaism a part of the rhythm of their lives.

Since 1990, there has been tremendous growth in the number of programs and participants in family education in Chicago. In 1996-97, most schools affiliated with the Community Foundation For Jewish Education offer an average of six to eight annual programs or optional family tracks, compared with only one to two programs per year in 1990. This year, more than 6,000 families from over sixty schools and congregations have been involved in family education programs. These have provided, in single-session, multi-session, and family school tracks, parallel learning experiences and parent education classes. This compares with the 500 families from twenty schools who were involved in holiday-centered, single-session programs in 1990. This tremendous growth represents a serious commitment on the part of Chicago synagogues and schools and on the part of the Community Foundation For Jewish Education. (CFJE) to preserving and strengthening Jewish families.

Community Commitment and Financial Assistance

The CFJE Department of Family Education is committed to providing synagogues and schools with program development, cutting-edge materials and resources related to family education, one-on-one assistance in planning family education, and funding in the form of subsidies. The 1996 CFJE Department of Family Education's budget line for subsidies was over $50,000. In order to qualify for a subsidy, the development, planning, and implementation of the proposed program must conform to the CFJE Criteria for Subsidies, which is our "Standards and Guidelines" instrument. Applicants must also have filled out the department's "Program Description" form for proposed programs. In this way, funded programs become part of the CFJE Family Education Program Bank for purposes of sharing them with others in the community. Schools and synagogues may also apply to the CFJE Grants Committee and to the Jewish Federation of Metropolitan Chicago for additional funding.

The tremendous growth in family education in Chicago has seen family thinking incorporated into the structure of many schools. It has become valued by religious school and synagogue lay boards of directors and budget committees. We work hand in hand with our educational directors in helping synagogue boards of directors recognize that more family education brings renewal even though it is labor intensive and time consuming. Our advocacy has resulted in additional funding being budgeted to provide for some part-time assistant educational directors or family educators to assist with family education. We have also seen significant changes in synagogue and school budgets, where added and/or increased monies have been designated for family educa- tion programs. Even so, the demand for family education programming in Chicago is still greater than the available resources. The response on the part of the Community Foundation For Jewish Education has been to make family education one of the top priorities for which we con- tinue to seek additional funds.

A Family Educators Coalition

In 1989, the agency established a Long Range Planning Committee to propose changes within the framework of our schools that would help Jewish education have a stronger impact on students and their families. This committee was to identify and define the problems, generate alter- native solutions, evaluate those alternatives, and make recommendations for implementing solutions. One conclusion drawn by this committee was that a crucial component of successful schools was the interrelations among teachers, school administrators, and parents. This conclusion was based, in part, on the committee's study of "The Effective School Movement" in general education. Members of the committee, agency board members and staff, and representatives from our affiliated schools asked key questions including the following: First, how do we go about making parents/families informed consumers of Jewish education? Second, shall we invest more resources in parent and family education? Third, how can we serve learners and their families more effectively and more directly? And fourth, how can we provide special innovative direct services to our affiliated synagogues and schools so that they can, in turn, provide family education to their families?

The committee concluded that unless we influence parents and the home there will likely be little long term, permanent effect from the Jewish education of their children. One outcome of the deliberations of the Long Range Planning Committee was the organization of a Family Educators Coalition charged with developing ways to empow- er parents with respect to their own Judaic studies and to develop joint programs with their children as well as assisting families in learning about and appreciating the intrinsic value of Jewish living. This Family Educators Coalition brought together educational directors, lay people, family education specialists, rabbis, teachers, and members of schools boards from our affiliated Reform, Conservative, and Reconstructionist synagogues and schools.

Significant Community Choices

The efforts of the Family Educators Coalition (FEC) were to be concentrated first on training and research in the field of family education, and then on the development, implementation, and dissemination of family education programs throughout the synagogue school community. The FEC decided that, during the course of the following year, the religious school educational directors responsible for family education would participate in an intensive training program in the field of family education. In subsequent years, this initial year-long training would be augmented by family education professional growth sessions and workshops in order that they could stay on the cutting edge of this emerging field.

We were aware that in some communities training programs for future full-time family educator positions were being initiated. We were afraid, however, that after the initial seed money ran out, positions for family educators would not be able to be absorbed by the budgets of our congregations who, in many cases, were hard pressed to provide budget lines even for full time religious school educational directors. Therefore, we consciously made the decision to target our present synagogue school educational directors rather than recruit and train new educators, hoping that there would be new, full-time family educator positions in the future.

We were also aware that some major communities were starting out by awarding thousands of dollars for the implementation of family education programming. Our decision was first to use the majority of our funds for training and only award small increments, hundreds rather than thousands of dollars, for implementation of programs developed as a result of training. The training program was partially funded by a special family education budget put in place by the agency. In addition, the synagogues and schools designated a percentage of their annual Congregational Enrichment Initiative Grant Fund from the Federation to the program.

Chicago Meets Whizin!

We developed a list of nationally known experts working in the area of family education as possible presenters in the Family Educators Coalition Training Program. The program was scheduled to begin in August, 1990. In January of 1990, at our annual Winter Institute, Harlene Appelman, the director of the JEFF family education program in Detroit, was invited to be the key note speaker. She shared with us her recent work in the field of family education. She noted how much she had already learned from working with key Chicago Jewish educators and mentioned the Whizin Summer Seminar, to take place in June at the University of Judaism in Los Angeles under the direction of Dr. Ron Wolfson.

After presenting at our Winter Institute, Harlene told Ron about Chicago's plans for family education. At that time, Whizin had been in existence for one year and was planning their second Summer Seminar. In talking with Ron, we discovered that Chicago's goals for placing a central emphasis on family education were the same as those of the Whizin Institute for Jewish Family Life. In addition, almost all of the Jewish educators we had thought of as presenters for our Family Educators Training Program were already part of the consulting staff of the Whizin Institute. It made sense for us to pool resources and work together. As a result, in the spring of 1990, a partnership and a reciprocal agreement was made between our agency and The Whizin Institute. This made additional funding and expert staff available for our Family Educators Training Program.

At the second Whizin Summer Seminar, I worked with the Whizin staff to develop our year-long training program for Chicago educators based on the subject matter covered at the five-day Whizin Summer Seminar. The thirteen training sessions to be held in Chicago included the Whizin staff as well as local professors from the University of Illinois, the University of Chicago, and Chicago's Adler Institute.[7]

A Curriculum for Training in Family Education

Participants brought to these sessions a wide variety of experiences in family education. Many were complete novices, but the director of an established Family School Track was also there. Educational directors, lay people, family education specialists, rabbis, teachers and members of synagogue school boards attended a three day institute in August, 1990, which opened the Family Educators Coalition Training Program. In the course of the year's training, participants were exposed to many aspects of dealing with families in the synagogue context, with a strong emphasis on theory preceding practice. The program created a family education networking structure that continues in place in our community today. One of the results of the program was the development of a Standards and Guidelines instrument for the planning of family education programs; it was the first of its kind in the country.

The curriculum for the training sessions held throughout the year addressed Jewish identity development in the family, family systems, family learning, group dynamics, goal setting for family education, and an in-depth examination and study of successful models of family education programs from all over the country.

A. Curriculum Topics

During the course of the year, topics for sessions included:

1. Family education as a field, not a fad or quick fix
2. Exploring learning experiences that occur within the context of the Jewish family
3. Stages of development of Jewish identity in infants, children, adolescents, and adults within the context of the family; and the role of rituals and symbols in identity formation
4. Family learning in relation to how families function as a system
5. Stages of the Jewish family life cycle
6. How behavioral change occurs in adults and in the home; what happens when children are more Jewishly knowledgeable than their parents; and how families function while also changing their practices
7. Parent empowerment and the transfer of learning. We asked: How can we help the family to transfer the knowledge and skills learned in programs to the realities of their home situation?
8. Family education and the family unit. Family education is concerned with the family as a unit. The whole family is "the client," not just the children and not just the adults

9. Establishing habits of family observance within the family: constancy and regularity, and the forces which may interfere with establishing these habits
10. Psychological barriers to parental change: for example fear, discomfort, and resistance to change based on parents' early experiences with Jewish education
11. The team approach to family education involving the educational director, teachers, family education specialist, rabbi, parents, school committee, and central agency family education consultant
12. The five levels of Jewish involvement in family education based on the work of Joan Kay
13. Marketing and the cost-benefit analysis of family education programs
14. Developing goals for family education

B. Goals for Family Education

During the course of the year-long training program, we identified the following goals:

1. To re-establish and strengthen the family as the center of Jewish identity formation (Jewish Identity)
2. To assist families in being the primary vehicle for the transmission of Jewish knowledge, values, culture and heritage from one generation to another (Family and Jewish Values)
3. To bring parents and children together for Jewish learning and Jewish living experiences. To enlist parents as partners in their children's Jewish education (Child's Jewish Education)
4. To encourage families to identify with their Jewish heritage and the Jewish community by developing a closer relationship with the synagogue and the Jewish community (Closer Ties to the Synagogue and the Jewish Community)
5. To foster a sense of community and encourage Jewish communal support of vital services to the Jewish community (Communal Support)

6. To encourage families to become lifetime Jewish learners; in addition, the goals included helping schools develop a holistic family education plan which addresses the enrollment of a family from the first day of religious school or Jewish pre-school, and takes into consideration all grade levels and the involvement of the entire family in the synagogue community (Lifetime Jewish Learning)

C. Family Education Standards and Guidelines

During the course of the year, I worked with our educational directors in developing a set of "Standards and Guidelines for Developing Family Education Programs." Chicago was the first in the country to develop such guidelines and, subsequently, we shared them with other communities. We also published a booklet describing our philosophy of Jewish family education, the goals we had developed, and a list of the piloted programs we had begun to experiment with. This booklet was distributed to members of the Chicago Jewish Educators Coalition and JESNA (Jewish Educational Services of North America) distributed it to agencies and educators across the country. The "Standards and Guidelines" are as follows:

1. Set goals with respect to school curriculum, Jewish content, generating interest in future or ongoing programming, and the end result of the program
2. Family issues, such as intermarriage, single families
3. The Judaic knowledge level of parents
4. How to provide opportunities for parents to be Jewish teachers and Jewish learners
5. How the programs might change parents' behavior at home, in the synagogue or in the community
6. School and synagogue involvement, such as how the proposed program will use the skills of the educational director, teachers, family education specialist, rabbi, parents, school committee and the central agency consultant
7. Evaluation, follow up and plans for assessment of whether or not the goals were met

D. Continuing the Training through Professional Growth
Currently, on an annual basis, an average of four to six professional growth sessions are offered throughout the year from within the agency and in cooperation with other community, agencies which relate to working with families. In addition, we have
experimented with teacher training sessions at particular schools
and the subject of family education was addressed as part of our
Master-Teacher Training Course. Educational directors, family
educators, lay leaders, and rabbis have participated in a wide
range of professional growth sessions following on our initial
training and development program. These sessions have helped
our community remain current about family education and
Jewish education.

Direct Service Planning: Family Education Programs

As part of our direct service, The Community Foundation For Jewish
Education's Department of Family Education plans, creates, designs,
and customizes family education programs for our affiliated synagogues
and schools. Resource materials, current thinking, and our expertise on
issues related to the planning and delivery of family education is available on a continuous basis.

During the spring and summer of each year, I develop a family education plan of action for the coming year with the educational directors and
family educators of our affiliated schools and synagogues. Additional
planning may take place with grade-level teachers, teams of teachers, lay
committees, or family education teams, depending on the framework and
structure of individual sites and considering informal and anecdotal evaluations. We recognize the need and value of formal evaluation instruments and feedback, and our work in developing evaluation instruments
for family education is an ongoing work-in-progress.

The programs may be designed for the entire family, for parents and
students of a particular grade or grade levels, for grandparents and grandchildren, or others. Programs range from school or community or grade-
level events to parallel learning family tracks, where parents and children
attend classes together on a regular basis throughout the year. Our families may also participate in ongoing projects and home study. The subject
matter includes: holidays, Shabbat, Torah, life cycle, family history,

Jewish history; Hebrew, mitzvot, values, morals and ethics; and specific issues in Jewish parenting. Our family education programs include learning stations, parallel learning, workshops, community events, large group activities, family retreats, multi-session, and home practices.

The CFJE Department of Family Education works with other CFJE departments but is primarily occupied with planning programs and activities in synagogue and religious/Hebrew schools from Kindergarten through seventh grade, and in day schools affiliated with our agency. The early childhood schools within the CFJE have made family education an integral part of everything they do. Their activities have always been responsible for planting the seeds of Jewish learning and Jewish living practices in young families and, in recent years, our Early Childhood programs have sparked more formal planning for family education including parent education.

At the other end of the age range are adolescents. Family education has become a regular part of the high school curriculum over the last three years. The CFJE High School Department works on new ways to include parents in its programming. As a beginning step, a family education orientation at this level has helped parents and teens to communicate more openly about their families and about Judaism. These programs have also given parents an opportunity to interact with other parents of teenagers.

A Family Education Program Bank

CFJE Department of Family Education intends to remain on the cutting edge of the family education field in order to provide high quality direct service to our schools. We have more than three hundred program descriptions in our Family Education Program Bank. We are currently rewriting these programs in a standardized format—program descriptions, goals, preparation, procedure, and evaluation—for the purpose of dissemination. We are the first agency in the country to have such an organized Family Education Program Bank. In addition, we recently completed *Family School: Six Models*, which details the family school models we have established or are currently piloting.

Family School: A School Within a School

Family schools are alternative schools designed to meet the individual needs of families established within the existing framework of religious schools. A family's decision to participate is optional. Thus, family schools are made up of self-selected groups of families. Several families decided to participate in a family school after attending family education programs over the years. These families want a more intense experience as they engage in study as a family.

Parents and children participating in family schools and attending classes together year-round on a regular basis is a relatively new, exciting concept in the field of family education. The CFJE and its affiliated schools are committed to experimenting with innovative family education models to provide significant options for families. The six Chicago models now in place reflect our intention to be open to innovative "next steps" in family education.

Students express delight at being with their parents within the family school. They are enthusiastic and motivated. Parents say they have a heightened interest in their own Judaic knowledge, have increased their own observance or level of discussion of Judaism within the home, want to continue to study, and experience a sense of community. These motivated families often become energizers of the synagogue and become more involved in congregational activities, services, leadership, and study.

Six Family School Models

1. Temple Sholom Family School, established 1985

"Jewish Education Family Style," a three year program, focuses on Jewish holidays in third; Israel in fourth; and Jewish Life Cycle in sixth grades. Parents attend with their children twice a month on Sunday mornings, first at a one-hour parallel study session in the classroom, and then at a one-hour parent session, studying at an adult level, followed by informal parent interaction.

2. Beth Emet Family School, piloted 1994

A participatory weekly two-year Shabbat morning program for fifth and sixth graders, including child-centered study, adult-centered study, children and adults together, and children and adults separately, with a curriculum of Shabbat worship and Torah study the first year and Shabbat workshop and Tanach study the second year. During the morning, the fifth and sixth graders study with their parents while their siblings attend a special class designed for them. Students do not attend school on Sunday.

3. Or Shalom Family School, piloted 1994

Parents join their third- through sixth-grade children for intensive parallel learning of Torah and Hebrew twice a month on Sunday mornings. Sessions include Jewish text study; Hebrew vocabulary and prayers; and creating art, drama, or music together. Families learn about the Shabbat evening service and then lead a service with explanations of specific prayers and comments about how learning together as a family this year has touched them.

4. Beth Israel, "K'hillat Shabbat," piloted 1994

"K'hillat Shabbat" is a community Shabbat and learning experience which includes community worship; study sessions for adults and children, together and apart; a communal Shabbat meal; and a weekend retreat. K'hillat Shabbat teaches about Jewish living in the context of a learning and practicing community. K'hillat Shabbat teaches participants how to recognize, acknowledge, and celebrate holiness in time, places, and relationships. The program is also open to congregational members without children.

5. Atz Hayim School for Jewish Living, piloted 1995

Pods of six families meet in homes throughout the year. Two pods meet weekly and one meets monthly. Students are from three- to twelve-year-olds. Parents research, plan, organize, and teach Judaic studies while Hebrew is taught by a tutor once per week. The school places responsibility for education, observance, Jewish behavior, discussion, and activities in the family squarely on the parents.

6. McHenry Congregation Family School, piloted 1995

Six sessions throughout the year replace the fourth Sunday of the religious school time slot. Of the fifty families enrolled in the religious school, twenty to thirty families choose to attend these sessions. Families with students in Kindergarten through eighth grade attend services together and participate in both student and parent education study. The curriculum is devoted to Tikun Olam and Jewish Holiday observance and celebration.

The Family as Our New Student

Six years ago, we involved parents because we wanted them to support their child's Jewish education. Now, we involve parents because we want to affect the life of the family. Today, the whole family system is our student. This is a major change in our perspective and in the notion of what Jewish education is about. The central feature of our expanded view of family education is that our target is the whole family, not the children alone and nor the adult alone. As a result of an intensive focus on family education, the nature of Jewish education in the metropolitan Chicago area is radically changing, especially in the synagogue setting.

Fundamental changes in many schools and synagogues integrate the family unit into the culture of the congregation and affect the overall approach to religious schooling and synagogue life. Family education has been a part of the school curriculum. Significant work has been done by lay committees in framing mission statements and articulating long term goals tailored to the needs of their constituencies. I have found that family education is most successful in those schools where synagogue lay leadership and professionals work together and family education is an integral part of the entire synagogue community rather than being relegated to the religious school.

Lay leadership support also has determined that in Chicago over the last six years family education has become a prominent line on most of our synagogue and school budgets. Lay leadership may also have an impact on programming itself. The expectations of those families participating in family education programs have also changed. In many cases, those "drop off" parents of yesterday have become the "drop in" parents of today. But "Family Education 101," over and over again, is not acceptable to them. As families become more sophisticated, programs must also become more sophisticated.

Success in Family Education

What is the definition of success in the field of family education? Do we want it to mean more support by parents of their children's Jewish education? Do we want it to mean that parents are more supportive of the religious school today than in the past? Do we want it to mean more partnerships with parents than before? Do we want it to mean more Jewish families living more Jewish lives? Does it mean that we are getting closer to achieving our goal of building a stronger sense of Jewish community? In my view, the answer to all these questions is, "Yes."

First, with respect to their children, parents involved in family education become role models for their children and give their children the message that Jewish education is valued.

Second, in relation to support for Jewish institutions, because more parents are physically present in the religious school, learning and participating in a variety of Judaic experiences, our religious school professionals are feeling supported for their teaching. Many of our family education parents further demonstrate their support for their school and synagogue by becoming more involved, whether by attending synagogue functions, volunteering to help in the school or synagogue, working on a committee, or taking a board position.

Third, in relation to Jewish learning and living, as our families begin to acquire Judaic skills and knowledge, we have noticed changes in their attitudes. Many families have begun to view Jewish learning as of value in their family's daily home-life. For example, in Bringing Shabbat Home, for four to six weeks, parents learn about Shabbat and about how to bring this celebration into their lives. They sign up to be hosts or guests at future Shabbat dinners.

Home study experiences contribute to helping families make Judaism part of the natural rhythm of their lives through reading Jewish books to young children and answering such questions as "Why do I have to go to Hebrew School?" and "Why should I have a Hebrew name?" Joint homework assignments encourage parent-child discussions.

Teach Them Diligently Unto Your Children

The old idea of family as central to Jewish life has not changed, but, as we have discussed, the lives of our families are constantly changing. Why are our families of the 1990s more receptive to family education than the families of the 1970s and 1980s? I believe the answer is their recognition that "quality time" together provides an opportunity to pass on their Jewish values and heritage from one generation to another. Many families have come to realize that the religious school and the synagogue environment can be places to spend precious family time together. Parents often come to our programs looking for opportunities to be together and to strengthen their families. Schools and synagogues that find ways to capitalize on this desire observe good participation in family education programs and parental transfer of what they experienced back into the home.

We cannot expect this to happen overnight; we must nurture and cultivate. Judaism offers a way of bringing families together, of providing a vehicle for parents to communicate with their children and pass their values on to them. Our endeavors in the field of family education have only just begun. As we enter the twenty-first century, "may we go from strength to strength"—V'Dor L'Dor—in our endeavors.

*N*ancy Bloom is assistant professor in the Benjamin S. Hornstein Program in Jewish Communal Service at Brandeis University where she is also the director of Field Work. She received her M.S.W. from the School of Social Work at Boston University.

Nancy Bloom

Marion Gribetz

*M*arion Gribetz is Family Education Consultant at the Bureau of Jewish Education of Greater Boston. She has directed the Jewish Family Educator Network of the Sh'arim Initiative since its inception in 1994.

*B*arbara Penzner is the rabbi at Congregation Hillel B'nai Torah in West Roxbury, Massachusetts. She received her ordination at the Reconstructionist Rabbinical College. She serves as a consultant to the Commission on Jewish Continuity in Boston.

Barbara Penzner

Not Pictured

*S*haron Jedel is the Bronfman Foundation Yozma Intern at the Shoolman Graduate School of Education at Hebrew College. She is a participant in the Family Educator program.

*H*arvey Shapiro is director of Educational Programs and assistant professor of Jewish Education at Hebrew College. He has directed the Family Education program there since its inception in 1993.

Boston: Planning, Supporting, Training

Nancy Bloom, Marion Gribetz, Sharon Jedel,
Barbara Penzner, Harvey Shapiro

This four-part article, written by multiple authors, offers a detailed analysis of Sh'arim and its components.[1] The first section provides an overview of Sh'arim. The second provides a brief time-line and an analysis of the complex planning process, including a description of the start-up of the Sh'arim initiative, its key elements, and a discussion of some of its successes. The third section includes a discussion of the support network for the project. And it describes the structures that helped participating institutions reflect on their family education programming and integrate a new professional into their institutions. The final section describes the training program at Hebrew College. It outlines the uniqueness of this training program for family educators; and describes a number of the courses offered in the program. Elsewhere in this volume, Susan Shevitz's article discusses the evaluation process connected with the Sh'arim project.

Overview

In 1993, the Boston Jewish community embarked on a path-breaking, comprehensive initiative in Jewish family education. Planfulness on the part of the entire community motivated this. It was the product of years of groundwork done in the community since the early 1980s.

In 1985, the Federation (Combined Jewish Philanthropies or CJP) commissioned its second ten-year demographic study. This study described two interesting phenomena in the Jewish community of greater Boston, a community of approximately 200,000. One was that eighty-five percent of Boston-area Jews were affiliated, at some point in their lives, with a synagogue—particularly when families had bar mitzvah-aged children. Secondly, the 1985 data showed that eighty-five percent of the children receiving Jewish education were enrolled in congregational schools. These two findings contributed to the call for a mutually beneficial partnership between the synagogues and the Federation.

In 1989, under the professional leadership of president Barry Shrage, CJP convened a Commission on Jewish Continuity (COJC). For the first time, the congregational movements were invited to send both lay and professional representatives to sit at the table along with representatives from CJP and its agencies. The congregations had been attempting to find a way to partake of community funds; and CJP was coming to understand that education was an arena in which it wanted to promote a particular vision. This alliance included representation from the key education agencies, Hebrew College, and the Bureau of Jewish Education. Other communal agencies, particularly the JCC and the Synagogue Council of Massachusetts and later the Jewish Family and Children's Service, were there as well. Key committee chairs from CJP disseminated the message of the Commission on Jewish Continuity throughout the CJP. The chairs of this commission reflected and supported the alliance of the synagogue and the Federation world.

The issues discussed in the early meetings of the Commission on Jewish Continuity centered on trying to identify modes of Jewish education which would best meet the changing needs of the community. These discussions preceded publication of the 1990 Council of Jewish Federations population study. Unprecedented findings in the CJF study highlighted the rapid rate of intermarriage nationally and became a call to arms for many communities. Nevertheless, while intermarriage in the Boston Jewish community may have been on the minds of many COJC participants, it did not become an explicit agenda item for the commission. As the COJC's planning process evolved, the two major themes that did emerge were the need to transform congregations and institutions, and the need to enrich and transform individuals' Jewish lives.

In 1992, the COJC enlisted the assistance of a skilled Jewish education consultant from outside the community to help clarify and plan for these goals. The consultant provided the language that has since been used by those involved in the initiative. Lay leaders and professionals took ownership of the language and of the agenda of transformation.

A combination of complimentary forces propelled the COJC forward. In concert, the commission, the professional educators, and members of the community all began to talk about the importance of family education. This confluence led to Sh'arim: Gateways to Jewish Living as the first vehicle for the COJC's goals. The Sh'arim initiative proposed the creation of a new profession, that of the family educator. This initiative would require not only funding for salaries, benefits, and programming but also training, ongoing support, and evaluation of the initiative itself.

The Sh'arim Initiative—The Time Line

Jewish continuity, as an agenda item, arrived in Boston in 1989 and built on the foundation of previous communal work in Federation-synagogue relations, Jewish education issues, and a nascent family education effort. The Commission on Jewish Continuity created a "wall-to-wall" coalition, representing a first for Federation-synagogue relations on a formal level, especially given the fact that funding from the CJP would become available to congregations for the first time.

The original COJC consisted of more than sixty members, including rabbis, educators, and lay leaders from the movements and synagogues; professionals from the Jewish educational establishment (Bureau of Jewish Education, Hebrew College, faculty of the Hornstein Program in Jewish Communal Service at Brandeis University); professionals from other Federation-supported agencies (JCCs of Greater Boston, Synagogue Council of Massachusetts, and later the Jewish Family and Children's Service); and Federation lay leaders. This group brought together agencies and individuals with an interest in Jewish education, thereby creating from the outset an educational focus and direction for the group. This was not accidental; it reflected support by CJP president Barry Shrage and by the planner responsible for staffing the COJC, Dr. Sherry Israel.

The COJC devoted a year to listening to reports about Jewish education in the Boston area and sharing views on the issues of Jewish education before it began to tackle aspects of the problem in small task groups. At the same time, Barry Shrage, the president and the executive director of the Combined Jewish Philanthropies, published several papers and spoke publicly of his own vision for Jewish education. Thus, while the commissioners were engaged in a process intended to develop trust, to become better-educated about Jewish education, and to develop a sense of communal purpose, a communal vision was also being proposed. Family education was a key component, if not the primary thrust, of that vision.

The COJC agreed to focus on three target populations: (1) pre-school and elementary school children; (2) adolescents; and (3) college-age and young adults. The commission divided into smaller task groups, which met for a year to consider goals and strategies for improving Jewish education in each of these categories. The task groups' composition needed to achieve representation balanced between the Federation and the congregational world, between lay and professional leaders, among educational agencies, and across movements.

At the end of the year's deliberations, each task group shared its work with the COJC. Out of that work came lists of ideas such as creating traveling educational curriculum units and consultants for local schools and synagogues, enhancing the Jewish content in summer camps, and establishing a "storefront" drop-in center in downtown Boston for young adults. These provided program ideas for institutional use; but because they represented more of a "wish list" than a document reflecting consensus, they were neither discussed nor voted on but left in "draft" form without further dissemination.

This exercise in "dreaming" served to stimulate thinking in the education community and helped to develop a shared sense of the potential of Jewish education. The process was successful in floating ideas in a larger arena—some of which have since been adopted outside the formal COJC process. The commission's work may have been less successful in creating an overall sense of "ownership" for the final outcome. For example, some people complained that the agenda had been set up to highlight family education, and therefore, none of the recommendations should be taken seriously. It was true that, without a major endowment and the many hours needed for discussion, only one or two major initiatives could reach the drawing board in 1993.

Each task group had been challenged to develop priorities and to make number one choices. The Pre-school/Elementary Task Group endorsed a Family Educator Initiative to provide trained family educators to congregations, day schools, and JCCs. The Adolescents Task Group supported a Youth Initiative to develop a cadre of professional youth workers. The recommendations of the College/Young Adult Task Group urged the national Council of Jewish Federations (CJF) to develop a national funding plan for campuses to respond to the cut backs in B'nai B'rith funding for Hillels, to recruit young adults to connect them to Jewish programs and institutions, and to develop a system of disseminating information to this population. These recommendations eventually landed in the hands of communal professionals outside of the COJC.

While these latter two initiatives constituted significant aspects of Barry Shrage's vision, it was the Family Educator Initiative which received across-the-board COJC approval due, in part, to widespread experience with family education in the synagogue community. Susan Shevitz's 1992 report on the implementation of earlier programs proposed by the Task Force on Supplemental Jewish Education had confirmed and publicized both the success and appeal of family education programming and the urgent need for training professionals in family education to extend its impact. Many of the educators serving on the COJC knew the power of family education first-hand and were eager to broaden community support, financially and substantively. With all this in mind, the COJC director was able to encourage the Pre-School/Elementary Task Group to endorse family education almost unanimously.

In the third year of the COJC's work, two implementation committees met to develop a plan for making the recommendations a reality. These two committees, focusing on service delivery and personnel respectively, were composed of commissioners as well as non-commissioners, reflecting great concern for "balanced representation." This balance, though essential, sometimes became cumbersome and over-politicized, impeding real progress. To overcome these obstacles, the Service Delivery Committee eventually directed three smaller working groups to actually hammer out the work plans required for implementation of the family educator initiative, later named "Sh'arim: Gateways to Jewish Living." One working group developed the bare bones structure for the training program, a second drafted a proposal for evaluation, and a third struggled mightily to outline conditions and standards of "readiness" for applying to and being accepted into Sh'arim.

By the time the working groups' reports had been prepared and approved by the COJC, the CJP Social Planning and Allocation Committee, and the CJP Board, it was April, 1993. COJC participants were eager to begin implementation. With tight budget deadlines and hiring schedules, the entire community mobilized to apply for and select the first Sh'arim sites, to structure the training program, and to recruit and hire candidates for the family educator positions. While enough may not have been done to create and evaluate "readiness," and while some early mistakes may have been made, it was difficult to imagine delaying the initiative for yet another year. In a spirit of experimentation and with the desire to capitalize on momentum and excitement, eight sites came on board as a result of this push for implementation.

The initiative has gone on to involve two JCC's, two day schools, and thirteen congregations during its first three years. In addition to the training program at Hebrew College, which certifies family educators, the initiative has also spawned a series of professional development workshops, which began in 1996-97, for professionals seeking to learn more about family education from congregations unlikely to enter Sh'arim. The Commission is currently imagining new models to reach sites not likely to have the funds or the awareness to make a commitment to Sh'arim. While it remains the flagship of COJC initiatives, Sh'arim is also feeding into other COJC-sponsored programs, creating a dynamic climate of commitment to Jewish education throughout greater Boston among professionals and lay leaders in synagogues and the Federation alike.

Reaching Communal Consensus

The role of the congregations in Boston's vision for the Commission on Jewish Continuity has been prominent from the outset. Over the years, one primary goal of the COJC's efforts has become "transforming the congregation." Often stated implicitly, rather than explicitly, the possibility of such a transformation has been assumed whether talking about family education, adolescents, or universal adult Jewish literacy.

Buying into the vision of transformation has often proved more difficult than buying into family education. Transformation has been hard to define, entailing restructuring of professional roles and responsibilities in response to changing needs of congregants of all ages in the late twentieth century. The idea of transforming congregations has created tensions with other agencies, such as day schools and JCCs. Nonetheless, it is a frequent topic of conversation among professionals on the COJC and the idea stimulates thought throughout the community.

Most people on the COJC had set their sights on programs rather than on goals. As the banner project espoused by Barry Shrage, the Federation President, family education was an obvious priority. As noted above, funding for family education had been growing for five years prior to the implementation of Sh'arim. Aaron Wildavsky, in *Speaking Truth to Power*, (1979) emphasizes that "to understand where future policies are likely to lead us, we need to know about past policies." Susan Shevitz's evaluation of the several programs of the Task Force on Supplemental Jewish Education, which included family education programming grants, indicated that the congregational lay and professional leaders were deeply invested in family education, supported it, wanted more of it, and in many cases, were ready to move to a new level. Based on these findings, Shevitz recommended establishing family educator positions in congregations and schools, along with providing training in the field. Such extended involvement over time led to the implementation of a far-reaching program like Sh'arim.

Some have questioned whether the COJC functioned as a community coalition with a common purpose or whether it was a representative committee in which each member protected his or her vested interests. At times, the denominational movements and congregational participants complained about what they considered a misnomer, that is, that the COJC was a "partnership," given its commanding role in staffing and funding commission efforts. Certainly, COJC's work would have been less directed without Barry Shrage's clear commitment to a few key objectives.

In general, the consensus model of decision-making, which characterizes federations, tends to minimize the amount of change possible in these settings. But federations' influence can be countered; creative and dedicated participants have added elements or changed directions in unexpected ways. Nevertheless, a federation remains a powerful convener for a diverse community. Over time, vested interests in the Boston community, having achieved many of their goals, have given themselves over to a shared vision. As implementation advances, the political maneuvering has diminished. Professionals and lay people have come to appreciate both the communal contribution of Sh'arim to their individual institutions and have recognized the added value of sharing with their colleagues.

Key Features of Sh'arim

Sometimes committees can be the death of an initiative. Tedious hours of discussion can drive good ideas into the ground. The COJC experienced some attrition, particularly among lay leaders who lost interest or felt left out of professional-level discussions. Yet, a complex, comprehensive program like Sh'arim,—considered by some to have sought implementation too hurriedly—requires considerable reflection. Though many questions of policy remained, and still remain, unanswered, participants did their homework in predicting the challenges of implementation.

Any plan for improving, strengthening, or enhancing Jewish education must consider the quantity and quality of available personnel. In developing such a plan, therefore, a community must consider where the personnel will come from to carry out the plan, what recruitment and training will be necessary to implement it, and what salary and benefits will be offered to make the positions attractive. Such personnel considerations must include educators on-the-ground, those involved in the new training program, in consultation and evaluation, and in professional development for educators, rabbis, and lay leaders needed to support the initiative in each site where a family educator works.

The COJC built into its planning a salary range to attract and retain high quality professionals. Sh'arim provides significant funding to congregations, JCCs, and day schools so that they may engage a family educator. Initial support provides fifty percent of a half-time or more family educator position, to a total of $17,500 (or one-half of a salary of $35,000). Funding is available for salary but not benefits, programming, or the capital expenditures which may accompany the new staff person. Funding is assured over time, with a promise that decreases will not exceed ten percent per year, and that a floor of twenty-five percent funding will be maintained as long as the Sh'arim initiative is in effect.

In the first three years, funds were available for the fifty percent subsidy. However, this subsidy system failed to take into account either cost-of-living or merit increases. The burden of negotiating raises with employing institutions rests solely on the shoulders of the individual family educators. As the COJC reduces the amount of communal funding, this tension will likely increase.

Sh'arim provides a two-year training program at Hebrew College, culminating in a certificate in Family Education. This training is part of the family educator's work load, regardless of whether the person is in a full or part-time position. Any family educator working in a Sh'arim setting receives free tuition, funded by the COJC. One of the Commission's underlying motives in creating a training program for family educators was the general need for more skilled professionals in the field of Jewish education. Although an attempt is made to seek individuals who will remain committed to their jobs and their communities long-term, we are aware that many who enter family education have or will develop higher ambitions for careers in the Jewish community. In fact, many factors, including personal life changes, professional ambitions, and incompatibility between family educators and employers, created a number of transitions in the first three years of the initiative. Thus, training becomes an ongoing process which expands to include other professionals in the community as well as the replacements for those who leave their positions. Remarkably, however, nine of the original family educators from the first two years have remained in the initiative. Additionally, one of the family educators from the original 1993 cohort has been appointed education director at her Congregation as of September 1997.

The COJC built into the Sh'arim initiative consultants for schools and for the JCCs to help them create the "institutional readiness" required when taking on a family educator. Also built in was ongoing consultation to evaluate progress, reexamine the original objectives, and troubleshoot. Consultants from the Bureau of Jewish Education make themselves available on an ongoing basis. Neither the commissioners nor the applying institutions had any idea of the dramatic changes that a new professional would generate. An important message that the availability of ongoing consultation was intended to communicate was that experimentation and failure were acceptable aspects of change. The Commission's attitude was to create an environment for success. As we learn more and reflect on successes and failures, we continue to fine-tune policies, standards, consultation, and training to seek the best results. We continue to strive for a program which has an impact on institutions as well as on the individual families who are the clients of family education.

Institutional responses to consultation have ranged from great enthusiasm to rare contact. Recognizing that each site responds in accordance with its particular culture, the consultants have experimented with different strategies to reach out to the professionals and lay leaders in a non-threatening way. One consultation team achievement was to create a Family Educators' Network. The Network meets during the training program and continues after graduation, to enable family educators to speak freely, share philosophical and practical issues, and continue their professional development in an informal atmosphere.

Sh'arim sites fulfill obligations to the community in return for funding and other resources. They must create a workable job description for their family educator which permits that person to attend courses. They must participate in the evaluation project. They must acknowledge the COJC's contribution in all their publicity. The family educators submit mid-year and year-end reports to the COJC documenting their work.

Boston is unique in having a rich academic environment, including the resources of Brandeis University. The COJC drew on professionals from the academic world, both Jewish and general, in its early and ongoing deliberations. Many experts continue to serve in advisory functions or in active consultation to Sh'arim sites, others in preparation and implementation of evaluations, and still others in ongoing policy discussions.

The elements of Sh'arim outlined above are continually analyzed and subjected to searching questions, such as: What are the components of change, and how can family educators share the burden of transforming their institutions? What role do other professionals, especially the rabbi and educator, play in supporting, advocating for and enhancing family education? What is the role of lay leadership and how can they be recruited, trained and involved most effectively? What mechanisms are essential for assessing the needs of the clients in the community? What exactly are the sites' and the family educators' obligations to the broader community which funds them so heavily? How should the community deal with a site regarding its own internal funding for the initiative? How can family education develop a stronger content base and a curricular foundation?

What Constitutes Success?
Everyone wants to know if Sh'arim will succeed and how we define and measure success. The evaluation component of Sh'arim will determine success from the perspective of its impact on individuals and on institutions. However, the work of COJC and its initiatives has already produced other kinds of successes. One success of the planning phase was that COJC achieved its process goals:

1. To build a "wall-to-wall" coalition
2. To unite the coalition around the issue of Jewish education
3. To develop and implement a communal plan to enhance Jewish education

Many participants and observers credit the entire Boston community for this achievement, which came about both through the sensitivity of COJC leaders to process issues and through the prior history of coalition-building in the community, which nourished a climate of trust among participants and between the federation and synagogue communities.

Even before Barry Shrage brought his own vision of federation-congregation relations to the Boston Federation and community, such discussions had already taken place and, some say, had led to the selection of Barry Shrage as president of CJP in 1987. The existence of an active and creative Synagogue Council had laid the groundwork for both increasing inter-movement cooperation and raising the profile of movements and congregations within the community. Forums organized through the Bureau of Jewish Education, Hebrew College, and Brandeis University, furthermore, had brought together the various religious streams and their adherents. All these efforts had built connections among lay people, educators, movement directors, and rabbis which led to successful collaboration on the COJC.

Another success has to do with the participation of congregational educators. Among the most active participants in the Commission process, and often its most ardent supporters, were congregational educators. The presence and contribution of these educators was a major factor in the success of the process. The educators became COJC's sales force in the community. Their involvement can be seen as a success on two fronts: it signaled community recognition of the value and status of Jewish educators, and it developed and enlarged the educators' knowledge base of the communal process.

A third success, already evident, is the presence of institutional self-assessment and reflection, rare in Jewish educational circles. The process of project implementation entailed a concerted effort to assist participating institutions to understand the program, begin self-assessment (including creating an educational and financial plan as well as establishing and prioritizing goals and objectives), and developing a mutually beneficial evaluation system which would provide feedback to participating institutions to help them meet their objectives while keeping track of Sh'arim's progress for the community.

And finally, I believe that all of Jewish education in Boston is gaining new status, and more positive attention. Throughout the community, people are talking about professional development, personnel recruitment, content and curriculum. Many are gravitating to adult education in many forms. Success can be measured in a change in the zeitgeist as well as in specific impact on individuals. While not every program is a winner and not every site has a sophisticated understanding of the potential of family education, the level of the discussion in the community is, on the whole, more sophisticated. What characterizes this change is a commitment to ongoing reflection, fine-tuning, and a growing boldness in demanding higher standards which many are eager to meet, or perhaps, even exceed.

A System for Professional Support

The Scene: Boston, August, 1993: Eight newly-hired, full-time family educators are meeting for their first training session. Seven are working in congregations; one is at the Jewish Community Center. These family educators have just completed the hiring process in their respective institutions. Each institution had created a job description for its new professional and had recruited from within the community and beyond. The family educators are supported by their own institution and by matching funds from the Combined Jewish Philanthropies through the Commission on Jewish Continuity. The COJC had sent application guidelines to institutions that wanted to be partners in this experiment and receive funds for their new family educator's salary. Eight institutions met the required guidelines, received the grants, and hired individuals to help create a new profession in Jewish education in Boston.

The COJC said that its goals for the family educators were that they should be the implementers of institutional and family change. The planners on the COJC had outlined a number of ingredients for this experiment. These included:

1. Training for family educators
Although the new family educators may have come with expertise in the subject matters of Jewish education, adult education, Jewish education for children, social work, or Jewish

communal service, the integrated knowledge and skills needed for this new profession were seen as unprecedented. A two-year training program was to serve as an "early service" program for the new profession.

2. An institutional team

The concept of a "team" was vaguely defined as consisting of relevant professionals (e.g., rabbi, educational director) and a few key lay leaders who would create the vision and encourage its implementation.

3. A family education lay committee

In the institution, this committee would represent various constituencies in the design, integration, and monitoring of the new staff person and the new programs.

4. An intake interview process

It was hoped that the family educator would introduce the practice of conducting individual interviews with each member family, especially new members. This would help professionals ascertain the needs, interests, and backgrounds of the congregants and help them feel a personal connection to the institution.

5. Supervision

As a new professional in a newly-created field, supervision of the family educator by one of the other professionals was seen as essential to effective priority setting, learning, and growth.

6. Evaluation

It was thought that the institutions should know their demographics at the start of this process and continually assess their own work. In addition, the community should be able to learn about how the assumptions underpinning family education worked in reality. Thoughtful documentation and a plan for evaluation were part of the Sh'arim initiative.

During its planning process, the COJC outlined these six requirements. In their individual applications, the institutions had to address what they would do in each of the six areas. Acceptance into the initiative was predicated upon the promise of using these six principles as guides for work in family education.

Despite all the years of discussions, meetings, research, planning, and documentation, it was not possible to address all the specifics of exactly what impact the family educators would have on their institutional settings and the larger community. And, in spite of their common willingness to use the COJC's six principles, each of the eight sites brought their own histories, personalities, and constituents to their understanding of the endeavor. As the first year of the project unfolded, a number of challenges emerged and a great deal of learning occurred on everyone's part.

Throughout the year, the family educators felt under extreme pressure "to produce" in order to justify their new positions. "To produce" translated into running numerous programs which were well attended. Little attention was placed on individual families. Congregations were eager to show that the new professional was touching many people and creating lots of opportunities for family education. Yet very few family educators or others in the institutions understood how to develop and use family intake interviews in a way that was comfortable and seemed worthwhile.

The hours spent at the Hebrew College training program added to, rather than reduced, the stress on the new family educators. Institutions did not free their family educator to do less work because of the time they were required to spend in courses and in preparing for them. The family educators badly needed additional time, beyond that spent in formal learning, in which to share information about programs and resources. They also needed to feel that their personal anxieties were not unique. Since the training program was organized on an academic model, the educators had no forum or time in which to do professional sharing. Also, the courses offered in the training program met the needs of some of the new family educators, but not all, because everyone came with differing experiences and prior training.

Even though their application documents were carefully prepared, the institutions were not nearly as "ready" as they appeared on paper. Some lacked clear goals for family education; others did not agree on the populations to be served; still others had unclear channels of communication or undefined roles for their committees and board support. Often committees were not in place, teams did not exist, and in some cases, it was unclear who was to supervise the family educator. Also, the role of the lay leadership in each institution was critical but poorly understood or underdeveloped. Developing lay leadership structures was yet another responsibility of the new family educator. As a result, for the most part, "teams" were seen as a creation of the COJC and not an organic entity that would naturally encompass the new family educator. These problems made it difficult for the family educator to know just where and how to begin, and they felt pulled in many directions.

For their part, supervisors, most often the education directors, had hoped for quick relief from the overwhelming job of directing the school and, at the same time, planning and running the new family education programs. Yet many also felt ambivalent about losing control over the exciting new programs they had just created. The supervisors needed the opportunity to reflect upon their role, upon the issues arising from these changes, and upon ways they could continue their own learning about Jewish family education, and they needed the support to do so.

By the spring of 1994, eight dedicated, but rather frustrated, individuals were struggling as Jewish family educators in Boston. They knew that they could share ideas and support each other, but their demanding schedules often did not allow time for these activities. They needed a community.

The Bureau of Jewish Education (BJE) Jewish Family Educator Network: The Challenge

The challenge going into the second year of the Family Educator Initiative was to create an atmosphere in which professionals would feel safe to seek support and guidance for their ongoing professional development. During the first year of the initiative, the family educators had encountered both frustrations and triumphs. They were creating successes in their institutions and were reporting back to the community on their progress. Nevertheless, during the first year, there was also dissonance for the family educators because they were both a part of their own institutions and one part of a communal process. The new family educators were trying to create links to many families, to communicate with their boards and committees, and to integrate themselves into the professional structure already in place in their institutions. They were caught between the demands of the COJC and their need to create a space for themselves in their home institutions. They were challenged by the COJC's conception of this new profession as one which would create change for families as well as change for institutions.

The "early service" training program, which used an academic model at an academic institution, created additional stress and dissonance for the family educators. During the program's first year, with the exception of one retreat at the beginning of the year, there was no time provided for the new professionals to share their experiences with each other. This became particularly troublesome as the year progressed. As the year drew to a close, many of the family educators had to think about negotiating salaries and conditions of future employment. Some were still without offices, computers, or phones, not to mention professional benefits.

Setting up the Network

The Commission on Jewish Continuity thought that a professional network for the new family educators would augment the service provided by the community to the family educators, and by extension, would enhance service to the sites in the initiative. All of the individuals and partners on the COJC had their own idea of what such a network would bring to the project.

As the network unfolded, it became clear that it would become a safe and nurturing place for the family educators to share with each other. The network also provided the time to grow professionally beyond the course work in the "early service" training program. The first year the network was in place coincided with the conclusion of the first cohort of family educators' course work at Hebrew College. As they left the structure of the training program, the network became a suitable arena for the family educators' continued professional growth.

The new professional network was characterized by a good balance between the group's ability to set of its own agenda for each meeting and the BJE consultant staffing the network, who also had the ability to identify important issues. The network operates with trust and respect for all and with confidence that specific issues can be brought up for analysis and assistance with problem solving.

Suggestions come out of the network meetings. One of the first network accomplishments was the decision that the BJE consultant would act as a clearing house and create an annotated listing of individuals and resources in the community. The family educators were so busy learning their new jobs and producing a demanding schedule of programs and events for their institutions that they were unable to compile such a resource for themselves. They never even had the time to give one another the names of particular facilitators, storytellers, musicians, and the like, who had been particularly helpful in various programs.

As the network has grown, the group has begun to work collaboratively and to apply many of the ideas discussed at network meetings in their own institutional settings. For example, one of the family educators described a school/community collaborative Tzedakah Fair; this led to a remarkable collaborative proposal to the CJP. Five family educators prepared a community-wide Tzedakah Fair for the entire greater Boston community to be held on Super Sunday. The fair is now a model family education program. At the fair, members of the community learn with their families from the text sources for tzedakah; they learn how to enhance their celebration of bar/bat mitzvah with tzedakah projects; and they meet "tzedakah heroes" and create tzedakah crafts for their homes. As the Boston community undertook its annual fund raising campaign, family education enjoyed a primary role in the fund raising festivities.

In summary, the Jewish Family Educator Network has created both time and space for the Jewish family educator to grow professionally through sharing and networking. The issues raised by this group become the basis for reflection, dialogue, action plans, and learning opportunities. The network addresses the need which all professionals have for contact with others who share similar settings and confront similar struggles and successes—a need all the more critical in a newly created profession.

The Hebrew College Family Educator Program

The family educator program of Hebrew College prepares family educators to service multiple generations of Jews in synagogues, day schools, and Jewish community centers. The program is part of Sh'arim, the Commission on Jewish Continuity's large scale initiative to promote Jewish literacy and Jewish consciousness for all family members.

The curriculum is geared to the particular circumstances surrounding the family educator's position in their institutions and in the field. The institutions themselves have created something new—the position of family educator. In addition, most of the individuals in these positions have not previously held a family educator position. Thus, everyone is defining both the role and its relationships as they go. Finally, the field of family education as a professional enterprise is a relatively new arrival on the landscape of Jewish education. Given these considerations, the program at Hebrew College tries to provide guidance and support to family educators, in newly created positions, new to their institutions, and in a newly-emerging field. This threefold "newness" has several important implications for the Hebrew College program.

Consider the differences between this professional development program and more customary efforts to prepare and support professionals. First is the understanding of the role. In the synagogue, for example, the positions of rabbi, cantor, educator, and synagogue administrator all have a built-in set of overall definitions that allow each synagogue to reach consensus, either tacit or explicit, on the nature of the role and the expectations for it in its own setting. Numerous colleagues and mentors are available to support one another in these more-established careers. Professional identities are therefore grounded in long-standing practices and conceptions. This is not the case for family educators.

A second difference between this program and more customary professional development efforts is that this program is serving family educators who are already working in full- or part-time professional positions. This makes the program unlike that of other professional preparation programs, which may be characterized as pre-service, in that they provide instruction for individuals before they assume their first position in the field. The program is also different from conventional in-service training programs, which normally train established professionals who wish to learn new techniques, theories, and insights in their field. The Hebrew College program differs from this in-service model because it relates to professionals who are at a very early stage in developing their professional roles.

The family educator program may thus be characterized as an early service professional development program. As such, it seeks to develop a common language for the field, to share a variety of practical and theoretical models for conducting family education, and to help the key stakeholders in their institutions develop a viable vision for the family educator position.

For two years, participants in the family educator program gather one full morning per week at Hebrew College. During this time, they learn how to shift their overall perspective about the role of the student. Rather than considering the families who will be their students as objects of their educational endeavors, the family educators come to view their students as subjects. If viewed as an object, the student role would be to benefit from learning experiences designed by the educator and to imbibe the knowledge which the instructor imparts. If viewed as a subject, the student role is to be the proactive initiator of learning experiences and imparters of their own knowledge. An important goal of family education, then, is to help everyone make this shift, as learners, from being receivers of knowledge and experience to being providers of knowledge and experience.

Family educators explore ways to facilitate this shift for the families they deal with and especially for the parents, who will take on new roles in the Jewish education of their family. The extent to which families can increasingly take on a proactive role in initiating Jewish experiences and learning in the home and in the synagogue or school is one measure of the family educators' success. Thus, family educators in the Hebrew College program are learning how to design experiences and curricula that will allow families to grow Jewishly and to become increasingly independent and proactive.

Hebrew College faculty, as well as faculty from Brandeis University and Harvard University, teach a multi-dimensional curriculum encompassing study of Jewish texts, theory and practice of family education, and specific background disciplines.

In about half of the courses, students study and analyze Jewish sources. Often entering the program with a master's degree in Jewish education or its equivalent, family educators study both classical and modern Jewish texts. The rationale behind this component of the curriculum is twofold: to further strengthen the educators' Judaic knowledge and to model approaches to teaching Jewish sources in an adult setting. Dr. Marc Brettler, Associate Professor of Hebrew Bible at Brandeis University and a faculty member in the Hebrew College program, offers an additional justification: to help the educator transcend the Bible's ancient near-eastern context by highlighting the similarities of family issues in the twentieth century to those found in biblical narratives. During the program's three week intercession in January, Professor Brettler introduces a biblical narrative with particularly intriguing family dynamics and relationships. For example, students have explored the story of Joseph and his brothers, the story of Ruth, and the story of Samson. Family educators have found the issues of matrilineal descent, intermarriage, and parent-child relationships continued in these selections remarkably germane and in fact parallel to the issues they encounter in their own settings. Confronting and dealing with these circumstances has become a natural component of class discussions.

Family educators also develop their skills at interpreting traditional Jewish sources in The Seventy Faces of Torah. This course enhances their hermeneutic skills by looking at the numerous ways in which the Torah can be understood. Closely examining selected chapters from Genesis and Exodus, students compare the methods of both traditional and modern commentary, as well as literary analysis. In doing so, family educators specifically focus on how women can relate to these diverse approaches. Dr. Judith Kates, the course instructor, considers the emphasis on women-centered interpretations invaluable to the field of family education. She notes that, in their work, family educators are increasingly encountering adults who "have the impression that the Torah subordinates women. This notion is a major source of problems and alienation for many women."

The family educator's study of Jewish sources continues in courses such as The Family in Modern Jewish Literature, an examination of the portrayal of the Jewish family in Hebrew, Yiddish, and American literature, and The Jewish Journey of Faith, a historical exploration of Jewish faith in biblical, rabbinic, medieval, and modern periods.

In addition to looking at sources and at modes of interpreting them, students study the foundations and practice of family education. They examine a variety of educational models such as parallel learning for parents and children, the role of parents as teachers, the creation of Jewish role models, and the enhancement of home observance. A course on curriculum development helps them link programs and classes based on the notion that education should not occur as single, isolated events but as integrated experiences occurring over a long period of time.

Family educators also study the differences between the various institutions in which they work. A course on Contexts of Jewish Family Education, taught by Dr. Joseph Reimer, the former director of Brandeis' Hornstein Program for Jewish Communal Service, helps them recognize the particularities of the own contexts.

During the second year, the family educators participate in an intensive workshop dealing with case studies in family education. Each person proposes a dilemma or challenge which they have encountered in their work. With the guidance of experts, they construct alternative ways to define and deal with what they confront.

A third component of the family education program—in addition to the first two of text study and the theory and practice of family education—is attention to cognate fields such as human development, family systems and family dynamics, organizational behavior and change, and evaluation and needs assessment. For example, in a course taught by Dr. Robert Kegan, a professor of Developmental Psychology at Harvard University, students focus on the life cycle from a developmental perspective. They examine how people at different life stages make sense of new knowledge, obligations, and relationships. According to Dr. Kegan,

> Many Jewish adults have continued to grow psychologically beyond the Jewish selves they were as children. They have not yet had the opportunity to make sense of these old Jewish experiences through the new selves they have become. Thus, they have often thought about religion in terms of how they experienced it as a child and as something merely for children. They don't know how Judaism can be meaningful to their own lives.

The Hebrew College family educator program in Boston, which provides a certificate at the end of a two-year course of study, is one of many efforts throughout the country that help educators reconnect adults and families with their Jewish identity and thus ensure Jewish continuity.

Endnotes

1. Barbara Penzner authored the "Sh'arim Initiative" section of this article; Nancy Bloom and Marion Gribetz, the section entitled "A System for Professional Support;" Sharon Jedel and Harvey Shapiro, the section entitled "The Hebrew College Family Educator Program."

Jeffrey Schein

Jeffrey Schein received his rabbinical ordination from the Reconstructionist Rabbinical College in Philadelphia in 1977 and his doctorate in education from Temple University in 1980. Between 1971 and 1991, he was principal for three different religious schools in Philadelphia and California. Between 1991 and 1993 he developed Project Mishpacha, the Philadelphia community's initiative in Jewish family education. He is presently associate professor and director of Community Family Education programs at the Cleveland College of Jewish Studies. He also serves as National Education Director for the Jewish Reconstructionist Federation.

Cleveland: Planning and Spontaneity
Jeffrey Schein

Cleveland is a community with complex initiatives in Jewish family education (JFE), many of which come out of the "granddaddy" of continuity commissions, our Commission on Jewish Continuity (COJC). In 1988 the COJC completed a three-year study by initiating ten major new programs in the community, six of which addressed aspects of Jewish family education. Looking at such centralized planning, it might be easy to miss the insight Joe Reimer had, when surveying the field nationally, that Jewish family education is a "grass-roots phenomena...Jewish family education in Cleveland was influenced by the work of rabbis and educators who were ahead of the communal planning process in their own thinking and programming."[1]

There was JFE activity in Cleveland which predated the recommendations of the Commission on Jewish Continuity. Throughout the 1970s and early 1980s, Jewish educators had been acting on intuitions the COJC later articulated into a formal declaration of the importance of Jewish family education. For example, one congregation had done a great deal of grade-level family programming and also offered an alternative post b'nai mitzvah class where families could learn together in a ḥavurah-style home setting. Actually, then, the COJC report of 1988 built on a foundation that already existed in the community. The report articulated three broad areas of emphasis in addressing what they saw as the crisis of Jewish continuity: first, personnel development, which encompassed the recruitment, training, and retention of staff needed to maintain Jewish continuity activities; second, "beyond the classroom" opportunities that included a range of informal educational programs and activities; and third, family and parent education to enhance the effectiveness of educational experiences for children and adults.

The COJC planning process, 1986-1988, produced a set of community-wide initiatives to support existing JFE efforts and nurture new ones. COJC dramatically expanded the Congregational Enrichment Fund's resources to support growth in JFE programming and other experiences beyond the classroom. The Cleveland Fellows Program—a four-year program designed to develop fifteen master's-level Jewish educators—contained an extensive training component in family education. Further, a JFE specialist was invited to assume a clinical professorship position as part of the Cleveland Fellows Faculty of the Cleveland College of Jewish Studies. Also, the newly formed Retreat Institute, which was commissioned to foster informal retreats as part of Jewish educational programming and was to house the Jewish Community Center, made family education retreats a major part of their work. And third, Project Curriculum Renewal (PCR) of the then Bureau of Jewish Education (now Jewish Education Center of Cleveland) incorporated family models and modules in developing their new curricula for schools.

The pace of activity in JFE intensified greatly in the early 1990s. The evolving force of grass roots programs—now grown from two to eight congregations—combined with the planned COJC initiatives to create a kind of JFE greenhouse. Imagine, for instance, four summer vignettes, all prior to, and in preparation for, the consummate act of running a JFE program in the fall. First, an education director reapplies to the community Congregational Enrichment Fund, administered by the Jewish Education Center of Cleveland, for money to help her run an ambitious set of some fifteen JFE programs the following year. Second, a rabbi, an education director, a family educator (a graduate of the Cleveland Fellows Program), and a faculty member of the Cleveland College of Jewish Studies' Center for Jewish Education meet to review the revisions to the proposed next year's work of their full-time family educator. Third, faculty members from a congregation begin studying Jewish texts with a staff member from the Retreat Institute in order to generate the theme for this congregation's family retreat next November. And fourth, a congregational family educator meets with the community consultant for the Melitz Numbers Two Thousand Project to incorporate this six-week period of family study into next year's curriculum.

These are just a few of the Cleveland JFE scenarios which took place during the early- and mid-1990s. One might speculate that such diversity of activity was generated in no small measure because the Commission on Jewish Continuity had decided in 1988 that no single institution would shape JFE in Cleveland. Their centralized planning process was intended to empower a number of different agencies with responsibility for JFE. Why and how this decision came about is "over-determined." Many different forces were at work in the community, each exerting an influence that will be understood differently depending on one's own position in the community. A range of motives were undoubtedly at work.

The COJC hoped that a "thousand flowers" would bloom. They felt that the community would benefit more from a wide variety of approaches to JFE than it would from any single approach. The COJC may also have had respect for the wisdom of "good practice," and wanted to encourage actual track records in staging successful JFE programs and events. Finally, pure political "sekhel" was probably operative. The Cleveland College of Jewish Education, the Bureau of Jewish Education, and the Jewish community centers all had already laid claims to the field. Declaring one winner among these competitors might have shaken the consensus necessary to move forward with the entire scope of the community's plan for Jewish education.

The COJC 1988 decision dramatically influenced the field of Jewish family education in Cleveland. The sheer number of new initiatives proposed in JFE challenged congregational and educational leadership to sift through their priorities in integrating new programs. The professionals heading these initiatives had to learn to work together amidst ambiguity about overall communal responsibility for JFE. I remember well how one congregational professional, in the hot-house atmosphere of new initiatives, had forgotten that she had contracted with two different agencies for the same work.

With hindsight, this 1988 decision of the COJC seems to have been the right one. The field of JFE in Cleveland has prospered. A Community Task Force in JFE, convened in 1994 by the Jewish Education Center of Cleveland, was charged with the responsibility of evaluating JFE progress over the six years since the COJC report and of formulating recommendations for the continued growth of the field. Its final report of January,

1996, attributes many of the new creative opportunities and challenges that will face the community over the next decade to having been built upon the success of the "let a thousand flowers bloom" strategy. Not surprisingly, this report also urges better tending of the JFE garden and further integration of JFE resources in the community. Eight years later we can see that a rational planning model might have hindered the development of JFE in Cleveland if it had been introduced in 1988, but now some elements of rationality seem essential. What follows is a discussion of the 1994 Cleveland Community Task Force Report that also points to general issues in the national field of JFE.

The Evolved Goals of JFE—Then and Now

Because JFE is a very rapidly-developing field, the Community Task Force felt that it should reexamine the mission statement of the COJC in light of six years of local and national JFE experience. The Community Task Force studied newly-emerging frameworks and definitions of Jewish family education and wrote the 1996 mission statement. Both the 1988 and 1996 statements are presented below along with a brief analysis of how differences reflect broader developments in the field of JFE.

In 1988, Jewish family education was defined to include any program or process that strengthened the religious and spiritual character of the Jewish home; provided parents with new opportunities to develop, on an adult level, the Jewish skills and knowledge they might not have received as part of their own Jewish education; provided parents with the resources to serve as the primary transmitters of Jewish learning and celebration; and enabled parents to become partners with schools in their children's Jewish education.

In reviewing this statement, the Community Task Force saw that their reformulation of these goals required greater study of JFE at a number of different levels. They met with Dr. Ron Wolfson of the Whizin Institute to hear an updated report on current national developments in JFE. They reviewed a survey of current JFE programming in the community. Focus groups of educators, rabbis, and parents were convened. After integrating their ongoing deliberations with these new sources of information, the Community Task Force restated the 1996 goals of JFE for the Cleveland community as follows:

One of the great challenges of Jewish education is empowering the Jewish family to serve as a primary center for Jewish experience and informal facilitator of Jewish learning. Therefore, we should utilize communal educational resources to support and motivate Jewish families to lead full Jewish lives and make informed Jewish choices in their homes in order to strengthen the religious, spiritual, and cultural character of the Jewish home.

Thus, the community ought to develop creative and varied venues that will: provide parents with opportunities to expand their Jewish skills and deepen their Jewish knowledge; promote the sharing of quality Jewish time for families; increase the Jewish knowledge, identification, and commitment of parents and children as they learn together as a family; and consolidate the partnership between the home and the educating institutions in the life of the child.

The earlier and the current statements are similar to one another in emphasizing the centrality of the family to the larger process of Jewish education and the importance of strengthening the religious and spiritual character of the Jewish home. In the 1996 statement, adding the cultural to the spiritual and religious character of the home, however, was more than semantics. This definition of education represented a conscious effort of the part of the committee to align itself with the widest variety of Jewish identities within the community. The Workmen Circle's school, with its strong Yiddishist orientation, for instance, more easily moves within the orbit of the 1996 statement than the 1988 definition.

The statements differ from one another in ways that reflect the evolution of the field. In 1988, the mere existence of programs were—perhaps naively—thought to be sufficient to bring about changes in Jewish family life. In the 1996 statement, programs are more clearly conceived of as only one means to that same end. The emphasis on multiple ways in which the sum of JFE initiatives actually affects the qualities of Jewish celebration and family home life reflects the community's sense that it is ready to move to a new stage of JFE.

Programs—Then and Now

To support this emphasis on really making a difference in the home life of Jewish families, a new set of grants were created for programs providing intensive JFE experiences for smaller groups of families. These Shoresh grants for 1996-97 were competitive. Five grants, with funding of up to $5,000 for the first year, were made available. The criteria established to receive a grant were taken from the vision statement of the Community Task Force with only minor adaptations.

The Shoresh grant criteria required that institutions pay much greater attention than previously to the way in which they formulated goals for their JFE program, ascertained and addressed the needs of a particular Jewish population, and discussed how they would evaluate the programs proposed. To get a Shoresh grant institutions would need to stretch. A grant-winning JFE idea would need a strong supporting cast of educational actors.

Professional and lay leaders voiced some concern about the more stringent nature of Shoresh requirements. Would anyone apply for the Shoresh grants under such conditions? Since Cleveland had, in the past, given out educational funds based on equity rather than excellence (for example, congregational enrichment funds are allocated on the basis of the number of students in the educational program) would only a very few submit proposals for the Shoresh grants? To our surprise and delight, however, eleven grant proposals were submitted. The five awards included a program for working more intensively with the bar/bat mitzvah age population; a program for teaching Jewish sources to high-school families based on a collaboration between a Reform and Conservative congregation and the Judaic and Education faculties of the Cleveland College of Jewish studies; a proposal at a day-school to extend the Shabbat celebration of a group of families by creating a se'udah-shleesheet/havdal ḥavurah; and proposal to establish a parenting center at an Orthodox day school.

Team-Building and Goals—Then and Now

Joan Kaye discusses elsewhere in this volume the multiple points of entry into the process of family education employed by different communities. Clearly, Cleveland's initial emphasis was on two of the four "P's" of Jewish family education: programming (through the Congregational Enrichment Fund) and personnel (through the Cleveland Fellows program). The other two P's of family education—philosophy and process—received less emphasis. Our experience in Cleveland, however, teaches us that wherever you may begin, in the end all four dimensions are critical and require attention. Communities, as well as individuals, need to attend to their "shadow" or less-developed sides.

We have tried to wrestle with the underlying philosophical issues of JFE in various ways. In the spring of 1996, we engaged seven congregational teams in the process of goal charting by utilizing the publication of JESNA and the Jewish Reconstructionist Federation *Targilon: A Workbook for Charting the Course of Jewish Family Education*. In January, 1997, we have a JFE course that will unpack the underlying conceptual and valuation differences between a "grade-level" and "whole-family" approach to Jewish family education.

In Cleveland, paying better attention to process has meant devoting greater attention to building the JFE team. Understanding and planning for the JFE role of teachers, parents, and lay-leaders has been a critical point of discussion during the past seven years. We have been aided in this process by two national organizations, one Jewish and one secular. In the Jewish sphere, the connections of the Cleveland community with the Whizin Institute and University of Judaism, in Los Angeles, have provided significant opportunities for developing JFE teams. In addition, the Cleveland community hosted Dr. Joyce Epstein, the director and chief researcher of The Center for School, Family, and Community Partnerships of Johns Hopkins University. Dr. Epstein heads an international coalition of schools committed to effective school-family-community partnerships called Partnership 2000. Initially a project for the public domain, Partnership 2000 has now invited "private" schools to join the project. The centerpiece of this effort is a framework, developed through Dr. Epstein's research, that delineates six significant domains of interaction among parents, schools, and communities. Utilizing this framework requires the establishment of a team at each school or congregation. It appears that one day school, our community Hebrew school, and five of our congregations will be joining Partnership 2000.[2]

Personnel in JFE—Then and Now

The 1988 Continuity Commission had created the Cleveland Fellows Program as a way of developing fully-trained professional family educators for the community. By 1995, the Cleveland College of Jewish Studies had trained twelve individuals at a masters level. Ten were serving primarily as family educators at congregations and communal institutions. Their presence led to a welcome and anticipated increase in the number and quality of JFE programs.

The personnel needs of the community in JFE had, by 1996, become more differentiated. The community needed to bring new professionals, particularly teachers, into the field as members of the teams led by the family educators; it needed to provide continuing opportunities for reflection and skill development for those rabbis, educators, and lay leaders who play critical JFE roles in their congregations and the community; and its needed to provide our previously-trained and most "senior" (a funny word, perhaps, for a field so new) family educators with new challenges for their professional growth.

To meet these new needs, we have established family education certification programs connected to the National Board of License and the local Cleveland Board of License, a program of guest scholars to bring the most creative family educators from across the country to Cleveland, and several new networking schemes, including a video-conference hook-up between Cleveland and Milwaukee family educators.

Perhaps the most significant of these in terms of the field is the one addressed to "senior" full-time family educators in the field. Seven such family educators have been invited to participate in the Cleveland Fellows-Whizin Colloquium on research and evaluation in Jewish family education, a collaboration between the Cleveland Fellows Program and the Whizin Institute of the University of Judaism in Los Angeles, California. There is a two-year commitment on the part of seven individuals and the cooperating institutions to help participants deepen their skills as evaluators and researchers in JFE. Participants receive an honorarium for their weekly participation in the colloquium over a two-year period. The colloquium is presently engaged in a collaborative research program on parents' perceptions of the new roles suggested or demanded by the focus on family education in Jewish life. The ongoing work of the colloquium is also designed to address a newly-emerging set of questions about evaluation: How do we measure the quality of a JFE program? Can we find out whether the cumulative impact of these programs—even if individually evaluated as excellent by participants—actually makes a difference in the Jewish home life of the family?

These are questions that could hardly have been imagined more than eight years ago when the Commission on Jewish Continuity made its initial report. Then it would have been dayenu to have mustered enough resources to have put together a few decent programs. Perhaps we all ought to recite the sheheheyanu, not for having reached our ultimate goal, but rather for having moved along to a new stage in the journey of JFE in Cleveland.

Endnotes

1. Joe Reimer, "Family Education," in *What We Know About Jewish Education.* Los Angeles: 1992.

2. Information about Partnership 2000 may be obtained through the Johns Hopkins Center for School, Family, and Community Partnerships.

Carol Press Pristoop

Carol Press Pristoop has served for ten years as director of The Jack Pearlstone Institute for Living Judaism, an endowed program of THE ASSOCIATED: Jewish Community Federation of Baltimore. In this capacity, she helped found The Pearlstone Coalition for Jewish Family Education, a resource service for congregations and schools. Carol is a former director and graduate of the Baltimore Institute for Jewish Communal Service and has earned master's degrees in Modern Jewish History, English Literature, and Social Work. She is the wife of Allan and the mother of Rafi, Eli, and Rebecca.

Baltimore: How It Goes
Carol Press Pristoop

Imagine having the opportunity to design and implement a Jewish family education service delivery system entirely from scratch when money is no object. A pipe dream? Not in Baltimore. Thanks to the vision and commitment of community leaders Richard and Esther Pearlstone, under the auspices of The Jack Pearlstone Institute for Living Judaism, an endowed program of THE ASSOCIATED: Jewish Community Federation of Baltimore, the Baltimore Jewish community was able to do just that.

In 1992, in collaboration with Dr. Ron Wolfson and his outstanding cadre of consultants at the Whizin Institute for Jewish Family Life at the University of Judaism in Los Angeles, California, a select local team comprised of synagogue, Federation, agency, lay, and professional leaders carefully crafted the design of The Pearlstone Coalition for Jewish Family Education (Pearlstone Coalition). Incremental implementation began in 1992, and by 1993, the Coalition was having a positive impact on congregations, schools, and families in Baltimore. Subsequently, the Coalition has been used as a prototype for community-based interagency programs in a number of other cities around the country.

Background
Jewish family education (JFE) was first identified by educational and congregational representatives to be an area of interest during the Federation's strategic planning process of 1989. In 1990-91, special subcommittees were convened to further refine and prioritize these areas. The subcommittees requested that a new entity be created to preside over the Federation's entire Jewish educational enterprise before any of the previously-identified interest areas could be pursued. This new entity, to be called the Center for the Advancement of Jewish Education (CAJE), was

also commissioned to develop an Endowment for Jewish Education to fund any new initiatives that would emerge from the strategic planning process. It soon became apparent that the introduction of new initiatives would be a slower process than anticipated.

Fortuitously, at the same time as the Baltimore community was engaged in the establishment of funding priorities for Jewish education, Richard and Esther Pearlstone had asked the director of The Pearlstone Institute to initiate a country-wide search for a "cutting-edge" funding focus for the Institute. Established in 1987 as a "retreat center without walls," The Pearlstone Institute had been supporting a variety of projects that enriched Jewish identity through experiential, informal programs such as Israel trips and teen mitzvah projects. The Pearlstone family next wanted to concentrate their efforts in one specific program area to make a meaningful and substantial impact. After an extensive literature search, numerous conversations with key educators across the country, and an exciting meeting in the fall, 1990, with Ron Wolfson and Harlene Appelman, in consultation with Federation professional leadership, it was determined that family education met the criteria established by the Pearlstones. The decision was made to develop a comprehensive proposal for their consideration and to utilize the consultation services of the Whizin Institute in the proposal design.

The selection of family education as a funding priority at this juncture was both Federation staff and donor driven. Yet, since this programmatic area had been identified by a representative lay/professional committee as part of a community-wide and mandated strategic planning process, and since it dove-tailed with the latest educational concepts being advocated nation-wide, we felt that we had sufficient justification to proceed. Given the nature of the Federation planning process, we knew it would be two or three years before implementation could begin on the sub-committee's recommendations. In that time, funds for an endowment would have to be raised. In contrast, the Pearlstone Family viewed their money as an opportunity to take risks. If Jewish family education were to turn out to be less beneficial than everyone believed, the general community's endowment resources would not have been wasted.

At this point we faced a great challenge. How were we to develop a detailed-enough proposal to give donors a real feel for the objectives, staff, and fiscal needs of the project, while at the same time, leave enough flexibility for community institutions to feel authorship and ownership? Also, since the idea had not yet been broached with the donors, there was a real concern about raising expectations among the various institutions we hoped would be our partners. The planning for the basic design of the program was not a group endeavor. However, there was a "collaborative spirit" in that, before putting pen to paper, the Pearlstone director quietly shared the vision and the concept with several key agency executives and rabbis in the community and promised to keep them informed of developments.

A proposal was drafted by the Pearlstone director and Dr. Ron Wolfson describing a comprehensive, integrated, community approach to Jewish family education. Two key factors fueling this design were the cordial and cooperative relationships among the personnel of the Federation agencies and the amount of Pearlstone money available. The innovative features of what was to become the Pearlstone model were a comprehensive design, an interagency approach, and the placement of a family education initiative within a Federation endowment rather than with any particular agency. We hoped to promote a community-wide team of equal partners. The Federation viewed this program as an opportunity to reach out directly to congregations, thus promoting closer synagogue/Federation relationships, and as a way of making our agency personnel more accessible to the community. Basically, the proposal projected a representative entity that would provide consultation services and in-service training to area congregations and schools. This entity would also fund educational materials, financial grants to individual congregations, and community-wide family education initiatives. The acquisition of a community Jewish family educator was a central aspect of the plan design.

In the spring of 1991, Richard and Esther Pearlstone enthusiastically accepted the proposal and agreed to assume the challenge of creating and funding an entire delivery system for Jewish family education. The project was to be funded for a limited time with the understanding that, if successful, the system would be absorbed into the Federation infrastructure through the avenue created by CAJE and the new endowment.

Planning Process

Once we received the green light in the spring of 1991, we were left with just weeks to invite the agencies to be our partners in this new enterprise and to select a core group of people reflecting various aspects of what we hoped would become part of our "representative entity" to send to the second Whizin Summer Seminar in June at the University of Judaism in Los Angeles. The Whizin faculty was very excited about our idea of a community-wide approach to JFE, and they developed a community team track for their curriculum that summer.

With more time, we might have been able to mobilize an arguably more appropriate team of people, more appropriate in terms of their roles in their respective agencies and in the breadth of constituents represented. Nevertheless, this group of creative and committed people gave generously of their time and talent over the next several years to help design and implement what became The Pearlstone Coalition for Jewish Family Education.

The Pearlstone team consisted of seven people: a Jewish educator who was both a principal of an afternoon school and a staff member of the Board of Jewish Education (BJE) (later to become the Council for Jewish Education Services, CJES); a lay leader from the BJE; a staff member and a lay leader from Jewish Family Services; a congregational rabbi (representing the Board of Rabbis); a staff member from the Jewish Community Center; a staff member from Baltimore Hebrew University; and the director of The Jack Pearlstone Institute for Living Judaism.

By design, we did not meet as a group until we arrived at the Whizin Summer Seminar. It was hoped that, even though reaching this stage had been a Federation-driven process, our participation at Whizin would become a shared starting point and formative experience for the actual creation of the program. Our week at Whizin was all that we hoped it would be. We learned what comprises excellence in family education programming. We developed a blueprint for our organizational process: to create a mission statement, goals, and objectives and to go out and establish relationships with individual rabbis and education directors. We became friends who shared a dedication to the concept of Jewish family education. We went home to Baltimore all fired up.

We drafted a mission statement, articulated goals and action objectives, and then met with congregations. The Pearlstone director was the team manager. Members of the team were assigned congregations. We set out to meet with community rabbis and educators, enthusiastically armed with what we thought would be an eagerly-sought commodity. We soon lost our optimism. Typical responses to our presentation were:

Why, out of all the priorities enumerated in the Strategic Plan, did you select family education? Why not teacher health benefits?

This is another example of the Federation telling us what to do.

We're already doing family education programs, and no one comes.

We in the Orthodox community don't need family education; our families are already educated.

What do you mean? I have to have a social worker as part of a team to teach a b'nai mitzvah family program?

You're asking me as a rabbi to spend my time on a week-end retreat? What about the other family who has a bar mitzvah at the shul that Shabbat? Are they going to be happy with my absence?

Some people interpreted the language in our mission statement as arrogant, giving the impression that the Federation was "empowering" congregations and that family education was previously unknown to Baltimore. The "staff-driven" beginnings of our process came back to haunt us.

Chastened and enlightened, we processed their criticism and perspectives and went back to the drawing board. Our language became much more collaborative. The term coalition become part of our name. We also used phrases such as "the enhancement of existing programs." Our Mission Statement read:

Mission

1. To help families acquire the knowledge and skills of Jewish living and effective family functioning that will promote Jewish commitment and continuity.

2. To create a community culture that (1) recognizes the priority of Jewish family education (JFE), (2) acknowledges the necessity to view the entire family as the educable unit, and (3) is willing to commit significant time, energy and resources toward its implementation.

3. To enhance the ability of congregations, agencies and organizations in the Baltimore Jewish community to engage in Jewish family educational experiences and retreats through the provision of personnel, financial resources and effective materials.

As one of our first tasks, we compiled an inventory of current congregation JFE programs and publicized it in the educational community. We expanded our base of representation and convened an Advisory Council to validate our Mission Statement and to help develop a governing structure and operating policies.

We also realized that the educational community itself had to be exposed to the full potential of Jewish family education. We, as a Pearlstone Team, had "bought into" the Whizin concept of JFE—that "parents are not mere spectators and cheerleaders for their children, but should be engaged in serious learning." To that end, we brought Ron Wolfson to Baltimore on several occasions to conduct workshops for various congregations and agency staff. We also sent packets of new articles to rabbis and educators to heighten their awareness of the issues involved in JFE. And there were plenty to send. Coincidentally, in the fall of 1991, just after we had made our first disappointing round of visits to the congregations, the General Assembly of the Council of Jewish Federations (GA) took place in Baltimore. It was at this time that the alarming statistics on intermarriage were widely publicized, and a session was offered there entitled "Will Your Grandchildren Be Jewish?" The Pearlstone Institute sponsored David Hartman as the keynote speaker for the GA. In an electrifying moment, before he began his final speech to the Assembly, he said,

> The dominant buzz these last few days have been about the gloomy statistics and the question of Jewish grandchildren. I say to you, don't worry about your children and grandchildren, worry about yourselves. Are you leading the kind of lives that model Jewish behavior and precepts? Only that will save your children and grandchildren.

After the GA in Baltimore, Jewish family education became an easier "sell." To demonstrate its value, we selected a few congregations for pilot programs and began to implement them at once. The Pearlstone Institute director still assumed the major staffing for their formative efforts, but individual pilot programs were under the leadership of the interagency team and direct service staff they assigned to the projects. A search committee began the process of hiring a community Jewish family educator.

In all, we spent eighteen months, much longer than we had anticipated, in our "start-up" experience of gaining community support, team-building, assessment, experimentation, and the employment and placement of a Jewish family educator on the CJES staff. We ended calendar year 1992 with a Baltimore Whizin Conference. Nine members of the Whizin consulting team were in Baltimore for an intensive one and one-half days of workshops and congregational consultations. Over 120 rabbis, principals, lay leaders, and agency staff members participated. At that conference the grant applications and guidelines were distributed to the congregations. Finally, full-scale Jewish family education had begun.

In fiscal years 1993, 1994, 1995, and 1996, The Pearlstone Coalition for Jewish Family Education delivered services in the following areas: (1) consultative services to congregations; (2) in-service training for educators; (3) JFE program grants and subsidies; (4) community-wide family education initiatives; (5) the creation and provision of *The Alef Branch*, a family magazine supplement appearing quarterly in the *Baltimore Jewish Times*; and (6) an expansion of the JFE resource material collection at the CJES Resource Center.

Evaluation Process

Since the program is multi-faceted, we organized evaluation procedures on several levels. The Coalition Advisory Board, representing the various constituencies, participated in a self-study process after the first year of operation and suggested changes in its own composition and structure. The grant selection criteria and process was also revised with input from the community. Evaluation instruments were administered to participants of all the community-wide programs. Community educators completed annual questionnaires regarding *The Alef Branch* and a questionnaire was included in one issue to gauge reader satisfaction. The congregational grants process is closely monitored and evaluated. Submission of three separate process instruments are required from grant recipients during the year they receive a grant. Besides delineating their planning and implementation steps, these instruments ask for direct feedback from participants and teachers. Now that many congregations have from three to five years of experience with a given program, we are using a grant from the Crane Foundation to do comprehensive evaluations of the delivery system and individual programs and a longitudinal study of select families.

The Future

Nineteen-ninety-six represented the last year of a firm commitment by The Pearlstone Coalition to Jewish family education. From its inception, the Pearlstone family made clear that its intention was to turn over to the Federation the funding and operation of the Coalition so that the family could begin the next phase of their philanthropic strategy—the construction of a conference center for family education retreats. As part of its own strategic plan, the Federation made a commitment to establish an Endowment for Jewish Education with the Coalition, presumably funded from that source. Unfortunately, the endowment was not yet in a position to begin funding any projects. As the 1997 budgeting season began, and community educators realized that The Pearlstone Coalition was in jeopardy, the religious school principals sent a petition to the Council of Jewish Educational Services (CJES) with copies to the Federation president, to express their support for its continuation. The principals stressed the importance of JFE programming in their schools and congregations and identified the grants and counsel of The Pearlstone Coalition as being the major factors for their success. They indicated that their congregational leadership had come to value JFE programs and that they were ready to allocate funds to them. The loss of the grants were not the complaint; the principals were most concerned that the community Jewish family educator position continue at CJES. They considered the consultation, support, and resources provided by the staff people to be essential and invaluable to them. The Pearlstone family agreed to continue funding for the educator position and some of the community-wide programs. The Blaustein Foundation and the Crane Foundation picked up minor program pieces as well. For 1997, the entire program remained intact although without congregational grants.

As the 1998 budgeting season approached, JFE was reaffirmed as a top priority by the Federation's educational planning entity, the Center for Advancement of Jewish Education (CAJE). They recommended the JFE initiative to a newly-established Federation Priority Review process that, it is hoped, will result in the establishment of JFE program funds in the base budgets of appropriate agencies.

Observations

Our experience in Baltimore reflects a significant dilemma at the forefront of communal resource development in the North American Jewish community. As generic campaign dollars become scarce, Federations look to special interest donors and endowments for partners in the provision of essential services. In one respect, as we have demonstrated, this is wonderful. Through partnership with an endowment willing to experiment and risk money in a start-up phase, we were able to test and fine-tune our delivery system. Now the community can assume responsibility for the JFE program at the peak of its productivity. From another perspective, however, as we have also experienced, partnerships with endowments can pose challenges. Endowments often have stipulations and restrictions and cannot or do not want to be permanent funders.

During the 1990s, Jewish "continuity" has jumped to the top of our national communal agenda. The identification of JFE as a powerful entry point and foundational component of the Jewish continuity effort is also finally accepted. But the majority of these programs are supported by the "soft money" of interested donors. All of our federations must begin the difficult process of re-prioritizing, consolidating, and shifting allocations of resources from the base budgets of affiliated agencies to synagogue and home settings, where the most effective family learning can take place. This is a problematic paradigm: agencies have public accountability and unrestricted access; synagogues have closed books and denominationally restricted memberships. Yet this is a vital issue with which all of our communities must grapple. As the Pearlstone model in Baltimore has demonstrated, the results can be rewarding. Our collaborative effort has enhanced synagogue/federation relationships and provided new opportunities for synagogues and synagogue families to interact on a city-wide level. It has been a true community-building experience.

In Baltimore, we have focused on families affiliated with congregations. Our project preference has been for programs integrated into the classroom curriculum and spaced throughout the academic year. We have not funded one-shot holiday extravaganzas. The reason for this emphasis is two-fold. When we suggested "out-reach to the unaffiliated" during our start-up phase, the community rabbis noted that, from their perspective, their concern was in-reach. Secondly, we are committed to the institution of the synagogue. We firmly believe that Jewish identity has to be nourished by its spiritual institutions. The institution of the synagogue is uniquely suited to support the various components that contribute to identity; religious, spiritual, educational, social, and service. School-based JFE programs provide a sense of relatedness and reinforcement. They complete the picture: You are not just Jewish in a Hebrew school, you are not just Jewish in the synagogue, you are not just Jewish at the family seder, but you are Jewish all the time—in these settings as well as in your own home and in your daily public life.

Having stated all of the above, however, we know that the warm and fuzzy holiday-focused, experiential programs that occur in shopping malls or the JCC's are unbeatable as a tool for out-reach to marginal Jews. And so, we urge outreach to the unaffiliated. If American Jews can spend millions of dollars in the Soviet Union to resuscitate that community, why can't we spend communal dollars on lapsed Jews in the United States? The other branches of Judaism should take a leaf from the Orthodox *Keruv* movement and begin creating its own non-threatening situations that encourage estranged Jews to re-enter the mainstream. If synagogue membership and its conventions are off-putting, the congregations and their denominational leaders may have to find small satellite settings—home-based or storefront—in which to locate programs that will slowly spark involvement. We have to meet people where they are in order to help rekindle their Judaism. In many communities, some rabbis may warily view Jewish community centers and family service agencies as less-costly substitutes for synagogue-affiliation, rather than as conduits to congregational membership. We have to work on overcoming the tensions that surround this issue.

Rabbinic involvement is key to any JFE endeavor. Not only must the rabbi be supportive in general and be an active proponent in board proceedings which allocate funds to synagogue priorities, but the rabbi has to be actively involved in and visible during the implementation of the program. The ultimate factor in reinforcing Jewish identity is the positive feeling derived by being connected to a people and a community. For many people, the rabbi symbolizes Judaism. It is very important for them that the rabbi know who they are and applaud their involvement in Jewish family education programs. We have heard so often from family educators, as well as from active parents, that no one knows or appreciates the wonderful things they are doing and the impact the programs are having. If the rabbi does not value JFE, can it really be of value?

Some useful concepts to remember in navigating the politics and turf-consciousness of the Jewish communal world: (1) always have a classic primer on community organization at hand; (2) do not skimp on doing the basic ground-work of establishing a common starting point; (3) establish channels of communication early and use them frequently; (4) allow plenty of start-up time—institutional inertia is not a myth, and change most often happens in minute increments; (5) be sensitive, responsive, and thick-skinned at the same time; (6) generate excitement in the face of ambivalence—pilot a program in one congregation, then after it is a success, everyone will want to come aboard.

Closing

In a time of growing assimilation and shrinking financial resources, The Pearlstone Coalition developed a comprehensive model that effectively delivers Jewish family education to a variety of synagogue settings. This model successfully minimized the degree of service duplication in Federation agencies, while maximizing the use and accessibility to agency professionals by community congregations and their membership.

The promotion of JFE as an essential component of life-long affiliation to Judaism by The Pearlstone Coalition has had a profound impact on our community. Beth El, one of the largest Conservative congregations, restructured and rewrote its religious school curriculum and currently provides a special JFE track. Many other congregations designated specific staff members as family educators. Coalition projects have been accorded enthusiastic and grateful reception on the part of educators, students, and especially parents. Congregations value the encouragement, expertise, and funding. They view the process as an example of positive synagogue/Federation relations. Community-wide events and *The Alef Branch* have provided a feeling of unity and cohesiveness for our diverse Baltimore Jewish population. Whatever the immediate future for the status of the Coalition, the concept and the commitment to JFE as an essential vehicle for Jewish continuity has been universally accepted by the Baltimore Jewish community.

Cecile Jordon

C*ecile Jordan received her Ed.D. from the University of Houston in Educational Administration and Supervision in 1986. Cecile has an M.A. from New York University in Jewish Education and an M.A. from the University of Bridgeport in Elementary Education. Her B.A. degree in Social Studies is from Case Western Reserve University. Certified to teach grades K-12, Cecile has also been a principal of a supplementary school and a day school. She has been executive director of the Agency for Jewish Education in San Diego, California, since 1986.*

San Diego: Collaboration, Outreach, Inreach
Cecile Jordan

Overview

In 1991, when the Agency for Jewish Education (AJE), San Diego, California, began its strategic planning process, Jewish family education (JFE) was already a concept in the minds of many of us. As the Planning Committee sifted though various ideas about future directions, it became clear that we needed more understanding of what comprised Jewish family education. A year later, as the goals and objectives for our strategic plan were being finalized, we decided that Jewish family education was one area in which the AJE would take a lead position. Now, family education has become a buzz-word throughout the San Diego Jewish community. It stands for interactive, exciting, multi-generational Jewish educational programs. More than 300 educators have been trained in Jewish family education and over 5,000 families have participated in at least one family education program with approximately 4,100 participating in several.

The staff of the AJE in San Diego consists of a full time executive director, a full time high school principal and three part-time professionals, including a director of family education. As the executive director, I was the lead staff person for the Strategic Planning Process and for the Jewish Family Education Project until it received sufficient funds to pay its own director. In this chapter, I will describe what has happened in family education in San Diego County over the course of the previous five years and what we have learned from our experiences.

Background

San Diego has a burgeoning Jewish community of approximately 70,000 Jews with nineteen synagogues (four Reform, three Orthodox, one Reconstructionist, five Conservative and six Chabad), four day schools, sixteen preschools, two Jewish Community Centers, a Hebrew

Home for the Aged, Jewish Family Service branch offices in multiple locations, a Hillel Foundation at each of the two major universities, a Jewish Federation and an Agency for Jewish Education. (AJE) The AJE, which serves the entire Jewish population, is located within twenty minutes of any Jewish building and a block away from the Federation.

More than 4,200 children in San Diego receive some Jewish education each year. They are taught by approximately 350 educators. Seven hundred thirty-two children are in pre-schools, 980 students attend day schools, 2,340 take part in supplementary school classes and 248 participate in the High School of Jewish Studies, a community supplementary school administered by the AJE for affiliated and unaffiliated students.

San Diego began its formal commitment to Jewish family education in 1992 while the AJE was engaging in its strategic planning process. During the previous year, as we conducted focus groups of teachers, principals, parents, heads of agencies, Federation lay and professional leaders, and rabbis, family education had been mentioned frequently. People wanted the AJE to help them learn more about family education.

After doing a telephone survey to ascertain what others around the country were doing, the Strategic Planning Steering Committee decided that family education should become one of our six priority areas as we prepared to enter the twenty-first century. The other areas were: (1) educational planning; (2) improved public relations, publicity, and increased fund raising; (3) expanded use of our Teachers Center, Media Center, and Library; (4) expanded professional services for educators; and (5) a more diversified curriculum at the community High School of Jewish Studies.

As we look back on our last five years, we realize that family education programming has helped us achieve the other goals. In addition to leading the San Diego Jewish community into family education, we are now both a resource for and a provider of family education programs. Family education programming has caused the AJE professional staff to become more aware and savvy about publicity, marketing, and public relations. Educators in schools working on family education programs use our professional and physical resources even more than previously. We are often invited to JCC and Federation events to provide the family education component. Sometimes at these events, we do an entire outreach program—one year we set up ten different stations to teach about the fall holidays, another year we provided programs to teach about Shabbat.

Planning to Plan

Based on what we had read, seen, and learned from our own and other communities, AJE believed that family education could link the generations and was, perhaps, the key to keeping families Jewish. It became a top priority for us and prompted us to learn how to create partnerships for family education projects.

Partnerships were entirely new to us. During the winter of 1992, we invited Dr. Ron Wolfson, the director of the Whizin Institute, to speak with significant leaders in the San Diego community. Lay people and professionals from Federation, JFS, JCC, day and supplementary schools, synagogues, and the Jewish Community Foundation were all impressed by the possibilities that family education programming might provide.

Ron suggested we bring a team to the 1992 Whizin Summer Seminar on family education "to scout out the land." Three people attended—myself from the AJE, a school principal who was also president of the Principals Council, and a member of the Russian émigré community. These three became part of an expanded team that met the following year to think about strategic directions for Jewish family education.

After the 1992 Whizin Summer Seminar, we talked informally with principals, parents, lay leaders, and national leaders in the field and framed the following objectives for our Jewish family education initiative: (1) to teach teachers and principals new methods that they could use in their schools and synagogues; (2) to provide Jewish family education school consultations; and (3) to establish a Jewish Family Education Program Bank at the AJE which the entire community could use.

Financing such a project was a little scary, but we jumped in feet-first in our search for partners and invited other agencies and schools to join with us. And they did. This was how we came to learn how a multi-disciplinary team could have a far greater impact on the community than an educators-only team. And we also learned that decision making becomes more complicated when multiple agencies and priorities are involved.

Mobilizing for Action

We wrote a grant to the Jewish Community Foundation of our United Jewish Federation and requested financial support to enable us to send a very large team to the 1993 Whizin Summer Seminar. Our very supportive Foundation granted us $10,000. We invited day schools, synagogue schools, pre-schools, the two JCC's, and the JFS to join the team and attend the 1993 Whizin Summer Seminar. We offered to pay for one person from each location and suggested that schools and agencies send another person or a site team to be part of this large San Diego Whizin group. We also took the principal of the High School of Jewish Studies, one member of the émigré community, two teachers who were to teach a family education program to the émigré community, the AJE Staff member who was to be our Family Education director, the president and executive director of the AJE, and the director of the Continuity Task Force of the United Jewish Federation. Twenty-six people went, representing four agencies, two pre-schools, seven supplementary congregational schools, and two synagogues. We were teachers, principals, social workers, lay people, rabbis, and émigrés from the former Soviet Union.

We assembled our coalition and decided that, since the purpose of our family education project was to encourage and teach families how to make their own Jewish memories, we would call what we were doing Making Jewish Memories (MJM). We developed a logo and ordered T-shirts for everyone. We selected community JFE chairpersons. Yet, in a way, our project at this stage was like the emperor's new clothes—we had obtained the money to bring our team to Whizin, but we did not yet have funding for a program and a director. What were we to do?

We did two things. We applied to the Continuity Task Force of the United Jewish Federation for funding for our JFE program, and we invited the Federation's Continuity Task Force to join our Jewish Family Education Coalition. Since the Continuity Task Force was charged with developing and funding programs to provide connections to the Jewish community for Jews who were barely or not yet connected, AJE proposed that we provide family education outreach programs to both unaffiliated and affiliated members. We would also provide family education newsletters, *The Parent Connection*, for families, and *Making Jewish Memories*, for educators. In addition AJE would develop a JFE Program Bank for the entire community. All of these would be continuity projects run by the AJE. The twenty-six people on the Whizin Team would design and staff the MJM outreach programs for the first two years.

Our bargain changed our original design for family education. We had first planned to learn how to do family education ourselves and then help those in the community we could interest in family education use it in their own settings. Our new partnership meant that, although we would still be helping members of the community do their own JFE programs, the AJE was going to be putting primary emphasis on using family education as an outreach tool for the community.

Team-Building

The grants AJE received from the Jewish Community Foundation of the United Jewish Federation and from the Continuity Task Force of the United Jewish Federation encouraged us to learn to work as a team because one stipulation of the grants was that there be lay chairpersons for the team. Over the next two years, AJE struggled to balance the needs and priorities of multiple schools, synagogues, and agencies with the wishes of our funders. We learned about creating consensus, how difficult it is to get volunteers, and how impossible it is to work without them.

Although we had had one group meeting before we went to Whizin, we had not established sufficient clarity of purpose to allow us to reach decisions later that were well accepted by everyone. There were times when the Making Jewish Memories team thought it had made a good decision—but within a day discovered that genuine differences still remained, and we had to come back to the table and renegotiate.

During the first year, we grappled non-stop with creating meeting, personal, and communal agendas. The support from the Jewish Community Foundation of $10,000 and from the Continuity Task Force of $28,000 made our visions a reality. The clout of the newly formed Continuity Task Force helped us market Jewish family education. Jewish family education was about to become reality in San Diego County.

Each individual who attended Whizin as a member of our community team signed a document which committed them to participate in community family education planning and programming for the following two years and to work on at least two community family education programs during that time. We knew that our initial programs were too ambitious to undertake without a large group of committed individuals willing to devote ideas, time, and lots of hard work.

The entire twenty-six-member Whizin team met several times during our initial two years to help plan and execute all the MJM outreach programs. These meetings gave team members the opportunity to develop new ideas together. Participants were also able to talk about how they were using the knowledge and skills learned at Whizin in their own work. Our expectation was that such team activities would sustain an ongoing dialogue about family education. They have. Some participants now lead family education programs in their own school or synagogue settings. Others helped with community outreach programs for several years.

The 1993 Whizin Summer Seminar
We proudly wore our Making Jewish Memories T-shirts to dinner the first night at Whizin. Our motto, "Our community is too heavy for any one individual to carry alone." (Deuteronomy Rabba 1:10), was on the back. We listed the organizations that had already funded the MJM community team because we knew that our goals for family education could only be carried out if there was even more widespread support in the community. Our quote and the shirts were not merely for community spirit. Without obtaining the financial support of the Whizin Institute, the Jewish Community Foundation of the United Jewish Federation, the Continuity Task Force of the United Jewish Federation, the Agency for Jewish Education, and the Émigré Task Force of the United Jewish Federation, the Agency for Jewish Education would not have been able to begin this very ambitious, wide reaching community project.

Jewish Family Education Programs, Year by Year
Upon our return from Whizin in July, 1993, and after additional consultation with Whizin faculty and others, members of the MJM team and the AJE began piloting two different outreach programs. The MJM outreach programs were administered by AJE for the Continuity Task Force of the UJF. The MJM outreach programs for émigré families were administered by the AJE for the Émigré Task Force of the United Jewish Federation. In addition, we wrote our *Making Jewish Memories* newsletter for educators. By June 1994, each of the Making Jewish Memories programs was up and running. The émigré MJM program had seventy individuals attending every other Sunday afternoon. The other MJM outreach programs were off to a somewhat slower start; only two programs had taken place—and four had been approved by the committee for the following year. The Continuity Task Force also invited the AJE to pilot a Pathways to Judaism program, a family education program for interfaith unaffiliated families, for the next year.

By June 1995, AJE had done two years of MJM programs for émigrés, four MJM outreach programs for the general community, four newsletters for educators, one newsletter for parents, and one year's worth of weekly Pathways to Judaism (PTJ), a family education program for thirty unaffiliated, interfaith families. By September 1995, the community MJM planning team had finished their two-year commitment and were using the skills they had acquired in their own schools, synagogues, and centers. By June 1996, AJE had run Pathways to Judaism for two years, published six family education newsletters for educators, six for parents, produced twenty-one programs for the community, developed the Family Education Program Bank, taught the MJM Émigré Outreach program for three years, and was invited to do JCC and Federation programs on a regular basis.

Family Education for Outreach to Unaffiliated Families

AJE has direct responsibility for three major family education outreach programs: Pathways to Judaism, MJM for Émigrés, and MJM Outreach to the Unaffiliated. During the first two years, our community-wide Jewish Earth Day gala attracted over five hundred people, most of whom were affiliated with a synagogue. During our first four years, our More Than Matza Passover programs, which were held simultaneously at three synagogues, attracted forty-one percent unaffiliated families and thirty-four percent intermarried families. The remaining twenty-five percent of the families were affiliated with synagogues. Our fall holiday program, Apples and Honey and Much, Much More, attracted a similarly non-affiliated and intermarried group. We also tried out FIRST (Families Interested in Reading Stories Together), a family reading program for Jewish holidays. We learned that even though we advertised for unaffiliated people, a good program attracts affiliated people as well.

We began the FIRST program because we wanted to see where ongoing contact with families with children between three and eight years of age might lead. The goal was to bring small groups of families together to learn about the holidays through story telling, craft projects, and, of course, food. Eighty percent of the participants were not affiliated with synagogues. We discontinued the program after one year because our Continuity Task Force wanted us to focus on large-group outreach.

In the second year of Making Jewish Memories we began Chailights, a summer reading program; its aim was to encourage unaffiliated families to borrow and read Jewish books. Although people could read any Jewish book they wanted, many of the books borrowed from the AJE library were part of The Parent Connection, a family education project in which each book also contains discussion cards to stimulate family interaction. Chailights also had four story hours so that families could meet and talk with each other and so that AJE could stay connected with these families and be able to give them information about the availability of seats for the High Holidays and general information about the Jewish community.

During our third year, we organized two additional MJM outreach programs. To celebrate the 3,000th anniversary of the City of David, a Jerusalem A-Fair was organized at the Jewish Community Center. One hundred forty-five people, fifty-one families, mostly affiliated, attended and learned about archaeology, Hezekiah's Tunnel, the meaning of a hamsa, and the eight gates of the city of Jerusalem. As they learned about the place of the Western Wall in our tradition, participants could send faxes to the Kotel. Our other new program, Jonah and the Whale and other Jewish Tails, was held at our local aquarium. This program taught about kashrut and attracted mostly affiliated families.

Next, we tried out a program for teens and their families. We piloted the Jewish Civics Initiative Course (JCI) with a small group of families of tenth and eleventh graders. This course was to have eight meetings during the year for the families. Then the teens were to participate in a JCI trip to Washington. Upon their return, the teens were to perform thirty hours of volunteer work in agencies with their goal "to help repair the world." We spent a lot of money on publicity but did not recruit a sufficient number of families to make this family education program viable.

Now, three years later, we are beginning to see some trends and draw some tentative conclusions about family education outreach programs.

1. We think that non-holiday programs attract families who are already members of synagogues because these families look for new and varied Jewish family experiences. On the other hand, unaffiliated families may not know what to make of a program called Jewish Earth Day, a Jerusalem A-Fair, or Jonah and the Whale and Other Jewish Tails. Titles like these may not "speak to them" as clearly as do holiday programs.

Our Jewish Baby Fair, presented during the fourth year of MJM programs, probed this further. One hundred individuals participated in the fair and attended the eight Jewish content and parenting workshops. Since more affiliated than unaffiliated families attended, our thesis that affiliated families look for new and varied Jewish family experiences tended to be supported. Perhaps the unaffiliated may not know enough, or care enough, to attend a program which is not holiday based.

Nevertheless, since our plans and our advertising for the Jewish Baby Fair included a lot of education on health related issues, we thought we would draw the unaffiliated in larger numbers. It is interesting to note that half of the unaffiliated families who attended the Baby Fair were interfaith families.

The Jewish Baby Fair was our first attempt at having a corporate sponsor defray some of the costs of the booths and vendors providing information about babies and young families.

2. We also need to probe the question of site location. Most of our programs took place at Jewish sites. We had originally supposed that using a non-Jewish site might be less threatening to the unaffiliated and therefore would attract more unaffiliated families. Jonah and the Whale and Other Jewish Tails was a story telling/singing/and general Jewish information program that took place at the Aquarium. Most of those who attended were affiliated with synagogues. Since our publicity was widespread, we think we may have been incorrect in assuming that a secular site would attract the unaffiliated to MJM programs. Jonah, at the aquarium, seemed to appeal mostly to the affiliated.

3. We learned that we may not yet know how to market effectively to teens and their families based on our experience with the JCI family education program. Had we received many inquiries and few enrollees, we would have assumed that we knew how to market, but that our product was not appealing. We received few inquiries, however, and since this program was popular and successful in our high school, either it is not a great program for families or we do not know how to market to families of teens.

4. We have been reinforced in our conjecture that families will not pay a lot of money for MJM programs. We charged about $3.00 per adult and $2.00 per child for each program. For a

family with three children this is about $12.00 for a two hour program. Since families told us that they would not pay much more than this, we never tried charging more.

5. We also learned how difficult it is to collect evaluations after outreach programs such as these. Picture, if you will, a family leaving our More Than Matza program. In their hands the parents have at least one tired child, a seder plate they have crafted, the charoset they have made, a matza cover they designed, and several copies of the Hagaddah used for our model seder. If they agree to our request to fill out, in legible handwriting, the evaluation form, we have to hold not only the children, but also the artifacts. And what if six families are leaving at the exact same time? This is highly staff/volunteer intensive, and we have never had adequate people for this part of the project. We considered adding $3.00 to the cost of each family's admission and returning it to families who legibly completed the evaluation form. But we did not try it because we wanted to defray the cost of the program. Were the program to be run again, we should probably budget evaluation costs and use the method suggested here.

Family Education for Unaffiliated Interfaith Families

AJE has provided Pathways to Judaism classes to interfaith, unaffiliated families for three years. About thirty families attend a two-hour class every week during the school year. There are separate classes for children and for adults and a monthly family event. During the year there are also Shabbat dinners and other special programs. The mid-year and final evaluations from this program have been outstanding, and we have found that many participants are making Jewish choices for their families as a result of this family education program. Forty-five percent of the families from the first two years joined synagogues, one child was enrolled in a day school, several families are seriously "synagogue shopping," and one father is enrolled in a conversion class. After the year-long program, interested families usually form a havurah, staffed by the PTJ director, to maintain their friendships and their connections to the Jewish community. Fifty percent of the families usually join the havurah.

We find the Pathways participants by placing ads in the local secular press. The marketing budget for this program is $5,000 and families pay approximately $95.00 per person to participate in it. During each of our first three years, more than two hundred individuals called for information about the program.

We have learned the following from our PTJ programs:

1. It is exceedingly important to listen to participants. We hand out formal written evaluations twice a year but we also talk a lot, one-on-one, to current and former students. One discussion taught us that we should provide some unstructured time each week for participants to visit together or ask questions. The adult program now lasts an additional thirty minutes after the two-hour formal teaching class ends. That way participants have time to get to know each other and to talk informally about whatever is on their mind. Another discussion made us realize we should have past participants on our PTJ committee. We now do!

2. One discussion with participants led us to revamp the preschool portion of the PTJ program. We now provide music, art, and story telling for the two to four year olds instead of just baby sitting. The children hear holiday stories, do holiday crafts, and learn holiday songs.

Family Education for New Émigrés

The Émigré MJM program had a record attendance of seventy people at each class during the first two years. During that time, San Diego had a large influx of émigrés each year. Families met together every second Sunday afternoon for a year to learn about and experience Jewish holidays, holy days, and Jewish history and culture. They loved Israeli dancing, made many elegant ritual objects for use in their homes, acted out Purim plays, and attended Shabbat dinners together. As part of Shabbat study, the participants took home an audio cassette of Shabbat prayers and blessings and a laminated place mat of Shabbat prayers and songs in Hebrew with Russian transliteration. At the end of the program, each family also took home a Making Jewish Memories family photo album so they had a record of the Jewish memories they had made together. Assessments from the first and second years of this program were superb. We learned a great deal from doing this program.

1. We learned to involve our Russian community in all of our planning and all of our teaching. And we learned to ask a lot of

questions from those in other communities who had experience with programming for new émigrés.

2. We learned that our original decision to take new émigrés, and others who would be teaching the émigrés, with us to the Whizin Summer Institute and to include them in all of our discussion and planning was a sound and helpful decision. One of the new émigrés still helps with the weekly teaching and serves as the Russian secretary for the program.

3. We learned that our method of teacher selection was great. We would recommend it to others. We invited a teacher who knew some Russian to be our lead teacher and paired her with a member of the Russian community for informal Russian lessons during the summer before our program began. Our émigré teacher was likewise paired with a knowledgeable Jewish teacher and tutored on Judaism during the summer before we began our program. Both these individuals are still teaching in the program.

4. We learned to adjust our program according to need and finances. As emigration to San Diego declined, MJM attendance declined as well. In its third year, the MJM program only had thirty people at each bi-weekly session. Due to inadequate funding during the fourth year (1996/97), the MJM program had only eight sessions. Still, the monthly classes were very well attended by sixty to seventy percent of the new émigré families.

Family Education Inreach: Support for Jewish Institutions

Our AJE goal, to make family education a community reality, took hold. Our Family Education director (who was fondly known as "Marcia from Making Jewish Memories") maintained a bank of family education programs, newsletters, and other information. She worked with and advised synagogue educators planning family education programs. AJE published a family education newsletter, *Making Jewish Memories*, for educators, three times a year, so that educators could share their programs and ideas.

AJE also published *The Parent Page*, a family education newsletter for families, three times a year. Beginning with the 1996/97 school year, synagogue schools agreed to become our partners in distribution. AJE produced *The Parent Page*. Synagogue schools made copies and distributed it to all their families.

After the first two years, MJM was funded by the UJF as a Continuity spin-off program. Although we did not need approval from the Continuity Task Force to do our programs, each fall we consulted with the director and the chairperson of the Continuity Task Force about our ideas and tried to obtain "buy in."

Impact of Family Education

Since beginning our family education programming, we have all learned a great deal. Although the JFE outreach programs did not continue to be funded by the United Jewish Federation after the first four years, Jewish family education is permanently in place in San Diego. Every synagogue and school is working on Jewish family education programs either as part of their regular curriculum or as special additional programs. Teachers and principals use AJE resources for family education on a regular basis.

Our day schools and synagogue schools are growing increasingly interested in JFE. AJE hosted one day of training by the Whizin staff for two-hundred-fifty school staff members. Two day schools received Family Education Grants (Avi Chai Foundation and Torah u'Mesorah). One day school has engaged a family education coordinator and JFE programs are a regular part of the school. Another day school has increased its parent education programs several fold. One synagogue school received a grant from a congregant to do family education programs at all grade levels. Two more synagogues have ongoing family programs for holidays and for special topics in their regular supplementary school curriculum. Several synagogue bulletins have monthly family education columns.

AJE expects the number of JFE programs to increase each year. Although most of our AJE outreach programs were "one shot" events, our experience with the FIRST Program, the Émigré Program, the Chailights Reading Program and the Pathways to Judaism Program has led us to believe that unaffiliated Jewish families might commit to "mini" courses on popular Jewish themes. Since we were unable to obtain funding to provide Jewish family education mini courses to the community, we did not have the opportunity to test this hypothesis.

We understood that every project we worked on would not come to fruition, and we managed to learn throughout the process. For example, the AJE director of Family Education spent six months working with several principals who were considering piloting a family education strand in their Sunday schools to replace regular classes for some children. After months of planning and researching, the principals decided not to try the new program, but everyone learned from the time and research that went into the planning. And the materials remain in our program bank.

We found out that it is very useful to run good ideas past people outside our own agency. They bring a fresh perspective; outsiders can bring up issues agency staff might not have ever considered or encountered. At the same time, we became aware that it is far more difficult to work with a group of individuals who have different mind sets than it is to work with a group of like-minded individuals. Interagency cooperation is easier said than done, especially if not all agencies are created equal. During the first two years of our program, our community team was often unsure about whether the team or the funder was to make the final decision. For example, who decides if a family education program should be done? The interagency group? The agency who runs the program? The funding agency? Who decides if a family education program is worthwhile and if it will be continued? These issues not only concern substance but also concern the process of decision making.

AJE was accustomed to working with schools and synagogues, with principals and rabbis, and with the Federation. But working with professionals from many other agencies, and all at the same time, was somehow different. During our first two years our group spent a lot of time clarifying feelings and testing the waters. Eventually we learned how to plan programs together.

Our Whizin experiences gave us entree to professionals with expertise in teaching and evaluating Jewish family education, and we learned to enlist the advice of those outside of our community for ideas and support. The Whizin consultants taught us the principles, theory, and content of Jewish family education programming and also about the use of consensus techniques when working with a large community group. Whizin also helped us connect with Jewish family educators all over the United States.

We still struggle with the concept of using Jewish family education programs as a vehicle for outreach to unaffiliated families. We see how successful such programming is within the context of our synagogues and schools. And we realize the great potential of such programs as a vehicle for outreach. But the outreach issue has an additional marketing overlay, and this is complicated. For example, when one plans a synagogue program, after checking the synagogue calendar and perhaps the community calendar, all that remains is to plan carefully and publicize the event. If you have a record of good programs, your families will come. Determining how much content should be taught versus how much time should be spent in getting to know other participants is always a difficult balance to decide. And almost no one registers in advance, so planning is very difficult.

It seems impossible to do sufficient marketing no matter how large the marketing budget. We have had a budget of $5,000 for marketing each year since the program began. During the third year, when we piloted the program for families of teens, we had to add $1,000 to the marketing budget. And in the fourth year we tried using a corporate sponsor to help stretch the marketing budget even further. One item regarding marketing is very clear: in the four years since MJM began outreach programs, advertising rates have increased. Therefore if our marketing budget did not increase each year (which it did not), we had to do less marketing or less programming and spend more funds on marketing. This was a dilemma we should have been able to solve, but could not.

Another big challenge for MJM outreach programming was funding. Once the program passed its two years as a Continuity Pilot Program, it was given to the AJE to run. But the allocation was a "special one," and we never knew until June each year if MJM was funded for the coming year. What would have been very helpful would have been to receive a five-year commitment for the MJM outreach program, so that a schedule of programs could be planned for the future.

When we began the MJM outreach program the Continuity Task Force and the AJE hoped that we would be able to find individual donors to fund each program. We envisioned the *Schwartz* More than Matza Program and the *Cohen* Apples and Honey Celebration. This type of long range funding could have insured the continuation of MJM outreach programs.

All these remain challenges for the AJE and the UJF. Nevertheless, the time, funds, and energy that AJE and the UJF have invested to bring Jewish family education to San Diego has been very well spent. Thousands of families have had the opportunity to participate in Jewish family education programs, making Jewish memories for adults and children together.

Sandy Waldman Dashefsky

Sandy Waldman Dashefsky is assistant executive director of the Commission on Jewish Education of the Jewish Federation of Greater Hartford and is an instructor at Hebrew College, Hartford Branch. She is also staff consultant to the Federation's Council on Jewish Continuity. Sandy has co-authored many articles and has been a consultant to many organizations and a presenter at national and local conferences. Presently, she is studying for her doctorate in Educational Leadership.

Hartford: Collaborative Endeavors
Sandy Waldman Dashefsky

A community is too heavy for anyone to carry alone.
Midrash Rabbah Deuteronomy

The Greater Hartford Jewish Community: An Old New Community

The Greater Hartford Jewish community is a long-established, traditional community that has undergone substantial geographic expansion in the past generation. Estimates are that in the 1930s the Jewish population in the city of Hartford was fifteen to twenty percent of the total population, making it one of the most densely populated Jewish cities in the United States at that time. By 1982, the *Greater Hartford Jewish Population Study* (Abrahamson 1982) indicated that the Jewish population had remained fairly stable at about 26,000 people and that the proportion of the Jews in the larger metropolitan area was 3.5 percent, well above a national metropolitan average of 2.2 percent given by the *1990 National Jewish Population Survey (NJPS)*. (Kosmin, et al. 1991)

Today, the Greater Hartford Jewish community is widely distributed throughout thirty-two towns and is served by twenty-three congregations (5 Orthodox, 11 Conservative, 5 Reform, and 2 Independent) and the local Federation. As noted by Dalin and Rosenbaum, "In the half century after World War II, Hartford Jewry transformed itself. From an insular community generally confined to the city's boundaries, a regional center encompassing almost all of central Connecticut emerged."(Dalin and Rosenbaum forthcoming) There are several ramifications of this spread. First, within the greater Hartford Jewish community, people are now more physically isolated from each other than they used to be, making effective Jewish community building a greater challenge. Second, it is now more demanding and costly to distribute Jewish educational services efficiently and effectively over such a wide area.

The composition of the Jewish community of Greater Hartford differs from that of the national sample. There is a higher proportion of Jewish children in the Hartford population, where children constitute twenty-eight percent of the Jewish population, compared to twenty percent nationally. (Kosmin, et al. 1991) In addition, a larger proportion, forty-two percent, are receiving a Jewish education than the overall rate of thirty-six percent. These Greater Hartford statistics indicate that there is fertile soil here in which to plant innovative educational initiatives.

As part of the Jewish philanthropic community, Hartford's Federation has had a long-standing reputation for successfully raising funds for local, national, and oversees needs. In the 1980s, Hartford was one of the most highly-rated Jewish philanthropic communities in America. In the 1990s, because of major economic recessions, Hartford suffered losses; nevertheless, even in these financially difficult times, the organized community increased its commitment to Jewish education, which Dalin and Rosenbaum argue, "represents one major promising trend."

Family Education in Hartford: A New Outlook

A Family Education Task Force is Formed

Jewish Family Education for the Hartford community began in the mid 1980s with an evolving partnership between talented professionals and ardent lay leadership at the Commission on Jewish Education (CJE), the Federation, the Jewish Community Center, Jewish Family Service, and local synagogues and schools. From the beginning, with the establishment of a Community Task Force on Family Education, under the direction of the CJE, there was broad-based cooperative planning. Initially, the task force established a set of goals for planning and then proceeded to survey Hartford-area institutions in order to describe characteristics, needs, and programs in preparation for setting a meaningful agenda for the future.

The Community Task Force on Family Education (or Family Education Task Force) believed that parents, lay leaders, and educators must work in partnership to educate children. To develop new visions and arrangements for alternative learning modes, everyone had to view both parents and children as the "clients" to be served. We hoped that the development of family education would increase student and parent satisfaction with the culture and institutions of Jewish life and expand their involvement as well. Since it is widely acknowledged that the Jewish family has always been a major factor in the transmission of Jewish ethnic and religious identity (Dashefsky and Shapiro 1993/1974), the Task Force asserted that family education offered a vehicle for increasing Jewish involvement and helping to ensure Jewish continuity for the future.

New Planning and Programming
The Family Education Task Force and the CJE began experimenting with a variety of community-wide celebrations, including Fathers and Toddlers programs, Tzedakah and Bible Fairs, and retreats at the JCC Camp Sholom. Also, my CJE colleague, Dr. Judith Epstein, and I started assisting synagogue schools and day schools in establishing family education programs and planning structures for their institutions, and we created and collected materials for our resource center.

Family Education In-service
In the late 1980s, recognizing that staff training in family education was critical to its success, the CJE, the Jewish Educators Council, and the Rabbinic Fellowship developed in-service opportunities for rabbis, principals, teachers, and agency professionals. Hartford-area professionals also attended national conferences on family education and family systems. In 1991, I and two colleagues from CJE and JFS received a grant to participate in the first inter-agency track at the Whizin Summer Seminar.

A Family Education Network
The early 1990s brought new developments, including the formation of a Family Education Network, coordinated by the CJE, consisting of professionals from schools, synagogues, JCC, JFS, and Federation. Dr. Judith Epstein and I served as teachers and facilitators at the bi-monthly network sessions, where everyone shared discussions on family education issues, goals, and programs, including successes and concerns. In addition, the network worked in partnership with the Family Education Task Force in visioning and planning. This framework would later expand into a mentoring project and formal classes in family education.

A Grants Process
The early 1990s saw the establishment of five or six small annual family education grants, hundreds of dollars each, for creative initiatives in local institutions. These Dr. Alfred Weisel Family Education Grants, coordinated by the Task Force, were funded through the Endowment

Foundation of the Jewish Federation of Greater Hartford. Recognizing the importance of ongoing learning, grant recipients were required to initiate ongoing, multi-sessioned family education projects. In addition, grant goals encouraged parallel structures for separate adult and child study in the expectation that parents would become better able to teach their children if they were better informed. Thus, there was a strong emphasis on adult learning for parents as a component of these grants. Though small in dollars, these allocations precipitated many innovative ideas and brought visibility to family education. They proved to be stepping stones towards future initiatives.

Continuity Grants: New Collaborations and New Directions

A Council on Jewish Continuity is Established

The 1990, *NJPS* "drew a sociological picture of Jewish identity and religious observance that rocked the leaders of organized communal life" (Dalin and Rosenbaum forthcoming) In response to the threat posed by assimilation reported in the 1990 *NJPS*, the Jewish Federation of Greater Hartford, staffed by the Federation executive director, brought together community leadership from the synagogue and Federation worlds by establishing a Task Force in 1992. Through presentations from national leaders, this Task Force examined issues on Jewish education and assimilation. A key Task Force recommendation was the formation of a Council on Jewish Continuity (COJC) as an arm of the Federation, to represent all agencies, congregations, and organizations within the Jewish community. The COJC was initially funded with $250,000, to be spent over two years on grants to projects fostering Jewish identity and continuity in the spirit of communal cooperation. The COJC spent a year researching and planning the framework and focus of these grants. A synagogue-Federation cabinet of rabbis, synagogue presidents, and Federation leaders was established to serve as COJC advisory board.

After listening to national leaders and engaging in lively discussions of various perspectives and visions, the COJC selected four target areas: (1) family education for affiliated families with children from pre-school to twelve years of age; (2) lay leadership; (3) teens; and (4)outreach to interfaith families. These were considered "gateway" areas, regarded as the community's best hope for fulfilling its mission to bring renewed vigor to the enjoyment, study, and observance of the Jewish cultural and religious heritage. The grants were also meant to strengthen the commitment of Greater Hartford's Jews to existing Jewish institutions; allocations were to support those projects which strengthened the linkage between members and their institutions and increased the number of affiliated individuals. The annual funding of $125,000 from campaign dollars for these continuity grants was especially notable in light of the major decline in the 1990s Federation campaign in Hartford, as noted above.

Here we will deal with only the first COJC target area, family education. The goals were to assist parents, as well as children, to view Jewish learning and living as a life-long process; to build community; to provide quality programs to stimulate Jewish identity, knowledge, and commitment; and finally, to bring Jewish living and learning back into the home.

Collaboration is the Key

One requirement of the grants program was that proposals demonstrate cooperative efforts among and between congregations and Jewish Federation agencies. My role, as staff from CJE, was to bring together organizations with similar proposals to assist congregations and agencies to combine efforts.

The decision to require collaboration meant that no one institution could receive a COJC grant. This was a great challenge for the community and has had a significant impact on the grant development process and outcome by stimulating new collaborations within and between congregations, schools, and agencies. The philosophy of the council was that the community would accomplish more through a synergistic, cooperative effort than through individual initiatives. This brought to the Greater Hartford community a new way of thinking about structures, directions, and ways of sharing community resources. As Jonathan Woocher wrote,

> New institutional relationships are an indispensable element of the community building agenda. Pragmatically, we will need not just the involvement of multiple institutions but also their collaboration and multiple sources of support if we are to have a sufficient number of high quality contexts and programs for identity development and expression.(Woocher 1995)

The past four years have witnessed a variety of new initiatives in teamwork among institutions and their lay leadership, parents, and professionals. Synagogues have shared scholars, artists, and storytellers and have had joint congregation shabbatonim. Congregations, day schools, and agencies have joined our community Tikkun Olam and tzedakah projects.

Even more significant, however, were the unexpected ripple effects—the formation of lay and parent committees from different congregations, day schools, and agencies, who planned joint projects and studied Torah together. Workshops on leadership development were designed for lay leaders and parents from many different institutions. Young parents from varied backgrounds developed new parent and child play groups. Family educators transported ideas from place to place, including models of alternative family schools and Shabbat dinner ḥavurot. The synergy that this collaboration created in Greater Hartford has forged new links among families, synagogues, local agencies, and the Federation.

Initiatives

From 1993 to 1997, with the grants from the Federation-funded Council on Jewish Continuity, projects in family education grew to twelve. The largest of these grants, the Jewish Family Educators Initiative, established partnerships among community day schools and local congregations. To date, four family educators, funded through COJC, work with professionals, lay leaders, and parents in two or three institutions to assess needs, establish goals, develop creative ongoing family education projects, and build community collaboration. The Family Educator Initiative also established an intensive mentoring component where I meet monthly with family educators as a team to practice self assessment.

Recognizing the need to raise the number and caliber of professionals, Hebrew College, Hartford Branch, developed a two-year academic program culminating in a Family Education Certificate. Approximately twenty people, including family educators, aspiring family educators, rabbis, principals, teachers, agency professionals, and lay leaders take courses each semester. Instructors have been drawn from the CJE staff (Dr. Judith Epstein and myself), and from locally and nationally known educators. In addition, the students meet annually, in teams, with seventy other educators and lay leaders at a Family/Adult Education Institute that includes national leaders from the Whizin Institute and other pioneers in this new field. This program, initiated by the CJE, the Jewish Educators Council, and the Rabbinic Fellowship, was funded through COJC. Other COJC initiatives included Jewish curriculum expansion at the JCC's Early Childhood Center to connect young families to Judaism and expose them to day school options; a Shabbat Kodesh program focused on creating meaningful Shabbat experiences and learning materials for interfaith families; and a Jewish Birth Baskets project, coordinated by the JCC and Federation, which gave parents of new babies small gifts, information about local resources, and an ongoing play and support group.

Assessment: What Have We Learned?

What impact have the Family Education Continuity grants had? First, we learned that the reorganization of institutions and communities is challenging work. We also understand that the Council on Jewish Continuity's decision that grants be awarded collaboratively was critical to the process. Developing new coalitions within institutions and developing multi-institutional partnerships has seemed difficult at times, requiring consistent negotiating to build and rebuild relationships and structures. Success varied. Some institutions "bought in" more readily than others. Difficulties included families' resistance to traveling beyond their own institution; family educators' initial lack of true investment in the collaborative process; institutions that desired only a "silent" partner in order to receive grant funds; denominational differences about Jewish observance; and complications of coordinating calendar dates between institutions.

We learned that change takes time. Still, we can see that in four years a greater comfort level, and trust of collaborative ventures and an unfolding of new cooperative skills have slowly developed. As families experienced quality programs in other congregations, their attendance in joint endeavors increased. Also, family educators, now realizing advantages of planning together, initiated in 1997 a community-wide Tzedakah exhibit. Without doubt, the collaborative funding requirement stimulated these institutions and their constituents to experiment.

The grants process assessment was done through preliminary, mid-year, and year-end reports and through ongoing dialogue among grantees, the Council on Jewish Continuity, the CJE, and Federation staff. To evaluate the impact of projects on parents and children, we relied on individual self-evaluations, interviews, and observations. We also created a structure for "reflective practice," in which family educators engage in ongoing self-assessment. I have worked with Federation and the Council on Jewish Continuity to guide this formative stage of evaluation. It has been difficult wearing the hat of guide and evaluator while trying to remain unbiased in the grants process.

Our evaluation reports indicate general satisfaction and dedicated participation by seventy-five to ninety percent of the participants in the COJC funded programs. We have also seen increased enrollment in adult education over this period. We have new models of community collaboration and involvement. Over one hundred Jewish educators and lay leaders have expanded their knowledge and developed new skills through participation in Jewish family education courses or institutes. Most importantly, as a result of the COJC initiatives, there is heightened awareness of the importance of Jewish living and learning within the Greater Hartford community. Over 2,000 families from ten congregations (of 7,000 families representing 23 congregations) together with two day schools, the JCC, and JFS have been involved with the Federation and its CJE in these COJC initiatives.

We are aware that our local research effort is limited, as is national research in Jewish family education. We do not yet have the longitudinal studies needed to assess the long term effect of family education on parent and child behaviors and attitudes. As Reimer (1992) states, "The field is still in an early stage of trial and error, but until the current experiments are monitored, it will be very hard for educators to learn from mistakes and build confidently on successes." In an important step, an outside evaluator has been engaged to provide a summary evaluation for a more complete, unbiased picture.

From Family Education to Organizational Change: Min Hekal El Hakaved (From the Easy to the Hard)

Beyond developing multi-institutional partnerships between and among organizations, our grants set the stage for new directions within institutions. Because of the COJC grant mechanism, new coalitions of stakeholders were created with school, adult education, ritual, youth group, and finance representation. The grants process led recognition that, for real organizational change to occur, "none of these individuals or groups is isolated: all are part of the synagogue 'system' and must work together if they are to create a whole which is greater that the sum of its parts." (Tigay 1994/5754)

As a result of this insight, a new pilot program, the Synagogue Initiative Project (SIP), initiated by the CJE and funded by the Endowment Foundation, began in the spring of 1996. Its purpose was to develop a collaborative, process-oriented strategy to explore and learn about organizational change. This initiative provided intensive consultation to all lay and professional elements in two synagogues, selected for their organizational readiness, so each could develop a shared vision for the future. Working with consultants, I facilitated collaboration among all segments of the two synagogues, e.g., youth, school, adult education, ritual, and membership, so that each can successfully design and implement its own action plans.

We anticipate that this SIP pilot will be followed by a much larger Federation-funded synagogue transformation project, which will stimulate major, system-wide rethinking and re-engineering of congregations, schools, families, and members. Such an initiative, Aron states, "represents a first step in the process of re-conceptualizing congregational education and translating the new conceptions into working models. This process will be long and arduous…it also will be invigorating and exciting." (1995) This endeavor will make available to participants of all ages the tools to experience the beauty and richness of Jewish life—in the school, in the synagogue, and at home. The Greater Hartford Jewish community is still at the beginning of its journey. While much work is yet to be done, we take comfort from Pirke Avot, "You are not required to complete the work, but neither are you free to evade it."

References

Abrahamson, M., *A Study of the Greater Hartford Jewish Population* (Connecticut: Greater Hartford Jewish Federation and the Endowment Fund of the Greater Hartford Jewish Federation, 1982).

Aron, I., "From the Congregational School to the Learning Congregation," In Aron, I., Lee, S., Rossel, S., eds., *A Congregation of Learners.* (New York: UAHC, 1995) 56-77.

Dalin, D. and Rosenbaum, J., *From Congregation to Community: Hartford Jewry, 1843-1993* (New York: Holmes and Meier, forthcoming).

Dashefsky, A. and Shapiro, H. M., *Ethnic Identification Among American Jews,* (Lanham, MD: UPA, 1993/1974).

Kosmin, B., Goldstein, S., Waksberg, J., et al., *Highlights of the CJF 1990 National Jewish Population Survey* (New York: Council of Jewish Federations, 1991).

Reimer, J, "What We Know About Jewish Family Education," in Kelman, S., editor, *What We Know About Jewish Education* (Los Angeles: Torah Aura, 1992) 177-185.

Tigay, H., "Focusing on the Whole: The 'Systems Approach' in Jewish Schools," *Highlights,* (Winter, 1994/5754) 4-5.

Woocher, J, "Toward a 'Unified Field Theory' of Jewish Continuity," In Aron, I., Lee, S., Rossel, S., eds., *A Congregation of Learners* (New York: UAHC, 1995) 14-55.

Victoria Koltun Kelman began her journey into Jewish education the summer her parents announced that she and her sister would be going to a "Hebrew speaking camp" (Ramah). Exactly thirty summers later, she created and directed the first Family Camp at Ramah in California. In between, she collected three degrees, made a specialty of teaching teenagers in Jewish schools, and became a curriculum developer for the Melton Research Center. Her long work in classrooms led her to realize the urgency of engaging parents in the Jewish educational enterprise. Her first foray into this then-nameless field was Together: A Child-Parent Kit, *published by Melton in 1984, followed by* Windows *and five summers of Family Camp at Ramah in California.*

Victoria Koltun Kelman

   A founding member of the Whizin faculty, she is now director of the Jewish Family Education Project, a collaboration between the Jewish Community Federation and the Bureau of Jewish Education of the San Francisco Bay Area, a capacity-building project mentoring family education in synagogues, JCCs, and day schools.

Nechama Tamler is director of Jewish Continuity Planning for the Jewish Community Federation of San Francisco, the Peninsula, Marin, and Sonoma Counties, where she has been employed for fifteen years. She holds a master's degree in Marriage, Family and Child Counseling and spent a year in Jerusalem in 1993 as a Jerusalem fellow. She has worked with intermarried couples and Jewish feminist concerns for many years in a variety of settings, including JCCs, synagogues, and Hillels. She taught in afternoon supplementary schools for over a decade and has worked with adult learners in synagogues and the Federation, concentrating on the Book of Genesis.

Nechama Imberman Tamler

   One of her current interests is contemporary midrash in poetic, dramatic, and prose formats. Nechama lives in Palo Alto with her husband, Howard Tamler. They have two sons, a daughter, and a daughter-in-law. She is constantly amazed by how much more there is to learn about subjects she loves. Hobbies: voracious reader, gardening, writing and reading poetry, hanging out with friends.

San Francisco: Strategy and Serendipity

Victoria Koltun Kelman and Nechama Tamler

Inspired by Kohelet's teaching, "To everything there is a season," (Ecclesiastes 3:1) and William Shakespeare's "the readiness is all," we have come to understand that, as there are auspicious times in a person's life, so there are auspicious times in the life of a community. At such times, forces are optimally aligned to make something new and unprecedented possible. In San Francisco, in fall 1993, a number of factors helped create a climate conducive to launching a Jewish family education initiative.

The View from the Federation—

A Strategic Planning Process Begins with a Demographic Study

When an organized Jewish community is able to build on previous efforts it is not necessary to begin with *aleph*. In the late 1980s, the Jewish Community Federation of San Francisco, the Peninsula, Marin, and Sonoma Counties, along with the Federations of Greater San Jose and the Greater East Bay commissioned a demographic study. This study was used as the basis for an extensive strategic planning institute with the Jewish Community Federation of San Francisco, the Peninsula, Marin, and Sonoma Counties (JCF), completed in 1990. One key feature of the strategic plan (the Wornick Plan) was that it highlighted community development and "continuity issues" as key concerns. It also acknowledged the pivotal role of synagogues in continuity issues and in Jewish identity building. To follow up on the Wornick plan, JCF leadership determined that its next step was to explore avenues for JCF-synagogue collaborations and to foster improved relations between these two worlds.

The Task Force on Synagogue-Federation Relations

In the fall of 1992, an exploratory task force was created. A chair, who had been a synagogue president and was a federation leader in the planning process, was appointed to head this task force. The task force conducted a series of eight group conversations with lay and professional synagogue leadership in order to hear directly what areas they identified as prime targets for JCF help and support to synagogues.

The areas identified by these small groups were (1) building strong communities and (2) "continuity with content." The discussions helped the task force articulate a vision of an ideal Jewish community as one in which "Jews are well educated Jewishly, committed to life-long learning, observant in their homes, actively involved in synagogue life, tolerant and appreciative of diversity of practice."[1] This vision specified as priority areas: family education, the creation of regional Jewish high schools, the recruitment and training of Jewish professionals, and the increased accessibility of Israel trips for Jewish teens.

Multiple mentions were made of family: the need for places where parents can spend time with, and do Jewish things with, their children; the need for parents to explore their own Jewish commitments while they are involved in their children's upbringing; the need to pass on to children a strong sense of Jewish identity, history, and a love of Klal Yisrael and Am Yisrael. The work of the Synagogue Federation task force led to creation of the Family Education Task Force (FETF).

Initial Funding for Jewish Continuity

In June 1992, the Jewish Community Endowment Fund of the Jewish Community Federation had already set aside $100,000 for use in Jewish continuity programs with special emphasis on JCF-synagogue partnerships. There was a certain feeling of security engendered by the existence of this fund. Because the money had already been set aside, the task force was free of constraint in brainstorming about potential programmatic use of the money.

The Family Education Task Force became the next step because family education was seen as important and as having the potential to generate enthusiasm. It was seen as more do-able and was judged to be able to generate results faster than the other areas identified. The other areas were also perceived as having more complicating factors in terms of the community's attitudes, structures, and history. Family education could serve everyone equally without raising turf issues or stepping on toes.

The Family Education Task Force:

The Family Education Task Force was convened by the Planning and Allocations Department of the JCF. It was composed of key lay leaders and professional educators. It was not conceived as a "wall-to-wall" coalition but rather as a representative one. The lay leaders were active volunteers from various synagogues, some of whom also served on the boards of the BJE or the JCF. The professionals included the director of the Endowment Fund of the JCF, the director of the BJE, the head of the largest day school in the area, the director of a coalition of JCCs, the staff of a private family foundation very involved in funding projects in the Jewish community, the staff from Planning and Allocations and the senior rabbi of one of the larger congregations in the area.

From the outset, the task force saw itself as a coalition that considered family education to be the key to strengthening the capacity of families to live according to Jewish values and ethics and to affirm Judaism as a way of life. The initial proposal for planning sent to task force members in late November 1993 stated:

> Jewish family education has been recognized among experts as fundamental to Jewish continuity. Without parents as equal partners in the Jewish educational process, much of Jewish education is ineffective since it is isolated from the reality of the home and the rest of a child's life. Jewish family education involves parents in Jewish activities with their children and brings Jewish living into the home and into quality family time...the goal of the task force is to determine how the community can strengthen existing programs and stimulate new ones. The end result will be a specific recommendation for a Jewish family education initiative in this community. The recommendations will be sent on to the Planning and Allocations steering committee and will include funding recommendations to utilize funds already set aside by the Jewish Community Endowment Fund.[2]

The first meeting of the Family Education Task Force was held in January 1993. Task force members prepared by reading background articles about family education. The chair emphasized the need to think "out of the box" and encouraged the task force to dream, to think big. This first meeting featured a presentation by a prominent practitioner in family education along with a presentation by the Federation staff of the "best practices" in family education, developed based on a series of phone interviews with family education personnel at key sites in Boston, Detroit, Philadelphia, Baltimore, and MetroWest (New Jersey).

At its succeeding four meetings, the task force listed components of successful family education programs culled from national interviews and conversations within the community with educational personnel already engaged in family education. The committee did an environmental scan, listing unique characteristics of the San Francisco community which might be important to consider before adapting models from other communities. For example, in the Bay Area, synagogue affiliation rates are lower, and the Orthodox community represents a smaller percent of the affiliated community than in any of the other cities consulted.

In March, the task force drafted a two-year plan submitted as a grant request to the Jewish Community Endowment Fund as a seed project. A job description for a community family education specialist or consultant was part of this document. In addition, it was decided that the $100,000 allocated at the outset for synagogues was now to be incorporated in this draft proposal as grant money for Jewish family education programs in synagogues. When the subject of governance was raised, there was a strong consensus that, during the first two "seed" years of this project, an oversight committee would best be comprised of key stakeholders, similar in make-up to the task force, rather than having the project in one agency under the direction of a single agency board.

In April, the seed grant proposal was submitted, and in May, the Endowment Fund approved a grant of $80,000 to establish the Jewish Family Education Project and supported the use of the original $100,000 for grants to synagogues for family education purposes.

A New Strategic Direction for The BJE

In 1993-4, the Bureau of Jewish Education (BJE), a key institutional stakeholder in the community, was in the midst of a strategic planning process. Following a period of some turmoil, a new director was in place, who, along with a new president, undertook a planning process which also set Jewish family education at the top of the agency's priorities. This change opened a unique window of opportunity. The new director of the BJE, who began in San Francisco in the summer of 1993, was not entrenched in maintaining the status quo. He worked closely with a new president, who also played a key role at the Federation. He was open to new directions and was committed to a communal planning process. These factors contributed to making this the season for family education in San Francisco. Changes in the community and the wave of continuity-based concerns created a spirit of collaboration and contributed toward blurring traditional boundaries. Planning and serendipity were catalysts for the speed with which this communal initiative was launched. A director was hired for the Jewish Family Education Project. A serendipitous aspect of this process is that a leading national figure in family education, a person who had served as a consultant early in this process, was available to fill the position. She began work on August 15, 1994, less than a year after the initiation of the Family Education Task Force.

The View From Inside the Jewish Family Education Project

The Jewish Family Education Project (JFEP) came into existence on August 15, 1994, as the culmination of this multi-year process. It began with an operating budget of $80,000 and $100,000 to be distributed to synagogues for family education programs, one full time staff member, a one-third time secretary, and a two-year life span. At this writing, the project has an operating budget of almost $250,000.[3] It also has a professional staff of two; a more than half-time support staff; two library bookcases overflowing with family education resources; a track record of fifty programs underwritten in synagogues, day schools, and JCL; an ongoing family series held in conjunction with the Jewish Community Library; and two Israel trips under its belt—one for family educators and one for families. Approximately five hundred families each year have participated in Jewish family experiences underwritten or encouraged by the JFEP.

The JFEP was designed to be a capacity-building project with a mandate to foster family education in all interested institutions in the community served by our Federation. This is done by developing the capacity of each site to provide Jewish experiences for its families. Toward this end, the project has four central undertakings: (1) professional development in family education; (2) consultation services; (3) organization and dissemination of print resources in and for family education; and (4) allocation of grant monies to underwrite worthwhile programs for families.

It came into being in the space left between community agencies—it belonged neither to the Federation nor to the BJE, although it was located at the Bureau and the executive director of the Bureau is the supervisor of the project. It had its own advisory committee, which was composed of lay leaders and professionals, and it stood on its own, not answering (in a hierarchical or structural way) to either of the above arms of the community, yet it was closely affiliated with both. As the director of the Jewish Family Education Project, I, Vicky Kelman, worked closely with Nechama Tamler in Planning and Allocations, as I did with Bob Sherman, the executive director of the BJE.

When my work began, I embarked on two different fact-finding missions—one internal and one external. I began, in the short window of freedom one has in a new community, to be an ethnographer of the San Francisco Jewish community. Building on the process begun by the Family Education Task Force, which interviewed local practitioners and did an environmental scan, I met with and asked many questions of almost everyone thought to be pivotal in the enterprise of Jewish education and Jewish communal structure. I was able to probe and pry with questions ranging from "Who holds the power in the community?" to "How would you say the Bureau is viewed in the community?" and included many "Can you say more about..." and "Tell me about...." In a fairly short time I had gained a very rich picture of how the community ticks, and although I still am surprised from time to time, I have found this early phase of my work exceedingly valuable and exceedingly true.

My second ethnographic excursion was to the family-education land beyond my community. Using my extensive network from the Whizin Institute in Los Angeles and CAJE, I began to telephone every city that I knew had committed resources to family education so as to do extensive phone interviews. These sites included Boston, Detroit, Baltimore, Philadelphia, Washington, D.C., Hartford, New York City, and Chicago. Later the list came to include Cleveland and Columbus and led to the organization at the Whizin Summer Seminar of the Community Family Educators' Network, which has met annually there for three years. In the fall of that same year, I traveled east and interviewed community family educators in Washington, D.C., Baltimore, and Philadelphia.

In gathering this information, I was the fortunate inheritor of previous pioneers' accomplishments as well as goofs. I am exceedingly grateful to all of my colleagues who shared openly of their own experiences. Slowly but surely I was able to begin to weave an approach to capacity-building in family education which would suit my new community. I felt that JEFF would not be the model for such a project on a limited budget. I also felt that the early Boston model of large competitive grants would not root family education widely enough here because we did not yet have enough professionals sufficiently skilled in family education. And so I amassed details, and wove my new knowledge into a fabric which would complement my own community's texture.

The two most pivotal decisions, made early on by the project's advisory committee, were: (1) use a "let a thousand flowers bloom" approach to allocating grant money—to give more smaller grants, rather than a few large ones, in order to help institutions to become successful in the grant process and to spread the money over two years; and (2) to link engagement in professional development to eligibility for grants.[4] [5]

The grant requirements were created by the JFEP Advisory Committee in the fall, 1994, and have guided the process, with minor fine-tuning, for the three years over which the $100,000 was distributed. Underlying these requirements are two prerequisites. First, for change to happen in an institution, several "champions" are needed who will advocate, articulate, and argue for it. Long-lasting, deep-rooted change cannot be brought about by one person alone. Second, family education is a specialty which demands unique skills, attitudes, beliefs, and philosophies from practitioners. It was recognized that without these two, champions and prepared professionals, the grant money would be like throwing seeds at parched desert soil. The grant requirements included:

1. Filing a Letter of Intent to Apply
2. Creating a family education "team" on site to be composed of the rabbi, the educational director, and at least one lay leader, preferably someone on the board of the synagogue
3. Having this team attend the JFEP mini-conference[6]
4. Having the team meet with the director of JFEP for a two-hour consultation
5. Having the whole team amass a specified number of professional development hours

The grant proposals themselves were expected to include a substantial amount of intra-family interaction, the centrality of important Jewish ideas, and complementarity with the mission of the sponsoring institution. It is important to note here that our community has no one whose job definition is solely that of "family educator." We have some people for whom that is one of the hats they wear. Most of our family educators are school directors; others are lay leaders, rabbis, cantors, and teachers.

During the early phases of this process, we wondered whether institutions would be willing to devote energy to fulfilling all these steps for what, for some, amounted to a relatively small sum of money. There was initially much excitement about the availability of money on a non-competitive basis, but it took much hand-holding and many reminders to keep everyone on track with dates and deadlines. Sixteen synagogues of a possible twenty-five, completed the process during the first year.[7]

The ability of sites to continue in subsequent years was related to the internal coherence of the site as it organized itself for family education. At sites with insufficient or troubled infrastructures and at sites whose team members were assembled for a one-time-only meeting to meet the "letter of the law" of the consultation requirement, involvement in the project could not be sustained after the first year. It is true that the grants were smaller in the following two years and therefore may have constituted less of an incentive, but this did not seem to be the deciding factor for those synagogues which chose not to continue in succeeding years.[8]

There were some "grumblings" about "a lot of hoops to jump through for a few thousand bucks." Still, for many synagogues, this grant constituted the difference between having a family education program or having nothing at all. As participants (rabbis, school directors, teachers, and lay leaders) began to attend professional development seminars and the annual mini-conference, doubts receded as they realized that the "hoops" offered substantial learning opportunities related to new skills and attitudes to inform their practice. Across the board, participants felt that the two-hour consultation with the director was the most valuable aspect of the time they spent fulfilling the requirements.

This structure remained in place for the initial three years of the project. When the two years of seed funding ended, the Jewish Community Endowment Fund extended the funding and additional foundation grants were secured in amounts sufficient to maintain the pre-existing structure. At the end of two years, the Bureau also received $25,000 from the annual campaign of the JCF for the JFEP, which began to shift the locus of the project to the BJE itself. As the fourth year began, the BJE received sufficient funding from the annual campaign so that the core funding of salaries and some administration was placed within the BJE's operating budget. In a way, this culminated the process begun with the demographic study, as the JFEP was recognized as "ours" by the community, outgrowing its "seed/trial" phase and becoming a permanent part of the community's priorities for ongoing funding.

In addition to the various programs developed at participating sites, two direct programming ventures were created: One was Booktime for Families and the other was several small projects linking families and Israel. Booktime for Families, now in its fourth year, is a collaboration of the Jewish Community Library, part of the BJE, and the JFEP. It is a series of two-hour programs at the library for families with elementary school-aged children. In February, 1997, we took a group of twenty-one educators to Israel so that they could study, plan, and recruit for family Israel experiences. Participants agreed to work toward creating and recruiting a family Israel trip in their home institution as one requirement of this trip, which was partially underwritten by a gift secured by the endowment fund. The first family trip which sprang from this endeavor has already taken place and several others are on the drawing board. Working with the JFEP, a group of ten San Francisco families in Israel for the Wexner Heritage Institute organized a four-day family Israel experience in the northern Galilee during the summer of 1997. As a community partner, the JFEP has also been involved in the Bereavement Camp, a weekend for families who have suffered a loss, created by Camp Tawonga; Jewish Healing Month, sponsored by Ruach Ami/The Bay Area Healing Center; and the creation of F.Y.I., Families of Youth traveling to Israel, a series of pre- and post-Israel trip programs for teens and their families.

Looking ahead—The Short View
(Jewish Year 5758 / School Year 1997-98)

In its first three years, JFEP's time and resources were divided between program grants to sites and professional development. The grants process was the core, and professional development was tied to it. When the original $100,000 set aside for synagogues was almost depleted, the focus then shifted to professional development. Now professional development is at the core and program money is linked to it.

Next year, in addition to Booktime for Families, the Family Educator Israel Network, and additional Israel experiences, the JFEP will include:

1. A Case Writing project
Twelve family education practitioners, a group which includes a rabbi, two cantors, several school directors, several lay people, and an early childhood educator, will be working with a consultant to write up cases which illuminate issues in the practice of family education. Learning will come from the development, writing, and analysis of cases; the casebook which results can be used for the next year's professional development; a grant from the Bernard Osher Jewish Philanthropic Fund will cover consultant expenses, retreat expenses (the project starts off with a day and a half retreat), and stipends for participants.

2. Common Ground
A collaborative study group for people involved in family education; its purpose is an ongoing learning conversation built around reflection on practice, text study, and joint planning for a family education event to be held next summer at each participant's site. A grant from the Bernard Osher Jewish Philanthropic Fund will provide grants to cover the cost of the program which emerges.

3. Family Room
Extend Family Room into six sites and provide orientation for facilitators and monthly colloquia for leaders as they launch their groups in the winter; A grant from the Walter and Elise Haas Fund is underwriting facilitator salaries and program costs.

4. Family History Video Project PLUS
An enhancement to a popular decade-old sixth grade family history curriculum (published by our BJE) will enrich the family portion of this curriculum and provide for increased professional development and for a city-wide event, a family folklore festival, for all participating classes; a grant from the Righteous Persons Foundation is covering the curriculum revision, teacher stipends for added professional development and the festival.

On the Horizon
We are just beginning to study the results of a wide-ranging evaluation which queried all participants and many professionals at almost all of our sites. The report is not yet complete, but early results point to a significantly greater impact for programs which involved families in multiple

sessions over an extended period of time over those where people attended only one-time events. This greater impact shows up on measures of increased Jewish activity in families' "private life" as well as on stronger commitment to the sponsoring institution. If this turns out to be the case when the evaluation is concluded, this finding will influence the future direction of program funding as well as professional development.

We are currently working on a five-year plan to establish a professional development certificate or degree-granting program to prepare family educators for our community. Several possible models are on the table and include formal relationships with institutions of higher learning, long-distance learning, internships, mentoring, and summer intensives. Part of our vision involves subsidies for full-time family educators who complete the program and who might divide their time among several institutions close to one another. Along with this "dream," we will work on acquiring long-range, secure funding for our next phase of growth.

We look forward to a time when providing Jewish experiences for families is just "what we do," from pre-school through Israel trips. As a lay leader said recently, "Wouldn't it be funny if when our children are parents of children in synagogue schools, twenty years from now, family learning would be so routine and accepted that some one might say, 'Hey—isn't this an odd idea? Did anyone ever consider dividing learners by age and having them in classrooms with their own teachers?' "

Endnotes

1. Family Education Task Force minutes.
2. Proposal sent to Task Force members.
3. Composed of $125,000 from the Federation Campaign, now a permanent part of the BJE budget, and the remainder from a series of private foundation grants covering several professional development projects.
4. The first year's grants, allocated in spring 1995 for the 1995-96 school year, were for $3000. In the second year, grants for $2000 had to be matched with $500, and in the third year, grants were $1000, which had to be matched with $1000.
5. They were actually spread over three years as a result of subsequent decisions made by the Advisory Committee.
6. A half-day conference held on a Sunday afternoon in February.
7. The original $100,000 had been set aside expressly for synagogues, making it unavailable to JCCs and day schools. We were able to secure an additional grant to offer small grants ($500-$1000) to those sites. Four JCCs and two days schools participated. All other services and resources of the JFEP were available to them as well.
8. In the second year, 13 synagogues participated; 13 participated in the third year.

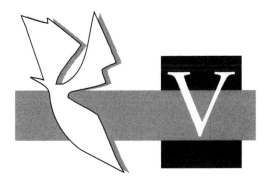

Breaking New Ground

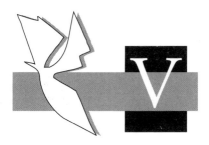

Introduction: Breaking New Ground

These articles provide a sample of sources that might continue to nourish Jewish family education in the future. Each author connects expertise to elements already present in this emerging field: the enriching variety of sources and multidisciplinary perspectives from Jewish religious writings to educational theory and practice on to the insights of sociology, developmental psychology, and organizational behavior.

Joel Lurie Grishaver, in *Towards a Theology of the Jewish Family*, gives us a collage of snapshots—quick portraits of his students, personal impressions, commentary on texts, and introspective musings. As we read, these short takes illuminate both the exuberance and the confusion of our time.

In *Evaluating Communal Initiatives: Facts Can be Friendly*, Susan L. Shevitz describes the intention of family education planners in Boston to learn about whether the components they had designed were succeeding in real life. They insisted that systematic evaluation activities accompany each step of the process. As the evaluator, Susan reflects on what happened and what she discovered about "fact gathering" along the way.

Harlene Winnick Appelman and Joan S. Kay, in *Curricularizing Jewish Family Education*, suggest that the family constitute the lens through which many educational activities be viewed. They propose that family educators move beyond one-shot programs and think—comprehensively and for the long-term—about sequences of "beginner-to-advanced" courses of study to accompany families through successive stages.

In *Interagency and Multidisciplinary Collaboration: A Win-Win Strategy*, Sally Weber points out that Jewish family education is not only the province of educators and schools or of rabbis and synagogues but also of social workers and agencies that deal first hand with the challenges faced by families today. She looks specifically at Jewish Family Service and its professional staff and suggests how fruitful relationships between that agency and other institutions engaged in family education might be initiated and sustained.

Diane Tickton Schuster, in *Adult Development and Jewish Family Education*, presents psychological research that portrays adults not as fully-formed, static personalities but rather as life-long learners who change and grow in relation to the stresses, needs, and challenges in their lives. She says that, in order to make the parent-oriented aspects of family education rich and rewarding for adults, educators should learn how to listen in on and be responsive to individuals at different stages in their adult development.

Betsy Dolgin Katz, in *Adult Education and Jewish Family Education*, argues that the principles of adult education are essential tools for family educators. She notes that, although family educators usually regard the entire family, rather than individual adult, as the "student," the interactive instructional techniques common to adult education are very useful, regardless of whether parents, children, or perhaps grandparents are learning together as a family or whether parents are learning for their own sake or to become better teachers of their children.

Family education, as a newcomer in the Jewish communal world, is often supported by grant dollars from foundations or individuals. Acquiring these dollars and negotiating the arrangements by which professionals and donors will work together on the funded project may require new skills that people have not previously exercised. Rachel Sisk, in *Funding Family Education Can Leave You Breathless*, provides a case story to illustrate the emerging field of Jewish family education funding.

Esther Netter, in *Spreading Success*, details the specifics of how a small family education project within a large institution grew, prospered, and became very successful. Esther observes how the very same techniques which contributed to the success of the small project had to be used again to manage a successful new relationship with the parent institution.

Joel Lurie Grishaver is a teacher of Jew-ish texts to adults and teenagers, a writer, a cartoonist, and an innovative Jewish thinker. He has degrees from Boston University and the University of Chicago and has done extensive course work at the Hebrew Union College and the University of Southern California. His more than fifty published books include Learning Torah, Shema is For Real, And You Shall Be A Blessing, 40 Things You Can Do To Save the Jewish People, *and* The Bonding of Isaac. *His recent*

Joel Lurie Grishaver

articles have appeared in Jewish Spectator, Hadassah, The Baltimore Jewish Times, Jewish Education News, Jewish Family, *and* Manna.

Joel is the creative chairperson of both Torah Aura Productions and the Alef Design Group. He is the creator and co-editor of Learning Torah With…, A Facsimile Dialogue on the Weekly Torah Portion, Bim Bam, C.Ha *and* <shabbas.doc.>. *He is a just-retired faculty member of the Los Angeles Hebrew High School and is still active on the faculty of the Department of Continuing Education at the University of Judaism. He is also a consultant to the Whizin Institute for Jewish Family Life.*

Towards A Theology of The Jewish Family:
The Dysfunctional Myth of the Functional Family
Joel Lurie Grishaver

An Insight: Here is my latest vision of the truth: everyone, at least everyone I know, has two families. One is our real family, our birth family (or if you prefer "our family of origin"). It is the one in which we feel stuck. Our real families frustrate and anger us, embarrass us, challenge our individuality and maturity—yet we know that they are always there. Each of us also recruits and adopts a "pseudo-family," a group of friends who feel like family. We celebrate our holidays with this pseudo-family (when we can get away with it), we confide our inner lives to them, telling them all the things our real families wouldn't understand. We share vacations and joys with our pseudo-families; yet, we live with a deep insecurity (a hidden, inner knowledge) that ultimately our pseudo-families will drift away on the winds of mobility, lifestyle change, economic evolution, or just disappear because of the currents of time. It is the very rootedness of our real families which generates much of the tension. We live with the dual knowledge that they will always be there for us—no matter what, and that we can never escape them—no matter what. Likewise, it is the very ad hoc status of our pseudo-families which allows the intimacy and safety—and in turn the deeper sense of ultimate loneliness. Pseudo-families, in an ironic sense, offer all the freedom and angst of a one night stand.

My friend Adrianne Bank argues that this paper should speak of three families—adding "the ones we create." She argues that I am speaking as "author-as-child" and ignoring "author-as-parent." I believe that stuck is stuck. I hear her truth. I acknowledge it, but it is not mine to speak.

Our family lives are lived suspended between two poles: the classic, mythic roots of the family, with all its tension and darkness, and the "colorized" illusions of the Louis B. Meyer idealized "Andy Hardy," all-American family, which has tried to digitize away all the shadows. Pseudo-families try to recreate the illusion that our real families cannot but fail to actualize. We are trapped between the "dark" myths of ancient Greece and the "lie" modernist truths of a popular culture now passing.

Think Oedipus! Think Demeter! All that stuff. Wicked step mothers, absent or impotent fathers, jealous siblings, mad progenitors, witches, demons, giants, and capricious monarchs are the things which animate the families in "real" fairy tales; these are the mythological family truths. They stand in marked contrast to the free market illusion of hands with better cuticles thanks to liquid dishwashing detergent. Oedipus is not the "Ultimate Bob" 50s advertising icon Dad with a pipe in his mouth. We live at a time when all the cracks in our real families have broken through our facades. Of the 1950s illusion of 2.2 children, two parents and a dog, nothing remains but the mirage evoked by retro-suburban chic. It never was. It never will be. Families are not exclusively happy, sunlit, endlessly joyous places that can solve every problem with a punch-line in twenty-two minutes. No one lives at Club Med. Family is not a vacation.

The darkness which motivates Dan Quayle's attack on *Murphy Brown* is also a fear that motivates Jewish family education. Both flow from a panic that families do not appear stable enough to bear the weight we wish to place upon them. So Dan Quayle argues that we must insist upon "family values" because they appear to be vanishing. And the popular voice of the Jewish community is chanting *family education* to sustain a sense of Jewish family, which seems to be all but gone. This is the ultimate darkness—the vortex of our unspoken night terrors. We are all deep into denial, not that the family of our dreams is dying, but that finally we must admit that it never was at all.

We now live in a moment where there are no families which live up to the Hollywood myths. Any of the families you think you know that do are actually the exceptions that prove the rule or the ones with great camouflage. It is a time where all that seems to have been stable in our culture is disintegrating. Into that void, the family educator has charged. We do not know whether he or she is Don Quixote or Diogenes or Sisyphus or Persephone—the beginning of the end or the end of the beginning.

Pre-Text: Village Power

A child lay in a cradle
The messenger stood beside the cradle
Villagers formed a ring around them both

Who takes responsibility for this child?

Two parents came into the circle
We will feed and clothe
Bathe and protect
Teach and love the baby
The siblings came into the circle
We will tell the baby the story of our family
And ease the child into the routine

The elders stepped into the circle
We will pass on the history of our people
And give guidance to the parents

The neighbors stepped into the circle
We will watch out for the child
When he leaves the home
And wanders along his life journey

The community stepped into the circle
We will guard the path of the child
Guiding the steps on the pavement
Offering the knowledge we have stored

The children stepped into the circle
We will show the baby how to be a child
Making discoveries
Learning all that we can

The messenger rocked the cradle
And smiled
For the circle on the outside
Had become the inside

Leaning into the cradle he whispered
"I am leaving you to the care of the village.
Your life will be rich."
And his job being done
He left the child
With the village

The fires of the village need rekindling
We must return to the rearing by the village
The cries of the families are growing louder
Let the talking drums speak
Speak to the needs of the village
Bring the babies to the village
Let the rearing begin
With the love of the village! [3]

Now this essay can begin...

Prologue:

Snapshot: It is after class and I am talking to "the kid" again. Usually we do a couple of rounds of My Father the Fascist, starring "the kid" as The Prisoner in the Iron Mask Who Was Eternally Grounded. It is a great Oedipal struggle between father and son: epic in its angst, classic in its form, and a lot of fun to empathize with and smile at. (Knowing that both of them will eventually outgrow it—somewhat) It is the stuff that the first few teen years are made of—especially for boys in the prime of their puer. I do my ritual intervention: "He's a father, that is what he is like. You have a lot of other feelings toward him, but you also love him—learn to live with it. Parents are like that."

Today, it is different. Today, "the kid" is crying and mumbling to his shoes. From the sounds that emerge, one can detect evidence of a fight between parents that had evoked the abhorred curse word, *divorce*. "The kid" is in terror. He nobly proclaims that he will stop it. That he will be better behaved—a better student—that he is the only one who can hold it together—that he will stay home from camp—that he will never leave home. This, too, is classic, but I am too close to the situation—too into empathy—to think that this round is cute. Eventually, he faces up to the fearful decision: *the choice.* His answer, a shock to me only at first reflection, is that he will go with his father. I respect him too much to try to wipe away his tears or tell him it will be better. When a pause finally invites my comment, I tell him, "I actually think the fighting is a good sign." His father had been ill for almost a year. While his father's actual life had never really been at risk, the family had been living with the fear of his dying. This fight was an omen of good health. It said, "Now we have enough faith to break out of mourning mode and have fights over the anger and fear we've been saving up." He cried some more. Then we hugged. Then he went home. A week later, all I heard of the resolution was, "It's better." Then we went on to other conversations—safer stuff.

Snapshot: I go to Seattle and make seder with my friend Carol. We clean, cook, actually see a movie in the afternoon before first seder. Everything is great. Second seder is designed to be an instant replay. It spins into a huge fight. Probably it is my fault—that is what the Russian judge says. Late at night, after the mixed-multitude has returned home, the tears and the screams break forth. It is as bad as the Thanksgiving from Hell, my worst adult attempt to return to the nurturing bosom of my birth family. It was the one time I took the words of Rabbi Shimon seriously. He said, "When three eat together at the same table and have not spoken words of Torah there, it is as they had eaten dead bodies."[4]

That year, by the time the ritual arguments involved in the preparation had taken place, the turkey tasted like something the undertaker had rejected. Maybe it was a cornerstone. Carol and I yelled and blamed each other, then hugged and made up, knowing that perhaps the "adoption" had taken—we had blended into a real family, perfectly accessorized with family feuds. We were now a real family, no matter what the fight, a resolution would always follow. We, too, could safely be hurt and petulant and needy, and have the fights and gaps of silent self-righteousness every family needs. The Thanksgiving from Hell was the last time I ever went home. I swore to myself that this was the case. I have been there many time since. It is an annual pilgrimage. I earn lots of frequent fighter miles.

Snapshot: I am having dinner with another one of "my kids." His parents have just separated. This meal becomes a game called Which One Shall I Choose? (He named the game—not me!) In between trips to the salad, pasta, and dessert bars, I listen and ask just enough questions to allow him to continue uninterrupted. I learn of the bribes each parent is offering. Bottles of wine (for an eighth grade party), relaxed curfews, confusion. These stories are intermixed with stories of strictness—when, instead of trying to induce the child's affection, each parent is proving to the other their ability to impose stability. When it all comes down to it, the choice is simple—the boy who is just growing his first pubic hairs chooses to be with the father who is losing most of his hair and who has again taken to wearing gold chains. Adolescence springs eternal. All this takes place between gulping handfuls of colored sprinkles intended to be sprinkled on the soft ice cream. He just keeps eating them.

A couple of weeks later the couple has reconciled. It is just another offering in the salad bar of family life. I suspect that "the kid" will not look back too unfondly on this as some of his pasta days.

Snapshot: My own mother and her husband come to visit. They spend eight days. It is my feeling that we usually do well for about three days together. We go to Palm Springs for the weekend. If Robert Conrad could survive his Palm Springs Week-End, so could I. The trip tests the limits. On day six we are eating lunch. I complain that, given the cost of housing in California, I will never be able to afford a home. I state, not complain, that, "In this day and age, 'homefulness' is an inheritance, not a right." My mother's husband then let's go with both barrels. He means well. I know he means well. It is important that I tell you he meant well at that moment. Even then, when his words were hurting me, I knew part of his motivation was fondly paternal—part was Oedipal—I'm never sure of the difference. My mother's husband kindly tells me, "I don't want to tell you how to live your life, but it seems to me that it's time you stopped wasting your time with this fantasy business and earned a real living—then you can move out of that hell hole where you live into a real place."

I was good. I gently protested, asserting pride in my career and accomplishments, but I don't fight back. Later my mother cried, apologizing for him. At the time, though, she said nothing. He never apologized himself.

The next day, again out of love and concern, my mother asks me about my business partners—my "real" (read "self-chosen") family (in contrast to my relatives)—suggesting that they are taking advantage of my skills and creativity. I again let it pass in relative silence. I assert the facts (my view of them) and then drop into silence. The rest of their visit is tense. My mother calls crying the day after she returns. She tells me, "I love you," followed by a lot tears and a lot of testimonies of affection. I tell her, "I love you. too, I just don't like you a lot at the moment." This cycle goes round a lot of times. I assure her that I will not abandon her. It makes her unhappy that I don't allow my feelings of hurt to dissipate quickly and conveniently. For me, love doesn't conquer gross insensitivity.

The night after my mother and her husband leave, I call "the kid." He is the one person I know will really understand. I tell him we are going to reverse parts. I tell him the story of my Palm Springs Week-End. He responds with the appropriate responsive rituals. "They are parents, that is what they are like. You have a lot of other feelings toward them, but you also love them—learn to live with it. Parents are like that." I wonder how long it will be before the next time I will never spend time with my parents again. I wonder how long before "the kid" tells his father, "I love you, I just don't like you a lot at the moment."

Snapshot: I sit at a conference on Jewish family education at the Whizin Institute with the world's leading experts. It is lunch. We wind up in a strange kind of confessional. I tell the story of My Parents Visit and the story of retelling My Parents Visit to "the kid." The flood gates break. Everyone tells the "real" story of the skeleton in his or her own family educator closet. We are a perfect family collection, with rebellious out-of-control kids, disintegrated marriages, difficult relationships with our own parents—the whole litany. We are anything but a Quaker Oats commercial—therefore, we have the perfect background to work with real Jewish families. We all breathe deeply—we have confessed one shared dark secret.

To unpack this notion of *function* versus *dysfunction*, let's braid two post-modern texts together and make family midrash.

Torah Text: "Whatever trouble he's in, his family has the right to share it with him. It's our duty to help him if we can, and it's his duty to let us, and he doesn't have the privilege to change that."[5]

Proem Verse: *Lyman*: Oh. Actually, though, why do we think of monogamy as a higher form of life? *Theo*: Well, it implies an intensification of love. *Lyman*: But how does that make it a higher form? *Theo*: Monogamy strengthens the family; random screwing undermines it. *Lyman*: But as one neurotic to another, what's so good about strengthening the family? *Theo*: Well, for one thing it enhances liberty. *Bessie* (Puzzled): Liberty? Really? *Theo*: The family disciplines its members; when the family is weak, the state has to move in; so the stronger the family, the fewer the police. And that is why monogamy is a higher form. *Lyman*: Jesus, did you just make that up?[6]

[1] Rabbinic Visions of the Family

Let's go from an idea we understand to one which may be new. Classical Jewish theology teaches that God created people in God's image (Gen. 1.27). Does that mean people are Godlike? No, it means, given a lot of work, people can become Godlike. How so? What we need to do is take "God's image" and modify it with, "You shall be holy, for I, Adonai your God, am holy. Each of all of you shall awe your mother and your father—

and my shabbatot you shall keep" (Lev. 19.2). In other words, "God's image" contains the raw material to be Godlike, but to manifest it—and "be holy," takes a lot of work, a lot reflection, a lot of mitzvot.

Essentially, "holiness" is a fantasy—a mystical quality like an "aura," like "the shining," like "talent," in fact like "God," whose attributes can be described, but whose essence is illusive. We can look at whether or not a person does things we predefine as holy, whether or not a person seems to have a sense of the holy, but there is no holiness meter. Likewise, "functionality" is a similar construct. It has become a mystical essence like "chi" or "the right stuff," which families can seem to possess. If I were a therapist or a sociologist, an anthropologist or a statistician, I might try to elucidate a formal definition. But, my role is that of social commentator, and I am interested, in this essay, in the popular fantasy of "functionality" that—like the Holy Grail, like all the black and white ghosts which still haunt us from the golden age of television—families can find a state of grace we call functionality. (The acid test, if I had to give you one, is that functional families can solve all problems from drug addiction to halitosis in thirty minutes with time left over for two commercial breaks.) Here, we are talking about the "idea of the functional" and the "myth of the dysfunctional." We are not interested in their truth, but in their mythic role, the way they have worked into the fabric of contemporary thinking as the Valhalla and Hades of post-shag-rug America.

This is the idea which may be new: I've come to suspect that the "Live up to God's Image" principle can be applied to families. (Because in many ways covenant theology turns God and Israel into a family unit.) Families have the potential for functionality—but it is an act of work, not grace, to achieve it. Families come with tidal forces. Every couple—no matter how much in love, no matter how committed—fights battles between intimacy and freedom. All children—no matter how close—have moments of the Cain and Abel thing. Children regularly accuse parents of the "Saturn/Kronos eats his children" syndrome when they demand an independence for which parents are not yet ready. Simultaneously, parents describe it as a moment when Daedalus needs to warn Icarus not to head too close to the sun. Families always have mythic proportions.

In our times, the *National Inquirer's* dream family nightmares are becoming real, ordinary, and everyday. Just ask the Royal Family of England. Ask the cast of *The Brady Bunch*, or your next door neighbor, or just look in your own family's closet. Families just don't seem to be what they used to be. The only problem is, families are actually just what they always were—bonded groups of people who both soar together and who equally often ravage each other. The ancient stories, whether Greek or biblical, Chinese or African, understand the duality of the family— arenas of light and arenas of shadow—the solarium and the root cellar.

Modernity fostered the illusion that penicillin would conquer disease. But, we now know all about penicillin-resistant bacteria—and even British flesh-eating bacteria. We fostered the illusion that first radio, then television, and now computers would educate the masses. We ignored the fact that two weeks after the discovery of each new communications technology, we have had to face its use as a vehicle for the distribution of pornography. Printing brings the Bible to the masses. Printing makes *Playboy* possible. Modernity, with its illusions about nature and technology—with its fantasy that "everything is getting better and better every day"—thought it could recreate the family in its own image—only light, only functionality. It believed that poverty and disease were the external sources of darkness. In the new womb of suburbia (freed of the evils of city life), with all needs only a short drive away, families could not fail to grow and prosper. The myths—meaning stories to teach truth—of the modern era really believed that love and science conquered all. Therefore, family life was triaged (in popular usage) into the functional—that which is the manifestation of Dan Quayle's "Family Values"—and dysfunction—that which a mental health professional is hired to exorcise.

What was forgotten was that the soul of the family—like the soul of an individual—has moments of sunrise and of midnight. What is dysfunctional (unproductive for health and prosperity) is the fantasy that most families should never know profound pain, loneliness, jealousy, suffering—that only "bad families" have divorces, addictions, and eating disorders. Even though we now know better (because many of us get to talk about it with our twelve-step groups, our therapists, or our favorite talk radio host) we still feel the guilt—and suffer the pain for being more like the Cramdens than the Cleavers. Mythic truth is that we all have moments of being Hamlet, of acting like Lady Macbeth, and of being Lucy—of having our impulses destroy our best intentions. The nice thing about *I Love Lucy*, by the way, is that every episode is the affirmation of the possibility of repentance.

Thomas Moore comments: "When I see those three letters 'dys' in dys-functional, I think of 'Dis,' the old name for the mythological under-world. Soul enters life from below, through cracks, finding an opening into life at the points where smooth functioning breaks down….In study-ing the mythologies of the world, you always find evil characters and some sort of underworld: the same is true in the family. It always has shadow, no matter how much we wish otherwise. Its functioning is always soiled by Dis." [7]

Family comes from the Latin word *familia*. "This famous word…is inseparable from the idea of land settlement, and is therefore essential-ly the house itself, with the persons living in it. And thus the religion of the familia will be a religion of practical utility, of daily work, of strug-gle with perils. It is not the worship of an idea of kinship." [8] As James Hillman observed:

> The notorious "nuclear" family of statistics, sermons and adver-tisements—two parents, two siblings, a family car and a pet—does not correspond with the Latin word from which family derives. *Familia*, familias to the Romans, meant primarily "a house and all belonging to it." In fact, a domesticated animal was often considered a familiar. Living together in a familiarity as a psycho-economic organism—such is the meaning of family. Even the Greek word *oikonomia* (from which come economy and economics) means household management or housekeeping.
>
> The family is a function of the house, rather than vice versa. [9]

This notion of family as bayit, as house, is one which we see the Jewish tradition also echoes. The first bottom line is that kinship is over-rated. The second bottom line is that ancient families knew that their "homes" had dungeons and demons.

> Various gods and goddesses lived with the ancient family: Vesta at the hearth (focus is the Latin word) who must be acknowl-edged first and daily or the else the central bonding flames must go out; Janus at the gates so one remembered the different faces required for inside and outside….The ancient house gave plenty of place to the invisibles that lived with a family, propitiating and domesticating its daimones, which it acknowledged as rightfully belonging. [10]

Ancient cultures knew that families had shadows. This truth we hid from ourselves, replacing it with a false myth of automatic familiar functionality. What has been shattered in our age is merely the freckled Norman Rockwell illusion of wholesome family life. Here are three simple pieces of evidence to think about.

A. Look at any of the family stories from the Torah. They have all of the family's greatest shadows—rape, incest, adultery, favoritism, sibling rivalry—all of the dark side.

B. Look at fairy tales. Before you get to "live happily ever after," there are wicked stepmothers, absent and weak fathers, evil siblings, and a whole host of demons, dragons, giants, and other dangers to get through.

C. Look into your own heart and feel all the ambivalence family in the specific generates when you contrast it with family in the ideal. Every Cleaver clan has Charley Addam's family living in the closet, attic, or basement.

James Hillman teaches a number of important lessons. First, he says there are no actually "normal" families left in America. Seventy-five percent of family units are not nuclear, normal families. (Ninety-four percent of all families may be "dysfunctional"). Twenty-five percent of all households are people living alone. Twenty-five percent of children are now born out of wedlock Fifty percent of new marriages now end in divorce. Thirty-three and three-tenths percent of those treated for mental disorders in hospitals are teenagers. Three out of every one hundred adult males in the United States are in the correctional system. Three out of five children born will spend part of their childhood in a single parent household. In the State of Virginia, forty-four percent of children prefer the company of the television set to that of their fathers. The family home is the most dangerous place you can be (it is where you are most likely to be killed or injured—and the perpetrator is usually a relative).[11] And we are now smart enough not to protest with, "But Jewish families are different!" We know better. Thomas Moore reaches the same conclusion this way:

Today professionals are preoccupied with the *dysfunctional family*. But to some extent all families are dysfunctional. A family is a microcosm, reflecting the nature of the world, which runs on both virtue and evil. We may be tempted at times to imagine the family as full of innocence and goodwill, but actual family life resists such romanticism. Usually it presents the full range of human potential, including evil, hatred, violence, sexual confusion, and insanity. In other words, the dynamics of actual family life reveal the soul's complexity and unpredictability; any attempts to place a veil of simplistic sentimentality over the family image will break down.[12]

E. B. Howe gets this irony down just right when he says: "The worst thing in the world is the homesickness which comes over a man when he is at home." Moore writes:

> Some people believe the images of normality and maintain the secret of their family's corruption, wishing they had been born elsewhere in a land of bliss. But recovery of soul begins when we can take to heart our own family fate and find in it the raw material, the alchemical prima materia, for our own soul work. For this purpose, 'family therapy' might take the form of simply telling stories of family life, free from any concern for cause and effect or sociological influence. These stories generate a grand local, personal mythology.[13]

Rabbi Lawrence Kushner regularly teaches that "[T]he Torah is the collective unconscious of the Jewish people." Let's use some Torah (oral and written) to find and tell some stories which reveal the real Jewish vision of the family. Let's use a Mishnah (Bava Metzia 1.5) to understand part of the rabbinic vision of family:

> An ownerless object found by one's minor son or daughter; an ownerless object found by a man's Canaanite male slave or female slave,
> An ownerless object found by his wife—these belong to him.
> An ownerless object found by one's adult son or daughter,
> An ownerless object found by a man's Jewish manservant or maidservant,
> An ownerless object found by a man's ex-wife whom he divorced, but whom he has not yet given her ketubah to her—these belong to them.

Commentary: First let's redefine family. Let's think walls—not blood. Rather than think of a family as being a kinship group—part of the fantasy of the Norman Rockwell Universe—family was once, and is again, a psycho-economic unit that lived and struggled to survive together. The slave, the cow, and even the furniture were part of "the family." That is the Scottish idea of "The Keep." Home is not where the heart is—the heart is, rather, connected to those who live in the home. Familiarity breeds family! That is the Torah of Stephen Stills: "If you can't be with the one you love, love the one you're with." And like all good and true emotions, home feeling/family love is ambivalent. A son cannot love a mother without simultaneously struggling for freedom from her. Husband and wife cannot love each other without simultaneously—and often deep in places that are hard to admit—nursing their unfulfilled needs. In each of our relationships we struggle with the no-reality of platonic relationships (the cave, not the friendship) while falling back into being (at best) only the best possible relationship we can manage.

This Mishnah reaches into that ambivalence and paints an interesting portrait of a family. This is the story! A son finds a coin and tries to keep it. The father feels that he is struggling to maintain the whole family, that he needs the coin and every resource in order for the family to make it, and that the lazy son doesn't do enough to support the family anyway. The son, meanwhile, feels put upon, robbed and infantilized all at once. They yell at each other. They do a tug of war with the coin. Perhaps they throw things. Maybe doors are slammed. Finally, when there is no reconciliation, they take the matter to the Bet Din. The rabbis give a ruling: "If the kid is a major, he can keep it. If the kid is a minor, Dad gets it."

The matter went to court. How do we know that? Simple, the Mishnah made the ruling. Things that don't need verdicts aren't made into mishnayot. If there is a Mishnah, then there were court cases. It's that simple. The Mishnah is basically a guide book for rabbis acting as judges. Why did the matter get to court? Whenever I teach this text, someone, usually a woman, says: "They should just give the money to charity." She doesn't get it. This is not fifty cents or ten dollars, this is the mythic million-dollar briefcase no one can trace, and the family has been reduced, as the rabbis knew that many families are reduced, to a pair of two year-olds each screaming, "Mine." Why didn't good conversation work things out? The answer is simple: in real families, fathers don't always know best—and when they do, it is rarely acknowledged. Conversations don't always work out. The Mishnah is written for such eventualities and for times when families haven't yet climbed up to hyper-functionality. The Mishnah knows what Louis B. Meyer denied: families often need family courts. (Even then some Judge Hardys molest Judy when Andy isn't looking.) As Tom Bodett teaches, "What do sex, rock and roll, and family secrets have to do with growing up? Just about everything."[14]

But the universe of family strife is not just between fathers and sons. In this passage, we have arguments between husbands and wives, between masters and servants, between fathers and adult children, between separated and divorced couples. Here is a world where Shakespeare would feel comfortable. A lot of family comedy—and family tragedy—all are situations which take more than twenty-eight-and-one-half minutes to resolve—a lot of winters of our discontent. (By the way, if you can't see all that in those few lines of Mishnah, you've got to learn a little about unpacking Rabbinic texts.) Remember, the whole world is a Mishnah, and the people merely actors....

The Gemara (Bava Metzia 12a ff) goes even deeper. In it, a precocious twelve-year-old yells at the court, "I am no minor." Like Macaulay Culkin, he argues, "Judaism needs a Coogan Law—I am earning enough money to be treated like an adult. I take care of Dad (who is the fat, lazy—and perhaps alcoholic—cretin who regularly spends my money). Dad doesn't take care of me! I am an orphan with an abusive father."

Slowly the argument (which I will nor reconstruct here) evolves a new concept—m'p'nai darkhei shalom—compromises for the sake of family peace. This Gemara is worth studying on its own—both for the insights and for the compromises. But the story of our father and son needs an ending. The verdict goes this way: the concept of being an adult is redefined by economic status rather than age. An adult child is "someone who no longer eats at the family table (on a regular basis)." Anyone who still sits at the table—even though they have the "legal right" to keep what they find—are told by the rabbi/judge m'p'nai darkhei shalom, not to push the point, but to give in. And we learn the deep lesson: when it comes to family, being right isn't always smart. That is the Torah of m'p'nai darkhei shalom—compromises for the sake of family peace.

Davar Aẖer: A Different Truth: And then my friend and teacher Sally Weber will always add that darkei shalom (family peace) also can be the gag used to mask a lot of family abuse. Families' souls have shadows and light, just like the rest of us.

In this passage, we see that family membership deals with economic interdependence and proximity—not just blood. (Think of the parallel inclusion of slaves, servants, children, and wives). More than that, we see the rabbinic perception of "dysfunctionality" as normative, a perception that is clarified by the amount of "family law" they make explicit—and the centrality they place on learning it. The rabbis know and understand the kind of family diversity and potential darkness that Thomas Moore and James Hillman describe. After our fight between father and son—after the chorus of "Mine"—they still are a family. They are just a stressed family. They know Jared Barkley's truth: "Whatever trouble he's in, his family has the right to share it with him. It's our duty to help him if we can, and it's his duty to let us—and he doesn't have the privilege to change that."[15] Stuck is stuck. That is the Torah of m'p'nai darkhei shalom. That is Robert Frost's truth: "Home is the place that when you have to go there, they have to take you in."

Imagine This Situation: A twenty-three-year-old daughter, post-college, moves back home. She has a fight with her mother and retreats to her room. She blasts some loud, ugly music on her stereo. The mother yells at her to turn it down. She yells back, "It's my room." The mother yells again, "Not in my house it isn't." The mother enters the room—without knocking, and without permission—to continue the fight. She sees on the wall a recently-done graphic painting (composed by the daughter as a mural) of a couple engaged in a rather athletic act of intercourse (think gymnasts doing it in space). The mother yells, "Get that off my walls." The daughter yells, "Get out of my room." And in our world—as Mishnaic as this situation is—there often is no longer the knowledge that a Bet Din exists—no longer the sense that a "rule" in Jewish Law prescribes a needed compromise. The yelling continues for awhile. Then the two find their own kind of reconciliation—usually. That is the kind of Mishnaic stage most of our families act out.

My friends and teachers, the Wollins, tell this story: Their seventeen-year-old daughter left for college in a huff of blame and chastisement. As she left, she revealed to her parents all the ways in which they had limited, ruined, and devastated her life. Then she was gone. The next night they returned home from dinner out to find this message on the answer phone: "Where are you? I called and you were gone!" The Wollins—here and elsewhere in their writing—reveal a lot about the two-stepped tango of the family. They understand that to be family, to live together, is always to be trapped in the dual-edged feelings of protection and confinement, or love and resentment. The very act of living together with one set of people generates the fantasy that there are others with whom we could bond more easily. That is the duality of the tango between families real and adoptive. The Wollins, in their book *The Resilient Self,* are the first to suggest this notion of the "adoptive family." The Wollins write:

> Is it true that for every resilient survivor there is at least one caring, strong adult who makes a critical difference? I am invariably asked this question. My problem with the question is not with the content, it's the emphasis that makes me uncomfortable. I have heard resilient survivors attribute their endurance and determination to a "life-saving" figure who came to their aide [The 'Adopter']. But like all stories, the one about the caring grown-up and the hurt child can be told from other perspectives; some slants are better for survivors than others. The version I prefer least revolves on the theme of generosity. A reframed version of the "Save-the-child" [story is] "The Appealing Child Meets the Potentially Interested Adult." This script depicts relationships as the fruits of your own labor, a rich yield, carefully and deliberately cultivated in the soil of despair.[16]

The Wollin's model originates in pathology (in response to their studies of addiction). I, like most post-modernists, suggest that a good dose of pathology is always normative and that psychogenic truth generalizes into our own everyday understandings. We can sing Stephen Stills' chorus: *If you can't be with the one you love, love the one you're with.*

There are moments in our life where we, faced with Tennessee William's mother as our own mother, flee to Glenda the Good Witch to protect us—only to find that she really doesn't care the way that "Mom Williams does." As Hillman puts it, in family "[N]o one is at fault, no one is kicked out, no one can be helped. In the paralysis lies the profoundest sense of acceptance. Grampa can go on grumbling, brother attacking the administration, sister introvertedly attending her exacerbating eczema, and mother goes on covering up with solicitous busy-ness. Everyone goes down the drain because family love allows family pathology; an immense tolerance for the hopeless shadow in each, the shadow that we carry as a permanent part of our shadow and that we unpack when we go back home."[17] Some Thanksgivings we eat the bear. Some Thanksgivings Kronos eats us. Or as Jonathan Omer-Man teaches: "God was gracious for giving us so many nights of Passover, so that each side of our family can stage their own psycho-drama." We can just imagine Shakespeare's quartet of seder questions.

Davar Aher: Another Version of this Lesson: We could have learned that lesson as easily from the Torah itself. My friend and teacher, Peter Pitzle, has enabled the spinning of a multi-verse of insights and rethinkings of the biblical text both with his writing and his facilitating of biblical psychodrama. His work can be found in his book, *Our Father's Wells,* and his influence is all over.

There is no absolute truth in a family system, only the truths of the participants. These truths are often unspoken, sometimes only partially conscious, and conditioned by the perspective and histories, illusions and convictions, of each family member. Indeed, to be a member of a family is to live with secrets, hidden motives, suspected alliances, painful exclusions. Psychodrama, by its ability to voice all the various perspectives that conspire in the family, allows us to explore the family system and attend at any moment to its strange polyphony.[18]

But let's work with a micro example. The story of Cain and Abel begins with an innocent line, which seems just to be pro forma narration (Don Pardo with his hand over his ear). Worked as a "psychodrama" open to the world of human experience cum midrash, it becomes something else. The Torah says (Genesis 4.1), "Adam knew his wife Eve. She became pregnant and gave birth to Cain. She said, 'Cain means I got a man with God's help.'" When I asked the group to "become" Eve and tell us the "story" behind the naming, the following diverse family truths emerged.

- Birth was such a miracle.
- God takes away and God gives. God kicked us out of the garden, but God gave us a kid. When we saw the first smile on Cain's face, all the work and all the pain was more than worth it. God is great! Cain is better than free fruit.
- After the Garden thing, there was so much distance between Adam and me that I thought a child would bring us together. I asked God for that blessing. I got the child, but it didn't work for very long. Soon, Adam again was remote, but at least God blessed me with a companion. I got a new man to replace the one who virtually left me.

- It hurt so damn much to give birth, I though I was going to die. I was all alone. (I had to bite through the umbilical chord with my teeth.) Adam was busy working his field, too far to hear my shouts. And neither of us knew what to do—or what was happening. But, I got through it because God was my co-pilot.
- Hey, we were young. We hadn't yet connected our nights of pleasure to something that happened nine months later. The stork myth hadn't been invented yet, so who else were you going to blame for this crying thing which oozed fluids at all orifices. But Cain was cute to start with.

Is all of this in the Torah? Perhaps. But regardless of your fantasies of revelation and the connection between oral and written Torah, this much is clear: the Torah's content, and its literary style of allusion and silence, invites exactly such participation. For the past fifteen years or so, Torah teacher after Torah teacher has remarked, with the surprise of discovery, that biblical families are "dysfunctional." These days, at those instances, I smile and say, "Of course, biblical families are families like all other families, struggling up from their worst tendencies towards Kedushah (holiness/functionality)."

Davar A<u>h</u>er: Another Version of this Lesson: I am in Chicago with a <u>H</u>avurah called Eitz Hayyim and we are studying the Torah portion of the week. We find this passage (Genesis 33:1-2), "Jacob lifted up his eyes and saw that Esau was coming with four hundred men. So he divided his children among Leah, Rachel, and the two maids. He put the maids and their children first, Leah and her children were behind them, and Rachel and Jacob behind them...." Jacob is using a King's India Defense. Next Esau arrives and introductions are made. The text reads, "Then the maids approached. They and their children bowed low. Then Leah and her children approached and bowed low. Last, Joseph and Rachel approached and bowed low" (33:6-7). Rashi reads the passage and asks: "Why did Joseph step in front of Rachel?" As usual, Rashi answers his own question. "Joseph knew Esau's reputation, and stepped in front of his beautiful mother to protect her." We study the passage. We study Rashi's reaction, and the group evolves this insight. Joseph and Rachel behave in a way we recognize. They are like a single parent mother raising a son. They are sometimes like lovers, sometimes like siblings, sometimes like parent and child—each sometimes being the parent in the dyad. Jacob is such an absent parent, and Rachel and Joseph are so estranged from the rest of the camp, that they are behaving the way many mothers and the sons they are raising alone behave. There is a lot of Richard the Third in the Torah.

[2] Can the Reality of Family Support the Fantasy of Family Values, Family Education, and Family Whatever...?

Family education is the latest Messiah in the Jewish war against the demographics of assimilation. It is very likely to become the next in a long-standing series of failures, each predicated on a different mythic vision of Jewish survival. In essence, it is a question of cloning. We are trying to "clone" Jewish life, creating new Jews in an artificial and partial environment. We are constantly seeking the minimum amount of ethno-genetic material necessary to spontaneously generate Jewishness. We are looking for an easy way to say: "Let there be Jews" and have there be Jews. We would like all of our family education to be a G.T.H.B.A.—a "Good Time Had By All"—education, to cure the world by blessing and ceremony, never getting our hands bloody, never crawling into the mud.

Once Judaism, Jewish Identity, Jewishness, and Jewish Survival were an organic whole. Judaism was a closed ecology—it was a living organism. The idea of factoring out individuals or individual elements was not a consideration. Only when we put a little "English" on the ball and ricocheted ourselves off the bumpers of modernity did pieces begin to break off. First, following Martin Luther's path, we affirmed the individual in his or her individual relationship to God, Torah, and Israel. Catholic Israel was no more. Slowly, we have learned that "individual" interventions, that working with individuals—especially kids—has failed to generate enough new Jews. Philosophy, identity, consciousness—all are, along with spirituality, great tools. They are not, however, the penicillin of Jewish survival. (Remember, bacteria learns....) Moreover, individualism stands in dynamic tension with the centrality of family—that is the story of ego development. To be a rebel, to be a hero, you have to leave home— even if you eventually return. Individualism demands space—you can't do it when five people have to get through the bathroom every morning. Moses didn't take his family up Mt. Sinai and let the kids enjoy the experience. Revelation isn't a family vacation.

Emphasize individual identity and personal need and you destroy family. Family is inherently balanced on uneasy compromise and self-effacement. Family, so goes the developmental tale, is only the beginning, a necessary evil, which, like all beginnings, must be left behind. An adult has grown up, declared his independence, and his life and liberty are dedicated to the pursuit of his own happiness....Psychoanalysis has swallowed whole the myth of the individual's development away from family. Everyone who buys an hour of analysis buys into this myth called "strengthening the ego."[19]

David Elkind clarifies the progression of family from modern to postmodern and beyond. "Around the '50s, most of us lived in nuclear families. We operated under the assumptions that women should stay home, men should be the providers, and the children should be protected." Since then, that image had been broken down.

> Couples used to believe in romantic love—that there was just one person in the whole world who was for you...second there was the notion of maternal love, the belief that women possessed a maternal instinct to be with their children at all times...to make a nest, and that if they didn't something was wrong with them...a third sentiment of the nuclear family was domesticity and the idea that the home was the center of one's life. That really grew out of the movement into cities and industrialization. The factory was a cold, hard place, and the factory worker was a cog in the machine. In contrast, the home was a warm, welcoming place in a heartless world. And in that home, mother was the center.

Then came the transformation. "The industrial revolution robbed women of their creative outlets. Women were told not to grind their own coffee because they could buy vacuum packed....Women were turned into consumers, which eventually contributed in a very important way to the woman's movement."

In this economic transformation, other values changed too. Among others, virginity has lost its value. "The implicit contract based on an exchange of virginity for commitment no longer exists. The basis of the contract has become consensual. Marriage is an agreement between two equals, with the idea that we'll stay in this relationship as long as it serves our purposes and needs." As marriage changed, the family changed.

Parents today have to protect themselves first, much as in an airplane they must put the breathing masks on themselves before they put it on their children. To make sure that their children are provided for, they devote tremendous time to working and refurbishing their skills. So, too often, parents are focused on their own activities, forcing their kids to be autonomous as well—to be much more independent, to be home alone, to get their own meals, to organize their own time.

This has big fall out. "The family meal has gone by the board. It used to be a gathering place for the nuclear family. Today, soccer practice or a business meeting takes precedence over dinner because personal needs are more important than the family."

In this article, I have often pointed out that every truth and its opposite are often simultaneously true—as each over-reaction invites the next pendulum swing. So Elkind points out: "Statistics show that young people are marrying later and are having fewer children. They are trying not to make the mistakes in their own lives that their parents made. They don't want to go through divorce. When they get into a relationship they want to make it work. This bodes well for the family."[20]

Some families now "abandon family" in order to participate as "individuals" in communal activities. Some families now have returned to nesting—devoting almost exclusive time to the family—and shunning outside involvements. Strong families eat away at community. Ask the Hatfields and the Capulets. Families breed nepotism. It is definitional. Community demands equality. Think about it. It is the same issue. The naive vision that strong individuals join together to create families which breed new, strong individuals is indeed just a naive vision. It is a small part of a larger pathogenic truth. Adding the demands and tidal pulls of community involvement only complicates the picture. We live in an age where community is eroding from just these forces.

Consider this Truth: There is striking evidence that the vibrancy of American civil society has notably declined over the past several decades….It is not just the voting booth that has been increasingly deserted by Americans…the number of Americans who report that "in the past year" they have "attended a meeting on town or school affairs" is down by more than a third…both religious service groups and church-related groups have declined modestly (about one-sixth), and while more

Americans are bowling today than ever before, bowling in organized leagues has plummeted in the past decade or so (forty percent). The traditional form of civic organization whose decay we have been tracing have been replaced by vibrant new organizations (like the Sierra Club, the National Organization for Women, and the AARP)...where the only act of membership consists in writing a check.[21] To a large degree, this is what Christopher Lasch describes in *The Culture of Narcissism.*

> The new narcissist is haunted not by guilt but by anxiety. He seeks not to inflict his own certainties on others but to find meaning in life...superficially relaxed and tolerant, he has little use for dogmas of racial and ethnic purity but at the same time forfeits the security of group loyalties and regards everyone as a rival for favors conferred by a paternalistic state.[22]

Why would someone join a synagogue with 3,000 members, a swimming pool, and sixteen rabbis on staff? Lasch argues that such institutions are a perfect narcissist's choice because they have the resources to meet needs on demand, yet they provide great anonymity. He argues that, like someone trained in karate, the narcissist knows that his own "leanings" can be used against him. Therefore, being known, belonging in reality and not just on a membership list, means that demands can be placed on her or him. That is why today, much which looks like affiliation and membership is really just the purchasing of services from a vending institution. "He [the narcissist] extols cooperation and teamwork while harboring deeply antisocial impulses. He praises respect for rules while secretly believing that they do not apply to himself. Acquisitive in the sense that his cravings have no limits, he does not accumulate goods and provisions against the future, in the manner of nineteenth century political economy, but demands immediate gratification and lives in a state of restless, perpetually unsatisfied desire."[23]

Recently a Reform rabbi found one of his bar mitzvah students wearing a cross during a Torah reading rehearsal. He asked for explanation and the boy, from an intermarried home, explained that he was to be confirmed a few weeks after his bar mitzvah. When the rabbi asked the father for an explanation, the father replied, "We wanted our son to have the protection of both religions." Often what looks like belonging is just paying dues. "The narcissist has no interest in the future because, in part, he has so little interest in the past. Impending disaster has become an everyday concern, so commonplace and familiar that nobody any longer gives much thought to how disasters might be averted. People instead busy themselves with survival strategies, measures designed to prolong their own lives, or programs guaranteed to ensure good head, and peace of mind."[24] In other words, while some new people have gotten really excited about joining bowling leagues, more people are bowling alone.

Home Alone is one of today's myths. It is the story of the competent child who is forced to raise himself. He is the suburban and urban feral child—king of the latch key. He or she is the child of lessons, carpools, and quality time. That is one new American myth; Linda and Richard Eyre are creating one of the others. They are Mormons, family educators who have made it to the best seller list with books entitled *Teaching Your Child Values, Teaching Your Child Responsibility*, and *Teaching Your Child Sensitivity*.[25] In these books they propose intensive family processes which literally take five to ten hours of "family work" every week. Included on their list is a family night, a family court, a family bank, a repentance bench, a family "value of the week," which is studied, a unique and different birthday celebration for each and every family member, and a weekly parents' night out (to review and log the family plan for each child). All-but-absent-parenting and hyper-parenting coexist.

But in general, we are in the midst of an era of nesting and comfort food. We live in a post-Einsteinian reality where time is collapsing—not so much from traveling faster than the speed of light, but from down-sizing. We are at a moment where the dissipation of the myth of "quality" time is generating a new gaggle of stay-at-home mothers who shun baby sitters, where professionals are refusing to move for promotion so that their children can know their grandparents. Having pushed family to the brink—having seen its impending destruction—we have backed off. We have recentered ourselves in home and family. We have invested in couch-based memberships and participate in a virtual community. This is a moment when Martha Stewart is big time. Still, the reaction formation is growing, formulating, and on the rise.

Since Lakeville, since Marshall Sklare's first lists of Jewish behaviors, we've wanted to reduce Jewish identification to a series of observable and reportable actions and attitudes. At first we tried to influence individuals to perform more of these behaviors—now we believe the Jewish future can best be served by modifying, or at least reinforcing, family performance of these symbolic factors. Over-simplified, but not untrue, we see the Jewish future directly connected to the number of Jewish families who light Shabbat or Hanukkah candles. We assume that Shabbat candles are a direct step towards in-marriage. The numbers have already proved those assumptions wrong, but understanding why is important. It is a "black box" problem.

Jeremiah Johnson was a great early Robert Redford character. He was a mountain man who inherits a Native American wife and a deaf-mute son. They build a life together They transcend the cultural issues. They overcome communication difficulties. They build a common life, common accomplishments, and common life rituals. For Jeremiah Johnson it ends by attack from the outside: his family is killed by marauders. But it would have ended anyway. Mythic marauders would have eventually disrupted the isolated mountainside. The Wilderness Family always returns home. Ultimately, the kid would have run away—with or without permission—the log cabin becomes claustrophobic and the sirens of the outside world beckon. Often, family education strives to create Jewish families which light their candles and say their blessings and feel their identity alone on the mountainside. When the kids age, they must leave home to reproduce. Families, except for where incest is involved, are sterile—it takes outside blood. Only the active and meaningful involvement of the family in the Jewish community dramatically increases the odds of in-marriage. Family is clearly a desirable condition for Jewish survival, but it is not a sufficient condition. In other words, as Vicky Kelman teaches in the name of the Torah of Africa, "It takes a whole village to raise a child." She was quoting it years before Hillary Clinton did.

Each of us needs a collection of peers (to pressure us differently than the way our family does) and mentors to help us reflect on our family condition. The growth curve of the human soul requires breaking with a family in order to achieve enough independence to then return to that family as an adult. The rabbinic tradition always balanced the mitzvah of marriage and home with the insight: "Get yourself a teacher and find yourself a haver [a best friend/Torah partner]." For home to work, there always needs to be a place away from home. You can learn this lesson from Dorothy. You have to leave Kansas to realize "There is no place like home." That is something you can never see from Kansas. But for Jewish life to be a closed environment—to keep our futures from the demographic truths of the Little Mermaid—a community relatively confluent to our family values must be the place we to which we go to escape our family when the pressures build. "The grass is always greener in the other fellow's yard…unless they are part of the eruv [those who live within the Shabbat fence], not the eruv rav [the wild hoard/mixed multitude]."

Davar Aḥer: Thomas Moore writes: "Loneliness, and God knows we are all lonely, can be the result of an attitude that community is something into which one is received. Many people wait for members of a community to invite them in especially after they have paid the dues, and until that happens, they are lonely. There may be something of the child here who expects to be taken care of by the family. But a community is not a family. It is a group of people held together by feelings of belonging, and those feelings are not a birthright. 'Belonging' is an active verb, something we do positively."[26] His message is clear and significant. Community is not one big happy family (we have already learned that no family is ever just one, big happy family). Community makes different demands. Community requires different skills. Davening in a minyan is far more dynamic and takes greater skill than lighting a ḥanukkiyah. Just as pre-school takes a lot more education to actualize its full potential, so, too, must family education lead to a yet undefined process—community education. And we must remember that community skills are more complex, less obvious, and harder to "amass" than are family skills. Ducklings don't imprint on board meetings. *Robert's Rules of Order* are not natural law.

Adrianne Bank reads and asks, "Are you equating community with your previously alluded to 'pseudo-family?'" No, but yes. While there can be aspects of "pseudo-family" that emerge from participation in community (ḥavurot being a good indicator), community is of a different scale. Communities don't fit in living rooms. Communities can't be moved or influenced by a single dining table conversation. Communities are public domains—families (real and pseudo) are private domains. Communities and families take different outfits and different masks.

The two-fold of conclusion of this article is therefore:
1. To be a true Jewish family educator, one must always paint a realistic, rather than romanticized, vision of the family; and
2. To actualize Jewish family education, one must always educate towards community.

So much for praxis, now back to theology.

[3] Towards a Redemptive Vision of Dysfunctionality

Tom Bodett (the Motel 6 guy) is actually a brilliant storyteller whose Alaskan tales convey a deep sense of the mythic as manifest in modern American life. I use several of his stories as focal points—texts—in my teaching of the life cycle. He introduces his new audio novel with these words: "That's what the. . .odyssey is all about—leaving home and coming home, and trying to understand the difference."[27] This is another expression of the family tango—the dance that we all do, moving towards and away from family simultaneously. We are always Jacob fleeing from family and visioning ladders reaching to heaven. We are always Jacob finding our way home and wrestling with dark angels at midnight. A proactive theology of family needs to include both. And the roots of that theology are present in the origins of the biblical text itself.

In lectures glossing the work of Lawrence Stager, William G. Dever, a leading figure in biblical archeology, spoke of the unique difference between late Bronze-era Israelite and Canaanite settlements:

A typical peasant farm house can be related to the biblical bet ha-av usually translated literally as 'the house of the father,' but in sociological terms a descent group or 'nuclear family.' And clusters of these houses at the sites we have surveyed then reflect the biblical mish-pah-<u>hah</u>, to be understood as an extended or multiple family. This approach yields the best evidence yet that the new archeology can deal with ethnicity....Modern archeology begins to give Israelite 'ethnicity' a real definition, both in terms of distinctive material, cultural traits, and in terms of the patterns of behavior they reflect.[28]

Based on archaeological evidence, he implies that what made the Jewish people unique (different from other people in the Land of Canaan) was their sense of family. Their living space was designed to enforce and establish a sense of "family connection."

Let's compare Dever's reflections with the work of Mark S. Smith:

Early Israelite culture cannot be separated easily from the culture of Canaan. Canaanite and Israelite material culture cannot be distinguished by specific features in the period of the judges [the same time frame Dever discusses]. Items such as the four-room house, collared-rim store jar, and hewn cisterns, once thought to distinguish the Israelite culture of the highlands from the

Canaanite culture of the coast and valleys, are now attested on the coast, in the valleys, or in Transjoran. [However], from evidence that is available, one may conclude that although largely Canaanite according to currently available cultural data, Israel expressed a distinct sense of origins and deity and possessed largely distinct holdings in the hill counties. Israel inherited local cultural traditions…and its culture was largely continuous with the Canaanite culture of the coast and valleys during the Iron I period. The realm of religion was no different.[29]

Smith argues that Israel was initially monolatrous (worshipping only One God but not denying the existence of others.) Early Israelite culture tolerated (and occasionally participated in) the worship of minor deities, while holding that their God was the central, most powerful force in the universe. Smith argues that only later, in the period of the monarchy, did this ethnically unique monolatry shift to monotheism (more through political than religious process).

What seems to evolve as Israel's monotheistic theology can be described as "mono o'mono," monotheism engineered to protect and sustain the monarchy. The one true God protected and sustained the one true king. The worship of the One was an act of fealty to the other. Both benefited from the elimination of competition. Monogamy came as an interesting side benefit to this process—one that prophets like Hosea exploited to the hilt (2:21-22): I [God] will betroth you [Israel] to me forever, and I will betroth you to me with righteousness, justice, kindness, and mercy. I will betroth you to me with fidelity, and you shall know Adonai." Here, Hosea and many other prophets use the metaphor of marital fidelity as an expression of Israel's relationship with God. Hosea's story is this (Chapter 2): When Adonai first spoke to Hosea, Adonai said to Hosea, "Go and marry a hooker and adopt the whore's children [as a metaphor for the way the land will stray from following Adonai]….He went and married Gomer." He has three kids with her whom he names, in order, Jezreel (for Bloody deeds at Jezreel), Lo Ruhamah (I show no mercy), and Lo Ami (Not of My people). Then he breaks out in prophecy:

Rebuke your mother, rebuke her
For she is not my wife
And I am not her husband—
Have her stop being a whore—it shows on her face

Take away the adultery from her breasts
Otherwise I will strip her naked
And leave her as on the day she was born. . . .
Thus I will punish her. . . .

Hosea goes on ranting and raving for a while, then comes reconciliation:

And when that day comes—says Adonai
You will call me your ish [husband]
And no longer your baal [master/husband/pagan god]
For I will remove the names of the baalim [pagan gods]
From her mouth
And they shall never be mentioned by name any more. . . .

Hosea then describes a covenant made with birds and beasts and people:

I [God] will betroth you [Israel] to me forever,
And I will betroth you to me with righteousness, justice, kindness,
and mercy.
I will betroth you to me with fidelity,
And you shall know Adonai.
Then comes the final reconciliation:
I will answer from the sky
And I will answer to the earth
And the earth will answer back
With new grain and wine and oil
And Jezreel will be answered.
I will sow for her the land as my own
And return Lo Ruhamah to favor
And I will say to Lo Ami, "You are my people."
And he will respond, "You are my God."

Here, the saga of family becomes metaphor for a relationship with The Divine. Hosea tells us that dealing with God is also the family tango—Tom Bodett's "Leaving home and coming home." Just as our story as a people of faith struggling with fidelity to the One God is a story of failure, forgiveness, and reunion—a story of exile and return—it is also a family story. So, too, are the struggles to be family, with its moments of creation and corruption, revelation and rebellion, redemption and destruction, and issues of theology as well as therapy. It is a rich irony that David (whose lack of fidelity is legendary) had a political agenda of monarchy which made Hosea's theology of family monogamy desirable.

Both in the biblical text itself, and in the probable reconstruction of its origins—we find the same eternal duality.

Dever, in his argument, doesn't suggest what is cause and what is effect. But to us, the possibilities are interesting. What is the connection between monotheism and a strong sense of family? Especially in the tales in Genesis where we see an emphasis on fidelity and monogamy. Each of the stories where monogamy does not actualize is seen ironically as exceptional. We explain why Abraham takes another wife—it is not an obvious action. It is infertility, not lust or greed. We justify Jacob's multiple partners because of family politics and find a way to understand that strange practice. There is an active apologia going on relative to polygamy—an apologia which in the long run teaches a monogamist ideal—long before Rabbi Gershom's taḥannah.[30] What is the connection between monogamy and monotheism? Which is the chicken? Which is the egg? I suspect monogamy is at the core. Jews have always lived with the ideal of family, all the time knowing that like the speed of light, that sunlit ideal vision of family can be approached but not attained.

That echoes precisely one of the dual truths which began this proem, taught by Theo in Arthur Miller's play: *Lyman:* Oh.—Actually, though, why do we think of monogamy as a higher form of life? *Theo:* The family disciplines its members; when the family is weak the state has to move in; so the stronger the family the fewer the police. And that is why monogamy is a higher form. *Lyman:* Jesus, did you just make that up?[31]

Families, despite their weaknesses, tend to move us toward higher values (and in turn—find the confinement suffocating and occasionally regress toward their perversion). David, who established monotheism in the name of monarchy, is a big abuser of human rights. We know that the "God's Image" piece, which is big in his public theology, doesn't play out in his interpersonal relationships, despite Natan's bedtime counting of sheep. In community, as in family, as in any psychologically true theology, we can't forget that every castle has dungeon. Every yetzer ha-tov (good urge) has a yetzer ha-rah (evil inclination). Where there are giants, dwarfs will also be found. Nothing is absolute, except the eternal duality of bipolar paired truths. This is the teaching of Rabbi Tarfon, "You are not expect to finish the job—but you can't give up the ghost, either."[32] (Something like that!) One is always leaving home. One is always coming home. And Adrianne Bank would add, "one is always building or remodeling the home from which others leave and return."

Thomas Moore teaches: To care for the soul of the family, it is necessary to shift from causal thinking to an appreciation for story and character, to allow grandparents and uncles to be transformed into figures of myth and to watch certain familiar family stories become canonical through repeated retellings. If we were to observe the soul in the family by honoring its stories and by not running away from its shadow, then we might not feel so inescapably determined by family influences.[33]

This is indeed the universe of Genesis—the deep process of Truth we should acquire from all those wonderful stories of strong families in stress and dynamic tension. We need to learn to do the same exegesis of our own family stories—to live family aggadah and make family midrash. I'd love to do a Midrash on the time Nana dragged an iron bunk bed home on her back on the MTA (Poor Old Charlie). And such is a path towards a workable family education—and a workable community education— one which deals with light and with shadow. A true theology of family is therefore a study in quanta. Functionality and dysfunctionality are, not actual places, but probable instances which can be recalled. They are wave and particle in the struggle to become family. A true theology understands that "being a family" is simultaneously something we are (without escape) and something we approach (without being able to reach).

Davar Aher: The Other Side of the Duality: Hillman:The measure of a families' magnanimity is not measured by what it gives to charity, but rather its capacity to shelter the shadows of its members. Charity begins at home. Hillman, who is a Jungian, attacks the Freudian fixation on the battle between ego and family. He suggests that the psychoanalytic myth blames the family for everything. It believes that the "child is father to the man" and that our upbringings tend toward pyschic-predetermination. He suggests that it is much more important to view family relationships archetypically, to relish their ambivalence. He says: "We go back home because it is a regression and rejects the independence which is the heroic thing. The purpose of family is to provide shelter for the regressive needs of the soul. Everyone needs a place to crawl and lick his wounds. A place to hide and be twelve years old, inept and needy. The bar, the bed, the board room and the buddies do meet the needs which always limp along behind the myth of independent individuality. Families are unreal, he teaches, because they live in the fantasies of each of the individuals.

Families are creatures of myth, not of rational reality or even direct causality. Homelife is always lived in mythical proportions."[34]

In other words, the shattered, stretched families we keep in the closet are real Jewish families. They struggle with Haggar and don't always reach a perfect accommodation. They hate the little brat Joseph, but still find that they need him. Jewish fathers, like Jacob, split emotional loyalty, but still seem to manage to hold together a vision and process of family. Jewish families have always done the best they can. They don't live in Mayberry. Norman Rockwell didn't paint Tamar in action. Kids always want to keep the coins fathers believe they need. The family path to redemption is a balancing act, a tight rope—always stretching between the idealized vision of the "adoptive" family and the stuckedness of the "actual" family in which we find ourselves confined. Our walls have hearts—and hearts do bleed as well as beat. The family path to redemption lies at Le Grange points, at a synchronous orbit between the needs of the individual and the demands of the community. Family not only enables and confines, supports and burdens, it also mediates and mitigates—providing shade, sometimes within its walls, sometimes in its shadows.

A theology of family is very useful. It allows us to tell of how our hearts can point in two directions at once. It lets us know that when we leave home, we can always return. And, it lets us know that when we return, we can always leave. Our life experience, and our tradition, provide us with both stories. The need, a la Tom Bodett, is "trying to understand the difference."

Epilogue

We know that family is not the instant cure to the Jewish future. Even if family was all that Louis B. Meyer hoped it was and wasn't, it couldn't do it alone. *Little House on the Prairie* isn't Jewish, it takes Walnut Creek and the Olsons to make a shtetle. Individualism, family, and community will always be involved in interrelated dynamic tension—simultaneous attraction and opposition. Now that we've reinvented the Jewish family, we need to think about jump-starting our sense of community as well—otherwise it will be another all-or-nothing dead-end.

We also need to know that family is a fantasy. It is a construct made up of the perceptions and projections of each of the participants—it is a mythical reality—not a state of fact. Rationality has nothing to do with it. Family is a midrashic realm—it goes way beyond the p'shat (the literal meaning) of any of the interactions. We need to broaden and deepen our vision of family back to what it always was—chaotic tensions dreaming of an ultimate monotheistic monogamy. When we do this, we will validate all kinds of interdependent psycho-economic living units and good and authentic batim—Jewish families.

A Family Midrash: Once I saw Sonny and Cher on the Mike Douglas Show, back in their *I Got You Babe* days, when the beat still went on. They got into a disagreement. Sonny looked at the camera and said, "And you thought it was all sunny and Cher?" It was a great moment. Families are stuck together, their histories inescapably bound up together. Jarod Barkley is right: whatever trouble he's in, his family has the right to share it with him. It's our duty to help him if we can and it's his duty to let us, and he doesn't have the privilege to change that. But Arthur Miller is right, too, family is only a "socially" useful manipulation, a lessening of police power, unless its vision empowers fantasies we can realize. We have to bring the Addam's Family up from the dungeon and take them to Club Med once in a while.

My mother called today. She was worried about me in the latest earthquake. We had to settle up bills from the Palm Springs vacation. It wasn't an easy conversation. Everything wasn't sunny and Cher. But, we'll talk again next week. Families are like that.

Endnotes

1. Reprinted and amended by permission of the author.
2. "Myth" in this essay is used in a Jungian sense of archetypal truth, rather than in the colloquial understanding of "false assumption." It is best understood within Robert Bly's chosen explanation, "a myth is a truth frozen in a story."
3. An anonymous poem typed on the back of a flyer and tacked to the bulletin board in my loft complex.
4. Avot 5:4
5. Jarrod Barkley, in *The Big Valley*. Jack Mingo and John Javna. 1989. *Primetime Proverbs: The Book of TV Quotes*. Harmony Books.
6. Arthur Miller, *The Ride Down Mt. Morgan*. Unpublished, 1992. The author was good enough to fax me a couple of pages of the script to allow for inclusion here.
7. Thomas Moore. 1992. *Care for the Soul*. Harper Collins.
8. W. W. Fowler, *The Religious Experiences of the Roman People*. Macmillan.
9. James Hillman. 1989. *A Blue Fire, Selected Writings*. Harper Perennial.

10. Hillman, 1989. "Mythology as Family", in *A Blue Fire.*
11. James Hillman, 1991. *Myths of the Family.* Sound Horizons Audio Video, Inc.
12. Moore, *Care for the Soul.*
13. Moore, *Care for the Soul,* 26.
14. Tom Bodett. 1995. *The Free Fall of Webster Cummings.* Nova Audio Book.
15. Barkley. *The Big Valley.*
16. Steve and Sybil Wollin. 1993. *The Resilient Self: How Survivors of Troubled Families Rise Above Adversity.* Vilard.
17. Hillman. *A Blue Fire,* 201.
18. Peter Pitzele. 1995. *Our Fathers Wells: A Personal Encounter with the Myth of Genesis.* Harper.
19. *A Blue Fire,* 196-7.
20 Quoted material from David Elkind. 1996. "A Conversation With David Elkind," *Educational Leadership,* April 1996.
21. Robert D. Putnam. 1995. "Bowling Alone: America's Declining Social Capital," *Journal of American Democracy.* 6:1.
22. Christopher Lasch. 1978. *The Culture of Narcissism: American Life in an Age of Diminishing Expectations.* W. W. Norton.
23. Lasch, 1978.
24. Lasch, 1978.
25. Eyre, Linda and Richard. 1993, *Teaching Your Child Values*; 1994, *Teaching Your Child Responsibility*; 1995, *Teaching Your Child Sensitivity,* Simon & Schuster.
26. Moore, *Care for the Soul,* 94.
27. Bodett, 1995.
28. William G. Dever, 1990. *Recent Archeological Discoveries and Biblical Research,* 171. University of Washington Press.
29. Mark H. Smith, 1990. *The Early History of God, Yahwah, and the Other Deities in Ancient Israel,* 1-3. Harper & Row.
30. A tahannah is an improvement in the Jewish tradition. Circa 1000, Rabbi Gershom ruled that Jewish (Ashkenazim) men could no longer have more than one wife.
31. Miller, 1992.
32. Pirke Avot 2.
33. (Ibid., 28-30
34. *A Blue Flame,* 199-200.

Susan L. Shevitz is director of the Hornstein Program in Jewish Communal Service at Brandeis University, where she teaches courses in organizational behavior and Jewish education. Holding undergraduate degrees from Columbia University and the Jewish Theological Seminary of America and a doctorate from Harvard University in Administration Planning and Social Policy, Susan works with a wide range of communal and educational agencies on innovation and change.

Susan L. Shevitz

For the last decade she has been responsible for the evaluation of Boston's Jewish family education initiatives for the Boston BJE. Susan enjoys the challenge of helping groups root innovations in their settings and is fascinated by how systems adapt. This includes her own family system, since she is the mother of two teenage sons.

Evaluating Communal Initiatives: Facts Can be Friendly

Susan L. Shevitz

Introduction

Program evaluators who fear that what they learn through their research will not be used productively or even worse, will be used to harm a program, may be heartened by Carl Roger's observation that "facts are friendly." As the evaluator of the Boston Jewish community's large-scale, long-term family education initiatives, I have often chanted Roger's phrase to myself as if it were a mantra, particularly when people objected to one or another aspect of what my colleagues and I were doing.[1]

Still, when I reflect on our overall experience of the last decade, it is clear to me that the process of conducting program evaluations and applying what has been learned through them has helped the Boston Jewish community forge and improve its approach to family education. Perhaps, most importantly, this experience has helped change the organized Jewish community's attitude towards evaluating Jewish educational initiatives. Today, I believe that there is a general and growing acceptance of the value of evaluation on the part of most stakeholders in Boston's Jewish education system. This is a marked difference from fifteen years ago, when the Bureau of Jewish Education began this work. Facts have become, if not close friends, than certainly helpful comrades.

This article details the chronology of how one community, Boston, incorporated evaluation into its communally-sponsored family education initiatives. These initiatives were developed and organized through its Commission on Jewish Continuity, a joint project of Boston's Combined Jewish Philanthropies and its agencies, Union of American Hebrew Congregations, United Synagogue of Conservative Judaism, the Council of Orthodox Synagogues, and the Synagogue Council of Massachusetts.

Evaluating a community-wide project sponsored by the Commission has not been easy and has at times raised poignant dilemmas.

I also speculate on the next stages in this community-wide educational evaluation and raise some cautions about what might happen. This is not to suggest that the problems I discuss will inevitably occur. However, there is enough history in the field of educational evaluation to be aware that program evaluations, whatever their technical quality, can be left unused or misused. Evaluations can fail to improve a project or, to use Robert Stake's phrase, they may even "quiet reform." This latter point is particularly relevant whenever an activist educational agenda, such as that of Jewish family education, is under scrutiny.

In this article I argue that, although educational evaluation may sometimes generate controversy, Boston's evaluation process has produced four very significant outcomes.

1. It has influenced subsequent policy decisions because information gathered during the evaluation was made known to program funders at critical times, and thus it helped shape their subsequent policy decisions.

2. It has improved the original initiative because those responsible for policy or program had access to evaluation information.

3. It has stimulated systematic information gathering because institutions had to collect systematic information about themselves—in and of itself a powerful and positive intervention—and, as a result, they acquired significant insights which helped them plan for family education.

4. It has increased awareness of evaluation's potential benefits. Because of the community's ongoing insistence on evaluation in communally funded projects, there is greater acceptance of the potential benefits of evaluation on the part of the stakeholders.

I hope this story of the Boston community enables other communities to learn from its pioneering efforts and encourages them to undertake systematic evaluation.

Phase I: 1984-1993

In the mid-1980s the Boston Federation—the Combined Jewish Philanthropies (CJP) of Greater Boston—started a planning process in order to identify its key priorities. Three of the five priorities specified by the Communal Objectives Committee related to Jewish education: the first was to improve supplemental education; the second, to assist and strengthen the Jewish family; and the third, to encourage greater collaboration in planning and programming among agencies and between agencies and synagogues. These priorities led to the establishment of the CJP Task Force on Supplemental Education.

After working for eighteen months, this CJP Task Force framed initiatives which it believed would make a difference to supplemental schools.[2] These fell into two categories: one was for "beyond the classroom" initiatives and the second for professional development.

Among the "beyond the classroom" initiatives was Jewish family education. This was not surprising. The Task Force was looking for projects to yield palpable and encouraging results and family education seemed a natural area. People sensed that something exciting was happening in this area in a few trail blazing local sites.[3] The executive director of the Bureau of Jewish Education (BJE), Danny Margolis, had already encouraged consultant Joan Kaye to learn about family education so that she would be poised to take a leadership role. Many educators advocated for family education by citing its potential benefits, which ranged from increasing parental support for school goals to fostering better family relationships. Also, Barry Shrage, the Federation's executive, was an early and staunch advocate of family education. He forcefully promoted a vision among the Federation's constituents of what its future might be.

Over the life of the Task Force (1987-1992), $496,000 was allocated to fund family education. The Task Force spent another $450,000 on projects not related to family education. The most significant of these were the full time educator ($210,000) project and a research and evaluation project ($72,000).

Family education funding was handled through a three-tiered system of grants to experimenting sites. Lighthouse Grants of up to $5,000 were awarded for innovative projects offering "experimentation in new forms and/or methods and anticipated having significant impact on the school." Smaller School-Initiated Grants, of up to $2000 each were awarded for original programs "consistent with the school curriculum" and other grants of up to $2,000 were allocated for programs prepared by the BJE or other centralized sources. Forty schools received grants; many received several over the five-year period, accounting for a five-year expenditure of $256,000.[4] The BJE also received funds to provide consultation services to the sites.

The Federation's investment in family education was unique, and so it insisted that all Task Force projects be evaluated. In the words of the Task Force chair, "We wanted to know whether what we would be doing would make a difference." The BJE was designated as the agency responsible for the evaluation. Since the Jewish educational community did not keep systematic records about programs or participation—data crucial to any attempt to understand what was happening—we, as evaluators, needed to find a way to get schools to gather and then share such information.[5] Discovering who was attending what kinds of programs was the first step in the evaluation process. The second step was getting specific information about how family education was being instituted at each site. The evaluation process itself was regarded as exploratory. It relied throughout on regular, self-reporting mechanisms and focus groups.

In many ways, what we did in Boston was more documentation than evaluation. In a system made up of autonomous schools that had rarely provided data other than enrollment figures to a BJE or a Federation, there was no easy way to modify this nor were there sufficient funds for an in-depth assessment of what was happening at each school. Most sites were not ready to admit outsiders, who might see weaknesses as well as strengths. The residue of historical mistrust between the congregations and denominational bodies, on the one hand, and the BJE and Federation, on the other, was substantial enough to preclude that sort of relationship. This distrust stemmed from earlier times when the synagogue and communal spheres of the Jewish community—nationally, regionally, and locally—were conceived as separate domains. At that time communal funding was not provided to religious institutions and communal agencies eschewed a religious perspective.[6]

The Bureau, charged with the responsibility of evaluating all five Task Force initiatives, had to help schools learn to keep records and document what they were doing. This was an arduous task. Accustomed to operating informally, the schools and congregations needed help to figure out what information to keep and how to gather it. Workshops and consultations were held to help sites develop strategies for obtaining and organizing the information. There were also workshops on program evaluation in order to encourage practitioners and provide them with some basic tools with which to analyze their own programs.

Our efforts paid off. The sites gradually began to provide information regularly in reports and interviews. Gathering data and reporting on it slowly became routine. By the time the project entered its fourth year, important basic questions were emerging about some aspects of family education. Separate focus groups were held with parents, family education practitioners, principals of schools experimenting with family education, and rabbis of sponsoring congregations. These focus groups probed stakeholders' perspectives. What was difficult and what was easy for the front-line practitioners? Other staff? Parents? Children? How did family education impact other aspects of the congregation such as the school, worship, youth group, or committee structures? What did principals need to know and do to institute family education? From parents' perspectives, what was more and less useful? What experiences seemed to have a positive and lasting impact?

As the Task Force work proceeded, the Federation was simultaneously paving the way for deeper involvement in the world of the synagogue and Jewish education. By the end of the decade, plans existed for a "wall-to-wall coalition," which intended to forge a working partnership between synagogues and Federation.[7]

By 1990, CJP had organized this coalition in the form of the Commission on Jewish Continuity. It began identifying priorities. CJP continued to fund projects initiated under the Task Force's auspices, and the community wanted a five-year assessment of these projects. Data from the sites were compiled and analyzed. This information was discussed with professional and lay leaders and released in a BJE report, *What We Have Learned: The Projects of CJP's Task Force on Supplemental Education, 1987-1992.* The focus was on learning from their experience since it was assumed that the Continuity Commission's initiatives, as well as other educational innovations, would benefit from understanding the Task Force projects' strengths and weaknesses.

This report was released with much fanfare. Professional and lay leaders, because of the Task Force's commitment to evaluation, had been kept informed throughout these years about what was happening. Further, there were concrete and impressive achievements which could be celebrated. Findings about two of the projects—family education and the full-time educators—were pivotal to the community's conception of what the Continuity Commission should be doing in its own work.

Findings Influence Communal Plans

The report contained considerable evidence that schools participating in the full-time educator project had changed in some important ways.[8] Congregants' expectations had increased. They were pleased that an educator was at the helm rather than a part-time administrator who could only give a few hours a week. There was persuasive evidence that the school, and perhaps the entire congregation, was significantly strengthened by making available a full-time educator who worked closely with a BJE consultant.[9]

Findings about the family education project were also intriguing. Forty schools had received grants to do family education programming. The larger schools with full-time educators developed the more ambitious programs. Smaller schools were less likely to be involved in family programming; and when they were, they generally used packaged programs the BJE made available. The community was astounded by the large numbers of people, more than 5,000 families, who attended all kinds of programs—from single-session holiday celebrations to multi-session parent classes coordinated with religious school content. Many people had assumed that families would only come to one-shot programs, but numerical evidence supported the anecdotal evidence that some families were coming to serious, ongoing, learning programs. And those congregations with strong family education programs seemed to be growing.[10]

With this success came other insights, which without the evaluation process, might not have been adequately noted or legitimated. First, the principals developing family education faced an impossible dilemma. They quickly found that family education was a full-time job on its own. How could they run the school and do family education at the same time? Most decided that the school could be left on the back burner for a year or two while the family education program was developing, but they recognized that this was not a long-term solution.[11] A second insight was equally troubling: there were too few people, even among trained educators, who could comfortably "do" family education. Even talented practitioners talked of the difficulties of this new work.[12] Their insights surfaced through the evaluation and could not be easily dismissed.

Because of these findings, combined with what people already believed, the Continuity Commission continued its support of family education. Why abandon a locally popular initiative which was catching on throughout the country, which had already garnered considerable investment, and which was beginning to demonstrate success? Shrage continued to advocate for family education and other initiatives which supported meaningful Jewish living for adults and families. The question for the Continuity Commission was not whether to support family education but, rather, how to fund and develop it further.

In 1992-93 the Continuity Commission shaped "Sh'arim: The Family Educator Initiative" as "one vehicle of the continuity agenda whose purpose is to make significant impact on the lives of Jewish families who enter the major gateways to the Jewish community."[13] The Commission worked through committees made up of professionals and lay leaders. It defined family education broadly as:

1. An instrument for dealing with intake of new members and families
2. A set of educational processes which work with families and groups in contrast with working with individuals
3. A way of demonstrating how Jewish observances can enrich family functioning
4. A context for adult Jewish learning
5. A means of working with adults and children to prepare them for future roles in Jewish life

The Commission acknowledged that other formulations of family education goals were likely to emerge from the sites. In order to be inclusive of the ideologies and capabilities of the diverse players and institutions, the Commission's goals were phrased in general terms; that is, participating institutions were to develop their "own individual goals, objectives, and strategies" while drawing on the following precepts:

1. Involve family members in their children's Jewish education;
2. Establish contexts for family members' Jewish learning;
3. Establish programs for joint family involvement in Jewish

learning;
4. Build community among families;
5. Adapt Jewish learning to the home.[14]

The Commission expected that families and institutions would change as a result of these activities. The kinds of changes were left to be decided by individual institutions. While this formulation made Sh'arim politically and pragmatically viable, it did pose difficulties in determining the criteria for success for the communal evaluation.

Three important findings which had already emerged from the evaluation helped to shape Sh'arim: the benefits derived from having full-time professionals; the need to prepare family education specialists; and the desirability of committing to ongoing research and evaluation. Accordingly, the Federation was to fund fifty percent (decreasing over subsequent years to a minimum of twenty five percent) of the cost of a full-time family educator in appropriate schools, congregations, and Jewish community centers. When hired, each family educator would receive two years of training at the local Hebrew College on a part-time, in-service basis and receive ongoing assistance from BJE consultants. Also, each site would participate in the research and evaluation component mandated by the Commission.

Would the Continuity Commission have decided to continue to fund family education without the evaluation of the Task Force projects? Probably, yes. At that moment family education was a popular educational intervention which had caught on throughout the country and had local prominence. Leaders in the Boston Jewish community had been aggressively promoting the vision. Would the project have taken on the contours it did? Perhaps, no, but ideas confirmed or revealed through the evaluation process shaped the thinking of those persons influencing the process and making decisions. This is what Perrow calls a "third order control;" one in which the assumptions that people bring to decision-making powerfully shape their subsequent decisions.[15] The assumptions that full-time, trained professionals were needed in schools and that they would be able to stimulate significant changes were so well established that they shaped many subsequent decisions about Sh'arim.

Another clear effect of having evaluated the Task Force's initiatives should not be overlooked. The community was becoming accustomed to providing information and receiving feedback. There was very little resistance to this second round of evaluations, that is, the evaluation of Sh'arim as the Continuity Commission's work went forward.

Phase II: 1992-1996[16]

The Task Force's work was the precursor to Sh'arim, which was seen as the "big time." From its start in the 1993/94 school year through June 1996, Sh'arim has received close to two million dollars from Federation endowment funds. This covers its share of costs for family educators at sixteen sites, the training program offered at the local Hebrew College, BJE consulting time, and funds for evaluation.[17] The sixteen sites cover the costs of the remaining salary and of program expenses. There is no predetermined ending date for this initiative.

By now accustomed to receiving systematic information about Jewish educational innovations, many decision-makers wanted the evaluation to tell them whether "the initiative was working." The Boston Jewish community was now ready to go beyond documentation. The Continuity Commission wanted to know about impact: What effect would the intervention have on families? On institutions? It wanted a way to determine whether the funding for the family educators was indeed justified.

The BJE was asked to be responsible for Sha'arim's evaluation. As a senior consultant for research and evaluation (on a part-time basis), I was to develop and implement the project. The process was to be consultative and iterative; preliminary evaluation plans went to the Continuity Commission, educators at the sites, and a committee of professionals from the agencies involved with Sh'arim. We believed that it was important to gain up-front commitment to the evaluation plan.

The overall evaluation plan was prepared with the active involvement of a Professional Advisory Group of evaluation experts from local universities and non-profits as well as representatives from the Conservative and Reform movements.[18] Independently of the Commission, the Professional Advisory Group dealt with messy methodological, political, and epistemological issues and provided valuable guidance. It helped develop a sampling strategy, for example, that made sense given both the sites' diversity, and the stipulation that data collection not be too burdensome for sites or participants. This group helped conceptualize and review the survey instruments. Due to financial

as well as political realities, the plan called for a communal evaluation—
that is, a look at impact across sites, rather than at individual sites. The
plan had several inter-related components and ultimately relied, of
course, on the cooperation of the sites. Negotiating the evaluation design
evaluation instruments and with the Commission and the involved sites
took almost two years.

The Evaluation Design

The formative evaluation component collects ongoing data to improve
the initiative as it unfolds. Primary data sources include mid-year and
year-end written reports filed by the sites; systematic interviews with family educators, their supervisors, and others; and observations by family
education consultants. These written reports yield information about
program types, participation, work of family education teams and staff,
new ideas, governance issues, and other data which show how the initiative is proceeding. Findings focus on assumptions, procedures, problems,
and opportunities encountered as Sh'arim develops.

All of this is fed back into the community in several ways. Feedback is
privately shared with each relevant institution. Problem-solving deliberations are held with key professionals and, if appropriate, lay leaders.
General discussions of the critical issues are scheduled with groups such
as the family educators or BJE consultants. Periodic written reports are
prepared for the community. These play an especially important role
because, in addition to charting trends and accomplishments, they focus
on central issues facing the project and thereby legitimate the need for
ongoing deliberation and modification.

Some Early Findings

Reports prepared during the first year show problems typical of a start-
up period: the need to improve coordination, specify goals, clarify expectations, do more training as well as longer range planning. This information was not publicly released; instead the evaluator worked privately with involved agencies to discuss the data and consider alternatives.
This behind-the-scenes work had major advantages: agencies, schools
and synagogues could examine problems without fear of embarrassment and explore solutions without undue attention. Based in part on
feedback from the evaluation, the BJE restructured its consulting
processes and established a network for the family educators. The

Hebrew College significantly changed its training program. The Commission staff modified some activities. Private consultation had one important disadvantage, however. It was hard for the community to identify exactly what was being accomplished.

By the end of second year of the initiative, 1994/95, several themes were becoming clear. They were summarized, along with the many accomplishments of Sh'arim, in a BJE publication.[19] Programs were attracting a great many participants and family educators were finding their institutional niches. There were success stories about families' excitement and involvement. Other patterns also surfaced. For example, there were some problems with intake interviews. Many practitioners acknowledged that they did not know how to do them, or when they did them, how best to use the resulting information. Not all lay/professional teams functioned effectively and, in some places, teams were neglecting the slow work of building support throughout their institutions. When the range of programs and the populations served by them was analyzed, questions surfaced about unserved populations and the programmatic mix. There was a tendency to offer many basic courses and activities, although some sites did experiment with serious, ongoing courses. Institutions were challenged to "curricularize" their approaches by thinking systematically about sequence, scope, goals, and populations.

Based on these early findings, the Continuity Commission is rethinking the notion of teams and what is needed to support teams in institutions unaccustomed to ongoing teamwork. It must grapple with the question of whether all sites really should have lay/professional teams. Similarly, because of the identification of programmatic and curricular trends, important new questions could be raised: Why is this so? Is it appropriate? What other approaches might be attempted?

Data suggested that in their first year the family educators focused on programming because they acutely felt the need to produce visible results. Recognizing this, we could then raise to everyone's awareness the importance of infrastructure. What needed to be done to gain long-term support? With this in mind, the BJE and HC staff could begin to help family educators develop the perspectives and skills to do internal organizational work at their sites.[20] By uncovering these problems, typical of the early stages in a project, the community could take actions based on what it had learned. Practitioners could use ideas which had surfaced from elsewhere. This could all be achieved without exposing any particular site.

The Summative Component:

In addition to this formative evaluation, a long-range-impact study is being undertaken. This will document how families and institutions change over time as a result of Sh'arim. The evaluation design assumes that there will be different effects on different families. It assumes that site-based behavior will be the easiest to influence and that home-based behavior the most difficult. Thus, if successful, family education will likely stimulate increased participation in site-based family education activities. This participation, in turn, will lead some families to other site-based activities such as attending adult education classes or services. Some families may become more involved in Jewish activities elsewhere in the community. Finally, some may change their behaviors at home, whether in terms of ritual practice, Jewish cultural pursuits, family interactions, and the like. It is also expected that participants will feel an enhanced sense of "belonging to a community" as a result of their involvement.

The anticipated changes expected at Sh'arim sites are: (1) enhanced member intake and retention procedures resulting in improved membership retention and increased involvement at the sites; (2) institution of comprehensive, systematic planning for family education; (3) provision of focused family education offerings; (4) development of committees dealing with family education; and (5) changes in the governance structure to bring family education into alignment with other aspects of education at the site.

Inventory of Institutional Characteristics

Developed with input from the sites, this inventory of institutional characteristics asks about members' demographic characteristics, all current formal and informal Jewish educational programs at the site as well as a description of the organizational structure of the educational system. This is information which a synagogue, school, or JCC should have in order to plan its own approach to family education even through maintaining such up-to-date, centralized information is not yet a high priority in most of these places. This data will provide everyone with a baseline. By again looking at these indicators after five and ten years, people will be able to see how schools and congregations change and whether family education activities are brought into alignment with other activities at the site. Getting this base-line data proved more difficult than we anticipated. Information within congregations and schools is diffuse. No single person or group possesses all the knowledge, although well-placed members, rabbis, executive directors, and educators might together be able to piece together much of it. Recognizing the complexity of amassing this information, we recommended that each site appoint a volunteer research coordinator—a member who appreciates the need for information and could organize effective ways of getting it. This was a highly effective tactic at many sites. The professionals were already over-burdened and it seemed reasonable to ask members to aid in the effort. Members, whether researchers, statisticians, engineers, marketing consultants or teachers were pleased to help. At some sites the family educator retained responsibility for this function.

A few sites were reluctant to provide information to a central source. They argued that the information was highly sensitive and obtaining it would intrude on family privacy. Despite reassurance that the data would be used only in evaluation and released only in aggregate, some refused to comply until pressure from the Commission was brought to bear.

At other sites, however, collecting the data and finding out new things about themselves proved to be a powerful intervention. These schools, congregations, and JCCs learned much about their own populations and programs, sometimes confirming what they had suspected, in other cases discovering important new things. Some found that they served fewer single-parent families, for example, than they had assumed. Another learned how many member units resided in each zip code, enabling the congregation to develop more easily neighborhood clusters. By asking about the governance structure—which committees deal with youth, adult, family education either formally or informally—sites could reconsider the relationships among the various committees and their functions.

Survey of Family Attitudes and Behaviors
The insight from the survey of family attitudes and behaviors is even more profound. The survey was administered to parents of second and fifth grade students in late autumn 1995 and winter 1996. The survey asks about Jewish educational and demographic background, family involvement in Jewish study, worship, Jewish cultural activities, ritual

practice, social action, and other indicators of how they live their lives Jewishly. There are also questions about attitudes and feelings about being Jewish. To permit comparability, many of the questions are derived from the 1995 demographic study of Boston Jews conducted by CJP or the 1990 *National Jewish Population Study* conducted by the Council of Jewish Federations.

Recognizing how this information might help them, several sites were eager to cooperate with this research. They requested that we report findings back to them. We had originally planned only to report aggregated funding but happily re-adjusted our plans to honor these requests. A few sites were opposed to asking questions directly of their families; gaining their cooperation was more difficult. In most places, the questionnaires were distributed in person when the parents of each grade gathered for another reason. Many parents enjoyed thinking about the questions and a few expressed pleasure that someone was interested in their Jewish lives. The surveys were administered to almost five hundred families who will be surveyed again in later years.[21]

A complementary, in-depth, qualitative component to the evaluation began in 1997. It explores the ways in which Sh'arim has affected people and institutions. Data sources will be observations, individual interviews, group interviews, and written analyses and descriptions from participants.

As this article is being completed, the results of the survey of families' attitudes and behaviors are being tabulated. A full report is being prepared and will soon be available from the BJE of Greater Boston.

1996 And Beyond: How Will Ongoing Evaluation Affect Sh'arim?

Evaluation is a set of techniques of systematic data collection, analysis, and interpretation. In part, it is also a political act which can help rally a community to support or disavow a particular program. When the Task Force's projects were documented in 1992, the community felt proud of its achievements and reassured that its sense that educational interventions could be effective was accurate. This bolstered its resolve to move ahead. That evaluation did not look at impact on participants over time. The current one does. This is a critical difference. We are documenting that more people are, in fact, coming to programs at sites, and we can feel justifiably proud of this. What is not yet known, but will ultimately be more important to know, is how these programs affect participants' Jewish identities and how institutions can become better at providing conditions which enhance participants' Jewish identity. Sh'arim also aspires to change institutions in ways which may be uncomfortable or not desired by some people in those institutions.[22] The challenges of influencing deeply embedded personal and institutional patterns and tracing what happens over time lead me to a consideration of several issues which may have to be faced in the near future.

Will the information be acted upon in forceful and effective ways? So far, discussion concerning the hard issues uncovered through the evaluation process has been interesting but it has not yet yielded new approaches. There are several possible explanations for this. First, it may be too early in Sha'arim's life to solve certain kinds of problems since basic procedures and policies are still being ironed out. Second, it may be that the problems, though acknowledged, might not seem as significant to the practitioners who are doing the work as they are to the evaluators. Cooper observes in a recent article, "Speaking Power To Truth: Reflections of an Educational Researcher After Four Years of School Board Service," that until a problem-solving discussion corresponds to how people experience the problem, not much will happen. Knowledge generated through social science research, in this case our evaluation, is but one way of knowing. Everyday experience is another. As Lindblom and Cohen argue, "Information and analysis provide only one route [for solving social problems] because...a great deal of the world's problem solving is, and ought to be, accomplished through various forms of social interaction that substitute action for thought, understanding and analysis."[23]

Social science inquiry can reshape, somewhat, "the mountain of ordinary knowledge" and perhaps that is what the findings from this evaluation will do if practitioners start to experience problems with teams, intake, infrastructure, and curriculum.[24] While intake procedures and team building were central to those who conceptualized Sh'arim, practitioners are more focused on everyday challenges such as developing programs, designing publicity flyers, creating a job niche for themselves, marketing, recruiting families, providing resources, or locating program facilitators. For the first two years of Sh'arim, the family educators were acclimating to their positions, finding a balance between the demands of the training program and their jobs. They also felt personally responsible for the success of the initiative and indeed, for all of "Jewish continuity."[25] Problems about infrastructure, team building, and the like may have seemed remote.

A third possible explanation of why changes have not yet been made is suggested by studies of educational change. The power of an institution's way of doing things derives from its "unverbalized, culturally determined assumptions that guarantee that when pressures for change do arise they will be assimilated in ways that confirm the adage 'the more things change the more they stay the same'."[26] Changing the relationship among professionals and laity, or dealing differently with members certainly challenges the institutions' regularities, their preferred way of doing things. Few institutions are prepared to challenge their own basic assumptions and change how they do their work, especially if things are functioning reasonably well. If this is the case, they might not want to engage with the problems of teams or of intake. If this inattention persists, Sarason's general observation may be appropriate: "[W]hen efforts at educational change repeatedly founder, despite everyone's good intentions, it is safe to assume that we are prisoners of ways of thinking that seem so right, natural and proper that we never critically examine them."[27]

It is too early to know whether some sites will be prisoners of existing ways of thinking. It is certainly possible that if the new ideas challenge the sites' regularities—their accustomed ways of doing things—the new ideas, rather than the regularities, will be modified or abandoned.

What Ought to be the Orientation of the Evaluation?

A second set of issues stems from early decisions about the orientation of the evaluation itself. Boston has led the North American Jewish community in its commitment to funding ongoing educational evaluation. Political exigencies, fiscal constraints, and policy questions caused this particular evaluation to focus on communal rather than institutional trends; that is, trends across sites rather than at individual sites are being studied. The evaluation's sponsor, the members of the Continuity Commission, are policy-makers rather than practitioners. While it can be argued—rightly I believe—that this is the best approach for this community at this time, the approach has produced two interesting tensions.

One tension relates to the audience for the evaluation. While some of what we are learning is indeed helpful to the family educators, the kind of information which would most directly guide them in doing family education is not being regularly collected. For example, we might have included in-depth studies of curriculum, program approaches and best practices, or psychological studies of family interaction. Instead, we chose to focus on more general measures of interest to policy makers. This is common practice in multi-site studies, especially where site contexts and program goals differ from one another. Stake, in his powerful analysis of the evaluation of the federal Cities-in-Schools programs, notes that what the evaluators focused on for policy purposes actually demoralized the line staff who thought that other things were more important.[28] There is no evidence that this has yet occurred with Sh'arim, but it is not impossible to imagine that it might, if what is learned from the institution has little salience for practitioners.

Related to this is a second tension connected to the utility of the evaluation for solving problems. Some problems can be addressed in an across-the-board manner, but the real challenge is to help each site best develop what it is doing. This would require more staff time and expertise than is currently available, as well as ready access to sites.[29] Nevertheless, as noted earlier, merely administering the inventories and surveys in institutions which had not previously generated or used data for systematic planning was, in and of itself, a powerful intervention. Several sites have asked for more rather than less involvement. They want "their" data to be presented to them, and they want assistance thinking through the implications of what is found. The survey of family attitudes, for example, represents the first time a congregation, school, or JCC can get a reasonably comprehensive view of members' Jewish attitudes and practices. Congregations are coming to see this as an opportunity to learn about their populations and want help in thinking through the implications of their data. This is a very significant, unintended consequence!

What Will Happen if the Data are not Immediately Encouraging?

The question of what will happen if "bad news" emerges is especially relevant to the longitudinal impact study. The expectation is, of course, that over the next few years we will find that those families more involved with family education will in some ways be "more Jewish" than those who were less involved. The underlying assumption is that some families will participate more in their site activities and elsewhere; and that a small group will actually change their home practices.

But what if this is not the case? With investment in Sh'arim reaching three million dollars by the time the study is completed, how would the Boston community react to such news? With the community's high expectations, would modest results seem good enough? Findings of modest or no effects are not necessarily bad, but as Stake showed regarding the Cities-in-Schools project, in a political climate which wants dramatic results, "modest or no effects at this time" may be interpreted as program failure. In a climate where "continuity" is the buzz word and "family education" has been cast as a solution to the "continuity problem," anything other than large, positive effects might diminish the incentive to proceed. So there does exist the possibility, unlikely but real, that the results of the evaluation may unwittingly serve to quiet reform.

Of course there will be success stories, whatever the overall results of the impact study. With multiple data sources, we may be able to identify critical success factors. The qualitative study of participants will provide an understanding of how some families change, Jewishly, over time. These findings will be helpful to the Jewish educational community and can inform family education initiatives here and elsewhere. And there is a good probability that the evaluation will find strong positive impacts. Then, the worrisome issues I've discussed will be of no consequence.

Whatever the outcome, the Jewish community, whether local, regional, national, or international, should be committed to learning about the impact of what it does. In an age of quick information, competing priorities, and limited resources, the systematic information provided by an evaluation is crucial. We expect that the evaluation of Sh'arim will leave those in charge of designing and delivering Jewish educational initiatives in a better position than they would have been without it. Other communities have already turned to Boston in order to model their own evaluative work on what has been done here. Just as evaluating educational programs has changed our own local community's attitude towards evaluation, it is influencing other communities as well. Boston has been a pioneer in family education and in synagogue-Federation collaboration. It is a now a pioneer in its commitment to educational evaluation. The stance we have taken is that facts are indeed our friends. They help us thrive over the long haul.

Endnotes

1. (Carl Rogers, 1961, 25). Thanks to my colleague and friend, Sherry Israel, for introducing me to this essay by Carl Rogers. I would like to note here that without the work of many others, the evaluation of Jewish family education described in this article would not be taking place. The family educators at Sh'arim sites have been educational pioneers of the best sort; their ability and commitment propels the project. I also want to acknowledge my colleagues at the Continuity Commission and the Boston Bureau of Jewish Education whose innovative work has enabled the evaluation to go forward. This includes: Combined Jewish Philanthropies' (CJP) president, Barry Shrage; Dr. Martin Abramowitz, CJP's vice president for Planning and Agency Relations, who organized CJP's Communal Objectives Committee; staff directors of the Commission on Jewish Continuity, Dr. Sherry Israel (1988-1991) who also staffed the Task Force on Supplemental Education; Rabbi Barbara Penzner (1991-1993); Carolyn Keller (1993-present). At the Boston Bureau of Jewish Education: Dr. Daniel Margolis, executive director; family education consultants and staff members Joan Kaye (1986-1991), Carolyn Keller (1988-1993), Naomi Towvim (1993-present), Marion Gribetz (1994-present), Nancy Bloom (1993-1996), Rabbi Barbara Penzner (1995-present), Debbie Yoburn (1995-present). I appreciate the responses of many colleagues to earlier versions of this paper and especially want to thank Drs. Martin Abramowitz, Amy Sales, and Daniel Margolis for their careful reading and suggestions. While I have tried to incorporate others' viewpoints in this essay so that the events are represented fairly, any errors or misinterpretations are entirely my own.
2. For a more detailed account of the thinking and politics behind the Task Force's operation and decisions, see Sherry Israel, "Some Key Issues in Federation Funding of Congregational Schools," 1988.
3. This included Cherie Koller Fox at the Harvard Hillel Children's School (now Congregation Eitz Chayim), Lois Edelstein at Temple Isaiah, Serene Victor at Temples Ohabei Shalom and Emunah, and others.
4. Shevitz 1992: 18-19.
5. This is also true for the other sectors of Jewish communal life, such as health, welfare, advocacy, social services.
6. Shevitz 1986: 47-51.
7. Shrage 1992: 321-330.
8. Funds were provided to congregations which had part-time principals to fund full-time positions. In the first year of a congregation's participation, through the Task Force CJP provided fifty percent of salary and benefits; this decreased each year until, by the fourth year, the congregation footed the entire bill. The educator and school committee worked with the BJE during this entire time to develop its educational approaches. Shevitz 1992: 44-48.
9. Shevitz 1992: 18-34. This suggests a particular dynamic: some of the most competent religious school principals, supported by congregations committed to education, were the ones experimenting with family education. The constellation of effec-

tive personnel and programs creates fertile conditions for many congregations.

10. Shevitz 1992:27.
11. Shevitz and Kaye, 289.
12. Penzner, 1.
13. Penzner, 1.
14. Penzner, 3. Each goal was further detailed though not in terms of educational out-
    comes or measurable results.
15. Perrow, in Wilkins, 6.
16. This article discusses what has occurred through Spring, 1996.
17. The Orthodox were not represented because Sh'arim did not involve any Orthodox
    schools.
18. There is an ongoing tension between spending time on "process" (i.e., developing
    an infrastructure to support family education at the site and in the community) and
    "producing product" (i.e., family programs).
19. Shevitz and Kapel 1995.
20. These were from nine sites: the day schools and several congregational schools were
    on hiatus from the program and the two JCCs are being handled separately with a
    survey modified for their context.
21. The focus on institutional change has been a source of controversy. Some believe
    that Sh'arim should be "transformative," and help institutions to change in signifi-
    cant ways. Others argue for a less ambitious formulation and never bought into the
    "transformation agenda." This is one of the tensions with which the Continuity
    Commission deals.
22. Lindblom and Cohen 10.
23. Lindblom and Cohen 14.
24. Based on presentation by Nancy Bloom, Marion Gribetz and Marilyn Stern at the
    Sherman Conference on Research in Jewish Family Education, Brandeis University,
    June 19, 1996.
25. Sarason, 87.
26. Sarason, 88.
27. Stake, 42.
28. Guba and Lincoln, 254-5.

References

Cooper, Harris. "Speaking Power to Truth: Reflections of an Educational Researcher
    After Four Years of School Board Service." *Educational Researcher*, 25, Jan.-Feb. 1996.
Commission on Jewish Continuity, Barbara Penzner, staff. (March 1993).
    Sh'arim/Gateways to Jewish Living: The Jewish Family Educator Initiative. Boston:
    Combined Jewish Philanthropies.
Guba, Egon and Yvonna Lincoln. *Fourth Generation Evaluation.* Sage: Newbury Park,
    CA, 1989.
Israel, Sherry. "Some Key Issues in Federation Funding of Congregational Schools." In
    David Resnick (ed.), *Communal Support for Congregational Schools.* New York:
    JESNA, 1988.

Lindblom, Charles E. and David K. Cohen. *Usable Knowledge: Social Science and Social Problem Solving.* New Haven, Conn.: Yale University Press, 1979.

Rogers, Carl. *On Becoming a Person.* New York: Houghton Mifflin, 1961.

Sarason, Seymour. *Revisiting the Culture of the School and the Problem of Change.* New York: Teachers College Press, 1996.

Shevitz, Susan. "Communal Responses to the Teacher Shortage." *Studies in Jewish Education,* Vol. III, Jerusalem: Magnes Press, 1988.

Shevitz, Susan (1992). *What We Have Learned: The Projects of CJP's Supplemental School Task Force, 1987-1992* (Research Report #2). Boston: Bureau of Jewish Education.

Shevitz, Susan and Debbie Karpel. (1995) *Sh'arim Family Educator Initiative: An Interim Report of Programs and Populations.* (Research Report #3,). Boston: Bureau of Jewish Education.

Shevitz, Susan and Joan Kaye. (1991) "Writing for Sesame Street, Directing Traffic, Marketing a Product, and Saving Souls: Jewish Family Educators Describe Their Practice." *Journal of Jewish Communal Service,* Vol. 67, No. 4.

Shrage, Barry. (Summer 1992) "The Communal Response to the Challenges of the 1990 CJF National Jewish Population Survey: Toward a Jewish Life Worth Living." *Journal of Jewish Communal Service,* Vol. 68, No. 9.

Stake, Robert. *Quieting Reform: Social Science and Social Action in an Urban Youth Program.* Urbana and Chicago: University of Illinois Press, 1986.

Wilkins, Alan. "Organizational Stories Which Control the Organization." Unpublished paper, Brigham Young University, 1980.

*H*arlene Winnick Appelman is director of Field Services for the Whizin Institute for Jewish Family Life. She has created and directed many family education programs in Detroit, Michigan. Among them are the highly regarded Jewish Experiences for Families, affectionately known as JEFF; Family Camp; and Jewish Acculturation Programs for Russian Newcomers.

Currently, Harlene is director of Community Outreach for the Detroit Federation and consultant to the Appelbaum Family Center of Detroit's Shaarey Zedek Congregation. She received the Covenant Award from JESNA for her outstanding contributions to Jewish education.

Harlene Winnick Appelman

*J*oan S. Kaye, an original member of the Whizin faculty, graduated magna cum laude and Phi Beta Kappa from Boston University and completed an M.A.T. at the Harvard Graduate School of Education. Her first experience with Jewish education was as chairperson of the school committee of Congregation Beth El of the Sudbury River Valley. Many years, many ulpanim, and many courses in Jewish studies later, she became director of the Brandeis Jewish Education Program.

In 1981, she went to the Boston Bureau of Jewish Education (BJE) as Director of High School Programs. In her five years in that position, she established the BJE as the foremost producer of Jewish high school materials, co-authoring six curricula including Why be Good?

Joan S. Kaye

and The Power to Lead. In 1986, Joan became director of the BJE's newly formed Division of Community Education and Planning through which she created the one of the first Bureau family education departments. She also authored The Parent Connection. In 1991, Joan moved to Newport Beach, California, to become Executive Director of the Orange County Bureau of Jewish Education and is currently engaged in a community-wide professional development initiative funded by the Covenant Foundation.

Curricularizing Jewish Family Education
Harlene Winnick Appelman and Joan S. Kaye

Introduction

Family education has become a fact of Jewish educational life. There are few synagogues or Jewish centers which don't have at least one family program; and there are many institutions around the country with full-time family educators who provide great numbers of family programs.

Our task, in this article, is to encourage thinking that goes beyond programming so that educators will ask not, What should the fourth grade family education program be? but questions such as, What does my school, my synagogue, or my center want to offer families? What sets of experiences can we provide that will enable us to reach our vision of what Jewish families can be? What skills must families have? In what order should they get them? How do we plan a structure within which all this can take place?

This article is not an essay on how to develop curriculum. It contains no scope and sequence charts, no K-12 behavioral objectives; rather, it offers a way of thinking about family education curriculum and some possible paths to explore along the route.

A Philosophy Of Family Education

Jewish family education has been perceived by some as a threat to formal Jewish education and by others as a panacea for the problems of intermarriage. We believe it is neither. Rather, it is one of the pieces of the contemporary Jewish education puzzle. Just as formal education, camping, and an Israel experience each play their respective roles in the development of thoughtful, intentional Jews, so too does family education.

Jewish family education (JFE) creates a framework by which parents can become Jewish teachers to their children and families can learn to live

Jewish lives together. Family education occurs through family experiences. Sharing these together in an interesting, productive, and fun-filled manner will lead to lasting positive memories. Whether by teaching a new skill, demonstrating how to observe a new ritual to deepen holiday observance, or by stimulating a fascinating discussion, the goal of family educators is to help families engage with our Jewish heritage in a manner meaningful to the whole family and, at the same time, to empower parents so that they can teach their children Jewishly.

In some family education programs, the teaching of adults and children will take place in parallel, separately but simultaneously. Adults and children may be exposed to separate experiences and then reunited and encouraged to share their reactions either in a structured session, when driving home in the car together, or at a special family time at home.

In other family education programs, all members of the family will have the same experience at the same time. This might occur in a single morning or afternoon. More often, learning will take place at several sessions over several weeks or months.

Adults can also come together to learn by themselves, in order to bring back to their families new skills and rituals with which to enrich their Jewish home lives. Nevertheless, unlike traditional adult education, family education for adults is always designed to impact the life of the family, rather than provide benefit only for the adult learner.

The real challenge for all of these methods is to create instances when parents and children learn from one another through discovery and dialogue and are supplied with the information and resources necessary for them to turn these pleasurable experiences into regular behavior. The real challenge for educators is also to combine these experiences and programs into a meaningful whole, develop a framework and then fill it in with specifics: in short, to curricularize the work of Jewish family education.

The Experience Of Family Education

Family education is a way in which all of Jewish living might be taught and, indeed, probably was, at one time in our history. John Dewey provides a wonderful insight into what family education is about: "If an experience arouses curiosity, strengthens initiative and sets up purposes that are sufficiently intense to carry a person over dead places in the future, continuity works in a very different way. Every experience is a moving force. Its value can be judged only on the ground of what it moves toward and into."[1] We assert that any family education curriculum (or ordered sets of experiences) should be based on the two criteria suggested by Dewey: arousing curiosity and strengthening initiative. One important goal of family education is surely "carrying people over dead places in the future." And its ultimate goal is clearly "the ground of what it moves toward and into."

The R.E.A.C.H. Model

The R.E.A.C.H model provides one paradigm for "moving forward and into." It constitutes a framework for planning Jewish family education, as well as a tool for determining the appropriateness of specific family education experiences. The R.E.A.C.H. model consists of a series of steps designed to lead families to the ultimate goal of Jewish family education: Jewish living.

Recognition

Jewish families often do more Jewish things than they think they do. By helping families to recognize the Jewish behaviors that are already part of their lives, we, as educators, can encourage them to take their next steps. What are some of these behaviors? For example, almost all of the families we come in contact with give to charity, give tzedakah. We can encourage the adults to share that experience of giving with their children. Parents might be encouraged to tell their children about the work of the organizations to which they write checks. They might actually form a family tzedakah collective to decide where to contribute. When the adults or the family visits someone in a hospital or invites a new neighbor to dinner, we might give the adults, who in turn might give their children, the words to understand that they are doing the mitzvah of bikkur holim or hakhnasat orhim. We might help them understand that it makes a difference to a child when parents say not only that they are going to a meeting but explain that they are going to a meeting at the synagogue to discuss their child's Jewish education.

Enhancement

Educators might help families look at their own customs and practices and think either about how to add a Jewish component to what they already do or about how to intensify an already existing one. For example, many parents read to their children. They might be given Jewish books to read. They might be urged to take the weekend family walk or bike ride and turn it into a "mitzvah walk/ride." They might be encouraged to say a berakhot for the wonderful things they encounter together as a family. Many families already light Hanukkah candles and pass out presents, but they may not know what else to do. Educators might help them create family activities for each of the eight days of Hanukkah. Or, if families are beginning to set aside Friday nights as a time to be together, they may be ready to learn how to turn those experiences of togetherness into meaningful observances of Shabbat.

Adoption

This is the level at which families might begin to incorporate Jewish behaviors into everyday life and begin to experience a conscious desire for Jewish living that comes from inside themselves rather than from outside expectations. Families may move to a level where they mark the year by the Jewish calendar and the New Year is experienced as Rosh ha Shanah rather than January 1. When families reach this stage, they understand and live the Shabbat that comes to them every week, not at the once-a- month family service. The family education curriculum, at this stage, becomes that of providing them with the resources and sets of experiences that will encourage them to maintain and deepen that commitment. For example, Ron Wolfson's *The Shabbat Seder* would be a wonderful resource for enriching the lives of families beginning to celebrate Shabbat on a weekly basis.

Community

Jewish families who have been engaged in learning and sharing family experiences can begin to form communities which provide support at times of crisis and of celebration, simha. They may turn to one another for the help they need, and they may begin to see this as taking place within a Jewish context. Adults at this stage begin to move beyond the needs of the family to seek out personal means of spiritual growth. It is essential that the resources be made available for them, by family educators or others to do so—either through the synagogue or in the wider community.

Hevrah

This is the highest level, the goal for families to which all Jewish family education should aspire. Families, at the beginning of their journeys, may not be able to articulate this. They may only say that they want something "meaningful" to do with their children once a month, a way of connecting to other families, or some activities to make their seders more fun for the kids. But as they move from stage to stage, as their involvement deepens, so, too, will their needs. The R.E.A.C.H. model is predicated on the belief that one stage leads to the next. In using it, we have discovered that, not surprisingly, families who have good experiences in one family program will ask for more. As families experience the richness that Judaism can bring into their lives, the more deeply will they want to become involved. In traditional terms, mitzvah goreret mitzvah—one mitzvah leads to another.

At the stage of ḥevrah, families will find support in their communities, not only for personal events, but also for Jewish living. There will be other families' sukkah to visit on Succot, other families with whom to share Shabbat. When children grow up and go off to college, their Jewish holiday celebrations will not disappear because there will be a flourishing community to support them. The Jewish growth of the children will not disappear because parents will have developed in them the habit of looking to their community to meet their spiritual and intellectual, as well as emotional and celebratory needs.

Family education curricula should lead to the formation of Jewish habits, through a combination of knowledge, skill, and motivation, beginning with, as Dewey said, arousing curiosity and strengthening initiative.

Toward A Definition Of Jewish Family Education

Put six Jewish educators in a room together and you will hear twelve different definitions of Jewish family education. We believe that we educators need not agree on specific definitions, but rather, that we should understand the elements essential to the practice of Jewish family education. We believe that these are some of the important elements.

- JFE defines the family qua family as the educable unit and asserts that the entire family should be involved in Jewish experiences. This element is built on a Jewish view of everyday life, and it helps to make daily life take on a Jewish perspective. It also enables families to make Jewish choices which lift them out of the pattern of everyday American life.
- JFE empowers parents to be Jewish role models for their children. It helps them attain the tools, props, skills, and

information for their own Jewish living.

- JFE is radically different than other kinds of education. While it seeks to impart skills and transfer information, JFE's basic goal is to change behavior.

- JFE is a perspective with a large plan. It is not limited to a particular age group. Good family education provides experiences for growth so that families are continually engaged in new explorations that stretch their Judaic/Jewish curiosity. It meets the "human" as well as the Jewish needs of families. It includes a good balance of many types of experiences and environments and views the entire community as its domain. It also includes means for follow up, feedback, and evaluation on a timely basis.

- JFE is based on Jewish family interactions continuing in the setting unique to each family, their homes. JFE, when provided within an institutional setting, often includes thoughtful, attractively packaged materials to take away and use at home, so that Jewish experiences continue at home.

- JFE builds comfortable, safe Jewish learning environments in which all kinds of families are welcome.

By design, family education should include many types of learning opportunities: intellectual, recreational, experiential, prayerful, and more. Uni-dimensional education doesn't work well with families. There are too many personalities and learning styles as well as motivations for educators to offer only one approach. Contemporary society is based on choice, and it behooves us, as educators, to offer as much variety as we can as long as what we offer reflects careful thought and is part of a larger plan.

Developing Curricula For Jewish Family Education

What should a "Jewishly educated" family know, understand, and be able to do? At a minimum, family members would feel comfortable in the synagogue of their choice and be able to participate in Shabbat and holiday services. They would understand the basics of the Jewish calendar and have a sense of the progression of the year. They would be able to observe Shabbat and each of the major holidays and festivals in a manner appropriate to their communities. Their homes would be readily identifiable as Jewish from the ritual objects, books, and magazines displayed.

They would understand the rituals surrounding life-cycle events and be able to engage in them as active participants. Mitzvot such as tzedakah, gemilut ḥesed and talmud torah would be regular and integral parts of their lives. They would have a basic knowledge of Jewish holy books and know where to look for answers to their Jewish questions. They would be part of a community actively engaged in living and growing Jewishly.

The above list deals with Jewish family education goals related specifically to Jewish growth. In addition, there is another set of goals which promote the well-being of the Jewish family as a family. Clearly, both sets of goals are essential: without the latter, the former is unlikely to occur. The following section on Sources for Jewish Family Education Curriculum incorporates both types of goals.

Sources for Jewish Family Education Curriculum

There are numerous sources from which to derive Jewish family education curricula. Six sources, more fully described below, include:

1. The current school curriculum.

2. The Jewish calendar. This includes knowledge about holiday celebrations, as well as skill-building for observing the rituals as well as sessions on the parenting demands that holidays evoke.

3. Life-cycle events. Programs can be designed to meet the needs of families at specific life-cycle points such as helping them cope with, and plan for, events such as the birth of a new baby or a bar or bat mitzvah.

4. The questions people ask. By identifying and helping families search for Jewish answers to questions such as how to deal with violence in the media or the ethics of in vitro fertilization, JFE strengthens the linkages between Judaism and daily life.

5. Historical and contemporary Jewish issues (such as local, national, or world events, or books, movies, television, and newspapers). Either the anniversary of the expulsion from Spain or the latest crisis in Israel, for example, might be the spark that leads to the development of such curricula.

6. The physical environment of the congregation—or of the entire community. People respond to, and can be prompted

by, their every-day surroundings. Encounters with open spaces, with architecture, and with nature can be utilized to evoke specifically Jewish responses.

1. School-Curriculum-Based Family Education

Family education might be organized as an expansion of subject matter that a school has already deemed valuable. It would make sense, depending on the depth of adult knowledge, that much of what is important to teach a child is equally important for his or her parents. Furthermore, family experiences can deepen and reinforce classroom learning. Many educators feel that a family education curriculum directly parallel to the basic school curriculum is very worthwhile. This means that the curriculum for families is sequenced according to what the children are learning.

Schools can choose from a number of published written curriculum designed for families or create their own experiences for families. Before choosing a curriculum, however, it is essential to begin with questions about the role of families in the educational program and synagogue.

- Should family experiences be designed to maximize the educational impact on the student by soliciting parental support for the child's learning; or should the experiences be designed to exert an impact on the life of the whole family?
- Should parents be invited into the school as witnesses or observers of their children or should they participate with their children?
- What must be done to help parents feel welcome? What do they see when they enter the building? Who greets them? What kind of ongoing communication is fostered with their youngsters' classroom teachers?
- How will the synagogue become more "family-friendly?" Will all activities continue to be divided by population (Sisterhood? Brotherhood? Youth?) or is there a way of providing activities for family units?
- Who will be responsible for organizing the learning of the adults? (The adult education committee? Rabbi? School?)

We could speculate that if educators were not to adopt the child's existing school curriculum but, instead, were to create a curriculum in which the family, rather than the child, was the focus of attention, they really would have an exciting opportunity to take a new look at, and perhaps revise, the school curriculum from a family development viewpoint. A wide range of interesting educational experiences might be created which would address the family as a unit in its evolving Jewish identity. Let's look at some of the possibilities.

(a) Primary Level

When families with young children enter a family school, everyone might immediately become engaged in learning and practicing a set of Jewish behaviors designed to capture the hearts and minds of the children and develop their lifelong habits. Such behaviors are teachable, manageable, and parents really can feel successful doing them. They incorporate principles which constitutes good education: frequency, constancy, and intensity.

- Parents learn to read Jewish books to their children.
- Parents learn to say the Shema with a child before he/she goes to bed.
- Families begin to acknowledge Shabbat on a weekly basis.
- Parents learn the concepts of tzedakah and gemilut ḥesed and incorporate them into family life.

One might ask why these, rather than other, behaviors? We think it is because these behaviors have common characteristics: through routinization they can be learned fairly simply; they occur daily, weekly, or periodically throughout the year; they reflect the regular behaviors to which many families aspire; and finally, they are really not remarkable nor surprising to many parents enrolling their children in a religious school.

(b) Elementary Level

One of the next building blocks in a school curriculum for families with children in the middle elementary school (grades 3-6) could be based on the following comment by Amitai Etzioni.

It took me a long time to understand it, but the psychological trait you need to be an effective person and a moral person has one common denominator—that is, you must control your impulses.

A moral person is somebody who, when he or she feels an impulse, can defer responding long enough to pass judgment about the appropriateness of the action. That's what separates us from the animals. The animals give in to their impulses; we pass judgment. All the rest is details.... Now, the capacity to defer impulses is exactly what you need to do math and reading and writing and be a good worker. The capacity to defer impulses is half of what we should teach; the other half is to be sympathetic to others.[2]

Or, expressed in Jewish terms: "Who is strong? That person who can control his impulses (desires, etc.)."[3]

These years provide opportunities to involve the family in classes and conversations about delayed gratification. Included in these lessons could be the values we learn from tzaar baalei ḥayim (or the appropriate treatment of animals) the power of berakha and the acknowledgment that we need to pause to say thank you and appreciate before we enjoy the gifts God has given us. The concepts of tzedakah and gemilut ḥesed introduced in earlier years could be expanded and deepened at this time to incorporate the idea of putting aside our needs to serve others. In a more concrete manner, this orientation provides the perfect opportunity to involve entire families in a variety of social action projects. These projects are likely to be particularly successful if families are clustered into small helping groups. As families often need the power of the group to get started doing these activities, these small groups not only accomplish important social action goals but are another way of building community.

(c) Junior High and High School Levels

At the junior high and high school levels, there are two key elements: involve families in action-oriented tasks that are highly valued by them and deal with issues arising from the process of separation and individuation. For example, CPR is something that every family could use and the skill itself is a Jewish one, for "if you save one life, it is as if you've saved the entire world." Other examples may be asking parents and teens to engage in dialogue about "Why be Jewish?" or helping parents create an ethical will. Clearly, issues of self image and personal affirmation versus social pressure might be tackled as well as concerns about anorexia/bulimia, sexuality and responsibility, and substance abuse.

One more element that should not be overlooked is that of giving comfort. In today's society where intimacy and human contact are on the wane, we are called upon to help families learn how to give comfort. This may take the form of hospital visits, shiva calls, or leading a minyan. On a day-to-day basis, this may have to do, also, with comforting peers. This topic works well for children as well as for adults.

All of these examples point to the need for opportunities to explore the realm of ethical decision making within a Jewish framework. *Why Be Good*, a curriculum published by the Boston Bureau of Jewish Education, is an excellent compilation of the issues, although some sections may be somewhat dated. Originally designed for high school students, it easily lends itself to use in a parent/teen setting.

Every school can create its own pathway for reaching out to families. As R. S. Barth wrote in *Improving School from Within: Teachers, Parents and Principals Can make a Difference*, "the problems of education are usually universal, but their solutions are (almost invariably) unique." At its best, such a family education curriculum would enhance the quantity and quality of family interactions within the school, the congregation and the community.

2. The Jewish Calendar: Holiday Workshops

Holiday workshops can have many different formats. The purpose of any holiday workshop is to divide the information, skills, and tools that one might need to celebrate a holiday at home into small, accessible units. Information presented in such manageable formats is easy to learn and not overwhelming to the novice, whether parent or child. In workshops for parents and pre-schoolers, each piece of information is paired with an experiential opportunity or project such as a craft activity, cooking, music, or a game. The information is joined to an action which generally requires conversation between parents and child. This is important. The more that parents and children talk about what it is they are doing, the more likely they are to remember it.

As children become older, or families become more experienced, workshops may become less project oriented. Nevertheless, our experience is that even parents and teenage children enjoy creating something beautiful and worthy of use in the home. The key is to make certain that whatever the educator asks parents and/or children to do, it is attractive and interesting for both.

For teenagers, task-oriented lessons are most successful. Giving both parents and teens something meaningful that must actually get done is the best way to involve families with teenagers in family education.

3. Life-Cycle Curricula: Life-Cycle Events

Inspiration for curriculum frequently comes from the life experience of the family educator. For example, when a family educator's child gets his/her driving permit, the educator will instinctively search the tradition for appropriate pieces and develop a program for parents and teens living through this same difficult experience. When an educator's daughter has her first baby, all the issues of long-distance grandparenting surface and lead to a special grandparent program. A family educator should be constantly aware of not only his or her own personal situation but also what is going on in the community and in the world. There is nothing that does not have potential for family education. All that is required is the imagination to transform it.

A curriculum need not be limited to enrollment in a month- or a year-long course. Family education curricula can span a person's lifetime. Adults are often motivated to learn and to make changes for themselves when they feel stressed by life situations. Many do not have the luxury of taking courses for a distant purpose in the future. For example, there is usually little interest in pre retirement planning, including financial planning, much ahead of time—not until children are grown and people are within ten years of retirement; and engaged couples are not usually attracted to programs designed to prevent marital problems.[4]

In today's world, however, community and its Jewish iteration, hevrah, (see R.E.A.C.H. model above) are commodities that, when offered honestly, can be irresistible. Family education and its perspective can be pivotal in making "community" happen. Exploration of life-cycle issues present opportunities for community building. If a group of people contemplating marriage is formed for information and education, then it seems logical to offer that same group an opportunity to continue to meet simply for a Shabbat dinner, or more elaborately, as a havurah. For a class of expectant parents, a later get-together as a play group or a post-natal support group makes good sense. In a society of high mobility and isolation from extended family, classes that bring people together as a common interest group or to form new relationships draw people to them.

Life-cycle events classes, except in the case of b'nai mitzvah, may be for adults only. They take into consideration the issues that adults are facing and frame them in Jewish terms. Children can and should be involved, from time to time, where appropriate. Classes can range from "So You're

Going to Be a Jewish Parent"—a class for the about-to-be Jewish parent, or the grandparent—to workshops on the Jewish way of mourning.

As families approach and pass through each stage, whether or not that stage is marked by tradition or ritual, three issues seem to recur for people: communication, intimacy, and finances. These issues should be part of every life-cycle curriculum. Although we have not repeated them each time, these are fundamental to each of the following areas from which a curriculum could be built. So in each stage listed below, some discussion time should be devoted to: How will communication among or within families change? How will this stage affect patterns of intimacy, both physical and verbal? How will this stage be financed?

1. For couples contemplating marriage, topics might include: Jewish marriage ceremony; ketubah; traditional responsibilities of spouses to one another; Taharat Hamishpa<u>h</u>ah (family purity).

2. For people expecting babies, topics might include: naming; Brit Milah and Simhat Bat; blessing your child; creating a Jewish home.

3. For people enrolling their children in school for the first time (religious and/or public school), topics might include: tzelem Elohim (child's self image) and expectations; parents' and teachers' expectations; parental involvement—how little? how much? rituals for starting school; creation of family rituals around school.

4. For families with a child joining a residential camping program, topics might include: freedom and independence; peer pressures; learning to cope; re-entry issues.

5. For families with bar/bat mitzvah, topics might include: changes in responsibilities; peer pressures; mitzvah projects; parsha projects; group holiday celebrations; Tallit projects, Sim<u>h</u>a stress—extended family expectations, keeping battles off the bima, celebrations in the face of changing families; se'udat mitzvah (appropriate ways of celebrating a mitzvah).

6. For families with a new driver, topics might include: responsibility and freedom; T'fillat HaDere<u>h</u> (Traveler's Prayer); financial planning; What new mitzvot can I do now

that I have a car? How can I put the car tzedakah use?

7. For families with a child leaving for Israel, topics might include: safety, responsibility, and freedom; geography of Israel, as well as coping with "re-entry" issues; T'fillat HaDere*h* (Traveler's Prayer); financial planning and who should pay—child, family, community?

8. For families with a child leaving home (for a life on their own, college), topics might include: "Burn the mortgage and shoot the dog;" empty nest issues around Jewish celebration; creating connections between the absent adolescent/adult; and Jewish celebration.

9. For families with children getting married, topics might include: permeable, impermeable, and semi-permeable boundaries; financial planning; Sim*h*a stress—extended family expectations, keeping battles off the bima, celebrations in the face of changing families; se'udat mitzvah (appropriate ways of celebrating a mitzvah).

10. For families becoming grandparents, topics might include: expectations—theirs and ours; responsibilities—theirs and ours; permeable, impermeable, and semi-permeable boundaries; long-distance grandparenting; financial planning—What do I pay for? How much is too much? What about day school tuition?

11. For families dealing with aging parents, topics might include: expectations—theirs and ours; responsibilities—theirs and ours.

12. For families who need comforting, topics might include: illness and healing; death and mourning practices.

From this brief outline, a curriculum could be developed through partnerships among local congregations and agencies such as Jewish Family Service. For example, a year of activities for parents and their pre-bar or bat mitzvah child, with good stress relief and sports activities as well as interesting discussions, could be designed with the Jewish Community Center. Life-cycle issues might be done team style, with interdisciplinary input, so that participants discover a variety of ways of looking at the same topic. Sessions might be single evening programs or a series. Lay committees are crucial for making certain that appropriate issues are addressed.

4. Identifying and Answering Questions People are Currently Asking—the Needs They are Trying to Fill

This is an area in which it is essential to customize the curriculum. Curriculum designed to meet expressed needs may need continuing modification to meet the new, often emerging needs of the group. It is often desirable to mix life cycle, holiday, cooking, or communication topics. In these settings, participants learn from one another's experiences. Personal "story telling" is really important. For instance, what is sometimes caustically referred to as gastronomic Judaism takes on a very different tone when the cooking class is taught by seasoned congregants or respected community personalities who fill the sessions with stories of the origins of the recipes. It is in such informal settings that participants gain the courage to ask the questions that are really on their minds. Learning how to weave, do calligraphy, or crochet a kippah are all opportunities to transmit important Jewish lessons. It simply requires educators to have an openness and ability to hear the questions as they are being asked.

5. Reaction To Contemporary Issues

Topics for family education sometimes grow out of a need to inform people about the most recent issues and events affecting them. For example, events in the Middle East, changes in the neighborhood, or an outbreak of anti-Semitism in a local high school may each be the impetus for a Jewish family education program. Programming with local authors or local celebrities make exciting Jewish family education opportunities. Although this type of programming is reactive rather than proactive and cannot always be planned months in advance, these programs are popular, interesting, and informative.

6. Using the Jewish Environment as Family Education

Family education can occur with every visit to the congregation or other Jewish institution. For example, the gift shop is an ideal place. If ceremonial items had notes of explanation for the purchaser, then education in a very non-threatening way could occur. In fact, much like knitting shops that sell wool and teach people to knit, a variety of family classes could be offered by the gift shop based on the items for sale (particularly with new Judaic software, family genealogy software, etc.) Another catalytic environment for family education curriculum opportunities is the congregational library. Still another is in the synagogue pews where interesting interactive explanations about Shabbat services can be placed, so that families bringing young children to services will have easy access to the answers to questions children ask. Such informational pieces eliminate embarrassment for parents who might not know the Jewish answers. By looking around their buildings or exploring the land on which the synagogue sits, educators can find innumerable ways to weave family education into the environment. Jewish gardening, including the origins of tzedakah, holidays, and Shabbat as well as the Jewish origins of ecological concerns, could be used to turn the congregation grounds into congregational gathering sites. If there is a zoo in the community, educators could use it to plan a family experience for the week when parashat Noah is read. If the community is lucky enough to have a planetarium, Jewish family educators might incorporate star-gazing into a community-wide havdalah service. This curriculum is as limitless as one's imagination.

Conclusion

These six sources are possibilities from which to derive Jewish family education curriculum. Creative family educators will find many more from their own particular settings and from the needs of families with whom they are in contact. Each source presented here might be used to generate a single program or become the entire framework within which a curriculum is designed. The sources themselves can be mixed and matched. Whether one chooses one source or many and what to do with them depends on a variety of factors. It depends heavily on who is developing the curriculum.

We have focused on a number of sources which can be used as an organizing framework with which to build curriculum. For two sources, that of the school and that of life cycles, we have provided outlines which can be developed into full family education curricula. When developing curricula, the R.E.A.C.H. model can be used to match each piece to the Jewish developmental stage of the family.

We have tried to stress the importance of determining goals and of making decisions about the role family education will play in your institution. We have encouraged you to see families as they are, to listen to their needs, and to dream with them about what their Jewish lives could be. Most of all, we want to open your eyes to the myriad possibilities that exist for creating Jewish family education curriculum and the many paths that can be taken on the road to doing so. The greatest piece of advice we can offer is to start the journey somewhere that is important to you and keep taking the next steps. It will prove most worthwhile.

Endnotes

1. John Dewey. 1925. *Experience and Education*, 38.
2. Amitai Etzioni, "On Transmitting Values," *Educational Leadership*, November, 1993.
3. Pirke Avot
4. Kathryn Apgar and Jane Kane Coplon, "New Perspectives On Structured Life Education" *Group Social Work*, March-April 1985.

Sally Weber, LCSW, is Regional Director of the San Fernando Valley Office of Adult and Children's Services, Jewish Family Service of Los Angeles. She has been a faculty member of the Whizin Institute for Jewish Family Life since its inception and is a lecturer at the Graduate School of Jewish Communal Service at Hebrew Union College.

Sally has served as program consultant to agencies and synagogues locally and nationally. She has fostered many inter-agency and inter-disciplinary projects in Los Angeles

Sally Weber

particularly focused on the needs of the changing Jewish family. She has authored professional articles on this topic and is coauthor of Shalom Bayit A Jewish Response to Child Abuse and Domestic Violence. *She was awarded the 1996 Career Achievement Award from the Jewish Communal Professionals of Southern California.*

Interagency and Multidisciplinary
Collaboration: A Win-Win Strategy[1]
Sally Weber

Intra- and inter-institutional collaboration is of great importance in an era of shrinking resources. Social workers and educators bring different and complementary skills to Jewish family education, and a team effort would enhance such programs. The outcome of such a collaborative effort is a strengthening of our agencies, disciplines, and in turn, the Jewish Family.

The unique challenge to all concerned with the future of American Judaism and the American Jewish family is how to best join our professional resources to provide a broad menu of creative, welcoming, informative, and helpful services to our community. Our mandate for the twenty-first century is to address the ways in which such collaboration can enhance our ability to serve the Jewish community and the Jewish family. The challenge of how to intensify Jewish identity, behavior, education, and continuity of children, adults, and families does not involve only one profession or one institution within our communities. It requires all of us.

Those now working in the field of Jewish family education have come from many disciplines, including social work, education, communal service, and the rabbinate. Some of our institutional settings such as synagogues already include within them a wide range of professionals. In such settings, there are natural capacities to meet with colleagues with diverse skills and perspectives. In other, more homogeneous settings such as day schools, where everyone has had similar training, we must intentionally create opportunities to meet with prospective partners in other institutions.

We should not minimize the difficulties of either intra- or inter-institutional professional collaboration. We each have professional orientations and languages that give us a particular focus; and our institutions have their own missions and interests. Sometimes, we find ourselves guarding that turf. Sometimes we compete for limited dollars. In an era of shrinking resources, we all struggle with smaller staffs, fewer dollars, and greater demands. All the more important, then, that we find ways in which to join with one another to advance the work to be done.

This article focuses on interdisciplinary collaboration between educators and social workers as a model for discussing collaboration in general. It examines the Jewish Family Service Agency—not a traditional educational setting, but one with a long record of working with the Jewish family in a variety of modalities—and how its staff of social workers and family educators work as partners in the field of Jewish family education. The article explores commonalties and differences among educators and social workers linked to training, mandate, and what we bring to planning for the Jewish family. Collaboration itself is an area that requires "capacity building"—building the capacity both of individual professionals to understand one another's work and of institutions to create and share common goals. Therefore, this article looks at training issues—not only how to work together but how to develop a common language with which to build programs and create services for our families.

Social Workers, Educators, and Jewish Families

Social workers and educators are natural partners in the field of Jewish family education. The main difference between them lies in their starting focus: whereas Jewish family educators start with the "J" and see "Jewish" as their focus, Jewish Family Service workers start with the "F" and see "Family" as theirs. The educational goal of educators, whether in synagogues or in schools, is an increase in the Jewishness of families. In contrast, the social work goal of a Jewish Family Service program is to meet the needs of the family—but, except for specifically designated programs, not necessarily to address the *Jewishness* of Jewish families.

Table 1 was developed at a Think Tank meeting of Bureau of Jewish Education community educators and Jewish Family Service family life education specialists at the 1996 Whizin Seminar on "Reaching and Teaching the Jewish Family" in Los Angeles. It illustrates the skills different disciplines bring to the collaborative table and the complementary skills required to ensure that the collaboration will be successful.

Table 1. Collaboration in Jewish Family Education

What Educators Bring to Collaboration with Jewish Family Service Agencies.	What Jewish Family Service Workers Bring to Collaboration with Educators.
Educational know-how and an educator's mind-set toward new learning	Understanding of family dynamics, social issues, and life-cycle issues and/or interpersonal and intra-personal issues
Judaic knowledge and a wide range of Judaic dimensions and disciplines	Experience with group dynamics
Direct contact and familiarity with congregations and families	A very broad understanding of diversity
	The ability to see people in the broad context of family, social, and professional environments; the understanding of systems, including family systems and the implications of change within a family
Awareness of communal needs outside of the Jewish Family Service sphere	The understanding of when an issue of family identity or life cycle touches deeper levels of feelings that may require other forms of help, i.e., a therapeutic intervention
Wide access to people and academic institutions in the community	An ability to enter the world of others in a non-judgmental way; an ability to help people make changes
Experience with institutional collaboration	A knowledge of community resources
	Experience with advocacy for clients

What Jewish Family Service Workers Need From Educators to Collaborate in Jewish Family Education	What Educators Need From Jewish Family Service Workers for Collaboration
Teaching methods and classroom techniques, especially with children	Clinical and developmental know-how regarding individuals, families, and groups
Judaic knowledge and resources	Experience with group process and skills as potential facilitators
A place for Jewish Family Service clients to affiliate, i.e., schools, synagogues, and JCCs	Sensitivity to ethnic and cultural aspects of Jewish identity
Families—a "captive audience" available in a school or synagogue setting	The social worker's systems approach and knowledge of Jewish community sociology and demography
	Knowledge of what to do if someone is in emotional trouble
	The JFS worker's inside-outside participant/observer perspective
	Network of national collaboration; grants know-how
	Experience in volunteer training and coordination

Despite different starting places, there are several synergies between the attributes of Jewish community educators and of Jewish Family Service professionals. The discussion of similarities at that Think Tank led to recommendations of partnered programs around interfaith issues, Jewish Lamaze, and Jewish parenting, single-parent issues, and the Jewish life cycle. We are, however, at the very beginning of understanding one another's institutions and vocabulary. Because of its complexity, it is important to understand the scope of Jewish Family Service programs in order to know how and where Jewish family education fits into its mandate.

Most Jewish Family Service agencies receive funding from the United Way, from government and foundation grants, and from Jewish community sources. Therefore, those services that receive funding from non-Jewish sources must be non-sectarian—open to everyone who applies and is qualified to receive the services. The receipt of non-sectarian funding differentiates JFS agencies from many potential partners, particularly synagogues, JCCs, and Bureaus of Jewish Education.

Family Life Education (FLE), Jewish Family Life Education (JFLE), and Jewish Family Education (JFE): Similarities and Differences

Family Life Education (FLE) programs address issues of family life: parenting, coping with change and loss, and managing stress. These programs are often funded by non-Jewish sources and are open to everyone. They usually do not have a Jewish context or content, although Jewish or religious issues sometimes arise in discussion. They focus on *enhancing the quality of family life and providing families with skills for daily life.*

Jewish Family Life education (JFLE) programs, in contrast, address *Jewishly-related family issues.* Some provide the setting for Jews coping with similar issues to come together for support and education. Although the *context* of the group is Jewish, the content may or may not be. An example of this type of program is a separation and divorce program for Jewish participants. Offering this in a Jewish agency can provide a greater level of comfort and familiarity for single Jews than a similar group in another, non-Jewish setting such as a community center or YMCA.

Other JFLE programs may include Jewish content: for example, "How to Raise a Jewish Child" or a premarital program that uses Jewish texts to help explore issues of mutual respect, communication, sexuality, and intimacy in marriage. Even divorce and separation groups sometimes deal specifically with the changing responsibilities for Jewish ritual. Who lights the Shabbat candles in Dad's home? Who says Kiddush in Mom's? And what does Judaism say about the nature of family? The focus of JFLE programs in on the *Jewish life of the family.*

Jewish Family Education (JFE) programs are usually offered not by Jewish Family Service agencies but by Jewish educators in school or synagogue settings. The JFE focus is on imparting Jewish content and increasing Jewish behavior and observance. Programs may be multi-generational (parents and children together) or designed for either parents or children, but the context of these educational programs is always the family. The focus of JFE programs is on the *Jewish education of the family.*

Jewish Family Life Education and Jewish Family Education, although similar in some ways, are very different from one another. JFLE programs begin with a life situation or experience: for example, adolescence or bereavement. These address behavior and values and may include some Jewish educational component; however, they are driven by the norms and values of social work. Although their desired outcomes may include imparting Jewish skills, behaviors, and values as tools for growing, learning, and coping, their primary intention is to understand the feelings and issues that arise as families or individuals cope with change.

In contrast, JFE programs are driven by the norms and values of education. It begins with a Jewish experience, for example, bar/bat mitzvah, and then deals with what a family needs to know Jewishly, as well as what might be family and developmental issues. Although dealing with the individual family's values may be a significant piece, the bottom-line intention is that the family will acquire tangible Jewish knowledge. For example, whereas a JFLE program beginning with issues of adolescent development might use the bar/bat mitzvah experience as an example of a life-cycle milestone, a JFE program beginning with a focus on the bar/bat mitzvah might also introduce issues of adolescent development.

JFE and JFLE, similar in their goals of affecting behavior and creating and maintaining healthy Jewish families, differ in emphasis. These differences are clarified by the following examples, using an educational model, a social work model, and a combination of both. In these examples, the participants are young teenagers and their parents.

1. Social Work Model, Family Life Education Program (FLE)

This program offers parents or parents and teens an opportunity to explore adolescence as a gateway to adulthood and presents information about adolescent development within the family. Participants explore areas of growing independence during the teen years and the symbols of such independence: for example, driver's licenses, later curfews. Participants learn how to discuss these issues at home and analyze what would encourage and what might impede negotiations around adolescent independence (good grades? proven responsiveness to existing rules of curfew? attentiveness to family responsibilities?) Families leave the program with information and strategies for negotiating with adolescents in their own families.

2. Education Model, Jewish Family Education (JFE)

Synagogues and schools often sponsor programs for bar/bat mitzvah families. In a JFE approach, a year-long series of programs is offered for parents and bar/bat mitzvah age students to learn together as families about the bar/bat mitzvah ceremony, and the Torah and Haftorah portions each child will be learning. They learn ways of maximizing family involvement with the child in Jewish learning. The JFE program also incorporates issues of adolescence development and family life passages to help parents and children develop a fuller understanding of what the family may experience during this period. The goal of such a program is to enable the pre-bar/bat mitzvah family to experience this significant Jewish life-cycle passage more richly and knowledgeably.

3. Social Worker/Educator Model, Jewish Family Life Education (JFLE)

A Jewish Family Life Education approach focuses on a particular kind of family—separated, divorced, or remarried—and examines their particular concerns. One such program in Los Angeles is Celebration and Negotiation: How to Keep the Battle Off the Bima. In conducting this program, the Jewish Family Service social worker must be knowledgeable about the bar/bat mitzvah service, but has as another primary task helping families resolve conflicts over who will attend, how honors will be dispersed between the two families, who will pay for what, how reception seating will be arranged, and how invitations will be worded, while still keeping the simha (celebration) central to the day.

Each program represents a different approach. In examples 2 and 3, the collaborative effort of a team of educators and social workers would be salutary. All team members would benefit from the combined expertise: the educators in Jewish content, teaching know-how, and programming expertise; and the social workers in group process facilitation, understanding of family systems, and sensitivity to issues of family diversity.

Both the JFE and JFLE programs described here have a great deal in common. Families are not the "subject" of the program but are active participants. Both programs have built-in mechanisms to encourage families explore values, make decisions, and effect change. And both underscore the importance of family. The difference lies in the goals: for JFE, to impart Jewish knowledge in the context of the family; for JFLE, to impart skills in coping as a family within a Jewish context.

The curriculum of the Jewish Family Life Education program, in particular, could be expanded to incorporate Jewish texts as examples for decision-making, parenting and responsibility toward children. A partnered leadership of social worker, Jewish educator and, in some instances, rabbi, could expand how these programs address the needs of families within a Jewishly grounded curriculum.

Social Workers and Jewish Family Life Education: Capacity Building

Any program that proposes to train Jewish Family Service workers in Jewish Family Education/Jewish Family Life Education must address many issues of Jewish knowledge.

1. Personal issues around Jewish identity

Personal journeys are a crucial part of our Jewish identities. Social workers specialize in journeys—in helping people tell and understand their stories. As most of them have chosen the field of social work, not necessarily Jewish social work, helping them relate their Jewish journeys to their professional work is part of "capacity building."

Social workers entering the field of Jewish Family Life Education are often concerned about weaknesses in their Jewish backgrounds. During a focus group discussion on working with interfaith families, several social workers in my agency expressed concern about their own lack of Jewish education. They worried that they would not have the appropriate background or knowledge to be helpful to their clients. Sometimes, these issues overwhelm a social worker's sense of professional competence, highlighting what they don't know *as Jews* rather than what they *do know* as clinicians. These feelings are shared by many members of the community. Many American Jews are highly capable, successful, and educated in the secular world, but still see themselves as children Jewishly; and this sense of childishness results in embarrassment and ultimately a great reluctance to be involved in Jewish life for fear that their lack of competency will be exposed.

How do we address the diverse levels of Jewish knowledge and experience of our workers? The reality is that many Jewish Family Service workers come from richly textured and knowledgeable Jewish backgrounds; that many, although lacking the teaching tools of Judaism, have experience in the practice of Judaism; and that many would (and do) eagerly participate in Jewishly based programs as long as they do not need to be the Jewish expert. Some staff members are personally observant, others are culturally or politically identified but non-religious. In fact, the range of Jewish knowledge and commitment among Jewish Family Service staff varies as greatly as the level of group process skills and interest in working with adults and families varies among our educators.

As is discussed in the section on staffing, not all Jewish Family Service workers are suited to the work of Jewish family education. Our training programs give us an opportunity not only to train our staffs but to assess the interest, willingness, and ability of individual staff members to work in this methodology. We must remember to be above-board with our training goals: if we are training social workers to work with issues of Jewish content and Jewish identity, then we must say so and indicate in what settings these new skills might be used. Doing so not only defines the nature of the training goals but also helps workers conceptualize program goals, thereby giving them a greater sense of ownership in the Jewish programming in which they will be involved.

2. Professional Issues and Personal Values

In social work practice, a core issue is when and under what circumstances is it appropriate for social workers to be involved in value-laden and Jewish outcome-related work. Although quite comfortable with the value of preserving the family, clinical social workers are trained to avoid making judgments about the attitudes and behaviors of individuals and families. At times, this neutral stance may seem at odds with programs advocating for specific Jewish outcomes.

One goal of in-house training programs is to help social work staff explore both their training and attitudes regarding this stance and to help them envision professionally appropriate ways to move into Jewish advocacy programs. Respect for social work training, coupled with the opportunity for JFS professionals to participate in both defining and expanding the boundaries of Jewish programming within JFS, is crucial in that it enables the social work staff to become full partners in what for many is a new professional modality.

Jewish Family Services and Jewish Family Life Education: Institutional Issues Involved in Collaboration

I. Settings

In some clinical settings, social worker *advocacy* for Jewish identification, growth, and outcome is not considered professionally acceptable. For example, if an interfaith couple comes to our agency for marital therapy, a clinical social worker providing therapy will raise issues of religious identification and other possible tension points in the relationship. The therapist will provide information and resources as appropriate but must accept the clients' decisions regarding religious identification, whatever they are. The therapist's mandate is to be certain that they are *informed* decisions. Informed decisions may or may not result in positive *Jewish* choices, just as they may not result in positive choices for other aspects the couple's relationship. The focus in the clinical setting is on the health of the family and encouraging as much understanding and communication between spouses as possible to help clarify their decision making.

Similarly, a program on "How to Parent Your Preschooler" should deal with the role of ritual in transmitting family values. Rituals include everything from bedtime and dinner rituals to life-cycle and holiday celebrations. In such a setting, a Jewish family discussing their enjoyment of celebrating Christmas may well set off some feelings within the Jewish social worker, but it would not be appropriate for the social worker to express personal feelings in this setting. It is important that our agencies do not "bait and switch," that is, offer parenting programs that are actually intended to be programs to promote Jewish identity.

In contrast to the above parenting program, a Jewish Family Service class on "How to Raise a Jewish Child" has the clear goal of reinforcing Jewish identity and participation. First, families attending such a program understand its purpose and stance. Second, the person facilitating such a program is seen not simply as a facilitator but as a role model—someone who *advocates* for the outcome of establishing a Jewish home. A discussion within this context of what it means for parents to celebrate Christmas would be central to the purpose of the program. And although the social worker's stance would not be judgmental in terms of "you're a good parent or a bad parent," he or she would be expected to identify issues of conflicting values and the implications of these choices in terms of the family's stated goal of raising a Jewish child.

There *is* a difference between the work social workers do behind closed clinical doors with individuals, couples, and families, and the work they do in group programs specifically labeled as Jewish Family Life Education. *Where* they offer these programs often helps define the nature of the program. For example, programs held in synagogues, Jewish Community Centers and Jewish schools—in other words, in Jewish membership organizations—have a clear-cut mandate for Jewish advocacy. In this instance, there are two clients: the sponsoring institution and the program participants. A social worker facilitating a program commissioned by one of these institutions and advertised as addressing Jewish issues is "starting where the client is," and the Jewish outcome goals of are an open part of the agenda.

When Jewish Family Service social workers and educators work together, it is important to think through the goals of their programs and choose environments appropriate to those goals. Overtly Jewish settings may provide "freeing" options not available in clinical offices.

II. Staffing

Not all social workers want to do or are suited for JFLE/JFE work for either personal or professional reasons, and staffing patterns vary by agency. In some agencies, such as Jewish Family Services in Albany, New York, staff members are hired with the expectation that they will participate in Jewish Family Life Education programming. Albany's primary program—a supplemental school program for parents and children offered in several congregations throughout the city—is staffed by a Jewish Family Service worker with an M.A. in education. Other Jewish Family Service agencies hire non-social workers to do their Jewish Family Life Education programs. In Minneapolis, the JFLE director has workers on staff with strong Jewish backgrounds. However, the director does not use clinical staff by themselves for JFLE projects, but teams them with either educators or social worker/educators. In Philadelphia, the JFLE director hires outside consultants from a variety of professions for special projects, such as their synagogue-based bar/bat mitzvah project.

At Jewish Family Service in MetroWest (New Jersey), a "menu" of Jewish Family Life Education programs to be offered at synagogues was passed around for sign-up, and clinical social workers were asked if they were comfortable doing this work and what they would like to do if they received proper training. The agency expectation was that, with appropriate training, all workers could and would work in this milieu. Sometimes Board members at MetroWest are trained as co-facilitators for JFLE programs. The executive director finds that this adds to the "culture of the institution." Working in teams results in what he describes as "a positive sense of contagion—the more people participate, the more others want to as well!" However, he adds that it is important to have clarity regarding roles: "The most appropriate Jewish Family Life Education person may not always be a clinician."

Jewish Family Service of Central Maryland has different staffing requirements for different programs. Their Jewish Family Life Institute provides programs designated specifically for Jewish participants. Only Jewish staff (social workers and educators) are hired for these programs. Part-time or contract workers must attend an orientation where they agree to incorporate Jewish content components into their programs and to observe kashrut if food is served at the events.

III. Funding

Jewish Family Service agencies are increasingly becoming fee-for-service agencies. As both Jewish community and United Way monies shrink and grants become more competitive and difficult to obtain, significant portions of JFS budgets must come from fees. All Jewish Family Service agencies provide sliding scales for clinical services. In many agencies, Jewish Family Life education programs are loss leaders; that is, although there may be a fee for programs, they rarely cover the agency's expenses for providing them. However, these programs do benefit the agency by providing visibility for its other services.

The reality is that professional collaboration—using two staff members instead of one—usually costs more. Fortunately, the current trend among Jewish funding sources (foundations and federations) is to encourage interagency or synagogue/agency collaboration. However, an important part of partnered planning is to look at where the continuing dollars will be coming from and to clarify from the outset what each agency's financial needs will be.

IV. Jewish Content and Jewish Learning

As noted earlier, Jewish Family Service workers come from diverse personal and professional backgrounds. Many Jewish Family Service workers already have strong Jewish backgrounds, and many are themselves educators.

There are a variety of ways in which new Jewish learning and knowledge can be introduced in Jewish Family Service agencies. Guidelines for helping social workers gain Jewish learning are not very different from guidelines for helping families enter Jewish Family Education. The information itself must be provocative, informative, and interactive. It must respond not just to what the trainers want to teach but to what learners want to learn. And the learning experience must help move participants to positive anticipation of the next learning session.

Ten years ago, as a result of a Board retreat staffed by Dr. Norman Linzer, past dean and currently the Samuel J. And Jean Sable Professor of Jewish Family Social Work at the Wurzweiler School of Social Work of Yeshiva University, New York, Jewish Family Service of Central Maryland instituted a "J in JFS" Committee. The retreat, which used case studies to explore issues presenting potential conflicts between Jewish values and social work values for the professional staff, provided a context within which to continue exploring these issues—not just whom they serve but how they serve. This staff-led committee, co-facilitated by an Orthodox social worker and a religiously liberal social worker, working in conjunction with rabbis and educators in the community, provides seminars, staff retreats, printed materials, and the opportunity for case presentations that address challenges for Jewish programming and Jewish social work. It also provides training in Jewish holidays, traditions, and culture for the largely non-Jewish case management staff.

Multi-disciplinary collaboration is a wonderful tool for Jewish learning if the right person is chosen. At our recent ḥanukkat ha bayit (dedication) of our new office, the rabbi invited to speak explained the Shma in the mezuzah—teaching it paragraph by paragraph, relating it to the work of clinical social workers through the words of "hearing," "loving," and "teaching." His explanation was so accessible, so in tune with the staff members assembled, that he was welcomed back at staff meetings to do ongoing teaching—this time, on Jewish family issues in the Torah. This rabbi has also been actively involved in bringing a group of rabbis together each summer to study family dynamics and crisis intervention with a social worker/psychologist team. Once you have studied with someone whom you respect and who respects you in return, once you've built a trusting personal and collegial relationship, collaboration is not only a natural but an obvious outcome.

From Jewish learning that is skillfully provided, we can well anticipate a change by social workers, especially increased interest in exploring how Jewish materials and ideas can be used within Jewish Family Service. Training, then, helps build a core of Jewish Family Service staff members who are able to become active partners in JFE and JFLE programs.

V. Training and Collaboration

Social workers have a keen sense of their own professional abilities and an equally keen sense of what others have to offer. Educators and rabbis, natural partners for Jewish Family Life Education, are also natural partners for Jewish learning. Many Jewish Family Service agencies have a close relationship with the Board of Rabbis in their communities; many have specific rabbis with whom they have close working relationships and use those rabbis to offer staff development sessions around such issues as mourning and loss, ethical dilemmas, pregnancy and child-rearing.

Relationships are reciprocal. As Rabbi Ed Feinstein of Valley Beth Shalom in Encino, California, has observed, "The lines between rabbis and social workers blur. People come to rabbis with counseling issues; they come to social workers with Jewish issues. Rabbis need more pastoral skills—social workers can help us with that. Social workers need more neshama (Jewish soul) because people come to social workers with Jewish questions when they're too threatened by coming to the rabbi. We can help social workers with that." Similarly, Jewish educators have knowledge and expertise to share, coupled with a desire to learn more about family systems and group dynamics. Opportunities abound.

Case Study: Jewish Family Service of Los Angeles and Interfaith Families

In 1994, the Board of Directors of JFS/LA established a lay/professional task force to explore how to address the agency issues raised by working with interfaith families: particularly, how prepared [trained] were JFS workers to deal with interfaith family issues and what were the workers' needs for training.

Focus-group discussions within the agency, bringing together staff from the Departments of Adult and Children's Services, Senior Services, and Immigration and Resettlement, as well as separate focus groups of agency social work managers and clinical supervisors, in one case, and in another case, social workers, managers, rabbis, and educators, explored interdisciplinary collaboration.

On a personal level, many workers revealed stories about their own children and other family members who had intermarried. They spoke of their own need, at various points of their lives, to talk about this with others struggling with similar situations. Most workers commented that they rarely or never had the opportunity to do this in a professional setting. Similar sentiments were expressed by both of the other focus groups. Everyone supported Task Force recommendations that such discussions be integrated into training or consultation programs.

Many social workers voiced concerns about the nonsectarian mandate of the agency but were also eager to entertain the idea that there are settings where it is appropriate and helpful for Jewish Family Service workers to participate in Jewish advocacy work with interfaith families.

Social workers were reassured to learn that there is a body of knowledge available about how interfaith issues affect the family and that there are "experts" in the community who can provide staff development in this area. The social workers also requested training in developing further their "Jewish psycho/educational skills." If they could now provide straightforward parenting classes, what additional skills would they need to offer programs on how to raise a Jewish child? How could they be helped to combine materials traditionally used in parenting classes with materials expanding the content into Jewish parenting concerns?

The focus group also discussed the nature of social work-educator collaboration. What do we need to know about each other's skills and role boundaries in order to work together effectively? How can we expand our own ability to create and facilitate programs that address the needs of Jewish families by collaborating with colleagues whose skills complement ours and whose values parallel ours?

The Task Force worked for three years. During that time, many collaborative programs developed among various participants. For example, funding was received for a joint synagogue-JFS program for parents of children who intermarried; one JFS office was asked to co-facilitate a synagogue program addressing issues of interdating; and a multi-disciplinary community forum, "Two Part Harmony," was held to begin delineating ways in which Jewish Family Service, schools, synagogues and JCCs can work together to train staff and develop programs for addressing the issues of interfaith families.

The agency planning process not only led to program development but also to the ability of staff members to participate in the development and facilitation of these programs.

Conclusion

Interdisciplinary collaboration is one of the great resources available to us in the Jewish community. Like many resources, it is often overlooked. Sometimes it has been set aside because of history, personality, or turf. More often, we have not taken the time in our home communities to explore what we have to offer each other *and* what we need from each other. As Jewish professionals, we are also a family. We can learn from one another, strengthen one another, and grow together, respecting our similarities and our differences. The ideal outcome is a strengthening of our agencies, institutions, and disciplines so that, in turn, we can help strengthen the Jewish family—both in its identity as a family and in its identity as a member of the Jewish community.

Endnotes

1. Originally published in the *Journal of Jewish Communal Service*, Winter/Spring 1996/97. Reprinted by permission.

Diane Tickton Schuster

*D*iane Tickton Schuster, Ph.D., is a developmental psychologist currently writing a book about the growth and learning of contemporary American Jewish adults. An adjunct faculty member at the Claremont Graduate School and California State University, Fullerton, Diane has taught and consulted for numerous Jewish adult learning programs. Her book, Women's Lives Through Time: Educated American Women of the Twentieth Century (Jossey-Bass, 1993), reflects her ongoing interest in adults' life stories, career and family development, transitions, and patterns of lifelong learning. She and her husband, Jack, have raised two daughters, Jordana and Ariana, in Claremont, California, and maintain an active involvement with Temple Beth Israel of Pomona.

Adult Development
and Jewish Family Education
Diane Tickton Schuster

On a Sunday morning in October, a new round of Jewish family education activities is about to begin. As Ruth, the educator, gets out of her car
in the temple parking lot, she is approached by Brenda, a congregant who
has participated in family education activities ever since the first of her
three children entered preschool. Ruth is delighted to see Brenda. At a
meeting for parents of second graders to be held during religious school
today, she plans to introduce a program for a family shabbaton scheduled
for late fall. She is confident that she will be able to count on Brenda to
take on much of the "administrivia" that is always a part of any such large
group function. As Ruth moves to greet Brenda, she notices that Brenda
is pulling out her car keys. Surprised, she asks her, "Aren't you coming to
the meeting?" "Not this time," Brenda replies. "I've got work I brought
home from the office, and we still haven't finished building our sukkah.
And anyway, Ruth, I don't think I can put up with one more 'how-to-do-
holidays' program. I need to get beyond that. I want to think more deeply
about Judaism and prayer, how I feel about Israel today, and what these
things mean to me as an adult first. You know, I'm realizing that family
education isn't really Jewish adult education."

Ruth is stung by Brenda's remarks. She understands all too well what it
is like to juggle competing demands, and she knows that Brenda and her
family lead busy, active Jewish lives. But Brenda's words present a challenge that makes Ruth feel defensive. What does Brenda mean when she
says that she can't put up with another holiday program? Ruth thinks that

these programs are the best part of her curriculum. She has worked long and hard to develop activities appropriate for parents and children together. In fact, many parents have assured her that the availability of repeated programming has increased their awareness of the Jewish calendar and helped them to sustain celebration in their homes. And besides, today's meeting wasn't going to focus on another "holiday" anyway. The idea for a shabbaton originally stemmed from people like Brenda, who expressed interest in experiential activities that involved the whole family learning together. Disturbed by Brenda's comments, Ruth asks herself, "Isn't family education adult education?" "Aren't they really the same thing?"

How do family educators respond to Ruth's questions? On the one hand, helping parents learn about Jewish life and practice is at the center of the Jewish family education (JFE) agenda. In JFE, adult education is going on all the time. Family education is meant to educate adults. Teaching Jewish parents is one key to teaching their children. And in turn, children teach their parents as they learn. Still, JFE is not what most people think of when they consider adult education. They see classes for adults, focused on adult interests, and designed with adult learning needs in mind. JFE programs typically do not begin with the experiences of grown-ups; rather, they start with the age or developmental stage of the child. Since children have specific learning needs, capacities, and interests, JFE educators may not even consider parents' characteristics and differences when they envision an interesting program or activity. There is only so much an educator can do to meet the diverse needs of all the people participating in JFE programs. Given this, adult education understandably becomes a by-product, rather than the heart of most JFE programming. Nevertheless, the challenge Brenda offered must be confronted. Jewish family educators like Ruth know that they must think more deeply about adults whose learning interests and needs are not adequately addressed by intergenerational, child-centered programs.

What does Ruth need to understand about the adults in her programs? She proceeds into the second grade parents' meeting, eager to tell the group about her aspirations for the shabbaton. When everyone is seated she notices several new faces in the room and decides to spend some time getting acquainted—even though many parents already know one another. As the introductions—actually Jewish mini-autobiographies—begin,

Ruth realizes that she is listening with "a new set of ears." Brenda's concerns are on her mind. Suddenly she hears the parents' stories in a different way. She finds herself thinking about these people as adults first. Listen to what these parents say:

Deborah: *Hello. I'm Deborah. I grew up in a secular household. My parents never joined a synagogue and some years bought a Christmas tree. My ex-husband was raised Orthodox, but the more he studied science, the less he was interested in anything religious. I joined the synagogue so that my son, Adam, would meet other Jewish children and not feel so alone on Sundays. All the kids in my neighborhood go to church on Sundays. I'm not sure what kind of Jewish home or community I can sustain for my child, especially since I may have to move with my company to a part of the state where there are very few Jews. But I'm eager and ready to learn. I mean, look, I'm a thirty-three year old with a master's degree who's used to being a quick study. What I want to know is: what books should I buy and where do I begin?*

Harold: *Hi there. My name is Harold. My wife, Judy, hoped to come this morning, but she had a patient in labor and had to go to the hospital. We were really disappointed not to be here together, because, finally, at age forty-four, we've decided that we want to get more involved in family education activities. Actually, I'm here because I lost my father last spring, and since that time I've been thinking a lot about my life as a Jew. You know, I was really involved with my temple's youth group when I was a kid, and I was so good at Hebrew that I even thought about becoming a rabbi. But in college I got turned off by my parents' pressure to marry a Jewish girl and for a long time I rejected anything Jewish.*

Funny thing, though, I did marry a Jewish girl, and now that our kids are studying Hebrew, we want to learn it—really learn it—too. We've even been thinking about having Judith's mother move in with us, which means we'd have to keep kosher. We realize that we've been giving our kids mixed messages about being Jewish. We want our whole family to lead a more deliberately Jewish life.

Irina: *Hello everyone. I am Irina and this is my husband, Sacha—Alex. We are from Russia and our daughters come here to the temple. We want to know more about Jewish things, about what Jews believe. In our country in the 1950s, when our parents were growing up, no one ever told them anything good about being Jewish. When we came to the U. S. and studied computers in the 1980s, we felt shy about going to meet American Jewish people. We didn't understand anything about Jewish prayers or even what a Shabbat is. And now our daughters know what it is to be Jewish, and they try to teach us. We wish we had more to teach them!*

Mel: *I'm Mel. I'm here because my life partner, Dan, has a son, Josh, who has just begun to spend every other weekend with us. As Dan will tell you, he converted to Judaism when he married Josh's mother. Even though they are now divorced, Dan wants Josh to grow up with a really positive sense of Jewish family on both sides. That's great for me, because Jewish family life was what mattered most in my background. I hated Hebrew school and never really learned much about Jewish texts, but I liked being Jewish and now want to get clearer on what Jewish philosophy, history, and law are all about. Right now, though, Dan and I are feeling really isolated in the temple. Because we're gay, we aren't taken seriously as a Jewish family. Our parents still think that they should be hosting all holiday meals instead of ever coming to our house. We are concerned that people here at the synagogue will give Josh the message that because his family life is "different," he doesn't really belong. We both want to become involved and known here for who we are.*

These stories—and every family educator's version of them—are case studies about Jewish adult development and learning. Embedded in them are many of the issues that confront Jewish family educators today. After they have achieved initial success with intergenerational-yet-child-oriented programs, many JFE educators do not know where next to take the JFE experience. And if Ruth is typical of her professional peers, she has not had much experience with or preparation for thinking about Jewish adults and their lives. What should she infer from these stories? What do they suggest about the needs of adult participants in Jewish family education programs? What does Ruth need to know about adulthood and learning in Jewish adult life to begin thinking about future JFE programs?

Adult Development: Issues to Think About

During the past twenty years, the study of adult development by social and behavioral scientists has provided a rich literature about what happens to healthy people over the course of the adult life cycle. (Kastenbaum 1993; Kimmel 1989) Contrary to earlier beliefs about human development, this new literature consistently points out that adulthood may not be the time of continuity, commitment, stability, or even predictability that earlier conventional wisdom had assumed. Earlier "continuity theory" asserted that growth and change were the hallmarks of early childhood and that an individual's ability to learn new ways or try new approaches diminished significantly during the adult years. (Atchley, 1989) Adults who changed marital partners, careers, lifestyles, and even religions were seen as "outside the norm" and as not fully functional in grown up roles. This notion posited that the "good life" for adults replicated the values and institutions of the preceding generation.

Recently the parameters of what constitutes a healthy adulthood have been reframed, due to many factors. First, people are living longer and healthier lives. Whereas in 1900 the average life expectancy for white men was 46.6 years and for women 48.7 years, projections for midlife adults today anticipate that the majority of both men and women will live well into their seventies. (Sheehy 1995) Moreover, the more affluent and better educated a population group, the more likely the group members are to use medical treatment, which also prolongs life. Thus, longer life expectancy is readily available for certain segments of the population.

Second, because of a rapidly changing social climate, adults today are expected—even encouraged—to see the adult years as a time when change is both acceptable and beneficial. No longer do adults routinely anticipate having only one career, one employer, one geographic location, a fixed lifestyle, or even one spouse or family. Transitions are common in contemporary life, and a measure of adult well-being is how able the individual is to cope with the ups and downs of ongoing change. (Bridges 1980; Schlossberg 1989) Moreover, research has demonstrated that adults are extremely resilient, able to overcome losses and reinvent themselves in the face of major upheaval. Consequently, adulthood is seen as a time of "multiple selves," wherein by necessity or by choice, adults may lead several different lives in succession.

Third, in terms of cognitive capacity, researchers have found that, barring health problems, an individual's ability to learn and retain new ideas and information continues throughout adulthood. (Tennant and Pogson

1995) Old dogs can and do learn new tricks. The more an adult is challenged intellectually, the better able he or she is to maintain cognitive flexibility. Cognitive flexibility—considering alternatives, trying new approaches, taking risks—motivates adults to explore learning areas they never before considered. Also, if adults see the relevance and applicability of what they are learning, their motivation to learn increases significantly. Adult learners respond especially well to learning situations that empower them to use what they are learning in everyday life.

Fourth, America is a "learning society" in which education is considered beneficial and desirable for every age group. (Apps 1989; Merriam and Caffarella 1991) Enrollments in adult education and college reentry programs have risen steadily since the 1960s. Technological advances now require retooling in every career field. As adults engage more in new learning activities, they begin to see themselves as lifelong learners. Moreover, it has been found that the more adults learn, the more they want to learn.

Fifth, adults who are in the process of ongoing change and learning tend to broaden their sense of purpose and to diversify their sources of personal meaning. The adult years have been described as a time of generativity—the stage at which the individual passes on what he or she has learned to members of the next generation. (Erikson 1982; Kotre 1984) Although adults continue to do much of their generative work in occupational and family settings, there is new appreciation of other ways that people find to "leave their mark"—by being creative, altruistic, or involved in spiritual pursuits.

Finally, in recent years, a new appreciation has emerged with respect to the diversity of adult experience within every segment of the population. (Kimmel 1989) Ongoing changes in the social and economic climate of the country, compounded by constant geographical and occupational mobility in the American populace, have provided vast numbers of adults with opportunities to redirect the course of their adult years. Sociologists thus report extraordinary "varieties of human experience" in contemporary American culture.

This considerable variability notwithstanding, social historians have noted that each "birth cohort"—people born at a particular time in history—share common experiences that will shape how they see adulthood and what they expect of themselves and their communities during the adult years. (Stewart and Healy 1989) Accordingly, each birth cohort has a set of unique developmental issues and learning needs that will emerge over time. An example of this is the cohort of individuals who were born between 1946 and 1964—the baby boomers—who came of age in the 1960s and 1970s. As a group, these adults, especially if they were in the middle class, experienced a series of social and economic transformations that resulted in later timing of marriage and parenthood, longer years in higher education, and fuller involvement by both women and men in the full-time work force. Baby boomers also were shaped significantly by such phenomena as the technological revolution, environmental pollution, and the globalization of the marketplace. In the 1990s, it appears that these social conditions have prompted many baby boomers to raise questions about the predictability and security of their future, as well as other "spiritual" questions about the meaning of their lives. (Roof 1993)

Jewish Adulthood: Other Things to Keep in Mind

Just as there are new insights about what characterizes healthy adulthood today, there also are issues about Jewish adult life that merit consideration. Jewish adults, like others in American society, are growing, changing, learning individuals forging new identities and opportunities for themselves. The lives of Jewish adults today are not static and cannot be explained solely in terms of the experiences or values of their parents or grandparents. Yet Jewish adults do carry forward religious, ethical, and communal legacies from earlier generations. And despite national trends toward disengagement from the organized Jewish community, many Jewish adults are eager to learn more about themselves as Jews and to become comfortable with their Jewish identity. Increasingly, these adults are expressing the desire to find continuity along with change. They are looking for ways to develop Jewishly. Increasing numbers are turning to Jewish institutions with new energy and curiosity, hoping to find learning communities that will welcome them and bring them in closer to Jewish life.

To date, little has been written about the psychological or intellectual development of these Jewish adults. Research and theory-building are just beginning to evolve as a new generation of Jewish scholars and practitioners bears witness to the increased involvement of Jewish adults in Jewish learning programs. Much of what is known is anecdotal—like the stories that Ruth heard in the family education gathering. But within these stories, several themes about Jewish adult life emerge, themes that express the complexities of contemporary Jewish life and offer windows on what today's Jewish adults want and need. Let's return to focus on four themes found in the stories Ruth has heard.

Theme One: Hineni

In each of the stories Ruth hears is a wake-up call by a Jewish adult who is saying "I am here. I am ready. I want to learn." This readiness to learn stems from what appears to be a new consciousness among American Jewish adults about Jewish identity. Unlike the generation of adults of the 1950s and 1960s, who sought to blend into the larger American culture, the new cohort of Jewish adults are "wearing" their Jewishness with increased openness and pride. The multiculturalism of the 1980s and 1990s has encouraged the current generation to adopt a more informed approach to Jewish identity and practice. Accordingly, like Deborah—the single parent from a secular background who is raising her son among non-Jews—there are hundreds of adults now actively seeking to know themselves Jewishly. These women and men are open-minded learners who find themselves eager to "find a way in" and receptive to taking concrete steps to consolidate their Jewish experience.

Many adults discover their readiness to learn at the time of a life-cycle event that they associate with being Jewish. This might be the case for Harold, whose father just died; midlife loses frequently prompt adults to reclaim their sense of Jewish involvement. Life-cycle phenomena could also be motivating Mel, who has only recently become a parent to a Jewish child, or Deborah, who is beginning a new life as a single parent. The readiness to learn tends to be accompanied by an openness to new commitment, which is an important part of how individuals forge new Jewish identities. Identity formation is an ongoing developmental experience, and commitment or re-commitment to Judaism can occur throughout adult life.

Jewish family educators are in a position to hear the needs and commitment-making of Jewish adults who are ready to learn. Autobiographical introductions like the ones Ruth heard provide information about the past, but they also provide clues to each individual's learning priorities and goals. For example, in her introduction, Deborah asks for books, which is a common request from college-educated adults, who are accustomed to starting learning endeavors by going to the bookstore. Deborah needs a "shopping list," especially one that is annotated with explanations of which books address which issues in Jewish life. Deborah might be willing to help organize a workshop on "Building Your Jewish Library," or she might be interested in a book discussion group for Jewish adults from secular backgrounds. This woman also indicated that weekends in their non-Jewish neighborhood are hard for her son; she and Adam might appreciate being paired with another Jewish single parent family for Shabbat or for attending Jewish community outings.

In Harold's story there are messages about issues that could be translated into a specific, tailor-made Jewish curriculum for Harold and his whole family. Such a family curriculum would address issues of kashrut, Hebrew, interfaith dating, and cross-generational communication. Harold is looking for substantive content and continuity in Jewish family education; like Brenda, the woman in the parking lot, he is not coming to family education solely because of his children, but he may want to involve his children (and even his mother-in-law!) in a Jewish life program that anticipates their growth and development over time.

Jewish adult stories such as these provide important indicators about what educators can offer adults who are growing and deepening their Jewish lives. Asking Jewish adults for their stories is a way to begin program planning and curriculum development that derives from who the adults are rather than what the educator believes the content should be.

Theme Two: Fear and Trembling

Jewish adults who are ready to learn tend to be highly motivated, but many are also very vulnerable. Some, like Mel, previously have had negative religious education experiences and assume that Jewish learning will once again cause them to feel inadequate, incompetent, or stupid. Others, like Irina, lack a Jewish knowledge base and assume that without rudimentary understanding they cannot even begin to study. Still others, like Harold, are overwhelmed by what seems to be an endless set of rules and practices that require a lifetime to learn. In some respects, these adults are not unlike schoolchildren who suffer from learning disabilities; they lack a fundamental literacy and may see themselves as incapable of Jewish learning—especially Hebrew. Often they hold tightly to old, sometimes simplified, impressions of what Judaism is, and in their concreteness they cannot imagine the scope of the tradition or its relevance to contemporary life. Some Jewish adults carry negative images of Judaism and Jews, and their stereotypes interfere with their being open to exploring Jewish practice or ideas. Many approach Jewish institutions with a heavy dose of skepticism and self-protectiveness, determined to avoid further damage to their already low Jewish self esteem. In their wariness, they may have no idea that there are hundreds of other Jewish adults who feel just as insecure, intimidated, and uncomfortable as they do.

How can Jewish family educators best respond to adults who carry so much "baggage"? This is a particular challenge for Jewish professionals who already live in a Jewish world and feel comfortable with their own Jewish identity. They may find it hard to identify with the issues or the emotionality that the disaffected or vulnerable adult is presenting; they also may feel that they are being asked to defend Judaism or "sell" Jewish life to a resistant consumer. What are some ways to cut through the charged energy of Jewish adults who are filled with "fear and trembling?"

A starting point is for the Jewish family educator to acknowledge that it is difficult for many people to become involved in Jewish life and invite parents to talk about their ambivalence, doubts, negative associations, anxieties, and concerns about Jewish identity. While this may seem like a negative place to begin, the reality is that Jewish adults who are already skeptical actually find positive benefits when their concerns are taken seriously. They appreciate the validation of their feelings and of their right to question and wrestle with Jewish issues. What Jewish family educators may not realize is that there are many intelligent, critical-thinking Jewish adults who have no idea that Judaism supports, even encourages, discourse and debate—or that dialogue about Jewish values is a healthy dimension of Jewish family life.

A key aspect of inviting discourse—and of reducing fear—is the facilitation of trust building. Typically we think of trust as a developmental task of very early childhood, but the reality is that any time people enter into new learning situations, they revisit the question of trust. Part of the challenge of entering into new learning is figuring out whether or not the learning environment is safe, whether one can risk exposing one's ignorance without being shamed, and whether the teacher will be accepting of whatever limitations the learner brings to the situation. Because many

Jewish adults are very embarrassed by their needs, and also feel isolated by their ignorance, lack of skills, and inexperience as successful Jewish learners, they are especially vulnerable to feeling judged by educators and other professionals in the Jewish community. They worry that they will be asked to give of themselves before they receive—and this in turn may stir up stored defensive feelings about being Jewishly inadequate and alone. Accordingly, although these adults want to come in closer to Jewish life, they may not have found safe places—sanctuaries—where they can explore their Judaism, take small steps toward Jewish ritual or observance, sort through their questions, or genuinely begin to learn.

Jewish family educators who are attuned to the anxieties of Jewish adults can create sanctuaries for Jewish adult learning by communicating such messages as: "It's all right that you do not already know how to do things Jewishly," or "Your most basic questions are appropriate and worthwhile," or "Of course you will need to 'practice, practice, practice' Judaism—feeling authentic as a Jewish adult doesn't happen overnight." These messages can even be presented as discrete workshop topics. They certainly should be communicated and stated to individuals and groups on a continual basis.

To help Jewish adults overcome their feelings of "fear and trembling," Jewish family educators must be willing to offer sincere nurturance and support and to create a "sense of home" in the learning environment. Once this sense of home—an atmosphere of secure attachment—is established and sustained, the educator will find that Jewish adult learners quickly begin to trust themselves, take learning risks, and discover their capacity to think about Jewish life and learning in new ways. More significantly, when these adults become part of a trusting process, they receive important reinforcement for developing into trustworthy partners with educators, collaboratively helping to build Jewish family education programs for themselves and for other people.

Theme Three: Being a Stranger in the Jewish World

The experience of "otherness" has long been part of the universal Jewish experience, and Jewish adults today typically report that part of being Jewish is still the feeling of "being different." Yet, in the stories many family educators hear, the issue of alienation refer specifically to experiences with fellow Jews. This is clearly the case with Mel and his partner, Dan, who feel rejected by the Jewish community. It also is an issue for Irina and Sacha, who bear the scars of anti-Semitism in Russia and now have to cope with being uninformed and inadequately socialized into American Jewish life. It likely is a concern for Deborah, who may have felt a keen sense of otherness with her Orthodox ex-in-laws and who still lacks basic information about how to participate in the Jewish community in a meaningful way. For Jews who feel like "strangers" in the Jewish world, the need for welcome by Jewish professionals is of utmost importance.

The job of welcome is an interesting challenge to many Jewish family educators, because it involves anticipating the needs of adults rather than just children. The protocols of adult-adult welcoming frequently are not well understood. Unlike children, who are accustomed to the idea that newcomers need help, adults who enter into unfamiliar territory tend to be extremely boundary-conscious and reluctant to intrude on others or even ask for assistance. And although these adults may be outgoing and open about themselves in other situations, in Jewish settings they become shy and self-conscious, embarrassed by their ignorance or lack of famil-iarity with the Jewish world. Thus, when these adults attend services at a new synagogue, they don't introduce themselves to old members; when they join a congregation, they don't assume that they can be included on committees. They do not know how to become involved, and many find it extremely hard to turn to their age peers for guidance.

Jewish family educators can play a vital role in the socialization of adults who feel like Jewish strangers: they can help them to understand the "lay of the land" in a congregation or community. Socialization activities help people learn the language, customs, rules, and expecta-tions of whatever society they are joining. In JFE, these activities may take the form of intake interviews, new JFE member groups or pro-grams, old member/new member mentoring arrangements, adopt-a-grandparent programs, and the like. Whatever the form, the content and spirit of these activities must sensitively anticipate the needs of the new-comer and help participants find common ground, mutual support, and resources for ongoing connection.

Theme Four: Linking Generations

Historically, a defining characteristic of Jewish adulthood was the obliga-tion of one generation to pass down to younger people the lessons of

Jewish history and experience. Thus, in earlier times, providing for Jewish continuity was a fundamental dimension of responsibility taken in adult life. Extended families offered children and grandchildren a range of resources for Jewish learning. If, by chance, a family was fractured or unstable, the community assumed responsibility for transmitting knowledge to people who lacked Jewish family education from within.

Today, as seen in the examples in Ruth's group of second grade parents, there are many Jewish adults who are not part of multigenerational families that can provide a sense of continuity or transmit Jewish learning or experience. Like Deborah (the woman who grew up with Christmas trees), some of these people may be three or four generations removed from active Jewish involvement and do not have Jewish parents or other family members who give them a sense of positive Jewish identification. Or, because of immigration or other family upheaval, they are—like Irina and Sacha—"Jewish orphans" who have endured many years feeling cut off from their roots. Or, like Mel and Dan, they may be eager to assert themselves as Jewish adults, but their families—and potentially their community—resist accepting them or their right to create a fully functioning Jewish home.

Intergenerational linkages can be tremendously valuable to Jewish adults and their children. They provide a sense of continuity over time, and they help people of all ages to feel less fragmented in Jewish life. Jewish family educators are in a wonderful position to address the intergenerational needs of Jewish adults by offering programs that foster the development of new friendships and connections, encourage the formation of surrogate Jewish families, and assist the building of networks for shared Jewish learning and support. By acknowledging that Jewish adults need family—and that with family begins community, which also assures Jewish continuity—family educators can help adults to see themselves as linked to all Jewish generations across time.

The starting points for thinking about intergenerational programs are first, to recognize that JFE is relevant to adults of all ages; and second, to begin to systematically include older adults in JFE activities. Invite older adults to discuss their needs as grandparents, in-laws, and members of "changing families." Arrange for adults from different generations to exchange their stories, traditions, recipes, and other aspects of their Jewish lives. Match "grandparent-less" children with individuals who are willing to serve as surrogate grandparents. Ask children in Hebrew classes to teach prayers and songs to older adults who may have had no Hebrew education. Encourage multigenerational groups to do mitzvah projects and document these projects by assembling scrapbooks, photo albums, or videos that highlight how members of extended families collaborate and learn from one another. Communicate the messages that Jewish families need one another and can educate one another, and that JFE is a place where teachers and learners of all generations can come together to share Jewish life.

It is Sunday afternoon and Ruth is walking to her car after a busy morning of Jewish family education. "Or," Ruth asks herself, "was it Jewish adult education?" Ruth realizes that she has found a new challenge: during the coming year, she will try to listen to adults with a greater consciousness of adult development issues. She will reflect more deliberately on the particular concerns and needs of Jewish adults in contemporary America. She will begin to do more systematic information gathering, asking parents about their Jewish adult development and learning experiences. With more information, she will be able to think about future program and curriculum planning that will be specifically responsive to what parents in her community want and need. As part of the information gathering process, she might invite parents like Brenda to speak publicly about their journeys as Jews and as Jewish parents. Or she could offer a parents' workshop on "Jewish questions everyone's been too embarrassed to ask." Or maybe she could invite parents to come together to discuss designing a curriculum tailored to their individual or group learning needs. Or she could ask parents who have become involved in the larger synagogue or Jewish community to help shy newcomers make connections. Or she could do a Shabbat workshop where grandparents and grandchildren teach one another how to do blessings.

Or, then again, perhaps Ruth realizes that she, too, is a Jewish adult who is growing and changing, learning from experiences, eager to stretch and take risks. For her, personally, Jewish family education is an opportunity for her own adult education. She is excited to see new possibilities, new resources, new ways to serve her diverse adult learning population. Ruth looks across the parking lot and sees Brenda returning to pick up her children. "Hey, Brenda," she cheerfully calls out. "I love your questions. And my answer is: Jewish family education certainly can become Jewish adult education too. Let's begin."

References

Apps, Jerold W. (1988). *Higher Education in a Learning Society*. San Francisco: Jossey-Bass.

Atchley, Robert C. (1989). "A Continuity Theory of Normal Aging." *The Gerontologist*, 29, 183-190.

Bridges, William. (1980). *Transitions: Making Sense of Life's Changes*. Reading, MA: Addison-Wesley.

Erikson, Erik. (1982). *The Life Cycle Completed*. New York: Norton.

Kastenbaum, Robert. (Ed.) (1993). *Encyclopedia of Adult Development*. Phoenix, AZ: Oryx Press.

Kimmel, Douglas. (1989). *Adulthood and Aging* (Third Edition). New York: Wiley.

Kotre, J. (1984). *Outliving the Self: Generativity and the Interpretation of Lives*. Baltimore: Johns Hopkins University Press.

Merriam, Sharan B. and Caffarella, Rosemary S. (1991). *Learning in Adulthood*. San Francisco: Jossey-Bass.

Roof, Wade C. (1993). *A Generation of Seekers: The Spiritual Journeys of the Baby Boom Generation*. San Francisco: Harper San Francisco.

Schlossberg, Nancy K. (1989). *Overwhelmed: Coping With Life's Ups and Downs*. New York: Lexington.

Sheehy, Gail. (1995). *New Passages*. New York: Random House.

Stewart, Abigail J. and Healy, Joseph M., Jr. (1989). "Linking Individual Development and Social Changes." *American Psychologist*, 44, 30-42.

Tennant, Mark and Pogson, Philip. (1995). *Learning and Change in the Adult Years : a Developmental Perspective*. San Francisco: Jossey-Bass.

Betsy Dolgin Katz is the North American director of the Florence Melton Adult Mini-School, a two-year Jewish school for adults located in twenty-six communities across North America. Betsy is a part-time staff member of the Chicago Community Foundation for Jewish Education, where she now does work in adult learning and where she has, in the past, served in the areas of school consultation, teacher development, and family education.

Betsy Dolgin Katz

Betsy teaches adult education classes in Chicago and has written and spoken on the subject extensively, including teaching both at the University of Judaism and the Jewish Theological Seminary. She is a member of the Board of Directors of the Covenant Foundation. Having served as the director of Family Education at North Suburban Synagogue early in her career, she has always maintained her interest in the field. She and the staff of the Florence Melton Adult Mini-School, in cooperation with the Community Foundation, are developing a Parent and Family Education Program called DVASH for the parents of the Chicago Solomon Schechter Schools.

Adult Education and
Jewish Family Education
Betsy Dolgin Katz

Introduction: The Context

As the field of Jewish family education matures by defining and refining itself, family educators have looked to related disciplines for insight into practice and expansion of theory. One such field is adult development and learning. All parents and grandparents are adults, and when they learn within the varied contexts of family education, the principles and practices of adult learning can contribute to how they understand the experience.

A family educator is responsible for creating learning opportunities in a variety of settings all of which are part of family education. To list a few: (1) families participating in formal learning in groups; (2) families learning informally in their homes; (3) parenting classes on how to be good parents; (4) parents learning about what their children are doing in school; (5) parents studying Judaism to become teachers of their children and role models for them. Unlike in adult learning settings, the parents involved in family education are motivated to share, apply, and transfer what they learn to their children. They anticipate that what is learned will suffuse their home and family environment. Still, whatever their motivation, they are fundamentally adults involved in the process of learning. Knowing more about adult development, adult learning theory, how to teach adults, and how adults learn can provide guidance for family educators that will enrich the excellent work they are already doing.

What Is Adult Learning?

The field of adult learning is still a new one. Scholars have defined the field in a number of ways. Some have described what they consider to be unique qualities of adult learners. Others have differentiated adult learning from the learning of children by looking at motivation or adult life situations. Still others focus on consequences or on changes in learner consciousness.

For our purposes in the family education setting, the most meaningful definition of adult learning describes what happens to the adult learner and/or the family during the learning process. This definition encompasses two levels of interaction between the learner and the subject matter. Drawing on the work of the philosopher Jurgen Habermas and on that of the educator Paulo Freire, we can see that there are two phases to the learning process, the second resulting from the first, that elucidate what can happen to adults when they enter a family education program.

Practical Learning

Although some parents attend family education programs out of obligation to school, teacher, or children, more enter as consumers. They expect that they will receive specific knowledge and skills useful in their lives. This practical knowledge consists of pieces of information about Jewish life and beliefs. The learners see their task as understanding their heritage and what comprises Jewish life today. They want to know what others have said and done that they can emulate in being good parents and good Jews. It is easy for parents, as voluntary learners, to move in and out of such practical learning settings. If the "product" offered is what parents want, they will continue. If the nature, presentation, or quality of what they learn does not meet their needs, they will leave. We have found that parents often do want to learn to observe Shabbat and holidays with their children. They do like to learn how to tell Jewish stories or how to talk about God with children. They do benefit from learning about the obligations that parents have to children or that children have to parents in Jewish tradition.

Emancipatory Learning

The insights gained from the writing of Paulo Freire are of particular interest here. His work concerns both the larger framework of social change and the learning process itself. His theories have contributed to literacy education and have much to say to family educators concerned with Jewish literacy. Education, according to Freire, can either oppress or liberate. In his terms, we can envision family education as creating a deepening awareness of the reality that shapes our lives—in our case Judaism—and at the same time, of our capacity to transform that reality. Adult learning is a process that should empower adults to think critically and to transform life creatively.

Families may enter family education to obtain a tangible product, but as time passes, they are likely to gain the capacity to incorporate that new knowledge into their lives. As this occurs, they enter into the Jewish conversation that has been going on for thousands of years. They wrestle with ideas, examine practices, question beliefs, and contribute to Judaism by shaping it to their own families. We hope this will also allow them to shape the nature of Judaism in their community.

Before entering into such an education process, parents may have had no voice. They may have been unable to participate in Judaism fully or to make it part of their lives or their children's lives. When they begin to learn, they only want answers to the questions, "What is Judaism?" and "What does it offer us?" In the second stage of the process, parents become free to contribute to that Judaism, and they have a greater ability to make themselves understood by their children, their extended family, and their community. They have acquired the freedom, the joy, and the opportunity to make Judaism a part of their lives. Now they ask, "What does Judaism mean to us?" and "What do I have to contribute to the nature of Judaism?" Learning helps in discovering meaning and transforming one's life. It often becomes a habit at this point. Families will design their own Shabbat or Passover seder; they will create their own sukkah, or write their own Jewish stories and transmit them to their children; they will think knowledgeably, creatively and deeply about God and about their role as Jewish parents. When family educators encourage this and provide families with knowledge, resources, and moral support, they help move families into creative, productive Jewish living.

It should be noted that many parents in synagogue and day school settings who attend these education programs want to enrich that which already exists in their homes. They may already be deeply committed to

Jewish learning and practice, but they, too, desire to deepen their under-standing and to be part of a learning community of parents.

How Should Knowledge of Adult Development Inform Family Education?

Up until a short time ago, someone entering adulthood was considered a finished product, the end result of childhood and adolescence, which would alter little throughout the rest of his or her life. Fortunately, research now recognizes that significant growth and change occurs throughout adult life. Countless numbers of recent books have been written on the stages of adulthood and the transitions that take place between them.

Parents who attend family education programs are at a particular point in their own identity development. Regardless of age, they are in their child bearing and child raising years, which Erik Erikson describes as the period in which the dilemma one confronts and must resolve is that of generativity versus stagnation. Parents in this stage take their place in society and help in the development of the next generation. They assume their role in bearing, nurturing, and guiding those who will succeed them in their family, in the community and, in our case, in the Jewish world.

This is not to say that we are working with a homogenous group of individuals. We have individuals and couples coming to learn who are living their day-to-day lives while wrestling with vastly different life issues. Many are dealing with concerns arising out of their roles as spouses or ex-spouses, as adult children of aging parents, or as friends. They experience tensions from the world of work—relationships with co-workers and supervisors, success or failure in the workplace. Other matters in their lives that could affect their educational experience may include the following.

Transitions

Moving, job changes, divorce, death of spouses or parents, illness, conversion, new children are all events that create instability and anxiety. Most peoples' lives follow a sequence that alternates between stability and transition. Personality, social structure, culture, social roles, major life events, and biology contribute to the character of one's life, to the stable periods and to the transitions. Interestingly, parents may turn to educational experiences at either time. In a period of stability, when they are feeling in control, they have the energy to devote to learning and growth. In times of instability, many adults take a class in the hope that their learning will allow them to regain control and make effective decisions in this aspect of their lives. Knowledge of the learners' situations can guide the selection of classroom content and activities as well as the expectations of what can be accomplished.

Jewish Seekers

Besides describing the adult stage as periods of generativity versus stagnation, Erikson also delineates an earlier stage that may be relevant to that of family educators. This stage, referred to as that of identity versus role confusion, describes individuals in their late teen and middle years. Many adults with whom family educators work have a clear sense of identity regarding their occupations, sex roles, or politics. But, because of a lack of Jewish education and experience in their late teen years, the clarifying of their Jewish identity has been delayed. The resulting confusion as adult Jews may prevent them from transmitting a clear Jewish identity to their children. As a consequence, they may be seeking adult or family education activities to achieve a sense of who they are as Jews. This search for identity may include learning about Jewish history, literature, practices, and beliefs. It may be part of their search for meaning in life. It can be a spiritual search to fulfill their longing for a relationship with God and with those things in life that extend beyond the material world.

Community

Some are searching for a sense of connection to a community. The community can be perceived as being the Jewish people, K'lal Yisrael, or simply a group of individuals who share an interest in Judaism and in Jewish family activities. Family education can become the entry point for those wishing to become part of this Jewish community, to share a vision of Jewish learning and living. Families new to the city or the school look for a way to belong. Individuals who have felt outside of the Jewish community seek meaningful affiliation with others interested in Jewish life. This makes the social dimension of family education a very significant aspect of the program. Family education responds to these dimensions of adult development almost unconsciously. To bring these to a conscious level can increase the effectiveness of what is done by family educators.

How Should Knowledge of how Adults Learn and Change Influence Family Education?

Active Participation

One strong assertion, since the earliest formulation of theories on adult education practice, is that adults learn better when they are active participants in the learning process. This has two important implications.

First, adult learners should be involved in the planning of what is to be learned and how it is to be learned. This allows them to express goals and needs that will shape their learning experience. Those responsible for the program should become acquainted with participants so that the family education program will build on their reality. Adults bring a rich set of life experiences to the classroom. They can share these with other learners and benefit from the experiences of their peers. Background questionnaires can be designed to inform leaders about the nature and the interests of the families involved in their programs. Information on what families already enjoy doing together and what they want to get out of the program can be helpful in designing activities. Some ongoing family education programs involve selected parents and children on a planning committee for direct input into what is done and for leadership at events.

Second, strategies in the classroom should encourage interaction between teacher and learner and among the learners themselves. Teachers of adults should use various forms of collaborative learning. Small group work, guided inquiry, case studies, and problem solving encourage critical thinking and active involvement. There are times when lecturing may be appropriate, but the goal should be to encourage learner involvement and independent thinking.

Learning and Transformation

One of the objectives of Jewish family education is to build the confidence and competence of Jewish parents for the purpose of enabling them to transmit knowledge and practices to their children. Those responsible for family education are undeniably working to transform Jewish lives. The issue is how learning leads to transformation of lives.

1. The first part of the learning process is gathering information. There are countless sources of information within the family and within parent education programs: reading and interpreting texts, lectures, computer, media, dialogues and discussions.

Through these a body of knowledge emerges. It is important that information acquisition be at a high level, a challenging adult, not a pediatric, experience. "Doing it for the kids" does not necessarily mean participating in a program on a child's level.

2. Taking in information does not constitute learning. It is necessary to reflect upon what is learned. The new information must be placed within a framework of existing knowledge. Some prior knowledge may be sophisticated; some may be underdeveloped. Some pre-existing knowledge may even include wrong information. The learner comes to question and evaluate previously held assumptions. Misconceptions may need to be confronted and corrected. Negative attitudes must be overcome or altered. Such reflection can be a difficult process. People tend to maintain old understandings and beliefs and to resist change. Arguing and defending one's ideas will strengthen some and eliminate others.

3. New ideas are formed during the evaluation and questioning process. The learner creates new meanings and builds new assumptions based on newly acquired knowledge. In other words, learning is not just adding new information. It involves questioning existing beliefs and changing some of them.

4. An important step in transformation is trying out one's ideas on others. This becomes a way to gain confidence and to confirm new ways of thinking and acting. One applies knowledge to life to examine it more fully. A learning community is essential for this process. Learning with a group is more effective than studying alone. Change is more easily accomplished with others who are also in the process of change. This is one reason why effective parent or family education should involve both parents.

5. The final step in personal transformation is acting upon new ideas. One strength of successful education is that it provides new opportunities for families to practice what they have learned. They actively make decisions about how to express themselves as Jews. One can study the Passover seder and then create it, study the Shabbat worship service and then attend one, learn about Hebrew names and participate in a naming ceremony.

What Learning Environments Support Adult Learning?

At this point it is important to indicate that many of the observations and recommendations made about adult learning in family education hold true in other educational settings as well. The following summarizes the characteristics of optimal learning environments.

An adult learning environment is welcoming and affirming. Adults frequently enter these learning situations apprehensively. They are not accustomed to feeling incompetent or ignorant. It is important that they be accepted whatever their entry point and be respected for who they are and for wanting to learn and grow. Jewish parents may begin with a lack of Jewish knowledge, but they all bring expertise in other areas of life. Discovering their individual strengths and allowing them to contribute to the program is one way to confirm who they are and what they can do. A travel agent can help parents plan a pretend or actual trip to Israel. A musician can talk about Jewish music. A teacher can teach about Egyptian civilization at the time of the Exodus. Someone who enjoys cooking can share Jewish recipes.

The atmosphere should be positive, exciting and fun and yet reflect a seriousness of purpose. This is not entertainment. Study requires involvement and commitment and the subjects studied are an important part of life.

The environment must be one that encourages and supports questions. Adults want to analyze, argue, and debate. It should be acceptable to experiment with ideas and to put out assumptions to which others can react. Accordingly, making mistakes is just a part of learning. The learning place is one where the learner can be nurtured and can grow. One way this manifests itself is in insuring development from being a dependent learner (a consumer) to one who has the knowledge, competence and self-esteem to discover new meaning and to teach others (an emancipated learner). The teacher nurtures this independence by providing guidance and encouragement as well as opportunities for the adult to learn independently and to teach others. Thus, providing the resources and support that enables parents to teach their own children is one of the goals of the family educator.

One Final Word From An Adult Educator

There is one more important message that the field of adult learning offers the field of family education: family and parent education must be viewed as one part of the process of lifelong learning. Since our earliest history as Jewish learners, perhaps since Sinai, we have been taught to see learning as an activity that extends throughout the cycle of life. At each point, we are ready to learn new and different things and each person continually reevaluates what he or she knows in light of new knowledge made available to them.

There is a danger in linking adult learning only to benefits for children. When the children are out of school and out of the home, parents may assume that their own needs to learn have been fulfilled. If the rewards and pleasures of learning depend only on responses from children, adult incentive for life-long learning can be lost. If, however, these qualities have been embodied in parent or family education programming, adults' motivation to continue to study will exist independently of whatever their children are doing. Adult education as a dimension of both family and parent education can be a driving force. It can assure that the learning so vital to Jewish community will continue throughout everyone's lifetime.

References

Erikson, E. H. *Childhood and Society.* New York: Norton, 1950 (Reissue 1963)

Freire, P. *Pedagogy of the Oppressed.* New York: Seabury Press, 1970.

Habermas, J. *Knowledge and Human Interests.* Boston: Beacon Press, 1970.

Knowles, M.S. *The Modern Practice of Adult Education: From Pedagogy to Andragogy.* New York: Cambridge Books, 1980. (2nd ed.)

Mezirow, J. *Fostering Critical Reflection in Adulthood: A Guide to Transformative and Emancipatory Education.* San Francisco:Jossey Bass, 1990.

Rachel Sisk is director of Family Education at the Central Agency for Jewish Education in Miami, Florida. She holds a master's degree in Social Work from the University of Southern California, a master of arts in Jewish Communal Service from the Jewish Institute of Religion at Hebrew Union College, and a certificate of advanced graduate study in Jewish Family Education from the University of Judaism.

Rachael received her B.A. from the University of California, Los Angeles, in Sociology and Social Psychology. She has been involved in Jewish family education programming and training at camps, community centers, day schools, synagogues, Jewish museums, and the Whizin Institute. Her most important influences in family education come from memories she shares with her family and from her own family experiences.

Rachel Sisk

Funding Family Education Can Leave You Breathless
Rachel Sisk

Grants are good.... Breathe.... Grants are good.... Breathe....
I find myself chanting this mantra every time somebody mentions grants. It helps me to calm my nerves and focus. As both a family education programmer and an administrator, I have experienced grants from two sides of the funding process. I have had the breath taken away by the excitement of someone believing in my ideas enough to give me the money to support them. I have also had my breath knocked out of me by the responsibility of having to put one more thing on an already over-full plate when the grant money "came through" for a program or event. I am cautious, now, of both aspects, but I am also challenged by them. It is thrilling to take an idea and run with it; and despite the trials that accompany them, grants are wonderful opportunities for growth, creativity, and learning. As long as you remember to breathe.

As a Jewish family educator, I know that family education is still often thought of as an "extra," which means that money for staff and supplies are difficult to come by. Institutions therefore must turn to the outside to seek funding for family education. And this means that professionals must learn about grants. Working with outside sources of funding requires negotiation and understanding among the parties involved in the process. In Jewish family education (JFE), at least five groups of stakeholders have needs, interests, concerns, and agendas that professionals must consider when developing grant proposals.

1. The Grant Seekers
These are professional administrators in Jewish communal institutions who often generate ideas for family education programs. When they write grant proposals, they represent their organization.

2. The Grant Givers

These are the individuals, organizations, or foundations able to fund family education projects. They have their own ideas about how things should be done—their own interests and conditions for disbursing funding.

3. The Lay People

These are the backbone of Jewish communal institutions and organizations. They are the policy-makers, ultimately accountable for the well being of the fund-seeking agency and highly invested in its success.

4. The Staff

Administrators are lucky if they have staff with whom to work to implement exciting and innovative programming. They will most likely be responsible for carrying out the funded program.

5. The Families

These are the beneficiaries of family education grants in action.

With all these stakeholders, agendas and egos engage in a delicate balance of power. To make outside funding work, grant recipients must have the organization and communication skills to facilitate cooperation and coordination between stakeholders. Patience, good will, the ability to listen, a belief in teamwork, and a clear vision must be present all around. Here is an example of a grant funded family education project:

Dr. Rosh, headmaster of the Bet Shammai Community Day School, followed educational trends closely. He was a devoted and knowledgeable administrator and attended conferences regularly. One winter, he returned to school from a conference energized and excited about Jewish family education. He decided to obtain funding for a family education program for the following year. His first step was to write a grant proposal, which he sent to several funding sources. In the spring, he found a funding partner: the Ma'asim Tovim Foundation, a private philanthropy devoted to Jewish educational causes. Dr. Rosh was thrilled with the money he received and made a presentation to the board of directors of the school, telling them of the good news.

Over the summer, Dr. Rosh searched for a new staff person to implement the funded proposal. In the fall, Ms. Kahal, who was new to the community but experienced in Jewish family education, was hired for the part-time job. She received copies of the grant proposal and the paperwork from the Ma'asim Tovim Foundation and went to work getting to know the school. She scheduled appointments with board members, teachers, and the PTA presidents as a way of introducing herself to the school community. At each meeting, however, she was surprised to find only a handful of people who knew about the grant project or about her job; and even after explaining, she received little support. Following these meeting, Ms. Kahal sent a survey to parents detailing the types of programs she could offer, only to have them again respond with little interest. Next, she created an advisory committee and started with minimal programming such as family Torah study classes, a family reading project, and a take-home family newsletter. Her goal was to begin to meet parent's needs while spreading the word about the new program.

Midway into the grant year, the Ma'asim Tovim Foundation requested a progress report. They expressed concern over differences between what had been written in the grant proposal and what was happening at the school. Ms. Kahal and the Foundation had several conversations about the process of change, the definition of Jewish family education, the needs of the school, and how progress should be measured. Opinions differed on all of these issues. They reached an impasse, and each felt unsure of how to proceed without compromising their integrity. Dr. Rosh stepped then joined in the discussion and offered a solution for how the school would meet the requirements of the Ma'asim Tovim Foundation. By the time he finished presenting his solution, the Foundation felt better about the project, and the school had a new plan of action for the remainder of the grant cycle. Ms. Kahal continued her family education programming at Bet Shammai until funding for the project ended.

Now here's a look at what they might have done differently if they had remembered that:

1. Knowledge is empowering.

Rather than developing an idea and a grant proposal for the school's family education program by himself, Dr. Rosh might have created a more widely accepted proposal if he had worked with a team of primary stakeholders—teachers, board members, and parents. Their input would have created buy-in from the outset, and set a tone of inclusion and teamwork for the remainder of the project. The teachers would not have been surprised with new responsibilities and new demands on their time at the beginning of the school year; and word-of-mouth would have spread information among families, generating enthusiasm and ownership.

2. Lay people are the lifeblood of an organization.
Rather than informing the board of the grant after the money had been awarded, the board could have provided insight into the needs of the community and its potential response to the proposal. As the school's representative body, a board's opinions and reactions are important guideposts for programmatic and institutional success. If informed, they could have developed a family education committee to support both the project and the new staff person and to generate ideas and enthusiasm for Jewish family education at the school.

3. Sharing information eliminates surprises.
Rather than having Ms. Kahal work in a vacuum, separated from the entire school, she could have been introduced as part of the staff even before her arrival and then publicly welcomed when she assumed her duties. If staff members had been told of their responsibilities to her, they most probably would have felt less defensive, reactive, or insulted about their new obligations. If parents had been given prior information, they, too, could have begun to think about the type of programming that they would find most useful to their families, and they could have anticipated and planned for the start of something new. If Ms. Kahal had known that she was supposed to consider the terms of the grant proposal as binding, she might have followed it more literally and avoided engaging in frustrating mid-grant discussions with the Ma'asim Tovim Foundation, or she could have engaged in an exploration of the Foundation's expectations earlier in the process. If Dr. Rosh had discussed his ideas with Ms. Kahal before she spoke with the Foundation, she could have participated in his solution, used different terminology to express what she had been doing, or adjusted her program development to come closer to the terms of the grant.

4. Visibility is a key to success.
Rather than greeting Ms. Kahal's hiring with silence, the staff of the day

school could have responded in advance by making an announcement to the teachers, by sending a press release to the local paper, or by sending a newsletter home to every family. They could also have arranged meetings in advance where she have introduced herself and the new program. After the completion of this "getting to know you" phase, continued visibility would keep enthusiasm high and generate additional word-of-mouth publicity. Also, if a family education committee had been put in place at the beginning of the grant writing process, they could have generated immediate lay support for the project once it was funded.

5. Know your funders.

Rather than assuming that the grant proposal was merely an outline for how the school would proceed in the field of Jewish family education, Ms. Kahal could have set up lines of communication with the Foundation early on so that she would have understood their expectations. Instead, miscommunication ensued, followed by frustration and disappointment on both sides. Ms. Kahal could have eliminated or reduced this if she had been aware of the Foundation's expectations before she began the process of program implementation. Dr. Rosh could have been more forthcoming in providing helpful information about the Foundation that he had gained during his initial search for funding for the proposal.

6. Support is serious business.

Rather than becoming involved only after a crisis developed, Dr. Rosh could have actively and publicly supported Ms. Kahal and communicated with her from the day she was hired. If she had received constant, visible, and consistent support from Dr. Rosh from the beginning of the implementation phase, many of the uncomfortable situations in which she found herself would have been eliminated or been less problematic. His authoritative presence would have helped legitimize Ms. Kahal's role within the school. In contrast, his sporadic presence actually served to undermine the respect she might have developed within the school community or with the Foundation. By pulling rank and intervening in her discussions with the foundation, and by silencing her part in the conversation, he infantilized her and undermined her credibility. By not supporting her with teachers, he gave the impression that her work was of little importance.

7. Time is money.

Rather than allowing Ms. Kahal to develop the program at a relaxed pace, either Dr. Rosh or the Foundation could have suggested a time frame for how they expected her to proceed or they could have asked her to develop time-related goals for the program. The amount of time for which a grant project is funded should be clear from the beginning, and what is expected to happen upon completion of the grant cycle should be considered before it ends. If Dr. Rosh really wanted family education to become a regular and successful part of the day school, he either needed to find a way to write it into the budget at the end of the funding cycle or to begin to look for other sources of funding to compliment the original grant or to seek renewal of the original grant before the money ran out or ask for time to promote ongoing funding for the program before accepting the initial grant money.

Grants are a tricky business. They are today's hot commodity in Jewish family education. Everyone wants them. And everyone has different expectations of what they will provide. Many stakeholders bring many differing agendas to the same table. Our goal as Jewish family educators is to reach, teach, and serve families. On the roller coaster to securing outside funding, we must weigh our own options carefully while we decide how much compromise we can afford. Accepting funding for new Jewish family education is wonderful only if we can use it for effective process as well as for the creation of innovative products. Also, it must be acceptable to refuse outside funding if the risk it presents is too great. For if we damage ourselves or our relationships along the way to creating a program, or if we set ourselves up to fail, we will be unable to serve anyone effectively. But most of all, whether we say "Yes, please," or "No, thank you," to the exciting possibilities outside funding can bring to Jewish family education, we must think positively and *remember to breathe.*

Esther Netter is executive director of My Jewish Discovery Place Children's Museum and Cultural Center of Jewish Community Centers of Greater Los Angeles, an innovative and interactive museum for children and families which has become a model for the nation. During 1997, its traveling exhibits were in more than thirty Jewish communities including London and Warsaw. Esther also serves as the assistant executive director of Jewish Community Centers of Greater Los Angeles.

Esther Netter

Esther is on the faculty of the Whizin Institute for Jewish Family Life at the University of Judaism and a member of the clinical faculty of the Rhea Hirsch School of Education at Hebrew Union College. She lectures and teaches about museum education and informal education in North America, Europe, and Israel.

Esther received her undergraduate degree in Jewish studies from the University of California, Los Angeles, and her master's degree in Jewish education from the Jewish Theological Seminary in New York. She is the mother of three innovative and interactive children, Elisheva, Moshe, Shira.

Spreading Success
Esther Netter

Whatever your project, wherever your position, you never work in a vacuum. Small projects are part of larger entities. Departments are part of institutions, which in turn, are part of federations, which in their turn, are part of communities. Individuals alone cannot move projects; they need partners, collaborators, and supporters. So do institutions. To paraphrase a quote recently made famous: it takes a whole village to raise a program and a whole community to maintain it. Four years ago, a local Jewish Community Center (JCC) decided to take a small amount of money and establish a new Family Experience Project to include family retreats, a family holiday series, family heirloom art workshops, and Shabbat Shalom family programs. This is the story of how the project started, became successful, and then had to handle carefully its success.

Finding the Chair

To insure that the Family Experience Project would be a high priority within the JCC, it was important to select the right chairperson. At a meeting of the JCC's executive director, president, and Family Experience director, lists of possible community leaders were spread on the table. A discussion of each person's talents led to the formation of the criteria for this particular chairpersonship. To establish this as a strong new project, the chairperson would need many skills and resources. After much searching, a chair was selected who met the criteria. She was a respected member of the Jewish community, committed to the project, and understood its vision as well as the mission of the JCC. She was, in addition, a person of influence and means, a person with a broad social network, someone who had access to many facets of the Jewish and general communities. This chairperson was to work very closely with the

Family Experience director, also a member of the JCC executive staff.

Building the Board

Quickly, the executive director and new chair began to develop the structure and the plan for the Family Experience Project. They built a board of directors, established institutional coalitions, formed partners, and found advisors. Individuals were invited to serve on the Family Experience Board only after they had become enthusiastic about the Family Experience Project and its mission. Since the JCC was under tight budgetary limitations, everyone who became involved in the Family Experience knew that each step in developing the project had to be handled planfully and judiciously. Therefore, everyone who was asked to participate felt lucky to be able to be part of this innovative project. Everyone also realized the important role finances would play in the development of the project. The director worked diligently to find meaningful, personalized connections for each board member—to create project involvement that extended beyond financial and time commitments. For this project to succeed, board members had to grow Jewishly themselves, and find new ways to contribute their own knowledge and expertise.

Establishing the project's board and personalizing their relationships strengthened the fabric of the project as a whole. Because the chair, understood how important the board selection process was and how valuable it was to make the invitation to serve on the board an individual one, she courted, in the best sense of that term, each potential board member. Whether in her own living room, at the country club, in the foyer of a local arts museum, or in the still-empty space dedicated to the future Family Experience Project, she let each individual know how valuable their involvement would become to them and to their own families.

Next an advisory group was created to bring together people with expertise in early childhood education, Jewish family education, museum education, Judaica, arts, and culture. This group was to work with the board and staff to insure high quality programs and educational materials. These individuals saw, as did the board, that their involvement was a way to enrich their own families and themselves Jewishly.

As the board matured, it became clear that, in order to maximize each board members' contribution, subcommittees with different responsibilities should be formed. The executive director's conversations with board members always included both a statement and a question: "We are thrilled that we will be working together to develop the Family Experience. What are your ideas and thoughts even at this early stage?"

Inevitably, responses were something like: "I think that marketing is the key." "Have you thought of working with synagogues?" "I know someone with Disney and they could do…." "Could you call so and so? They would be very interested in getting involved." I would like to offer my home for a parlor meeting…." "Have you thought of doing a newsletter? I would be happy to be the editor." "There was never anything like this for my family when I was raising my kids. I'd love to help get this going for my grandchildren." "How about a music program?" I worked in New York with the symphony, and I'll call the Los Angeles symphony…." I'll sleep on it and call you tomorrow with a list of ideas."

Out these conversations came the first subcommittees—public relations, fund raising, programming, and family learning. Others followed as new individuals joined the board. As the project proceeded, the ongoing education and training of the board became a priority, parallel to the creation of the Family Experience Project itself. Staff time was divided among working with the board, creating the project, and raising the funds to continue it beyond its first year. Regular meetings between the lay chairperson and the Family Experience director often consisted of setting the agenda of board meetings. The director would say, "The board should get together, see one another, share what is going on in one another's lives, and, yes, it also needs to make some decisions." Working with board members and their families became its own family experience. The chair played an important role, having board members and their families for Shabbat dinners, holiday celebrations, and Passover seders.

Creating the Program

Ideas for the Family Experience Project accumulated quickly. The next step was to create a permanent, dedicated space for the project and its related programs and special events. The host JCC allocated a small but adequate space in which to begin the project. With a board selected and space to use, the process of creating programs could begin.

From the very beginning, board members acted as members of design teams, and team-building became as important as the end result. The board sought additional institutional partners. The same team work that took place on the board, the advisory board, and among JCC staff was also taking place with representatives of the Bureau of Jewish Education, the Federation, synagogues, and other communal institutions. These replicated the now-identifiable culture of the board of the Family Experience Project, thus defining and underscoring the way in which the project was creating itself. No matter what the particular agenda was, finding partners, working together, and ensuring that all contributors gained something for themselves and their families became the underlying theme of all meetings. Each planning meeting and each fund raising lunch was seen as a step towards the realization of the bigger picture, the new Family Experience Center. But even the Family Experience Center itself was seen as only one small step towards reaching the even bigger picture of involving Jewish families in the larger community.

The "Ask"

It was difficult to build the new Family Experience Center. In a time of depleted resources, it was hard to ignite people's passions, to spark their interest, and procure the necessary funds. The director and the chair constantly invoked the vision of the project to motivate and focus people. The chair constantly practiced what she preached. She believed in the center, contacted new people, and empowered them to make decisions. Most important, she obligated them, in turn, to involve others. That obligation added an energy, motivation, and dynamism to the project.

Seeking funds required effort. The chair, on many occasions, would say "I don't want to make any more calls. It's too hard. Stay, hold my hand." The director also disliked asking for funds but kept her eye focused on the long-term goal. Together, the director and chair would conduct direct solicitations. One would hold the other's hand when continuing the "ask" seemed to become too difficult. While one did the asking, the other would be the keeper of the dream and the vision of the completed Family Experience Project.

In nine months their combined energy had built a strong board and turned the Family Experience into a project much larger than originally expected. The Family Experience Project embodied the mission of its parent agency more clearly and with greater intensity than any other single JCC project. The JCC's mission to reach Jewish families, strengthen identity, build community, and insure Jewish continuity was being actualized through this Jewish Family Experience. And in the process, the project brought new leadership and participants to the JCC.

Growing Pains

The Jewish Family Experience Project had its logical home in the agency that fostered it. The JCC has expertise in informal, experiential Jewish education, cultural arts, and community outreach. The JCC relies on strong lay-professional relations and partnerships to run its institutions. It is, by definition, pluralistic, serving as port-of-entry for everyone in the Jewish community. After achieving early prominence, the Jewish Family Experience Project had a strong, overwhelmingly successful first year. The chair and director won local and national recognition, which brought prestige and acclaim not only to the project but also to its parent agency, the JCC. The following year, the Family Experience Project became a national prototype to be installed at other JCC's. The director became a national consultant to help new communities create their own Family Experience projects. At this time of growth, attention was paid to nurturing the Family Experience Project itself, since it was taking off on all fronts. Less attention was being paid to integrating this new, larger Family Experience Project into the larger JCC, its parent organization.

During the second year, the project's relationship with the larger JCC became complicated. The Jewish Family Experience, with its high profile board, was perceived by many at the JCC to be more influential than the JCC and its own board. Due to the Family Experience Project's success and reputation, it received an inordinate amount of good publicity and visibility. The Family Experience board felt that the publicity also included acclamation for the JCC, since the Family Experience was part of the JCC. For the Family Experience board, their success in reaching and involving new families was also a success for its parent agency.

At JCC executive board meetings, the Family Experience was repeatedly held up as an example of successful board development, new leadership training, fund raising, coalition building, and innovative Jewish family programming. Other program staff began to feel judged for not having raised new dollars or for not having involved new leaders on their respective boards. Among the JCC executive staff, the same dissonance began to surface; similar conversations took place on a lay level. Center presidents were directed to look closely at the work of the chair of the

Family Experience Project and to emulate her. Congratulations for the success of the Family Experience Project were tinged with jealousy: success was both positive and negative. It pulled the Family Experience closer to the JCC while simultaneously pushing it away from its parent body.

Early in the second year, these problems surfaced. The JCC approached the director and the board with conflicting messages. On the one hand, it wanted to support the Family Experience Project in growing and expanding its programs. On the other, it seemed to want to discourage further visibility. While the JCC board appeared to woo the Family Experience chair, she was not included in JCC leadership meetings. It became clear that better integration was needed so that the projects' laity would become part of the parent organization. The JCC lay leadership needed to understand and embrace the benefits of the Family Experience and not to feel threatened by the its success. A way had to be found to minimize conflict, jealousy, and misunderstanding. Similarly, there was jealousy among the JCC executive staff, and the Family Experience director had become a target of that jealousy. As the Family Experience continued to be highly visible and to receive positive coverage in the press, comments were made about the director such as "He's only out for himself." "All he cares about is the Family Experience, not the JCC." "Why isn't he bringing new leaders into the JCC?" "If he can raise so much money for this project, why doesn't he do it for the whole agency?"

Spreading Success

A short time later, the approach used to build the Family Experience Project's board was used again to resolve these intra-organizational tensions. Establishing a shared vision, building partnerships, empowerment, ownership, and a sense of obligation became the framework for bringing JCC laity and professionals into conversation with the Family Experience Project's laity and professionals. Just as the Family Experience board's initial development process had taken a year, so too, these repair and prevention processes between the Project and the JCC are likely to continue long term. Years two and three for the Family Experience Project focused on expansion, growth, replication, resource development, and leadership development. At the same time, building connections and understandings with the JCC was a major priority.

Only time will reveal the ultimate success or failure of this process in building and maintaining this unique Family Experience Project. Time will also reveal whether one city's experience can guide other cities as additional JCC's begin to develop their own Family Experience Projects.

Lessons Learned

What can we learn now from this case about Jewish family education that can be applied to other situations? What general issues surface from exploring this particular instance? Here are some that come to mind:

1. The role of lay leadership is central and, in particular, the role of the lay chair is critical in the successful start-up of Jewish family education projects and programming.
2. The ongoing independence of lay leadership in supporting Jewish family education as it grows and affects institutions and communities is crucial.
3. Nurturing and fostering the relationship between small projects and their larger institutional homes must happen on a continual and continuing basis.
4. The balance between innovative and successful "sexy" projects and ongoing core, pre-existing programs needs to be constantly re-evaluated and readjusted.
5. The pros and cons of fast-paced, high-profile achievement versus slower, gradual growth should always be considered.
6. Juggling and managing the internal and external perceptions of a project is the duty of professional and lay leadership. Managing the "reflected glory" of one part and making sure it is shared with the whole is part of what is needed.
7. Perceived competition between a project and its larger parent institution can place ongoing support of the project at risk.

Epilogue

Much has transpired during the four years since the Jewish Family Experience Project began. Even with changes in JCC executive leadership and with new people coming into professional and lay roles, the Family Experience Project has been integrated into the JCC and enjoys its institutional commitment. The Family Experience lay leadership and professional staff hold positions of importance in the JCC and are viewed as valuable partners. The Family Experience is a leading project of the Jewish Community Center, with local, national, and international boards and a catalogue of successful programs.

Postscript

Somehow, I know that my parents, Shirley and Arthur, of blessed memory, are very pleased with the articles in the preceding pages. This harvest of *First Fruit* from the wonderful folks who make up the Shirley and Arthur Whizin Institute for Jewish Family Life provides ongoing evidence of my parents' life long devotion to the future of Jewish life in America and Israel.

My father and mother were born in 1906 and 1909, respectively, in Brooklyn, New York. The similarity ends there. My mother, a Cohen, was raised Orthodox, and my father was as secular as they come. Each moved to Boyle Heights in Los Angeles during their teens, but here, also, there were great differences in the way that happened. My mom moved west with her family, and by the age of sixteen, was a student at UCLA. My dad had quit school when he was twelve and by the age of fifteen was Texaco Oil Company's chief diesel mechanic on Long Island, New York. At the age of sixteen, he started out for California in his own car, with his older brother Charlie. But somewhere around St. Louis, Charlie drove the car off a bridge, and they wound up taking the bus the rest of the way.

When my dad arrived on the West Coast, he expected to go to work for Texaco. But when he arrived, there was no work. So, instead, he went to work driving a truck and delivering pies to restaurants. Six months later, he bought his own pie truck and went into business for himself— all this while he was still only sixteen years old. Five years later, in 1927, he was twenty-one and had $10,000 in the bank. To give you some perspective on how much that was, eggs were then two cents a dozen. He went to night school at Roosevelt High and got his high school diploma.

My father met my mother when she was seventeen and he was twenty. The story varies, but it was either just before, or just after, she had won the Miss Los Angeles Beauty Pageant. Though they were different in many ways, one of their similarities was her beauty and his good looks. (My dad was even more handsome than Rudolph Valentino.) My mom had a lot of boys hanging around the house, but my dad, (again, so the story goes) was the only one working, so he won out. She quit school, and they got married. They opened their first restaurant in 1929, the TNT Cafe on Pico Boulevard. My dad was the cook and dishwasher; my mom, the waitress. The cafe had four stools and a very small kitchen.

In 1931 they opened their first Chili Bowl restaurant right during the heart of the depression. My mom was no longer "in the business" because she was pregnant with me. I was born on March 5, 1931. At that time, a huge bowl of chili and beans, with all the French rolls you could eat, was ten cents. People have come up to me to say that the huge amount of food for that price actually saved their lives. One man told me he had twenty-five cents a week to eat on, so one week he would eat two meals and the next week, three.

By 1940, Mom and Dad had twenty-one restaurants spread out all over the city. Those pieces of property were the early start of my dad's real estate investments. He owned them because of something that happened to him at the end of the first year's lease on his first Chili Bowl. The lease was going to expire; the landlord saw the big business being done on his property and decided not to renew it. My dad had three-hundred dollars invested in the building itself. He bought a piece of property one block away, moved the building, and decided he would never again open a business unless he owned the property it stood on outright with no mortgage. He always told me, "If you owe money, sooner or later, if times are bad, the banks will own what you have spent your life acquiring."

He was right. During World War II, he had to close all but two of the Chili Bowls because workers went into the army or off to work in the war effort. Later, he was able to keep only one restaurant open, working it by himself, so he was able to pay the taxes on the other pieces of property.

In the late forties he started selling the properties. This was the source of what was to become the significant estate that would eventually fund the Whizin Foundation, the Shirley and Arthur Whizin Center for the Jewish Future, the Shirley and Arthur Whizin Residential Campus at the University of Judaism, the Shirley and Arthur Whizin Biotechnology Center at Technion, the Israel Institute of Technology, and all of the other charities we now support.

In 1937, my parents were among the founders of the Valley Jewish Community Center, which became Adat Ari El, in North Hollywood. That's when their Jewish communal life began. They were also among the founders of the University of Judaism, Camp Ramah in California, and many other local Jewish institutions. For fifty years, until my mom died in 1986, they were active in every facet of Jewish community life. After my mom died, my dad withdrew into seclusion; he never came out. Then he, too, died in December, 1994.

In the early 1970s my folks had decided, with my enthusiastic support, to put most of their estate into a charitable entity in order to "help preserve the Jewish future." Shortly after my mom died, my dad got macular degeneration in both eyes, which meant he could no longer read. As a result, I started helping him with these matters. One day my dad and I were talking about his and mom's plans to establish the Whizin Center at the University of Judaism. They had never really had a clear picture of what the center should do, only that it should help to preserve the Jewish future. Spontaneously, I looked at him and said, "You don't know what you want to do so why don't you let me see to it that your and mom's dreams come true." Little did I know that from that moment on, my own life and Shelley's would forever-more be involved almost totally in Jewish communal service.

In these few paragraphs, I have tried to sketch my folk's varied, intense journey so that you might get some feel for them as people. If you have read *Weathering the Storms*, the article I wrote for this collection, you know some of my puzzlement over my own Jewish upbringing. Let me state here that I am truly my mother's and my father's son. I would not be who, what, or where I am if it were not for what they gave me, physically, emotionally, and mentally. Although I didn't get everything from them, they are the base from which I started, and I am grateful to them both. They were extraordinary people—not perfect, flawed as we all are—but they filled me with the concept of service to one's city, country, and people, especially the Jewish people.

This anthology, the Whizin Center, the Whizin Institute for Jewish Family Life, the Synagogue 2000 Institute, the Whizin Foundation, the Biotechnology Center, and all of the other wonderful things Shelley and I are now involved in, would not exist were it not for Art and Shirley's life-long labor. The hundreds of thousands of Jews who have benefited, and who will continue to benefit, from the programs already created, being created, and yet to be created, would never have done so were it not for Shirley and Art.

Mom, and Dad: Shelley and I are so happy for the life we are leading, doing the work we are doing, and we owe it all to you. We know you are as pleased as we are. We love you. b'shalom.

Bruce Fabian Whizin